Making Sense of Search and Seizure Law

Making Sense of Search and Seizure Law

A Fourth Amendment Handbook

Second Edition

Phillip A. Hubbart

Carolina Academic Press
Durham, North Carolina

Library of Congress Cataloging-in-Publication Data

Hubbart, Phillip A., author.
Making sense of search and seizure law : a Fourth Amendment handbook / Phillip A. Hubbart. -- Second edition.
pages cm
Includes bibliographical references and index.
ISBN 978-1-61163-615-4 (alk. paper)
1. Searches and seizures--United States. 2. United States. Constitution. 4th Amendment. I. Title.

KF9630.H83 2015
345.73'0522--dc23

2015003668

Carolina Academic Press
700 Kent Street
Durham, North Carolina 27701
Telephone (919) 489-7486
Fax (919) 493-5668
www.cap-press.com

Printed in the United States of America

Summary of Contents

Contents

Part II · Substantive Law of the Fourth Amendment

Foreword

The fifty-four words of the Fourth Amendment have "both the virtue of brevity and the vice of ambiguity."[1] This combination results in a vast jumble of judicial pronouncements that is not merely complex and contradictory, but often infuriatingly perverse. This Amendment is one of the most controversial in the Bill of Rights, and among the most frequently adjudicated.

While Fourth Amendment jurisprudence has evolved over two centuries, the avalanche began when *Mapp v. Ohio* applied the exclusionary rule to the states. It is a daunting task for the trial or appellate lawyer—or even a trial or appellate judge—to master the history and scope of this body of law. Yet it falls to the busy lawyer and judge to make sense of seemingly inconsistent and irreconcilable cases in their daily work—whether in a persuasive trial memo, brief, or legal opinion. Rarely do they have either the time or the patience to struggle through a vast library of cases, treatises, and law review articles.

Phillip Hubbart designed *Making Sense* for the overworked and overwhelmed lawyer and judge. We need a trustworthy guide to navigate this maze and Hubbart has the broad experience necessary to write this book. He has studied the Fourth Amendment from different points of view as a defense lawyer, public defender, appellate court judge and law school professor. He has carefully crafted this book, however, not through the lens of an advocate, but rather in a clear-eyed, neutral, non-argumentative exposition of what the Fourth Amendment law is, not what he thinks it should be.

This book organizes the material in an efficient way that makes it is easy to follow and keeps it to one volume rather than in an unwieldy multi-volume encyclopedia. Yet in this one volume Hubbart manages to cover every Fourth Amendment decision decided by the Supreme Court, over 430 such decisions, and puts useable quotations from the opinions in footnotes.

The book is divided into two parts: first the historical background and then the substantive law. Hubbart advises lawyers that they can skip over the detailed history behind the Amendment in Part I, Chapters 2 to 5, and go directly to Chapter 6 and then on to the modern cases. But if you do, you will miss a great read.

Part I, which is divided into 6 chapters, provides an in-depth, deeply contextual reading of the history of the Amendment and demonstrates how it has heavily influenced the development of search and seizure law. Most treatises give short shrift with a couple of paragraphs while *Making Sense* gives the full history down to the judicial roots from the English cases. I am a legal history buff yet I discovered numerous new gems in this part.

The exclusionary rule was once considered the seminal bright-line rule in Fourth Amendment jurisprudence, but alas no longer. It is slowly being eroded, perhaps into ir-

---

1. Jacob W. Landynski, Search and Seizure and the Supreme Court 43–44 (1966).

relevance. The limitation of *Mapp* by the good faith exception from *United States v. Leon* is by far the most important issue covered by the book but not the only one. The book also covers the lesser exceptions such as the independent source doctrine, the inevitable discovery rule, impeachment of the testifying defendant and others.

The upgrade to this new edition focuses on this frightening trend. Chapter 17 covers the historical development, purpose, and substantive law of the judge-made exclusionary rule. Importantly, Hubbart demonstrates that the framers never thought the Amendment was just an admonition or aspiration but rather that it would be enforced by judges.

The Court has complicated the application of the good faith exception by developing a balancing test to determine whether the rule or the exception is applicable in a given case. This "case by case" analysis requires mastery of all the cases. Fortunately Hubbart has done the work for us—and it is not simple, as he describes the Court's cases at times as following a "zig-zag course."

The lodestar of all Fourth Amendment litigation, including the exclusionary rule, is the unreasonableness requirement for a violation. A great constitutional right is written in principled terms that are not self-executing and are open to intense debate. The Amendment purposefully doesn't define "unreasonable," so it is up to judges and lawyers to put a gloss on it.

But is it reasonable for a law enforcement officer to be mistaken about facts of the case and ignorant of the law? So long as the police act with an objectively "reasonable good-faith belief" that their conduct is lawful the Court is willing to excuse them. *Making Sense* analyzes in detail, with copious illustration, the theories and canons of construction used by the Supreme Court to decide these thorny issues. It is crucial for the litigator to have command of them.

The value of any book is determined by the benefit we get from it. By that standard, it is hard to find one as useful as *Making Sense of Search and Seizure Law*. This is a volume I will turn to over and over again in my professional practice. But it is more than that—it is also a joy to read.

Roy Black
March 30, 2015

Preface to the Second Edition

A decade has passed since the first edition of this book was published in 2005. During this period, some significant changes in Fourth Amendment law have occurred. Annual supplements to the book have grown to over 100 pages.

Among other things, the Fourth Amendment exclusionary rule, covered in Chapter 17, has undergone some remarkable revisions that have further constricted the reach of the rule. Indeed, liberal critics of the Roberts Court have charged that the Court has pushed the exclusionary rule to the brink of extinction—a view that I have some sympathy with, but ultimately do not share.

To accommodate all the Court's Fourth Amendment decisions in the past ten years, a second edition of the book has been published.

The book's overall purpose, however, remains unchanged: to restate existing Fourth Amendment law, as announced by the U.S. Supreme Court's 430-plus decisions on the subject, in an organized and lucid fashion, true to its historical origins—so that the entire structure hangs together and makes sense.

I have poured a great deal of my 50-year professional career into this endeavor—as an appellate judge, public defender, adjunct law professor, and legal writer.

Some critics may say that I have embarked on an impossible task, that Fourth Amendment law is a crazy-quilt of conflicting principles and holdings that cannot possibly be reconciled. They argue that Fourth Amendment decisions are entirely dependent on the judicial philosophy of the individual justices on the Court, who can manipulate the law any way they please—so that the end result is a bundle of confusing contradictions.

Not only do I disagree, but practicing lawyers and judges can hardly afford the luxury of this academic point of view. They are required to look up the applicable law on a search-and-seizure point when the issue arises and to apply it in a given case. The judicial philosophy of the Court that rendered a particular decision is irrelevant to this very practical endeavor.

Moreover, the public has a right to expect that the Supreme Court is a court of law that follows its past precedents while adapting the law's basic principles to the rapidly changing country in which we live. Indeed, the Court's credibility depends entirely on its ability to do just that. Cynical views that the Court is really a political institution like the Congress or the presidency undermines the Court's otherwise fragile authority in our constitutional system—something, I think, the Court is painfully well aware of.

Thus, the reason for this book—to make sense of Fourth Amendment law by discovering its controlling rules and principles as an organized whole, true to its historical roots.

To accomplish this purpose, I have, among other things, provided relevant quotations from the Court's decisions to support both the organizational structure and the statements of law in the text. Given the complexity of this law, readers, in my view, are entitled to an accurate, yet clear hornbook on the subject—not my subjective views. I hope this volume satisfies that requirement.

As for lower federal and state court cases on search and seizure, I have supplied frequent references to Professor Wayne LaFave's magisterial six-volume work on the subject, *Search and Seizure: A Treatise on the Fourth Amendment* (*5th ed.*, 2012)—as well as relevant West Digest key numbers that collect the cases on point.

Moreover, the historical background that led to the Fourth Amendment, and the theories of constitutional construction followed by the Court in interpreting the Amendment, have been augmented in this edition with more recent authorities and works.

And, as with the first edition, this work will be annually supplemented with the most recent U.S. Supreme Court decisions.

A variety of professionals should find this book useful: prosecutors, private criminal defense lawyers, public defenders, judges, law professors and their students—as well as political science and criminal justice professors and their students.

Also American history buffs may find particularly interesting Chapters 2–6 of the book which covers the stirring historical background that led to the Fourth Amendment (1761–1791).

I thank my friend Judge Charles Edelstein for reviewing and proofreading this second edition of the book, as he did the first edition—and for offering many valuable suggestions that have helped improve the text.

My thanks also go to Keith Sipe and Linda Lacy, the publisher and senior editor, respectively, at Carolina Academic Press, for agreeing to publish a second edition of this book. I will always be indebted to the fine people at this marvelous publishing house for all their encouragement and support over the years.

Phillip A. Hubbart
Miami, Florida
March 30, 2015

Preface to the First Edition

Fourth Amendment law is both fascinating and inspiring—dealing, as it does, with a fundamental human right, the denial of which was one of the leading causes of the American Revolution. I greatly admire this body of law, and I hope the reader shares my enthusiasm.

But this law can also be extremely confusing. Indeed, the Fourth Amendment is easily the most complicated, sprawling and misunderstood of all the freedoms guaranteed by the Bill of Rights. Perhaps this has made the subject all the more challenging, as it cannot be easily mastered.

Accordingly, the purpose of this book is to make sense of this subject. The work tries to organize and explain Fourth Amendment law, as announced by U.S. Supreme Court decisions, so that it is understandable and coherent. In particular, it concentrates on U.S. Supreme Court case law, relies heavily on the historical background of the Fourth Amendment upon which much of this law is based, and cites to the relevant treatises and West key numbers when dealing with the leading decisions of the lower federal courts and state courts.

A thorough understanding of this law and its historical roots is especially timely today—as we approach the many constitutional issues raised by the USA Patriot Act and the country's other efforts to track down and punish terrorists.

Although of interest to the country as a whole, the book is written primarily for the criminal justice community, namely:

- Judges, prosecutors, public defenders, and private criminal defense lawyers as they confront Fourth Amendment issues at the trial and appellate levels;
- Law enforcement personnel, police legal advisors, and academy instructors as they confront the same issues in the field and in the classroom;
- Law professors and law students in their study of criminal constitutional law, of which the Fourth Amendment is a vital part; and
- Professors and students at the undergraduate level in various criminal justice courses that cover the law of arrest and search and seizure.

The book, however, is not slanted in anyone's favor. Its sole purpose is to re-state Fourth Amendment law as objectively as I am able.

I am not, of course, the first to try to fathom this daunting subject. There are other splendid treatises that have been written in the field, principally Professor Wayne LaFave's magisterial work on the subject[1]—and a treasure trove of law review articles. Many of these works are cited in this book and are well worth consulting.

1. 1–6 Wayne LaFave, Search and Seizure (5th ed. 2012).

The treatises, however, tend to be encyclopedic reference works—valuable, but covering many volumes, with innumerable cases discussed at the federal and state levels. Something most professionals do not have the time to read in depth. They are also highly critical on occasion [often brilliantly so] of the existing law, sometimes endorsing the views of dissenting Justices—again valuable and fascinating, but not terribly helpful to the busy professional seeking to understand the law as it is. And finally these works do not appear to organize the law around a principled or historical basis—understandably so, given the apparent crazy-quilt of decisions in this field. Enter the avalanche of law review commentary which, in part, attempts to supply this perceived vacuum with various theories that the Court is urged to adopt.

By way of contrast, I have tried in a *single volume* to restate the mass of Fourth Amendment law in a way that makes sense, has practical application, and is readable. I have not tried, however, to advocate alternative theories, criticize decisions as erroneous, or impose a new order on this body of law. That effort has an esteemed place in our legal literature, but that has not been my task.

Instead, I have tried to restate the content, order and principled basis of Fourth Amendment law that are found in the myriad of U.S. Supreme Court decisions on the subject—a painstaking operation that requires infinite time and patience in order to plumb the depths of these decisions. Something most busy judges, prosecutors, public defenders, private defense lawyers, law enforcement officials, and even some law or undergraduate professors do not have the luxury to do. I can assure the reader that I have done just that. Indeed, it has taken me twenty-five years to complete this work.

Justice Holmes once described the "ocean of law" as laden with "a thick fog of details" engulfed by "a black and frozen night," but nonetheless "human ... a part of man, and of one world with all the rest." "There must be a drift to it," he said, "if one will go prepared and have patience which will bring one out to daylight and a worthy end."[2]

Likewise, I think there is a certain drift to Fourth Amendment law with all its complexities—which, if a person perseveres, will also bring one out to daylight and a worthy end. This work is dedicated to that proposition.

Phillip A. Hubbart
Miami, Florida
June 30, 2005

2. The Mind and Faith of Justice Holmes 36 (Max Lerner ed. 1943) (speech by Justice Oliver Wendell Holmes at Brown University Commencement 1897).

First Edition Acknowledgments

I am indebted to many people for helping me complete this book.

In particular, I thank my close friends and current law partners Gerald Wetherington [former Chief Judge of the Eleventh Judicial Circuit in Miami, Florida], and Herbert Klein [former Associate Chief Judge in the same court] for their constant encouragement, helpful advise, and understanding nature on my long journey to complete this book. Judge Wetherington, in particular, has been of invaluable assistance in helping me sort out difficult Fourth Amendment issues relating to the exclusionary rule, as well as many other aspects of search and seizure law.

Fred Lewis [a good friend and former Dean of the University of Miami Law School] gave me some critical advice in the late 1970s when he encouraged me to write a national work on the Fourth Amendment, rather than continue my then limited project on Florida search and seizure law.

My close friends Judge Charles Edelstein [former prosecutor and former county judge in Miami], Judge Arthur Rothenberg [former assistant public defender and current circuit court judge in Miami], and Michael Genden [former practicing lawyer and current circuit judge in Miami] have long encouraged me to continue this work. Judge Daniel Pearson [my good friend and former appellate court colleague in Miami] did the same with his constant encouragement and wry humor—but unfortunately passed away before the book was accepted for publication.

Judge Edelstein, in particular, was kind enough to read my initial draft manuscripts and offered invaluable comments for improvement of the text.

Roy Black, Jack Denaro and Stephen Lipton—all distinguished Florida attorneys—were also kind enough to read my initial manuscript and offer valuable advice as to suggestions for change. All three worked for me as assistant public defenders in the 1970s when I was the Public Defender in Miami-Dade County, and have since gone on to successful legal careers.

Professor Michael Graham of the University of Miami Law School—himself an accomplished author on the Federal Rules of Evidence as well as many other evidence treatises—was instrumental in helping me focus my work, secure a suitable title, put the final manuscript into understandable form, and find a publisher. Moreover, Professor Norman Lefstein of the University of Indiana Law School and my former college debate partner, suggested that I contact Carolina Academic Press which, fortunately for me, ultimately became the publisher of this work.

My thanks also go to my professors at Duke University Law School, Robinson Everett and Francis Paschal, who in the late 1950s and early 60s kindled a life-long fascination with Fourth Amendment law. And while I was serving as an appellate court judge in Miami 1977–96, Judge Charles Moylan of the Maryland Court of Appeals particularly inspired me to learn this daunting subject with his insightful and sparkling lectures on the Fourth Amendment to judges and police.

Hugo Black, Jr. [son of the great Supreme Court Justice and a highly accomplished trial lawyer in Miami], Gerald Kogan [former Chief Justice of the Florida Supreme Court and of counsel to my law firm], and Myles Tralins [a prominent trial lawyer in Miami]—were all very supportive in my efforts to complete this work. Mr. Tralins unfortunately was killed in a tragic automobile accident before the book was published.

My special thanks also go to Robert Conrow and the other editors at Carolina Academic Press for agreeing to publish this work and for their unfailing efforts in putting the final manuscript together. I will always be grateful to them.

My brother, Judge Gerald Hubbart, a former assistant state attorney, assistant public defender and current circuit judge in Miami, was always there when I needed him to share my dreams for this work and my disappointments at its glacial progress. My son Ted Hubbart also offered his brand of confidence and humor as I slogged through this project. And my many law students over the years have helped me to better organize and simplify the basic principles of Fourth Amendment law.

Of course, I take full responsibility for what is ultimately written in this work. The many people who have helped and encouraged me played an important role in the development of this book, but I alone take responsibility for the material I have placed in it.

Finally, I cannot put into words how much I owe my devoted and talented wife Martha. So I will not try—except to thank her for her expert proofreading work on this book, and for enriching my life for over forty years.

Phillip A. Hubbart
Miami, Florida
June 30, 2005

About the Author

Phillip A. Hubbart holds a Juris Doctor from Duke University Law School and a LL.M. from Georgetown University Law School. He is a member of the Florida Bar and the District of Columbia Bar.

He served for nineteen years as a judge on the Third District Court of Appeal in Miami, Florida (1977–96), including two and a half years as Chief Judge of that Court (1980–83). Before that, he served six years as the elected Public Defender of Miami-Dade County, Florida (1971–76); five years as an assistant defender in the same office (1965–69); two years in private practice in Miami, Florida (1964–65, 1969–70); and two years in public defender work in Washington, D.C. (1961–63) as a lawyer for the Legal Aid Agency for the District of Columbia (now the Public Defender Service), and as an E. Barrett Prettyman Fellow at Georgetown Law School. He has also taught criminal-law-related courses as an adjunct law professor for nearly thirty years—including a seminar on the Fourth Amendment. For over fifteen years, he has practiced appellate law as a member of the law firm of Wetherington, Klein and Hubbart in Miami, Florida.

He is a joint author of *Florida Evidentiary Foundations* (Michie 2d ed., 1997), and a joint author of the practice commentaries to *Florida Criminal Practice Service, vols. 1–5* (Lawyers Coop., 1993). He is also a life member of the American Law Institute.

Plan of the Book

Here, in brief, is how the book organizes the vast legal materials on Fourth Amendment law.

• **Introduction.** The first chapter comments on the importance and limit of Fourth Amendment freedom, outlines the three distinctive parts of Fourth Amendment law, surveys the growth of Fourth Amendment decisions, notes other sources of search and seizure law besides the Fourth Amendment, and ends with a short framework for analyzing a Fourth Amendment question on a motion to suppress in a criminal case.

• **Historical background and purpose.** Part I, Chapters 2–6, examine in depth the historical background and purpose of the Fourth Amendment, covering the formative Revolutionary Period of American history (1761–91). This is done because much of Fourth Amendment law has been influenced by and is based on the original understanding of the Framers.

• **Substantive Law.** Part II, the balance of the book, examines the *substantive law* of the Fourth Amendment. As a preface to this analysis, Chapter 7 surveys the three basic approaches that the U.S. Supreme Court has employed in interpreting the Fourth Amendment to produce this body of law: an historical approach, a balancing approach, and a common law reasoning approach.

Thereafter, Part II divides into three Subparts, which discuss the three distinct divisions of Fourth Amendment law: (1) the "Standing Requirement," (2) the "Unreasonableness Requirement," and (3) the Exclusionary Rule.

1. **The "Standing Requirement."** Subpart A analyzes the constitutional requirement that there must be a "search" or "seizure" of the complaining party's "person, house, papers [or] effects." There can be no Fourth Amendment violation unless this requirement is met. This requirement has three elements:

    - **A Personal Standing Element**, discussed in Chapter 8;
    - **A Governmental Action Element**, also discussed in Chapter 8; and
    - **A Search or Seizure Element**, discussed in Chapters 9 and 10.

2. **The "Unreasonableness Requirement."** Subpart B analyzes the "Unreasonableness Requirement" of Fourth Amendment law: the constitutional requirement that the search or seizure in question must be "unreasonable." There can be no Fourth Amendment violation unless this requirement is also met.

    - **General rules and principles.** Chapter 11 initially surveys the *general rules and principles* of Fourth Amendment unreasonableness—including the general rule that a search of private premises [particularly the home] must be conducted with a search warrant.

• **Unreasonable seizures and searches.** The balance of this Subpart deals first with *unreasonable seizures*, and second with *unreasonable searches*, each of which is analyzed separately by U.S. Supreme Court decisions.

– **Unreasonable seizures.** Chapter 12 covers arrests and temporary detentions of persons, as well as full-blown and temporary seizures of personal and real property.

– **Unreasonable searches.** Chapter 13–15 examines searches of real and personal property [such as a home, business, or motor vehicle], as well as searches of persons.

♦ **Searches with a search warrant.** Chapter 13 deals searches conducted *with a search warrant*

♦ **Searches without a warrant.** Chapters 14–15 cover searches conducted *without a search warrant*, concentrating on the many *exceptions* to the search warrant requirement rule.

* **Criminal exceptions.** Chapter 14 covers the *criminal exceptions* to the search warrant requirement rule—i.e., search incident to a lawful arrest, stop-and-frisk search, moving vehicle search, consent search, and exigent circumstances search.

* **Civil or special needs exceptions.** Chapter 15 deals with the *civil or special needs exceptions* to the search warrant requirement rule—i.e., inventory search, border search, administrative inspection search, probationer home search, public student search, drug testing search, airport or public building electronic search, and others.

– **Special Problems.** Chapter 16 examines special "Unreasonableness Requirement" problems, so that the reader can see how the various strands of Fourth Amendment law apply in concrete and often recurring factual scenarios.

3. The Exclusionary Rule. Finally, Subpart C reviews the *Weeks-Mapp exclusionary rule* adopted by the U.S. Supreme Court to enforce the Fourth Amendment. The applicability of this rule has long been treated as a separate issue apart from whether there has been a Fourth Amendment violation. Chapter 17 discusses the historical development and rationale for the exclusionary rule, covers the substantive law of the exclusionary rule, and ends with a treatment of miscellaneous procedural and appellate considerations.

List of Abbreviations

R. Brown	Richard Brown, Revolutionary Politics in Massachusetts (1970)
W. Cuddihy	William Cuddihy, The Fourth Amendment: Origins and Original Meaning 602–1790, Oxford University Press (2009)
H. Gray	Horace Gray Jr., Quincy's Massachusetts Reports 1761–72, Appendix I (1865)
O.M. Dickerson	O.M. Dickerson. "Writs of Assistance as a Cause of the Revolution," The Era of the American Revolution (Richard Morris ed. 1939)
J.R. Frese	Joseph R. Frese, "Writs of Assistance in the American Colonies 1660–1776" (Harvard Univ. Doctoral Dissertation 1951)
J.R. Frese, N.Eng.Q.	Joseph R. Frese, "James Otis and the Writs of Assistance," 30 New England Quarterly 498 (1957)
J. Landynski	Jacob Landynski, Search and Seizure and the Supreme Court (1966)
N. Lasson	Nelson Lasson, The History and Development of the Fourth Amendment to the United States Constitution (1937)
L. Levy	Leonard Levy, Original Intent and the Framers' Constitution (1988)
Perry and Cooper	Richard L. Perry and John C. Cooper, Sources of Our Liberties (ABA 1959)
Quincy	Quincy's Massachusetts Reports 1761–72 (1865)
M.H. Smith	M.H. Smith, The Writs of Assistance Case (1978)
C. Rossiter	Clinton Rossiter, 1787 The Grand Convention (1966)
R. Rutland	Robert Rutland, The Birth of the Bill of Rights (rev. ed. Northeastern paperback 1983)
B. Schwartz	Bernard Schwartz, The Bill of Rights: A Documentary History (1971) vols. I & II
F. Siebert	Fredrick S. Siebert, Freedom of the Press in England 1476–1776 ch. 18 (1952)
T. Taylor	Telford Taylor, Two Studies in Constitutional Interpretation (1969)
C. Van Doren	Carl Van Doren, The Great Rehearsal (1948)
Wroth and Zobel	L. Kinvin Wroth and Hiller B. Zobel, 2 Legal Papers of John Adams (1965)

The Fourth Amendment

The right of the people to be secure in their persons, houses, papers and effects against unreasonable searches and seizures shall not be violated, and no warrants shall issue, but upon probable cause, supported by oath or affirmation, and particularly describing the place to be searched, and the persons or things to be seized.

Making Sense of Search and Seizure Law

Chapter 1

Introduction to Fourth Amendment Law

Section 1. The Importance and Limit of Fourth Amendment Freedom

One of America's great achievements, perhaps its greatest and most enduring, has been the United States Constitution—in which the democratic ideal of individual freedom and equality under the rule of law was given a concrete reality. Indeed, the leaders of the American Revolution literally invented a nation based on this great ideal. They first announced it to the world as a fighting faith in the Declaration of Independence, and later gave it the force of law in the United States Constitution, particularly the Bill of Rights.

But the marvel is that they did it all within a republican governmental structure, heretofore unknown in modern history, that created a nation out of autonomous states with the power to govern and thereby "check the very forces they unleashed."[1] In so doing, they avoided the later chaos and internal bloodbaths of the French Revolution and the countless other unrestrained revolutions and uprisings that followed.[2] As the historian Richard Hofstadter has stated, "[t]here is common agreement among modern critics ... that the Constitution itself is one of the world's masterpieces of practical statecraft"[3]—a masterpiece that elevated the common man in an ordered society and gave this country its lifeblood. In Justice Hugo Black's words, "I think this country has lived because of its Constitution and its laws and its ideals of liberty and equality and freedom."[4]

To be sure, the adoption of the Constitution in the late eighteenth century did not establish individual freedom and democratic rule where there was none before. Indeed, 170 years of limited colonial self-government, with qualified rights under English law, preceded the American Revolution. Nor did the Constitution initially extend the full range of freedom to all Americans: African-American slaves, native Americans, women, indentured servants, and property-less whites being notable exceptions. But the Founders in one masterstroke swept away all vestiges of monarchical rule and aristocratic society, created the first modern democratic state in the history of the world, and guaranteed greater freedom for more people than had ever before existed in history.

---

1. Forrest McDonald, E Pluribus Unum 371 (2d ed. 1978); see also Joseph J. Ellis, Founding Brothers 8–9 (2000).
2. Forrest McDonald, E Pluribus Unum 371 (2d ed. 1978).
3. Richard Hofstadter, The American Political Tradition 15 (1948).
4. 1968 television interview of Justice Hugo Black with Martin Agonsky and Eric Sevareid, as quoted in Roger Newman, Hugo Black: a Biography 586 (1994).

Moreover, and perhaps of utmost importance, these leaders unleashed the ideal of individual freedom and equality under law that soon took on a life of its own. It served as the rallying cry for the further political and social democratization of the country—including the abolition of slavery, the emancipation of women, the universal extension of adult suffrage, the rise of free capitalism and labor, and the civil rights and other liberation movements of the mid- to late twentieth century and early twenty-first century.[5] Indeed, it was this relentless drive toward democratization and equality that Alexis de Tocqueville, in the 1830s, accurately saw as the inherent and central characteristic of American democracy and of democracy generally.[6] Even in its initial stages, this remarkable egalitarian development both astonished, and at times even dismayed, many of the revolutionary generation.[7]

As a consequence, this country under the Constitution has evolved over two centuries, and continues to evolve, into a more democratic society, with greater protections for individual freedom for more people, than that which existed at its beginnings.[8] All of which is not surprising because democracy is the only form of government in history that grows into its full existence, albeit with force of arms sometimes used along the way, while the ways of democracy are learned by its people.[9] Moreover, this development into a robust democratic state with strong egalitarian tendencies is surely a remarkable achievement—particularly when viewed against the backdrop of the troubled twentieth century with its brutal dictatorships, its ruthless disregard of human rights, and its millions of tortured and dead.[10] As the philosopher William Barrett has noted, "[t]he best argument for freedom is the horror of the world without it,"[11] an argument that has proven irresistible to so many people around the world, as shown by the ultimate collapse of the Soviet empire and the rise of democracies the world over.[12]

---

5. Gordon Wood, The Radicalism of the American Revolution 1–8 (Vintage Book ed. 1993) ("It was the Revolution, more than any other single event, that made America into the most liberal, democratic, and modern nation in the world." id. at 7).

"The noblest ideals of Americans—the commitments to freedom, equality, constitutionalism, and the well-being of ordinary people—came out of the Revolutionary era. The Revolution gave Americans the consciousness that they were a people with a special destiny to lead the world toward liberty.... It was the Revolutionary experience and the ideals and beliefs flowing from it that have held Americans together and made them think of themselves as a single people." Gordon Wood, The Great Republic: A History of the American People, "Framing the Republic 1760–1820" 229 (1977).

6. Alexis de Tocqueville, Democracy in America 3, 479–82 (1835) (Mansfield-Winthrop translation 2000).

7. Gordon Wood, The Radicalism of the American Revolution 365–69 (Vintage Book ed. 1993).

8. See Edmund S. Morgan, The Birth of the Republic 1763–89 155 (Univ. of Chicago paperback rev. ed. 1977).

9. R.M. MacIver, The Web of Government 132 (Free Press rev. ed. 1965).

10. It has been estimated that Communist regimes in the twentieth century—principally the Soviet Union and China—have caused the death of nearly 100 million civilians through horrific human rights abuses. Stephane Courtois, The Black Book of Communism, "Introduction: the Crimes of Communism" 4 (1999). Similarly, the Nazi regime in Germany in the 1930s and 1940s executed a ghastly policy of genocide against European Jews killing an estimated 5,933,900 people. Lucy S. Dawidowicz, The War Against the Jews 1933–1945 403 (1975).

11. William Barrett, The Illusion of Technique 325 (Anchor Books ed. 1979).

12. Joseph Ellis, The Founding Brothers 4 (2000) ("The republican experiment launched so boldly by the revolutionary generation in America encountered entrenched opposition in the two centuries that followed, but it thoroughly vanquished the monarchical dynasties of the nineteenth century and then the totalitarian despotisms of the twentieth, just as Jefferson predicted it would.").

The right of the people to be free from unreasonable searches and seizures guaranteed by the Fourth Amendment ranks as one of the great freedoms established by the American Bill of Rights. It is surely indispensable to a free society. Although the right of free speech under the First Amendment may constitute the cornerstone of a free society, this freedom would be greatly diminished if there was no guaranteed zone of privacy, such as the home, for a person to retreat to and speak openly, free of arbitrary governmental intrusion and retribution. The Fourth Amendment guarantees precisely this kind of privacy.

It prohibits warrantless, non-consensual, electronic surveillance by the government of people's conversations in their homes, as well as the ominous knock on the door as a prelude to arbitrary search and arrest that has so terrorized millions of people in the twentieth century. In Judge Jerome Frank's words, the privacy of the home is "a sizeable hunk of liberty worth protecting from encroachment," as "[a] sane, decent, civilized society must provide some such oasis, some shelter from public scrutiny, some insulated enclosure, some enclave, some inviolate place which is a [person's] castle."[13] Surely, it is in the home—more than any other place on earth—where a person can withdraw to find solace in an often frantic world, to experience "the sweetness of companionship and the joy of understanding hearts,"[14] and most important, to express one's true self.[15]

Although a deep commitment to individual liberty and a strong aversion to governmental power remain an indelible part of the American Creed, thc "felt necessities of the times" have forced Americans in the twentieth century, at times reluctantly, to accept a greater role for the government, federal and state, in order to deal with the pervasive problem of crime. Electronic searches of air travelers as they board commercial air flights have become commonplace to protect against aircraft hijacking. The same type of electronic searches have been accepted as people enter certain public buildings, such as courthouses, to protect against armed attacks. Court-ordered wiretapping and electronic eavesdropping have been accepted to crack down on organized crime and terrorism. A limited degree of blanket drug testing has been accepted to combat drug use by minors and by people in sensitive public positions. Similarly, unobtrusive vehicle checkpoints to prevent drunk driving and promote highway safety have general public support. And wider search and seizure powers accorded to law enforcement authorities to deal with street crime, illegal drug traffic, and terrorism enjoy wide-spread public acceptance.

Still, Americans generally—whether Democrat, Republican, independent, liberal, conservative, moderate, libertarian or non-political—have long been nineteenth-century Jeffersonian liberals at heart in that they are anti-statist and individualistic.[16] To be sure, there have been sharp disagreements among Americans on law-and-order issues over the years, with American "liberals" generally favoring the individual and American "conservatives" generally favoring the government. Indeed, in 1968, President Richard Nixon made the "liberal" U.S. Supreme Court largely appointed by Democratic presidents

13. Quoted in Silverman v. United States, 365 U.S. 505, 511 n.4, 81 S.Ct. 679, 5 L.Ed.2d 734 (1961).

14. Reinhold Niebuhr, The Essential Reinhold Niebuhr 73 (1986).

15. "The Fourth Amendment protects '[t]he right of the people to be secure in their ... houses, and it is beyond dispute that the home is entitled to special protection as the center of the private lives of our people." Minnesota v. Carter, 525 U.S. 83, 119 S.Ct. 469, 142 L.Ed.2d 373, 386 (1998) (Kennedy, J. concurring), quoted with approval in Georgia v. Randolph, 547 U.S. 103, 126 S.Ct. 1515, 1523, 164 L.Ed.2d 208 (2006).

16. Seymour Lipset, American Exceptionalism 20, 31 (1996).

a campaign issue. And upon his election, he appointed a series of "conservative" U.S. Supreme Court Justices who proceeded to cut back on many of the "liberal" Warren Court criminal justice decisions.[17]

In recent years, however, this general alignment in the law-and-order debate has become somewhat blurred, with the "liberal" Democratic party becoming more sympathetic to the government, and the "conservative" Republican party becoming more attuned to the individual. This is seen, for example, in the debate on gun control, and the crackdown on abortion clinic bombings and right-wing terrorist groups. Moreover, the controversies over the Waco assault, the Ruby Ridge shooting, and the Elian Gonzalez Miami home invasion further illustrate this remarkable shift in position—with liberals generally defending the use of governmental search and seizure power, and conservatives generally condemning the use of such power.

Beyond that, there is the strange emergence of the economically conservative Libertarians as a third party movement that fiercely opposes all forms of governmental interference in people's lives, including law enforcement authority, particularly the federal government's "war on drugs." In this respect, they resemble the liberal-leaning American Civil Liberties Union which has a long record of defending individual rights in court against unduly intrusive law enforcement activity.

The attack on the World Trade Center and the Pentagon in 2001, however, seemed to have temporarily united both liberals and conservatives alike against the threat of domestic terrorism with the subsequent passage in Congress [almost unanimously] of the hard-line USA Patriot Act. Even there, a debate is slowly beginning to emerge that returns us, in part, to older alignments—with some liberal constituencies opposing certain provisions of the Act as draconian, and traditional conservative constituencies generally defending the Act as proper and necessary.

Of course, a cynic might suggest that it all depends on whose ox is gored when a Fourth Amendment freedom is proclaimed. If search and seizure power is directed against the urban poor and powerless minorities to stamp out illegal drug use or street crime, it is usually the liberal constituencies who protest and speak glowingly of Fourth Amendment freedoms. Conservative constituencies, on the other hand, usually approve such police action, warning of a breakdown in "law and order" and the "shackling of the police" if the civil libertarians prevail. On the other hand, if this power is being directed against large corporate interests to enforce tax, business regulation, environmental or gun control laws, it is usually the conservative constituencies who denounce such governmental interference and invoke Fourth Amendment rights. Liberal constituencies, on the other hand, generally applaud the use of such governmental power.

It is only when the country itself is attacked, as it was on September 11, 2001, that these constituencies seem to unite, if only temporarily, to empower the government to hunt down America's enemies until the threat is over or subsides. Admittedly, there is an uncomfortable degree of truth in all of this. Perhaps pragmatic self-interest guarantees, if nothing else, that Fourth Amendment freedoms will survive and flourish.

More to the point, however, is the often-unrecognized truth that freedom is indivisible in a democratic society where the rule of law governs: when the freedom of one person

17. "During the 1960s, the Warren Court emphasized protection of citizens from unwarranted governmental intrusion. More recently, during the 'war on drugs,' the Burger and Rehnquist courts have favored aggressive law enforcement." Thomas Y. Davies, The Oxford Companion to American Law 719 (Kermit L. Hall ed. 2002).

is violated, the freedom of all is diminished. A haunting passage attributed to Pastor Martin Niemoller makes this point chillingly clear. As a Lutheran minister in Nazi Germany in the 1930s, Niemoller witnessed the gradual breakdown of democratic freedoms in that country and was eventually arrested by the Gestapo and taken to Dachau concentration camp. He reportedly described this ghastly era in these stark terms:

> In Germany, they came first for the Communists, and I didn't speak up because I wasn't a Communist. Then they came for the Jews, and I did not speak up because I wasn't a Jew. Then they came for the trade unionists, and I didn't speak up because I wasn't a trade unionist. Then they came for the Catholics, and I didn't speak up because I was a Protestant. Then they came for me, and by that time no one was left to speak up.[18]

University of Pennsylvania historian Thomas Childers draws a similar lesson from the devastation left by the Nazi Third Reich:

> Be vigilant about your rights. Care about the rights and fundamental human dignity of others. When the rights of any group, no matter how small or how marginal, are violated, your liberty is put at risk.... Forewarned, let us hope, is indeed forearmed.[19]

Nonetheless, whether based on pure idealism or self-interest or encrusted political sympathies or a mixture of some or all the above, it remains true that the American people as a matter of principle have generally distrusted the concentration of governmental power, clung to a belief in limited government, and passionately prized their individual freedom as part of the American Creed.[20] Justice Robert Jackson, who was America's chief prosecutor at the Nuremberg War Crimes trial in 1946, speaks to this great heritage in his eloquent and oft-quoted tribute to Fourth Amendment freedoms:

> These, I protest, are not mere second class rights but belong in the catalog of indispensable freedoms. Among deprivations of rights, none is so effective in cowing a population, crushing the spirit of the individual and putting terror in every heart. Uncontrolled search and seizure is one of the first and most effective weapons in the arsenal of every arbitrary government. And one need only briefly to have dwelt and worked among a people possessed of many admirable qualities but deprived of these rights to know that the human personality deteriorates and dignity and self reliance disappear where homes, persons, and possessions are subject at any hour to unheralded search and seizure by the police.[21]

Still, one should not be carried away in a utopian civil libertarian dream. Merely because a Fourth Amendment claim is made in a given case does not mean that the claim must be accepted, else the cause of liberty will be dishonored. Surely, Fourth Amendment

---

18. Bartlett's Familiar Quotations 684 (16th ed. 1992). Niemoller made this famous statement, apparently in various forms, at the end of speeches he gave during a tour of the United States just after World War II. Franklin H. Little, Exile in the Fatherland vii–viii Forward (1985) (slightly different version quoted).

19. Thomas Childers, "A History of Hitler's Empire," Lecture 8 (The Teaching Co. 1995).

20. The theologian Reinhold Niebuhr summarizes this part of the American Creed in a single aphorism: "Man's capacity for justice makes democracy possible; but man's inclination to injustice makes democracy necessary." Reinhold Niebuhr, The Children of Light and the Children of Darkness xiii (1960).

21. Brinegar v. United States, 338 U.S. 160, 180–81, 69 S.Ct. 1302, 93 L.Ed.2d 1879 (1949) (Jackson, J. dissenting).

freedoms would become trivial, lose all public respect and ultimately collapse if virtually any such claim, no matter how dubious, were accepted and made a part of our law. All freedom presupposes the existence of an ordered society in which that freedom can flourish; indeed, this country could use a healthy dose of communitarian values to offset an often exaggerated commitment to rampant individualism. It therefore follows that legitimate governmental interests in enforcing federal and state criminal law has long been, and should continue to be, an important consideration by the U.S. Supreme Court in determining the limit of Fourth Amendment freedoms. Indeed, under this Amendment, the people are protected from *unreasonable* governmental searches and seizures, not *all* governmental searches and seizures.

On the other hand, one should not be carried away on a righteous moral crusade to enforce our criminal law at virtually any cost—whether against street felons, drug traffickers, white collar offenders, or terrorists. Merely because a Fourth Amendment claim, if accepted, will free a criminal wrongdoer and make it more difficult to enforce our criminal law in the future, does not mean that the claim should be rejected, else an ordered or just society will be endangered. Indeed, "there is nothing new in the realization that the Constitution sometimes insulates the criminality of the few in order to protect the privacy of us all."[22] Stalin, Hitler and Mao maintained a rigidly ordered society in pursuit of perceived governmental interests, but at a terrible human rights cost. Surely, no thoughtful American wants such a result here.[23] To the contrary, as the political scientist Herbert Muller has stated, "[t]here has seldom been too much freedom for too many individuals, nor is such freedom the great menace today," and that "given all the political and cultural pressures for conformity even in the advanced democracies, the final stress should be on the claims of the individual, the ideal of freedom to think and act for oneself."[24] It has therefore been the U.S. Supreme Court's interpretive task to define in a given case what constitutes an *unreasonable* search or seizure under the Fourth Amendment, as opposed to a *reasonable* one, so as to maintain the delicate balance between freedom and order that the American revolutionary generation called liberty.

Section 2. Basic Principles and Organizational Structure of Fourth Amendment Law

The Fourth Amendment is the primary source of search and seizure law in this country. It contains fifty-four words, has two clauses and provides as follows:

---

22. Arizona v. Hicks, 480 U.S. 321, 107 S.Ct. 1149, 94 L.Ed.2d 347, 357 (1987).

23. Admittedly, the current terrorist danger presents a temptation to start down the totalitarian road. But Richard Clarke, the top counter terrorist official in the Clinton and Bush II administrations, has cautioned:

"We must also defend the Constitution against those who would use the terrorist threat to assault the liberties the Constitution enshrines. Those liberties are under assault and, if there is another major, successful terrorist attack in this country there will be further assaults on our rights and civil liberties. Thus it is essential that we prevent further attacks and that we protect the Constitution ... against all enemies."

Richard A. Clarke, Against All Enemies xiii (2004).

24. Herbert Muller, The Uses of the Past 73 (Mentor Book ed. 1952).

> The right of the people to be secure in their persons, houses, papers and effects against unreasonable searches and seizures shall not be violated; [**search and seizure clause**]
>
> and no warrants shall issue, but upon probable cause, supported by oath or affirmation, and particularly describing the place to be searched, and the persons or things to be seized. [**warrants clause**]

The U.S. Supreme Court, following various theories of constitutional construction, has built a large and complicated body of constitutional law on this Amendment. In order to fully understand this complex subject, however, it is essential at the outset to review some basic principles of Fourth Amendment law, and to examine, as well, the organizational structure of this body of law.

a. Applicability of the Fourth Amendment to searches and seizures conducted by federal and state officials

It is well settled that the Fourth Amendment, as part of the original Bill of Rights, applies to the federal government—that is, to the actions of any agent of the federal government.[25] The Fourth Amendment also applies to the states—that is, to any agent of the state, county or municipal government—through the Due Process Clause of the Fourteenth Amendment.[26] Federal constitutional standards under the Fourth Amendment, as established by the U.S. Supreme Court, govern in determining whether not only federal, but also state or local officials have complied with the Fourth Amendment.[27] Accordingly, when interpreting the Fourth Amendment, state courts, like lower federal courts, are bound to follow U.S. Supreme Court opinions interpreting the Fourth Amendment—and cannot interpret the Fourth Amendment inconsistent with Fourth Amendment federal standards, even when that interpretation is more restrictive on police activity and gives the individual greater constitutional protection.[28]

---

25. Weeks v. United States, 232 U.S. 383, 391–92, 34 S.Ct. 341, 58 L.Ed. 652 (1914); Bivens v. Six Unknown Named Agents of the Bureau of Narcotics, 403 U.S. 388, 392, 91 S.Ct. 1999, 29 L.Ed.2d 619 (1971); see Barron v. Baltimore, 32 U.S. (7 Peters) 243, 8 L.Ed. 672 (1833).

26. Mapp v. Ohio, 367 U.S. 643, 655, 81 S.Ct. 1684, 6 L.Ed.2d 1081 (1961); Wolf v. Colorado, 338 U.S. 25, 27–28, 69 S.Ct. 1359, 93 L.Ed.2d 1782 (1949); Stanford v. Texas, 379 U.S. 476, 481, 85 S.Ct. 506, 13 L.Ed.2d 431 (1965).

27. "We reiterate that the reasonableness of a search is in the first instance a substantive determination to be made by the trial court from the facts and circumstances of the case and in the light of the 'fundamental criteria' laid down by the Fourth Amendment and in opinions of this Court applying that Amendment. Findings of reasonableness, of course, are respected only insofar as consistent with federal constitutional guarantees. * * * The States are not thereby precluded from developing workable rules governing arrests, searches and seizures to meet 'the practical demands of effective criminal investigation and law enforcement' in the States, provided those rules do not violate the constitutional proscription of unreasonable searches and seizures and the concomitant command that evidence so seized is inadmissible against one who has standing to complain." Ker v. California, 374 U.S. 23, 33–34, 83 S.Ct. 1623, 10 L.Ed.2d 726 (1963); see Oregon v. Hass, 420 U.S. 714, 719, 95 S.Ct. 1215, 43 L.Ed.2d 570 (1975).

28. "[A] state may not impose greater restrictions [on police activity] as a matter of federal constitutional law when this Court specifically refrains from imposing them." Oregon v. Hass, 420 U.S. 714, 719, 95 S.Ct. 1215, 43 L.Ed.2d 570, 576 (1975), rejecting as "not the law" the following pronouncement of the Oregon Supreme Court: "[W]e can interpret the Fourth Amendment more restrictively than interpreted by the United States Supreme Court." 420 U.S. at 720 n. 4, 43 L.Ed.2d

But when the state courts are not interpreting the Fourth Amendment, and instead are interpreting their own state constitutional guarantee on search and seizure or their own state statutes or procedural rules on search and seizure, a slightly different rule prevails. Accordingly, a state court may *not* interpret its own constitution and laws to give the individual *fewer* rights than those guaranteed by the Fourth Amendment, as a contrary rule would allow the states to undermine guaranteed Fourth Amendment freedoms.[29] But, in a bow to federalism, a state court is privileged to interpret its own constitution and laws to give the individual *greater* rights than those guaranteed by the Fourth Amendment, as interpreted by the U.S. Supreme Court.[30]

Given its pervasive applicability to all governmental activity in the country, it is clear that the Fourth Amendment sets the *minimum* standard for searches and seizures conducted by agents of all American governmental entities—federal, state and local.

b. Two broad requirements of substantive Fourth Amendment law

In interpreting the Fourth Amendment, the U.S. Supreme Court has developed two broad requirements that must be met before it can be successfully claimed that a person's Fourth Amendment rights have been violated. Both requirements are separate and distinct and both must be shown before a Fourth Amendment violation is established.

The first Fourth Amendment requirement is a threshold "Standing Requirement"—that is, in the language of the Fourth Amendment, the party complaining must show that a"search[] [or] seizure[]" of his or her "person[], house[], papers [or] effects" has been conducted by an agent of the government.[31] The term "standing" is used here in a Fourth

at 576. Arkansas v. Sullivan, 532 U.S. 769, 121 S.Ct. 1876, 149 L.Ed.2d 994 (2001) (follows Oregon v. Hass and reverses the Arkansas Supreme Court for interpreting the Fourth Amendment to give the individual greater protection than prior U.S. Supreme Court precedent interpreting the Fourth Amendment). "State courts, in appropriate cases, are not merely free to—they are bound to—interpret the U.S. Constitution. In doing so, they are not free from the final authority of this Court." Arizona v. Evans, 514 U.S. 1, 115 S.Ct. 1185, 131 L.Ed.2d 34, 43–44 (1995).

29. "New York is, of course, free to develop its own law of search and seizure to meet the needs of local law enforcement [citation omitted], and in the process may call the standards by any names it may choose. It may not, however, authorize police conduct that trenches upon Fourth Amendment rights, regardless of the labels which it attaches to such conduct." Sibron v. New York, 392 U.S. 40, 61, 88 S.Ct. 1889, 20 L.Ed.2d 917 (1968).

30. "Individual States may surely construe their own constitutions as imposing more stringent constraints on police conduct than does the Federal Constitution." California v. Greenwood, 486 U.S. 35, 106 S.Ct. 1809, 100 L.Ed.2d 30, 39 (1988). "Our holding, of course, does not affect the State's power [under state law] to impose higher standards on searches and seizures than required by the Federal Constitution if it chooses to do so." Cooper v. California, 386 U.S. 58, 62, 87 S.Ct. 788, 791, 17 L.Ed.2d 730, 734 (1967). Oregon v. Hass, 420 U.S. 714, 719, n. 4, 95 S.Ct. 1215, 43 L.Ed.2d 570, 575 (1975) approving as "good law" the following pronouncement of the Oregon Supreme Court: "We can ... interpret[] Article 1, § 9 of the Oregon constitutional prohibition of unreasonable searches and seizures as being more restrictive than the Fourth Amendment."

"States can afford more protection to individuals [under their state constitutions] than the Fourth Amendment does but if the state constitution is construed to offer less, the Fourth Amendment serves as a floor. Hence, for state judges, the question is whether the state constitution should be construed to afford more protection to individuals than the Fourth Amendment." Thomas K. Clancy, The Fourth Amendment: Its History and Interpretation 20 at n. 75 (2008) (internal citation omitted).

31. The Fourth Amendment "Standing Requirement" is discussed at Chapters 8–10 of this work in which relevant U.S. Supreme Court cases are collected and analyzed.

Amendment, substantive law context, as it is derived from the language of the Fourth Amendment itself. Although the U.S. Supreme Court has disapproved the use of this term insofar as it designates something other than a constitutionally-based meaning,[32] it is nonetheless helpful as a shorthand reference to describe a separate and distinct branch of substantive Fourth Amendment law.[33]

This "Standing Requirement," in turn, breaks down into three separate elements: (1) it must be shown that the Fourth Amendment rights of *the party complaining* has been invaded, rather than that of a third party;[34] (2) it must be shown that this invasion was conducted by an agent of the government, rather than by a private person with no governmental involvement;[35] and (3) it must be shown that a "search[] [or] seizure[]" of the complaining party's "person[], house [], papers, [or] effects" has taken place.[36] When all three elements of this constitutional requirement are satisfied, the party complaining has the Fourth Amendment "standing" to attack the search or seizure in question as being "unreasonable."

The second Fourth Amendment requirement, which represents the bulk of search and seizure law, is the "Unreasonableness Requirement"—that is, in the language of the Fourth Amendment, the complaining party must show that the search or seizure in question was "unreasonable."[37] The Court generally focuses on the *initial* Fourth Amendment intrusion, whether it be a search or a seizure, and has devised a number of principles and rules in determining whether this intrusion, as well as all subsequent searches and seizures, are reasonable or unreasonable in the Fourth Amendment sense. Seizures are treated differently from searches and generally require a showing of individualized wrongdoing [whether based on probable cause or articulable suspicion] in order to be reasonable, at least when the government is engaged in ordinary criminal investigation. A balancing of the relevant interests in favor of the government, however, is generally required for seizures of the person to be reasonable when the government is engaged in a civil or administrative

32. Rakas v. Illinois, 439 U.S. 128, 139–40, 99 S.Ct. 421, 58 L.Ed.2d 387 (1978) ; see Minnesota v. Carter, 525 U.S. 83, 119 S.Ct. 469, 142 L.Ed.2d 373, 379 (1998) ("Central to our analysis [in Rakas] was the idea that in determining whether a defendant is able to show the violation of his (and not someone else's) Fourth Amendment rights, the 'definition of those rights is more properly placed within the purview of substantive Fourth Amendment law than within that of standing.' ").

33. "In my view, Rakas v. Illinois ... recognized two analytically distinct but 'invariably intertwined' issues of Fourth Amendment jurisprudence. The first is 'whether [a] disputed search or seizure has infringed an interest which the Fourth Amendment was designed to protect.' The second is whether 'the challenged search or seizure violated [that] Fourth Amendment righ[t].'* * * [I] do not read today's decision, or Rakas, as holding it is improper for lower courts to treat these inquiries as distinct components of a Fourth Amendment claim. Indeed, I am convinced that it would invite confusion to hold otherwise." Rawlings v. Kentucky, 448 U.S. 98, 111–12, 100 S.Ct. 2556, 65 L.Ed.2d 633, 646 (1980) (Blackmun, J. concurring) (internal citations to Rakas omitted).

34. The personal standing element of the Fourth Amendment "Standing Requirement" is discussed at Chapter 8, Section 1 of this work in which relevant U.S. Supreme Court cases are collected and analyzed.

35. The governmental action element of the Fourth Amendment "Standing Requirement" is discussed at Chapter 8, Section 2 of this work in which relevant U.S. Supreme Court cases are collected and analyzed.

36. The search or seizure element of the Fourth Amendment "Standing Requirement" is discussed at Chapters 9 and 10 of this work in which relevant U.S. Supreme Court cases are collected and analyzed. Chapter 9, in particular, deals with the "seizure" component of this element; while Chapter 10 deals with the "search" component of this element.

37. The Fourth Amendment "Unreasonableness Requirement" is discussed in detail at Chapters 11–16 of this work in which relevant U.S. Supreme Court cases are collected and analyzed.

endeavor.[38] Searches, on the other hand, generally require a search warrant issued in compliance with the Warrants Clause of the Fourth Amendment in order to be reasonable, subject to a series of criminal and civil or special needs exceptions.[39] The criminal exceptions generally require some showing of individualized criminal wrongdoing, while the civil or special needs exceptions generally require a balancing of the relevant interests in which the scales are tipped in favor of the government.[40]

If the "Standing Requirement" of the Fourth Amendment is not met and there has been no governmental search and seizure of the complaining party's person, house, papers or effects, the Fourth Amendment is *inapplicable* to the challenged activity—no matter how unreasonable or outrageous the methods employed to secure the challenged evidence.[41] If, on the other hand, the "Standing Requirement" is met, but the second "Unreasonableness Requirement" of the Fourth Amendment is *not* met and the challenged search or seizure is a reasonable one, the Fourth Amendment is *satisfied* and no violation of this Amendment has occurred.[42] As Judge Charles Moylan has analyzed it, the first requirement is concerned with the threshold question of whether the Fourth Amendment is *applicable* to the activity challenged by the complaining party; and the second requirement is concerned with whether the Fourth Amendment has been *satisfied,* in the sense that the challenged search or seizure passes a constitutional test of reasonableness.[43]

c. Enforcement of the Fourth Amendment

Given a showing that the Fourth Amendment rights of the party complaining have been violated by an unreasonable governmental search and seizure of the person, house, papers or effects, the U.S. Supreme Court has next considered the issue of how best to redress this Fourth Amendment violation. In the process, the Court has formulated a distinct body of law that is concerned solely with the sanctions to be imposed in the event of a Fourth Amendment violation. Although a civil remedy of damages has been accorded to the victim of the unreasonable search or seizure as against the offending governmental officials,[44] the primary remedy fashioned by the Court has been a judicially-created exclusionary rule of evidence. This rule bars the government from using the fruits of an

---

38. The unreasonableness rules related to seizures of persons and property are discussed at Chapter 12 of this work in which relevant U.S. Supreme Court cases are collected and analyzed.

39. The Fourth Amendment search warrant requirement rule is discussed at Chapter 11, Section 1 of this work. And the unreasonableness rules related to searches conducted with a search warrant are discussed at Chapter 13 of this work. Relevant U.S. Supreme Court cases are collected and analyzed therein.

40. The criminal and civil or special needs exceptions to the Fourth Amendment search warrant requirement rule are analyzed, respectively, at Chapters 14–15 of this work in which relevant U.S. Supreme Court cases are collected and analyzed.

41. There may be, however, a substantive due process violation under the Fourteenth Amendment if the conduct in question is so arbitrary that it "shocks the conscience" and violates the "decencies of civilized conduct." County of Sacramento v. Lewis, 523 U.S. 833, 118 S.Ct. 1708, 140 L.Ed.2d 1043, 1057–58 (1998); Rochin v. California, 342 U.S. 165, 172–73, 72 S.Ct. 205, 96 L.Ed. 183 (1952).

42. See generally Rawlings v. Kentucky, 448 U.S. 98, 111–12, 100 S.Ct. 2556, 2565, 65 L.Ed.2d 633 (1979) (Blackmun, J. concurring).

43. Charles Moylan, "The Fourth Amendment Inapplicable vs. The Fourth Amendment Satisfied: The Neglected Threshold of 'So What,'" 1977 So.Ill.L.J. 75 (1977).

44. The civil remedy fashioned by the U.S. Supreme Court to enforce Fourth Amendment guarantees is discussed at Chapter 17, Section 6g of this work.

unlawful search or seizure at a federal or state criminal trial against the victim of the search or seizure, subject to certain important limitations and exceptions.[45]

Section 3. Growth and Complexity of Fourth Amendment Law

Over 430 cases on the Fourth Amendment were decided by the U.S. Supreme Court from 1791–2014.[46] Only five of these cases were decided prior to 1900,[47] and only 91 were decided in the twentieth century prior to the landmark decision of *Mapp v. Ohio*,[48] which applied the Fourth Amendment exclusionary rule to the states. The balance, over 300 cases or 75% of the total, are post-*Mapp* decisions rendered during the 54-year period 1961–2014.[49] No doubt this trend will continue well into the twenty-first century. As Dean Erwin Griswold has accurately observed:

> For more than a century, this provision [the Fourth Amendment] was a sleeping giant.... Except for the Boyd case, virtually no search and seizure cases were decided by the Supreme Court for the first 110 years of our existence under the Constitution, that is, up to the year 1900.... Except for a few cases arising out of the federal courts, the active history of the Fourth Amendment did not begin until 1961, when the Court decided the case of Mapp v. Ohio.... The result has been—as in so many areas in recent years—a great torrent of litigation.[50]

There are many reasons for the dormancy of Fourth Amendment law during the period 1791–1900, the gradual growth of such law during the period 1900–61, and the virtual explosion of such law since then.

First, Fourth Amendment issues generally arise in a criminal case in which the defendant challenges the legality of an arrest or search by government officials and seeks to suppress any incriminating evidence obtained thereby. In the nineteenth century, the federal courts had little or no criminal statutes to enforce, and, for most of this period, the Supreme

45. The *Weeks-Mapp* exclusionary rule is discussed at Chapter 17 of this work, in which relevant U.S. Supreme Court cases are collected and analyzed.

46. The exact case count is 433 and is current through the end of December 2014. The count, however, includes some older wiretapping, electronic eavesdropping, and search warrant execution cases which have Fourth Amendment implications but technically were decided under federal statutes. All references to Fourth Amendment case counts should be read with this caveat in mind.

47. The two most important cases were: Boyd v. United States, 116 U.S. 616, 29 L.Ed. 746, 6 S.Ct. 524 (1886); In re Jackson, 96 U.S. 727, 24 L.Ed. 877 (1877). The remaining cases were of lesser significance: Murray v. Hoboken Land & Imp. Co., 59 U.S. 272, 18 How. 272, 15 L.Ed. 372 (1855); Ex Parte Burford, 7 U.S. 448, 3 Cranch 448, 2 L.Ed. 495 (1806). There were no Fourth Amendment decisions rendered in the brief period between 1791–1800.

48. 367 U.S. 643, 81 S.Ct. 1684, 6 L.Ed.2d 1081 (1961).

49. In the preface to the first edition of his Fourth Amendment treatise published in 1978, Professor LaFave notes that "[a]t least in the years following the Supreme Court's landmark decision in Mapp v. Ohio in 1961, it is beyond question that the Fourth Amendment has been the subject of more litigation than any other provision of the Bill of Rights." 1 Wayne LaFave, Search and Seizure v (1st ed. 1978). Moreover, in the fifth edition of the same treatise published in 2012, Professor LaFave comments that the flow of Fourth Amendment decisions "has in no sense diminished over the past thirty-four years." 1 Wayne LaFave, Search and Seizure: v (5th ed. 2012).

50. Erwin Griswold, Search and Seizure: A Dilemma of the Supreme Court 2, 7 (1975).

Court had no right to hear criminal appeals from the few federal criminal convictions that were returned.[51] Not surprisingly, then, there were only five Fourth Amendment decisions in the nineteenth century, and only two of these were criminal cases.[52] Moreover, the Fourth Amendment applied only to the federal government at that time and was not held applicable to the states where most criminal cases were heard.

Second, beginning at the end of the nineteenth century and continuing at an increasing pace ever since, Congress has passed a long line of federal criminal statutes, including contraband drug and alcohol statutes. As a result, a number of federal criminal cases involving Fourth Amendment issues have reached the Supreme Court in the twentieth century.[53] In the 1914 case of *Weeks v. United States,*[54] a unanimous Court announced an exclusionary rule of evidence, so that thereafter a federal criminal defendant could successfully move to suppress at trial any evidence seized by federal officials in violation of the defendant's Fourth Amendment rights. The *Weeks* decision, plus the expansion of federal criminal cases reviewable in the Supreme Court, account for the steady rise in Fourth Amendment decisions from 1900–61. Still, the *Weeks* exclusionary rule applied only to the federal government and, as a result, the number of Fourth Amendment decisions rendered by the Supreme Court was limited to 91 for the period 1900–61.

Finally, the U.S. Supreme Court in the criminal law revolution of the 1960s decided three cases of great significance that largely account for the explosion of Fourth Amendment decisions in the latter half of the twentieth century. In 1961, the Court decided *Mapp v. Ohio*[55] which held that the *Weeks* exclusionary rule of evidence applied to the states under the Fourteenth Amendment, so that a state criminal defendant could thereafter move to suppress at trial any evidence seized by state or federal officials in violation of the defendant's Fourth Amendment rights.[56] In 1963, the Court decided *Gideon v. Wainwright*[57] and *Douglas v. California*[58] which held that an indigent criminal defendant was entitled to the appointment of counsel in a state felony case, both at trial and on appeal. The net effect of these decisions was profound, as (a) Fourth Amendment issues could now be raised in the state courts where most criminal cases are tried, and (b) every defendant was guaranteed counsel to raise these issues at trial and potentially appeal their cases to the

51. J. Landynski at 49 (1966). The right to appeal to the Supreme Court was not granted by statute until 1891. Id. "It is not surprising to find that during the [nineteenth] century following the adoption of the Federal Constitution and its first ten amendments, only a few cases involving interpretation of the Fourth Amendment reached the Supreme Court. During this period, the limited criminal jurisdiction of the Federal Government was not exercised by Congress except in minor instances." N. Lasson at 106 (1937).

52. See cases collected at footnote 46. The two criminal cases were habeas corpus matters: Ex Parte Burford, 7 U.S. 448, 3 Cranch 448, 2 L.Ed. 495 (1806); In re Jackson, 96 U.S. 727, 24 L.Ed. 877 (1877).

53. "But finally, with the extension of the criminal jurisdiction of the United States over such matters as the sale of narcotics and intoxicating liquors, the Fourth Amendment became one of the most prominent and litigated provisions of the Bill of Rights." N. Lasson at 106 (1937).

54. 232 U.S. 383, 34 S.Ct. 341, 58 L.Ed. 652 (1914).

55. 367 U.S. 643, 81 S.Ct.1684, 6 L.Ed.2d 1081 (1961).

56. The Court in Wolf v. Colorado, 338 U.S. 25, 69 S.Ct. 1359, 93 L.Ed. 1782 (1949), held that the right of privacy, the core of the Fourth Amendment protection, was applicable to the states under the Fourteenth Amendment, but not the exclusionary rule of evidence. Mapp, however, overruled Wolf and applied the Fourth Amendment in its entirety to the states, including the exclusionary rule of evidence.

57. 372 U.S. 335, 83 S.Ct. 792, 9 L.Ed.2d 799 (1963).

58. 372 U.S. 353, 83 S.Ct. 814, 9 L.Ed.2d 811 (1963).

Supreme Court. As a result, over 300 Fourth Amendment cases have been decided by the Supreme Court during the period 1961–2014, many involving state criminal cases in which the defendant was represented by appointed counsel.

As might be expected, lower federal court and state court decisions on search and seizure have experienced a similar growth pattern over the past two centuries for much the same reasons—although the sheer number of these cases is staggering when compared to the favored few that have reached the Supreme Court. Prior to 1900, only a scattering of lower federal court and state court decisions were rendered on the subject of search and seizure.[59] Since then, however, the search and seizure cases have steadily increased, with a virtual avalanche of such decisions having been rendered after 1961.[60] The steady increase in criminal cases, the growth in state constitution exclusionary rules, the national extension of the exclusionary rule in *Mapp*, and the guarantee of counsel in *Gideon* and *Douglas*—all account for this twentieth-century growth pattern.

Given the gradual increase in Fourth Amendment cases from 1900–61 and the enormous expansion in such cases since 1961, it is not surprising that Fourth Amendment jurisprudence is often complicated and at times difficult to understand. The commentators, individual Supreme Court Justices, and even the Court itself have, on occasion, commented on the complex and often confusing nature of this body of law.[61] Professor Wayne LaFave's standard treatise on the subject comprises six volumes covering a widely divergent set of Fourth

---

59. Sixteen lower federal court cases and 123 state court cases were decided prior to 1900 on the subject of search and seizure. Many of the state court decisions interpret state constitutional provisions on search and seizure. 43 Am. Decennial Digest 1658–1896 "Searches and Seizures" 2803–2816 (1903); First Decennial Digest 1897–1906 "Searches and Seizures" 30–36 (1910).

60. The search and seizure cases decided by the lower federal courts and state courts from 1900–2010 are collected in 15 decennial digests under three main topics: (1) arrest, (2) searches and seizures, and (3) criminal law § 394. First-Twelfth [part 2] Decennial Digests (1897–2010). There are also a large number of General Digest volumes covering these same topics beginning in 2010, which will continue until the Eleventh Decennial Digest [part 3] is published covering 2010–13.

There is no way to determine accurately the total number of these lower court search and seizure cases short of conducting a tedious hand count through each page of the above digests—which may vary from 10–20 case entries per page, with a single case often appearing several times under different key numbers. But a digest page count alone tends to demonstrate the gradual increase of lower court search and seizure cases from 1900–61, and the literal explosion of such cases since the Mapp case was decided in 1961. Under the three search and seizure topics stated above, there are 692 such pages in the six decennial digests between 1897–1956—and an astounding 11,883 pages in the nine decennial digests between 1956–2010, with the vast majority of those pages devoted to cases decided since 1961.

61. *Commentators*: See, e.g., 1 John Wesley Hall, Search and Seizure § 1.1 at 3 at 1.01 (5th ed. 2013) ("Nowhere in the law have so few words [as contained in the Fourth Amendment] generated so much litigation and confusion."); Thomas K. Clancy, The Fourth Amendment: Its History and Interpretation xix (2008) ("[T]he [Fourth] Amendment is the most commonly implicated and litigated part of our Constitution."); Anthony Amsterdam, "Perspectives on the Fourth Amendment," 58 Minn. L.Rev. 349 (1974); Lloyd Weinreb, "Generalities of the Fourth Amendment," 42 U.Chi.L.Rev. 47, 49 (1974); Ronald Bacigal, "The Fourth Amendment in Flux: the Rise and Fall of Probable Cause," 1979 U.Ill.L.Forum 763; Wayne LaFave, "Fourth Amendment Vagaries (Of Improbable Cause, Imperceptible Plain View, Notorious Privacy, and Balancing Askew)" 74 J.Crim.L.& Criminology 1171 (1983); Craig Bradley, "Two Models of the Fourth Amendment," 83 Mich.L.Rev. 1468 (1985). *Supreme Court Justices*: Robbins v. California, 453 U.S. 420, 430, 101 S.Ct. 2841, 69 L.Ed.2d 744 (1981) (Powell, J. concurring); Coolidge v. New Hampshire, 403 U.S. 443, 490, 91 S.Ct. 2022, 29 L.Ed.2d 564 (1971) (Harlan, J. concurring); Chimel v. California, 395 U.S. 752, 770, 89 S.Ct. 2034, 23 L.Ed.2d 685 (1969) (White, J. dissenting); Davis v. Mississippi, 394 U.S. 721, 728, 89 S.Ct. 1394, 22 L.Ed.2d 676 (1969) (Black, J. dissenting); Elkins v. United States, 364 U.S. 206, 238–39, 80 S.Ct. 1437, 4 L.Ed.2d 1669 (1960) (Frankfurter J. dissenting). *Supreme Court*: Arkansas v. Sanders, 442 U.S. 753, 757, 99 S.Ct. 2586, 61 L.Ed.2d 235 (1979); Cady v. Dombroski, 413 U.S. 433, 714, 93 S.Ct. 2523, 37 L.Ed.2d 706 (1973).

Amendment subtopics and a large number of decisions rendered by the U.S. Supreme Court, the lower federal courts and the state courts.[62] John Wesley Hall's work on the same subject comprises two volumes covering an equally diverse set of topics.[63] Thomas K. Clancy's one-volume Fourth Amendment work is more concise, but also covers a broad range of topics and cases.[64] Still, there is a good deal of predictability and clarity to many aspects of the subject, and much of its doctrinal basis seems firmly rooted in the historical background and principles that led to the adoption of the Fourth Amendment.

Section 4. Other Sources of Search and Seizure Law

Although the Fourth Amendment is the primary source of search and seizure law in this country, there are other secondary sources for such law that should be briefly mentioned. This work does not examine these secondary sources in any detail, but occasional reference will be made to them when necessary to supplement fundamental Fourth Amendment doctrine and law.

a. State constitutions

One of the more important secondary sources of search and seizure law is the constitutional guarantees against unreasonable searches and seizures that are found in the state constitutions of the 50 states. The overwhelming majority of these state constitutional provisions were modeled after the Fourth Amendment, although a few actually predate the Fourth Amendment and influenced its adoption.[65]

The states are permitted, as a matter of federal constitutional law, to interpret their own constitutional provisions and statutes as to impose *more restrictive* standards on state police activity in conducting searches and seizures than that required by the Fourth Amendment as interpreted by the U.S. Supreme Court,[66] and some states have done so

62. 1–6 Wayne LaFave, Search and Seizure (5th ed. 2012).

63. 1–2 John Wesley Hall, Search and Seizure (5th ed. 2013).

64. Thomas K. Clancy, The Fourth Amendment: Its History and Interpretation (2008).

65. In a separate 1947 opinion, Justice Frankfurter collected all 48 of the state constitutional provisions on search and seizure as they originally appeared in their respective state constitutions. Harris v. United States, 331 U.S. 145, 161 n. 5, 91 L.Ed. 1399, 67 S.Ct. 1098 (1947) (Frankfurter, J. dissenting). When Alaska and Hawaii were later admitted to the Union in 1959 as the forty-ninth and fiftieth states, their state constitutions also contained search and seizure guarantees similar to the Fourth Amendment. Art. I, Sec. 14, Alas.Const. (1959); Art. I, Sec. 5, Haw.Const.(1959).

66. "Individual States may surely construe their own constitutions as imposing more stringent constraints on police conduct than does the Federal Constitution." California v. Greenwood, 486 U.S. 35, 106 S.Ct. 1809, 100 L.Ed.2d 30, 39 (1988). "Our holding, of course, does not affect the State's power [under state law] to impose higher standards on searches and seizures than required by the Federal Constitution if it chooses to do so." Cooper v. California, 386 U.S. 58, 62, 87 S.Ct. 788, 791, 17 L.Ed.2d 730, 734 (1967). Oregon v. Hass, 420 U.S. 714, 719, n. 4, 95 S.Ct. 1215, 43 L.Ed.2d 570, 575 (1975) approving as "good law" the following pronouncement of the Oregon Supreme Court: "We can ... interpret[] Article 1, § 9 of the Oregon constitutional prohibition of unreasonable searches and seizures as being more restrictive than the Fourth Amendment."

in select cases.[67] The states, however, cannot interpret *the Fourth Amendment* to accomplish this result.[68]

Moreover, Florida has a unique constitutional provision on search and seizure that requires it be interpreted in *conformity* with the Fourth Amendment as interpreted by the U.S. Supreme Court.[69] In any event, no state is privileged to interpret its own constitution and laws so as to authorize police conduct that *abridges* Fourth Amendment rights.[70]

b. Federal and state statutes and rules of procedure

Another important secondary source of search and seizure law is represented by federal and state statutes and rules of procedure. There are a number of federal statutes on the subject of search and seizure, including arrest statutes,[71] search warrant statutes,[72] electronic eavesdropping and wiretap statutes,[73] customs search statutes,[74] and mail search statutes.[75]

---

67. See cases collected at 1 Wayne LaFave, Search and Seizure § 1.5(b) at 206–10 (5th ed. 2012), and 1 John Wesley Hall §§ 11.03–11.17 at 11.7–11.9 (5th ed. 2013).

68. "[A] state may not impose greater restrictions [on police activity] as a matter of federal constitutional law when this Court specifically refrains from imposing them." Oregon v. Hass, 420 U.S. 714, 719, 95 S.Ct. 1215, 43 L.Ed.2d 570, 576 (1975), rejecting as "not the law" the following pronouncement of the Oregon Supreme Court: "[W]e can interpret the Fourth Amendment more restrictively than interpreted by the United States Supreme Court." 420 U.S. at 720 n. 4, 43 L.Ed.2d at 576. "The Arkansas Supreme Court's alternative holding, that it may interpret the United States Constitution to provide greater protection than this Court's own federal constitutional precedents provide, is foreclosed by *Oregon v. Hass* ..." Arkansas v. Sullivan, 532 U.S. 769, 121 S.Ct. 1876, 149 L.Ed.2d 994, 998 (2001) (Arkansas Supreme Court interpretation of the Fourth Amendment to give greater protection to the individual than that afforded by a U.S. Supreme Court decision interpreting the same Amendment is disapproved).

"State courts, in appropriate cases, are not merely free to—they are bound to—interpret the U.S. Constitution. In doing so, they are not free from the final authority of this Court." Arizona v. Evans, 514 U.S. 1, 115 S.Ct. 1185, 131 L.Ed.2d 34, 43–44 (1995).

69. Art. I, Sec. 12, Fla.Const., 25A Fla. Stat.Anno. 471 (1968); see Bernie v. State, 524 So.2d 988 (Fla.1988); State v. Ridenour, 453 So.2d 193 (Fla. 3d DCA 1984).

70. "New York is, of course, free to develop its own law of search and seizure to meet the needs of local law enforcement [citation omitted], and in the process may call the standards by any names it may choose. It may not, however, authorize police conduct that trenches upon Fourth Amendment rights, regardless of the labels which it attaches to such conduct." Sibron v. New York, 392 U.S. 40, 61, 88 S.Ct. 1889, 20 L.Ed.2d 917 (1968). "Our holding, of course, does not affect the State's power [under state law] to impose higher standards on searches and seizures than required by the Federal Constitution if it chooses to do so." Cooper v. California, 386 U.S. 58, 62, 87 S.Ct. 788, 791, 17 L.Ed.2d 730, 734 (1967). Oregon v. Hass, 420 U.S. 714, 719, n. 4, 95 S.Ct. 1215, 43 L.Ed.2d 570, 575 (1975) approving as "good law" the following pronouncement of the Oregon Supreme Court: "We can ... interpret[] Article 1, § 9 of the Oregon constitutional prohibition of unreasonable searches and seizures as being more restrictive than the Fourth Amendment."

"States can afford more protection to individuals [under their state constitutions] than the Fourth Amendment does but if the state constitution is construed to offer less, the Fourth Amendment serves as a floor. Hence, for state judges, the question is whether the state constitution should be construed to afford more protection to individuals than the Fourth Amendment." Thomas K. Clancy, The Fourth Amendment: Its History and Interpretation 20 at n. 75 (2008) (internal citation omitted).

71. 18 U.S.C. §§ 3045, 3047, 3049–50, 3051–53, 3055–56, 3061–63.

72. 18 U.S.C. §§ 3103a, 3105, 3107, 3109.

73. 18 U.S.C. Ch. 119, §§ 2510 et.seq.

74. 19 U.S.C. §§ 1581–1582.

75. 39 U.S.C. §§ 603–605.

In addition Rules 12(b)(3(C)), 41(h) of the Federal Rules of Criminal Procedure provide for a pre-trial motion to suppress evidence obtained through an unreasonable search and seizure.[76] Most states also have arrest statutes,[77] search warrant statutes,[78] and electronic eavesdropping and wiretap statutes;[79] they also have rules of procedure on pre-trial motions to suppress unlawfully seized evidence.[80] These statutes and rules may supplement and give greater rights to the individual than that accorded by the Fourth Amendment, but in no event may such laws abridge Fourth Amendment rights.[81]

Section 5. General Framework for Analyzing a Fourth Amendment Question in a Criminal Case

Most Fourth Amendment questions arise in the context of a criminal case in which the defendant moves to suppress as evidence the fruits of an alleged unreasonable search or seizure. Based on the three-fold organizational structure of Fourth Amendment law as discussed at section 2 above, the following is a framework of analysis for determining whether the motion to suppress is well-founded. In accord with this framework, one should take the following analytic steps.

First, determine whether there is a Fourth Amendment search or a Fourth Amendment seizure in the fact pattern—that is, whether the "Standing Requirement" of Fourth Amendment law has been satisfied.[82] If so, identify all the Fourth Amendment searches and Fourth Amendment seizures involved in the case in *chronological order*, and proceed to the second step below. On the other hand, if there are no Fourth Amendment searches or seizures in the case, the motion to suppress should be denied, as the Fourth Amendment is inapplicable to the case.

Second, focus on the *initial* Fourth Amendment intrusion [whether it be a Fourth Amendment search or a Fourth Amendment seizure], and determine whether this search

76. Fed.R.Crim.P., 12(b)(3)(C), 41(h).

77. See, e.g., Cal. Penal Code, §§ 834–851.5; Fla.Stat.Anno. Ch. 901; Ill.Comp.Stat.Anno. Ch. 725, Art. 5-107; 11A McKinney's Consol. Laws of N.Y. Anno., Criminal Pro. Law, §§ 120.10–120.90, 140.05–140.55; 1A, 1B Tex. Code Anno, Code of Crim.Pro. Chs. 14–15.

78. See, e.g., Cal. Penal Code §§ 1523-42 ; Fla.Stat. Anno. Ch. 933; Ill. Comp. Stat. Anno. Ch. 725, Art. 5-108-3-108-14; 11B McKinney's Consol. Laws of N.Y. Anno., Crim. Pro. Law §§ 690.05–690.55; 1A Tex.Stat.Anno., Code of Crim.Pro.Art. 18.01-18.10..

79. See, e.g., Cal. Penal Code, Ch. 1.5 §§ 630 et. seq.; Fla.Stat. Anno. Ch. 934; Ill.Comp. Stat. Anno. Ch. 725, Art.5-108A–108B; 11A McKinney's Consol. Laws of N.Y. Anno., Crim. Pro. Law §§ 700.05–700.70, 705.00–705.35; 1A Tex.Stat.Anno.,Code of Crim.Pro., Art. 18.20-18.21.

80. See, e.g., Fla.R.Crim.P. 3.190(h), 33 Fla.Stat.Anno., Supp. at 112 (2014).

81. Almeida-Sanchez v. United States, 413 U.S. 266, 272, 93 S.Ct. 2535, 37 L.Ed.2d 596, 602 (1973) (Act of Congress cannot authorize law enforcement conduct that violates a person's Fourth Amendment rights); Sibron v. New York, 392 U.S. 40, 61, 88 S.Ct. 1889, 20 L.Ed.2d 917 (1968) (New York law cannot authorize police conduct that violates a person's Fourth Amendment rights).

82. The "Standing Requirement," in turn, consists of three elements: (1) a personal standing element, (2) a governmental action element, and (3) a search or seizure element. The first two elements are discussed at Chapter 8 of this work. The third element is discussed at Chapters 9 [seizures of persons and property] and 10 [searches of persons and property] of this work. When all three elements are satisfied, a *Fourth Amendment search* or a *Fourth Amendment seizure* has taken place.

or seizure is *reasonable or unreasonable* in the Fourth Amendment sense—that is, whether the "Unreasonableness Requirement" of Fourth Amendment law has been satisfied.[83]

- If *unreasonable*, determine whether the Fourth Amendment exclusionary rule is applicable to the case, which it usually is.[84] If so, the motion to suppress should be granted; if not, the motion to suppress should be denied.
- If *reasonable*, determine whether each of the *successive* Fourth Amendment searches and Fourth Amendment seizures [if any] are *also* reasonable in the Fourth Amendment sense, which is usually the case.[85] If so, the motion to suppress should be denied.
- If, however, *any* of the successive Fourth Amendment searches or Fourth Amendment seizures are *unreasonable* in the Fourth Amendment sense, determine whether the Fourth Amendment exclusionary rule is applicable to the case, which it usually is.[86] If so, the motion to suppress should be granted; if not, the motion to suppress should be denied.

83. The "Unreasonableness Requirement," in turn, consists of (1) a set of rules applicable to Fourth Amendment *seizures* [of persons and property] discussed at Chapter 12 of this work, and (2) a set of rules applicable to Fourth Amendment *searches* [of persons and property] discussed at Chapters 13 [searches with a warrant], 14 and 15 [searches without a warrant]. In addition, Chapter 11 discusses general principles of unreasonableness applicable to both Fourth Amendment searches and Fourth Amendment seizures—and Chapter 16 discusses special "Unreasonableness Requirement" problems also applicable to Fourth Amendment searches and Fourth Amendment seizures.

84. The Fourth Amendment exclusionary rule, in turn, is discussed at Chapter 17 of this work.

85. See footnote 81 for the rules on whether a Fourth Amendment search or a Fourth Amendment seizure is reasonable or unreasonable.

86. The Fourth Amendment exclusionary rule, in turn, is discussed at Chapter 17 of this work.

Part I

Historical Background and Purpose of the Fourth Amendment

Introductory Note

The historical background that led to the adoption of the Fourth Amendment spans a thirty year period of American history (1761–91) and a corresponding eight year period of English history (1762–70). It is truly an inspiring era. Indeed, "[t]he triumph of individual liberty against government power [during this time] is one of history's noblest themes, epitomized by the [American] Bill of Rights."[1] Because this history has played such an important role in Fourth Amendment decision-making by the U.S. Supreme Court, it is important for student and practitioner alike to have a working knowledge of the subject. The reader has two options here.

1. If the reader wishes to study a *detailed* narrative history of the Fourth Amendment, Chapters 2–5 cover this subject. In particular, Chapter 2 deals with the American colonial experience with the general writs of assistance 1761–76. Chapter 3 discusses the English experience involving the general warrants controversy 1762–70. Chapter 4 examines the American state constitutional provisions on search and seizure 1776–84. And Chapter 5 concludes with the adoption of the U.S. Constitution and Bill of Rights [including the Fourth Amendment] 1787–91.

2. On the other hand, if the reader wishes to study an *abbreviated version* of this narrative history that moves directly to the two historical purposes of the Fourth Amendment, Chapter 6 deals with this subject. Of course, the detailed reader is also invited to read Chapter 6, as it links the prior narrative history with the historical purposes of the Fourth Amendment.

---

1. Leonard Levy, Origins of the Bill of Rights 12 (Yale Univ. paperback 2001).

Chapter 2

The American Colonial Experience: General Writs of Assistance Controversy 1761–76

Section 1. Introduction

The American historical experience that led to the adoption of the Fourth Amendment grew largely, although not entirely, out of the efforts of the English government in the period 1761–76 to enforce the highly unpopular trade and navigation acts in the American colonies by the use of general writs of assistance.[2] The trade and navigation acts, passed by the English Parliament largely in the 1760s, imposed a series of import duties on goods imported into the colonies, as a means both of raising revenue and to prevent the colonies from trading outside the British Empire.[3] The general writs of assistance were used in a largely unsuccessful effort to enforce these import duties by ostensibly helping crown officials locate uncustomed goods that had been smuggled into the colonies.

These writs were separately issued by the colonial courts to individual customs officials in the port cities of the American colonies. They empowered these officials to search houses, vessels, warehouses, shops, and all other places for uncustomed goods. This blanket authority lasted for as long as the life of the then-reigning English sovereign, plus six months thereafter, and was not confined to any particular case; the general writ could be used in connection with any and all investigations which a customs official chose to undertake during this time period. No evidentiary showing was required for the issuance of the general writ; no description of the place to be searched and things to be seized was required on the face of the general writ; no return was required to be filed with the court

---

2. See, e.g., Jacob Landynski, "Search and Seizure," The Rights of the Accused 30 (Stuart Nagel ed. 1972); Leonard Levy, Origins of the Bill of Rights 150, 158 (Yale Univ. paperback 2001); Edward Corwin, The Constitution and What it Means Today 301 (Chase and Ducat rev. ed. 1974); Stanford v. Texas, 379 U.S. 476, 482, 85 S.Ct. 506, 13 L.Ed.2d 431 (1965). One Fourth Amendment scholar, however, has questioned this conventional view—contending that the English legal struggle against the general warrant (1762–70), discussed in Chapter 3 of this work, was the primary impetus that led to the Fourth Amendment. Akhil Amar, "The Fourth Amendment, Boston and the Writs of Assistance," 30 Suffolk L.Rev. 53, 76–80 (1996); Akhil Amar, The Bill of Rights, ch. 4 "Searches Seizures, and Takings" 66 at * fn. (1998).

3. Chief among these acts were the Sugar Act of 1764 and the Townshend Act of 1767. There were also other acts that pre-dated the 1760s, including the Molasses Act of 1733. Richard Morris, The American Revolution: A Short History 15–17, 26–27 (1955); Samuel Morison, The Oxford History of the American People 182–83, 189–94 (1965).

issuing the general writ itemizing the property seized. In sum, the general writs of assistance were warrants in name only because they gave the customs officials general exploratory search powers and were automatically issued as a mere formality to such officials by virtue of their office.[4]

The general writs of assistance were so named because the customs officials to whom they were issued "possessed the legal authority to command the assistance of a peace officer and the assistance, if necessary, of all nearby subjects, in [their] execution of the writ."[5] A sample general writ of assistance used in colonial Massachusetts in the 1760s is included in the appendix to this work.

The import duties imposed by the trade and navigation acts were extremely unpopular in the American colonies, formed the basis for much popular protest and open defiance, and significantly contributed to the movement for independence.[6] The general writs of assistance, which were used to try to enforce these duties, were equally unpopular. They aroused widespread opposition among the colonial bench and bar, the colonial merchants, and the emerging colonial leadership. Indeed, the controversy stirred by the general writs of assistance has been cited as one of the leading causes of the American Revolution.[7]

Section 2. Relevant English Statutes

To understand the legal controversy engendered by the general writs of assistance in the period 1761–76, it is first necessary to examine the relevant English statutes pertaining to such writs. These statutes were enacted by the English Parliament for the express

---

4. Leonard Levy has accurately called the general writ of assistance "a long-term hunting license for customs officers." L. Levy at 227. Cuddihy further states:

"The [general] writ of assistance was among the routine administrative paraphernalia that a customs official received on assuming office. He obtained the writ at about the same time as his commission and in much the same, automatic fashion that modern police officers receive uniforms and badges."

W. Cuddihy at 490–91. For a general discussion of the characteristics of the general writs of assistance, see N. Lasson at 53–55.

5. Leonard Levy, Origins of the Bill of Rights 156 (Yale Univ. paperback 2001).

6. See generally Allan Nevins and Henry Steele Commager, A Pocket History of the United States 61–62 (9th rev. ed. 1992); Brendan McConville, "Revolutionary War," Oxford Companion to United States History 666 (2001).

7. "American histories without exception list writs of assistance as one of the active causes of the American Revolution." O.M. Dickerson at 40. "The right to be taxed only by the representatives of one's choice was the great right whose violation helped cause the [American] Revolution. British attempts to enforce tax measures by general searches also occasioned deeply felt resentments that damaged relations between England and the American colonies and provoked anxious concerns that later sought expression in the Fourth Amendment." Leonard Levy, Origins of the Bill of Rights 150 (Yale Univ. paperback 2001).

"Our cases have recognized that the Fourth Amendment was the founding generation's response to the reviled 'general warrants' and 'writs of assistance' of the colonial era, which allowed British officers to rummage through homes in an unrestrained search for evidence of criminal activity. Opposition to such searches was in fact one of the driving forces behind the Revolution itself." Riley v. California, 574 U.S. ___, 134 S.Ct. 2473, 2494, 189 L.Ed.2d 430 (2014). "The [Fourth] amendment was in large part a reaction to the general warrant and the warrantless searches that had so alienated the colonies and had helped speed the movement for independence." Chimel v. California, 395 U.S. 752, 760–61, 89 S.Ct. 2034, 23 L.Ed.2d 685 (1969). "Historically we are dealing with a provision of the Constitution [the Fourth Amendment] which sought to guard against an abuse that more than any one single factor gave rise to American Independence." Harris v. United States, 331 U.S. 145, 159, 67 S.Ct. 1098, 91 L.Ed. 1399 (1947) (Frankfurter, J. dissenting).

purpose of authorizing the seizure of uncustomed goods located in various places in England and throughout the British Empire.

The first statute on this subject [12 Car.II, c.19, 7 Pickering Statutes At Large 460–61 (1660)] authorized a customs officer to conduct daytime searches of "houses" for uncustomed goods pursuant to a "warrant" issued by "the lord treasurer, or any of his barons of the exchequer or chief magistrate of the port or the place where the offense shall be committed, or the place next adjoining thereto," "upon oath thereof" presented to the official issuing the warrant. It further provided that no house could be entered unless done within one month after the offense suspected had been committed; also civil penalties were provided for as against an informer who gave false information for the issuance of a warrant. In sum, the statute provided for the substance of what we have now come to accept as a specific warrant based on sworn proof of wrongdoing.

The second relevant statute [13 and 14 Car.II, c. 11, 8 Pickering Statutes at Large 78, 80–81 (1662)], passed two years later, empowered a customs official to conduct daytime searches of "any house, shop, cellar, warehouse or room or other place" for uncustomed goods when "authorized by [a] writ of assistance under seal of his majesty's court of exchequer." It also authorized a customs official to board and search "any ship or vessel" for uncustomed goods. The statute, however, did *not* provide that the writ could only issue upon sworn proof of wrongdoing—as did the prior 1660 statute for customs official "warrants" aimed at precisely the same wrongdoing. [12 Car II, c. 19].

The final relevant statutes are also of importance. 1 Anne c. 8, 10 Pickering Statutes at Large 414, 416 (1701), provided that a writ of assistance that was in effect upon the death of an English king or queen continued in full force and effect until six months had elapsed thereafter. 7 and 8 Wm.III, c. 22, 9 Pickering Statutes at Large 428, 431 (1696), extended to American colonial customs officers the same authority held by English customs officers. And in the midst of the general writs controversy in America, 7 Geo.III, c. 46, 27 Pickering Statutes At Large 505, 512 (1766), was passed which empowered the American colonial courts to issue writs of assistance in the colonies.

The bench and bar of the American colonies, including Tory judges who were loyal to the Crown during the American Revolution, almost unanimously took the position that only a *specific*, not a *general* writ of assistance could issue under the 1662 statute. This conclusion was reached by reading the statute *in pari materia* with the 1660 statute, and against a common law background that required *specific* warrants upon sworn proof of wrongdoing in stolen goods cases. Under this view, the writ could only issue upon sworn proof of wrongdoing and had to order the search of specific premises and the seizure of specific goods.

On the other hand, the Crown's customs officials argued that they were entitled, by the literal terms of the 1662 statute and established English legal practice, to a *general* writ from the court, based on no sworn proof of wrongdoing, which would authorize them to search virtually any place in their discretion for uncustomed goods. This disagreement, in turn, led to a series of legal controversies in the American colonial courts beginning with a celebrated Massachusetts case in 1761.

Section 3. 1761 Boston Writs Case

The first legal challenge to the general writs of assistance in the American colonies came in 1761 in Boston, Massachusetts. Prior thereto, the several writs of assistance which had been issued, first by the colonial governor of Massachusetts Bay Province, and later by the Superior Court of the colony, had gone unchallenged.[8] The stage was set for a test case on the general writs, a case as it turned out of historic importance when on October 25, 1760, the reigning English sovereign, King George II, died.[9] Under then existing law and practice, the general writs heretofore granted by the Superior Court of Massachusetts Bay Province expired six months after the death of the king.[10] As such, new general writs of assistance had to be re-issued by March 25, 1761, else their general writ authority would lapse.

a. Petitions to court

The British Crown's customs officers, accordingly, petitioned the Massachusetts Superior Court to re-issue the general writs of assistance and addressed the matter for the court's consideration during the court term beginning the third Tuesday of February, 1761. The primary petition was filed by Thomas Lechmere as Surveyor General of the Crown's customs office for the Northern District of America. The petition was unsworn to, contained no showing that uncustomed goods were located in Boston or elsewhere, was unconnected with any particular case, and simply requested that the "Writs of Assistance may be granted to him and his Officers as usual."[11] Prior thereto, 63 Boston merchants had petitioned the Massachusetts Superior Court to hear arguments against the general writs.[12]

b. James Otis Jr.'s oral argument

The case came on for an oral argument before the Massachusetts Superior Court in February 1761 as requested. Representing the Massachusetts provincial government which sought the issuance of the writs was Jeremiah Gridley, the attorney general of the colony; representing the Boston Merchants were James Otis, Jr., and Oxenbridge Thatcher, both prominent Boston lawyers.[13] Otis, in fact, had resigned his lucrative crown position as advocate general of admiralty in order to avoid representing the government in this controversy.[14] Thomas Hutchinson, the lieutenant governor of the colony, sat as chief justice of the Massachusetts Superior Court; as an aside, he was a merchant and not a lawyer.[15]

---

8. N. Lasson at 55–56; J. Landynski at 31–32; H. Gray at 401–06; W. Cuddihy at 757–61.

9. N. Lasson at 57. According to Cuddihy, Boston did not hear of the king's passing until December 27, 1760. W. Cuddihy at 763, n. 20.

10. 1 Anne stat. 1. C. 8, 10 Pickering Statutes At Large 414–17 (1701); see N. Lasson at 57.

11. H. Gray at 413–14.

12. H.Gray 412–13; Cuddihy at 764.

13. James Otis Jr. (1725–83) was one of the leading political figures in the American colonies in the 1760s. He was a member of the Massachusetts colonial legislature (1761–69), helped organize and was a delegate to the inter-colonial Stamp Act Congress to protest the Stamp Act (1765), and wrote a series of political pamphlets that represented the fundamental political documents in the early part of the revolutionary struggle. Encyclopedia of American History 1097 (7th ed. 1996; Richard and Jeffrey Morris eds); Merriam-Webster's Biographical Dictionary 790 (1995). One of those pamphlets was "The Rights of the British Colonies Asserted and Proved" from which the revolutionary slogan "no taxation without representation" may have been coined. The Debate on the American Revolution 68–69 (Max Beloff 2d ed. 1960) (Otis wrote: "The sum of my argument is ... that no parts of his Majesty's dominions can be taxed without their consent.").

14. J. Landynski at 33; N. Lasson at 57–58.

15. N. Lasson at 56–57; J. Landynski at 33.

Gridley argued that general writs of assistance were legally authorized by 13 and 14 Car.2, c.11 (1662), and that the Massachusetts Superior Court had jurisdiction as a court of the exchequer to issue such writs.[16] Thatcher urged that the Massachusetts Superior Court had no jurisdiction to issue general writs of assistance because it did not possess the powers of the English court of the exchequer.[17] Otis' argument, in turn, sets out the central legal arguments that were later urged by the American bench and bar from 1761–76 against the general writs of assistance.[18] Indeed, it is oft-cited as an authoritative expression of basic Fourth Amendment doctrine.[19]

At the outset of his argument, Otis denounced the general writ of assistance:

> I will to my dying day oppose, with all the powers and faculties God has given me, all such instruments of slavery on the one hand, and villainy on the other, as this writ of assistance is. It appears to me ... the worst instrument of arbitrary power, the most destructive of English liberty, and the fundamental principles of the constitution, that was ever found in an English law-book.[20]

And throughout the argument, he continued his denunciation of the general writ:

> It is a power that places the liberty of every man in the hands of every petty officer.[21]
>
> Now one of the most essential branches of English liberty, is the freedom of one's house. A man's house is his castle; and while he is quiet, he is well-guarded as a prince in his castle. This writ, if it should be declared legal, would totally annihilate this privilege. Customs house officers may enter our houses when they please—we are commanded to permit their entry—their menial servants may enter—may break locks, bars and every thing in their way—and whether they break through malice or revenge, no man, no court may inquire—bare suspicion without oath is sufficient.[22]

---

16. Gridley's argument appears at H. Gray at 479–81, as reprinted in Wroth and Zobel at 136–38. For a discussion of this argument, see W. Cuddihy at 770–73.

17. Thatcher's argument appears at H. Gray at 482, and is reprinted at Wroth and Zobel at 138–39. The argument has no historical importance for Fourth Amendment doctrine purposes but was significant at the time. 7 Geo.III, c.46, 27 Pickering Statutes At Large 505, 512 (1766), passed by the English Parliament subsequent thereto, was designed to answer this argument by specifically authorizing the colonial courts to issue writs of assistance. For a discussion of this argument, see N. Lasson at 61–62 and W. Cuddihy at 773–76.

18. Otis' argument appears in various sources in slightly different forms and are all based on John Adams' original abstract of the argument prepared shortly after the argument from contemporaneously taken notes. The basic text, however, as it appeared in the Massachusetts Spy on April 29, 1773 at p. 3, cols. 1–3, is reprinted at Wroth and Zobel at 139–44, and appears in the appendix of this book. See also Wroth and Zobel at 134, n. 103. Leonard Levy states that Adams' abstract of Otis' argument takes about twenty minutes to read, although Otis' argument itself lasted four or five hours in court. Leonard Levy, Origins of the Bill of Rights 158 (1999). In an era of no shorthand court reporters to transcribe court proceedings, unavoidably much is left out of the Otis argument.

19. See, e.g., Stanford v. Texas, 379 U.S. 476, 481–82, 85 S.Ct. 506, 13 L.Ed.2d 431 (1965); Frank v. Maryland, 359 U.S. 360, 364, 79 S.Ct. 804, 3 L.Ed.2d 877, 881 (1959); Boyd v. United States, 116 U.S. 616, 624–25, 6 S.Ct. 524, 29 L.Ed. 746, 749 (1886); Harris v. United States, 331 U.S. 145, 157–59, 67 S.Ct. 1098, 91 L.Ed. 1399, 1409–1410 (1947) (Frankfurter, J. dissenting). "[A] straight line of progression runs from Otis' argument in 1761 to Adams' framing of Article XIV of the Massachusetts Declaration of Rights to Madison's introduction of the proposal that became the Fourth Amendment." Leonard Levy, Origins of the Bill of Rights 158 (1999).

20. Wroth and Zobel at 139–40.

21. Wroth and Zobel at 141–42.

22. Wroth and Zobel at 142.

> It is the business of this court to demolish this monster of oppression, and tear into rags this remnant of Starchamber tyranny.[23]

Otis argued at length that English law only authorized *special,* not *general,* writs of assistance issued by a court upon sworn proof of wrongdoing directing the search of specific places for smuggled goods which required a filed return with the court after the search.

> ... I will admit, that writs of one kind, may be legal, that is, *special writs, directed to special officers,* and to search *certain* houses &c, especially set forth in the writ, may be granted by the Court of the Exchequer at home, *upon oath made* before the Lord Treasurer by the person, who asks, *that he suspects such goods to be concealed* in THOSE VERY PLACES HE DESIRES TO SEARCH. The Act of 14th Car. II which Mr. Gridley mentions proves this. And in this light the writ appears like a warrant from the justice of the peace to search for stolen goods. Your Honours will find in the old book, concerning the office of justice of the peace, precedents of general warrants to search for stolen goods. But in more modern books you will find only special warrants to search such and such houses specially named, in which the complainant has before sworn he suspects his goods are concealed; and you will find it adjudged that only *special warrants are legal.* In the same manner I rely on it, that the writ prayed for in this petition being general is illegal.... I say I admit that *special* writs of assistance to search *special* houses, may be granted to certain persons under oath; but I deny that the writ now prayed for can be granted.
>
> But these prove no more than what I before observed, that *special* writs may be granted *on oath* and *probable suspicion.* The Act of 7th and 8th of William III. that the officers of the plantations shall have the same powers, &c. is confined in this sense, that an officer should show probable grounds, should take his oath on it, should do this before a magistrate, and that such magistrate, if he thinks proper should issue a *special warrant* to a constable to search the places.[24]

Finally, he argued that to the extent that the 1662 Act of Parliament did authorize a general writ of assistance, the statute was contrary to the constitution and was therefore void[25]—an argument that is one of precursors of the doctrine of judicial review later established in *Marbury v. Madison.*[26]

This specific-warrant view of English law was, at the time, almost universally accepted by the American colonial bench and bar, including Tories who were loyal to the Crown during the American Revolution. As stated by Dickerson:

> The lawyers and judges in the American colonies knew only the practices of the courts of common law. Under such courts, search warrants were issued only on specific information, supported by oath or affirmation, and returnable to the court of issue. There was no other practice known to the law courts in America. * * * American judges had no occasion to study the procedure of the Exchequer Court in England because the customs laws of England did not apply in the colonies. *Consequently, when the American judges and lawyers were confronted*

23. Wroth and Zobel at 144.

24. Wroth and Zobel at 141–142, 144 (emphasis and capital letters in original).

25. "No Acts of Parliament can establish such a writ; Though it should be made in the very words of the petition it would be void, 'AN ACT AGAINST THE CONSTITUTION IS VOID.'" Wroth and Zobel 144 (caps in the original).

26. 1 Cranch (5 U.S.) 137 (1803).

> *with a form for a writ [of assistance] prepared by the customs officers, fundamentally different from the established practices of the courts of common law and apparently in direct conflict with 12 Car. II, c. 19, they could not avoid the conclusion that it was novel and entirely unsupported by law.*[27]

Although Fourth Amendment scholars differ as to whether Otis's argument had a sound basis under English law and practice,[28] the near unanimous American view of English law at the time was that the Otis argument was correct—a view that was later given the force of law by the Fourth Amendment.[29]

Beyond this, it is plain that Otis' argument was not a dry legal affair. To the contrary, it was "one of the most celebrated speeches ever delivered in an American court of law"[30] and no doubt moved many in the courtroom audience.[31] But none was more stirred among the courtroom spectators than John Adams,[32] who was then a young man of 25,[33] just recently admitted to the bar,[34] but later to become one of the principal architects of American independence.[35] As an elder statesman in 1817–18, Adams was to recall Otis' argument in vivid terms as being, in effect, the first shot fired in the American Revolution:

---

27. Dickerson at 47–48. Horace Gray [later a Justice of the U.S. Supreme Court] echoes the reasonableness of this point of view in an early 1865 work on the general writs of assistance:

"As general warrants were not authorized by the common law, Otis argued that the writ of assistance mentioned in St.13 & 14 Car. 2, must be special, according to St. 12 Car. 2. This seems to have been considered at the time of the argument and afterwards the most important point; and upon ordinary rules of interpreting statutes *in pari materia* together, and according to the rule and reason of the common law, the conclusion of Otis seems inevitable."

H. Gray at 531–32.

28. Taylor, Cuddihy and Smith conclude that the 1662 Act of Parliament authorized general writs of assistance and that Otis' contrary argument on this point was wrong. T. Taylor at 35, 37; W. Cuddihy at 385; M.H. Smith at 384–85. Frese takes a contrary view. Frese at 1–2. Landynski states that Otis' view of English law was at least arguable. J. Landynski at 32. Wroth and Zobel state that the intent of Parliament on this issue was unclear. Wroth and Zobel at 108–09.

29. Leonard Levy states that Otis, in urging this view of English law, was really inventing new American search and seizure rights which led directly to the Fourth Amendment. L. Levy at 227–28 (1988). Indeed, "Otis had been among the first to challenge the constitutional authority of Great Britain in language that undercut any and all attempts to exercise arbitrary power; the principle he defended in the Writs of Assistance Case was later enshrined in the [fourth] amendment to the United States Constitution." Joseph Ellis, Passionate Sage 103 (1993).

30. James Thurlow Adams, The Adams Family 21 (1930) (author no relation to John Adams).

31. N. Lasson at 58; J. R. Frese, N.Eng.Q at 496; I Page Smith, John Adams 55–56 (1962); but cf. O.M. Dickerson at 42–43.

32. "Adams ... would remember it [the Otis argument] as one of the inspiring moments of his life, a turning point for him as for history." David McCullough, John Adams 62 (2001). "Adams was stirred in his deepest being, swept by the speaker's power from all mooring of skepticism or hesitation, transfixed by Otis' masterful use of classical quotation, of common law, of history, and of Scripture. It is only given a man to be once so moved, so transported as John Adams was." I Page Smith, John Adams 56 (1962).

33. John Adams was born in Braintree, Massachusetts on October 25, 1735. I Page Smith, John Adams 3 (1962).

34. John Adams was admitted to the bar before the Suffolk County Inferior Court on November 6, 1758 upon the recommendation of Josiah Gridley and other attorneys. L. Kinvin Wroth & Hiller B. Zobel, Legal Papers of John Adams lv (1965). He was then admitted to the Suffolk County Superior Court in November 1761. Id at lviii.; see also David McCollough, John Adams 44 (2001) (stating that Adams was admitted "before the Superior Court at Boston on November 6, 1759.")

35. Richard Morris selects John Adams (1735–1826) as one of the seven most important leaders of the American Revolution. Richard Morris, Seven Who Shaped Our Destiny 72–114 (1973). As a leading member of the Continental Congress, he was on the drafting committee that produced the Declaration of Independence, served as a member of at least ninety Congressional committees, and was the chairman of some twenty-five of these committees; he helped negotiate the Treaty of Paris

> I do say in the most solemn manner, that Mr. Otis' oration against the writs of assistance breathed into this nation the breath of life. * * *
>
> American independence was then and there born: the seeds of patriots and heroes were then and there sown ... Every man of a crowded audience appeared to me to go away, as I did, ready to take arms against writs of assistance. Then and there was the first scene of the first act of opposition to the arbitrary claims of Great Britain. Then and there the child Independence was born. In 15 years, namely in 1776, he grew into manhood, and declared himself free.[36]

As an aside, the U.S. Supreme Court early echoed this assessment by describing Otis's argument "as perhaps the most prominent event which inaugurated the resistance of the colonies to the oppression of the mother country."[37] And more recently, the Court has reaffirmed this view:

> Our cases have recognized that the Fourth Amendment was the founding generation's response to the reviled "general warrants" and "writs of assistance" of the colonial era, which allowed British officers to rummage through homes in an unrestrained search for evidence of criminal activity. Opposition to such searches was in fact one of the driving forces behind the Revolution itself. In 1761, the patriot James Otis delivered a speech denouncing the writs of assistance. A young John Adams was there, and he would later write that "[e]very man of a crowded audience appeared to me to go away, as I did, ready to take arms against writs of assistance." 10 Works of John Adams 247–248 (C Adams ed. 1856). According to Adams, Otis' speech was "the first scene of the first act to the arbitrary claims of Great Britain. Then and there the child Independence was born." *Id.*, at 248 (quoted in Boyd v. United States, 116 U.S. 616, 625 (1886).[38]

Indeed, this evaluation was generally accepted by Adams' contemporaries at the time, as well as many historians today.[39] Without question, "John Adams surely is a competent

---

that ended the Revolutionary War; he was the country's first ambassador to Great Britain; and he served as the second president, as well as the first vice-president, of the United States. "Thomas Jefferson called him 'our colossus' in the independence struggle." John Ferling, "John Adams," The Oxford Companion to United States History 7 (2001).

36. 10 Works of John Adams 276, 247–48 (letters of John Adams to H. Niles January 14, 1818, and John Adams to William Tudor March 29, 1817) (Charles Francis Adams ed. 1856). Much earlier, on the eve of the Declaration of Independence, Adams as a young man similarly recalled the Otis argument—although in more somber language, when the life of the fledgling nation hung in the balance:

"When I look back to the year 1761, and recollect the argument concerning writs of assistance in the superior court, *which I have hitherto considered as the commencement of this controversy between Great Britain and America*, and run through the whole period from that time to this, and recollect the series of political events, the chain of causes and effects, I am surprised at the suddenness as well as the greatness of this revolution."

Henry Steele Commager and Richard Morris, The Spirit of Seventy-Six 321 (Bicentennial ed. 1975) (letter of John Adams to his wife Abigail Adams, July 3, 1776) (emphasis added).

37. Boyd v. United States, 116 U.S. 616, 625, 6 S.Ct. 524, 29 L.Ed. 746 (1886).

38. Riley v. California, 574 U.S. ___, 134, S.Ct. 2473, 2495, 189 L.Ed.2d 430 (2014).

39. "Contemporaries generally accepted it as a fact, and historians agree, that the controversy on this [writs] question which took place in Massachusetts in 1761, the first serious friction between the British custom officers and the colonists, was 'the first in the chain of events which led directly and irresistibly to revolution and independence.'" N. Lasson at 51, quoting from A. Hart, American History Leaflets, No. 33, Introduction (historical sources cited in footnote). "George Bancroft writes that John Adams, Governor Bernard, and Chief Justice Hutchinson all agree, especially the latter in his correspondence, that Otis' argument in the Writs of Assistance Case was the origin of the party of revolution. [citing History of the United States (Boston, 1852) IV, 416 n.]," N. Lasson at 51 n. 1; see

witness on the causes of the American Revolution,"[40] and more than that, its "premier political theorist"[41] whom historians often turn to when studying this issue.[42]

c. Court ruling

At the conclusion of the legal arguments in the case, the court was inclined to deny the general writs, according to Thomas Hutchinson, who was the presiding judge in the case.[43] The court, however, resolved on Hutchinson's advice to reserve ruling and to seek legal instructions from England.[44] Those instructions were later forthcoming and were favorable to the issuance of the general writs.[45] The case was later re-argued in the Mas-

---

Joseph Ellis, American Sphinx 252–53 (1997) (Jefferson in his post-presidential correspondence with Adams agreed that Massachusetts deserved the title of "the cradle of independence," and was not willing to dispute Adams' assessment that Otis was "the first American revolutionary"). "Otis's arguments created a local sensation, prompted popular demonstrations against 'tyranny,' and launched his career as a leader of the opposition in the General Court [the colonial legislature]. Moreover, they redefined politics in Massachusetts by simultaneously giving opposition politicians a cause (the protection of rights), a hero (Otis), and a set of enemies (the customs officers, Bernard and Hutchinson)." Fred Anderson, Crucible of War: The Seven Years War and the Fate of Empire in British North America (1754–1766) 520 (Vintage ed. 2001). "To recapitulate, Otis in his attack on the writs of assistance helped to lay the foundation for the breach between Great Britain and her continental colonies." Lawrence Henry Gipson, The Coming of the Revolution (1763–75) 39 (Harper Torchbook ed. 1962).

Some scholars, however, have questioned Adams' assessment of Otis' argument as exaggerated. John Ferling, Setting the World Ablaze 68–69 (2000); Akhil Amar, The Bill of Rights, ch. 4 "Searches, Seizures and Takings" 66, fn. (1998); Theodore Draper, A Struggle For Power 185–88 (1996); M.H. Smith at 7, 518. Nonetheless, Smith gives "[t]op marks to Adams as publicist for Massachusetts and James Otis, respectively seedbed and begetter of Revolution," M.H. Smith at 518, and further states that "[i]t was in the writs of assistance case in Boston in 1761 that the American tradition of constitutional hostility to general powers of search first found articulate expression.... It was an American original." M.H. Smith at 7. Moreover, "there is no doubt that the speech was remarkable and carried James Otis to a position of radical leadership." Hugh Brogan, The Penguin History of the USA 123 (2d ed. 1999).

40. Harris v. United States, 331 U.S. 145, 159, 67 S.Ct. 1098, 91 L.Ed.2d 1399 (1947) (Frankfurter, J. dissenting).

41. "Just as James Madison established a reputation as 'Father of the Constitution' because of his leading role in the Constitutional Convention of 1787, [John] Adams established his reputation as the premier political theorist of the American Revolution because of his leading role in the Continental Congress." Joseph Ellis, Passionate Sage 47 (1993) (Norton paperback).

42. "Thus, in attempting to explain the causes and meaning of the American Revolution, historians have often turned to [John] Adams because he is considered by many as its most thoughtful spokesman. If Samuel Adams or Patrick Henry represent the spirit of the independence movement, John Adams embodied the mind of the American Revolution." C.Bradley Thompson, John Adams and the Spirit of Liberty xiii (1998) (endnote no. 2 omitted citing evaluations of John Adams by Gilbert Chinard, Vernon Parrington, Harold Laski, Charles Warren, Clinton Rossiter, Joseph Charles, Gordon Wood, Pauline Maier, and J.M. Porter & R.S. Farnell. Id. at 281).

43. H. Gray at 415n (letter from Hutchinson to Secretary Conway October 1, 1765) ("the court seemed inclined to refuse to grant [the writs of assistance.]").

44. H. Gray at 415n (letter from Hutchinson to Secretary Conway October 1, 1765) ("I prevailed with my brethren to continue the cause until the next term, and in the meantime wrote to England, and procured a copy of the writ, and sufficient evidence of the practice of the Exchequer there...."); see also William Tudor, the Life of James Otis of Massachusetts 86 (1823) wherein it is reported that Hutchinson announced from the bench at the conclusion of the arguments that the court "thought it best to continue the question to the next term."

45. N. Lasson at 62–63. Hutchinson, however, wrote to a provincial agent who had once been a crown prosecutor in Massachusetts, rather than Charles Pratt who was then the Attorney General of England. Id.; J. Landynski at 35. Had Hutchinson referred the matter to Pratt, arguably a different result might have obtained because Pratt was later elevated to chief justice and authored decisions

sachusetts Superior Court in November 1761, after which the court entered an order granting the application for the general writs.[46]

On December 2, 1761, the first of the general writs of assistance was issued to Charles Paxton, a Boston customs official.[47] A number of other general writs were thereafter issued to other customs officials in Massachusetts.[48] Chief Justice Thomas Hutchinson's draft of the writ of assistance was used as the pattern for all of these writs, and is included in the Appendix to this work.

The writ ordered all persons to permit a named customs official "[1] by night as by day from time to time to enter and go on board any Ship Boat or other Vessel riding lying or being within or coming to the Port of Boston [or other named port] ... then and there found to search..., and also [2] in the day time to enter and go into the vaults cellars warehouses shops and other places where any prohibited goods wares or merchandizes or any goods wares or merchandizes for which the customs or other duties shall not have been duly and truly satisfied and paid and ... to inspect and oversee and search for the said goods wares and merchandizes ... [3] And we further strictly Injoin and Command you and every one of you that to the said [named customs official] ... from time to time be aiding assisting and helping in the execution of the premises as meet."[49] In sum, the writ granted the named customs official general exploratory search powers based on no proof of wrongdoing, with the authority to enlist the help of others [including local constables] in carrying out these duties. By implication, the writ also gave the customs official the power to *seize* uncustomed goods without describing same, and without requiring the official to file a return with the court after the search was conducted to account for what was seized.

Section 4. Aftermath in Massachusetts of Boston Writs Case

a. Immediate reaction

The case produced a considerable reaction in Boston at the time. Reports of the case appear in the Boston Gazette in November and December 1761 and January and February 1762.[50] John Adams' manuscript notes on Otis' speech were circulated among Adams' friends, and, along with Thatcher's speech, were shipped from colony to colony.[51] Moreover, copies of Otis' speech, which was later reprinted in the Massachusetts Spy in April 1773, were sent to the Connecticut Committee of Correspondence.[52]

---

striking down the general warrant in seditious libel cases. N. Lasson at 43–48, 63; see also Chapter 3, Section 2 of this work.

46. Quincy at 51–57; N. Lasson at 63.

47. H. Gray at 418–21.

48. Frese states that separate writs of assistance were issued to customs agents in Falmouth, Nantucket, and Boston from 1762–65. J.R. Frese at 200–01; see also H. Gray at 422–34 wherein the court papers concerning these writs are reprinted.

49. Wroth and Zobel at 147.

50. J.R. Frese, N.Eng.Q. at 499.

51. J.R. Frese, N.Eng.Q. at 498, 508.

52. J.R. Frese, N.Eng.Q. at 507–08.

On March 6, 1762, the Massachusetts General Court, the colonial legislature, passed a bill that completely nullified the general writs decision and authorized only special writs in accord with Otis' view on the subject.[53] Otis, in fact, was a member of the General Court at the time and undoubtedly participated in the debates which led to the bill. The colonial governor, Francis Bernard, subsequently vetoed the bill "as being plainly repugnant and contrary to the laws of England," upon receiving advice from the Massachusetts Superior Court, at his request, that the bill would prevent the Court from issuing general writs of assistance.[54] Moreover, the General Court further expressed its displeasure with the general writs decision by reducing by ten pounds the salary of the Superior Court judges and eliminating the extra allowance allotted to Hutchinson as chief justice of the Court.[55]

b. Futile enforcement efforts

It was one thing to issue general writs of assistance to customs officials in Massachusetts and quite another for those officials to enforce those writs and seize smuggled goods, much less institute successful criminal or forfeiture proceedings based thereon. From all accounts, customs officials were notably unsuccessful in using the general writs to seize much, if any, smuggled goods in Massachusetts; this was due to widespread popular resistance to such searches and a lack of cooperation by local officials who, no doubt, reflected popular sentiment.[56]

Indeed, in two particularly celebrated incidents in Swansea and Boston (1765–1766), customs officials attempted searches pursuant to general writs of assistance and all came up virtually empty-handed due to popular and local official resistance.[57] In another famous incident (1768–69) involving John Hancock,[58] where smuggled goods were seized from Hancock's sloop Liberty pursuant to a general writ of assistance, the ensuing forfeiture effort met with violent resistance and the companion criminal proceeding against Hancock, which was enormously unpopular in Boston, was eventually dropped after dragging on for several months.[59] In sum, popular opposition to the general writs of assistance became so strong in Massachusetts that these writs became virtually unenforceable.[60]

---

53. J.R. Frese, N.Eng.Q. at 499–50; J. Landynski, at 35; H. Gray at 495–96.
54. H. Gray at 497–98.
55. N. Lasson at 67; J.R. Frese, N.Eng.Q. at 499; W. Cuddihy at 404.
56. W. Cuddihy at 491. "The result [of the Massachusetts court ruling]—not surprisingly, given the intensity of merchant anxieties, the popularity of Otis' oratory, the political capital to be made by appeals to liberty, and the willingness of smugglers to protect their investments by extralegal means—was that merchant-inspired mobs intimidated the customs officers and in effect nullified the writs." Fred Anderson, Crucible of War: The Seven Years War and the Fate of Empire in British North America (1754–1766) 520 (Vintage ed. 2001).
57. For a detailed discussion of these incidents known as the Polly Affair, and the Malcomb Affair, see respectively: (1) J.R. Frese at 205–12; W. Cuddihy at 491–96; and (2) J.R. Frese at 213–20; W. Cuddihy at 496–501; N. Lasson at 68–69. For a discussion of two other similar incidents of lesser importance, see J.R. Frese at 213 (the Falmouth Incident); W. Cuddihy at 496 (the Isley Incident).
58. John Hancock served as president of the Massachusetts Provincial Congress (1774), president of the Second Continental Congress (1775–77), and Governor of Massachusetts (1780–85, 1787–93); he was also the first signer of the Declaration of Independence. Encyclopedia of American History 1040 (Richard and Jeffrey Morris eds.; 7th ed. 1996); Merriam-Webster's Biographical Dictionary 458 (1995).
59. For a detailed discussion of the Hancock incident, see Wroth and Zobel at 173–210; H. Gray at 456–63; N. Lasson at 72. John Adams represented Hancock in the criminal proceedings.
60. After 1767, the general writ of assistance "was no longer a factor to be reckoned with in Massachusetts." J. Landynski at 36.

Section 5. Writs of Assistance Outside Massachusetts

Except for New Hampshire which generally followed Massachusetts' court practice, the British customs officials were notably unsuccessful in securing general writs of assistance from the colonial courts outside Massachusetts.[61] Four separate efforts were made by the American Board of Customs Commissioners in Boston to secure such writs from these courts in the period 1768–73, all yielding little or no results.[62] The 1767 Townshend Act had created this Board to enforce the general writs, and expressly empowered the American colonial courts to issue such writs so as to negate Thatcher's troublesome argument to the contrary in the 1761 Boston Writs case; in so doing, the Act expanded what began as a local controversy in Boston to all thirteen colonies.[63]

When applications were made before the courts outside Massachusetts and New Hampshire after 1767, the requests were at various times refused, ignored, delayed, or granted only in part. No highly visible court cases were ever argued on such applications, but the legal basis given by the colonial judges to the customs officials for refusing to grant general writs of assistance was, in effect, the argument made by James Otis in the Boston Writs case of 1761: such general writs were unlawful under English law and only special writs or warrants based on sworn proof were legally authorized.[64] Indeed, this was the near unanimous legal view of the colonial judges—including Tory judges who were loyal to the English Crown during the American Revolution.[65]

---

61. "In Massachusetts resistance to the [general] writs came from the people; elsewhere from the courts themselves. Only in New Hampshire (which usually followed the practices of the Massachusetts courts) did the courts readily grant the [general] writ; in other colonies they appear to have refused it." J. Landynski at 36. In Delaware, North Carolina and New Jersey, however, "requests for [general] writs of assistance either did not occur, or the Commissioners of Customs thought them too inconsequential to record." W. Cuddihy at 1052.

62. Cuddihy and Frese recount these four unsuccessful, historical efforts in considerable detail, and the reader is referred to these works for a more extensive treatment of the subject. The first such effort was made in early 1768; the second effort in 1769; the third effort in the fall of 1771; and the final effort in the fall of 1772, continuing through part of 1773. W. Cuddihy at 508–26.; J.R. Frese at 225–93. "These four campaigns culminated in one of the most errant failures in American legal history. In only a few colonies did the courts issue the writs as general search warrants, and the massive searches that those writs authorized were never implemented on an effective scale." W. Cuddihy at 508–09. Dickerson also extensively analyzes the colonial experience with the general writ of assistance outside Massachusetts, and his work should also be consulted for a complete picture of this subject. O.M. Dickerson 48–75. The discussion which follows is based on all three of the above works.

63. Leonard Levy, Origins of the Bill of Rights 164 (Yale Univ. paperback 2001).

64. O.M. Dickerson at 47–48; John C. Miller, Origins of the American Revolution 46–47 (1943). Edward Thurlow, the Attorney General of England, in an opinion letter to the Lords of the Treasury dated August 31, 1771, reported this legal basis as the ground given by the colonial judges for refusing to grant general writs of assistance, namely:

"... most of the judges refused to grant such [general] writs alledging that no information had been made to them of any special occassion for such writ, and unless such Information was made to them on oath they could not legally grant them, it being unconstitutional to lodge such a Writ in the hands of the officer which gave him unlimited power to act under it according to his own arbitrary Discretion."

Quoted in O.M. Dickerson at 69. Edward Thurlow also served as Lord Chancellor in England (1778–83, 1783–92), presided at the impeachment trial of Warren Hastings [colonial administrator of India] (1788), and generally "favored coercion of [the] American colonies." Merriam Webster's Biographical Dictionary 1024 (1995).

65. "Save for South Carolina which finally yielded, every court south of Massachusetts wherein the [general writs] issue was raised refused to grant the writs. Tory judges were as determined opponents

In Pennsylvania, Virginia, and Georgia, the colonial courts flatly refused the customs officers' applications for general writs of assistance;[66] in Delaware, the colonial court followed Pennsylvania court practice in this respect.[67] In Connecticut, Rhode Island and Maryland, the colonial courts delayed and ultimately refused to rule on such applications.[68] In New York, the colonial court issued a limited writ of assistance that the customs officials considered inadequate, and thereafter refused further applications for a general writ.[69] In South Carolina, the colonial court refused to rule on such applications for five years, but finally approved a general writ after great political pressure was exerted on it by the Crown, in which one judge was removed from office and four new judges were installed.[70] Indeed, the Crown pressure on all these colonial judges during this period was considerable, which no doubt heavily influenced the revolutionary leaders of the period to create an independent judiciary free from political influence when the Constitution was later framed.[71]

In 1773–74, the Connecticut Committee of Correspondence corresponded with the Massachusetts and Virginia Committees of Correspondence on the issue of whether the colonial courts should issue general writs of assistance.[72] The Massachusetts Committee replied by sending a copy of the arguments of Otis and Thatcher in the Boston Writs case of 1761. The Virginia Committee returned a very complete reply, together with the Virginia court's specific writ of assistance, stating that only specific writs of assistance based on affidavit were authorized by the relevant acts of Parliament, notwithstanding what the

---

of the writs as were their Whig associates." Richard Morris, The American Revolution 28 (Van Nostrand paperback ed. 1955).

66. For an account of the refusals of general writs in these three colonies, see O.M. Dickerson at 58–61, 64–66, 67–73; J.R. Frese at 244–45, 264–71, 277–80, 288–89; W. Cuddihy at 515–16. 519–20, 521–23, 525–26. Although the courts in these colonies refused all applications for general writs of assistance, they stood ready to issue specific writs of assistance upon sworn proof in a particular case. In fact, the Virginia colonial court issued a number of specific writs of assistance. J.R. Frese at 268–70.

67. O.M. Dickerson at 49.

68. For an account of the delays in these three colonies, see: O.M. Dickerson at 49–54, 61–63; J.R. Frese at 236–42, 245–46, 258–62, 274–75, 280–86; W. Cuddihy at 514, 519, 520–21, 524, 525–26. Jonathan Trumbull, the Chief Justice of the Connecticut colonial court, informed the customs officials that the primary basis for the court's refusal to rule on the applications for general writs was that the court was uncertain of their constitutionality, and was otherwise unfamiliar with warrant applications except by special petition. O.M. Dickerson at 52.

69. For an account of the New York colonial courts' experience with applications for general writs of assistance, see J.R. Frese at 242–44, 263–64; O.M. Dickerson at 54–58.

70. For an account of the South Carolina colonial court experience with the applications for general writs of assistance, see N. Lasson at 75; O.M. Dickerson at 66–67. Subsequent to the issuance of the general writ, one of the judges on the South Carolina court, William Drayton, was removed from office for sending a letter in 1774 to the First Continental Congress protesting the issuance of general writs and urging that only special writs or warrants were lawful. N. Lasson at 75 & n. 81.

71. "It took courage for judges to refuse writs of assistance when demanded by customs officers, since they held their commissions at the will of the Crown and were dependent for their salaries upon the revenues collected by the Customs Commissioners. * * * This unsung record of courage and fidelity to what they believed to be the law of the land must be considered in any appraisal of the colonial judiciary. The courts had nothing to gain and everything to lose by the course they pursued. * * * The American determination to keep the courts free from executive control grows in no small degree out of this experience." O.M. Dickerson at 74–75. "This courageous action by the judges in most of the colonies in preserving the principles of the common law in the face of mounting pressure from the executive—which paid their salaries and could at any time remove them, or offer them preferment—was in no small part responsible for the later determination of Americans to secure an independent judiciary, free of political control." J. Landynski at 37.

72. For a detailed account of this exchange of correspondence on the general writs of assistance, see J.R. Frese at 280–85.

actual practice of the English court of the exchequer might be. This exchange and other similar ones which took place during this period further illustrate the resolve of the emerging colonial leadership to resist the general writs of assistance in favor of specific writs or warrants, much as the colonial courts had done.

Section 6. Revolutionary Events Leading to Independence

The import duties imposed by the trade and navigation acts, along with the general writs of assistance that the Crown persistently sought as a means to enforce these duties, caused considerable dissatisfaction in the American colonies, which, after 1772, grew steadily worse with each succeeding year. This dissatisfaction led directly to independence and the American Revolutionary War.

a. John Dickenson: Letters from a Pennsylvania Farmer

John Dickenson, often referred to as the "Penman of the Revolution,"[73] wrote a series of letters in 1767–68 that appeared in a local Philadelphia newspaper and later were reprinted in many other colonial newspapers. They were subsequently published in a pamphlet entitled "Letters From a Farmer in Pennsylvania to the Inhabitants of the British Colonies." In very moderate terms, the Letters argued the American colonial cause against Great Britain on the various political issues of the day, and were widely read and applauded throughout the colonies.

In one of the Letters, Dickenson condemned the general writs of assistance as being contrary to the rights of British subjects:

> I am well aware, that writs of this kind may be granted at home, under the seal of the court of exchequer: But I also know that the greatest asserters of the rights of Englishmen have always strenuously contended that such a power was dangerous to freedom, and expressly contrary to the common law which ever regarded a man's house as his castle or a place of perfect security.
>
> If such a power was in the least degree dangerous *there*, it must be utterly destructive to liberty *here*.[74]

The Letters helped unite colonial opposition to Great Britain and hasten the movement toward independence. Dickenson was actually one of the more conservative American revolutionary leaders of the period.[75] Consequently, his opposition to the general writs of

---

73. Dickenson was, among other things, the chief draftsman of the Articles of Confederation as well as a series of protest petitions to the Crown issued by the First Continental Congress and the Stamp Act Congress. 1 Vernon Parrington, Main Currents in American Thought: The Colonial Mind 219–20 (1927). "Professor Tyler has fastened upon him the title 'penman of the Revolution;' but a juster title, and more in accord with the facts, would be 'spokesman of the Colonial Whigs.'" Id. at 220.

74. John Dickenson, "Letters From a Farmer in Pennsylvania to the Inhabitants of the British Colonies," Letter IX, Empire and Nation 54 (2d ed. Forrest McDonald ed. 1999).

75. Although he supported the Revolution as a member of the Continental Congress from Delaware (1776, 1777, 1779, 1780), Dickenson argued for reconciliation with Great Britain to the end and actually opposed the Declaration of Independence, although he abstained from voting on it. Later he served as a Delaware delegate to the Constitutional Convention in 1787 and was one of the signers of

assistance lends further support to the view that such opposition was a generally held view throughout the colonies and was not confined to "radicals" like Otis in Massachusetts.

b. Boston Committee of Correspondence

On November 2, 1772, a town meeting was held in Boston at Faneuil Hall to inquire into a move being made at the time by the English ministry to have the salaries of the colonial judges paid by the Crown, rather than the Massachusetts colonial legislature.[76] This proposal greatly concerned the colonists because it would free these officials from any effective local control. Governor Thomas Hutchinson[77] previously had been asked by the town meeting if there was any truth to this report. He replied, in effect, that it was none of the town's business, and further refused to call the Massachusetts legislature into session to inquire into this matter.[78] Samuel Adams, one of the leading colonial agitators for independence,[79] then moved the town meeting that a committee of correspondence be appointed, consisting of 21 persons, to state the rights of colonists and communicate and publish this to the towns in Massachusetts and to the world.[80] The motion passed unanimously, and the historic Boston Committee of Correspondence was created, the first of its kind in the American colonies.[81] James Otis, Jr., was named chairman of the committee; the leading political figures in Boston were named as members of the committee, including Samuel Adams and Joseph Warren.[82]

On November 20, 1772, following certain meetings, the committee presented for approval to the town meeting a statement entitled "The Rights of the Colonists and a List of Infringements and Violations of Rights," together with an accompanying letter to the towns of Massachusetts.[83] Although Samuel Adams and Joseph Warren are said to be the principal draftsmen of the statement, it is probable that this document was the collective

---

the U.S. Constitution. Jack Rackove, The Beginnings of National Politics: An Interpretive History of the Continental Congress 72–73, 88–100, 151–58 (1979); Encyclopedia of American History 1011 (7th ed. Richard & Jeffrey Morris eds.1996).

76. For a discussion of this entire political episode, see R. Brown at 48–91; see also H. Gray at 466n.

77. Hutchinson had also served as chief justice of the Massachusetts colonial court in the Boston writs case. See Chapter 2, Section 3b of this work. At that time he was Lieutenant Governor of the colony (1758–71); he later served as Governor of the colony (1771–74). Merriam Webster's Biographical Dictionary 520 (1995).

78. R. Brown at 55–56; 1 B. Schwartz at 199.

79. "In the history of the rise of political democracy in America, Samuel Adams occupies a distinguished place. He was by no means the first American to espouse the democratic cause, but he was the first to conceive the party machinery to establish it in practice." 1 Vernon Parrington, Main Currents in American Thought: The Colonial Mind 233 (1927).

80. R. Brown at 57.

81. R. Brown at viii–ix, 57; Richard Morris, The American Revolution: A Short History 44 (Van Nostrand paperback ed. 1955).

82. R. Brown at 59, 62. Joseph Warren was later president pro tem of the Massachusetts Provincial Congress (1775) which framed the measures to prepare the colony for war. On April 18, 1775, as a member of the Boston Committee of Safety, he sent Paul Revere and William Dawes to Lexington to warn John Hancock and Samuel Adams that the British troops were coming, just before the Battle of Lexington and Concord. He was later commissioned a major general and was killed in the Battle of Bunker Hill. Encyclopedia of American History 95–96 (Richard and Jeffrey Morris eds.; 7th ed. 1996); Merriam-Webster's Biographical Dictionary 1078 (1995); David Fischer, Paul Revere's Ride 94–97 (1994).

83. R. Brown at 62–66; see also I B. Schwartz at 199–200.

work of many committee members.[84] The statement contains a lengthy protest against the general writs of assistance reminiscent of Otis' argument in the 1761 Boston writs case.[85] It concludes with this peroration:

> Thus our houses and even our bed chambers, are exposed to be ransacked, our boxes chests & trunks broke open ravaged and plundered by wretches, whom no prudent man would venture to employ even as menial servants; whenever they are pleased to say they suspect there are in the house wares &c for which the dutys have not been paid. Flagrant instances of the wanton exercise of this power have frequently happened in this and other sea port Towns. By this we are cut off from that domestik security which renders the lives of the most unhappy in some measure agreeable. Those officers may under colour of law and the cloak of a general warrant break thro' the sacred rights of the Domicil, ransack men's houses, destroy their securities, carry off their property, and with little danger to themselves commit the most horred murders.[86]

The town meeting, which was moderated by John Hancock, unanimously approved the statement and accompanying letter which, in turn, were sent to the selectmen of every town in Massachusetts asking that the matter be laid before a town meeting and soliciting a response.[87] Over a hundred towns responded favorably after holding town meetings and forming local committees of correspondence.[88] This turned out to be an action of historic importance as it set in motion the creation of similar committees of correspondence in most of the other colonies; these committees later formed, in part, the basic administrative machinery at the state and local level for waging the revolution when it came.[89]

c. First Continental Congress

On September 5, 1774, the First Continental Congress met in Philadelphia. It consisted of 55 members chosen by revolutionary conventions or committees in twelve colonies.[90] On October 14, 1774, the Congress approved a declaration that, among other things, called for the repeal of the Townshend Act [7 Geo. III. c. 46] [which authorized colonial courts to issue general writs of assistance, and established a board of customs commissioners to seek writs from the colonial courts].[91] On October 25–26, 1774, the Congress, as its last act of business, approved and signed "The Petition of the Continental Congress to the King" which listed as one of its top grievances that "[t]he Officers of the Customs are empowered to break open and enter houses without the authority of any civil Magistrate founded on legal information."[92] These actions by the Continental Congress further

84. R. Brown at 70 n. 27; H. Gray at 466n.

85. H. Gray at 466n; N. Lasson at 72.

86. 1 B. Schwartz at 206.

87. R. Brown at 66–68; Bernhard Knollenberg, Growth of the American Revolution 1766–1775 88 (1975).

88. R. Brown at 92; Bernhard Knollenberg, Growth of the American Revolution 1766–1775 88 (1975).

89. Richard Morris, The American Revolution 44–45 (Van Nostrand paperback 1955).

90. Samuel Morison, The Oxford History of the American People 207 (1965).

91. 1 B. Schwartz at 214, 218. There is also a reference in the preamble to this declaration stating that the British Parliament has "established a board of commissioners with unconstitutional powers," clearly referring to the American Board of Customs Commissioners which persistently pressured the colonial courts to issue general writs of assistance after 1767. Id. at 215.

92. Journal of Proceedings of the Congress, Held at Philadelphia, Sept. 5–Oct. 26, 1774, 116, 132, 135 at 136 (Wm. & Thoms. Bradford, London Coffee House pub. 1774). The Petition is ten

establish the American resolve against the general writs of assistance in favor of special warrants based on sworn proof of wrongdoing.

d. Declaration of Independence

Finally, war broke out in April 1775 at Lexington and Concord. The Second Continental Congress met in Philadelphia, and, by resolution passed on May 10, 1776, recommended that each of the colonies form its own independent government "where no government sufficient to the exigencies of their affairs has been hitherto established."[93] On July 2, 1776, the Congress by unanimous resolution declared formal independence from Great Britain on behalf of the American colonies.[94]

The Declaration of Independence, approved by Congress two days later, sets out the reasons for declaring independence, and protests the abuses wrought by the hated trade and navigation acts.[95] As to the general writs of assistance which were used in a largely futile effort to enforce these acts, the Declaration contains no direct reference. It does, however, condemn the English King for sending "swarms of officers to harass our people" and for making colonial judges "dependent on his will alone, for the tenure of their offices and the amount and taintment of their salaries."[96] These references, although indirect, appear to include the English customs officers who asserted arbitrary search powers in the colonies through the general writs of assistance, and the persistent pressure exerted by the Crown upon the colonial judges to legitimize these writs.[97] Indeed, the U.S. Supreme Court has stated that the Crown's use of general warrants or writs of assistance during this period "was a motivating factor behind the Declaration of Independence."[98]

---

pages long. Id. at 135–44. The quoted writs-of-assistance grievance is the seventh paragraph of the Petition, and is found on second page of the Petition. Id. at 136.

93. 1 B.Schwartz at 229. The body of the resolution was approved on May 10, 1776, and the preamble thereto on May 15, 1776. 1 B. Schwartz at 229–30.

94. Carl Becker, The Declaration of Independence 3 (Vintage paperback ed. 1958); Pauline Maier, American Scripture: Making the Declaration of Independence 143 (Vintage paperback ed. 1998).

95. Carl Becker, The Declaration of Independence 4 (Vintage paperback ed. 1958); Pauline Maier, American Scripture: Making the Declaration of Independence 150 (Vintage paperback ed. 1998). "Congress adopted independence on July 2, 1776. It issued the Declaration on the fourth. After New York came in [and voted for independence], the Congress then said, 'It is now a unanimous declaration of the United States of America' and ordered the document put on parchment. It was only after it was on parchment and brought back to Congress on August 2 that they formally signed the document." Pauline Maier, "Declaring Independence," Booknotes: Stories from American History 13 (Brian Lamb ed. 2001).

96. 1 B. Schwartz at 253.

97. O.M. Dickerson at 73; N. Lasson at 80 n.7. "It is significant that the writs of assistance ... were reflected in the clauses of the Declaration of Independence ... denouncing the King because he had made judges dependent upon his will alone for their tenure and their salaries...." Richard Morris, The American Revolution 28 (Van Nostrand paperback ed. 1955). Lasson does note, however, that it is surprising that there is no direct reference to the general writs in the Declaration. N. Lasson at 80.

98. Berger v. New York, 388 U.S. 41, 58, 87 S.Ct. 1873, 18 L.Ed.2d 1040 (1967).

Chapter 3

The English Experience: General Warrants Controversy 1762–70

Section 1. Introduction

While the controversy was going on in the American colonies over the general writs of assistance, a simultaneous fight was being waged in England over the general warrant, which greatly supported the colonists' cause against the general writs. The general warrant was, as a matter of practice, being issued in England by the Secretary of State in seditious libel cases. It was much like the general writs of assistance in that it was not based on sworn proof of wrongdoing and did not particularly describe the place to be searched and the things to be seized. In a celebrated series of English court decisions in the 1760s, the general warrant was struck down in seditious libel cases as unauthorized under English law.

The legal basis employed by the English courts in reaching this result was very similar to the reasoning relied on by the American colonists in opposing the general writs. The English courts reasoned, in essence, that the general warrant was not authorized by a specific act of Parliament in seditious libel cases, and was otherwise contrary to the common law which generally required specific search warrants for the search of private premises based on sworn proof of wrongdoing. The American colonists reasoned, in like manner, that the general writs were not authorized by a specific act of Parliament and were otherwise contrary to the above-stated common law on search warrants. These English decisions, together with a contemporaneous legislative drive in Parliament led by William Pitt, the Elder, dealt a limited blow to the general warrant in England, all of which was greatly approved in the American colonies. We turn now to a brief survey of this relevant English legal experience.

Section 2. English Decisions Condemning the General Warrant

In 1762–63 the English ministry decided to move against two radical and politically troublesome newspapers in London: the Monitor and the North Briton. These papers printed articles extremely critical of the Tory Ministry on a regular basis, which apparently the Ministry believed were not being adequately answered by other opposing London newspapers friendly to the Ministry. John Wilkes, a radical member of Parliament, was the anonymous editor and author of the North Briton articles; he was also a great friend of the American colonial cause.[1]

a. Issuance of general warrants

On November 6, 1762, Lord Halifax as Secretary of State issued a general warrant to four of the King's messengers for the arrest of John Entick, a writer on the Monitor, and for the seizure of his papers. The warrant was not based on any sworn proof of wrongdoing, did not particularly describe the place to be searched or things to be seized, and authorized the messengers to search and seize as their whims dictated. The warrant commanded these officials

> ... to make strict and diligent search for John Entick, the author or one concerned in writing of several weekly very seditious papers, intitled the Monitor, or British Freeholder, No 357, 358, 360, 373, 376, 378, 379, and 380 ... which contain gross and scandalous reflections and invectives upon his majesty's government, and upon both houses of parliament; and him, having found you are to seize and apprehend, and to bring, together with his books and papers, in safe custody before me to be examined concerning the premisses, and further dealt with according to law....[2]

A similar warrant was also issued for Arthur Beadmore, the editor of the Monitor, and for the seizure of his papers. On November 11, 1762, the warrants were served, and Entick and Beadmore were arrested. Entick's house was searched and his papers therein were seized. A week later, however, Entick and Beadmore were released from custody, and a prosecution for seditious libel was dropped.[3]

On November 18, 1762, Lord Halifax as Secretary of State issued a general warrant for the authors and publishers of the North Briton. This warrant, however, was never served for unknown but perhaps tactical reasons. The new session of Parliament opened on April 19, 1763, and shortly thereafter an anonymous article appeared in the North Briton no. 45 attacking the King's speech given at the opening of Parliament. The King was irate and the Ministry found its best excuse to move against the North Briton.[4]

On April 26, 1763, Lord Halifax as Secretary of State issued a general warrant to four of the King's messengers for the authors, printers and publishers of the North Briton no. 45 and the seizure of their papers.[5] Like the Monitor general warrant, this warrant was based on no proof of wrongdoing, did not particularly describe the place to be searched or things to be seized, and authorized the messengers to search and seize in their discretion. Moreover, it did not expressly name the person or persons to be arrested as the Monitor general warrant had done. The warrant commanded the messengers

---

1. F. Siebert at 376–77; John C. Miller, Origins of the American Revolution 321–22 (1943).
2. This warrant is reproduced in Lord Camden's decision in Entick v. Carrington, 19 Howell's State Trials 1029, 1034 (1765) and is contained in the appendix to this work.
3. This account is taken from F. Siebert at 377. The reason for dropping the Entick and Beadmore prosecutions is unknown. Siebert suggests that the government may have felt that it had insufficient evidence or perhaps decided that the North Briton was a more important paper to proceed against.
4. This account is taken from F. Siebert at 377–78. Cuddihy also states that Wilkes' article attacked the new Ministry of George Grenville. W. Cuddihy at 440 .
5. F. Siebert at 378.

> ... to make strict and diligent search for the authors, printers and publishers of a seditious and treasonable paper, entitled, 'The North Briton, No 45 Saturday April 23, 1763 printed for G. Kearsly in Ludgate Street, London;' and them or any of them having found, to apprehend and seize, together with their papers, and to bring in safe custody before me, to be examined concerning the premises, and further dealt with according to law.[6]

Under this "roving commission," the messengers proceeded to arrest forty-nine people in three days, conducted searches of numerous private premises and seized a quantity of the arrestees' private papers. Among those arrested and searched was John Wilkes, the anonymous author of the North Briton no. 45; Dryden Leach, one of the printers of the North Briton, but not no. 45; and one of Leach's employees, Huckle, also a printer.[7]

b. Wilkes cases

Within a month, civil actions sounding in trespass and false imprisonment were filed against the King's messengers by a number of people arrested and searched under the North Briton general warrant, including Wilkes, Leach and Huckle. Later Entick and Beadmore brought similar suits based on the Monitor general warrant. All the suits were successful, resulting in damages paid by the government estimated to be in excess of £100,000.[8] Only John Wilkes was prosecuted for seditious libel and was later convicted; Wilkes was also repeatedly expelled from Parliament despite being repeatedly re-elected.[9]

Charles Pratt, the Lord Chief Justice of the Court of Common Pleas, was the trial judge in these cases. He strongly rejected the defense proffered by the King's messengers: namely, that their actions were justified by Lord Halifax's general warrant. In Huckle's action against Money, one of the messengers, the jury returned a verdict for Huckle and awarded £300 in damages.[10] Pratt denied a subsequent defense motion for new trial attacking the jury award, and condemned the North Briton general warrant as unauthorized under English law. He stated that, despite the small amount of actual damage suffered by Huckle,[11] the jury

> ... saw a magistrate over all the King's subjects, exercising arbitrary power, violating Magna Charta, and attempting to destroy the liberty of the kingdom, by insisting upon the legality of this general warrant before them; they heard the King's counsel, and saw the solicitor of the Treasury endeavoring to support and maintain the legality of the warrant in a tyrannical and severe manner. These are the ideas which struck the jury on the trial; and I think they have done right in giving exemplary damages. *To enter a man's house by virtue of a nameless warrant, in order to procure evidence, is worse than the Spanish Inquisition; a law*

---

6. The North Briton general warrant is reproduced in Lord Mansfield's decision in Leach v. Money, 19 Howell's State Trials, 1001, 1008 (1765) and is contained in the appendix to this work.

7. This account is taken from N. Lasson at 43–44; F. Siebert at 378; and J. Landynski at 28. For a more detailed account of these arrest and searches, see W. Cuddihy at 440–43.

8. This account is taken from F. Siebert at 378–79.

9. F. Siebert at 380; N. Lasson at 46, n. 114.

10. Cuddihy reports that after an eleven-hour trial, the jury deliberated only eleven minutes before returning a verdict. He also states that, in addition to the damages award, the jury awarded Huckle £200 in costs. This amounted to a total of £500 in damages and costs, which was ten times Huckle's annual salary of £50. W. Cuddihy at 447, 447 n.39.

11. Cuddihy reports that the messengers detained Huckle for six hours and treated him to beefsteaks and beer. W. Cuddihy at 446.

> *under which no Englishman would wish to live an hour; it was the most daring public attack upon the liberty of the subject.*[12]

In Wilkes' action against Robert Wood, a secretary to Lord Halifax who had supervised the execution of the North Briton general warrant against Wilkes, the jury returned a verdict for Wilkes and awarded £1,000 in damages.[13] Pratt in his charge to the jury condemned the North Briton general warrant as "totally subversive of the liberty of the subject."[14]

In Dryden Leach's action against three of the King's messengers who had arrested and searched him under the North Briton general warrant, the jury returned a verdict for Leach and awarded £400 in damages. The King's messengers appealed to the Court of the King's Bench, and on June 18, 1765, the appeal was heard by Chief Justice Lord Mansfield and three other justices.[15] The court affirmed the judgment appealed from, and Lord Mansfield delivered a short opinion for the court.[16]

Mansfield based his decision on the narrow ground that the North Briton general warrant, by its express terms, did not justify the entry and search of Leach's premises.[17] In the course of the opinion, however, Mansfield observed that the North Briton general warrant was invalid as being unauthorized by either an act of Parliament or by the common law. He conceded that the common law gave authority for officials to arrest without a warrant in certain cases, and that certain acts of Parliament did authorize general warrants, but here "it is not contended that the common law gave the officer authority to apprehend; nor that there is any act of parliament which warrants this case." Consequently, he reasoned that the case must "stand upon principles of the common law," and these principles condemn such a general warrant for giving the executing officer general exploratory search powers. He stated:

> It is not fit, that the receiving or judging of the information should be left to the discretion of the officer. The magistrate ought to judge; and should give certain directions to the officer. That is so, upon reason and convenience.[18]

---

12. Huckle v. Money, 2 Wilson K.B. 206, 95 Eng.Rep. 768 , 769 (1763) (emphasis added) . Cuddihy reports that the jury was initially instructed to return a special verdict on whether the express terms of the warrant authorized Huckle's arrest; but when the jury objected, a general jury verdict was allowed. Cuddihy also reports that in response to a question from the jury, Pratt stated that the express terms of the North Briton warrant had not authorized Huckle's arrest because Huckle was not "the author, printer or publisher" of the North Briton no. 45 whom the warrant ordered to be arrested. W. Cuddihy at 896–98.

13. Wilkes v. Wood, 98 Eng.Rep. 489, 499, 19 Howell's State Trials 1153, 1168 (1763). Later, in 1769, Wilkes obtained a jury verdict of £4,000 against Lord Halifax. 19 Howell's State Trials 1406 (1769); Cuddihy at 456.

14. Wilkes v. Wood, 98 Eng.Rep. 489, 498, 19 Howell State Trials 1153, 1167 (1763). For a critical analysis of Pratt's reasoning in the case, see W. Cuddihy at 447–49.

15. T. Taylor at 31; W. Cuddihy at 449–51. Taylor describes Mansfield, a Scotsman, as "a mixture of politician and jurist, and by no means as adventurous a magistrate as Pratt." T. Taylor at 31. Mansfield (1705–93) was chief justice of the King's Bench from 1756–88 and is chiefly known for his contributions to commercial law. Merriam-Webster's Biographical Dictionary 747 (1995).

16. Leach v. Money, 19 Howell's State Trials 1001 (1765). Mansfield's opinion was delivered in two parts after hearing separate arguments of counsel; the opinion covers a total of two printed columns in Howell's reports. 19 Howell's State Trials at 1026–27, 28.

17. "For, here the warrant is to take up the author, printer, or publisher; but they took up a person who was neither author, printer, nor publisher.... This makes an end of the case." 19 Howell's State Trials at 1028. The North Briton general warrant ordered the arrest and search of "the authors, printers and publishers" of the North Briton no. 45. Although Dryden was a printer for the North Briton, he had not printed the North Briton no. 45. N. Lasson at 44, n. 109.

18. 19 Howell's State Trials at 1027. The three other justices in the case agreed that the North Briton general warrant was illegal and void. Id. at 1027. Over two centuries later, the U. S. Supreme

c. *Entick v. Carrington*

We turn now to John Entick's action against Nathan Carrington and the three other King's messengers who arrested and searched Entick pursuant to the Monitor general warrant. In that case, the jury returned a verdict in Entick's favor and awarded £300 in damages. Carrington and the other messengers appealed to the Court of Common Pleas sitting en banc. Pratt, now Lord Camden, heard the appeal as Chief Justice of the court, together with three other justices; he delivered the opinion of the court upholding the verdict.[19] It is an extensive opinion and the most influential of all the general warrant cases of the period.[20]

Taylor states, "[a]t once meticulous and sweeping, it was an opinion such as Brandeis might wish to have written."[21] Holdsworth calls it "a masterly performance—remarkable for the breadth and insight of its historical learning, and for its mastery of the principles of the common law."[22] Cuddihy says it "provided the definitive precedent on secretarial general warrants."[23] It had a considerable impact, both on the British Constitution and on the subsequent development of the Fourth Amendment. As stated by the United States Supreme Court in *Boyd v. United States*:[24]

> Lord Camden pronounced the judgment of the court ... and the law as expounded by him has been regarded as settled from that time to this, and his great judgment on that occasion is considered as one of the landmarks of British liberty. It was welcomed and applauded by the lovers of liberty in the Colonies as well as in the mother country. It is regarded as one of the permanent monuments of the British Constitution, and is quoted as such by the English authorities on that subject down to the present time.
>
> As every American statesman, during our revolutionary and formative period as a nation, was undoubtedly familiar with this monument of English freedom, and considered it as the true and ultimate expression of constitutional law, it may be confidently asserted that its propositions were in the minds of those who framed the Fourth Amendment to the Constitution and were considered as sufficiently explanatory of what was meant by unreasonable searches and seizures.[25]

Camden's opinion considers in detail the two defenses raised by the King's messengers to Entick's trespass action. The first defense was that the messengers were protected from

---

Court in United States v. United States District Court, 407 U.S. 297, 316, 92 S.Ct. 2125, 32 L.Ed.2d 752, 765–66 (1972), cited Mansfield's opinion in support of basic Fourth Amendment doctrine that a search warrant issued by a neutral and detached magistrate is generally required to search private premises:

"Lord Mansfield's formulation touches the very heart of the Fourth Amendment directive: that, where practical, a governmental search and seizure should represent both the efforts of the officer to gather evidence of wrongful acts and the judgment of the magistrate that the collected evidence is sufficient to justify invasion of a citizen's private premises or conversation."

19. Entick v. Carrington, 19 Howell's State Trials 1029, 2 Wilson K.B. 275, 95 Eng.Rep. 807, 1558–1774 All Eng. Rep. 41 (1765).

20. The opinion covers thirty pages [one column per page] in Howell's Reports. 19 Howell's State Trials at 1044–74.

21. T. Taylor at 34.

22. 10 William Holdsworth, History of English Law 672 (1938).

23. W. Cuddihy at 453.

24. 116 U.S. 616, 6 S.Ct. 524, 29 L.Ed. 746 (1886).

25. 116 U.S. at 626–27, 29 L.Ed. at 749–50.

suit under the Constable's Protection Act of 1750. For reasons that have no relevance to Fourth Amendment doctrine, Camden rejects this defense after a lengthy analysis.[26]

The second defense was that the Monitor general warrant, under which the messengers acted, was a lawful warrant which justified their entry and search of Entick's premises. Camden also rejects this defense in an analysis that gives the case its lasting importance as part of the historical background of the Fourth Amendment. Moreover, it was this treatment of the subject that was met with enthusiastic acclaim at the time both in England and the American colonies. Indeed, Camden characterized the issue raised by this defense as "the great question" and "the most interesting question in the cause."[27]

Camden concludes that the Monitor general warrant was totally unlawful because (1) it was unauthorized by any act of Parliament, and (2) it was unknown to, and unauthorized by the common law—precisely the legal position taken by Otis in his attack on the general writs of assistance. Camden considers three arguments urged by the defendant messengers in support of the general warrant, and rejects each of them.

First, the messengers urged that the general warrant was analogous to the common law on search warrants for stolen goods. Camden rejects this argument by pointing out that even if this were the case, which it is not, "we have no right, without an act of parliament, to adopt a new practice in the criminal law, which was never yet allowed from all antiquity."[28] He also recites the differences between the general warrant and the common law search warrant for stolen goods. In particular, at common law, the search warrant for stolen goods was a specific warrant and could only issue upon sworn proof from the owner that the stolen goods were located in a particular place; a general warrant, on the other hand, had none of these safeguards.[29]

Second, the messengers urged that general warrants had issued frequently since the Glorious Revolution of 1688 and that a practice tolerated for so long must be lawful. Camden rejects this argument on the ground that a practice of this sort acquires no legal strength by the mere silence of the courts—a silence occasioned because the victims of such warrants, a few criminal booksellers, have been afraid to dispute it. Camden then traces the history of the general warrant, noting that the Licensing Act of the Restoration Parliament, which gave the Secretary of State the power to issue general warrants, expired in 1695 and had not since been revived. He then concludes that the general warrant cannot be justified by the common law.[30]

---

26. The Constables Protection Act [24 Geo. 2 c. 44(1750), 18 Halisbury's Statutes of England 10 (2d ed. 1950)] rendered constables and other officers immune from suit for anything done when properly executing a warrant issued by a justice of the peace. See also 18 Halisbury's Statutes of England 10 (2d ed. 1950). Camden concludes that the Secretary of State was not a justice of the peace "within the equity of this act," and that, accordingly, the King's messengers were not entitled to immunity under the Act when executing a warrant issued, as here, by the Secretary of State. 19 Howell's State Trials at 1045–62. Camden further concludes that, in any event, the messengers did not strictly comply with the Secretary's general warrant as required by the Act. They did not bring a constable with them when conducting the search of Entick's premises as required by the warrant; they also brought Entick's seized papers to an assistant to Lord Halifax, rather than Lord Halifax himself as required by the warrant. 19 Howell's State Trials. at 1062–63.

27. 19 Howell's State Trials at 1045, 1063.

28. 19 Howell's State Trials at 1067.

29. 19 Howell's State Trials at 1067.

30. 19 Howell's State Trials at 1067–72.

Finally, the messengers urged that it was necessary for the ends of government to lodge such a general search power in the Secretary of State in order to prevent libelous publications. Camden rejects this argument on the ground that if Parliament be of that opinion, it may revive the Licensing Act; because it has not done so, he concludes that it is not of this opinion. As a corollary to this position, the messengers also urged that the general warrant was a means of detecting criminal offenders by discovering evidence. Camden rejects this position as unauthorized by the common law.

> It is very certain, that the law obligeth no man to accuse himself; because the necessary means of compelling self-accusation, falling upon the innocent as well as the guilty, would be both cruel and unjust; and it should seem, that search for evidence is disallowed upon the same principle. There too the innocent would be confounded with the guilty.[31]

Camden stated, in effect, that general exploratory searches for evidence of crime was disallowed at common law for "if suspicion at large should be a ground of search, especially in the case of libels, whose home would be safe?"[32]

In sum, Camden rejects the two defenses raised by the messengers and sustains the £300 jury verdict for trespass obtained by Entick. Camden's lengthy statement at the outset of his discussion of the messenger's second defense is oft-quoted and serves as a fair summary of his legal condemnation of the Monitor general warrant:

> This, though it is not the most difficult, is the most interesting question in the cause; because if this point should be determined in favor of the [government], the secret cabinets and bureaus of every subject in this kingdom will be thrown open to the search and inspection of a messenger, whenever the secretary of state shall think fit to charge, or even suspect, a person to be the author, printer, or publisher of a seditious libel.
>
> The messenger, under this warrant, is commanded to seize the person described, and to bring him with his papers to be examined by the secretary of state. In consequence of this, the house must be searched; the lock and doors of every room, box or trunk must be broken open; all the papers and books without exception, if the warrant be executed according to its tenor, must be seized and carried away; for it is observable that nothing is left to the discretion or to the humanity of the officer.
>
> This power so assumed by the secretary of state is an execution upon all the party's papers, in the first instance. His house is rifled; his most valuable secrets are taken out of his possession, before the paper for which he is charged is found to be criminal by any competent jurisdiction, and before he is convicted either of writing, publishing, or being concerned in the paper.
>
> This power, so claimed by the secretary of state, is not supported by one single citation from any law book extant. It is claimed by no other magistrate in this kingdom but himself: the great executive hand of criminal justice, the lord chief justice of the court of Kings bench, chief justice Scroggs excepted, never having assumed this authority.[33]

---

31. 19 Howell's State Trials at 1073.
32. 19 Howell's State Trials at 1073–74.
33. 19 Howell's State Trials at 1063–64.

Section 3. Impact of English General Warrant Decisions in England and America

a. In general

These decisions in the Wilkes and Entick cases (1763–65) were greeted with great acclaim in both England and America; the slogan "Wilkes and Liberty" became a popular byword of the times.[34] Charles Pratt became a national hero in England for his trial and appellate decisions striking down general warrants in seditious libel cases. He was elevated to the peerage as Lord Camden and was also honored in the American colonies.[35] Wilkes, on the other hand, became a popular folk hero in London with the merchant class and disenfranchised; he was also enthusiastically embraced by the American colonial leadership for leading the fight against the general warrant.[36] Indeed, the entire episode had a profound impact on the American colonies as it was fully supportive of the colonial opposition to the general writs of assistance.[37]

b. American gifts and support of Wilkes

Wilkes emerged as the most popular Englishman of his day in America.[38] Symbolic gifts were sent to him by various Americans expressing their support for Wilkes' cause in

---

34. "'Wilkes and Liberty' became the byword of the times even in faraway America." N. Lasson at 45–46.

35. N. Lasson at 45–46. As a member of the House of Lords, Camden attacked the Stamp Act which was eventually repealed as it was extremely unpopular in America. As lord chancellor, he opposed the policy of colonial taxation of America which led to his resignation from this position in 1770. T. Taylor at 184 n. 35; Merriam-Webster's Biographical Dictionary 846 (1995). "As an ardent and outspoken pro-colonialist, his name was taken by the cities of Camden, S.Car. and Camden, New Jersey." T. Taylor at 184 n. 35. Camden, Maine is also named for Lord Camden. Akhil Amar, "The Fourth Amendment, Boston and Writs of Assistance," 30 Suffolk L.Rev. 53, 65 (1996).

In addition, Camden issued a writ of habeas corpus to free John Wilkes from the Tower of London where Wilkes had been committed by the Secretary of State for refusing to answer questions concerning the no. 45 North Briton incident; the legal basis for doing so was Wilkes' privilege as a member of Parliament. F. Siebert at 378; T. Taylor at 183 n. 31.

36. Raymond W. Postgate, That Devil Wilkes 62, 171–72 (1929).

37. "The writs of assistance were anathema in the colonies, and Otis' argument against them was well known among the founding fathers. The common law was their heritage, and they vibrated in sympathy with the new libertarian trends in England. Colonial lawyers would naturally turn to the speeches of Pitt and the opinions of Mansfield and Camden—especially of the latter, whose pro-colonial speeches had won him high place in the hearts of American patriots—for eloquent exposition of English liberties, and weighty examination of the common law of searches and warrants." T. Taylor at 38.

38. Wilkes-Barre, Pennsylvania, and Wilkesboro, North Carolina, were both named after Wilkes. Raymond W. Postgate, That Devil Wilkes 171 (1929). "To Americans, Wilkes despite his unsavory private life was a martyr to freedom of the press and to the subject's right to resist oppression. Their newspapers endlessly detailed his activities; printers advertised an 'elegant copper' engraving of the man 'fit for framing,' as well as editions of his works; patriot diners toasted 'his noble Struggles in The Cause of Liberty;' and parents accorded their tribute at the baptismal font.... Until his political eclipse in the early 1770s, Wilkes was almost as great a popular darling in America as in Britain."Arthur Schlesinger, Sr., Prelude to Independence: The Newspaper War on Britain 35 (1971).

the entire affair of the North Briton, no. 45. Samuel Adams' Boston Sons of Liberty sent Wilkes two turtles, one weighing 45 pounds and the other weighing 47 pounds.[39] A Virginia group in 1770 sent Wilkes 45 hogsheads of tobacco as a "small acknowledgment for his sufferings in the cause of liberty."[40] Paul Revere made a silver punch bowl with engravings thereon stating "No General Warrants," "Wilkes and Liberty," and "No. 45."[41] In all, the number 45 became a fiery numerical slogan for the patriot cause in America.[42]

While Wilkes was serving a twenty-two-month prison sentence (June 1768–April 1770) for criminal libel and obscenity based on papers seized from him under the North Briton general warrant,[43] the members of the Boston Sons of Liberty sent a number of warm letters of encouragement and praise for him and his cause, expressing outrage at the way he had been treated.[44] A committee composed of John Adams, Joseph Warren, Benjamin Kent, Benjamin Church, Jr. and Thomas Young jointly wrote Wilkes two such letters.[45] Individual members also wrote such letters to Wilkes: Benjamin Kent, Thomas Young, Joseph Warren, Nathaniel Barber, and William Palfrey [Wilkes's most prolific correspondent].[46] Wilkes responded warmly to all of these letters.

Moreover, the South Carolina colonial legislature voted to send £1500 to an English radical group that supported Wilkes in order to frustrate "the unjust and unconstitutional measures of an arbitrary and oppressive ministry." The South Carolina colonial governor and his council, however, refused to accede to this grant—and the Crown issued instructions to the governor to consent to no more money bills until the legislature had

---

39. Samuel Morison, The Oxford History of the American People 193 (1965). William Palfrey, in the letter which accompanied these gifts, stated that the weights of the two turtles totaled 92, which, he said, was the Massachusetts patriotic number. William Palfrey to John Wilkes, July 26, 1769, 47 Massachusetts Historical Society Proceedings 204, 206 (1914).

40. John C. Miller, Origins of the American Revolution 323 (1943).

41. Samuel Morison, The Oxford History of the American People 193 (1965).

42. In 1766, 45 lanterns were strung in Boston to celebrate the repeal of the Stamp Act. In 1768, a group in Norwich, Connecticut, downed 45 patriot toasts at a dinner from plates marked "45," while a nearby Liberty Tree flew a flag inscribed "no. 45, Wilkes and Liberty." On the 45th day of 1770, 45 New Yorkers consumed 45 pounds of beefsteak from a 45-month old bull. Flagpoles 45 feet high were often constructed, and quilts with 45 patches of one color were often sewn, throughout the American colonies. W. Cuddihy at 540; Arthur Schlesinger Sr., Prelude to Independence: The Newspaper War on Britain 36–37 (1971).

43. Wilkes was charged and convicted in absentia on February 21, 1764, for criminal libel, based on the North Briton no. 45, and for obscenity based on a private poem entitled The Essay on Woman. He was also declared an outlaw, as he had fled to France in December 1763 and was absent from his trial. He later returned to London in February 1768, his outlawry was lifted on June 8, 1768, and he was sentenced by Lord Mansfield to twenty-two months imprisonment on June 18, 1768, on both charges. He served the sentence at Kings Bench Prison and was finally released on April 17, 1770. Raymond W. Postgate, That Devil Wilkes 67–68, 87, 89–90, 109, 135–39 (1929); Barbara Tuchman, The March of Folly 148–49 (Ballantine paperback 1984).

44. For a discussion of these letters, see Raymond W. Postgate, That Devil Wilkes 171–78 (1929).

45. Boston Sons of Liberty to Wilkes June 6, 1768, and October 5, 1768. Included in the June 6, 1768 letter was a copy of John Dickenson's Letter From a Farmer in Pennsylvania which, among other things, attacks the general writs of assistance in America and refers favorably to the general warrant decisions in England with which Wilkes was associated. 47 Massachusetts Historical Society Proceedings 191–92, 193–94 (1914).

46. Benjamin Kent to John Wilkes, October 5, 1768; Thomas Young to John Wilkes, July 6, 1768; Joseph Warren to John Wilkes, April 13, 1768; Nathaniel Barber to John Wilkes, July 11, 1770; and William Palfrey to John Wilkes February 21, 1761, April 9, 1769, June 13, 1769, September 9, 1769, October 21, 1769. 47 Massachusetts Historical Society Proceedings 194–96, 202–03, 199–200, 214–15, 196–97, 198–99, 200–02, 210, 211–12 (1914).

withdrawn its grant to Wilkes. The legislature refused and launched an attack on the government that kept the colony in turmoil for four years.[47]

Based on this enthusiastic support of Wilkes and his cause against the general warrant, it is plain that the American colonial leadership was outraged at Wilkes' treatment in the entire North Briton affair. American patriot leaders clearly regarded Wilkes' prosecution, conviction and imprisonment as a violation of his legal rights, inasmuch as it was based entirely on evidence seized pursuant to the hated and invalid general warrant. More to the point, however, Wilkes' cause against the general warrant greatly supported the American colonial cause against the general writs of assistance, as both fights were based on similar legal grounds.[48]

Section 4. Parliamentary Efforts to Abolish the General Warrant

While the above events were transpiring, a drive was launched in the House of Commons (1764–66), led by William Pitt the Elder,[49] to abolish the general warrant. This effort was largely the result of the Wilkes and Entick cases, as well as popular feeling on the subject.[50] It was, however, a largely symbolic gesture as it accomplished very little.

In April 1766, the House of Commons passed two resolutions declaring the general warrant unlawful in libel cases, and generally unlawful except in cases expressly provided for by an act of Parliament.[51] These resolutions, however, merely declared that it would be a breach of privilege for such a warrant to be served on a member of the House and had no effect beyond that. Moreover, when a bill to prohibit the seizure of persons by general warrant was actually introduced, it was defeated. Later the House of Commons did pass a bill restraining the issuance of general warrants to seize papers except in cases of treason and felony without benefit of clergy, but the House of Lords rejected it.[52]

---

47. This account is taken from John C. Miller, Origins of the American Revolution 323–24 (1943).

48. "John Wilkes's career was crucial to the colonists' understanding of what was happening to them; his fate, the colonists came to believe, was intimately involved with their own. * * * [H]e had entered the public arena first as a victim and then as the successful antagonist of general warrants, which, in the form of writs of assistance, the colonists too had fought in heroic episodes known throughout the land." Bernard Bailyn, The Ideological Origins of the American Revolution 110–11 (Belknap paperback rev ed. 1992). "Americans watched the [Wilkes] drama with fascination. It seemed their own battle, as indeed to some extent it was. Wilkes fight against general warrants was the same as their fight against writs of assistance." Hugh Brogan, The Penguin History of the USA 154 (2d ed. 1999).

49. William Pitt, the Elder (1708–88), had an illustrious career as a war minister and member of both the House of Commons (1735–66) and the House of Lords (1767–78). Known as the "Great Commoner," he was a brilliant orator, a strong supporter of the American colonial cause, and a man greatly admired by the American colonists. Winston Churchill ranks him with the Duke of Marlborough as "the greatest Englishman in the century between 1689 and 1789." 3 Winston Churchill, A History of the English-Speaking Peoples: The Age of Revolution 132 (Bantam paperback ed. 1963). His most significant achievement was his successful and brilliant prosecution of the Seven Years War against France as war minister (1756–61). The British historian George Trevelyan states that he surpassed even Lincoln as a great war minister. G.M. Trevelyan, 3 History of England 59 (Doubleday paperback ed. 1956).

50. N. Lasson at 48.

51. T. Taylor at 34–35.

52. N. Lasson at 49.

William Pitt played a prominent role in these debates and argued that "no general warrant to search universally without specification of name or place was allowable, even in cases of treason."[53] Scholars are divided, however, on whether his legendary proclamation that an Englishman's home is his castle was uttered during these debates or during the 1763 Parliamentary debates on the Cider Act which authorized home invasions to enforce the Act.[54] In any event, it seems clear that Pitt's classic speech was well-known to the American colonial leadership of the period as supporting the colonist's fierce opposition to the general writs of assistance,[55] and has since reverberated as a fundamental privacy principle throughout our entire national history.[56]

> The poorest man may, in his cottage, bid defiance to all the forces of the Crown. It may be frail; its roof may shake; the wind may blow through it; the storm may enter; the rain may enter; but the King of England may not enter; all his force dares not cross the threshold of the ruined tenement.[57]

---

53. W. Cuddihy at 960.

54. Cuddihy collects an extensive array of historical authorities indicating a division on the subject, but concludes that Pitt's pronouncement was "probably" made during the Cider Act debates. W. Cuddihy at 465, 466 n.151. Lasson states that the subject pronouncement was made during the general warrant debates. N. Lasson at 49–50.

55. See T. Taylor at 38. "There can be no doubt that Pitt's address in the House of Commons in March 1763 echoed and re-echoed throughout the colonies." Payton v. New York, 445 U.S. 573, 601, n. 54, 100 S.Ct. 1371, 63 L.Ed.2d 639 (1980).

56. "We have, after all, lived our whole national history with an understanding of the 'ancient adage that a man's home is his castle to [t]he point that the poorest man may in his cottage bid defiance to all the forces of the Crown.' "Georgia v. Randolph, 547 U.S. 103, 126 S.Ct. 1515, 1524, 164 L.Ed.2d 208 (2006), quoting from Miller v. United States, 357 U.S. 301, 307, 78 S.Ct. 1190, 2 L.Ed.2d 1332 (1958).

57. N. Lasson at 49–50; see also W. Cuddihy at 946 n. 151. This is the best-known version of Pitt's classic speech. There is, however, another less eloquent version which appears at W. Cuddihy at 465–66:

"It is ... a maxim of our law, that every Englishman's house is his castle. Not that it is surrounded by walls and battlements. It may be a straw built shed. Every wind of heaven may whistle through it. All the elements of nature may enter in. But the King cannot; the King dare not."

Chapter 4

American Constitutional History: State Constitutional Provisions 1776–84

Section 1. Introduction

In response to the May 1776 resolution of the Second Continental Congress recommending that each of the colonies form an independent government,[1] all of the original thirteen colonies—plus Vermont, whose territorial status was in dispute—formed separate, self-governing states. Twelve of these fourteen states adopted constitutions between 1776–84—all except Connecticut and Rhode Island, both of which elected to continue under their colonial charters.[2] Of the twelve states adopting formal constitutions, eight states included therein a formal bill of rights, each of which, without exception, contained a search and seizure guarantee: Virginia (1776), Pennsylvania (1776), Delaware (1776), Maryland (1776), North Carolina (1776), Vermont (1777), Massachusetts (1780), and New Hampshire (1784). These state search and seizure guarantees were the direct ancestors of the Fourth Amendment.[3]

Section 2. Virginia and North Carolina

Virginia was the first state to adopt a permanent constitution and a bill of rights.[4] On June 12, 1776, the Virginia constitutional convention, sitting in Williamsburg, adopted the historic Virginia Declaration of Rights which is still in effect today.[5] This Declaration

1. I B. Schwartz at 229–30. The body of the resolution was adopted on May 10, 1776, and the preamble thereto on May 15, 1776.

2. I B. Schwartz at 289.

3. W. Cuddihy at 603. "Like most of the provisions of the Bill of Rights, the Fourth Amendment was derived from provisions already existing in state constitutions." Minnesota v. Carter, 525 U.S. 83, 119 S.Ct. 469, 142 L.Ed.2d 373, 382 (1998) (Scalia, J. concurring).

4. R. Rutland at 39. As an aside, New Hampshire had adopted an incomplete provisional constitution [without a judiciary or a bill of rights] in January 1776 that was intended to serve the colony temporarily until reconciliation with England could be effected. When this arrangement proved unsatisfactory and independence was declared, a prolonged process of constitution-making began in New Hampshire in 1778; it ended in 1783 with the adoption of a complete constitution together with a bill of rights. R. Rutland at 74–76; 1 B. Schwartz at 374.

5. I B. Schwartz at 231, 241.

was drafted by a committee chaired by Archibald Cary and composed of twenty-eight delegates, including George Mason, Patrick Henry, Edmund Randolph and James Madison.[6] In the committee deliberations, George Mason assumed a leadership role and submitted a proposed draft that is almost verbatim what the convention eventually adopted. This draft, however, did not include a search and seizure guarantee; this guarantee was later added by the drafting committee and adopted by the convention.[7] Edmund Randolph, a member of the drafting committee, recalled thirty years later in an essay he wrote on the convention that the search and seizure guarantee "was dictated by the remembrance of the seisure of Wilkes's paper from a Secretary of State."[8]

Section 10 of the Virginia Declaration of Rights provides:

> That general warrants, whereby any officer or messenger may be commanded to search suspected places without evidence of a fact committed, or to seize any person or persons not named, or whose offence is not particularly described and supported by evidence, are grievous and oppressive, and ought not to granted.[9]

This constitutional guarantee is a direct outgrowth of the Virginia colonial court's consistent refusal to issue general writs of assistance (1769–73) in accord with its view of English law supported by the Wilkes' cases, and its persistent practice of issuing only specific writs or specific warrants upon sworn proof of criminal wrongdoing.[10]

The guarantee clearly outlaws "general warrants" such as those the Virginia bench and bar opposed in the general writs of assistance regime prior to the Revolution. By implication, warrants not suffering from such an infirmity were authorized, i.e., specific warrants commanding the search of premises and the arrest of named persons based on evidence of criminal wrongdoing. This was the normal method, according to the consensus American colonial view, for searching private premises and arresting persons in connection therewith under the English common law. Moreover, the reference to "messengers" in this guarantee makes clear that the framers were cognizant of the Wilkes's cases that Virginians fully supported.

The impact of the Virginia Declaration of Rights on future constitution-making in the colonies during this period was considerable. Copies of the Virginia Declaration were widely distributed throughout the colonies and were well known to the framers of the state constitutions that followed.[11]

On December 14, 1776, the North Carolina Provincial Congress, sitting in Halifax, adopted a declaration of rights for the North Carolina Constitution.[12] Section 11 of the North Carolina Declaration of Rights, still in effect today, contains a search and seizure guarantee that is virtually identical to the Virginia guarantee.[13] There is no evidence that the colonial customs officials ever bothered to apply for general writs of assistance in North Carolina. Its decision to follow Virginia's lead as to this guarantee was probably

---

6. R. Rutland at 31–32; B. Schwartz at 231.

7. N. Lasson at 79; I B. Schwartz at 232.

8. I B. Schwartz at 248. See Chapter 3, Section 2 a & b of this work for a discussion of the Wilkes general warrant cases in England.

9. I B. Schwartz at 235.

10. For a discussion of the Virginia colonial court's refusal to issue general writs of assistance, see Chapter 2, Section 5 of this work.

11. R. Rutland at 43–44.

12. Perry and Cooper at 352–53.

13. I B. Schwartz at 287.

no accident, given Virginia's similar refusal to issue such general writs and its own fierce insistence on personal rights.

Section 3. Pennsylvania and Vermont

Pennsylvania was the next state after Virginia to adopt a bill of rights. On August 16, 1776, the Pennsylvania Constitutional Convention, sitting in Philadelphia, adopted a declaration of rights that was patterned to a great extent after the Virginia Declaration.[14] Section 10 of the Pennsylvania Declaration of Rights, since amended,[15] provided for a search and seizure guarantee that was based on the Virginia model, but with some important changes:

> That the people have a right to hold themselves, their houses, papers and possessions free from search and seizure, and therefore warrants without oaths or affirmations first made, affording a sufficient foundation for them, and whereby any officer or messenger may be commanded or required to search suspected places, or to seize any person or persons, his or their property, not particularly described, are contrary to that right, and ought not to be granted.[16]

This guarantee, unlike the Virginia version, recognizes a general right to be "free from search and seizure," naming specifically people's "houses, papers and possessions" as the items to which this right attaches. In recognition of this constitutional right, general search and arrest warrants are prohibited in language taken in part from, but more descriptive than the Virginia provision. By implication, warrants not suffering from such an infirmity, i.e., specific warrants, based on sworn or affirmed proof of criminal wrongdoing and particularly describing the place to be searched and things or persons to be seized, did not offend this right.

The Pennsylvania guarantee constitutionalized the view of the Pennsylvania colonial court on searches and seizures. That court, like the Virginia colonial court, steadfastly refused to issue general writs of assistance—insisting that English law permitted only the issuance of specific writs or warrants, based on sworn proof of criminal wrongdoing, as the normal method by which searches of private premises could be conducted.[17]

On July 8, 1777, the Vermont Constitutional Convention, sitting in Windsor, adopted both a constitution and a declaration of rights.[18] Vermont had never been a colony, but nonetheless claimed the status of a state against contrary claims by New York and New Hampshire.[19] Section 11 of the Vermont Declaration of Rights, still in effect today, is virtually the same as its counterpart in the 1776 Pennsylvania Constitution discussed above.[20]

---

14. R. Rutland at 46. Indeed John Adams noted in his diary at the time that the Pennsylvania Declaration was "taken almost verbatim" from the Virginia Declaration. Id.

15. Pennsylvania's current search and seizure guarantee approximates the form of the Fourth Amendment. Art. I, § 8, Pa. Const. (1874).

16. I B. Schwartz at 265.

17. For a discussion of the Pennsylvania colonial court's refusal to issue general writs of assistance, see Chapter 2, Section 5 of this work.

18. Perry and Cooper at 360.

19. Perry and Cooper at 358.

20. I B. Schwartz at 323.

Section 4. Delaware and Maryland

Delaware and Maryland were the next states after Pennsylvania to adopt a bill of rights in their state constitutions. Like Virginia and Pennsylvania, the colonial court in Maryland also had refused to issue general writs of assistance for precisely the same reasons given by the Virginia and Pennsylvania courts—although the Maryland colonial court effected its refusal by declining to rule on applications for such writs. Delaware, on the other hand, followed Pennsylvania court practice and never issued a general writ of assistance, apparently for the same reasons given by the Pennsylvania colonial court.[21] It is therefore not surprising that these states were of a mind to constitutionalize the legal view of the colonial bench and bar on general writs of assistance when they undertook to write a search and seizure guarantee into their state constitutions.

On September 11, 1776, the Delaware Constitutional Convention, sitting in New Castle, adopted a declaration of rights containing a search and seizure guarantee.[22] The drafting committee that produced this declaration of rights was chaired by George Read, who was also the president of the convention. Similarly, on November 3, 1776, the Maryland Constitutional Convention, sitting in Annapolis, adopted a declaration of rights containing a search and seizure guarantee that was virtually identical to its counterpart in the Delaware Declaration.[23] The seven-man drafting committee that produced this declaration of rights included Matthew Tilghman, the convention president, and Samuel Chase, later a United States Supreme Court Justice.[24]

Section 17 of the Delaware Declaration of Rights, since amended,[25] provided:

> That all warrants without oath to search suspected places, or to seize any person or his property, are grievous and oppressive; and all general warrants to search suspected places, or to apprehend all persons suspected, without naming or describing the place or any person in special, are illegal and ought not to be granted.[26]

Section 23 of the Maryland Declaration of Rights, still in effect today, provides:

> That all warrants, without oath or affirmation, to search suspected places, or to seize any person or property, are grievous and oppressive; and all general warrants—to search suspected places, or to apprehend suspected persons, without naming or describing the place, or the person in special—are illegal and ought not to be granted.[27]

These provisions were patterned after the search and seizure guarantee in the Virginia Declaration of Rights in that they generally condemn general warrants, although this prohibition is accomplished with more specificity than the Virginia model. By implication, warrants not suffering from such infirmities are lawful.

---

21. For a discussion of the Maryland and Delaware colonial court treatment of general writs of assistance applications, see Chapter 2, Section 5 of this work.

22. I B. Schwartz at 276; Perry and Cooper at 332.

23. Perry and Cooper at 341–42.

24. Perry and Cooper at 341; R. Rutland at 48–49; Merriam-Webster Biographical Dictionary 206 (1995).

25. The amended version recognizes a general right to be free from unreasonable searches and seizures as provided in the Fourth Amendment. Art. I, §6, Del. Const. (1897).

26. I B. Schwartz at 278.

27. I B. Schwartz at 282.

Section 5. Massachusetts and New Hampshire

Massachusetts and New Hampshire were the last two states to adopt constitutions and declarations of rights. In both states the process of constitution-making was long and arduous.[28] In the end, however, these states adopted search and seizure guarantees, with New Hampshire copying the Massachusetts version.

On March 2, 1780, the Massachusetts Constitutional Convention, sitting in Cambridge, proposed a constitution with a declaration of rights containing a search and seizure guarantee, and copies of same were distributed to the towns in Massachusetts for a vote thereon.[29] Following a lively debate and a favorable vote of the people, the Convention reconvened on June 15, 1780, and formally ratified the constitution and declaration of rights.[30]

At the convention, a committee of 31 convention delegates, including John Adams and Samuel Adams, was appointed to draft both a constitution and declaration of rights.[31] According to John Adams' later account, the drafting committee after some weeks of debate appointed a smaller subcommittee composed of John Adams, Samuel Adams and James Bowdin to prepare a draft; John Adams was, in turn, commissioned to draft both a proposed constitution and declaration of rights.[32] Adams' draft was approved by the committee and, with some limited alteration, adopted by the convention.[33] The search and seizure guarantee contained in the Declaration of Rights was accepted as originally drafted with only one minor amendment, thereby making Adams the author of this guarantee.[34]

Article 14 of the Massachusetts Declaration of Rights, still in effect today, provides:

> Every subject has a right to be secure from all unreasonable searches, and seizures of his person, his houses, his papers and all his possessions. All warrants, therefore, are contrary to this right, if the cause or foundation of them be not previously supported by oath or affirmation; and if the order in the warrant to a civil officer, to make search in suspected places, or to arrest one or more suspected persons, or to seize their property, be not accompanied with a special designation of the

---

28. In Massachusetts, a first constitution adopted by the state legislature in February 1778 was overwhelmingly defeated by the voters by a five-to-one margin. Thereafter, town resolutions and a convention that met in Ipswich, Essex County, demanded that any new constitution contain a bill of rights. A constitutional convention was convened, producing in March 1780 a second proposed constitution with a bill of rights, which was officially approved by the voters in June 1780. Perry and Cooper at 368–70; R. Rutland at 65–73. In New Hampshire, three separate constitutions with a bill of rights were adopted by a constitutional convention, but defeated by the voters in the towns over the period June 1779–December 1782; finally, the towns officially approved the fourth constitution and bill of rights in October 1783. Perry and J. Cooper at 380; R. Rutland at 74–76.

29. Perry and Cooper at 370.

30. Perry and Cooper at 370; R. Rutland at 70–73.

31. R. Rutland at 68.

32. R. Rutland at 68–69.

33. I B. Schwartz at 377; I Page Smith, John Adams 440 (1962).

34. Compare the search and seizure guarantee as drafted by Adams and approved by the drafting committee [I B. Schwartz at 372] with the search and seizure guarantee as finally adopted. 1 B. Schwartz at 342. Only the term "man" was deleted from the Adams' draft and the term "subject" was substituted therefor. Wroth and Zobel give Adams the credit for substantially drafting the entire declaration of rights. Wroth and Zobel at 116, n. 30. Schwartz gives Adams credit for substantially drafting the entire constitution and declaration. I B.Schwartz at 337.

> person or objects of search, arrest, or seizure: and no warrant ought to be issued but in cases, and with the formalities, prescribed by the laws.[35]

This provision, like the Pennsylvania guarantee, recognizes a generalized search and seizure right. But while Pennsylvania guarantees a right to be "free from search and seizure," the Massachusetts version refines this by guaranteeing a right to be secure from "all *unreasonable* searches and seizures." This is the first appearance of the term "unreasonable" in the search and seizure guarantees of the state declarations of rights, and is an obvious precursor to the first clause of the Fourth Amendment. The Massachusetts guarantee as thus refined, coupled with the condemnation of general warrants, constitutionalizes James Otis' view on the existing English law of search and seizure requiring specific warrants—shared throughout Massachusetts and the American colonies generally—as first expressed nearly twenty years earlier in the Boston Writs case of 1761.[36] It is perhaps fitting that John Adams was the author of this guarantee in view of the enormous impact that Otis' argument made on him as a young man listening to the argument in court.

On June 2, 1784, the New Hampshire Constitution and Bill of Rights went into effect after being adopted by a constitutional convention sitting in Concord, and approved by a vote of the towns in the state.[37] Article 19 of the New Hampshire Bill of Rights, still in effect today, contains a search and seizure guarantee that is identical to the Massachusetts version adopted in 1780.[38] This is not surprising, as New Hampshire had long followed Massachusetts' lead in legal practices.

---

35. I B. Schwartz at 342.

36. For a discussion of Otis' argument in the Boston Writs case of 1761, see Chapter 2, Section 3 of this work.

37. Perry and Cooper at 380.

38. Perry and Cooper at 384.

Chapter 5

American Constitutional History: United States Constitution and Bill of Rights 1787–91

Section 1. Constitutional Convention and Aftermath

After the American Revolution had ended at Yorktown in October 1781, and a peace treaty was finally concluded in Paris in September 1783, the country continued to operate under the short-lived Articles of Confederation which had been established during the Revolution. When this arrangement proved unsatisfactory, the confederation congress called for a constitutional convention for the purpose of restructuring the government.[1] The convention met in Philadelphia from May 25–September 17, 1787, and was composed of fifty-five delegates from twelve states.[2] The convention produced our present Constitution, but without a bill of rights.

As it turned out later, this omission proved to be a political error of enormous proportions, as it resulted in the near defeat of the Constitution in the state ratification conventions that followed.[3] To defend this glaring omission, Alexander Hamilton was later to argue in the Federalist Papers that a bill of rights was both unnecessary and dangerous because under the Constitution the central government had only *delegated* powers, none of which included the power to infringe individual rights.[4] But this position proved to be unpersuasive, and the Federalists eventually had to compromise on the issue in order to win ratification of the Constitution.[5]

---

1. C. Van Doren at 7. The Congressional resolution stated the Convention was to be held "for the sole and express purpose of revising the Articles of Confederation." C. Van Doren at 264. As it turned out, however, the Convention "revised" the Articles by wholly supplanting it with a new constitution.
2. Samuel Morison, The Oxford History of the American People 305 (1965). Rhode Island declined to send any delegates to the convention.
3. Edmund S. Morgan, The Birth of the Republic 154 (Univ. of Chicago paperback rev. ed. 1977).
4. The Federalist, No. 84 (Hamilton) 555–61 (1788) (Modern Library ed. 1937) "I go further, and affirm that bills of rights, in the sense and to the extent in which they are contended for, are not only unnecessary in the proposed Constitution, but would even be dangerous. They would contain various exceptions to powers not granted; and, on this very account, would afford a colorable pretext to claim more than were granted. For why declare that things shall not be done which there is no power to do." Id. at 559. This argument echoed a similar argument made by James Wilson, a prominent Pennsylvania delegate, in a public speech to citizens in Philadelphia shortly after the Convention had adjourned. I B. Schwartz at 528–29.
5. "'Why declare that things shall not be done for which there is no power to do?' Hamilton asked, but in this case his answer failed to resolve serious misgivings by many fair-minded persons." Richard

The subject of a bill of rights came up almost as an afterthought toward the end of the Constitutional Convention, five days prior to adjournment. On September 12, 1787, George Mason, the primary author of the Virginia Declaration of Rights and a delegate from Virginia, stated that he wished the Constitution would be prefaced by a bill of rights which, he said, could be drawn up in a few hours—and added that he would second a motion to that effect. Elbridge Gerry, a Massachusetts delegate, thereupon made a motion for the creation of a committee to prepare a bill of rights, which was seconded by Mason. A short debate followed; whereupon a vote was taken and the motion was defeated. Two days later, an effort by Gerry and Charles Pinckney of South Carolina to insert a guarantee for freedom of the press was also defeated. Beyond that, there is no other mention of a bill of rights in the convention proceedings.[6]

On September 17, 1787, the Constitution was formally signed by all the delegates present, with three illustrious exceptions: George Mason, Elbridge Gerry and Edmund Randolph.[7] George Mason had previously prepared written objections to the Constitution the day after the bill of rights proposal was defeated, and these objections were widely circulated thereafter; his first and chief objection was that the Constitution lacked a bill of rights.[8]

Elbridge Gerry subsequently wrote to the presiding officers of the Massachusetts legislature and emphasized the omission of a bill of rights as one of his principal reasons for not signing the Constitution.[9] It was originally thought that he then published an attack on the Constitution during the ensuing ratification debates, reminding his fellow Massachusetts citizens of their long battle against the general writs of assistance and the need for a federal bill of rights to guard against a recurrence of the abuses suffered under the general writs of assistance regime.[10] Subsequent historical scholarship has revealed, however, that the author of this tract was his friend Mercy Otis Warren, the sister of James Otis, Jr. and a prominent anti-Federalist.[11]

B. Morris, Witnesses at the Creation 226 (New American Library paperback ed. 1985). Indeed, Madison decisively answered this argument when he presented his Bill of Rights proposals to the House of Representatives in June 1789. See Section 3b of this chapter. Beyond that, the Federalists contradicted their position by guaranteeing certain individual rights in the original Constitution: the privilege of the writ of habeas corpus [Art. I, § 9, cl. 2, U.S. Const.], and the prohibitions against bills of attainer and ex post facto laws [Art. I § 9, c. 3; § 10, cl. 1, U.S. Const.].

6. This entire account is taken from 2 M. Farrand, The Records of the Federal Convention of 1787 (1911), as reported in I B. Schwartz at 438–39.

7. C. Rossiter at 234–37; Encyclopedia of American History 1079 (7th ed 1996; Richard and Jeffrey Morris eds). However, Edmund Randolph, a Virginia delegate and governor of the state, was somewhat reluctant in his opposition, and later changed his mind and supported the Constitution at the Virginia ratification convention. C. Rossiter at 234–37; C. Van Doren at 170–71.

8. I B. Schwartz at 443–45.

9. "My principal objections to the plan are ... that the system is without the security of a bill of rights." 1 The Debate on the Constitution 231–32 (Bernard Bailyn ed. 1993); see N. Lasson at 88–89.

10. II Federalist and Other Constitutional Papers 723 as quoted in N. Lasson at 89, n. 40.

11. Writing under the non de plume "A Columbian Patriot," Warren stated:

> There is no provision by a bill of rights to guard against the dangerous encroachments of power in too many instances to be named: but I cannot pass over in silence the insecurity in which we are left with regard to warrants unsupported by evidence—the daring experiment of granting writs of assistance in a former arbitrary administration is not yet forgotten in Massachusetts; nor can we be so ungrateful to the memory of the patriots who counteracted their operation, as so soon after their manly exertions to save us from such a detestable instrument of arbitrary power, to subject ourselves to the insolence of any petty revenue officer to enter our houses, search, insult and seize at their pleasure.

2 The Debate on the Constitution 293 (Bernard Bailyn ed. 1993) (pamphlet originally published

As its final official act, the constitutional convention, by resolution, sent the proposed Constitution to the confederation congress with the proviso that the subject document would go into effect when nine states had ratified it.[12] On September 20, 1787, the Constitution was laid before the confederation congress and was taken up for debate six days later.[13] Richard Henry Lee, a Virginia representative, took the lead in objecting to the Constitution as proposed. He submitted a bill of rights and several other amendments for congress to adopt before submitting the Constitution to the states.[14] The proposed bill of rights contained a search and seizure guarantee:

> That the Citizens shall not be exposed to unreasonable searches, seizure of their persons, houses, papers or property.[15]

This proposal was finally defeated, but, as a compromise, the Constitution was transmitted to the states for ratification, without recommendation, in accord with the resolves of the constitutional convention.[16] The following month Lee published a series of influential and widely circulated "Letters of the Federal Farmer" in which, among other things, he attacked the Constitution for its failure to include a bill of rights including a search and seizure guarantee.[17]

Section 2. State Ratification Debates

a. In general

In the debates that followed at the various state ratification conventions, the most powerful argument marshaled by the opponents of the Constitution was that the document lacked a bill of rights. This argument—which was made by such anti-Federalists as George Mason, Elbridge Gerry, and Richard Henry Lee, supported in Paris by Thomas Jefferson[18]—gained widespread acceptance and, in turn, provided the political impetus that

---

in Boston in February 1788). See Akhil Amar, The Bill of Rights 66 at n.* (1998).

Warren later published a three-volume History of the Rise, Progress, and Termination of the American Revolution (1805), that "defined the 'pure republicanism' interpretation [of the American Revolution], which was also the version embraced by the Republican Party and therefore called 'the Jeffersonian interpretation.'" Joseph Ellis, The Founding Brothers 13 (2000). Warren was a "friend and correspondent of leading political figures of her day including John Adams, Samuel Adams, Thomas Jefferson, and Elbridge Gerry." Merriam-Webster's Biographical Dictionary 1078 (1995). According to one historian, she was "the most formidable female intellectual in eighteenth-century America." Lester H. Cohen, Foreword, I History of the Rise, Progress and Termination of the American Revolution xvi (Liberty Fund 1989).

12. C. Van Doren at 310.
13. C. Van Doren at 176–77.
14. C. Van Doren at 176–77.
15. Quoted in N. Lasson at 87 n. 32.
16. C. Van Doren at 177–78.
17. In his fourth letter dated October 12, 1787, Lee stated:

"There are other essential rights, which we have justly understood to be the rights of freemen; as freedom from hasty and unreasonable search warrants, warrants not founded on oath, and not issued with due caution, for searching and seizing men's papers, property, and persons."

I B. Schwartz at 473; N. Lasson at 88 n. 37. Robert Rutland describes these letters as "one of the most respected offerings of the opposition press throughout the entire ratification period." Rutland at 126.

18. Jefferson was serving as U.S. minister to France at the time (1785–89), Encyclopedia of American History 1056 (7th ed. 1996; Richard and Jeffrey Morris eds.), and corresponded regularly

led directly to the Bill of Rights and the Fourth Amendment. As part of a political compromise to secure the Constitution's passage, the Federalists eventually agreed to a series of recommending amendments to the Constitution which the First Congress would take up as one its major orders of business. Accordingly, Massachusetts, South Carolina, Virginia and New York ratified the Constitution, but with such recommending amendments. Moreover, in Pennsylvania and Maryland, a minority report with recommending amendments was also filed by disgruntled delegates; and in North Carolina the ratification convention refused to approve the Constitution without the adoption of a series of preconditioning amendments. It was not the Framers, then, but the opponents of the Constitution who initially led the fight for a bill of rights.[19]

John Marshall, who was a delegate to the Virginia ratification convention, later summarized this period:

> Serious fears were extensively entertained that those powers which the patriot statesmen ... deemed essential to union, and to the attainment of those invaluable objects for which union was sought, might be exercised in a manner dangerous to liberty. In almost every convention by which the Constitution was adopted, amendments to guard against the abuse of power were recommended ... In compliance with a sentiment thus generally expressed, to quiet fears extensively entertained, amendments [to the Constitution] were proposed by the required majority in Congress, and adopted by the states.[20]

Altogether, a total of 210 amendments came out of these ratification conventions, involving nearly 100 substantive proposals.[21] Search and seizure guarantees were included in the amendments emanating from the Virginia, New York and North Carolina ratification conventions, as well as the minority reports of the Pennsylvania and Maryland conventions.

b. Pennsylvania

We begin with the minority report filed at the Pennsylvania Convention, which was the first state in which a real fight was waged over ratification. On November 21, 1787, the Pennsylvania ratification convention assembled in Philadelphia, composed of forty-six Federalist delegates and twenty-three anti-Federalist delegates.[22] The Federalist forces were led by James Wilson, who had been a Pennsylvania delegate to the constitutional convention and, next to James Madison, one of the principal architects of the Constitution.[23] The anti-Federalist forces were led by three delegates from western Pennsylvania: Robert Whitehill, William Findley, and John Smiley.[24]

---

with Madison and other leaders during this period. Jefferson was generally friendly to the Constitution, but regarded the lack of a bill of rights as a serious defect in the document and so stated his position in many letters to his correspondents in America. Merrill Peterson, Thomas Jefferson and the New Nation 357–61 (Oxford Univ. paperback 1970); Adrienne Koch, Jefferson and Madison: The Great Collaboration 39–55 (Oxford Univ. paperback 1973).

19. "It was the opponents of the Constitution who were most active in demanding such vital liberties as freedom of religion, freedom of speech and press, jury trial, due process, and protection from 'unreasonable searches and seizures.' These guarantees had to be incorporated in the first ten amendments because the [Constitutional] Convention had neglected to put them there." Richard Hofstadter, The American Political Tradition 11 (1948).

20. Barron v. Baltimore, 7 Peters 243, 249, 8 L.Ed. 672, 675 (1833).

21. II B. Schwartz at 983.

22. C. Van Doren at 182: C. Rossiter at 287.

23. C. Rossiter at 247–48, 287.

24. R. Rutland at 135.

At the time, the state was still locked in a bitter controversy over the 1776 Pennsylvania Constitution which the Federalists considered too radical, and the political quarrels engendered by that controversy were carried into the ratification convention.[25] Whitehill, Findley and Smiley had supported the 1776 Constitution, were outspoken anti-Federalists, and attacked the ratification of the Constitution on several grounds, including the lack of a bill of rights.[26]

On December 12, 1787, Whitehill offered fifteen amendments for the convention to recommend as part of the ratification process, which amendments included a bill of rights.[27] The fifth proposed amendment contained a search and seizure guarantee:

> That warrants unsupported by evidence, whereby any officer or messenger may be commanded or required to search suspected places, or to seize any person or persons, his or their property, not particularly described, are grievous and oppressive, and shall not be granted either by the magistrates of the federal government or others.[28]

Whitehill's motion to accept these amendments was defeated by a vote of 46–23, and the Constitution was thereupon promptly ratified by an identical vote.[29]

The disaffected anti-Federalist minority was bitter about this defeat and immediately held a rump convention.[30] On December 18, 1787, they issued a lengthy minority report setting forth their reasons for opposing the Constitution, one of which was the lack of a bill of rights.[31] Whitehill's proposed fifteen amendments, including the search and seizure guarantee, were also contained in the report.[32] Twenty-one of the twenty-three dissenting anti-Federalist delegates attended this rump convention, and all of them signed the report, including Whitehill, Findley and Smiley.[33]

c. Maryland

We next turn to the minority report filed at the Maryland Ratification Convention. On April 21, 1788, this convention met in Annapolis and sat only four working days.[34] By this time, the Massachusetts Convention had already met and ratified the Constitution by a narrow margin (187–168), but with a series of recommending amendments that was to set the precedent for future ratification conventions in South Carolina, Virginia, New Hampshire, and New York.[35] Not so in Maryland, however, as the Federalists were in firm control; after only a few days of debate, the convention ratified the Constitution by a 63–11 vote on April 26, 1788.[36]

A handful of aggressive anti-Federalist delegates was, nonetheless, determined to attach a series of recommending amendments to this ratification.[37] William Paca, a signer of the

25. Perry Cooper at 326; R. Rutland at 135.
26. R. Rutland at 135; C. Van Doren at 183.
27. II B. Schwartz at 658–60.
28. II B. Schwartz at 658.
29. II B. Schwartz at 660.
30. R. Rutland at 141.
31. R. Rutland at 141.
32. II B. Schwartz at 662–673, esp. 665.
33. R. Rutland at 141; II B. Schwartz at 673.
34. C. Van Doren at 207–08; C. Rossiter at 290.
35. C. Van Doren at 202; R. Rutland at 147–48.
36. C. Rossiter at 290.
37. R. Rutland at 154.

Declaration of Independence and later governor of Maryland,[38] was permitted after the ratification vote to present a general proposal that recommending amendments be attached; a thirteen member committee was thereafter appointed to draft such amendments and report back to the convention.[39] The committee, of which Paca was a member, subsequently met and approved thirteen proposed amendments, rejecting fifteen other proposed amendments.[40] Most of the approved amendments involved protections of individual rights, including a search and seizure guarantee:

> That all warrants without oath, or affirmation of a person conscientiously scrupulous of taking an oath, to search suspected places, or seize any person or his property, are grievous and oppressive; and all general warrants to search suspected places, or to apprehend any person suspected, without naming or describing the place or person in special, are dangerous and ought not to be granted.[41]

A majority of the committee, however, lost patience with the anti-Federalist minority on the committee probably because of the large number of proposed amendments; accordingly, the committee majority decided not to make a formal report or recommendation to the convention.[42] When the convention reconvened shortly thereafter, Paca himself read the thirteen amendments to the delegates, but the convention refused to approve them, and a vote thereon was not recorded; the convention then adjourned.[43]

Paca, together with three other members of the committee and eight members of the convention, then issued a minority report in pamphlet form setting forth the above proceedings; this report detailed the thirteen amendments agreed to by the committee.[44] As to the proposed search and seizure amendment, the minority commented that this proposal "was considered indispensable by many of the committee" because "Congress having the power of laying excises" under the constitution could expose "our dwelling houses, those castles considered so sacred by the English law ... to the insolence and oppression of office," through general warrants which, under the proposed amendment, "are also hereby forbidden to those magistrates who are to administer the general government."[45]

d. Virginia

We now turn to the recommending amendments that the Virginia Ratification Convention appended to its ratification of the Constitution. This convention met in Richmond from June 2–27, 1788, and of all the ratification conventions, it was the most dramatic, the most fully reported, and the most philosophical and wide-ranging in its debates.[46] It was also considered to be the most distinguished body ever to assemble in Virginia, numbering among its 173 members the outstanding leaders of the time.[47] The Federalist leaders included James Madison, Edmund Randolph, John Marshall, George Wythe, Henry Lee and Edmund Pendleton; the anti-Federalist leaders included Patrick

38. Merriam Webster's Biographical Dictionary 793 (1995).
39. C. Van Doren at 208; II B. Schwartz at 729, 731–32.
40. II B. Schwartz at 729–30, 732–35.
41. II B. Schwartz 733–34.
42. R. Rutland at 155; II B. Schwartz at 729, 737; C. Van Doren at 208.
43. II B. Schwartz at 729, 737; C. Van Doren at 208.
44. II B. Schwartz 729, 730–738; C. Van Doren at 208.
45. II B. Schwartz 734.
46. C. Rossiter at 291; C. Van Doren at 218.
47. Harry Ammon, James Monroe: The Quest for National Identity 70 (1971).

Henry, George Mason, James Monroe, William Grayson, Theodorik Bland, and Joseph Jones.[48]

One of the major issues debated at the convention was the lack of a bill of rights.[49] Although the anti-Federalists had other important objections to the Constitution, this was their most telling point and they made the most of it.[50] Patrick Henry led the fight on this and other issues—and, in so doing, was at the height of his considerable oratorical powers.[51] Among his many eloquent arguments on this issue, Henry urged on two occasions that the failure of the Constitution to contain a guarantee against general warrants was a fatal mistake.

First, he contended that, without such a guarantee as was contained in the Virginia Declaration of Rights, Congress could authorize its excise tax officers to ransack people's homes under a general warrant.

> In the present [Virginia] Constitution, they are restrained from issuing general warrants to search suspected places, or seize persons not named, without evidence of the commission of a fact &c. There was certainly some celestial influence governing those who deliberated on that [Virginia] Constitution; for they have, with the most cautious and enlightened circumspection, guarded those indefeasible rights which ought ever to be held sacred! The officers of Congress may come upon you now, fortified with all the terrors of paramount federal authority. Excisemen may come in multitudes; for the limitation of their numbers no man knows. They may, unless the general government be restrained by a bill of rights, or some similar restriction, go into your cellars and rooms, and search, ransack, and measure, every thing you eat, drink and wear. They ought to be restrained within proper bounds.[52]

This was the same argument made by the minority report at the Maryland Ratification Convention.[53]

Second, Henry argued that a search and seizure guarantee was also needed because the writ of habeas corpus was inadequate to protect people's rights from wrongful imprisonment under a general warrant because of the great distances many people had to travel in this country, as opposed to England, to obtain a judge for such a writ.

> I feel myself distressed, because the necessity of securing our personal rights seems not to have pervaded the minds of men [at the Constitutional Convention];

---

48. C. Rossiter at 291. The only Virginia leaders missing were George Washington, who had presided at the Constitutional Convention and had chosen to remain at Mount Vernon; Thomas Jefferson who was away in Paris as U.S. minister to France; and Richard Henry Lee who for reasons of health had chosen not to stand for election as a convention delegate. R. Rutland at 162; Merrill Peterson, Thomas Jefferson and the New Nation 357–61 (1970); Oliver Chitwood, Richard Henry Lee: Statesman of the Revolution 180 (1967).

49. II B. Schwartz at 762.

50. II B. Schwartz at 762.

51. II B. Schwartz at 762–63. "But they [the Virginia Federalists] were matched by one man: Patrick Henry, who rose to the occasion with the most dazzling performance of his life.... Every day the hall was packed with spectators, come to hear the most eloquent performance in the annals of forensic virtuosity. Spectators and delegates alike sat frozen, hypnotized, as Henry ranged on and on, now thundering, now whispering, now threatening, now pleading." Forrest McDonald, E Pluribus Unum 356, 357 (2d ed. 1979). "Jefferson, who was not a fan of Patrick Henry, once said that 'he spoke like Homer wrote.'"Andrew Burnstein, "Celebrating Fifty Years of Independence," Booknotes: Stories From American History 64 (Brian Lamb ed. 2001).

52. II B. Schwartz at 800 (Patrick Henry speech, June 14, 1788).

53. See Section 2c of this chapter.

> for many other valuable things are omitted: for instance, general warrants, by which an officer may search suspected places, without evidence of the commission of a fact, or seize any person without evidence of his crime, ought to be prohibited. As these are admitted, any man may be seized, any property may be taken, in the most arbitrary manner, without any evidence or reason. Every thing the most sacred may be searched and ransacked by the strong hand of power. We have infinitely more reason to dread general warrants here than they have in England., because there, if a person be confined, liberty may be obtained by the writ of habeas corpus. But here a man living many hundred miles from the judges may get in prison before he can get that writ.[54]

Clearly, Henry felt that a person imprisoned under a general warrant was entitled to be released from custody by a habeas corpus writ, but thought the remedy inadequate due to lack of immediate access to the courts for many people. A search and seizure guarantee, presumably, would prevent the issuance of the general warrant in the first instance and thus obviate the need for a subsequent habeas corpus writ. Without question, then, Henry contemplated no imprisonment whatever based on a general warrant.[55]

Edmund Randolph, a proponent of the Constitution, agreed that general warrants were odious and should not be granted. He urged, however, that the federal judiciary even without a bill of rights could prevent such practices—and failing that, the injured person could always obtain redress for his injury in the state courts.[56] He and Henry were, therefore, in complete agreement that the federal courts should have the power to prevent the issuance of general warrants and to afford relief to those who nonetheless were victims of such warrants.[57] Henry, however, felt that an express search and seizure guarantee was necessary to accomplish this result; Randolph disagreed.

As the convention wore on, however, the Federalists decided to compromise on the bill of rights issue and agreed to a series of recommending amendments in order to avoid a possible defeat of the Constitution or an indefinite adjournment of the convention.[58] On the other hand, the anti-Federalists leaders, such as Henry, would not accept this compromise and insisted that any proposed amendments be a *pre-condition* to ratification, rather than be recommending in nature.[59] On June 25, 1788, the issue came to a head, and a motion to ratify the Constitution with recommending amendments passed 89–79,

---

54. II B. Schwartz at 815 (Patrick Henry speech, June 24, 1788).

55. As will be seen later, the United States Supreme Court later chose a less drastic remedy for enforcing the Fourth Amendment's prohibition against general warrants: namely, the *Weeks-Mapp* exclusionary rule of evidence discussed at Chapter 17 of this work, rather than a complete discharge of the arrested man from custody under a habeas corpus writ. Nonetheless, this speech by one of the leading revolutionary leaders of the day indicates the deep aversion against general warrants entertained by the colonial leadership of the day and the tough enforcement measures they assumed were available against such warrants.

56. "That general warrants are grievous and oppressive, and ought not to be granted, I fully admit. I heartily concur in expressing my detestation of them. But we have sufficient security here also. We do not rely on the integrity of any one particular person or body, but on the number and different orders of the members of the government—some of them having necessarily the same feelings with ourselves. Can it be believed that the federal judiciary would not be independent enough to prevent such oppressive practices? If they will not do justice to persons injured, may they not go to their own state judiciaries, and obtain it?" II B. Schwartz at 805–06 (Edmund Randolph speech, June 15, 1788).

57. This is yet another expression of the wide-spread aversion to general warrants among the American colonial leadership of the period and the strong enforcement measures that everyone assumed the courts would adopt to prohibit them.

58. R. Rutland at 171–72.

59. R. Rutland at 173; II B. Schwartz at 762.

after defeating by a vote of 88–80 an anti-Federalist motion to require a declaration of rights and other amendments as a pre-condition to ratification.[60]

A twenty-member committee was then promptly appointed to prepare a series of recommending amendments in accord with the motion to ratify which had just passed.[61] On the committee was a fair cross-section of Federalist and anti-Federalist leaders including James Madison, Edmund Randolph, Patrick Henry, George Mason, James Monroe, and John Marshall.[62] On June 27, 1788, the committee reported to the convention a series of recommending amendments which included a comprehensive declaration of rights containing twenty separate articles.[63] A search and seizure guarantee was contained in these articles:

> That every freeman has a right to be secure from all unreasonable searches and seizures of his person, his papers and property; all warrants, therefore, to search suspected places, or seize any freeman, his papers, or property, without information on oath (or affirmation of a person religiously scrupulous of taking a oath) of legal and sufficient cause, are grievous and oppressive; and all general warrants to search suspected places, or to apprehend any suspected person, without specifically naming or describing the place or person, are dangerous, and ought not to be granted.[64]

As will be seen later, this proposal was the immediate model upon which the Fourth Amendment was eventually based.

On June 27, 1788, the convention approved all forty of the proposed amendments, prefaced by a statement urging the Virginia delegation to the First Congress to obtain ratification of these amendments.[65] The convention thereafter adjourned.

e. New York

On June 17, 1788, the New York Ratification Convention met in Poughkeepsie, New York, with only nineteen of the sixty-five delegates committed to ratification, and the balance being anti-Federalist.[66] The Federalists forces, led by Alexander Hamilton, John Jay and Robert Livingston, came largely from New York City;[67] the anti-Federalist majority was led by George Clinton, the governor of the state and chairman of the convention, together with Melancton Smith, John Lansing, and Robert Yates representing districts outside New York City.[68]

The contending forces clashed largely over the issue of a bill of rights and other amendments. The Federalists were agreeable to such amendments so long as they were recommendary in nature, while the anti-Federalists insisted that the amendments be a pre-condition to ratification. After a long series of debates in which Hamilton and Smith were the chief protagonists, after a strong recommending bill of rights was proposed, and after Hamilton had threatened that New York City and southern New York counties might

60. II B. Schwartz at 833–38.
61. II B. Schwartz at 838–39.
62. II B. Schwartz at 839.
63. II B. Schwartz at 840–42.
64. II B. Schwartz at 841–42.
65. II B. Schwartz at 840–45.
66. C. Rossiter at 293; C. Van Doren at 231.
67. R. Rutland at 177.
68. C. Van Doren at 231–32.

join the Union without the rest of the state—many of the anti-Federalists, including Smith, finally agreed to the Federalists' position.[69] On July 26, 1788, the convention ratified the Constitution by the slim margin of 30–27, together with a recommending bill of rights.[70]

Included in this bill of rights was a search and seizure guarantee similar to the Virginia recommending amendment:

> That every Freeman has a right to be secure from all unreasonable searches and seizures of his person his papers or his property, and therefore that all Warrants to search suspected places or seize any Freeman his papers or property, without information upon Oath or Affirmation of sufficient cause, are grievous and oppressive; and that all general Warrants (or such in which the place or person suspected are not particularly designated) are dangerous and ought not to be granted.[71]

f. North Carolina

North Carolina was the last state to hold a ratification convention prior to the establishment of the new federal government. On July 21, 1788, the North Carolina Ratification Convention met in Hillsboro and was from beginning to end overwhelmingly anti-Federalist.[72] Willie Jones, a Jefferson follower, was the acknowledged leader of the anti-Federalist forces.[73] James Iredale, who later served on the U.S. Supreme Court, was the spokesman for the outnumbered Federalist delegates.[74] As was true in Virginia, the central issue debated at the convention was the absence of a bill of rights.[75] Although the Federalists were willing to compromise on the issue with limited recommending amendments, this was unacceptable to Jones and the anti-Federalists, who favored extensive amendments as a pre-condition to ratification.[76]

The convention debates were rather short, as the result seemed a foregone conclusion. By August 1, 1788, Iredale and the other Federalists saw no point in continuing and submitted a pro forma motion to ratify the Constitution with six recommending amendments; this motion was defeated 184–84.[77] The next day the convention approved, by the same vote, a motion which called for the passage of a declaration of rights composed of twenty articles and twenty-six other amendments to the structure of government as a pre-condition to ratification of the Constitution.[78]

The proposed declaration of rights contained a search and seizure guarantee that was almost the same as the Virginia and New York recommending amendments on search and seizure:

> That every freeman has a right to be secure from all unreasonable searches and seizures of his person, his papers, and property; all warrants, therefore, to search suspected places, or to apprehend any suspected person, without specially naming or describing the place or person, are dangerous, and ought not to be granted.[79]

69. C. Van Doren at 231–34; C. Rossiter at 293–94.
70. C Van Doren at 234–35; II B. Schwartz at 854–55.
71. II B. Schwartz at 913.
72. C. Van Doren at 235.
73. R. Rutland at 182; C. Van Doren at 235–36.
74. II B. Schwartz at 932; C. Van Doren at 235.
75. II B. Schwartz at 932–33.
76. II B. Schwartz at 932.
77. II B. Schwartz at 932, 965–66, 971–77.
78. II B. Schwartz at 932, 966–71, 977.
79. II B. Schwartz at 968.

The convention thereupon passed a resolution that neither ratified nor rejected the Constitution, and then adjourned.[80]

Section 3. Formation of the New Government and Passage of the Bill of Rights

a. New government is established

After all the states, except North Carolina and Rhode Island, had ratified the Constitution, the confederation congress agreed to a timetable for the election of the president and vice-president, and established the time for the commencement of the new government in New York City.[81] When George Washington was elected and sworn in as president on April 30, 1789, the confederation congress officially passed out of existence.[82]

On April 1 and April 6, 1789, respectively, the House and the Senate convened,[83] and were in the hands of an overwhelming Federalist majority, with eleven framers of the Constitution sitting as senators and eight as representatives.[84] James Madison was one of the most prominent members of the new Congress. Although defeated in the Virginia Assembly for election to the Senate, he had been elected to the House from his district over James Monroe.[85] During the house campaign, Madison wrote to a follower in his district indicating his support for a bill of rights, including a search and seizure guarantee.[86]

The most significant action, in turn, of the first session of the first Congress—which acted almost as a second constitutional convention—was the passage of the Bill of Rights under the leadership of Madison.[87] George Washington in his first annual message to Congress had adverted to the necessity of possible amendments to the Constitution, but left it to Congress to determine what those amendments would be.[88] The congressional action that eventually resulted honored the unwritten Federalist pledge, made during many of the crucial ratification conventions, to pass a Bill of Rights as the first order of business of the new government.

Still, it was Madison, and Madison alone, who forced the Bill of Rights issue on a strangely reluctant House—as many Federalists, having won their ratification victory, were either opposed or apathetic to the proposal, and many anti-Federalists were similarly cool to the measure as they correctly feared that its passage would quiet popular fears about the new government and undermine their political drive for a second constitutional convention. Madison, however, would not be put off. He was belatedly persuaded by

---

80. II B. Schwartz at 932, 977.

81. C. Van Doren at 238; C. Rossiter at 300.

82. C. Rossiter at 300–01.

83. R. Rutland at 197.

84. C. Rossiter at 300, 301.

85. R. Rutland at 192, 195–96.

86. "[I]t is my sincere opinion that the Constitution ought to be revised, and that the first Congress meeting under it, ought to prepare and recommend to the States for ratification, the most satisfactory provisions for all essential rights, particularly the rights of Conscience in the fullest latitude, the freedom of the press, trials by jury, security against general warrants, &c." II B. Schwartz at 997 (James Madison to George Eve, January 2, 1789).

87. C. Rossiter at 301–02.

88. II B. Schwartz at 1011–12.

Jefferson that a Bill of Rights was required to protect individual freedom. Moreover, he was politically convinced that its passage would assure the entry of North Carolina and Rhode Island into the Union—and, of utmost importance, would destroy the anti-Federalist move for a second constitutional convention, which he feared might unravel the entire Constitution. Time and again he forced the issue on the House with his arguments, his proposals and his parliamentary maneuvers—until he could not be denied.[89]

The historian Leonard Levy best captures this political paradox:

> But for Madison's persistence the amendments would have died in Congress. Our precious Bill of Rights, at least in its immediate background, resulted from the reluctant necessity of certain Federalists to capitalize on a cause that had been originated, in vain, by the Anti-Federalists for ulterior purposes. The party that had first opposed the Bill of Rights inadvertently wound up with the responsibility for its framing and ratification, whereas the people who had at first professedly wanted it discovered too late that it not only was embarrassing but disastrous for their ulterior purposes.[90]

As a result, Madison's eventual victory "in the face of opposition and apathy entitles him to be remembered as the father of the Bill of Rights even more than as the father of the Constitution."[91] Indeed, "[o]f all Madison's achievements, the Bill of Rights remains his noblest heritage to the nation."[92]

b. Madison's Bill of Rights speech to the House

On June 8, 1789, Madison presented to the House his proposal for amendments to the Constitution which in large part became the Bill of Rights. He had gone over the 210 recommending amendments proposed by the state ratification conventions, the conditional amendments approved by the North Carolina convention, and the proposed amendments made by the minority at the Pennsylvania and Maryland conventions.[93] He derived his proposals, however, primarily from the forty Virginia recommending amendments[94]—and, in particular, proposed a search and seizure guarantee that in its language is taken in condensed form from the Virginia recommendation:

> The rights of the people to be secured in their persons; their houses, their papers and their other property, from all unreasonable searches and seizures, shall not be violated by warrants issued without probable cause, supported by oath or affirmation, or not particularly describing the places to be searched, or the persons or things to be seized.[95]

---

89. For a discussion of Madison's pivotal role in framing the Bill of Rights and in forcing the measure through the House, see Leonard Levy, Origins of the Bill of Rights 34–38 (Yale Univ. paperback 2001).

90. Leonard Levy, Origins of the Bill of Rights 43 (Yale Univ. paperback 2001).

91. Leonard Levy, Origins of the Bill of Rights 34 (Yale Univ. paperback 2001).

92. Richard B. Morris, Witnesses at the Creation 257 (New American Library paperback 1985).

93. Irving Brant, James Madison: Father of the Constitution 264 (1950); II B. Schwartz at 983.

94. Irving Brant, James Madison: Father of the Constitution 265 (1950); II B. Schwartz at 1007–09.

95. II B. Schwartz at 1027. The Virginia recommending amendment, in turn, was based on the Massachusetts state constitutional guarantee on search and seizure in the sense that the term "unreasonable searches and seizures" is derived from. Justice Frankfurter has therefore correctly stated that Madison based his search and seizure proposal on "the Massachusetts form." Harris v. United States, 331 U.S. 145, 158, 67 S.Ct. 1098, 91 L.Ed. 1399 (1947 (Frankfurter, J. dissenting).

Madison gave an historic speech to the House when he presented his bill of rights proposals. He proposed a series of eight amendments to be inserted at various points into the text of the Constitution, rather than being set apart at the end of the document.[96] In particular, Madison proposed that ten clauses be inserted in Article I, Section 9 of the Constitution containing what in large part later became the Bill of Rights, including the search and seizure guarantee.[97] After presenting these constitutional amendments, he then devoted the rest of his speech to defending the necessity for a bill of rights, during which he made two important points for Fourth Amendment purposes.

First, Madison answered the oft-repeated Federalist argument that there was no need for a bill of rights because the central government, having only enumerated powers, had no delegated power to trespass on anyone's rights.[98] Here Madison elaborated on an argument made by Patrick Henry at the Virginia Ratification Convention, as well as by the minority report of the Maryland Ratification Convention. He argued that under the Constitution, Congress had the power to make all laws which shall be "necessary and proper" for carrying into execution those powers that are otherwise vested in the government of the United States [Art. I, sec. 8, cl. 18, U.S. Const.]. He then reasoned:

> The General Government has a right to pass all laws which shall be necessary to collect its revenue; the means for enforcing the collection are within the direction of the Legislature: *may not general warrants be considered necessary for this purpose*, as well as for some purposes which it was supposed at the framing of their constitutions the State Governments had in view? *If there was reason for restraining the State Governments from exercising this power, there is like reason for restraining the Federal Government.*[99]

Plainly, Madison sought by the proposed search and seizure guarantee to prohibit Congress from passing legislation authorizing the use of general warrants to enforce its revenue measures by seizing untaxed goods and arresting its possessors. This had been the practice during the writs of assistance regime in the American colonies as well as the general warrants regime in England, and Madison's proposal was clearly designed to end this practice.

Second, Madison answered the argument that a bill of rights would be ineffectual and could be violated with impunity as had been the case under some of the state constitutions. In particular, he made the extremely important argument that the federal judiciary would have the power to enforce the Bill of Rights against any encroachments by the executive or legislative departments:

> If they [the bill of rights] are incorporated into the constitution, independent tribunals of justice will consider themselves in a peculiar manner the guardians of those rights; they will be an impenetrable bulwark against every assumption of power in the legislative or executive; they will be naturally led to resist every encroachment upon rights expressly stipulated for in the constitution by the declaration of rights.[100]

Without question, then, Madison intended that the proposed bill of rights was to be a series of legal guarantees, not mere admonitions, which would be enforced by the federal

---

96. II B. Schwartz at 1026–28.
97. II B. Schwartz at 1026–27.
98. See, e.g., The Federalist, no. 84 (Hamilton) 555–61 (Modern Library ed. 1937).
99. II B. Schwartz at 1030–31 (emphasis added)..
100. II B. Schwartz at 1031.

courts.[101] In this connection, Madison was undoubtedly influenced by his friend and political associate, Thomas Jefferson, who had written him from Paris just three months earlier:

> In the arguments in favor of a declaration of rights, you omit one which has great weight with me, the legal check which it puts into the hands of the judiciary. This is a body, which if rendered independent, and kept strictly to their own department merits great confidence for their learning and integrity.[102]

Moreover, Patrick Henry and Richard Henry Lee exchanged correspondence during this period and expressed, in effect, the same view.[103]

c. House debates and action

After some delays, Madison's proposed amendments were referred to a select committee of eleven, composed of one representative from each of the eleven states.[104] On July 28, 1789, the committee made its report to the House, recommending the Madison proposals without substantial alteration.[105] The proposed search and seizure guarantee, however, had been altered somewhat from Madison's proposal:

> The right of the people to be secured in their persons, houses, papers and effects, shall not be violated by warrants issuing without probable cause, supported by oath or affirmation, and not particularly describing the place to be searched, and the persons or things to be seized.[106]

On August 13–18, 1789, after further delays, the House resolved itself into the committee of the whole and took up the committee of eleven's report.[107] On August 17, 1789, the House committee of the whole briefly debated Madison's search and seizure guarantee and voted on a series of three amendments. Upon motion by Elbridge Gerry, the term "unreasonable seizures and searches" was inserted, along with a housekeeping change, so that the amendment was virtually identical to Madison's original proposal:

> The right of the people to be secure in their persons, houses, papers and effects against unreasonable seizures and searches shall not be violated by warrants issuing without probable cause, supported by oath or affirmation, and not par-

---

101. Later the U.S. Supreme Court fashioned a remedy to give the Fourth Amendment the force of law : the *Weeks-Mapp* exclusionary rule which will be discussed at Chapter 17 of this work. Indeed, in adopting such a rule in *Mapp v. Ohio,* 367 U.S. 643, 647, 81 S.Ct. 1684, 6 L.Ed.2d 1081, 1085 (1961), the Court quotes this passage from Madison's speech to support the conclusion—first expressed in *Boyd v. United States,* 116 U.S. 616, 630, 6 S.Ct. 524, 29 L.Ed. 746, 751 (1886)—that courts must have a "jealous regard for maintaining the integrity of individual rights."

102. II B. Schwartz at 620 (letter from Jefferson to Madison, March 15, 1789). Schwartz states that the statement in this letter "led Madison to emphasize, when he later presented his draft of the Bill of Rights to Congress, that the courts would enforce the limitations imposed in his proposed amendments." II B. Schwartz at 593.

103. Patrick Henry wrote: "The Judiciary are the sole protection against a tyrannical execution of the laws ... They [Congress] cannot depart from the Constitution; and their laws in opposition would be void." Richard Henry Lee, in reply, agreed: "Your observation is perfectly just; that right, without power to protect it, is of little avail." Charles Warren, Congress, the Constitution, and the Supreme Court 92 (rev ed. 1935) (ellipsis and brackets in original).

104. II B. Schwartz at 1050, 1057–61.

105. II B. Schwartz at 1050, 1061.

106. II B. Schwartz at 1112.

107. II B. Schwartz at 1050, 1062–1120.

ticularly describing the place to be searched, and the persons or things to be seized.[108]

Further, Egbert Benson, a representative from New York, moved to amend this proposal by striking the words "by warrants issuing" and substituting "and no warrant shall issue"; Samuel Livermore, a representative from New Hampshire, also moved to amend this proposal by striking the words "and not" between "affirmation" and "particularly."[109] Although at first defeated, these changes were ultimately adopted by the House on final passage.

On August 19–22, 1789, the House went out of the committee of the whole and proceeded to consider, as the House itself, the committee of the whole's report on amendments.[110] At the outset, Roger Sherman, a representative from Connecticut, made a motion that all amendments be placed at the end of the Constitution, rather than inserted within the text of the Constitution; the motion passed.[111] This was a crucial change, as it is doubtful whether the Bill of Rights would have attained its position as the vital center of our constitutional law if its provisions had been distributed throughout the Constitution as Madison had originally proposed.[112]

On August 20, 1789, the House approved the committee of the whole's proposed amendment on search and seizure.[113] Two days later, the House finished its debate on the committee's report, having modified several of the other proposed amendments; the House then approved these amendments, and appointed a committee of three representatives—Egbert Benson, Roger Sherman and Theodore Sedgwick—to draft a resolution containing the amendments previously approved.[114] On August 24, 1789, Benson, on behalf of this committee, reported to the House a proposed resolution setting forth seventeen articles to be proposed to the states as amendments to the Constitution.[115] Included in these articles is, in fact, the precise wording of what is now the Fourth Amendment; in an unorthodox move, the drafting committee had incorporated the changes previously proposed by Egbert and Livermore and inverted the term "unreasonable seizures and searches" to read "unreasonable searches and seizures."[116] Nonetheless, the House on that day approved the drafting committee's resolution as worded and sent it to the Senate.[117]

---

108. II B. Schwartz at 1112.
109. II B. Schwartz at 1112.
110. II B. Schwartz at 1125–38.
111. II B. Schwartz at 1121, 1125–26.
112. II B. Schwartz at 1121.
113. II B. Schwartz at 1112, 1127.
114. II B. Schwartz at 1138.
115. II B. Schwartz at 1122–24, 1138.
116. II B. Schwartz at 1123.
117. II B. Schwartz at 1121–22, 1122–24, 1138; Cuddihy at 1412–13; L. Levy at 244. Moreover, after the Senate approved its version of the Bill of Rights proposals and a conference committee worked out the differences with the House version, both the House and the Senate ultimately approved the conference committee's report incorporating the entire Bill of Rights proposals [including the final version of the Fourth Amendment] that was sent to the states. Accordingly, Lasson and Landynski conclude that it cannot now be claimed that the Amendment was improperly passed, notwithstanding the unauthorized alteration by the House drafting committee. N. Lasson at 102–03; J. Landynski at 42.

d. Senate action and final approval

There is no report of Senate debates on the Bill of Rights, because the Senate sat behind closed doors at that time and continued to do so until February 1794.[118] There are, however, some limited records from the Senate Journals and Annals of Congress that give a skeleton-like account of the Bill of Rights debate.[119]

On September 2–9, 1789, the Senate debated and made numerous changes in the House proposals, although it approved the search and seizure guarantee as it came from the House.[120] After a conference committee worked out the differences between the House and the Senate versions on the other amendments, a finalized version of twelve amendments was finally approved by the House on September 24, 1789, and by the Senate on September 25, 1789.[121] The sixth of these amendments was the search and seizure guarantee which later became the Fourth Amendment to the Constitution.[122]

e. Ratification by the states

On October 2, 1789, President Washington formally transmitted the proposed twelve amendments to the states for ratification.[123] This action, in turn, dislodged North Carolina and Rhode Island into formally ratifying the Constitution and officially joining the Union, as Madison had predicted it would.[124] And the anti-Federalist drive for a second constitutional convention soon collapsed, as popular fears of the new national government were allayed, and popular opposition to the Constitution virtually disappeared.[125]

Very little is known of the ratification debates on the bill of rights in the state legislatures, as there are little or no records of same.[126] From 1789–91, eleven of the fourteen states,[127] the required three quarters [Art. V, U.S. Const.], ratified ten of the proposed twelve amendments after no doubt some spirited debates.[128] The sixth of the ratified amendments was the search and seizure guarantee which became the Fourth Amendment.[129] On

118. II B. Schwartz at 1145.
119. II B. Schwartz at 1145.
120. II B. Schwartz at 1145–47, 1147–54.
121. II B. Schwartz at 1159, 1162–63.
122. II B. Schwartz at 1164–65.
123. II B. Schwartz at 1171, 1172.
124. On November 21, 1789, North Carolina approved the Constitution by a vote of 193–75 at a second ratification convention in Fayetteville. R. Rutland at 215–16; C. Rossiter at 303; C. Van Doren at 257. On May 29, 1790, Rhode Island approved the Constitution by a narrow vote of 34–32 at a ratification convention held in Providence. C. Rossiter at 303.
125. Leonard Levy, Origins of the Bill of Rights, 34, 43 (Yale Univ. paperback 2001).
126. II B. Schwartz at 1171.
127. In addition to North Carolina and Rhode Island, Vermont was also admitted to the Union during the ratification period on March 4, 1791. R. Rutland at 217.
128. II B. Schwartz at 1164,1171, 1202–1203. The two proposed amendments that failed ratification did not involve rights guarantees. The first proposed amendment dealt with a formula for apportioning representatives in the House. The second proposed amendment provided that "[n]o law, varying the compensation for the services of the senators and representatives, shall take effect until an election of representatives shall have intervened." Ironically, this proposed amendment was, in fact, ratified by the states two centuries later on May 7, 1992 and became the 27th Amendment to the Constitution. No time limit had been set by Congress in 1789 for the states to act on the proposed twelve amendments. The U.S. Constitution and Fascinating Facts About It 56 (7th ed. 2000).
129. II B. Schwartz at 1164–65.

December 15, 1791, Virginia became the eleventh and deciding state to ratify the Bill of Rights.[130] On March 1, 1792, Thomas Jefferson, as Secretary of State, officially announced the adoption of the Bill of Rights in a letter addressed to the governors of the several states.[131] Only Massachusetts, Connecticut and Georgia had failed to ratify these amendments, and they belatedly did so in 1941 to commemorate the 150th anniversary of the Bill of Rights.[132]

130. R. Rutland at 217.
131. II B. Schwartz at 1203.
132. R. Rutland at 217, n. 65.

Chapter 6

Historical Purpose of the Fourth Amendment

Section 1. Introduction

The preceding chapters have attempted to trace in narrative fashion the historical background of the Fourth Amendment from 1761–91. This chapter, on the other hand, attempts to draw inferences from this narrative history and ascertain the historical purpose of the Fourth Amendment. To accomplish this objective, however, it is necessary to refer briefly to various aspects of material already covered in greater detail. Because this necessarily involves some repetition, the reader's indulgence is requested. The repetition will be mercifully short as we move swiftly to the two purposes that the Framers wished to accomplish in adopting the Fourth Amendment. Those purposes were: (1) to end the abuse of general exploratory searches wrought by the general writs of assistance regime by constitutionalizing the special writs or special warrants practice of the common law; and (2) to empower the federal courts to enforce the Fourth Amendment as a legal guarantee.

Before treating these two purposes in depth, however, some introductory observations are in order. The Fourth Amendment, as drafted by James Madison and later modified by the House of Representatives, was derived from the recommendary amendment on search and seizure proposed by the Virginia Ratification Convention.[1] The Virginia amendment, however, was influenced by the search and seizure guarantees contained in the constitutions of the several states, particularly the Massachusetts guarantee which first recognized the right to be free from all "unreasonable searches and seizures."[2] Moreover, the last-minute alteration of Madison's proposal just before final passage in the House divided the Fourth Amendment into two clauses. The first clause guaranteed to the people an independent right "to be secure in their persons, houses, papers and effects against unreasonable searches and seizures." The second clause required warrants of search and arrest to be specific in nature and prohibited general warrants: "and no warrants shall issue, but upon probable cause, supported by oath or affirmation, particularly describing the place to be searched and things or person to be seized." Before this final revision, however, the last draft of the Amendment ran the two clauses together and provided, in effect, that the subject right could only be violated by the issuance of general warrants—thereby confining the guaranteed freedom to a prohibition against general warrants.[3] The final version, therefore, widened the scope of the guarantee to protect a general freedom

1. See Chapter 5, Sec. 3b of this work.
2. See Chapter 5, Section 3b of this work. See also Chapter 4 of this work, especially Section 5.
3. See generally Chapter 5, Section 3c of this work.

from unreasonable searches and seizures, and expressly outlawed general warrants as, in effect, an infringement of such freedom. As Cuddihy states: "The framers of the [Fourth] amendment were less concerned with a right against general warrants than with the broader rights those warrants infringed. * * * Privacy was the bedrock concern of the [Fourth] amendment, not general warrants."[4]

Similarly, after reviewing the above change in the draft of the Fourth Amendment in the House of Representatives, the Court in *Payton v. New York*,[5] stated:

> It is thus perfectly clear that the evil the [Fourth] Amendment was designed to prevent was broader than the abuse of a general warrant. Unreasonable searches or seizures conducted without any warrant at all are condemned by the plain language of the first clause of the Amendment.

It is a mistake, however, to focus exclusively on the exact words and grammatical construction of the Fourth Amendment—without reference to the overarching historical purpose it was designed to accomplish. Indeed, the historical purpose of the Fourth Amendment gives real meaning to the broad-based right to be free from "unreasonable searches and seizures," a point that Justice Frankfurter has emphasized[6] and the Court has expressly adopted.[7] Consequently, the extensive historical background of the Fourth Amendment covering a thirty-year period of American and English history (1761–91) is extremely important in understanding the content and meaning of the Fourth Amendment.

Section 2. First Historical Purpose: End General Exploratory Searches

The Fourth Amendment was primarily designed to end the abuse of general exploratory searches wrought by the general writs of assistance regime as practiced and asserted by the British customs officers in the American colonies in the period 1761–76.[8] Virtually

4. W. Cuddihy at 765–766.

5. 445 U.S. 573, 583–85, 100 S.Ct. 1371, 63 L.Ed.2d 639, 649–50 (1980).

6. "These words [of the Fourth Amendment] are not just a literary composition. They are not to be read as they might be read by a man who knows English but has no knowledge of the history that gave rise to the words.... Words must be read with the gloss of experience of those who framed them. Because the experience of those who framed the Bill of Rights was so vivid, they assumed that it would be carried down the stream of history and that their words would receive the significance of the experience to which they are addressed—a significance not to be found in the dictionary." United States v. Rabinowitz, 339 U.S. 56, 69–70, 70 S.Ct. 430, 94 L.Ed. 653 (1950) (Frankfurter, J. dissenting). "'Unreasonable' is not to be determined with reference to a particular search and seizure considered in isolation. The 'reason' by which the search and seizure is to be tested is the reason that was written out of the historical experience into the Fourth Amendment." Harris v. United States, 331 U.S. 145, 162, 67 S.Ct. 1098, 91 L.Ed. 1399 (1947) (Frankfurter, J. dissenting). "This bleak history of the past was living experience for Madison and his collaborators. They wrote that experience into the Fourth Amendment, not merely its words.... If the purpose of its framers is to be respected, the meaning of the Fourth Amendment must be distilled from contemporary history." Davis v. United States, 328 U.S. 582, 604, 605, 66 S.Ct. 1256, 90 L.Ed. 1453 (1946) (Frankfurter, J. dissenting).

7. "Mr. Justice Frankfurter wisely points out in his Rabinowitz dissent that the Fourth Amendment's proscription of 'unreasonable searches and seizures' must be read in the light of 'the history that gave rise to the words'—a history of abuses so deeply felt by the colonies as to be one of the potent causes of the Revolution." Chimel v. California, 395 U.S. 752, 89 S.Ct. 2034, 23 L.Ed. 685 (1969) (*Rabinowitz* and *Harris* overruled).

8. This view has frequently been expressed by United States Supreme Court decisions. Stanford v. Texas, 379 U.S. 476, 481–82, 85 S.Ct. 506, 13 L.Ed.2d 431 (1965); Frank v. Maryland, 359 U.S.

the entire American colonial leadership of the period, including the Framers of the Bill of Rights, intended by this Amendment to prohibit such searches by constitutionalizing the special warrants or special writs practice of the common law as an individual right—all in accord with the American understanding of existing English law on the subject. Stated differently, the Framers of the Fourth Amendment, along with the colonial leadership of the period, intended to prohibit all general warrants of search and arrest by requiring special warrants based on sworn proof of criminal wrongdoing that particularly described the place to be searched and the things or persons to be seized, as the usual method for the search of private premises by government agents—particularly homes, but also business establishments, warehouses, and other fixed premises.

This was done not as a pedantic legal exercise, but to protect an almost sacred right that the colonists felt about their privacy, particularly the privacy of their homes, but also their persons, businesses, and other private premises. The specific warrant procedure was seen as an independent judicial protection against a government that sought to intrude on this privacy for arbitrary and capricious reasons. The courts would stand as the bulwark against governmental encroachments of this precious freedom by requiring specific proof of criminal wrongdoing before a warrant would issue by a court for the search of specific private premises.

James Otis, Jr. first articulated this widely-held view in the Boston writs case of 1761,[9] and, as recounted in the preceding chapters, it was thereafter repeated in many different forms throughout the American colonies.[10] The Pennsylvania, Virginia, Connecticut, and Georgia supreme colonial courts either expressly refused, or declined to act on, applications for general writs of assistance, based on this view of English law, despite persistent pressure from the Crown to grant such applications. Although the supreme colonial courts of Massachusetts, New Hampshire, South Carolina and New York did issue such writs, this was done over often-persistent colonial opposition. Indeed, the Massachusetts colonial governor had to veto an act passed by the Massachusetts colonial legislature, after the 1761 Boston writs case, requiring specific warrants to search private premises based on proof of criminal wrongdoing.[11] And the New York and South Carolina colonial courts belatedly issued such writs only after many years of stalling. Moreover, the Virginia Committee of Correspondence expressed this view in its writings during the period.[12] Finally, the American colonists welcomed and were greatly supported in their view of English law by a series of analogous English court decisions striking down the general warrant in seditious libel cases in 1762–70.[13]

Beyond that, the controversy over the general writs of assistance, which were used to try to enforce the hated trade and navigation acts of the period, led in part to the American

---

360, 363–64, 79 S.Ct. 804, 3 L.Ed.2d 877 (1959); Weeks v. United States, 232 U.S. 383, 390, 34 S.Ct. 341, 58 L.Ed. 562, 58 L.Ed. 652 (1914); Boyd v. United States, 116 U.S. 616, 625–26, 6 S.Ct. 524, 29 L.Ed. 746 (1886). See also Jacob Landynski, "Search and Seizure," The Rights of the Accused 30 (Stuart Nagel ed. 1972) ("The Amendment was adopted in response to deep resentment against the general warrant (known as writs of assistance) used by British customs officials to search for goods smuggled into the colonies in violation of the trade and navigation acts, which severely restricted the ability of the colonies to trade with areas outside the empire."); Hugh Brogan, The Penguin History of the USA 213 n.16 (2d ed. 1999) ("The authors of the Fourth Amendment wanted to avoid any recurrence of the threat posed by writs of assistance.").

9. See Chapter 2, Section 3b of this work.

10. See Chapter 2, Section 5 of this work.

11. See Chapter 2, Section 4a of this work.

12. See Chapter 2, Section 5 of this work.

13. See generally Chapter 3 of this work.

Revolution. The American colonial view of English law on search and seizure was later written into the state constitutions adopted by eight states from 1776–84.[14] This included every state that chose to adopt a bill of rights during this period, counting among its number Massachusetts, Pennsylvania and Virginia where opposition to the general writs had been particularly fierce. It was finally inserted into the Fourth Amendment as part of the Bill of Rights at the insistence of strong political and popular pressure, which had demanded basic guarantees of personal liberty as a condition for ratifying the United States Constitution.[15]

The Fourth Amendment accomplishes this historical purpose in two clauses. The Warrants Clause of the Amendment clearly outlaws the hated writs of assistance and general warrants, as inveighed against by Otis and Camden, by proscribing the issuance of any warrant, save a specific one, one that the American colonial bench and bar had argued was required by English law to search private premises. Accordingly, the Amendment provides that "no warrant shall issue, but upon probable cause, supported by oath or affirmation, and particularly describing the place to be searched, and the persons or things to be seized."

The search and seizure clause of the Fourth Amendment, on the other hand, recognizes a general right of the people "to be secure in their persons, houses, papers, and effects, against unreasonable searches and seizures" and declares that this right "shall not be violated." Although phrased in principled language, this clause, when read in context with the basic purpose of the Fourth Amendment, guarantees what Otis and the American colonial bench and bar felt was already a recognized right under English law. This was (a) a right to demand a specific search warrant as a precondition for the search of one's private premises, particularly one's home, and (b) a right to refuse such a search where a specific warrant had not been previously issued authorizing such search.[16] Obviously, such a right would be violated where the sole authority of the search was a general warrant, as in the Wilkes-Entick cases, or a general writ of assistance as employed in the American colonies 1761–76. By implication, this right would also be violated by a search of private premises with no warrant at all, because that is what a general writ of assistance essentially was; it empowered customs officials with general exploratory search powers unconfined to any particular case for a virtually wide-open period of time.[17]

The private premises, in turn, to which the said right attached, is described in the Fourth Amendment as a "house[]" which plainly included one's home as the most sacred of all premises, but also one's business place and warehouse as well; moreover, the term

14. See generally Chapter 4 of this work

15. See generally Chapter 5, Sections 2 and 3 of this work.

16. "The other telling lesson of this [Fourth Amendment] history is that it was the common law warrant for stolen goods that embodied the requisites of 'reasonable' search. * * * [T]he basic 'original understanding' [of the Fourth Amendment] is plain enough and may be stated in this wise: 'The power to search, seize and arrest must be kept within reasonable bounds. Warrants have been issued to authorize dangerous and oppressive arrests and searches, and therefore we will now confine their issuance in line with specified requirements, developed for the common-law stolen-goods warrants with which we are all familiar and which have never given any trouble.'" T. Taylor at 39–40, 43–44.

17. Clearly, the Warrants Clause of the Fourth Amendment would be meaningless if such warrants were not otherwise required as a basic component of a "reasonable" search guaranteed by the Search and Seizure Clause of the Fourth Amendment. Indeed, "[i]t would be strange, to say the least, for the [Fourth] amendment to specify stringent warrant requirements, after having in effect negated these by authorizing judicially unsupervised 'reasonable' searches without a warrant. To detach the first [search and seizure] clause from the second [warrants] clause is to run the risk of making the second virtually useless." J. Landynski at 44.

"effects" in the Fourth Amendment no doubt covered vessels. This is so because these private premises were express targets of the general writs of assistance[18] that the Fourth Amendment was designed to prohibit. And, without question, the search and seizures outlawed were those conducted by governmental officials, not private parties, as the writs of assistance were all governmentally conducted.

All of this is not to suggest, however, that the right to be free from "unreasonable searches and seizures" forbade all searches and seizures conducted without benefit of a search warrant issued in compliance with the Warrants Clause of the Fourth Amendment. The pragmatic Framers of the Fourth Amendment were not doctrinaire about individual rights, and no doubt fully accepted the common law on searches incident to an arrest, which never required a search warrant.[19] Beyond that, the American colonists were primarily fighting the misuse of overly broad writs and warrants in private premises and never had occasion to focus on the lawful extent of warrantless searches outside of such premises.[20]

Properly viewed, then, specific warrants clothed with the protections of the common law were seen as the usual method for searching private premises, particularly the home, barring established exceptions such as hot-pursuit arrests and searches incident thereto. As to searches and seizures conducted outside private premises, warrants were probably not seen as necessary as they were not required by the common law. The only restriction seemingly intended is that such searches and seizures should not be "unreasonable" or arbitrary in nature. Moreover, these judicial protections for the search of private premises, as well as searches outside such premises, were seen as absolutely necessary to protect a deeply held and fiercely expressed right of privacy that the colonists entertained concerning their "persons, houses, papers and effects." This was particularly true as to the privacy of their homes which, in accord with an ancient English ideal, was their "castle," so eloquently expressed by William Pitt, the Elder in the English parliamentary debates of the 1760s.[21]

Section 3. Second Historical Purpose: Enforcement by Federal Courts

The Bill of Rights, including the Fourth Amendment, was not intended by the Framers to be a set of high-minded admonitions for government officials to aspire to in their discretion. Nor was this charter of freedom meant to be a series of rights that Congress at its option could implement by passing appropriate enforcement measures. To the contrary, the Framers intended the federal courts on their own to enforce the Bill of Rights as legal guarantees in adjudicating cases and controversies brought before them.

---

18. See Chapter 2, Section 3c of this work
19. T. Taylor at 39, 43.
20. T. Taylor at 41, 43.
21. See Chapter 3, Section 4, supra, of this work. As will be discussed later, this historical purpose fully supports the United States Supreme Court's subsequently announced rule that the search of private premises must, as a general rule, be accomplished with a search warrant issued in compliance with the Warrants Clause of the Fourth Amendment, subject to certain limited exceptions justified by necessity. For a discussion of the search warrant requirement rule, see Chapter 11, Section 1 of this work. The exceptions to this rule are discussed at Chapter 14 and 15 of this work.

Also this historical purpose fully supports the rule that the Fourth Amendment applies to governmentally-conducted searches and seizures, not purely private searches, as the exploratory searches that the Amendment was designed to end were all conducted by government officials. For a discussion of the governmental action rule, see Chapter 8, Section 2 of this work.

James Madison, the sponsor and principal draftsman of the Bill of Rights, in his June 8, 1789, speech to the House of Representatives clearly expressed this view when he presented his proposed amendments to the Constitution. In response to an argument that a bill of rights was unnecessary because it would be largely unenforceable, Madison stated that the federal courts, within their sphere of authority, would adopt whatever enforcement measures might be necessary to give these rights the force of law.[22] Indeed, Thomas Jefferson had expressed the same view in a letter to Madison three months earlier.[23] Moreover, this view was widely held by the American political leadership of the period, including the outstanding anti-Federalist spokesmen for a bill of rights including Patrick Henry and Richard Henry Lee.[24] Based on the historical evidence, Charles Warren has stated:

> [T]he question arises: what did the[] [Bill of Rights] framers and those who insisted on their adoption mean should be the effect? Once more it can be said emphatically that they were intended to be absolute legal guarantees to the citizens strictly binding upon every agency of the new Government, including the Congress and the Executive himself. They were declarations which were to be enforced. The radicals of 1788 knew full well that *only through the Courts of law could these rights be enforced.*[25]

Given this historical duty to enforce the Bill of Rights as a legal guarantee, Justice Hugo Black has similarly concluded: "I fail to see how courts can escape this sacred trust."[26]

Although it is uncertain what precise measures the Framers had in mind for the courts to utilize to enforce the Fourth Amendment in particular, it is abundantly clear that they intended these remedies to be extremely effective. They had just fought a revolution, in part, to guarantee Fourth Amendment freedoms to the individual and certainly were in no mood for pale measures when it came to giving these freedoms the force of law. Beyond that, certain *partial* indications of intent as to the strong measures they had in mind for Fourth Amendment enforcement can be gleaned from the thirty-year history that led up to the Amendment.

It seems quite clear, for example, that as to searches conducted pursuant to the hated writs of assistance and general warrants, the American colonial leadership and much of the populace rose up as one to condemn any arrests, criminal prosecutions and forfeitures based thereon—whether for smuggling, tax evasion, or criminal libel. The history of the Crown's largely futile efforts to enforce the general writs in Massachusetts from 1761–76 amply demonstrates this point. Time and again, the revolutionary leadership and local populace in Boston expressed their extreme opposition to the general writs, at times resorting to outright violence.[27] They thwarted the enforcement of such writs at every turn and loudly condemned the only criminal prosecution and forfeiture stemming from

---

22. See Chapter 5, Section 3b of this work. The Court in *Mapp v. Ohio,* 367 U.S. 643, 647, 81 S.Ct. 1684, 6 L.Ed.2d 1081, 1085 (1961), refers to this passage from Madison's speech to support the conclusion—first expressed in *Boyd v. United States,* 116 U.S. 616, 630, 6 S.Ct. 524, 29 L.Ed. 746, 751 (1886)—that courts must have a "jealous regard for maintaining the integrity of individual rights." This recitation also tends to support the *Mapp* Court's ultimate adoption of the exclusionary rule as a means of enforcing Fourth Amendment rights.

23. See Chapter 5, Section 3b of this work.

24. See Chapter 5, Section 2d of this work.

25. Charles Warren, Congress, the Constitution, and the Supreme Court 91 (rev. ed. 1935) (italics in original).

26. Hugo Black, "The Bill of Rights," 35 N.Y.U.L.Rev. 865, 880 (1960).

27. See Chapter 2, Section 4b of this work

a general writs seizure: the 1768–69 prosecution in Boston of John Hancock.[28] Moreover, the American colonial leadership's support of John Wilkes and his fight against the government in England during this time is further evidence of this same point. American leaders greatly applauded Wilkes' legal battles against the general warrant as supportive of their struggle against the general writs, enthusiastically embraced Lord Camden's legal judgments in the Wilkes-Entick cases condemning the general warrant in seditious libel cases, and were appalled by Wilkes' treatment at the hands of the government stemming from the general warrant searches conducted against him. While Wilkes was serving a twenty-two month prison sentence (1768–70) for criminal libel and obscenity based on evidence obtained by general warrant searches, the revolutionary leadership in Boston sent him warm letters of support that expressed their strong disapproval of Wilkes' prosecution and imprisonment.[29] In addition, the strong endorsement of the Wilkes-Entick court decisions in America tends to show that the leadership of the period accepted the remedy of civil suits as a means of redressing an invasion of private citizens' rights by a general warrant.

Beyond that, the ratification debates on the Constitution in 1787–88 and James Madison's speech presenting the Bill of Rights to the House of Representatives in June 1789 further demonstrate that criminal prosecutions and forfeitures based on a general writ of assistance or a general warrant were considered totally unacceptable by the political leadership of the period. Patrick Henry argued at the Virginia Ratification Convention that a bill of rights guarantee against general warrants was necessary lest an army of excise tax officers descend upon home owners armed with general warrants to seize property on which taxes had not been paid and make arrests.[30] The minority report of the Maryland Ratification Convention had previously made a similar argument;[31] and Madison repeated the argument when he presented his bill of rights proposals to the House of Representatives.[32] Clearly, tax evasion prosecutions and forfeitures of property based on general warrant searches were considered barred under a constitutional guarantee forbidding such searches.

Henry further insisted at the Virginia ratification debates that a search and seizure guarantee was needed as part of a bill of rights because the remedy of habeas corpus would be inadequate to protect people's rights against wrongful imprisonment based on general warrant searches.[33] Plainly, Henry contemplated no imprisonment whatever, and impliedly no criminal prosecution, based on general search and arrest warrants. Edmund Randolph immediately replied and agreed that general warrants were an anathema, but stated that the federal and state courts were sufficiently empowered to prevent such practices without a search and seizure guarantee in the federal constitution.[34] Clearly, Federalist (Randolph) and anti-Federalist (Henry) alike considered imprisonment and criminal prosecutions based on general warrant searches to be beyond the pale, with or without a bill of rights.

In sum, the Framers of the Fourth Amendment clearly intended the federal courts to enforce the Fourth Amendment as a legal guarantee. Arrests, forfeitures, and criminal prosecutions based on general warrant or general writ of assistance searches were considered strictly forbidden by the revolutionary leadership of the period. Civil suits brought by the

28. See Chapter 2, Section 4b of this work.
29. See Chapter 3, Section 3b of this work.
30. See Chapter 5, Section 2d of this work.
31. See Chapter 5, Section 2c of this work.
32. See Chapter 5, Section 3b of this work.
33. See Chapter 5, Section 2d of this work.
34. See Chapter 5, Section 2d of this work.

victims of general warrant searches were also looked upon with favor in redressing the wrong suffered by such searches. The American people had fought a revolution, in part, to guarantee Fourth Amendment freedoms to the individual and were unwilling to ratify the Constitution without a bill of rights containing such a guarantee; they further expected this right, which they had fought so hard for, to be given the force of law under the new national government. The federal courts were expected to carry out this constitutional mandate by adopting whatever enforcement measures might be necessary to achieve this objective when deciding cases or controversies under Article III of the Constitution.[35]

35. As will be discussed later, the *Weeks-Mapp* exclusionary rule of evidence adopted by the United States Supreme Court to enforce Fourth Amendment guarantees, along with certain limitations and exceptions thereto, is consistent with the original understanding of the Framers of the Fourth Amendment. See Chapter 17, Section 2 of this work.

Part II

Substantive Law of the Fourth Amendment

Introductory Note

As previously stated,[1] there are two requirements that must be met before it can be said that a person's Fourth Amendment rights have been violated.

(1) The first requirement is a threshold "Standing Requirement"—that is, the complaining party must show, in the language of the Fourth Amendment, that a "search[ ]" or a "seizure[ ]" of the complaining party's "person[ ], house[ ], papers, [or] effects" has been conducted by an agent of the government. If this requirement is *not* met, the Fourth Amendment is *inapplicable* to the challenged activity and no Fourth Amendment violation has occurred. On the other hand, if this requirement *is* met, the Fourth Amendment is *applicable* to the governmental action complained of—and it is necessary to determine whether the second Fourth Amendment requirement has been met.

(2) The second Fourth Amendment requirement is an "Unreasonableness Requirement"—that is, the party complaining must show, in the language of the Fourth Amendment, that the challenged search or seizure in question was "unreasonable." If this requirement is *not* met, the Fourth Amendment has been *satisfied*. On the other hand, if this requirement *is* met, the Fourth Amendment has been *violated*—and it is necessary to determine what sanction, if any, should be imposed for such a violation in a given case.

The chief sanction established by the U.S. Supreme Court for enforcing the Fourth Amendment has been the *Weeks-Mapp* exclusionary rule. That rule, save for certain limitations and exceptions, bars the government from using the fruits of an unreasonable search or seizure as evidence against the victim of the search or seizure in a federal or state criminal trial. The Court has also adopted a secondary civil damages remedy for Fourth Amendment violations.

The United States Supreme Court has followed certain theories of constitutional construction in developing these two Fourth Amendment requirements and the corollary exclusionary rule, which theories are briefly analyzed in Chapter 7. Subpart A [Chapters 8–10], Subpart B [Chapters 11–16], and Subpart C [Chapter 17] then discuss, respectively, the Fourth Amendment "Standing Requirement," the Fourth Amendment "Unreasonableness Requirement," and the *Weeks-Mapp* exclusionary rule.

---

1. Chapter 1, Section 2b of this work.

Chapter 7

Interpretation of the Fourth Amendment: Approaches to Constitutional Construction

Section 1. Introduction

This book is not a treatise on jurisprudence, and no effort is made here to advance a systematic theory of judicial review. Other works have been written in this field, and the reader is referred to them for a more formal treatment of the subject.[2] Instead, what will be developed here is a *description* of the various theories and canons of constitutional construction that the U.S. Supreme Court appears to follow when interpreting the Fourth Amendment. Working theories of this nature are necessarily eclectic and somewhat unstructured, but they are nonetheless important because they have proved useful over the years and enjoy a wide-spread judicial acceptance.

To begin with, the Court is presented with an obvious and unavoidable problem. The Fourth Amendment, like other provisions of the Bill of Rights, is largely framed in natural law language containing certain broad-based terms such as "unreasonable searches and seizures." This is not surprising, as no great individual right guaranteed by a constitution can be properly stated without using principled terms—terms that represent a dimension of justice, fairness or morality. Although these principled terms have great importance in that they point in broad general directions, they often do not dictate the outcome of close cases because they have no exact, positivistic meaning. Reasonable people of goodwill may differ as to their meaning and application in such cases.[3] This is not to say that the

2. See, e.g., Alexander Bickel, The Least Dangerous Branch (1962); Ronald Dworkin, Taking Rights Seriously (1977); Raoul Berger, Government by the Judiciary: The Transformation of the Fourteenth Amendment (1977); Jesse Choper, Judicial Review and the National Political Process: A Functional Reconsideration of the Role of the Supreme Court (1980); John Hart Ely, Democracy and Distrust: A Theory of Judicial Review (1980); Arthur Miller, Toward Increased Judicial Activism: The Political Role of the Supreme Court (1982); Michael Perry, The Constitution, the Courts and Human Rights (1982); Laurence Tribe, Constitutional Choices (1985); Antonin Scalia, A Matter of Interpretation(1997; Jeffrey Shamas, Constitutional Interpretation: Illusion and Reality (2001); Akhil Amar, America's Constitution (2005); Stephen Breyer, Active Liberty (2005). For a critique of such theories, see Daniel A. Ferber & Suzanna Sherry, Desperately Seeking Certainty: The Misguided Quest for Constitutional Foundations (2002).

3. As Justice Jackson has candidly stated:

"The Fourth Amendment first declares in bold terms: 'The right of the people to be secure in their persons, houses, papers, and effects, against unreasonable searches and seizures shall not be violated.... 'Our trouble arises because this sentence leaves debatable what particular searches are unreasonable

Framers somehow botched the job by not using exact, positivistic terms—for if they had, the right guaranteed would have been extremely limited and perhaps even trivial in nature. The irony—and herein lies the problem facing the Court—is that one cannot state a great constitutional right without using principled terms, but these terms, although greatly significant, have no obvious self-executing meaning and often excite considerable debate in given cases.[4]

It has therefore been necessary, as surely the Framers contemplated, for the Court to turn to certain theories and canons of constitutional construction in order to help give exact meaning to the Fourth Amendment and apply it in concrete cases. But these theories and canons are also somewhat principled in nature, and reasonable people of goodwill may at times apply them in given cases to reach different results. Ultimately, then, the Court cannot avoid making choices between conflicting, reasonable views in a given case, and must rest its decision on what appears to be the most reasonable legal position asserted. The Court necessarily assumes that there is a "right" decision in each case and relies on various theories, canons and modes of reasoning to help discover that decision and demonstrate its correctness. Happily, all constitutional questions may be reopened and reconsidered by the Court if the results reached do not in the long run stand the ultimate test of history, experience and reason.[5] It is one of our saving graces in this important but inexact craft of constitutional decision-making.

Generally speaking, the Court has relied on three theories of constitutional construction when interpreting the Fourth Amendment: (1) an historical approach, (2) a balancing-of-the-interests approach, and (3) a common law reasoning approach.

First, the Court has often turned for guidance to the extensive historical background, both American and English, that led to the adoption of the Fourth Amendment—and has attempted to construe the Amendment based on the historical purpose, fundamental

---

ones. Those who think it their duty to make searches seldom agree on this point with those who find it in their interest to frustrate searches." Harris v. United States, 331 U.S. 145, 195, 67 S.Ct. 1098, 91 L.Ed. 1399 (1947) (Jackson, J. dissenting).

4. See generally Ronald Dworkin, Taking Rights Seriously 131–37 (1977). "Our amended Constitution is the lodestar of our aspirations. Like every text worth reading, it is not crystalline. The phrasing is broad and the limitations of its provisions are not clearly marked. Its majestic generalities and ennobling pronouncements are both luminous and obscure. This ambiguity, of course, calls forth interpretation, the interaction of reader and text." Justice William Brennan, "The Constitution of the United States: Contemporary Ratification," Interpreting the Constitution: The Debate Over Original Intent 23 (Jack Rakove ed. 1990).

"A constitution states or ought to state not rules for the passing hour, but principles for an expanding future." Benjamin Cardozo, The Nature of the Judicial Process 83 (1921).

"The Bill of Rights was drafted in broad, sweeping terms, allowing meaning to be developed in response to changing times and current problems." O'Connor, Sandra Day, The Majesty of the Law 60 (2004).

"But the meanings of the Constitution's words are especially difficult to pin down. Many of its most precise commands are relatively trivial—such as the requirement that the President must be 35 years old—while nearly all of its most important phrases are deliberate models of ambiguity. Just what does the Fourth Amendment prohibit as an 'unreasonable search?'" Laurence Tribe, God Save This Honorable Court 42 (1985).

5. See, e.g., Vasquez v. Hillery, 474 U.S. 254, 266, 106 S.Ct. 617, 88 L.Ed.2d 598 (1986) (the Court departs from a past precedent when necessary "to bring its opinions into agreement with experience and with facts newly ascertained" (quoting from Burnet v. Coronado Oil & Gas Co., 285 U.S. 393, 412, 52 S.Ct. 443, 76 L.Ed. 815 (1932) (Brandeis, J. dissenting).

values, shared understandings and underlying principles that prompted the Framers to adopt it. Part I [Chapters 2–6] of this work has already examined in detail this historical background and purpose. As a corollary to this historical approach, the Court has also utilized two canons of constitutional construction: (1) the canon of liberal construction in which the Court liberally construes the right guaranteed by the Fourth Amendment in order to effect the intent of the Framers, and (2) the canon of long usage in which the Court gives deference to practices long recognized and followed in our Anglo-American history, including "framing era" statutes and common law rules, as being consistent with Fourth Amendment guarantees.

Second, the Court, particularly in cases since 1961, has often relied on a balancing-of-the-interests approach in determining whether a given search or seizure is an "unreasonable" one. This approach has often been used in cases of first impression where the historical approach offers little guidance. Indeed, the term "unreasonable" in the Fourth Amendment virtually invites the Court to engage in some type of balancing process in which competing interests are considered. In so doing, the Court has tended to weigh (1) the high importance of individual privacy, together with the degree of official interference therewith represented by the search or seizure in question, as against (2) the gravity of the public interests served by the official intrusion. Obviously, this approach calls for an exercise in judgment, but it has helped to guide the Court's judgment in resolving difficult cases.

Third, the Court has relied on a common law reasoning approach when applying the rules announced in its prior Fourth Amendment cases—whether in unique or analogous fact patterns. The intervening history of court interpretations, once decided, obviously plays a most important role when the Court applies the Fourth Amendment in a given case. Here the Court turns to the both holdings and underlying reasoning process of past cases to determine whether the case falls within the reach of the rule, or of the underlying justification of the rule, previously announced. Also past cases frequently announce a series of governing principles that Court often turns to for guidance in deciding a given case. And in cases of first impression, the Court at times engages in principled adjudication reasoning, using public policy considerations to reach its result. Judges and lawyers instantly recognize this entire approach in constitutional decision-making, as it is the very essence of garden-variety legal reasoning.[6]

These three approaches to Fourth Amendment decision-making, it should be noted, are not watertight. Often, the Court has used more than one of these approaches in a given case.[7] Other times, only one approach has been used or primarily used to reach a given result. Moreover, the separate concurring and dissenting opinions of United States Supreme Court justices have also used one or more of these approaches in Fourth Amendment cases. At times, these separate opinions have proved most influential in the development of Fourth Amendment law and have even been adopted by the Court in later cases. We turn now to a more detailed analysis of each of these three approaches to Fourth Amendment decision-making.

6. See Edward Levi, An Introduction to Legal Reasoning (1949).

7. For a representative example of how the Court has used the historical approach, together with the common law reasoning approach (history of prior cases and principled adjudication), to interpret the Fourth Amendment, see: Virginia v. Moore, 553 U.S. 164, 128 S.Ct. 1598, 170 L.Ed.2d 559(2008) (historical approach: Part II of the opinion); (common law reasoning, past history of cases approach: Part IIIA of the opinion); and (common law reasoning, principled adjudication approach: Part IIIB of the opinion).

Section 2. The Historical Approach: The Original Understanding of the Framers

a. An overview to the historical approach

As previously stated, the U.S. Supreme Court in cases of first impression, and other cases as well, has at times turned for guidance to the extensive historical background, both American and English, that led to the adoption of the Fourth Amendment. In doing so, the Court has attempted to discover the "original understanding" of the Framers and to construe the Amendment based on the historical purpose, fundamental values, established practices, and underlying principles that prompted the Framers to adopt the Fourth Amendment. This historical approach is of long standing, as it derives from the nature of the Constitution itself, and has always enjoyed widespread public respect and acceptance.[8] As James Madison has written, "[if] the sense in which the Constitution was accepted and ratified by the Nation ... be not the guide in expounding it, then there can be no security for a consistent and stable [government], more than for a faithful exercise of its powers."[9] Although the "original understanding" of the Framers does not answer all questions of constitutional interpretation and is not useful in all cases, it has helped illuminate the endeavor and has often been the starting point of initial constructions of the Constitution. Stated differently, the Court has long consulted the intent of the Framers, although not slavishly so, as an important guide in interpreting the Constitution.[10] Justice William Brennan has described this flexible historical approach as follows:

---

8. Jack Rakove, Professor of History at Stanford University, raises the question: "Why, then, in a society not otherwise known to defer to past wisdom, do appeals to the original meanings of the Constitution and the original intent of its framers still play a conspicuous role in our political and legal discourse?" His answer: "For better or worse, the Revolutionary era provides Americans with the one set of political symbols that come close to universal acceptance." Jack Rakove, Original Meanings 366, 367 (Vintage paperback 1997).

9. 9 James Madison, The Writings of James Madison 191 (G. Hunt ed. 1900–10).

10. "In determining whether a search or seizure is unreasonable [under the Fourth Amendment], we begin with history. We look to the statutes and common law of the founding era to determine the norms the Fourth Amendment was meant to preserve." Virginia v. Moore, 553 U.S. 164, 128 S.Ct. 1598, 1602, 170 L.Ed. 2d 559 (2008). "To determine what is an 'unreasonable' search under the Fourth Amendment, we look first to the historical practices the Framers sought to preserve; if those provide inadequate guidance, we apply traditional standards of reasonableness."Arizona v. Gant, 556 U.S. 322, 129 S.Ct. 1710, 1724, 173 L.Ed.2d 485 (2009) (Scalia, J. concurring) ("Since the historical scope of officers' authority to search vehicles incident to arrest is uncertain, [citation omitted], traditional standards of reasonableness govern." id.)

"In deciding whether a challenged governmental action violates the [Fourth] Amendment, we have taken care to inquire whether the action was regarded as an unlawful search and seizure when the Amendment was framed." Florida v. White, 526 U.S. 559, 119 S.Ct. 1555, 1558, 143 L.Ed.2d 748 (1999). "In determining whether a particular governmental action violates this provision [the Fourth Amendment], we inquire first whether the action was regarded as an unlawful search or seizure under the common law when the Amendment was framed." Wyoming v. Houghton, 526 U.S. 295, 119 S.Ct. 1297, 3100, 143 L.Ed.2d 408 (1999).

"I join the Court's opinion with the understanding that history is meant to inform, but not automatically to determine, the answer to a Fourth Amendment question." Wyoming v. Houghton, 526 U.S. 559, 119 S.Ct. 1297, 3104, 143 L.Ed.2d 408 (1999). (Breyer, J. concurring). "We read [the Constitution's] words, not as we read legislative codes which are subject to continuous revision with the changing course of events, but as the revelation of the great purposes which are intended to be achieved by the Constitution as a continuing instrument of government." United States v. Classic, 313 U.S. 299, 316, 61 S.Ct. 1031, 85 L.Ed. 1368 (1941); see Raoul Berger, Government by the Judiciary:

> We current Justices read the Constitution in the only way we can: as Twentieth Century Americans. *We look to the history of the time of the framing* and to the intervening history of interpretation. But the ultimate question must be, what do the words of the text mean in our time? For the genius of the Constitution rests not in any static meaning it might have had in a world that is dead and gone, but in the adaptability of its great principles to cope with current problems and current needs.[11]

In its Fourth Amendment decision-making, the historical approach has particularly gained widespread acceptance by the Court for at least three additional reasons. First, there are extensive historical background materials, both American and English, for the Court to consult in determining the "original understanding" of the Framers. This has made the Court's task much easier than it has been when interpreting other provisions of the Constitution where the historical background materials are not that extensive.[12]

Second, virtually the entire revolutionary leadership of the period was of one mind when adopting the Fourth Amendment, as previously discussed in chapter six of this work. They entertained virtually no ambiguous ideas about what they, as framers and ratifiers, intended to accomplish in adopting the Fourth Amendment. Their intent, on the whole, is relatively plain as revealed by the historical materials.

Third, and perhaps most important, the "original understanding" of the Framers of the Fourth Amendment—particularly the Amendment's underlying principles and broad historical purpose—has long been considered by the Court as exceptionally relevant to modern times. Indeed, the Court has always considered Fourth Amendment freedoms to have a certain timeless quality in the historical struggle for freedom, and to be absolutely indispensable to a free society. If anything, the Court has viewed this "original understanding" to be even more relevant to modern times than it was when the Fourth Amendment was adopted in the late eighteenth century, given the greater threats to personal privacy in today's society.[13]

The Transformation of the Fourteenth Amendment 367 (1977) (In interpreting the Constitution, "it has been the Court's practice over the years to consult the intention of the Framers.").

"The study of history for the purpose of ascertaining the original understanding of constitutional provisions is much like the study of legislative history for the purpose of ascertaining the intent of the lawmakers who enact statutes. In both situations the facts uncovered by the study are usually relevant but not necessarily dispositive." Georgia v. Randolph, 547 U.S. 103, 126 S.Ct. 1515, 1528, 164 L.Ed.2d 208 (2006) (Stevens, J. concurring). See also Justice Scalia's discussion of originalism as applied to the Randolph case. 126 S.Ct. at 1539–41 (Scalia, J. dissenting).

11. William Brennan, "The Constitution of the United States: Contemporary Ratification," Interpreting the Constitution: The Debate Over Original Intent 27 (Jack Rakove ed. 1990) (emphasis added).

12. "Alone among those constitutional provisions which set standards of fair conduct for the apprehension and trial of accused persons, the Fourth Amendment provides us with a rich historical background rooted in American, as well as English, experience; it is the one procedural safeguard in the Constitution that grew directly out of the events which immediately preceded the revolutionary struggle with England." J. Landynski at 19.

13. "If times have changed, reducing everyman's scope to do as he pleases in an urban and industrial world, the changes have made the values served by the Fourth Amendment more, not less important." Coolidge v. New Hampshire, 403 U.S. 443, 455, 91 S.Ct. 2022, 29 L.Ed.2d 564 (1971). "It is always somewhat dangerous to ground exceptions to constitutional protections in the social norms of a given historical moment. The purpose of the Fourth Amendment's requirement of reasonableness 'is to preserve that degree of respect for privacy of persons and the inviolability of their property that existed when the provision was adopted—even if a later, less virtuous age should become accustomed to considering all sorts of intrusion 'reasonable.'" Richards v. Wisconsin, 520 U.S. 385, 117 S.Ct. 1416, 137 L.Ed.2d 615, 623 n. 4 (1997), quoting from Minnesota v. Dickerson, 508 U.S. 366, 380, 113 S.Ct. 2130, 124 L.Ed.2d 334 (1993) (Scalia, J. concurring).

b. The seminal case of *Boyd v. United States*

The historical approach in Fourth Amendment decision-making began with *Boyd v. United States*,[14] the first leading decision on the Fourth Amendment. The case was decided in 1886 and proved to be enormously influential as it laid down the basic historical framework for interpreting the Fourth Amendment that the Court has followed ever since, together with the corollary canons of liberal construction and long usage.[15] At issue in that case was the constitutionality of a federal statute that compelled a person to produce one's private books and papers on motion of the U.S. Attorney in all suits arising from the federal revenue laws—upon pain of admitting the truth of the U.S. Attorney's criminal allegations concerning the said books and papers. The case itself involved a civil forfeiture proceeding in which the government sought to forfeit thirty-five cases of plate glass on the ground that the goods had been imported into the country without paying the required import duties. The Court held that the claimants' compelled production of a certain invoice under the above statute violated the claimants' Fourth and Fifth Amendment rights, that the admission of the invoice in evidence at the forfeiture proceeding was error, and that the statute authorizing this procedure was unconstitutional. In interpreting the Fourth Amendment, the Court relied heavily on the intent of the Framers as revealed by the historical background that led to the Fourth Amendment.

In the early part of the opinion, the Court states:

> In order to ascertain the nature of the proceedings intended by the Fourth Amendment to the Constitution under the terms 'unreasonable searches and seizures,' it is only necessary to recall the contemporary or then recent history of the controversies on this subject, both in this country and in England.[16]

Then follows an analysis of the relevant American and English historical background to the Fourth Amendment which, the Court says, was "fresh in the memories of those who achieved our independence and established our form of government."[17] James Otis, Jr.'s legal argument against the writs of assistance in Boston in 1761 and the debate in which it occurred is referred to as "perhaps the most prominent event which inaugurated the resistance of the colonies to the oppression of the mother country."[18] The English battles against the general warrant in the 1760s are also recounted by the Court, with great stress being laid on the English case of *Entick v. Carrington*.[19] The Court states:

> As every American statesman, during our revolutionary and formative period as a nation, was undoubtedly familiar with this monument of English freedom, and considered it as the true and ultimate expression of constitutional law, it may be confidently asserted that its propositions were in the minds of those who framed the Fourth Amendment, and were considered as sufficiently explanatory of what was meant by unreasonable searches and seizures.[20]

---

14. 116 U.S. 616, 6 S.Ct. 524, 29 L.Ed. 746 (1886).

15. "The Boyd opinion has been the guide to the interpretation of the Fourth Amendment to which the Court has frequently recurred." Harris v. United States, 331 U.S. 145, 160, 67 S.Ct. 1098, 91 L.Ed. 1399 (1947) (Frankfurter, J. dissenting).

16. 116 U.S. at 624–25, 6 S.Ct. at 529.

17. 116 U.S. 625, 6 S.Ct. at 529.

18. Ibid.

19. 19 Howell's State Trials 1029 (1765). For an analysis of the *Entick* case, see Chapter 3, Section 2c of this work.

20. 116 U.S. at 626–27, 6 S.Ct. at 530.

The Court then quotes at length from Lord Camden's opinion in the *Entick* case, extracts certain principles from the decision, and concludes that in light of these principles the Framers of the Fourth Amendment would never have approved the statute in question.[21]

As a further corollary to this historical analysis, the Court also announces a canon of liberal construction in interpreting the Fourth Amendment so as to further the high purpose of the Framers. The Court considers, in this context, an objection that the statute in question did not authorize a technical search and seizure but only a compulsory production of books and papers, and therefore did not come within the literal terms of the Fourth and Fifth Amendments. The Court rejects this argument:

> Though the proceeding in question is divested of many of the aggravating incidents of actual search and seizure, yet, as before said, it contains their substantial purpose. It may be that it is the obnoxious thing in its mildest and least repulsive form; but illegitimate and unconstitutional practices get their first footing in that way, namely: by silent approaches and slight deviations from legal modes of procedure. This can only be obviated by adhering to the rule that *constitutional provisions for the security of person and property should be liberally construed.* A close and literal construction deprives them of half their efficacy and leads to gradual depreciation of the right, as if it consisted more in sound than in substance. It is the duty of the courts to be watchful for the constitutional rights of the citizen, and against any stealthy encroachments thereon. Their motto should be obsta principis [avoid beginnings].[22]

The oft-quoted canon of liberal construction of the Fourth Amendment was born in this paragraph and has since been relied on by the Court in a variety of cases.

Earlier in the opinion, the Court also examines, as part of its historical analysis, various customs statutes passed by Congress, to determine whether the present statute could be deemed reasonable by long usage. The Court relies on the canon of construction that "long usage, acquiesced in by the courts, goes a long way to prove that there is some plausible ground for it, in the historical facts which have imposed a particular construction of the law favorable to usage," but that "we do not find any long usage or any contemporary construction of the Constitution which would justify any of the acts of Congress now under consideration."[23] The Court particularly focuses on a customs statute passed by the First Congress as indicative of the intent of the Framers of the Fourth Amendment, inasmuch as the First Congress proposed the Fourth Amendment to the states. In so doing, the Court announces a variation on the canon of long usage. "As this Act," the Court states, "was passed by the same Congress which proposed for adoption the original Amendments to the Constitution, it is clear that the members of that body did not regard

21. "Can we doubt that when the Fourth and Fifth Amendments to the Constitution of the United States were penned and adopted, the language of Lord Camden was relied on as expressing the true doctrine on the subject searches and seizures, and as furnishing the true criteria of the reasonable and unreasonable character of such seizures. Could the men who proposed these Amendments, in light of Lord Camden's opinion, have put their hands to a law like those of March 3, 1863, and March 2, 1867, before recited? If they could not, would they have approved the fifth section of the Act of June 22, 1874 [the statue in question], which was adopted as a substitute for the previous laws. It seems to us that the question cannot admit of doubt. They never would have approved of them. The struggles against arbitrary power, in which they had been engaged for more than twenty years would have been too deeply engraved in their memories to allow them to approve of such insidious disguises of the old grievance they had so deeply abhorred." 116 U.S. at 630.

22. 116 U.S. at 635. (emphasis added).

23. Ibid.

searches and seizures of this kind as 'unreasonable,' and they are not embraced within the prohibition of the Amendment."[24] The Court concludes, however, that the 1789 Act afforded no precedent for the statutes under consideration.

c. Post-Boyd cases utilizing the historical approach

Although the narrow holding of the Boyd case has since been considerably eroded by more modern authorities,[25] its basic historical approach—together with the corollary canons of liberal construction and long usage—have since been followed by the Court as a major guide to interpreting the Fourth Amendment.[26] What follows is a brief review of the post-*Boyd* cases that have utilized this overall approach, although often combined with a common law reasoning or balancing approach as well, to support the Court's ultimate result.

(1) Historical analysis cases

There are many Supreme Court cases that have either engaged in a full-scale historical analysis of the Fourth Amendment, similar to the *Boyd* case, as the *primary* basis for the decision reached by the Court,[27] or have recited, in part, the historical background of the Fourth Amendment as *one* of the bases for the Court's ultimate decision.[28] A large number of other Supreme Court cases have relied on the historical purpose of the Fourth Amendment, variously stated, to support the result reached.[29] Moreover, there are many

---

24. 116 U.S. at 635.

25. See Fisher v. United States, 425 U.S. 391, 96 S.Ct. 1569, 48 L.Ed.2d 39 (1976); Couch v. United States, 409 U.S. 322, 93 S.Ct. 611, 34 L.Ed.2d 548 (1973).

26. Justice Brandeis has stated that the *Boyd* decision is "a case that will be remembered as long as civil liberty lives in the United States." Olmstead v. United States, 277 U.S. 438, 474, 48 S.Ct. 564, 571, 72 L.Ed. 944 (1928) (Brandeis, J. dissenting).

27. Stanford v. Texas, 379 U.S. 476, 85 S.Ct. 506, 13 L.Ed.2d 431 (1965); Marcus v. Search Warrant, 367 U.S. 717, 81 S.Ct. 1708, 6 L.Ed.2d 1127 (1961); Frank v. Maryland, 359 U.S. 360, 79 S.Ct. 804, 3 L.Ed.2d 877 (1959), overruled, Camara v. Municipal Court, 387 U.S. 523, 87 S.Ct. 1727, 18 L.Ed.2d 930 (1967).

28. Riley v. California, 574 U.S. ___, 134, S.Ct. 2473, 2494, 189 L.Ed.2d 430 (2014) (warrantless search of the digital data on a cell phone seized from an arrestee struck down as comparable to the unrestrained general writs of assistance against which the Founders fought a revolution to end); United States v. Jones, 565 U.S. ___, 132 S.Ct. 945, 181 L.Ed.2d 911,918, 919, 919 n.3 (2012) (government trespassory entry onto property is a "search" if it was so considered at time Fourth Amendment was adopted); Virginia v. Moore, 553 U.S. 164, 128 S.Ct. 1598, 1602–04, 170 L.Ed. 2d 559 (2008); Oliver v. United States, 466 U.S. 170, 104 S.Ct. 1735, 80 L.Ed.2d 214, 223 (1984); Steagald v. United States, 451 U.S. 204, 220, 101 S.Ct. 1642, 68 L.Ed.2d 38 (1981); Payton v. New York, 445 U.S. 573, 583–85, 100 S.Ct. 1371, 63 L.Ed.2d 639 (1980); Marshall v. Barlow's Inc., 436 U.S. 307, 311–12, 98 S.Ct. 1816, 56 L.Ed.2d 305 (1978); United States v. United States District Court, 407 U.S. 297, 316, 92 S.Ct. 2125, 32 L.Ed.2d 752 (1972); Henry v. United States, 361 U.S. 98, 100–01, 80 S.Ct. 168, 4 L.Ed.2d 134 (1959); Marron v. United States, 275 U.S. 192, 195, 48 S.Ct. 74, 72 L.Ed. 231 (1927); Weeks v. United States, 232 U.S. 383, 389–91, 34 S.Ct. 341, 58 L.Ed.2d 652 (1914).

29. United States v. Verdugo-Urquidez, 494 U.S. 259,110 S.Ct. 1056, 108 L.Ed.2d 222, 233 (1990) (purpose of Fourth Amendment was to protect the people of the United States against arbitrary action of the federal government, not to restrain the actions of the federal government against aliens outside U.S. territory); Brower v. County of Inyo, 489 U.S. 593, 109 S.Ct. 1378, 103 L.Ed.2d 628, 635 (1989) (Fourth Amendment is aimed against the intentional abuses of governmental power as seen in the writs of assistance and general warrants, not the accidental effect of otherwise lawful government conduct); Walter v. United States, 447 U.S. 649, 655 n. 6, 100 S.Ct. 2395, 65 L.Ed.2d 410 (1980) (Fourth Amendment directed against unrestricted search and seizure power as a means of press censorship); Arkansas v. Sanders, 442 U.S. 753, 759 n. 5, 99 S.Ct. 2586, 61 L.Ed.2d 235 (1979) (Fourth Amendment was product of colonial resentment against the writs of assistance); Lo-Ji Sales, Inc. v.

concurring and dissenting opinions authored by individual Supreme Court Justices that have adopted the historical approach to reach the result urged in the opinion—portions of which are, at times, cited by the Court in subsequent cases.[30]

(2) *Canons of liberal construction and long usage*

Many Supreme Court cases have used the canon of liberal construction, first announced in *Boyd,* to support the result reached. In each of these cases, the canon was used to justify an application of the Fourth Amendment in favor of the individual—at times in the context of rejecting an overly technical reading of the Fourth Amendment that would defeat the Amendment's primary purpose of protecting the privacy of the individual against intrusions by an overreaching government.[31]

New York, 442 U.S. 319, 325, 99 S.Ct. 2319, 60 L.Ed.2d 920 (1979) (Fourth Amendment intended to protect against the general warrant or writ of assistance of the eighteenth century); United States v. Chadwick, 433 U.S. 1, 7–8, 97 S.Ct. 2476, 53 L.Ed.2d 538 (1977) (Fourth Amendment grew out of the colonists' experience with the writs of assistance, which were often carried out in private residences, although not limited thereto); G.M. Leasing Corp. v. United States, 429 U.S. 338, 355, 97 S.Ct. 619, 50 L.Ed.2d 530 (1977) (one of the primary evils which the Fourth Amendment was designed to eliminate was the massive invasion of privacy undertaken in the collection of taxes pursuant to general warrants and writs of assistance); Chimel v. California, 395 U.S. 752, 89 S.Ct. 2034, 23 L.Ed.2d 685 (1969) (Fourth Amendment was a reaction to the general warrants and warrantless searches that had so alienated the colonists and helped speed the movement for independence); Berger v. New York, 388 U.S. 41, 49, 87 S.Ct. 1873, 18 L.Ed.2d 1040 (1967) (the underlying value which the Fourth Amendment seeks to protect is the right of individual privacy); Warden, Md. Penitentiary v. Hayden, 387 U.S. 294, 301, 87 S.Ct. 1642, 18 L.Ed.2d 782 (1967) (Fourth Amendment was a reaction to the evils of the general warrant in England and the writs of assistance in the colonies and was intended to protect against invasions of the home and other privacies of life from indiscriminate government searches); Silverman v. United States, 365 U.S. 505, 511, 81 S.Ct. 679, 5 L.Ed.2d 734 (1961) (Fourth Amendment was primarily designed to protect a person from unreasonable government intrusions into one's home); Trupiano v. United States, 334 U.S. 699, 710, 68 S.Ct. 1229, 92 L.Ed.2d 1663 (1948) (Fourth Amendment was designed to protect the innocent and guilty alike from unreasonable intrusions into individual privacy while leaving adequate room for the necessary processes of law enforcement); Go-Bart Importing Co. v. United States, 282 U.S. 344, 357, 51 S.Ct. 153, 75 L.Ed. 374 (1931) (purpose of Fourth Amendment warrants clause was to protect against all general searches); Burdeau v. McDowell, 256 U.S. 465, 41 S.Ct. 574, 65 L.Ed. 1048 (1921) (Fourth Amendment was intended to restrain government officials, not private individuals).

30. See, e.g., Justice O'Connor's dissenting opinion in *Vernonia School District 47J v. Acton,* 515 U.S. 646, 115 S.Ct. 2386, 132 L.Ed.2d 564 (1995), for an example of the use of the historical approach in a separate opinion by a Supreme Court Justice. See also Justice Scalia's dissenting opinion in Maryland v. King, 569 U.S. ___, 133 S.Ct. 1958 , 186 L.Ed2d 1, 32–33 (2013).

Clearly, the most comprehensive and influential set of separate opinions on the Fourth Amendment involving a full-blown historical approach was Justice Frankfurter's trilogy of dissenting opinions in *United States v. Rabinowitz,* 339 U.S. 56, 70 S.Ct. 430, 94 L.Ed. 653 (1950); *Harris v. United States,* 331 U.S. 145, 67 S.Ct. 1098, 91 L.Ed. 1399 (1947); and *Davis v. United States,* 328 U.S. 582, 66 S.Ct. 1256, 90 L.Ed. 1453 (1946)—which were eventually accepted in substance by the Court in *Chimel v. California,* 395 U.S. 752, 89 S.Ct. 2034, 23 L.Ed.2d 685 (1969). Also Justice Douglas' dissenting opinion in *Frank v. Maryland,* 359 U.S. 360, 79 S.Ct. 804, 3 L.Ed.2d 877 (1959), heavily relies on the historical approach in its reasoning process—which opinion was eventually accepted in substance by the Court in *Camara v. Municipal Court,* 387 U.S. 523, 87 S.Ct. 1727, 18 L.Ed. 930 (1967). Finally, Justice Brandeis' famous dissenting opinion in *Olmstead v. United States,* 277 U.S. 438, 48 S.Ct. 564, 72 L.Ed. 944 (1928), relies, in part, on the underlying historical purpose of the Fourth Amendment: to prevent every unjustifiable intrusion by the government, whatever the means employed, into the privacy of the individual—which opinion was eventually accepted in substance by the Court in *Katz v. United States,* 389 U.S. 347, 88 S.Ct. 507, 19 L.Ed.2d 576 (1967).

31. Schneckloth v. Bustamonte, 412 U.S. 218, 228–29, 93 S.Ct. 2041, 36 L.Ed.2d 854 (1973); Coolidge v. New Hampshire, 403 U.S. 443, 454, 91 S.Ct. 2022, 29 L.Ed.2d 564 (1971); Silverman v.

Many other Supreme Court cases have applied the canon of long usage first announced in *Boyd*, either explicitly or implicitly, to justify the result reached. Indeed, the Court has always given great weight to long-standing search and seizure practices as strong evidence of their reasonableness for Fourth Amendment purposes.[32] The Court has at times focused on the common law in effect at the time of the adoption of the Fourth Amendment as indicative of the intent of the Framers of the Fourth Amendment.[33] At other times, the Court has focused on statutes passed by the First Congress as indicative of the Framers' intent because this Congress also proposed the Fourth Amendment to the states.[34] Similarly, the Court has relied on congressional or state statutes passed at or near the Founding era and beyond to demonstrate an accepted and long-standing search and seizure practice—to give the practice some indicia of reasonableness.[35] Nonetheless, common law and other long-standing practices, although important in a Fourth Amendment reasonableness

---

United States, 365 U.S. 505, 511, 81 S.Ct. 679, 5 L.Ed.2d 734 (1961); Johnson v. United States, 333 U.S. 10, 17 n. 8, 68 S.Ct. 367, 92 L.Ed. 436 (1948); Sgro v. United States, 287 U.S. 206, 210, 53 S.Ct. 138, 77 L.Ed. 260 (1932); Grau v. United States, 287 U.S. 124, 128, 53 S.Ct. 38, 77 L.Ed. 212 (1932); Go-Bart Importing Co. v. United States, 282 U.S. 344, 357, 51 S.Ct. 153, 75 L.Ed. 374 (1931); Byars v. United States, 273 U.S. 28, 32, 33–34, 47 S.Ct. 248, 71 L.Ed. 520 (1927); Gouled v. United States, 255 U.S. 298, 303–04, 41 S.Ct. 261, 65 L.Ed. 647 (1921); see also Silverthorne Lumber Co. v. United States, 251 U.S. 385, 391–92, 40 S.Ct. 182, 64 L.Ed. 319 (1920).

32. United States v. Watson, 423 U.S. 411, 96 S.Ct. 820, 46 L.Ed.2d 598 (1976); Colonnade Catering Corp. v. United States, 397 U.S. 72, 90 S.Ct. 774, 25 L.Ed.2d 60 (1970); Elkins v. United States, 364 U.S. 206, 80 S.Ct. 1487, 4 L.Ed.2d 1669 (1960); Wolf v. Colorado, 338 U.S. 25, 69 S.Ct. 1359, 93 L.Ed. 1782 (1949), overruled, Mapp v. Ohio, 367 U.S. 643, 81 S.Ct. 1684, 6 L.Ed.2d 1081 (1961); Carroll v. United States, 267 U.S. 132, 45 S.Ct. 280, 69 L.Ed.2d 543 (1925); see also United States v. Edwards, 415 U.S. 800, 804 n.6, 94 S.Ct. 1234, 39 L.Ed.2d 771 (1974).

33. "In reading the [Fourth] Amendment, we are guided by 'the traditional protections against unreasonable searches and seizures afforded by the common law at the time of the framing,' since '[a]n examination of the common-law understanding of an officer's authority to arrest sheds light on the obviously relevant, if not entirely dispositive, consideration of what the Framers of the Amendment might have thought to be reasonable.'" Atwater v. City of Lago Vista, 532 U.S. 318, 121 S.Ct. 1536, 1543, 149 L.Ed.2d 549 (2001) (extensive analysis of English and American common law and statutes to reject claim that warrantless arrest for a misdemeanor not amounting to a breach of the peace is unreasonable under the Fourth Amendment); Wilson v. Arkansas, 514 U.S. 927, 931, 115 S.Ct. 1914, 131 L.Ed.2d 976 (1995); United States v. Watson, 423 U.S. 411, 96 S.Ct. 820, 46 L.Ed.2d 598 (1976); Gerstein v. Pugh, 420 U.S. 103, 95 S.Ct. 854, 43 L.Ed.2d 54 (1975).

34. United States v. Villamonte-Marquez, 462 U.S. 579, 103 S.Ct. 2573, 77 L.Ed.2d 22, 28 (1983) (statute passed by First Congress authorizing the naval boarding of vessels to examine the ship manifest—relied on to support the boarding of a vessel by U.S. Customs officers to inspect the vessel's documents, as authorized by a current congressional statute which is a direct descendent of the statute passed by the First Congress) (a statute passed by the same Congress that adopted the Bill of Rights has "an impressive historical pedigree"); United States v. Ramsey, 431 U.S. 606, 616–17, 97 S.Ct. 1972, 52 L.Ed.2d 617 (1977) (statute passed by the First Congress authorizing customs officials to conduct warrantless searches of vessels relied on to support warrantless search of first class mail coming into the United States).

35. Carroll v. United States, 267 U.S. 132, 45 S.Ct. 280, 69 L.Ed. 543 (1925) (statutes passed by the First, Second and Fourth Congress authorizing the warrantless searches of vessels—as well as other similar congressional statutes passed in the 19th century—relied on to support the warrantless search of an automobile); United States v. Ross, 456 U.S. 798, 820 at 26,102 S.Ct. 2157, 72 L.Ed.2d 572, 591 (1982) (*Carroll* analysis of congressional statutes relied on to support the warrantless search of a container found during an otherwise valid warrantless search of an automobile); Wyoming v. Houghton, 526 U.S. 295, 119 S.Ct. 1297, 143 L.Ed. 2d 408 (1999) (*Carroll* and *Ross* analysis of congressional statutes relied on to support warrantless search of purse found during an otherwise valid warrantless search of automobile, which purse belonged to a passenger in the automobile); Florida v. White, 526 U.S. 559, 119 S.Ct. 1555, 143 L.Ed.2d 748 (1999) (*Carroll* analysis of congressional statutes relied on to support warrantless seizure of automobile as forfeitable contraband); Atwater v. City of Lago Vista, 532 U.S. 318, 121 S.Ct. 1536, 1548–49, 149 L.Ed.2d 549 (2001) ("framing era"

inquiry, have not always been decisive and at times have been outweighed by other considerations.[36] Indeed, the Court has at times qualified the canon of long usage so as to reflect its important, but not decisive influence in interpreting the Fourth Amendment.[37]

Section 3. The Balancing of the Interests Approach

a. An overview to the balancing approach: comparison with historical approach

The balancing-of-the-interests approach to Fourth Amendment decision-making did not emerge in a single early case like *Boyd v. United States* which the succeeding cases have since followed and elaborated on, as is true of the historical approach. Instead, the balancing approach gradually emerged in a succession of cases in the late 1960s and has continued to the present as a means of dealing with certain non-traditional search or seizure cases for which the historical approach does not provide a ready analytic framework. Essentially, it attempts to define a reasonable search or seizure by balancing the degree of the intrusion into personal privacy or security represented by the search or seizure in question as against the gravity of the governmental need for such action, together with some showing indicating that such search or seizure is not arbitrary in nature.

This approach, however, is supplementary to and not inconsistent with the historical approach to Fourth Amendment decision-making. Indeed, the central terms of the Fourth Amendment—"unreasonable searches and seizures"—invite the Court to balance the relevant interests involved where the Framers, by their original understanding, have not already balanced these interests in a particular way that resonates with modern times. Surely, the Framers contemplated such a result because they could not have possibly anticipated every conceivable type of search or seizure, and accordingly they used a flexible rule-of-reason term requiring an exercise of balanced judicial judgment to restrain all

---

state statutes relied on to reject claim that a warrantless arrest for a misdemeanor not amounting to a breach of the peace is unreasonable under the Fourth Amendment).

36. See, e.g., Tennessee v. Garner, 471 U.S. 1, 105 S.Ct. 1694, 85 L.Ed.2d 1 (1985) (rejecting common law rule that the use of deadly force was justified to arrest a fleeing felon because the justifications for such a rule are no longer applicable today).

37. "It is true that this Court has often looked to the common law in evaluating the reasonableness, for Fourth Amendment purposes, of police activity. On the other hand, 'it has not simply frozen into constitutional law those law enforcement practices that existed at the time of the Fourth Amendment's passage.'" Tennessee v. Garner, 471 U.S. 1, 105 S.Ct. 1694, 85 L.Ed.2d 1, 10–11 (1985). "A longstanding, widespread practice is not immune from constitutional scrutiny. But neither is it to be lightly brushed aside. This is particularly so when the constitutional standard is as amorphous as the word "unreasonable" [in the Fourth Amendment], and when custom and contemporary usage play such a large role in constitutional analysis." Payton v. New York, 445 U.S. 573, 600, 100 S.Ct. 1371, 63 L.Ed.2d 639 (1980). "The common law may, within limits, be instructive in determining what sorts of searches the Framers of the Fourth Amendment regarded as reasonable. [fn] The significance accorded such authority, however, must be kept in perspective ... The common law rules governing searches and arrests evolved in a society far simpler than ours today. Crime has changed, as have the means of law enforcement, and it would be naive to assume that those actions a constable would take in an English or American village three centuries ago should necessarily govern what we, as a society, now regard as proper. Instead the [Fourth] Amendment's prohibition against 'unreasonable searches and seizures' must be interpreted 'in the light of contemporary norms and conditions.'" Steagald v. United States, 451 U.S. 204, 217 & n. 9, 101 S.Ct. 1642, 68 L.Ed.2d 38 (1981).

governmental searches or seizures. It is therefore not surprising that the first early hint of the balancing approach was stated in *Carroll v. United States*,[38] as an almost essential ingredient of the historical approach:

> The Fourth Amendment is to be construed in the light of what was deemed an unreasonable search and seizure when it was adopted and in a manner which will conserve public interests as well as the interests and rights of individual citizens.[39]

And in a more modern context, the Court has stated:

> When that [historical] inquiry yields no answer, we must evaluate the search or seizure under traditional safeguards of reasonableness by assessing, on the one hand, the degree to which it intrudes on an individual's privacy [or security] and, on the other, the degree to which it is needed to promote legitimate governmental interests.[40]

The basic difference between the historical and balancing approaches lies in the direction toward which the approach tends to point in terms of ultimate outcome. The balancing approach, when employed, has generally resulted in a decision in favor of the government over the individual. Indeed, it is surely no accident that this approach has come into its own during a distinctly "conservative" trend in Fourth Amendment decision-making in the period 1970–2000. To be sure, the approach is not formulated to load the dice in favor of the government's interests over individual interests, but the approach tends to regard the competing interests as at least equally important. Moreover, a single person's interests in the abstract may seem rather paltry when balanced against the interests of society as a whole, particularly during times when the demands for law and order have been particularly compelling. Thus, the very formulation of the balancing approach in various contexts, when divorced from the historical approach, tends indirectly to point in favor of the government.

On the other hand, the historical approach tends to point more in favor of the individual. This is so because the Framers, although hardly doctrinaire libertarians, intended it to be this way. The Fourth Amendment, after all, does not confer law enforcement power on any branch of government and was never intended that way. It carves out, instead, an individual right that the Framers intended to be enforceable in the courts as a legal right against government. James Madison plainly so stated when he presented his Bill of Rights proposals to the House in 1789. Thus, to consult the "original understanding" of the Framers of the Fourth Amendment is to visit a body of historical experience and thought that gives great emphasis to the individual as opposed to the government. It should come as no surprise, then, that when the historical approach has been used by

---

38. 267 U.S. 132, 45 S.Ct. 280, 69 L.Ed. 543 (1925).

39. 267 U.S. at 149.

40. Wyoming v. Houghton, 526 U.S. 295, 119 S.Ct. 1297, 1300, 143 L.Ed.2d 408 (1999); see Riley v. California, 573 U.S. ___ , 134 S.Ct. 2473, 2485 189 L.Ed.2d 430 (2014); Virginia v. Moore, 553 U.S. 164, 128 S.Ct. 1598, 1604, 170 L.Ed. 2d 559 (2008). As an aside, it should be noted that the Court has often used a balancing approach to decide a Fourth Amendment question without a preceding historical analysis of any kind. As pointed out by Justice Stevens, "[t]o my knowledge, we have never restricted ourselves to a two-step Fourth Amendment approach wherein the privacy and governmental interests at stake must be considered only if 18th Century common law 'yields no answer.'" Wyoming v. Houghton, 526 U.S. 295, 119 S.Ct. 1297, 1300, 143 L.Ed.2d 408 (1999) (Stevens, J. dissenting). Still, in these cases it may be assumed that the Court *sub silentio* has concluded that an historical analysis would be of no help and has accordingly not addressed the issue, but proceeded directly to a balancing approach.

the Court in Fourth Amendment cases, the decision has often [but not always] been in favor of the individual.

The two approaches, however, are not unconnected with one another. Indeed, the historical approach plainly sheds light on the value and weight to be accorded the individual interests at stake in the balancing approach. Stated differently, the balancing approach, properly viewed, must give proper historical deference to the great value accorded by the Framers to individual privacy and personal security interests whenever the government conducts a search or seizure against a single individual—a value of enormous importance that is even more relevant to modern times with its greater assaults on individual privacy than it was when the Fourth Amendment was originally adopted in 1791.

The balancing approach to Fourth Amendment decision-making has no particular canonical form and has been articulated by the Court in various ways. Essentially, the approach attempts to define a reasonable search or seizure by balancing two factors: (1) the high importance of individual privacy or personal security and the degree of intrusion into that interest represented by the search or seizure in question, as against (2) the promotion of legitimate governmental interests served by such intrusion. In striking the appropriate balance, the Court strives, where practicable, to avoid giving government officials the right to conduct searches or seizures at their absolute discretion—(a) by requiring some showing of individualized wrongdoing, or (b) by requiring the use of neutral criteria[41] for conducting the intrusion, or some other like safeguard—so that, upon either showing, there is an assurance that the invasion of individual privacy or personal security is not based on the arbitrary discretion of the government official conducting the search or seizure.[42] It should be noted, however, that "a generalized interest in expedient law enforcement cannot, without more, justify a warrantless search."[43]

As to the first factor stated above, the Court has recognized that there is a difference in the degree of initial intrusion into personal privacy represented by a wide range of

41. "Neutral criteria" consists of standards unconnected with criminal wrongdoing that guide law enforcement discretion in making certain civil or administrative seizures of persons, such as roadblock stops of motor vehicles [i.e stopping every vehicle or every other vehicle for a drivers license or DUI check]. See Chapter 12, Section 1n of this work.

42. For a representative statement of the balancing approach, see Delaware v. Prouse, 440 U.S. 648, 653–55, 99 S.Ct. 1391, 59 L.Ed.2d 660 (1979); and Brown v. Texas, 443 U.S. 47, 50–51, 99 S.Ct. 2637, 61 L.Ed.2d 357 (1979). For other statements of the balancing approach, see: Samson v. California, 547 U.S. 843, 126 S.Ct. 2193, 2197, 165 L.Ed.2d 250 (2006); United States v. Knights, 534 U.S. 112, 122 S.Ct. 587, 591, 151 L.Ed.2d 497 (2001); Wyoming v. Houghton, 526 U.S. 295, 300, 119 S.Ct. 1297, 143 L.Ed.2d 408 (1999); O'Connor v. Ortega, 480 U.S. 709, 107 S.Ct. 1492, 94 L.Ed.2d 714, 724 (1987); Tennessee v. Garner, 471 U.S. 1, 105 S.Ct. 1694, 85 L.Ed.2d 1, 7 (1985); United States v. Montoya de Hernandez, 473 U.S. 531, 105 S.Ct. 3304, 87 L.Ed.2d 381, 388 (1985); New Jersey v. T.L.O., 469 U.S. 325, 105 S.Ct. 733, 83 L.Ed.2d 720, 731–32 (1985); United States v. Place, 462 U.S. 696, 103 S.Ct. 2637, 77 L.Ed.2d 110, 118 (1983); United States v. Villamonte-Marquez, 462 U.S. 579, 103 S.Ct. 2573, 77 L.Ed.2d 22, 30 (1983); Bell v. Wolfish, 441 U.S. 520, 559, 99 S.Ct. 1861, 60 L.Ed.2d 447 (1979); Pennsylvania v. Mimms, 434 U.S. 106, 109, 98 S.Ct.330, 54 L.Ed.2d 331 (1977); United States v. Martinez-Fuerte, 428 U.S. 543, 554–55, 96 S.Ct. 3074, 49 L.Ed.2d 1116 (1976); Terry v. Ohio, 392 U.S. 1, 20–21, 88 S.Ct. 1868, 20 L.Ed.2d 889 (1968); Camara v. Municipal Court, 387 U.S. 523, 536–37, 87 S.Ct. 1727, 18 L.Ed.2d 930 (1967).

43. Georgia v. Randolph, 547 U.S. 103, 126 S.Ct. 1515, 1524, n. 5, 164 L.Ed.2d 208 (2006), citing": [T]he privacy of a person's home and property may not be totally sacrificed in the name of maximum simplicity in enforcement of the criminal law," Mincey v. Arizona, 437 U.S. 385, 393, 98 S.Ct. 2408, 57 L.Ed.2d 290 (19 78); and "The warrant requirement ... is not an inconvenience to be somehow 'weighed' against the claims of police efficiency." Coolidge v. New Hampshire, 403 U.S. 443, 481, 91 S.Ct. 2022, 29 L.Ed. 2d 564 (1971); Scott v. Harris, 550 U.S. 372, 127 S.Ct. 1769, 1778–79, 167 L.Ed.2d 686 (2007).

searches, as well as a similar degree of intrusion into personal security represented by a wide range of seizures. For example, a temporary investigative detention of a person by a police officer represents a lesser degree of intrusion into personal security than that represented by a full-blown arrest of the person wherein the officer takes the individual to the police station for questioning or books him.[44] Similarly, a pat-down search of the person for weapons following such a temporary detention represents a lesser degree of intrusion into personal privacy than a full-blown search of the inner recesses of a person's clothing or body. In such cases involving lesser intrusions, the Court has looked to the various degrees of the intrusion in the balancing process. The lesser the degree of intrusion into personal privacy or security, the lesser the justification required to sustain the intrusion. The Court has therefore recognized that a temporary detention and frisk of a person on the street requires a lesser evidentiary showing than that required to sustain a full-blown arrest of the person and a full-blown search incident to effecting that arrest.[45]

As to the second factor stated above, the Court tacitly tends to recognize a difference in degree of importance among the governmental interests served by various searches and seizures. Plainly, a given search or seizure must promote some legitimate governmental interest and, without question, most do; a search or seizure which failed this elementary test would surely be condemned as unreasonable. But there is at times a considerable divergence in importance among the governmental interests served by some searches or seizures, which may figure into the balancing process. For example, Justice Jackson has stated that there is a vast difference between setting up a roadblock to catch a kidnapper, as opposed to setting up a roadblock to catch a bootlegger.[46] Similarly, Justice Powell has commented on the grave nature of the governmental interests served by searches and seizures designed to stem the trade of deadly narcotic drugs.[47] One can, of course, carry this analysis to unacceptable extremes, but there is obviously an element of common

---

44. For cases distinguishing between an investigative detention and a de facto arrest, see United States v. Sharpe, 470 U.S. 675, 105 S.Ct. 1568, 84 L.Ed.2d 605 (1985); Florida v. Royer, 460 U.S. 491, 103 S.Ct. 1319, 75 L.Ed.2d 229 (1983); Dunaway v. New York, 442 U.S. 200, 99 S.Ct. 2248, 60 L.Ed.2d 824 (1979).

45. Terry v. Ohio, 392 U.S. 1, 88 S.Ct. 1868, 20 L.Ed.2d 889 (1968).

46. "If we assume, for example, that a child is kidnaped and the officers throw a roadblock about the neighborhood and search every outgoing car, it would be a drastic and undiscriminating use of the search. The officers might be unable to show probable cause for searching any particular car. However, I should candidly strive hard to sustain such an action, executed fairly and in good faith, because it might be reasonable to subject travelers to that indignity if it was the only way to save a threatened life and detect a vicious crime. But I should not strain to sustain such a roadblock and universal search to salvage a few bottles of bourbon and catch a bootlegger." Brinegar v. United States, 338 U.S. 160, 183, 69 S.Ct. 1302, 93 L.Ed. 1879(1949) (Jackson, J. dissenting).

47. "The public has a compelling interest in detecting those who would traffic in deadly drugs for personal profit. Few problems affecting the health and welfare of our population, particularly our young, cause greater concern than the escalating use of controlled substances. Much of the drug traffic is highly organized and conducted by sophisticated criminal syndicates. The profits are enormous. And many drugs, including heroin, may be easily concealed. As a result, the obstacles to detection of illegal conduct may be unmatched in any other area of law enforcement." United States v. Mendenhall, 446 U.S. 544, 561–62, 100 S.Ct. 1870, 64 L.Ed.2d 497 (1980) (Powell, J. concurring). Justice Blackman has expressed much the same views. Florida v. Royer, 460 U.S. 491, 513, 103 S.Ct. 1319, 75 L.Ed.2d 229 (1983) (Blackmun, J. concurring).

In this connection, there is an uncomfortable element of truth in the observation of many criminal defense lawyers in America that the Fourth Amendment has been virtually repealed in cases involving large-scale narcotics trafficking, given the understandable inclination of many federal judges to uphold governmental searches and seizures involving deadly narcotic drugs. See 1 John Wesley Hall, Search and Seizure xxxi (3d ed. 2000) ("At times, criminal defense lawyers felt like the Fourth Amendment was on life support and we were working under the conditions of doctors in a war zone performing sense that enters into the balancing process, which every trial and appellate judge will instantly recognize as perfectly legitimate. Searches and seizures to enforce criminal laws of lesser importance such as bootlegging, minor theft crimes, and certain traffic offenses carrying a jail term, do not serve great governmental interests and in otherwise close cases ought not be sustained. On the other hand, searches and seizures to protect people's very lives and safety, against such crimes as airline hijacking, kidnapping, armed robbery, or large-scale narcotics trafficking, serve grave governmental interests and in close cases ought to be upheld. To be sure, the Court has not as yet spelled out in any detail how this factor should be treated, but in the real world it is plainly an important if often unstated consideration in the balancing process.

In striking the appropriate balance, the Court has generally strived to make certain that searches and seizures not rest in the unfettered discretion of the governmental official conducting the search or seizure. Indeed, to do otherwise would be false to the underlying historical purpose of the Fourth Amendment as conceived by the Framers and would return us to a modern version of the general writs of assistance regime. Where the purpose of the search or seizure is to discover evidence of crime, this factor has generally required an objective evidentiary showing establishing sufficient justification for the search or seizure in question, whether it be probable cause or reasonable suspicion. On the other hand, where the purpose of the search or seizure is civil or administrative in nature, the Court has not required an objective standard of proof and has instead authorized the use of neutral criteria by law enforcement officers in carrying out limited intrusions of personal security, as, for example, police roadblocks for drivers license checks.[48] The Court, in considering this factor in the balancing process, has sought to prevent government officials from invading people's privacy or personal security based solely on their own discretion, and has generally required some evidentiary showing or the employment of neutral criteria that reasonably restrain this authority. Only an extremely compelling showing of overarching governmental interests or of the impracticability of employing neutral criteria to carry out the subject intrusion has caused the Court to abandon this requirement.[49] We turn now to a brief review of how the balancing approach has worked out in the cases in the post-*Mapp* era.

b. General applications of the balancing approach

(1) Searches and seizures falling short of a full-scale arrest, search or seizure

The balancing approach to Fourth-Amendment decision-making has found a frequent application in a broad class of cases wherein law enforcement officials have temporarily

triage, deciding what part of the Fourth Amendment we could save. The 'war on drugs' has literally become a war on the Fourth Amendment."). Also see Thomas Regnier, *The "Loyal Foot Soldier": Can the Fourth Amendment Survive the Supreme Court's War on Drugs?*, 72 U.Mo-Kan.City L.Rev. 631 (2004).

48. See Delaware v. Prouse, 440 U.S. 648, 663, 99 S.Ct. 1391, 59 L.Ed.2d 660 (1979); id. at 663–64 (Blackmun, J. concurring).

49. See, e.g., United States v. Villamonte-Marquez, 462 U.S. 579, 103 S.Ct. 2573, 77 L.Ed.2d 22 (1983), in which the Court looked solely to compelling governmental interests in sustaining a random stop of a vessel for a documentation inspection, and did not require an evidentiary showing or neutral criteria, as in the case of land-based vehicles, where, in the Court's view, the employment of such criteria at sea would not have been practicable. The Court also relied on an historical approach to support its result. Also see the random drug testing programs that have been upheld by the Court. Chapter 15, Section 3e, infra, of this work, and cases collected.

detained a person—whether the person be on foot, in an automobile, or in a vessel—for some criminal investigative or administrative purpose. Often a limited search may follow such a detention—including a search of the person, of the conveyance in which the person is traveling, or of some effect the person is carrying. In each instance, however, the temporary detention has fallen short of a full-scale arrest or its equivalent and the ensuing search has often not amounted to a full-scale search. The purpose of the detention is to allow responsible officials to investigate further a criminal offense to determine if an arrest should be made—or to carry out some administrative purpose, such as conducting a drivers license check or a vessel document inspection. In these cases, the Court has used the balancing approach to define the constitutional limits of the intrusions into privacy and personal security. *Terry v. Ohio*[50] was the first case to employ a balancing analysis for this type of detention in a criminal investigative context, which was later followed by a series of other cases using the same balancing approach for similar detentions.[51]

It should be stressed, however, that the Court has rejected this approach where the seizure of the person goes beyond a temporary detention and amounts to full-scale arrest or its equivalent—as probable cause is always required for such an intrusion.[52] Beyond that, the Court has held that a balancing approach is generally not appropriate to decide a search or seizure issue where probable cause is, in fact, shown for the intrusion.[53]

The Court has also employed the balancing approach in several cases involving temporary detentions of persons by border patrol agents at or near the international border of the

---

50. 392 U.S. 1, 20–27, 88 S.Ct. 1868, 20 L.Ed.2d 889 (1968).

51. Maryland v. Wilson, 519 U.S. 408, 117 S.Ct. 882, 137 L.Ed.2d 41 (1997) (temporarily detained automobile passenger ordered to step out of the automobile); Pennsylvania v. Mimms, 434 U.S. 106, 98 S.Ct. 330, 54 L.Ed.2d 331 (1977) (temporarily detained automobile driver is ordered to step out of the automobile); Brown v. Texas, 443 U.S. 47, 99 S.Ct. 2637, 61 L.Ed.2d 357 (1979) (temporary detention for the purpose of ascertaining detainee's name and address); Michigan v. Summers, 452 U.S. 692, 101 S.Ct. 2587, 69 L.Ed.2d 340 (1981) (temporary detention of occupants of premises while premises are being searched for contraband pursuant to a search warrant); Michigan v. Long, 463 U.S. 1032, 103 S.Ct. 3469, 77 L.Ed.2d 1201 (1983) (temporary detention of the automobile driver followed by search of passenger compartment of automobile); United States v. Hensley, 469 U.S. 221, 105 S.Ct. 675, 83 L.Ed.2d 604 (1985) (temporary detention of automobile driver based on a police bulletin that driver was wanted on a felony charge); New York v. Class, 475 U.S. 106, 106 S.Ct.960, 89 L.Ed.2d 81 (1986) (temporary detention of automobile driver for a traffic offense followed by police intrusion into automobile to discover the automobile's vehicle identification number); see also Wyoming v. Houghton, 526 U.S. 295, 119 S.Ct. 1297, 143 L.Ed.2d 408 (1999) (balancing approach used as *secondary* basis to analyze whether police may search automobile passenger's purse during a valid probable cause search of an automobile during temporary detention of driver).

52. "Accordingly, we confirm today what our prior cases have intimated: the standard of probable cause 'applie[s] to all arrests, without the need to 'balance' the interests and circumstances involved in particular circumstances.' If an officer has probable cause to believe that an individual has committed even a very minor criminal offense in his presence, he may, without violating the Fourth Amendment, arrest the offender." Atwater v. City of Lago Vista, 532 U.S. 318, 121 S.Ct. 1536, 1557, 149 L.Ed.2d 549 (2001) (probable cause arrest for misdemeanor punishable solely by fine upheld as reasonable under the Fourth Amendment) (internal citation omitted); Dunaway v. New York, 442 U.S. 200, 213–14, 99 S.Ct. 2248, 60 L.Ed.2d 824 (1979).

53. "It is, of course, true that in principle every Fourth Amendment case, since it turns on a 'reasonableness' determination, involves a balancing of all relevant factors. With rare exceptions not applicable here, however, the result of that balancing is not in doubt where the search or seizure is based on probable cause." Whren v. United States, 517 U.S. 806, 116 S.Ct. 1769, 1776, 135 L.Ed.2d 89 (1996) (unnecessary to engage in balancing approach to determine the reasonableness of a traffic stop based on probable cause).

United States.[54] The balancing approach, however, has not been employed by the Court where the border patrol conducts a full-scale search of a person's automobile at or near the international border.[55] In another case, the Court used the balancing approach to determine the reasonableness of a temporary detention of an air traveler's suitcase at a metropolitan airport for the purpose of allowing a trained narcotics dog to sniff the subject suitcase for the presence of controlled substances therein.[56] Finally, the Court has employed the balancing approach to a random temporary stop of an automobile for a drivers license or vehicle registration check;[57] to a temporary stop of a vessel in waters having ready access to the open sea, for a vessel documentation check;[58] and to a temporary DUI roadblock stop of an automobile.[59]

(2) Unusual searches and seizures

There is another broad category of cases where the Court has used the balancing approach. For want of a better term, these cases present unusual types of searches and seizures that do not fit the traditional mold of the typical police search for evidence of crime. The Court has, accordingly, used the balancing approach to determine the reasonableness of health inspections of private homes,[60] safety inspections of private business places,[61] a home visit by a welfare worker,[62] wiretapping for domestic security purposes,[63] the surgical removal of a bullet from a person's body,[64] the use of deadly force by police to effect an arrest,[65] the workplace search of a public employee,[66] government drug testing in various contexts,[67] the inspection of Presidential papers and materials,[68] and searches

---

54. United States v. Brignoni-Ponce, 422 U.S. 873, 95 S.Ct. 2574, 45 L.Ed.2d 607 (1975) (temporary detention of automobile driver near the border, but not an established checkpoint); United States v. Martinez-Fuerte, 428 U.S. 543, 96 S.Ct. 3074, 49 L.Ed.2d 1116 (1976) (temporary detention of automobile driver at established checkpoint near border); United States v. Montoya de Hernandez, 473 U.S. 531, 105 S.Ct. 3304, 87 L.Ed.2d 381 (1985) (sixteen hour detention of traveler at border based on suspicion of alimentary canal drug smuggling).

55. United States v. Ortiz, 422 U.S. 891, 95 S.Ct. 2585, 45 L.Ed.2d 623 (1975) (traffic checkpoint search of automobile struck down as not supported by probable cause); Almeida-Sanchez v. United States, 413 U.S. 266, 93 S.Ct. 2535, 37 L.Ed.2d 596 (1973) (roving patrol search of automobile struck down as not supported by probable cause).

56. United States v. Place, 462 U.S. 696, 103 S.Ct. 2637, 77 L.Ed.2d 110 (1983).

57. Delaware v. Prouse, 440 U.S. 648, 99 S.Ct. 1391, 59 L.Ed.2d 660 (1979).

58. United States v. Villamone-Marquez, 462 U.S. 579, 103 S.Ct. 2573, 77 L.Ed.2d 22 (1983).

59. Michigan State Police v. Sitz, 496 U.S. 444, 110 S.Ct. 2481, 110 L.Ed.2d 412 (1990)

60. Camara v. Municipal Court, 387 U.S. 523,87 S.Ct. 1727, 18 L.Ed.2d 930 (1967).

61. Marshall v. Barlow's, Inc., 436 U.S. 307, 98 S.Ct. 1816, 56 L.Ed.2d 305 (1978).

62. Wyman v. James, 400 U.S. 309, 91 S.Ct. 381, 27 L.Ed.2d 408 (1971).

63. United States v. United States District Court, 407 U.S. 297, 92 S.Ct. 2125, 32 L.Ed.2d 752 (1972).

64. Winston v. Lee, 470 U.S. 753, 105 S.Ct. 1611, 84 L.Ed.2d 662 (1985).

65. Scott v. Harris, 550 U.S. 372, 127 S.Ct. 1769, 1778–79, 167 L.Ed.2d 686 (2007); Tennessee v. Garner, 471 U.S. 1, 105 S.Ct. 1694, 85 L.Ed.2d 1 (1985).

66. O'Connor v. Ortega, 480 U.S. 709, 107 S.Ct. 1492, 94 L.Ed.2d 714 (1987).

67. Ferguson v. City of Charleston, 532 U.S. 67, 121 S.Ct. 1281, 149 L.Ed.2d 205 (2001); Vernonia School District 47J v. Acton, 515 U.S. 646, 115 S.Ct. 2386, 132 L.Ed.2d 564 (1995); National Treasury Employees Union v. Von Raab, 489 U.S. 656, 109 S.Ct. 1384, 103 L.Ed.2d 685 (1989); Skinner v. Railway Labor Executives Ass'n., 489 U.S. 602, 109 S.Ct. 1402, 103 L.Ed.2d 639 (1989); see also Board of Education of Independent School District 92 v. Earls, 536 U.S. 822, 122 S.Ct. 2559, 153 L.Ed.2d 735 (2002) [balancing principles stated in Vernonia School District 47J v. Acton, supra, applied].

68. Nixon v. Administrator of General Services, 433 U.S. 425, 457–59, 97 S.Ct. 2777, 53 L.Ed.2d 867, 900–901 (1974).

of persons who are not the typical free adult—such as the search of a public school student on school grounds,[69] or a probationer,[70] or a parolee[71] or a pre-trial detainee,[72] or a prison inmate.[73] or an arrestee at time of booking (DNA sample taken).[74]

In these unusual types of cases, the balancing approach was employed to determine a variety of issues, including: (a) the type of probable cause showing for the issuance of a search warrant; (b) the type of evidentiary showing, if any, required to conduct a search or seizure of the person; and (c) whether an exception to the search warrant requirement rule should be recognized with respect to the search involved in the case.

c. Related balancing approaches in the administration of the exclusionary rule

In administering the exclusionary rule adopted to enforce the Fourth Amendment, the Court has used balancing-type approaches in its reasoning process that differ from, but are somewhat related, to the basic balancing approach employed to interpret the Fourth Amendment itself. When faced with the issue of whether to create an exception to the Fourth Amendment exclusionary rule, the Court has employed a cost/benefit type of balancing analysis. On the one hand, the Court looks to the societal cost of applying the exclusionary rule in the case presented, and invariably regards the cost as a grave one: usually the fact that the government is deprived of highly probative evidence of guilt. On the other side of the balance, the Court looks to the societal benefit of deterring future Fourth Amendment violations by applying the exclusionary rule as proposed, and generally has been skeptical of the rule's deterrent value outside the context of a criminal trial.[75] Moreover, the flagrancy of the Fourth Amendment violation weighs in favor of applying the exclusionary rule so as to deter such serious misconduct—while less egregious violations weigh against such application.[76]

Moreover, in determining whether to apply retroactively United States Supreme Court decisions that announce "new" standards in interpreting the Fourth Amendment and other

---

69. New Jersey v. T.L.O., 469 U.S. 325, 105 S.Ct. 733, 83 L.Ed.2d 720 (1985).

70. United States v. Knights, 534 U.S. 112, 122 S.Ct. 587, 151 L.Ed.2d 497 (2001).

71. Samson v. California, 547 U.S. 843, 126 S.Ct. 2193, 165 L.Ed.2d 250 (2006).

72. Bell v. Wolfish, 441 U.S. 520, 99 S.Ct.1861, 60 L.Ed.2d 447 (1979).

73. Hudson v. Palmer, 468 U.S. 517, 104 S.Ct. 3194, 82 L.Ed.2d 393 (1984).

74. Maryland v. King, 569 U.S. ___, 133 S.Ct. 1958 , 186 L.Ed2d 1 (2013).

75. Using the balancing approach, the Court has held that the exclusionary rule is inapplicable in a variety of contexts. Calandra v. United States, 414 U.S. 338, 94 S.Ct. 613, 38 L.Ed.2d 561 (1974) (grand jury proceedings); Stone v. Powell, 428 U.S. 465, 96 S.Ct. 3037, 49 L.Ed.2d 1067 (1976) (federal habeas corpus proceedings); United States v. Janis, 428 U.S. 433, 96 S.Ct. 3021, 49 L.Ed.2d 1046 (1976) (federal civil proceedings); INS v. Lopez-Mendoza, 468 U.S. 1032, 104 S.Ct. 3479, 82 L.Ed.2d 778 (1984) (deportation proceedings); United States v. Leon, 468 U.S. 897, 104 S.Ct. 3405, 82 L.Ed. 2d 677 (1984) (evidence seized pursuant to a law enforcement officer's reasonable good faith reliance on an invalid search warrant); Hudson v. Michigan, 547 U.S. 586, 126 S.Ct. 2159, 2165–68, 165 L.Ed.2d 56 (2006) ("knock and announce" violations).

In one case, however, the Court used a balancing approach to reject a proposed exception to the exclusionary rule. James v. Illinois, 493 U.S. 307, 110 S.Ct. 648, 107 L.Ed.2d 676 (1990) (impeachment of a defense witness with illegal statement obtained from defendant).

76. "The extent to which the exclusionary rule is justified by these deterrence principles varies with the culpability of the law enforcement conduct. As we said in Leon, 'an assessment of the flagrancy of the police misconduct constitutes an important step in the calculus' of applying the exclusionary rule. [citation omitted]." Herring v. United States, 555 U.S. 135, 129 S.Ct. 695, 701, 172 L.Ed.2d 496 (2009).

provisions of the Bill of Rights, the Court has employed a balancing-type approach in much of its reasoning process. In so doing, the Court has generally weighed three factors: (1) the purpose to be served by the "new" standard as announced by the decision in question; (2) the extent of reliance by law enforcement authorities on the "old" standard; and (3) the effect on the administration of justice of a retroactive application of the "new" standard. The first and leading decision to deal in depth with this issue and establish the basic balancing approach was *Linkletter v. Walker*,[77] followed by *Desist v. United States*.[78] Thereafter, the Court abandoned the balancing approach in Fourth Amendment cases of this nature and has generally followed a rule of law that Fourth Amendment decisions announcing a "new" standard do not apply retroactively.[79] Nonetheless, these are all cases that have *expanded* Fourth Amendment rights and have, accordingly, applied the exclusionary rule to suppress certain evidence. How this approach will work out when the Court is faced with whether to apply, retroactively, ground-breaking decisions that *narrow* Fourth Amendment rights and deny application of the exclusionary rule remains to be seen; it may be, however, that the balancing approach will be used to decide such a case.[80]

In addition, when faced with whether to apply the Fourth Amendment exclusionary rule to statements made by a defendant after being unlawfully arrested or detained, the Court has generally followed a balancing-type approach. Based on the fruit of the poisonous tree doctrine, the Court has treated such statements as being inadmissible in evidence unless the taint of the illegality has been dissipated after weighing certain relevant factors: (1) the flagrancy of the official misconduct involved in the case; (2) the temporal proximity between the illegal arrest or detention and the defendant's statements; and (3) the presence of intervening circumstances between the illegal arrest or detention and the subject statements.[81]

Finally, in determining whether the testimony of a live witness should be suppressed under the Fourth Amendment exclusionary rule when the identity of such witness was learned from an unreasonable search or seizure, the Court has adopted a similar balancing approach. Based on the fruit of the poisonous tree doctrine, the Court has declined to adopt a per se rule of exclusion, but instead has weighed two factors in deciding the issue: (1) the degree of free will exercised by the witness in the decision to testify; and (2) the

---

77. 381 U.S. 618, 85 S.Ct. 1731, 14 L.Ed.2d 601 (1965) (holding that Mapp v. Ohio, 367 U.S. 643, 81 S.Ct. 1684, 6 L.Ed.2d 1081 (1961), which applied the Fourth Amendment exclusionary rule to the states, did not apply retroactively).

78. 394 U.S. 244, 89 S.Ct. 1030, 22 L.Ed.2d 248 (1969) (holding that Katz v. United States, 389 U.S. 347, 88 S.Ct.507, 19 L.Ed.2d 576 (1967), which dispensed with the rule that a search and seizure required a trespass or physical penetration into a Fourth Amendment protected enclosure, did not apply retroactively).

79. See, e.g., Williams v. United States, 401 U.S. 646, 91 S.Ct. 1148, 28 L.Ed.2d 388 (1971); United States v. Peltier, 422 U.S. 531, 95 S.Ct. 45 L.Ed.2d 374 (1975); United States v. Johnson, 457 U.S. 537, 102 S.Ct. 2579, 73 L.Ed.2d 202 (1982). "[A]lthough the Court has been unwilling to conclude that new Fourth Amendment principles are always to have prospective effect, ... no Fourth Amendment decision marking 'a clear break from the past' has been applied retroactively." United States v. Leon, 468 U.S. 897, 104 S.Ct. 3405, 82 L.Ed.2d 677, 692 (1984). See Chapter 17, Section 6(f) of this work for a further discussion of this subject.

80. See 6 Wayne LaFave, Search and Seizure § 11.5(d) (5th ed. 2012).

81. Brown v. Illinois, 422 U.S. 590, 95 S.Ct. 2254, 45 L.Ed.2d 416 (1975) (defendant's statements excluded); Dunaway v. New York, 442 U.S. 200, 99 S.Ct. 2248, 60 L.Ed.2d 824 (1979) (defendant's statements excluded); Taylor v. Alabama, 457 U.S. 687, 102 S.Ct. 2664, 73 L.Ed.2d 314 (1982) (defendant's statements excluded); Rawlins v. Kentucky, 448 U.S. 98, 100 S.Ct. 2556, 65 L.Ed.2d 633 (1980) (defendant's statements not excluded). See Chapter 17, Section 3(b)(4) of this work for a further discussion of this subject.

great cost in barring live witness testimony—thereby necessitating a more direct link between the subject illegality and the live witness testimony, than the link required for other types of derivative evidence. Both these factors are clearly loaded in favor of not applying the Fourth Amendment exclusionary rule to live witness testimony.[82]

Section 4. Common Law Reasoning Approach

a. Introduction

By far, the most common form of reasoning used by the Court in interpreting the Fourth Amendment has been, for want of a better term, the common law reasoning approach which is characteristic of the general reasoning process used in all cases by common law courts in the English-speaking world.[83] This approach is found, at least in part, in virtually all Fourth Amendment decisions and consists, roughly speaking, of three broad categories: (1) the history of prior court decisions; (2) principled adjudication; and (3) a catch-all of various other devices.

b. History of prior court decisions

The most frequently employed method of common law reasoning is the history of prior relevant decisions of the Court, as it is based on the doctrine of *stare decisis* which lies at the center of all legal reasoning by common law courts. There is a narrow holding in every prior relevant U.S. Supreme Court case on the Fourth Amendment, and the Court is bound to follow that holding in future cases, absent a rare decision on its part to overrule the case. On occasion, the Court considers the case on all fours, and merely applies the holding of the prior case to reach its result.[84] At other times, a rule or rules

82. United States v. Ceccolini, 435 U.S. 268, 98 S.Ct. 1054, 55 L.Ed.2d 268 (1978) (refusing to apply the Fourth Amendment exclusionary rule to live witness testimony).

83. See Karl Llewellyn, The Common Law Tradition of Deciding Appeals (1960).

84. See e.g Michigan v. Fisher, 558 U.S., 130 S.Ct. 546, 175 L.Ed.2d 410 (2009) (applying Brigham City v. Stewart, 547 U.S. 398, 126 S.Ct. 1943, 164 L.Ed.2d 650 (2006); Kirk v. Louisiana, 536 U.S. 635, 122 S.Ct. 2458, 153 L.Ed.2d 599 (2002) (applying Payton v. New York, 445 U.S. 573, 100 S.Ct. 1371, 63 L.Ed.2d 639 (1980)); Arkansas v. Sullivan, 532 U.S. 769, 121 S.Ct. 1876, 149 L.Ed.2d 994 (2001) (applying Whren v. United States, 517 U.S. 806, 116 S.Ct. 1769, 135 L.Ed.2d 89 (1996) and Oregon v. Hass, 420 U.S. 714, 95 S.Ct.1215, 43 L.Ed.2d 570 (1975)); Flippo v. West Virginia, 528 U.S. 111, 120 S.Ct. 7, 145 L.Ed.2d 16 (1999) (applying Mincey v. Arizona, 437 U.S. 385, 98 S.Ct. 2408, 57 L.Ed.2d 290 ()); Maryland v. Dyson, 527 U.S. 465, 119 S.Ct. 2013, 144 L.Ed.2d 442 (1999) (applying Pennsylvania v. Labron, 518 U.S. 938, 116 S.Ct. 2485, 135 L.Ed.2d 1031 (1996)); Hayes v. Florida, 470 U.S. 811, 105 S.Ct. 1643, 84 L.Ed.2d 705 (1985) (applying Davis v. Mississippi, 394 U.S. 721, 89 S.Ct. 1394, 22 L.Ed.2d 676 (1969)); Thompson v. Louisiana, 469 U.S. 17, 105 S.Ct. 409, 83 L.Ed.2d 246 (1984) (applying Mincey v. Arizona, 437 U.S. 385, 98 S.Ct. 2408, 57 L.Ed.2d 290 (1978)); Michigan v. Thomas, 458 U.S. 259, 102 S.Ct. 3079, 73 L.Ed.2d 750 1982) (applying Chambers v. Maroney, 399 U.S. 42, 90 S.Ct. 1975, 26 L.Ed.2d 419 (1970)); Florida v. Meyers, 466 U.S. 380, 104 S.Ct. 1852, 80 L.Ed.2d 381 (1984) (applying Michigan v. Thomas, supra); Lanier v. South Carolina, 474 U.S. 25, 106 S.Ct. 297, 88 L.Ed.2d 23 1985) (applying Taylor v. Alabama, 457 U.S. 687, 102 S.Ct. 2664, 73 L.Ed.2d 314 (1982)); One Plymouth Sedan v. Pennsylvania, 380 U.S. 693, 85 S.Ct. 1246, 14 L.Ed.2d 170 1965) (applying Boyd v. United States, 116 U.S. 616, 6 S.Ct. 524, 29 L.Ed. 746 (1886)); Brinegar v. United States, 338 U.S. 160, 69 S.Ct. 1302, 93 L.Ed. 1879 (1949) (applying Carroll v. United States, 267 U.S. 132, 45 S.Ct. 280, 69 L.Ed. 543 (1925). Sometimes, however, there is considerable disagreement as to whether the prior case compels the result reached by the Court. See, e.g., Florida

announced in prior cases, as opposed to a narrow holding, are applied by the Court to the facts of the case at hand to reach the ultimate result.[85] On the other hand, where the prior case is factually not the same as the instant case, but is analogous thereto, the Court will apply and thereby extend the principle or reasoning of the prior case.[86] Where,

---

v. Riley, 488 U.S. 445, 109 S.Ct. 693, 102 L.Ed.2d 835 (1989) (5–4 decision) (applying California v. Ciraolo, 476 U.S. 207, 106 S.Ct. 1809, 90 L.Ed.2d 210 1986)); Taylor v. Alabama, 457 U.S. 687, 102 S.Ct. 2664, 73 L.Ed.2d 314 (1982) (5–4 decision) (applying Brown v. Illinois, 422 U.S. 590, 95 S.Ct. 2254, 45 L.Ed.2d 416 (1975) and Dunaway v. New York, 442 U.S. 200, 99 S.Ct. 2248, 60 L.Ed.2d 824 (1979)).

85. See, e.g., Missouri v, McNeely, 569 U.S. ____, 133 S.Ct. , 185 L.Ed.2d 696 (2013) (applying the totality of the circumstances rule of past cases to determine that there is no per se exigent circumstances exception to the warrant requirement in all drunk-driving cases);Bailey v. United States, 568 U.S. ____, 133 S.Ct. 1031, 185 L.Ed.2d 19 (2013) (applying the rule of Michigan v. Summers, 452 U.S. 692, 101 S.Ct. 2587, 69 L.Ed.2d 340 (1981), to limit temporary detentions incident to the execution of a search warrant to exclude persons outside the immediate vicinity of the searched premises) ; Safford Unified School District No. 1 v. Redding, 557 U.S. 364, 129 S.Ct. 2633, 174 L.Ed.2d 354 (2009) (applying the TLO standard for public school student searches); Arizona v. Johnson , 555 U.S. 323, 129 S.Ct. 781, 172 L.Ed.2d 694 (2009) (applying a line ot Terry v. Ohio cases in a traffic stop context); Brigham City v. Stuart, 547 U.S. 398, 126 S.Ct. 1943, 164 L.Ed.2d 650 (2006) (applying a line of U.S. Supreme Court cases upholding a warrantless entry onto private premises under exigent circumstances, regardless of the subjective motivations of the officers making such an entry); Davenpeck v. Alford, 543 U.S. 146, 125 S.Ct. 588, 160 L.Ed.2d 537 (2004) (applying the rule in Whren v. United States, 517 U.S. 806, 116 S.Ct. 1769, 135 L.Ed.2d 89 (1996), that an arresting officer's subjective state of mind is generally irrelevant in determining whether there is probable cause to arrest); Kaupp v. Texas, 538 U.S. 626, 123 S.Ct. 1843, 155 L.Ed.2d 814 (2003) (applying the rule of law established in Florida v. Bostick, 501 U.S. 429, 437, 111 S.Ct. 2382, 115 L.Ed.2d 389 (1991), and other cases defining when a Fourth Amendment seizure of the person takes place); United States v. Arvizu, 534 U.S. 266, 122 S.Ct. 744, 151 L.Ed.2d 740 (2002) (applying the totality-of-the-circumstances rule of past cases to determine whether reasonable suspicion existed for a temporary Terry stop); Kyllo v. United States, 533 U.S. 27, 121 S.Ct. 2038, 150 L.Ed.2d 94 (2001) (5–4 decision) (applying the rule of Katz v. United States and its progeny on what constitutes a Fourth Amendment search); Illinois v. Wardlow, 528 U.S. 119, 120 S.Ct. 673, 145 L.Ed.2d 570 (2000) (applying the rules in past Terry v. Ohio cases to reach result that unprovoked flight from the police in an area known for heavy narcotics trafficking constitutes reasonable suspicion for a temporary stop); United States v. Ramirez, 523 U.S. 65, 118 S.Ct. 992, 140 L.Ed.2d 191 (1998) (refining and applying the rules of two prior knock-and-announce, search warrant cases—to conclude that the lawfulness of a no-knock entry does not depend on whether the property is damaged in the course of the entry); Florida v. J.L., 529 U.S. 266, 120 S.Ct. 1375, 146 L.Ed.2d 254 (2000) (applying the rules of three Terry v. Ohio cases, along with principled adjudication to reject a proposed "firearms exception" to the Terry rule, to reach the result that an anonymous telephone tip did not constitute reasonable suspicion for a Terry stop); Michigan v. Chesternut, 486 U.S. 567, 108 S.Ct. 1975, 100 L.Ed.2d 565 (1988) (applying the test established by several past cases as to what constitutes a "seizure" of the "person" under the Fourth Amendment); Adams v. Williams, 407 U.S. 143, 92 S.Ct. 1921, 32 L.Ed.2d 612 (1972) (applying the stop and frisk rules previously announced in Terry v. Ohio, 392 U.S. 1, 88 S.Ct. 1868, 20 L.Ed.2d 889 (1968)); Fort Wayne Books, Inc. v. Indiana, 489 U.S. 46, 109 S.Ct. 916, 103 L.Ed.2d 34 (1989) (applying rules of past cases requiring the observance of procedural safeguards before books and films may be seized as obscene); Florida v. Wells, 495 U.S. 1, 110 S.Ct. 1632, 109 L.Ed.2d 1 (1990) (applying and refining the rule of Colorado v. Bertine, 479 U.S. 367, 107 S.Ct. 738, 93 L.Ed.2d 739 (1987), on the search of containers in an inventory search); Smith v. Maryland, 442 U.S. 735, 99 S.Ct. 2577, 61 L.Ed.2d 220 (1979) (applying the reasonable expectation of privacy test established in Katz v. United States, 389 U.S. 347, 88 S.Ct. 507, 19 L.Ed.2d 576 (1967), and its progeny to determine whether installation of a pen register on a telephone constitutes a Fourth Amendment "search"); Colorado v. Bannister, 449 U.S. 1, 101 S.Ct. 42, 66 L.Ed.2d 1 (1980) (applying the rule of past cases that an automobile may be searched without a search warrant after being seized and moved to the police station if the search is based on probable cause).

86. See, e.g., United States v. Biswell, 406 U.S. 311, 92 S.Ct. 1593, 32 L.Ed.2d 87 (1972) (applying by analogy Colonnade Catering Corp. v. United States, 397 U.S. 72, 90 S.Ct. 774, 25 L.Ed.2d 60

however, the Court sees important differences between the prior case and the instant case, the prior case will be distinguished, often clarifying or even altering its result in the process.[87]

Moreover, after a number of cases have been decided on a particular issue and various principles of law have been previously announced, the Court sometimes undertakes to re-state in hornbook fashion the controlling rules and principles of law that are relevant to the case at hand, frequently in a separate part of the opinion set out by a roman numeral or alphabetic letter. In so doing, the Court will at times "move the law along" a bit by announcing new rules derived from the reasoning or principles of prior cases. The Court will then apply the re-stated law to the facts of the instant case and reach its result.[88]

1970)); Maryland v. Buie, 494 U.S. 325, 110 S.Ct. 1093, 108 L.Ed.2d 276 1990) (applying the principles of Terry v. Ohio, 392 U.S. 1, 88 S.Ct. 1868, 20 L.Ed.2d 889(1968), and Michigan v. Long, 463 U.S. 1032, 103 S.Ct. 3469, 77 L.Ed.2d 1201 (1983)); New York v. Harris, 495 U.S. 14, 110 S.Ct. 1640, 109 L.Ed.2d 13 (1990) (applying by analogy the holding of United States v. Crews, 445 U.S. 463, 100 S.Ct. 1244, 63 L.Ed.2d 537 (1980)); Illinois v. Krull, 480 U.S. 340, 107 S.Ct. 1160, 94 L.Ed.2d 364 (1987) (applying by analogy the holding in United States v. Leon, 468 U.S. 897, 104 S.Ct. 3405, 82 L.Ed.2d 677 (1984)); Arizona v. Evans, 514 U.S. 1, 115 S.Ct.1185, 131 L.Ed.2d 34 (1995) (applying the reasoning of United States v. Leon, 468 U.S. 897, 104 S.Ct. 3405, 82 L.Ed.2d 677 (1984)); Maryland v. Wilson, 519 U.S. 408, 117 S.Ct. 882, 137 L.Ed.2d 41, 48 (1997) (relying on Michigan v. Summers, 452 U.S. 692, 101 S.Ct. 2587, 69 L.Ed.2d 340 (1981) "for guidance by analogy here."); United States v. Drayton, 536 U.S. 194, 122 S.Ct. 2105, 2112, 153 L.Ed.2d 242 (2002) (Court applies "the *Bostick* framework to the facts of this particular case," referring to Florida v. Bostick, 501 U.S. 429, 11 S.Ct. 2382, 115 L.Ed.2d 389 (1991)); Thornton v. United States, 541 U.S. 615, 124 S.Ct. 2127, 158 L.Ed.2d 905 (2004) (applying the reasoning of New York v. Belton, 453 U.S. 454, 101 S.Ct. 2860, 69 L.Ed.2d 768 (1981) to extend the Belton holding to analogous facts).

87. See, e.g., Fernandez v. California, 571 U.S. ___, 134 S.Ct. 1126, 188 L.Ed.2d 2014) (distinguishing the rule and modifying the dictum of Georgia v. Randolph, 547 U.S. 103, 126 S.Ct. 1515, 164 L.Ed.2d 208 (2006) in a consent search case involving co-occupants in which one occupant consents to the search while the other objects); Arizona v. Gant, 556 U.S. 322, 129 S.Ct. 1710, 172 L.Ed.2d 694 (2009) (distinguishing and modifying New York v. Belton, 453 U.S. 454, 101 S.Ct. 2860, 69 L.Ed.2d 768 (1981) as to the scope of search incident to the arrest of an occupant of an automobile); Scott v. Harris, 550 U.S. 372, 127 S.Ct. 1769, 1777, 167 L.Ed.2d 686 (2007) (distinguishing Tennessee v. Garner, 471 U.S. 1, 105 S.Ct. 1694, 85 L.Ed.2d 443, 455–56 (1985), in a § 1983 action involving alleged use of deadly force to effect an arrest); Illinois v. Caballes, 543 U.S. 405, 125 S.Ct. 834, 160 L.Ed.2d 842 (2005) (distinguishing Kyllo v. United States, 533 U.S. 27, 121 S.Ct. 2038, 150 L.Ed.2d 94 (2001), as to what constitutes a Fourth Amendment search in a narcotics "dog sniff" case); Ferguson v. City of Charleston, 532 U.S. 67, 121 S.Ct. 1281, 149 L.Ed.2d 205 (2001) (distinguishing a line of prior drug-testing cases); Bond v. United States, 529 U.S. 334, 120 S.Ct. 1462, 146 L.Ed.2d 365 (2000) (distinguishing two prior helicopter fly-over cases in which "open view" inspections were made by police of property below, from a federal agent's tactile manipulation of a canvas bag); Almeida-Sanchez v. United States, 413 U.S. 266, 93 S.Ct. 2535, 37 L.Ed.2d 596 (1973) (distinguishing prior automobile and administrative inspection search cases); Air Pollution Variance Board of Colorado v. Western Alfalfa Corp., 416 U.S. 861, 94 S.Ct. 2114, 40 L.Ed.2d 607 (1974) (distinguishing past administrative inspection cases); Illinois v. Rodriquez, 497 U.S. 177, 110 S.Ct. 2793, 111 L.Ed.2d 148 (1990) (distinguishing Stoner v. California, 376 U.S. 483, 84 S.Ct. 889, 11 L.Ed.2d 856 (1964) in a consent search case); Cooper v. California, 386 U.S. 58, 87 S.Ct. 788, 17 L.Ed.2d 730 (1967) (distinguishing Preston v. United States, 376 U.S. 364, 84 S.Ct. 881, 11 L.Ed.2d 777 (1964), in an automobile inventory search case).

88. See, e.g., Navarette v. California, 572 U.S. ___, 134 S.Ct. 1683, 188 L.Ed.2d 680 (2014); Minnesota v. Dickerson, 508 U.S. 366, 113 S.Ct. 2130, 124 L.Ed.2d 334 (1993); United States v. Hensley, 469 U.S. 221, 105 S.Ct. 675, 83 L.Ed.2d 604 (1985); Winston v. Lee, 470 U.S. 753, 105 S.Ct. 1611, 84 L.Ed.2d 662 (1985); United States v. Sharpe, 470 U.S. 675, 105 S.Ct. 1568, 84 L.Ed.2d 605 (1985); Arkansas v. Sanders, 442 U.S. 753, 99 S.Ct. 2586, 61 L.Ed.2d 235 (1979); United States v. Cortez, 449 U.S. 411, 101 S.Ct. 690, 66 L.Ed.2d 621 (1981); New York v. Belton, 453 U.S. 454, 101 S.Ct. 2860, 69 L.Ed.2d 768 (1981); Florida v. Royer, 460 U.S. 491, 103 S.Ct. 1319, 75 L.Ed.2d 229 (1983); United States v. Ventresca, 380 U.S., 102, 85 S.Ct. 741, 13 L.Ed.2d 684 (1965). See also

All of the above should come as no surprise, as it represents garden-variety legal reasoning that is so familiar to, and regularly employed by, judges and lawyers in common law countries. Needless to say, however, this method of reasoning is not mathematical in nature. Reasonable people, dealing with the same prior decisions may, and often do, arrive at contrary results in difficult cases. Indeed, in the problematic cases the Court usually grants review on, *the choice that the Court must make is which side has the better of the argument* in dealing with these past precedents, not which side is obviously right and which side is obviously wrong. For that reason, Fourth Amendment decisions of the Court often draw dissents from individual Justices on the Court.

Still, the framework of past Fourth Amendment decisions on a specific issue limits the choices that the Court can make in a given case, as the Court must necessarily make a reasoned case for accommodating the result it reaches in a way that logically appears within the scope of past case law. Stated differently, as a practical matter no Court, no matter what its judicial philosophy, can rewrite the law announced in its past cases without losing public confidence. Theoretically, of course, it has the *de jure* power to do so by overruling, artificially distinguishing or outright ignoring its prior relevant cases, willy-nilly. But if it did so, it would bring upon itself an avalanche of public and professional criticism that it could not possibly withstand. Indeed, impeachment proceedings might very well follow. The doctrine of *stare decisis* necessarily means that the Court's basic reasoning process must be deductive from, and therefore generally consistent with, its past relevant decisions. Although this framework is somewhat flexible in nature, it clearly has its limits which, as a practical matter, restrict the Court's decision-making process.

Indeed, any appellate judge at any level, federal or state, is well aware that his or her decisions must fit within a tradition of past case law, else one's judicial colleagues will rebel and refuse to sign extreme opinions reflecting only the judge's idiosyncratic views. Moreover, no judge and no Court wants to be embarrassed before the bench and bar, as well as the general public, by writing arbitrary, intellectually dishonest opinions that, in effect, disregard past relevant case law and thereby erode public confidence in the Court. Accordingly, in the real world, rather than the theoretical world, such case law exercises an enormous braking influence on the Court's decision-making process.[89]

c. Principled adjudication

Another form of common law reasoning that the Court at times employs is principled adjudication. In this variant of common law reasoning, the Court gives reasons for its holding based on considerations of logic, fairness and experience. This method of reasoning

---

Kentucky v. King, 563 U.S. ___, 131 S.Ct. 1849, 179 L.Ed.2d 865 (2011) (re-stating the law on the exigent circumstances exception to the search warrant requirement rule and extending this law using its past cases and principled reasons for doing so).

89. As Ronald Dworkin has accurately observed:

Judges may not read their own convictions into the Constitution. They may not read the abstract moral clauses [of the Constitution] as expressing any particular moral judgment, no matter how that judgment appeals to them, *unless they find it consistent in principle with the structural design of the Constitution as a whole, and also with the dominant lines of past constitutional interpretation by other judges.* They must regard themselves as partners with other officials, past and future, who together elaborate a coherent constitutional morality, and they must take care to see that what they contribute fits with the rest.

Ronald Dworkin, "The Moral Reading of the Constitution," XLIII New York Review of Books 46, 48 (March 21, 1996) (emphasis added).

is always mixed with a discussion of prior case holdings, rules and principles, but a significant part of the opinion is in the nature of a public policy justification for the result reached. This reasoning is found in part in many types of cases, but is primarily used where the Court is either overruling one of its past precedents[90] or deciding a major case of first impression.[91]

---

90. "Revisiting precedent is particularly appropriate where, as here, a departure would not upset expectations, the precedent consists of a judge-made rule that has recently been adopted to improve operation of the courts, and experience has pointed up the precedent's shortcomings." Pearson v. Callahan, 555 U.S. 223, 129 S.Ct. 808, 816, 172 L.Ed.2d 565 (2009) (giving principled reasons for overruling, in part, Saucier v. Katz, 533 U.S. 194, 121 S.Ct. 2151, 150 2L.Ed.2d 72 (2001), which had set up a mandatory two-step process for ruling on a defendant's motion for summary judgment based on the affirmative defense of qualified immunity in a civil rights action claiming a Fourth Amendment violation).

"The doctrine of *stare decisis* is, of course, 'essential to the respect accorded to the judgments of the Court and to the stability of the law,' but it does not compel us to follow a past precedent when its rationale no longer withstands 'careful analysis.' [citation omitted]. We have never relied on *stare decisis* to justify the continuance of an unconstitutional police practice."Arizona v. Gant, 556 U.S. 322, 129 S.Ct. 1710, 1722, 172 L.Ed.2d 694 (2009) (modifying New York v. Belton, 453 U.S. 454, 101 S.Ct. 2860, 69 L.Ed.2d 768 (1981) which had allowed an automatic police search of a vehicle whenever the driver or passenger of same was arrested).

"I recognize that stare decisis is not an inexorable command, and applies less rigidly in constitutional cases. But the Court has said that a constitutional precedent should be followed unless there is a special justification for its abandonment. Relevant factors identified in prior cases include whether the precedent has engendered reliance; whether there has been an important change in circumstances in the outside world; whether the precedent has proven to be unworkable; whether the precedent has been undermined by later decisions; and whether the decision was badly reasoned." Arizona v. Gant, 556 U.S. 322, 129 S.Ct. 1710, 1728, 173 L.Ed.2d 485 (2009) (Alito, J. dissenting) (internal citations and quotes omitted).

"Although we have recognized firmly that the doctrine of stare decisis serves profoundly important interests in our legal system, this Court has overruled a prior case on the comparatively rare occasion when it has bred confusion or been a derelict or led to anomalous results." California v. Acevedo, 500 U.S. 565, 111 S.Ct. 1982, 114 L.Ed.2d 619, 633 (1991) (giving principled reasons for overruling prior case holdings that a search warrant is required to search a closed container in a moving vehicle during an otherwise proper search of the vehicle).

See, e.g., Mapp v. Ohio, 367 U.S. 643, 81 S.Ct. 1684, 6 L.Ed.2d 1081 (1961) (giving principled reasons for overruling the holding of Wolf v. Colorado, 338 U.S. 25, 69 S.Ct. 1359, 93 L.Ed.2d 1782 (1949), that the Fourth Amendment exclusionary rule does not apply to the states); Elkins v. United States, 364 U.S. 206, 80 S.Ct. 1437, 4 L.Ed.2d 1669 (1960) (giving principled reasons for overruling the holding of Weeks v. United States, and its progeny, that the Fourth Amendment exclusionary rule does not apply to evidence illegally seized by state officials when introduced in a federal criminal trial); Warden, Md. Penitentiary v. Hayden, 387 U.S. 294, 87 S.Ct. 1642, 18 L.Ed.2d 782 (1967) (giving principled reasons for overruling the holding of Gouled v. United States, 255 U.S. 298, 41 S.Ct. 261, 65 L.Ed. 647 (1921), that the Fourth Amendment forbids the seizure of "mere evidence" by police); Chimel v. California, 395 U.S. 752, 89 S.Ct. 2034, 23 L.Ed.2d 685 (1969) (giving principled reasons for overruling the holding of Harris v. United States, 331 U.S. 145, 67 S.Ct. 1098, 91 L.Ed. 1399 (1947), and United States v. Rabinowitz, 339 U.S. 56, 70 S.Ct. 430, 94 L.Ed. 653 (1950), that after lawfully arresting a person, police may conduct a search of the entire area where the person is arrested); Camara v. Municipal Court, 387 U.S. 523, 87 S.Ct. 1727, 18 L.Ed.2d 930 (1967) (giving principled reasons for overruling the holding of Frank v. Maryland, 359 U.S. 360, 79 S.Ct. 804, 3 L.Ed.2d 877 (1959), that a warrant is not required for conducting a public health inspection of a dwelling); United States v. Salvucci, 448 U.S. 83, 100 S.Ct. 2547, 65 L.Ed.2. 619 (1980) (giving principled reasons for overruling the holding of Jones v. United States, 362 U.S. 257, 80 S.Ct. 725, 4 L.Ed.2d 697 (1960), that a person has "automatic standing" to challenge the reasonableness of a search merely if he is charged with criminally possessing the items seized in the challenged search).

91. See, e.g., Georgia v. Randolph, 547 U.S.103, 126 S.Ct. 1515, 164 L.Ed.2d 208 (2006) (giving principled reasons for striking down a warrantless search of private premises where one occupant of the premises consents to the search, but a physically present co-occupant of the premises expressly

d. Catch-all of various devices

Finally, there are a number of other devices which are occasionally used by the Court along with other approaches to justify its result. At times, the Court will rely on the holdings of relevant lower federal court and state court decisions,[92] apply a relevant federal statute or rule of procedure,[93] or invoke an appropriate canon of construction[94] to support its reasoning or result. At other times, the Court will announce rules that seem logical or fair but are introduced without much explanation or discussion as being self-evident and clearly correct.[95]

---

objects to the search); Schmerber v. California, 384 U.S. 757, 86 S.Ct. 1826, 16 L.Ed.2d 908 (1966) (giving principled reasons for upholding the warrantless, involuntary extraction of blood from a person lawfully arrested for DUI); Berger v. New York, 388 U.S. 41, 87 S.Ct. 1873, 18 L.Ed.2d 1040 (1967) (giving principled reasons for declaring invalid the New York Wiretap Act); Simmons v. United States, 390 U.S. 377, 88 S.Ct. 967, 19 L.Ed.2d 1247 (1968) (giving principled reasons for holding that defendant's testimony at a motion to suppress hearing is inadmissible at defendant's criminal trial as substantive evidence of guilt); Wyman v. James, 400 U.S, 309, 91 S.Ct. 381, 27 L.Ed.2d 408 (1971) (giving principled reasons for upholding a warrantless welfare home visit under New York welfare statutes and rules); Bivens v. Six Unknown Named Agents of the Federal Bureau of Narcotics, 403 U.S. 388, 91 S.Ct. 1999, 29 L.Ed.2d 619 (1971) (giving principled reasons for holding that a violation of the Fourth Amendment by a government official gives rise to a civil suit for monetary damages); Zurcher v. Stanford Daily, 436 U.S. 547, 98 S.Ct. 1970, 56 L.Ed.2d 525 (1978) (giving principled reasons for rejecting the holding of the courts below that a search warrant cannot issue for the search of private premises where the owner or possessor is not suspected of criminal wrongdoing); Franks v. Delaware, 438 U.S. 154, 98 S.Ct. 2674, 57 L.Ed.2d 667 (1978) (giving principled reasons for its holding that a search warrant cannot be based on a false affidavit where the false statements contained therein were knowingly or recklessly made and were essential to a finding of probable cause); Mincey v. Arizona, 437 U.S. 385, 98 S.Ct. 2408, 57 L.Ed.2d 290 (1978) (giving principled reasons for refusing to create a "murder scene" exception to the search warrant requirement rule); South Dakota v. Opperman, 428 U.S. 364, 96 S.Ct. 3092, 49 L.Ed.2d 1000 (1976) (giving principled reasons for creating an exception to the search warrant requirement rule for the inventory of impounded automobiles); Richards v. Wisconsin, 520 U.S. 385, 117 S.Ct. 1416, 137 L.Ed.2d 615 (1997) (giving principled reasons for rejecting a blanket exception for felony drug investigations to the general rule that police must announce their authority and purpose before forcibly entering a dwelling to execute a search warrant).

92. See, e.g., United States v. Banks, 540 U.S. 31, 124 S.Ct. 521, 157 L.Ed.2d 343, 353 n. 5 (2003); South Dakota v. Opperman, 428 U.S. 364, 96 S.Ct. 3092, 49 L.Ed.2d 1000 (1976); California v. Greenwood, 486 U.S. 35, 108 S.Ct. 1625, 100 L.Ed.2d 30 (1988); Nix v. Williams, 467 U.S. 431, 104 S.Ct. 2501, 81 L.Ed.2d 377 (1984); United States v. Edwards, 415 U.S. 800, 94 S.Ct. 1234, 39 L.Ed.2d 771 (1974); Bumper v. North Carolina, 391 U.S. 543, 88 S.Ct. 1788, 20 L.Ed.2d 797 (1968).

93. See, e.g., Jones v. United States, 362 U.S. 257, 80 S.Ct. 725, 4 L.Ed.2d 697 (1960) (Rule 41(e) of the Federal Rules of Criminal Procedure applied); Grau v. United States, 287 U.S. 124, 53 S.Ct. 38, 77 L.Ed. 212 (1932) (search warrant statute under the National Prohibition Act applied).

94. See, e.g., Federal Trade Commission v. American Tobacco Co., 264 U.S. 298, 44 S.Ct. 336, 68 L.Ed. 696 (1924) (Court will not read a congressional statute as authoring a search or seizure prohibited by the Fourth Amendment unless the statute explicitly so provides).

95. See, e.g., In re Jackson, 96 U.S. (6 Otto) 727 24 L.Ed 877 (1877) (announcing Fourth Amendment rules protecting letters in U.S. mails); Hester v. United States, 265 U.S. 57, 44 S.Ct. 445, 68 L.Ed.2d 898 (1924) (announcing rule that Fourth Amendment does not extend to the "open fields"); Fahy v. Connecticut, 375 U.S. 85, 84 S.Ct. 229, 11 L.Ed.2d 171 (1963) (announcing harmless error rule); Cooper v. California, 386 U.S. 58, 87 S.Ct. 788, 17 L.Ed.2d 730 (1967) (announcing rule that the states may impose higher standards on searches and seizures than that required by the U.S. Constitution); Lewis v. United States, 385 U.S. 206, 87 S.Ct. 424, 17 L.Ed.2d 312 (1966) (announcing rule that when a home is converted into a commercial center for the purpose of transacting unlawful business, it is entitled to no greater sanctity than if it were carried out in a store); Silverthorne Lumber Co. v. United States, 251 U.S. 385, 40 S.Ct. 182, 64 L.Ed. 319 (1920) (announcing "fruit of the poisonous tree" as part of the Fourth Amendment exclusionary rule).

Subpart A

The "Standing Requirement"

Introductory Note

The first requirement for a Fourth Amendment violation is a threshold "standing" requirement—that is, in the language of the Fourth Amendment, the party complaining must show that a "search[ ] [or] seizure[ ]" of his or her "person[ ], house[ ], papers or effects" has been conducted by an agent of the government. The term "standing" is used here in a Fourth Amendment, substantive law context as it is derived from the language of the Fourth Amendment itself. Although the U.S. Supreme Court has disapproved this term when used to mean something other than a constitutionally-based requirement,[1] it is entirely proper when referring, as here, to a separate and distinct branch of substantive Fourth Amendment law.[2] This constitutional "Standing Requirement" must be met in order to show that the Fourth Amendment is even applicable to the activity challenged by the complaining party.

The "Standing Requirement" breaks down into three elements: (1) a personal standing element, (2) a governmental action element, and (3) a search or seizure element. When all three of these elements are satisfied, the party complaining has the Fourth Amendment "standing" to attack the search or seizure in question as "unreasonable." If one or more of these elements is not satisfied, the Fourth Amendment is inapplicable to the case, no matter how outrageous the complained-of conduct might be—although there may be a substantive due process violation under the Fourteenth Amendment if the governmental conduct in question is so arbitrary that it "shocks the conscience" and violates the "decencies of civilized conduct."[3]

---

1. Rakas v. Illinois, 439 U.S. 128, 139–40, 99 S.Ct. 421, 58 L.Ed.2d 387 (1978) ; see Minnesota v. Carter, 525 U.S. 83, 119 S.Ct. 469, 142 L.Ed.2d 373, 379 (1998) ("Central to our analysis [in Rakas] was the idea that in determining whether a defendant is able to show the violation of his (and not someone else's) Fourth Amendment rights, the 'definition of those rights is more properly placed within the purview of substantive Fourth Amendment law than within that of 'standing.' "142 L.Ed.2d at 379).

2. "In my view, Rakas v. Illinois ... recognized two analytically distinct but 'invariably intertwined' issues of Fourth Amendment jurisprudence. The first is 'whether [a] disputed search or seizure has infringed an interest which the Fourth Amendment was designed to protect.' The second is whether 'the challenged search or seizure violated [that] Fourth Amendment righ[t].'* * * "[I] do not read today's decision, or Rakas, as holding it is improper for lower courts to treat these inquiries as distinct components of a Fourth Amendment claim. Indeed, I am convinced that it would invite confusion to hold otherwise." Rawlings v. Kentucky, 448 U.S. 98, 111–12, 100 S.Ct. 2556, 65 L.Ed.2d 633, 646 (1980) (Blackmun, J. concurring) (internal citations to *Rakas* omitted).

3. County of Sacramento v. Lewis, 523 U.S. 833, 118 S.Ct. 1708,140 L.Ed.2d 1043, 1057–58 (1998); Rochin v. California, 342 U.S. 165, 172–73, 72 S.Ct. 205, 96 L.Ed. 183 (1952).

Generally, the "Standing Requirement" is met in most search and seizure cases that arise in a criminal context. This is so because, typically, for search and seizure evidence to be incriminating against a defendant, it must be connected in some fashion with the defendant; most of the time, this essential evidentiary link will satisfy all the elements of the standing requirement. But not always. Consequently, a standing analysis is required in every case to determine whether the challenged activity is governed by the Fourth Amendment—and if so, to identify each of the one or more Fourth Amendment searches and seizures that may have been conducted in the case. This is necessary so that one can determine whether each of these searches or seizures was reasonable or unreasonable in the Fourth Amendment sense. Moreover, where the Fourth Amendment is applicable to only part of the activity challenged, it is essential to parse out of the case that part of the subject activity to which the Fourth Amendment is inapplicable so as not to employ an "unreasonableness" analysis to such activity.

Chapter 8

Preliminary Elements: Personal Standing and Governmental Action

Section 1. Personal Standing Element

a. Standing only to assert one's own Fourth Amendment rights

The United States Supreme Court has long held that a person making a Fourth Amendment claim has "standing" to make that claim only on behalf of himself or herself, and not on behalf of a third party.[4] This means that such a person must show, in the language of the Fourth Amendment, that his or her "person, house[ ], papers or effects" has been subject to a governmental "search[ ] or seizure[ ]." This is a rule with no exceptions, as there are no circumstances where this personal standing element may be waived.

A person is, accordingly, not excused from this personal standing element (1) because such person is criminally charged with possessing the evidence which he or she seeks to suppress [no "automatic" standing];[5] or (2) because the Fourth Amendment rights of a

---

4. Jones v. United States, 362 U.S. 257, 80 S.Ct. 725, 4 L.Ed.2d 697 (1960) ("In order to qualify as a 'person aggrieved' by an unlawful seizure, one must have been the victim of a search or seizure, one against whom the search was directed, as distinguished from one who claims prejudice only through the use of evidence gathered as a consequence of a search and seizure directed at someone else."); Alderman v. United States, 394 U.S. 165, 89 S.Ct. 961, 22 L.Ed.2d 176 (1969) ("[S]uppression of the product of a Fourth Amendment violation can be successfully urged only by those whose rights were violated by the search itself, not by those aggrieved solely by the introduction of damaging evidence. Coconspirators and codefendants have been accorded no special standing."); United States v. Padilla, 508 U.S. 77, 113 S.Ct. 1936, 123 L.Ed.2d 635, 640 (1993); ("It has long been the rule that a defendant can urge suppression of evidence obtained in violation of the Fourth Amendment only if that defendant demonstrates that his Fourth Amendment rights were violated by the challenged search or seizure."); United States v. Payner, 447 U.S. 727, 731, 100 S.Ct. 2439, 65 L.Ed2d 468 (1980) ("[A] court may not exclude evidence under the Fourth Amendment unless it finds that an unlawful search or seizure violated the defendant's own constitutional rights.... And the defendant's Fourth Amendment rights are violated only where the challenged conduct invaded his legitimate expectation of privacy rather than that of a third party."); United States v. Leon, 468 U.S. 897, 104 S.Ct. 3405, 82 L.Ed.2d 677, 690 (1984) ("Standing to invoke the [exclusionary] rule has thus been limited to cases in which the prosecution seeks to use the fruits of an illegal search or seizure against the victim of the police misconduct.").

5. United States v. Salvucci, 448 U.S. 83, 100 S.Ct. 2547, 65 L.Ed.2d 619 (1980), overruling the contrary holding of Jones v. United States, 362 U.S. 257, 80 S.Ct. 725, 4 L.Ed.2d 697 (1960). For a

co-defendant or co-conspirator in the case have been violated [no "derivative" standing];[6] or (3) because the person is the "target" of the criminal investigation that led to the search or seizure in question [no "target" standing].[7] In all cases, the person making the Fourth Amendment claim must affirmatively show that his or her protected interests as guaranteed by the Fourth Amendment have been invaded—as distinguished from the Fourth Amendment interests of a third party. Indeed, the Court has even refused to relax this personal standing element as part of the Court's supervisory power over the lower federal courts in a case where the search was conducted by government agents against a third party with full knowledge of the search's illegality in order to obtain evidence against the defendant.[8]

The effect of this personal standing element means that a defendant in a criminal case cannot move to suppress evidence seized in violation of the Fourth Amendment rights of a third party. It also means that such a defendant cannot complain that the evidence, which was used to form the probable cause to arrest or search the defendant, was obtained in violation of the Fourth Amendment rights of a third party. For example, where a co-defendant is illegally arrested and thereafter gives an incriminating statement to the police implicating the defendant in a crime for which the defendant is subsequently arrested and searched, the defendant can only claim that the subject statement contained insufficient facts to constitute probable cause to arrest and search the defendant, not that the police obtained this information in violation of the Fourth Amendment rights of the co-defendant; only the co-defendant has standing to complain about such an illegal arrest and to move to suppress the ensuing statement and any fruits thereof.[9] Moreover, even where this statement is suppressed upon motion of the co-defendant, it is suppressed only with respect to the co-defendant and cannot be suppressed with respect to the defendant.[10]

---

discussion of the rise and fall of the "automatic standing" rule of *Jones*, see 6 Wayne LaFave, Search and Seizure § 11.3(g) at 295–300 (5th ed. 2012).

6. Alderman v. United States, 394 U.S. 165, 89 S.Ct. 961, 22 L.Ed.2d 176 (1969); Wong Sun v. United States, 371 U.S. 471, 83 S.Ct. 407, 9 L.Ed.2d 441 (1963). The arguably contrary authority of McDonald v. United States, 335 U.S. 451, 69 S.Ct. 191, 93 L.Ed. 153 (1948), has been superseded by the *Alderman* decision. 394 at 173–74, n. 7. Moreover, a person's participation in a criminal conspiracy neither adds to nor detracts from such person's reasonable expectations of privacy and property interests protected by the Fourth Amendment. United States v. Padilla, 508 U.S. 77, 113 S.Ct. 1936, 123 L.Ed.2d 635 (1993) (disapproving a contrary line of decisions from the Ninth Circuit Court of Appeals). For a thorough discussion of the "derivative" standing issue, see 6 Wayne LaFave, Search and Seizure § 11.3(i) at 308–316 (5th ed. 2012).

7. Rakas v. Illinois, 439 U.S. 128, 99 S.Ct. 421, 58 L.Ed.2d 387 (1978). For a more thorough discussion of the "target" standing issue, see 6 Wayne LaFave, Search and Seizure § 11.3(h), pp. 301–308 (5th ed. 2012).

8. United States v. Payner, 447 U.S. 727, 100 S.Ct. 2439, 65 L.Ed.2d 468 (1980).

9. In *Wong Sun v. United States,* 371 U.S. 471, 83 S.Ct. 407, 9 L.Ed.2d 441 (1963), suspect no. 1 [James Toy] was illegally arrested in his bedroom and immediately made an oral statement implicating suspect no. 2 [Johnny Yee]. Suspect no. 2 [Johnny Yee] was then arrested based on this statement—and heroin was seized from Yee. Yee then stated that he got his heroin from suspect no. 3 [Wong Sun] who was then arrested.

The Court held that the initial illegally-obtained oral statement of suspect no. 1 [James Toy] and the heroin seized from suspect no. 2 [Johnny Yee] were the fruit of Toy's illegal arrest—and were therefore inadmissible solely against suspect no. 1 [James Toy]. But the Court further held that this same illegally-obtained heroin was admissible against suspect no. 3 [Wong Sun] because it was obtained solely in violation of suspect no. 1 [James Toy's] Fourth Amendment rights—not Wong Sun's Fourth Amendment rights. Stated differently, neither suspect no. 2 [Johnny Yee] nor suspect no. 3 [Wong Sun] could complain about the illegal arrest of suspect no. 1 [James Toy]; only Toy could complain about his illegal arrest.

10. Alderman v. United States, 394 U.S. 165, 173–74 & n. 7, 89 S.Ct. 961, 22 L.Ed.2d 176 (1969), distinguishing McDonald v. United States, 335 U.S. 451, 69 S.Ct. 191, 93 L.Ed. 153 (1948).

The underlying rationale for the Court's hard line adherence to this personal standing element appears to be rooted in the nature of constitutional rights. The Bill of Rights was generally designed to protect the rights of the individual, and it has therefore been thought axiomatic that when those rights are violated, only the injured individual should be in a position to complain, subject to very limited exceptions; stated differently, it is not generally thought necessary to vicariously vindicate the constitutional rights of a third party as that party may be relied on to assert such rights if and when it becomes important to do so. Beyond that, the Court has long considered the enormous social costs for imposing the Fourth Amendment exclusionary rule to greatly outweigh whatever deterrent benefits the rule would have if applied in this context.[11]

This view, however, has not gone unchallenged at the state level. The states are, of course, constitutionally free to interpret their own state constitutions to give greater rights to the individual than that guaranteed by the Fourth Amendment by abolishing this aspect of the standing requirement.[12] No less an authority than Justice Roger Traynor of the California Supreme Court authored the leading case that abolished the personal standing element in California,[13] although this decision was abrogated thirty years later under a 1982 state constitutional amendment.[14] Briefly stated, Traynor's view was that the government ought not be allowed to benefit from its own wrongdoing by basing a criminal conviction on illegally seized evidence whether that evidence was obtained from the defendant or third parties, that a contrary rule invites the police to violate the Fourth Amendment rights of a third party in order to obtain evidence to convict the defendant,[15] and that the deterrent value of the exclusionary rule is nullified by allowing the government to use illegally seized evidence obtained from third parties to convict anyone. This view, although applauded at the time by the commentators, has been consistently rejected by the United States Supreme Court and virtually all the states that have considered the issue for reasons already discussed.[16]

---

11. As stated by the Court in *Alderman v. United States,* 394 U.S. 165, 174–75, 89 S.Ct. 961, 22 L.Ed.2d 176 (1969):

"We adhere ... to the general rule that Fourth Amendment rights are personal rights which, like some other constitutional rights, may not be vicariously asserted. (citations omitted). None of the special circumstances which prompted NAACP v. Alabama, 357 U.S. 449, 78 S.Ct. 1163, 2 L.Ed.2d 1488 (1958), and Barrows v. Jackson, 346 U.S. 249, 73 S.Ct. 1031, 97 L.Ed. 1586 (1953), are present here. No rights of the victim of an illegal search are at stake when the evidence is offered against some other party. The victim can and probably will object for himself when and if it becomes important for him to do so. * * *

The deterrent values of preventing the incrimination of those whose rights the police have violated have been considered sufficient to justify the suppression of probative evidence [through the Fourth Amendment exclusionary rule] even though the case against the defendant is weakened or destroyed. We adhere to that judgment. But we are not convinced that the additional benefits of the extending the exclusionary rule to other defendants would justify further encroachment upon the public interest in prosecuting those accused of crime and having then acquitted or convicted on the basis of all the evidence that exposes the truth."

12. See Chapter 1, Section 4(a) of this work and cases collected.

13. People v. Martin, 45 Cal.2d 755, 290 P.2d 905 (1955).

14. In re Lance W., 37 Cal.3d 873, 210 Cal.Reptr. 631, 694 P.2d 744 (1985).

15. Indeed, the United States Supreme Court subsequently approved the admission in evidence of the fruits of just such an illegal, bad faith search directed against a third party when offered against a defendant. United States v. Payner, 447 U.S. 727, 100 S.Ct. 2439, 65 L.Ed.2d 468 (1980).

16. For a thorough discussion of the abolition of personal standing and its odyssey in California and elsewhere, see 6 Wayne LaFave, Search and Seizure § 11.3(j), at 317–321 (5th ed. 2012).

b. "People" entitled to assert Fourth Amendment claims

If a person whose Fourth Amendment rights have been violated is the only one who is entitled to complain of such a violation, the question arises as to what types of persons are entitled to make such a complaint. The Fourth Amendment guarantees to "the people" certain rights, and presumably any person falling within this broad ambit may complain about a violation of such rights. A plurality of the Court has interpreted the term "people" to mean "a class of persons who are part of a national [American] community or who have otherwise developed sufficient connection with this country to be considered part of that community."[17] Under this definition, it is clear that American citizens and resident legal and illegal aliens alike are "people" within the meaning of the Fourth Amendment where the search by government agents takes place within the territorial jurisdiction of the United States.[18] It is equally clear, however, that non-resident aliens are not included within the "people" protected by the Fourth Amendment where the search or seizure by government agents takes place outside the territorial jurisdiction of the United States,[19] although the result would appear to be different as to American citizens.[20] Corporations,

---

17. United States v. Verdugo-Urquidez, 494 U.S. 259, 110 S.Ct. 1056, 108 L.Ed.2d 222, 232 (1990). Although this was a 6–3 decision of the Court, the above definition of "people" was expressly adopted by only four Justices and is therefore a plurality opinion on this issue. Justice Kennedy in his concurring opinion states that his views "do not ... depart in fundamental respects from the opinion of the Court which I join," but later expresses the view that "I cannot place any weight on the reference to 'the people' in the Fourth Amendment as a source of restricting its protections" as such reference "may be interpreted to underscore the importance of the right rather than to restrict the category of persons who may assert it." 108 L.Ed.2d at 239, 240. Justice Stevens in his concurring opinion states that "aliens who are lawfully present in the United States are among those 'people' who are entitled to the protection of ... the Fourth Amendment," but otherwise declines to join "the Court's sweeping opinion." 108 L.Ed.2d 242–43. Justice Brennan in his dissenting opinion, joined by Justice Marshall, states that whenever the government, as here, seeks to apply its criminal law to an individual, that person, under the test announced by the Court, has a "sufficient connection" to the United States as he or she is "one of the governed" and therefore is among the "people" whom the Fourth Amendment protects. 108 L.Ed.2d at 243–45. Justice Blackmun in his dissenting opinion expressly agrees with Justice Brennan on this point. 108 L.Ed. at 253.

18. See, e.g., United States v. Verdugo-Urquidez, 494 U.S. 259, 110 S.Ct. 1056, 108 L.Ed.2d. 222, 236 (1990) ("[A]liens receive constitutional protections when they have come within the territory of the United States and developed substantial connections with this country."); United States ex rel. Bilokumsky v. Tod, 263 U.S. 149, 44 S.Ct. 54, 68 L.Ed 221 (1923); Fong Yue Ting v. United States, 149 U.S. 698, 13 S.Ct. 1016, 37 L.Ed. 905 (1893). "Numerous lower courts, however, have held that illegal aliens in the United States are protected by the Fourth Amendment, and not a single lower court has held to the contrary. See, e.g., Benitez-Mendez v. INS, 760 F.2d 907 (CA9 1985); United States v. Rodriguez, 532 F2d 834, 838 (CA2 1976); Au Yi Lau v. INS, 144 US App DC 147, 156, 445 F2d 217, 225, cert denied, 404 U.S. 864, 30 L.Ed.2d 108, 92 S.Ct. 64 (1971); Yam Sang Kwai v. INS, 133 US App DC 369, 372, 411 F.2d 683, 686, cert denied, 396 US 877, 24 L.Ed.2d 135, 90 S.Ct. 148 (1969)." United States v. Verdugo-Urquidez, 494 U.S. 259, 110 S.Ct. 1056, 108 L.Ed.2d 222, 244 (1990) (Brennan, J. dissenting).

19. United States v. Verdugo-Urquidez, 494 U.S. 259, 110 S.Ct. 1056, 108 L.Ed.2d 222 (1990) (Fourth Amendment held inapplicable to a search conducted by U.S. narcotics agents, together with Mexican police, in Mexico of two houses owned by a Mexican citizen residing in Mexico; the latter had been arrested in Mexico by Mexican officials, cooperating with U.S. officials, and involuntarily brought to the United States a few days prior to the subject search).

20. See, e.g., Reid v. Covert, 354 U.S. 1, 77 S.Ct. 1222, 1 L.Ed.2d 1148 (1957) (protections of the Fifth and Sixth Amendments held applicable to the overseas wives of American servicemen charged with murder before a U.S. military court). "Certainly nothing in the Court's opinion questions the validity of the rule, accepted by every Court of Appeals to have considered the question, that the Fourth Amendment applies to searches conducted by the United /States Government against United

as artificial entities, are also considered part of the "people" embraced by the Fourth Amendment and accordingly such corporations have standing to challenge the governmental seizure of their corporate books and records.[21]

The above results do not seem inconsistent with the "original understanding" of the Fourth Amendment and may even be supported thereby. Lasson argues that the use of the term "people" in the Amendment as opposed to "freemen"—which latter term appears in the search and seizure amendments proposed by the constitutional ratification conventions of Virginia and New York[22]—was inclusive enough to embrace slaves in the period before the Civil War.[23] Indeed, using such a term as "people," as opposed to "citizen" or "freeman," would seem to imply an intent to embrace all natural persons in the country including citizen and alien alike in today's world. As for the inclusion of corporations, it was probably unlikely that the colonial merchants in Boston and elsewhere who bitterly opposed the writs of assistance, ran incorporated businesses at the time, as corporations of this type were uncommon prior to 1800.[24] Still, it seems fair to assume that they regarded their businesses as being protected by English law against general search writs and no doubt would have been appalled at the thought that their businesses could be searched with impunity if corporately held. Plainly, the Framers of the Bill of Rights intended their businesses to be protected by the Fourth Amendment and would in all likelihood have thought it unimportant whether the businesses were incorporated or held as single proprietorships.

Section 2. Governmental Action Element

a. Search or seizure must be conducted by an agent of the government: private searches and seizures excluded

The second element of the "Standing Requirement" is that the search or seizure in question must be conducted by a governmental official—federal, state, or local—or by a private citizen acting as an agent of a governmental official. Searches or seizures conducted by private individuals acting on their own, however, are not governed by the Fourth Amendment—no matter how unreasonable the private search may be.[25] This basic Fourth

States citizens abroad." United States v. Verdugo-Urquidez, 494 U.S. 259, 110 S.Ct. 1056, 108 L.Ed.2d 222, 244, n. 7 (1990) (Brennan, J. dissenting), citing Conroy v. United States, 589 F.2d. 1258, 1264 (5th Cir.), cert denied, 444 U.S. 831, 62 L.Ed.2d 40, 100 S.Ct. 60 (1979); United States v. Rose, 570 F.2d 1358, 1362 (9th Cir. 1978).

21. United States v. Morton Salt Co., 338 U.S. 632, 651–52, 70 S.Ct. 357, 94 L.Ed. 401 (1950); Oklahoma Press Publishing Co. v. Walling, 327 U.S. 186, 205–06, 66 S.Ct. 494, 504, 90 L.Ed. 614 (1946); Silverthorne Lumber Co. v. United States, 251 U.S. 385, 40 S.Ct. 182, 64 L.Ed. 319 (1920): Hale v. Henkel, 201 U.S. 43, 75–76, 26 S.Ct. 370, 379–80, 50 L.Ed. 652 (1906). A corporation, however, is not protected by the self-incrimination privilege of the Fifth Amendment, which is confined solely to natural persons. Hale v. Henkel, 201 U.S. at 69–70.

22. See Chapter 5, Sections 2 d & e of this work for a discussion of the search and seizure amendments recommended by the Virginia and New York constitutional ratification conventions.

23. Nelson Lasson, The History and Development of the Fourth Amendment to the United States Constitution 117, n. 31 (1937).

24. Lawrence Friedman, A History of American Law 166–67 (1973).

25. "This Court has also consistently construed this protection [the Fourth Amendment] as proscribing governmental action only; it is wholly inapplicable 'to a search or seizure, even an unreasonable one, effected by a private individual not acting as an agent of the Government or with

Amendment principle was established by the Court in *Burdeau v. McDowell*,[26] wherein it was held that a search of a criminal defendant's office in a break-in by private detectives was a purely private search and seizure and was therefore not prohibited by the Fourth Amendment. This result is fully consistent with the "original understanding" of the Fourth Amendment, as clearly the Framers intended by this Amendment to restrain governmental officials, not private individuals, from engaging in the type of general search abuses committed by the colonial customs officials in the general writs of assistance regime. As the Court stated in *Burdeau*,

> The Fourth Amendment gives protection against unlawful searches and seizures, and as shown in previous cases, its protection applies to governmental action. Its origin and history clearly show that it was intended as a restraint upon the activities of sovereign authority, and was not intended to be a limitation upon other than government agencies; as against such authority it was the purpose of the Fourth Amendment to secure the citizen in the right of unmolested occupation of his dwelling and the possession of his property, subject to the right of seizure of process duly issued.[27]

The Fourth Amendment governs the actions of private individuals only when acting at the direction of and thus as an agent of government officials—as, for example, private telephone company employees who install electronic eavesdropping equipment on a person's telephone line at the request of law enforcement officials,[28] or private railroad officials who administer certain drug tests (blood, urine, breath) to railroad employees involved in certain train accidents when mandated by rules adopted by the Federal Railroad Administration or when authorized by such rules where the government encourages such tests and shares in their results.[29] Whether a private individual is an agent of the government for Fourth Amendment purposes turns on the degree of the government's participation in the individual's activity—a question that can only be resolved by all the facts and circumstances of the case.[30] Accordingly, where a private party with no prior government direction conducts a search or seizure of a person's private premises or property, the Fourth Amendment is inapplicable to such a search or seizure—as, for example, where a defendant's spouse turns over to the police "on a silver platter" the defendant's clothing and guns after the police come to the defendant's home to make certain inquiries of the spouse while the defendant is in police custody,[31] or where the employees of common carriers open in-transit packages entrusted to their care for delivery, discover contraband therein, and thereafter turn the contraband over to the police "on a silver platter."[32]

---

the participation or knowledge of a governmental official.'" United States v. Jacobsen, 466 U.S. 109, 104 S.Ct. 1652, 80 L.Ed.2d 85, 94 (1984) (quoted citation omitted).

26. 256 U.S. 465, 41 S.Ct. 574, 65 L.Ed. 1048 (1921) (defendant's pre-indictment motion for the return of books and papers taken from defendant's office in a break-in by private detectives was improperly granted by the District Court).

27. 256 U.S. at 475, 65 L.Ed. at 1051.

28. See Smith v. Maryland, 442 U.S. 735, 99 S.Ct. 2577, 61 L.Ed.2d 220, 226, n. 4 (1979).

29. Skinner v. Railroad Labor Executives Ass'n, 489 U.S. 602, 109 S.Ct. 1402, 103 L.Ed.2d 639 (1989).

30. Skinner v. Railroad Labor Executives Ass'n., 489 U.S. 602, 109 S.Ct. 1402, 103 L.Ed.2d 639, 658 (1989). For review of relevant state and lower federal court decisions on this issue, see 1 Wayne LaFave, Search and Seizure §§ 1.8(b)(c), at 370–407 (5th ed. 2012); also see cases collected at "Criminal Law" § 394.2(1), "Searches and Seizures" §§ 31.1, 33, 34, West Key Nos.

31. Coolidge v. New Hampshire, 403 U.S. 443, 91 S.Ct. 2022, 29 L.Ed.2d 564 (1971).

32. United States v. Jacobsen, 466 U.S. 109, 104 S.Ct. 1652, 80 L.Ed.2d 85 (). The fact that the carrier's employees notify police to confirm the presence of the contraband and to determine what to do with it does not convert the private search by the carrier into a governmental search governed

Nonetheless, it should be noted that the government's acceptance of this "silver platter" evidence usually constitutes a meaningful interference with the defendant's possessory interests in such property and is therefore a Fourth Amendment governmental seizure of the defendant's effects which requires a showing of probable cause to be reasonable.[33]

In this connection, it is often true that a given Fourth Amendment case may involve both private and governmental search and seizure activity. On occasion, a private party may initiate a search and seizure, discover evidence of crime, and call in the police who then take over and conduct further searches and seizures. In such a case, it is essential to parse out the non-governed private activity and determine that the governmental action element is met only with respect to the governed governmental activity. This becomes important when later determining whether the "Unreasonableness Requirement" has been met with respect to the identified governmental searches and seizures; the prior private searches and seizures are excluded from this determination because the Fourth Amendment is inapplicable to such activity. Moreover, that which is uncovered and shown to the police through a purely private search and seizure can constitute part of the evidentiary justification for any police search or seizure that follows.

b. Governmental agent may be criminal or civil official

The Fourth Amendment applies to all state, federal and local law enforcement officials in the United States and its territories.[34] The Amendment is not confined, however, to law enforcement officials, but also applies to government employees engaged in administrative or civil activity, such as public school officials,[35] building inspectors,[36] OSHA inspectors,[37] firemen,[38] public hospital employees,[39] and government employers and supervisors.[40] Although the Fourth Amendment was primarily directed at the pre-Revolutionary writs of assistance in which customs officers utilized the writs to search for smuggled goods, the Court has liberally interpreted the Amendment to apply to all forms of government action, whether the government's motivation is to investigate violations of criminal law or to carry out other types of civil or administrative activity. This interpretation is based on the theory that it was the abuse of governmental search and seizure power that the Amendment was adopted to correct, and that "it would be anomalous to say that an individual and his private property are fully protected by the Fourth Amendment only when the individual is suspected of criminal activity."[41]

---

by the Fourth Amendment. Illinois v. Andreas, 463 U.S. 765, 103 S.Ct. 3319, 77 L.Ed.2d 1003, 1009, n. 2 (1983).

33. For a discussion of what constitutes a Fourth Amendment *seizure* of personal property, see Chapter 9, Section 3 of this work; and for a discussion of what constitutes a *reasonable* Fourth Amendment seizure of personal property, see Chapter 12, Section 2 of this work.

34. See, e.g., Torres v. Puerto Rico, 442 U.S. 465, 99 S.Ct. 2425, 61 L.Ed.2d 1 (1979) (Fourth Amendment applies to Puerto Rican law enforcement officials).

35. New Jersey v. T.L.O., 469 U.S. 325, 105 S.Ct. 733, 83 L.Ed.2d 720, 729–31 (1985).

36. Camara v. Municipal Court, 387 U.S. 523, 528, 87 S.Ct. 1727, 18 L.Ed.2d 930 (1967).

37. Marshall v. Barlow's, Inc., 436 U.S. 307, 98 S.Ct. 1816, 56 L.Ed.2d 305, 311 (1978).

38. Michigan v. Tyler, 436 U.S. 499, 98 S.Ct. 1942, 56 L.Ed.2d 486 (1978).

39. Ferguson v. City of Charleston, 532 U.S. 67, 121 S.Ct 1281, 149 L.Ed.2d 205, 215 (2001).

40. National Treasury Employees Union v. Von Raab, 489 U.S. 656, 109 S.Ct. 1384, 103 L.Ed.2d 685 1989); O'Connor v. Ortega, 480 U.S. 709, 107 S.Ct. 1492, 94 L.Ed.2d 714 (1987).

41. Camara v. Municipal Court 387 U.S. 523, 530, 87 S.Ct. 1727, 18 L.Ed. 930 (1967); see also New Jersey v. T.L.O., 469 U.S. 325, 105 S.Ct. 733, 83 L.Ed.2d 720, 730–31 (1985).

Chapter 9

Search or Seizure Element: *Seizures* of Persons, Houses, Papers or Effects

Section 1. Overview of Search or Seizure Element

The third and most complex element of the Fourth Amendment "Standing Requirement" is the search or seizure element. In the words of the Fourth Amendment, it must be shown that the government activity being challenged was a "search[ ]" or a "seizure[ ]" of the complaining party's "person[ ], houses, papers or effects."

Although the Fourth Amendment uses the term "searches *and* seizures," the United States Supreme Court has not read the term literally to mean that there must be *both* a search and a seizure for the Amendment to be applicable. In accord with the principle of liberal construction, the Court has consistently held that a Fourth Amendment search and a Fourth Amendment seizure can exist quite apart from one another in that each invades different expectations and interests.[1] It is, accordingly, well-settled that the Fourth Amendment governs "seizures" although no search may be involved;[2]

1. "The Fourth Amendment prohibits both unreasonable searches and unreasonable seizures, and its protection extends to both 'houses' and 'effects.'" United States v. Jeffers, 342 U.S. 48, 52, 72 S.Ct. 93, 96 L.Ed. 59 (1951). "This text [the Fourth Amendment] protects two types of expectations, one involving 'searches,' and one involving 'seizures.'" United States v. Jacobsen, 466 U.S. 109, 104 S.Ct. 1652, 1656, 80 L.Ed.2d 85, 94 (1984). "The right to security in person and property protected by the Fourth Amendment may be invaded in quite different ways. A search compromises the individual interest in privacy; a seizure deprives the individual of dominion over his or her person or property." Horton v. California, 496 U.S. 128, 110 S.Ct. 2301, 110 L.Ed.2d 112, 120 (1990). "The Fourth Amendment guarantees the right to be free of unreasonable searches and seizures. A search may be of a person, a thing, or a place. So too a seizure may be of a person, a thing, or even a place. A search or a seizure may occur singly or in combination, and in differing sequence. In some cases the validity of one determines the validity of the other." Bailey v. United States, 568 U.S. ____, 133 S.Ct. 1031, 185 L.Ed.2d 19, 26 (2013).

2. It has been held that the removal of a house trailer from its foundations in a mobile home park to a neighboring property by a mobile home park owner with the assistance of police constituted a Fourth Amendment seizure of a home, although no Fourth Amendment search was involved. Sodal v. Cook County, 506 U.S. 56, 113 S.Ct. 538, 121 L.Ed.2d 450, 463 (1992) ("[S]eizures of property are subject to Fourth Amendment scrutiny even though no search within the meaning of the Amendment has taken place. More generally, an officer who happens to come across an individual's property in a public area could seize it only if Fourth Amendment standards are satisfied—for example, if the items are evidence of crime or contraband."). It also has been held that the Fourth Amendment governs the seizure of a person or a suitcase by police although what followed was not a Fourth Amendment

conversely, the Fourth Amendment governs "searches" although nothing is actually seized.[3]

A "search," of course, generally leads to a "seizure"—as, for example, when the police "search" a house and "seize" contraband therein. A "seizure" may also lead to a "search"—as, for example, when an individual is arrested by the police and his person is "searched" which, in turn, may lead to the "seizure" of physical items in the individual's pockets.

Indeed, a variety of chain reactions can be set off by a "search" or a "seizure." A "search" of a house may turn up a suitcase which is "seized"; the suitcase may then be "searched" and items of physical evidence therein may be "seized" which may include containers or packages which may be "searched" and items of physical evidence therein "seized." A "seizure," on the other hand, may lead to a "search"—as where a footlocker is "seized," opened and "searched"—which, in turn, may lead to a "seizure" of physical items of evidence therein. In short, there are often a series of searches and seizures in a given fact pattern—although the Court primarily focuses on the first such intrusion for purposes of Fourth Amendment reasonableness analysis.

It is not enough, however, that there be a governmental search or seizure of just anything before it can be said that the Fourth Amendment governs this activity. The search or the seizure must, in the words of the Fourth Amendment, be directed against the complaining party's "person[ ], house[ ], papers, [or] effects." The Court accordingly has focused on the search or seizure of one or more of these four items in determining the activity that the Fourth Amendment governs.

We turn first to a consideration of the *seizure* component of the search and seizure element. In the two remaining Sections of this Chapter, we will discuss (a) seizures of the person and (b) seizures of houses, papers and effects. In the next Chapter, we will cover the *search* component of the search and seizure element.

Section 2. Seizure of the Person

Because many Fourth Amendment issues start with an encounter between an individual and a government official such as a law enforcement officer, we begin our treatment of the search or seizure element with a discussion of Fourth Amendment seizures of the person. The Fourth Amendment protects the right of the people to be secure in their "persons" against "unreasonable ... seizures." There are, in turn, two types of Fourth Amendment seizures of the person: physical seizures and submission-to-authority seizures.

a. Physical seizure

Without question, a person is seized within the meaning of the Fourth Amendment when a government agent, such as a police officer, subjects that person to actual physical

---

search. Davis v. Mississippi, 394 U.S. 721, 89 S.Ct. 1394, 22 L.Ed.2d 676 (1969) (detained individual fingerprinted at police station); United States v. Place, 462 U.S. 696, 103 S.Ct. 2637, 77 L.Ed.2d 110 (1983) (detained suitcase subjected to narcotics dog sniff).

3. A civil damages suit lies against police based on a Fourth Amendment violation where police unreasonably search a person's home, but find nothing incriminating to seize. See Bivens v. Six Unknown Named Agents of the Bureau of Narcotics, 403 U.S. 388, 91 S.Ct. 1999, 29 L.Ed.2d 619 (1971).

restraint so that the person is not free to leave. "It must be recognized that whenever a police officer accosts an individual and restrains his freedom to walk away, he has 'seized' that person."[4] This is the case, for example, whenever the police perfect a routine arrest in which the arrestee is handcuffed, placed in a police car, and taken to the police station for booking.

Implicit in this definition, however, is that the police must *intentionally*, not accidentally impose this physical restraint. "A Fourth Amendment seizure [of the person] does not occur [unless] ... there is a governmental termination of [an individual's] freedom of movement through means intentionally applied."[5] Accordingly, a Fourth Amendment seizure of the person occurs when police physically detain a person for the purpose of ascertaining the person's identity,[6] or intentionally shoot and hit a fleeing suspect,[7] or intentionally set up and physically stop a fleeing suspect in a vehicle that crashes into a police roadblock;[8] or ramming a police car into a vehicle fleeing from police in order terminate the fleeing vehicle's freedom of movement. [9] On the other hand, it is not a Fourth Amendment seizure of the person for the police to stop a fleeing suspect by *accidentally* crashing into a vehicle driven by a suspect during a high speed automobile chase.[10]

b. Submission-to-authority seizure: contrast with "mere contact"

Difficult problems may arise, however, when a person is not subjected to intentional physical restraint, but instead is approached and questioned by a police officer. Undoubtedly, most people as good citizens feel a certain social pressure to remain and cooperate with the police when so questioned. But the Court has never held that such social pressure constitutes an official restraint on liberty. To the contrary, the Court has consistently held that police questioning of this sort, without more, does not constitute a Fourth Amendment seizure of the person.[11]

---

4. Terry v. Ohio, 392 U.S. 1, 16, 88 S.Ct. 1868, 20 L.Ed.2d 889, 903 (1968).

5. County of Sacramento v. Lewis, 523 U.S. 833, 118 S.Ct. 1708, 140 L.Ed.2d 1043, 1056 (1998).

6. Brown v. Texas, 443 U.S. 47, 99 S.Ct. 2637, 61 L.Ed.2d 357 (1979) (seizure held unreasonable).

7. Tennessee v. Garner, 471 U.S. 1, 105 S.Ct. 1694, 85 L.Ed.2d 1 (1985) (suspect's estate could maintain a Fourth Amendment civil rights suit against police).

8. Brower v. County of Inyo, 489 U.S. 593, 109 S.Ct. 1378, 103 L.Ed.2d 628 (1989) (suspect's estate could maintain Fourth Amendment civil rights suit against police). This physical seizure of the person is to be distinguished from a roadblock or checkpoint in which the motorist submits to the police show of authority and stops his car—in which event there is a Fourth Amendment submission-to-authority seizure of the person, to be discussed shortly in this chapter, rather than a Fourth Amendment physical seizure of the person.

9. "Scott [the police officer defendant] does not contest that his decision to terminate the car chase by ramming his bumper into respondent's [suspect's] vehicle constitutes a 'seizure [of the person].'" "'A Fourth Amendment seizure [occurs] ... when there is some governmental termination of freedom of movement by means intentionally applied'. [citations omitted]." Scott v. Harris, 550 U.S. 372, 127 S.Ct. 1769, 1776, 167 L.Ed.2d 686 (2007).

10. County of Sacramento v. Lewis, 523 U.S. 833, 118 S.Ct. 1708, 140 L.Ed.2d 1043 (1998).

11. "Our cases make clear that a [4th Amendment] seizure [of the person] does not occur simply because a police officer approaches an individual and asks a few questions." Florida v. Bostick, 501 U.S. 429, 111 S.Ct. 2382, 115 L.Ed.2d 389, 399 (1991). "[L]aw enforcement officers do not violate the Fourth Amendment by merely approaching an individual on the street or in another public place, by asking him if he is willing to answer some questions, by putting questions to him if he is willing to listen.... Nor would the fact that the officer identifies himself as a police officer, without more, convert the encounter into a seizure requiring some level of justification." Florida v. Royer, 460 U.S.

This obviously makes good sense. Police work involves a myriad of police-citizen contacts in which such questioning is generally either benign or otherwise absolutely essential to the job—whether in responding to calls for assistance or investigating possible criminal activity. Indeed, if all such police-citizen contacts were Fourth Amendment seizures of the person requiring some showing of individualized suspicion, the police could not constitutionally talk to possible crime victims, possible witnesses to crime, or people in need of emergency assistance—as there would be no basis for suspecting any of these people of a crime. Accordingly, voluntary encounters of this sort with the police—often referred to as "mere contacts"—are not governed by the Fourth Amendment.

On the other hand, when police approach and question someone whom they do suspect of a crime, either initially or at sometime during the encounter, more than social pressure may be brought to bear upon the individual. Accordingly, the Court has held that a Fourth Amendment seizure of the person occurs when the police exhibit a show of authority such that a reasonable person innocent of any crime would have believed that he or she (1) was not free to leave the officer's presence, or (2) was not free to refuse the government official's requests and terminate the encounter—providing the person yields to such authority and does not flee.[12]

"Obviously, not all personal intercourse between policemen and citizens involve seizures of the person. Only when the officer, by means of physical force or show of authority, has in some way restrained the liberty of the citizen may we conclude that a 'seizure' of the person has occurred."[13] With respect to a show of authority, "a person has been seized within the meaning of the Fourth Amendment only if, in view of all the circumstances surrounding the incident, a reasonable person would have believed that he [or she] was not free to leave [the officer's presence]"[14]—or was otherwise not free to refuse the government official's requests and terminate the encounter.[15] Moreover, a reasonable person under this objective test "presupposes an innocent person," not someone who is

---

491, 103 S.Ct. 1319, 75 L.Ed.2d 229, 236 (1983). "Law enforcement officers do not violate the Fourth Amendment's prohibition against unreasonable seizures merely by approaching individuals on the street or in other public places and putting questions to them if they are willing to listen. Even when law enforcement officers have no basis for suspecting a particular individual, they may pose questions, ask for identification, and request consent to search luggage—provided they do not induce cooperation by coercive means. If a reasonable person would feel free to terminate the encounter, then he or she has not been seized." United States v. Drayton, 536 U.S. 194, 122 S.Ct. 2105, 2110, 153 L.Ed.2d 242 (2002). "Asking questions is an essential part of police investigations. In the ordinary course a police officer is free to ask a person for identification without implicating the Fourth Amendment. 'Interrogation relating to one's identity or a request for identification by the police does not, by itself, constitute a Fourth Amendment seizure [of the person].'" Hiibel v. Sixth Judicial District Court, 542 U.S. 177, 124 S.Ct. 2451, 2458, 159 L.Ed.2d 292 (2004) (internal citation omitted).

12. See, e.g., Brendlin v. California, 551 U.S. 249, 127 S.Ct. 2400, 2405, 168 L.Ed.2d 132 (2007).

13. Terry v. Ohio, 392 U.S. 1, 19 n. 16, 88 S.Ct. 1868, 20 L.Ed.2d 889, 905 n. 16 (1968).

14. United States v. Mendenhall, 446 U.S. 544, 554, 100 S.Ct. 1870, 64 L.Ed.2d 497, 509 (1980); see INS v. Delgado, 466 U.S. 210, 104 S.Ct. 1758, 80 L.Ed.2d. 247, 255 (1984).

15. "A seizure of the person within the meaning of the Fourth and Fourteenth Amendments occurs when, taking into account all of the circumstances surrounding the encounter, the police conduct would have communicated to a reasonable person that he was not at liberty to ignore the police presence and go about his business." Kaupp v. Texas, 538 U.S. 626, 123 S.Ct. 1843, 1845, 155 L.Ed.2d 814 (2003) (citations and internal quotations omitted); United States v. Drayton, 536 U.S. 194, 122 S.Ct. 2105, 153 L.Ed.2d 242 (2002) (seated passengers in an interstate bus asked by police officer in aisle for permission to search passengers' luggage and person); Florida v. Bostick, 501 U.S. 429, 111 S.Ct. 2382, 115 L.Ed.2d 398, 400 (1991) (same, but involving search of luggage only).

guilty of a crime and who might very well overreact to otherwise non-threatening police behavior.[16] Not surprisingly, then, "[w]ith respect to a show of authority," no seizure of such a reasonable person occurs when "the subject does not yield" to such authority, but instead attempts to escape from the police.[17] In such a case, no Fourth Amendment seizure of the person occurs, only an *attempted* seizure—and "[a]ttempted seizures of the person are beyond the scope of the Fourth Amendment."[18] Accordingly, under this test, a person subjected to such a show of authority must, in fact, yield to that authority and not attempt to escape.

Based on this analysis, it is clear that a Fourth Amendment submission-to-authority seizure of the person occurs whenever police direct an automobile on the street to pull over, the driver complies and does not attempt to flee, and the police thereafter conduct a brief inquiry or issue a traffic citation.[19] The same is also true where police direct an automobile to stop at a highway checkpoint or roadblock, the driver complies and does not turn around or attempt to leave the area, and police thereafter conduct brief inquires of the driver or passengers.[20] Moreover, not only is the driver seized in these traffic stop scenarios, but also any passenger in the automobile.[21]

It is sometimes difficult, however, to draw the line between a Fourth Amendment seizure of the person and a mere police-citizen contact based on the submission-to-authority test. Each case tends to be fact-specific, although some broad guidelines have been laid down:

> Examples of circumstances that might indicate a seizure [of the person] ... would be the threatening presence of several officers, the display of a weapon by an officer, some physical touching of the person of the citizen, or the use of language

---

16. Florida v. Bostick, 501 U.S. 429, 111 S.Ct. 2382, 115 L.Ed.2d 398, 399 (1991).

17. California v. Hodari D., 499 U.S. 621, 111 S.Ct. 547, 113 L.Ed.2d 690, 697 (1991) (evidence discarded by defendant while in flight from police held admissible in evidence).

18. County of Sacramento v. Lewis, 523 U.S. 833, 118 S.Ct. 1708, 140 L.Ed.2d 1043, 1056 n. 7 (1998).

19. "There can be no question that the stopping of a vehicle [by police] and the detention of its occupants constitutes a 'seizure' within the meaning of the Fourth Amendment." Colorado v. Bannister, 449 U.S. 1, 101 S.Ct. 42, 66 L.Ed.2d 1, 4 at n. 3 (1980) (police direct an auto on the public streets to pull over and the driver complies; held Fourth Amendment seizure of the person); "The Fourth and Fourteenth Amendments are implicated in this case because the stopping of an automobile [by police] and detaining its occupants constitutes a 'seizure' within the meaning of these Amendments, even though the purpose of the stop is limited and the resulting detention quite brief." Delaware v. Prouse, 440 U.S. 648, 99 S.Ct. 1391, 59 L.Ed.2d 660, 667 (1979) (same); "Temporary detentions of individuals during the [police] stop of an automobile, even if only for a brief period and for a limited purpose, constitutes a 'seizure' of 'persons' within the meaning of the Fourth Amendment." Whren v. United States, 517 U.S. 806, 116 S.Ct. 1769, 1772, 135 L.Ed.2d 89 (1996) (same).

20. "Petitioners concede, correctly in our view, that a Fourth Amendment 'seizure' occurs when a vehicle is stopped at a [police] checkpoint." Michigan State Police v. Sitz, 496 U.S. 444, 110 S.Ct. 2481, 110 L.Ed.2d 412, 420 (1990). (DUI roadblock). "It is agreed that [government] checkpoint stops are 'seizures' within the meaning of the Fourth Amendment." United States v. Martinez-Fuerte, 428 U.S. 543, 556, 96 S.Ct. 3074, 49 L.Ed.2d 1116, 1127 (1976) (INS checkpoint near US-Mexican border). "It is well-established that a vehicle stop [by police] at a highway checkpoint effects a seizure within the meaning of the Fourth Amendment." City of Indianapolis v. Edmond, 531 U.S. 32, 121 S.Ct.447, 148 L.Ed.2d 333, 342 (2000) (narcotics roadblock).

21. "When a police officer makes a traffic stop, the driver of the car is seized within the meaning of the Fourth Amendment. The question in this case is whether the same is true of the passenger. We hold that a passenger is seized as well and so may challenge the constitutionality of the stop." Brendlin v. California, 551 U.S. 249, 127 S.Ct. 2400, 2403, 168 L.Ed.2d 132 (2007).

or tone of voice indicating that compliance with the officer's request might be compelled.[22]

It has been held that a police pursuit of a fleeing suspect does not constitute a Fourth Amendment seizure of the person—even when the police order the suspect to stop and the suspect continues to flee.[23] Similarly, it has been held that police officers in a squad car traveling alongside a suspect—who begins running upon observing the police—have not, without more, seized the suspect within the meaning of the Fourth Amendment.[24] Consequently, any incriminating evidence discarded by the suspect in these cases while in flight and later retrieved by the police is not subject to suppression.

In encounters of this sort, it is extremely important to know *when* a mere police-citizen contact begins—and *when* that mere contact ends and a Fourth Amendment seizure of the person begins. "What has evolved from our cases is a determination that an initially consensual encounter between a police officer and a citizen can be transformed into a seizure or detention within the meaning of the Fourth Amendment."[25] If the encounter is a "mere contact" at the time police learn certain information from the individual or obtain evidence pursuant to the individual's otherwise voluntary consent to search, the information learned and evidence obtained is not subject to suppression under the *Weeks-Mapp* exclusionary rule—provided any consent to search is otherwise freely and voluntarily given. Moreover, the police can use this mere-contact evidence and information as part of the "totality of circumstances" for justifying a subsequent temporary detention or arrest of the individual. But, on the other hand, if the encounter has already progressed into a Fourth Amendment seizure of the individual at the time this information is learned or such evidence obtained, that seizure must previously be "reasonable" under the Fourth Amendment—else it will generally taint and render inadmissible this information and evidence under the *Weeks-Mapp* exclusionary rule.

For example, federal and state narcotics agents have developed a practice of encountering persons who are suspected of transporting illegal drugs on commercial airline flights. These encounters usually take place at metropolitan airports as the suspect is about to board, or has just disembarked from a commercial airline flight. Typically, the agents will attempt to talk to the suspect, examine the person's airline ticket and identification papers, and obtain consent to search the person's luggage. If a consent to search the suspect's luggage is obtained during a "mere contact" before the suspect is seized within the meaning of the Fourth Amendment, the search is generally upheld provided the consent is voluntarily given.[26] Similarly, if a consent to search the suspect's luggage is obtained at the time the suspect is subjected to a *lawful* temporary detention or an arrest—that is, a "reasonable" seizure under the Fourth Amendment, the consent is generally considered "untainted" and the fruits thereof admissible in evidence, provided consent is otherwise voluntarily given. But if this detention or arrest is *unlawful*—that is, "unreasonable" under the Fourth Amendment, a contrary result is generally reached, as the unlawful seizure of the person usually "taints" and renders involuntary the consent to search.[27]

---

22. United States v. Mendenhall, 446 U.S. 544, 100 S.Ct. 1870, 64 L.Ed.2d 497, 509–10 (1980).

23. California v. Hodari D., 499 U.S. 621, 111 S.Ct. 547, 113 L.Ed.2d 690, 697 (1991).

24. Michigan v. Chesternut, 486 U.S. 567, 108 S.Ct. 1975, 100 L.Ed.2d 565 (1988).

25. INS v. Delgado, 466 U.S. 210, 104 S.Ct. 1758, 80 L.Ed.2d 247, 255 (1984).

26. United States v. Mendenhall, 446 U.S. 544, 100 S.Ct. 1870, 64 L.Ed.2d 497 (1980) (consent to search air traveler's luggage upheld; consent to search obtained during "mere contact" between federal narcotics agents and air traveler).

27. Florida v. Royer, 460 U.S. 491, 103 S.Ct. 1319, 75 L.Ed.2d 229 (1983) (mere contact between state narcotics agents and air traveler progresses into temporary detention and later into the functional

In these cases, it is important to know whether the narcotics agents obtained the air traveler's airline ticket during the encounter. If the ticket is examined and returned to the air traveler, this tends to show that a "mere contact" has taken place.[28] On the other hand, if the ticket and identification are retained by the agents and not returned to the air traveler, this generally means that the air traveler has been seized within the meaning of the Fourth Amendment—particularly where the air traveler is about to board a flight and needs the ticket to do so.[29]

A variation of these airport encounters is the commercial bus encounter. Law enforcement officers, on occasion, will board an interstate commercial bus as part of an interdiction effort to discover contraband narcotics or weapons, and ask seated bus passengers for permission to search the passengers' luggage or person. It has been held that this action, without more, does not constitute a Fourth Amendment seizure of the person[30]—and that when otherwise accomplished under non-coercive circumstances, such action is, in fact, not a Fourth Amendment seizure of the person.[31] Moreover, the Court has rejected a per se rule that law enforcement officers must advise passengers of their right to refuse to cooperate in these police-passenger bus encounters in order for the encounters to be voluntary[32]—although presumably the presence or absence of such a warning is a factor to be considered in determining whether the encounter amounted to a Fourth Amendment seizure of the person.

Finally, law enforcement officials sometimes will do more than approach and question a suspect in a public place. They may also request that the suspect accompany them to the police station where they may conduct an interview in private. Obviously, this may present a coercive situation depending on the circumstances, as the suspect may reasonably feel that he or she has no choice but to accede to this unusual police request; if so, the suspect is considered seized within the meaning of the Fourth Amendment.[33] Clearly, whether the suspect's "consent to accompany the [law enforcement] agents [to the police station] was in fact voluntary or was the product of duress or coercion, express or implied, is to be determined by the totality of the circumstances ... and is a matter that the Government has the burden of proving."[34]

---

equivalent of an arrest; held: reasonable suspicion shown for temporary detention, but probable cause not shown for "arrest" when consent to search luggage was obtained—thereby rendering the fruits of the search inadmissible).

28. United States v. Mendenhall, 446 U.S. 544, 100 S.Ct. 1870, 64 L.Ed.2d 497 (1980); Login v. State, 394 So.2d 183 (Fla. 3d DCA 1981).

29. Florida v. Royer, 460 U.S. 491, 103 S.Ct. 1319, 75 L.Ed.2d 229, 239 (1983); State v. Frost, 374 So.2d 593, 594 (Fla. 3d DCA 1979).

30. Florida v. Bostick, 501 U.S. 429, 111 S.Ct. 2382, 115 L.Ed.2d 389 (1991).

31. United States v. Drayton, 536 U.S. 194, 122 S.Ct. 2105, 153 L.Ed.2d 242 (2002) (officer spoke in low, polite tone of voice; did not block the aisle so that passengers could exit; asked every person on the bus for permission to check their luggage as part of security check for weapons and illegal narcotics; other two officers on bus did not block aisle; no weapons were brandished).

32. United States v. Drayton, 536 U.S. 194, 122 S.Ct. 2105, 153 L.Ed.2d 242 (2002).

33. Kaupp v. Texas, 538 U.S. 626, 123 S.Ct. 1843, 155 L.Ed.2d 814 (2003) (six police officers go to 17-year-old boy's home at 3 AM, are admitted by the boy's father, wake the boy up in his bedroom, one officer says: "We need to talk," and the boy replies, "Okay," the boy is handcuffed and led out of the house shoeless, clad only in his boxer shorts and t-shirt, and taken to the police station where he is questioned; held: Fourth Amendment seizure of the person requiring probable cause to justify).

34. United States v. Mendenhall, 446 U.S. 544, 577, 100 S.Ct. 1870, 64 L.Ed.2d 497, 511 (1980) (suspect's consent to accompany federal agents to DEA interview room in airport held voluntary); but see Florida v. Royer, 460 U.S. 491, 103 S.Ct. 1319, 75 L.Ed.2d 229 (1983) (contrary result). For a discussion of what constitutes a voluntary consent, see Chapter 14, Section 5 (a) of this work.

c. Temporary detention vs. arrest

As an aside, after a Fourth Amendment seizure of the person has been accomplished, whether an actual physical seizure or a submission-to-authority seizure, governmental officials may choose to make the seizure (a) a temporary one for a criminal investigative purpose or a civil or administrative purpose, or (b) a more extensive deprivation of liberty, such as a formal arrest.[35] As will be discussed later, temporary detentions that have a criminal investigative purpose require a showing of "reasonable suspicion," but not "probable cause" to be constitutionally reasonable.[36] Temporary civil or administrative detentions must satisfy a Fourth Amendment balancing test to be constitutionally reasonable.[37] And more intrusive or prolonged detentions, including arrests, generally require a showing of "probable cause" to be constitutionally reasonable.[38]

Section 3. Seizure of House, Papers or Effects: Interference with Possessory Interests Test

The Fourth Amendment also protects the right of the people to be secure in their "houses, papers or effects" against "unreasonable ... seizures." The term "papers" includes any printed matter—such as books, records, magazines, documents and the like—as well as first class mail.[39] The term "effects" means personal property, not real property.[40] This includes any motor vehicle such as an automobile,[41] a vessel,[42] personal luggage,[43] and any container such as a footlocker, a zippered leather pouch, or closed paper bag.[44] And a Fourth Amendment seizure of a "house[ ]"—although very unusual—includes any kind of enclosed structure, such as house trailer torn from its foundations in a mobile

35. For a discussion of the distinction between a temporary detention and an arrest, see Chapter 12, Section 1a of this work.

36. For a discussion of the reasonable suspicion standard for temporary detentions, see generally Chapter 12, Section 2e of this work.

37. For a discussion of the reasonableness standard for civil or administrative temporary detentions, see Chapter 12, Section 1n of this work.

38. For a discussion of the probable cause standard for arrests, see generally Chapter 12, Section 1e of this work.

39. See, e.g., United States v. Van Leeuwen, 397 U.S. 249, 90 S.Ct. 1029, 25 L.Ed.2d 282 (1970) (first class mail); In re Jackson, 6 (Otto) 727, 24 L.Ed. 877 (1877) (same).

40. "The framers [of the Fourth Amendment] would have understood the term 'effects' to be limited to personal property, rather than real property." Oliver v. United States, 466 U.S. 170, 104 S.Ct. 1735, 80 L.Ed.2d 214, 223 n. 7 (1984).

41. See, e.g., South Dakota v. Opperman, 428 U.S. 364, 367, 96 S.Ct. 3092, 49 L.Ed.2d 1000 (1976) (automobile); Cady v. Dombrowski, 413 U.S. 433, 93 S.Ct. 2523, 37 L.Ed.2d 706 (1973) (automobile); California v. Carney, 471 U.S. 386, 105 S.Ct. 2066, 85 L.Ed.2d 406, 411 (1985) (mobile motor home); Rios v. United States, 364 U.S. 253, 80 S.Ct. 1431, 4 L.Ed.2d 1688 (1960) (taxicab).

42. See, e.g., United States v. Villamonte-Marquez, 462 U.S. 579, 103 S.Ct. 2573, 77 L.Ed.2d 22 (1983); United States v. Lee, 274 U.S. 559, 47 S.Ct. 746, 71 L.Ed. 1202 (1927).

43. Bond v. United States, 528 U.S. 334, 120 S.Ct. 1462, 145 L.Ed.2d 365 (2000); see also Arkansas v. Sanders, 442 U.S. 753, 99 S.Ct. 2586, 61 L.Ed.2d 235 (1979).

44. United States v. Ross, 456 U.S. 798, 102 S.Ct. 2157, 72 L.Ed.2d 572, 592 (1982) (zippered leather pouch and closed brown paper bag); United States v. Chadwick, 433 U.S. 1, 97 S.Ct. 2476, 53 L.Ed.2d 538 (1977) (footlocker).

home park.[45] In turn, "[a] [Fourth Amendment] seizure of [such] property occurs when there has been some meaningful interference with an individual's possessory interests in the property."[46] Moreover, a person does not lose standing to object to a Fourth Amendment seizure of personal property because the property seized is contraband, such as illegal drugs.[47]

When a private person—as opposed to the police—meaningfully interferes with an individual's possessory interests in property, and turns that property over to the police on a "silver platter," the *acceptance* of the property by the police is generally treated as a Fourth Amendment seizure of the individual's property. This means that such seizure must be reasonable under the Fourth Amendment at the time of the acceptance—as, for example, where there is probable cause to believe that the property contains contraband drugs, based on the appearance of the property or information given by the private person to the police.[48]

On the other hand, an undercover police officer's purchase of magazines for sale at an adult book store during business hours is not considered a Fourth Amendment seizure of the magazines. Clearly, there is no meaningful interference with the book store owner's possessory interests in such magazines in these circumstances. The owner has voluntarily relinquished possession of the magazines upon payment therefor by the police officer—albeit in an undercover capacity.[49]

---

45. Soldal v. Cook County, 506 U.S. 56, 113 S.Ct. 538, 121 L.Ed.2d 450 (1992) (removal of house trailer from its foundations by police).

46. United States v. Jacobsen, 466 U.S. 109, 113, 104 S.Ct. 1652, 80 L.Ed.2d 85, 94 (1984).

47. United States v. Jeffers, 342 U.S. 48, 72 S.Ct. 93, 96 L.Ed. 59, 65 (1951).

48. United States v. Jacobsen, 466 U.S. 109, 104 S.Ct. 1682, 80 L.Ed.2d 85, 99 (1984).

49. Maryland v. Macon, 472 U.S. 463, 105 S.Ct. 2778, 86 L.Ed.2d 370 (1985).

Chapter 10

Search or Seizure Element: *Searches* of Persons, Houses, Papers or Effects

Section 1. Introduction

We turn now to the *search* component of the search or seizure element in the Fourth Amendment "Standing Requirement." The Fourth Amendment protects the right of the people to be secure in their "persons, houses, papers and effects against unreasonable *searches*."

Generally, there is no problem in determining whether a Fourth Amendment "search" has taken place in a given case. This is so because in most cases a traditional trespassory search of private premises or a person has taken place—as was prevalent during the general writs of assistance regime that the Fourth Amendment was designed to end. Such a search in this common-sense, historically-based meaning is unquestionably a Fourth Amendment search. Indeed, long before the modern test for a Fourth Amendment search was announced, it was axiomatic that a Fourth Amendment search took place whenever a government agent physically looked for evidence hidden from public view in an individual's home, business or automobile, or on an individual's person—a result that is fully embraced within the modern test that will be discussed shortly.[1] Moreover, the old trespass test for a Fourth Amendment search has itself been revived recently as a *secondary* test such a search—as will also be discussed shortly.

It is therefore in a rare case—usually one of first impression—where a problem is presented as to whether a Fourth Amendment search has occurred. It is only in these cases that the Court has resorted to an extensive analysis of the issue. This has occurred in cases involving (1) wiretapping, electronic eavesdropping or tracking devices; (2) the use of enhanced observation devices (i.e., a flashlight, searchlight, thermal imaging device or long-range photography); and (3) the trespassory entry onto an individual's yard or large tract of land. This has also occurred in cases involving Fourth Amendment searches of a person's home or vehicle in which other persons besides the owner or lessee are also located—and the issue has been whether a Fourth Amendment search has occurred with respect to these other persons.

---

1. Hale v. Henkel, 201 U.S. 43, 76, 26 S.Ct. 370, 50 L.Ed.652, 666 (1906) ("[A] search ordinarily implies a quest [for evidence] by an officer of the law, and a seizure contemplates a forcible dispossession of the owner ...").

Even in these unusual cases, it is unnecessary to go into an extensive analysis if the Court has clearly settled whether a particular government action is or is not a Fourth Amendment search as to a particular person. The Court simply follows the holding announced in the prior controlling case. With these caveats in mind, we turn now to the modern test of a Fourth Amendment search. Because this can get very complicated, an overview of what follows is in order.

- We will first examine in detail the *modern* test for a Fourth Amendment search: whether there has been a governmental invasion of the complaining party's reasonable expectation of privacy when directed against one's person, house papers or effects. Section 2 of this chapter covers this subject. As an aside, we will also briefly look at the older recently-revived trespass test for a Fourth Amendment search.
- We will then break the modern test down into two components and examine each part separately: (1) whether the *complaining party* has a reasonable expectation of privacy in one's person, house, papers or effects, and (2) whether the government by some action has invaded that reasonable expectation of privacy. Sections 3 and 4 of this chapter examine these two components.[2]
- In particular, Section 3 breaks down the first component of this *modern* test into three subsections: (a) the reasonable expectation of privacy enjoyed with respect to one's *person*; (b) the reasonable expectation of privacy enjoyed with respect to one's *house* [i.e., one's dwelling, business or place of employment, and other premises]; and (c) the reasonable expectation of privacy enjoyed with respect to one's *papers or effects* [i.e., one's personal property, including a motor vehicle, a vessel, a container, first class mail]. In the latter two subsections, we will also examine the complaining party's *connection or lack of connection* to the protected premises or property involved.
- Section 4, in turn, focuses on the second component of the *modern* test: the *governmental invasion* of this reasonable expectation of privacy. In particular, this section examines the *physical entry* of a governmental agent into protected private premises and personal property—as well as other *specialized governmental actions* such as "open view" sightings, electronic eavesdropping, and canine sniffs. Moreover, Section 5 of this chapter expands on these specialized governmental actions—and also covers governmental retrievals of abandoned property.

Section 2. General Test: Governmental Invasion of One's Reasonable Expectation of Privacy & Trespass Addendum

The U.S. Supreme Court has generally [although not exclusively] defined a Fourth Amendment "search" as a governmental invasion of one's reasonable expectation of pri-

2. The older recently-revived trespass test for a Fourth Amendment search is relatively straightforward and is not examined in detail, as its case law to date is rather limited.

vacy[3]—when directed against one's "person[ ], house[ ], papers or effects."[4] There are two interrelated components to this test:

1. The complaining party must have a reasonable expectation of privacy in one's person, house, papers or effects; and
2. A government official or agent must, by some action, invade this reasonable expectation of privacy.

If a government official or agent has invaded an individual's reasonable expectation of privacy as thus defined, this only means that a Fourth Amendment search has taken place. It does not mean that the individual's Fourth Amendment rights have been violated. The search must still be shown to be "unreasonable" in order to constitute a violation of the individual's Fourth Amendment rights.

The modern test has gradually emerged from the cases. But *Katz v. United States*,[5] particularly Justice Harlan's highly influential concurring opinion,[6] is the leading case—and

---

3. "A [Fourth Amendment] 'search' occurs when an expectation of privacy that society is prepared to recognize as reasonable is infringed." United States v. Jacobsen, 466 U.S. 109, 104 S.Ct 1652, 80 L.Ed.2d 85, 94 (1984); see also United States v. Karo, 468 U.S. 705, 104 S.Ct. 3296, 82 L.Ed.2d 530, 539 (1984). "We have recently held that 'the Fourth Amendment protects people, not places'... and wherever an individual may harbor a reasonable 'expectation of privacy'... he is entitled to be free from unreasonable governmental intrusion." Terry v. Ohio, 392 U.S. 1, 88 S.Ct. 1868, 20 L.Ed.2d 889, 898–99 (1968). "Since the decision in Katz v. United States ... it has been held that 'capacity to claim the protection of the Fourth Amendment depends ... upon whether the person who claims the protection has a legitimate expectation of privacy in the invaded place.'" Minnesota v. Olson, 495 U.S. 91, 110 S.Ct.1684, 109 L.Ed.2d 85, 92 (1990), quoting from Rakas v. Illinois, 439 U.S. 128, 143, 99 S.Ct. 421, 58 L.Ed.2d 387 (1978). "Capacity to claim the protection of the [Fourth] Amendment depends not upon a property right in the invaded space, but upon whether the area was one in which there was a reasonable expectation of freedom from governmental intrusion." Mancusi v. Deforte, 392 U.S. 364, 88 S.Ct. 2120, 20 L.Ed.2d 1154, 1159 (1968).

On the other hand, "[o]fficial conduct that does not 'compromise any legitimate interest in privacy' is not a search subject to the Fourth Amendment. We have held that any interest in possessing contraband cannot be deemed 'legitimate,' and thus governmental conduct that *only* reveals the possession of contraband 'compromises no legitimate privacy interest.' This is because the expectation 'that certain facts will not come to the attention of the authorities' is not the same as an interest in 'privacy that society is prepared to consider as reasonable.'" Illinois v. Caballes, 543 U.S. 405, 125 S.Ct. 834, 837–38, 160 L.Ed.2d 842 (2005) (internal citations omitted). Examples of such official conduct revealing *solely* the possession of contraband are (1) a narcotics "dog sniff" of a car, Illinois v. Caballes, supra; and (2) a chemical test of a powder to determine whether it is cocaine. United States v. Jacobsen, 466 U.S. 109, 104 S.Ct. 1652, 80 L.Ed.2d 85, 100–101 (1984). See Section 5c, infra, of this chapter for a discussion of narcotic "dog sniffs."

4. "The purpose of the Fourth Amendment is to prevent unreasonable governmental intrusions into the privacy of one's person, house, papers, or effects. The wrong condemned is the unjustified invasion of these areas of an individual's life." United States v. Calandra, 414 U.S. 338, 94 S.Ct. 613, 38 L.Ed.2d. 561, 575 (1974).

5. 389 U.S. 347, 88 S.Ct. 507, 19 L.Ed.2d 576 (1967). Although the term "reasonable expectation of privacy" does not appear in the Court's opinion, the general analysis presented concerning a Fourth Amendment search generally speaks in privacy terms. "For the Fourth Amendment protects people, not places. What a person knowingly exposes to the public, even in his own home or office, is not subject to Fourth Amendment protection.... But what he seeks to protect as private, even in an area accessible to the public, may be constitutionally protected." 389 U.S. at 351, 19 L.Ed.2d at 582.

6. The concept of a "reasonable expectation of privacy" was first stated in Justice Harlan's concurring opinion in *Katz*. "As the Court's opinion states, 'the Fourth Amendment protects persons, not places.' The question, however, is what protection it affords those people. Generally, as here, the answer to that question requires reference to a 'place.' My understanding of the rule that has emerged from prior

is now the primary touchstone of Fourth Amendment analysis with respect to searches.[7] This primary *Katz* analysis supersedes, but does not entirely abandon, older formulations relating to the scope of Fourth Amendment protection, so that the Fourth Amendment is no longer *confined under this test* to real or personal property interests or to common law concepts of possession or trespass;[8] nor can the Fourth Amendment be invoked thereunder solely because the person complaining is "legitimately on the premises" at the time of the alleged search of same.[9] The test under *Katz*, as to whether a Fourth Amendment search has occurred, is whether the challenged activity constitutes a governmental invasion of the complaining party's reasonable expectation of privacy—with real and personal property interests, common law concepts of possession and trespass, and legitimate presence on the premises, all being important but not decisive factors in determining whether there has been an invasion of one's reasonable expectation of privacy.[10] Other

---

decisions is that there is a two-fold requirement, *first that a person have exhibited an actual (subjective) expectation of privacy and, second, that the expectation be one that society is prepared to recognize as reasonable*. Thus, a man's home is, for most purposes, a place where he expects privacy, but objects, activities or statements that he exposes to the 'plain view' of outsiders are not 'protected' because no intention to keep them to himself has been exhibited." Katz v. United States, 389 U.S. 347, 361, 88 S.Ct. 507, 19 L.Ed.2d 576, 587–88 (1967) (Harlan, J. concurring). The Court has since fully accepted this formulation. See, e.g., Kyllo v. United States, 533 U.S. 27, 121 S.Ct. 2038, 2042–43, 150 L.Ed.2d (2001).

7. "Since Katz v. United States, 389 U.S. 347, 88 S.Ct. 507, 19 L.Ed.2d 576 (1967), the touchstone of [Fourth] Amendment analysis has been the question whether a person has a 'constitutionally protected reasonable expectation of privacy.'" Oliver v. United States, 466 U.S. 170, 104 S.Ct. 1735, 80 L.Ed.2d 214, 223 (1984), quoting from Justice Harlan's concurring opinion in *Katz;* see also California v. Ciraolo, 476 U.S. 207, 106 S.Ct. 1809, 90 L.Ed.2d 210, 215 (1986). For a more detailed discussion of the *Katz* reasonable-expectation-of-privacy test, see 1 Wayne LaFave, Search and Seizure § 2.1 (a)-(d) (5th ed. 2012).

8. "But 'the premise that property interests control the right of the Government to search and seize has been discredited.'... Once this much is acknowledged, and once it is recognized that the Fourth Amendment protects people—and not simply areas—against unreasonable searches and seizures, it becomes clear that the reach of that Amendment cannot turn on the presence or absence of a physical intrusion into any given enclosure." Katz v. United States, 389 U.S. 347, 353, 88 S.Ct. 507, 19 L.Ed.2d 576, 583 (1967), overruling Olmstead v. United States, 277 U.S. 438, 48 S.Ct. 564, 72 L.Ed. 944 (1928). "We are persuaded, however, that it is unnecessary and ill-advised to import into the law surrounding the constitutional right to be free from unreasonable searches and seizures subtle distinctions, developed and refined by the common law in evolving the body of private property law which, more than any other branch of law, has been shaped by distinctions whose validity is largely historical. Distinctions such as 'lessor,' 'licensee,' 'invitee,' and 'guest,' often only of gossamer strength, ought not be determinative in fashioning procedures ultimately referable to constitutional standards." Jones v. United States, 362 U.S. 257, 266, 80 S.Ct. 725, 4 L.Ed.2d 697, 705 (1960). "[L]egal possession of a seized good is not a proxy for determining whether the owner had a Fourth Amendment interest for it does not invariably represent the protected Fourth Amendment interest. * * * While property ownership is clearly a factor to be considered in determining whether an individual's Fourth Amendment rights have been violated..., property rights are neither the beginning nor the end of the Court's inquiry." United States v. Salvucci, 448 U.S. 83, 91, 100 S.Ct. 2547, 65 L.Ed.2d 619, 628 (1980).

9. Rakas v. Illinois, 439 U.S. 128, 99 S.Ct. 421, 58 L.Ed.2d 387 (1978), overruling in part Jones v. United States, 362 U.S. 257, 80 S.Ct. 725, 4 L.Ed.2d 697 (1960).

10. "Nonetheless, '[o]ne of the main rights attaching to property is the right to exclude others'..., and one who owns or lawfully possesses or controls property will in all likelihood have a legitimate expectation of privacy by virtue of their right to exclude." Rakas v. Illinois, 439 U.S. 128, 143, n. 12, 99 S.Ct. 421, 58 L.Ed.2d 387 (1978). "We do not question the conclusion in Jones that the defendant in that case [a guest occupant of an apartment] suffered a violation of his personal Fourth Amendment rights. Nonetheless, we believe that the phrase 'legitimately on the premises' coined in *Jones* created too broad a gauge for the measurement of Fourth Amendment rights.... We do not wish to be

factors may also include (a) the place where the individual is when the challenged government activity occurs—whether it be at home, at work, in a car or in a public place;[11] (b) the uses to which the individual has put the location where the search occurs; (c) the intention of the Framers of the Fourth Amendment,[12] (d) the right to exclude other persons from the premises which are searched,[13] and (e) general understandings that are recognized and permitted by society.[14] Stated differently, "in order to claim the protection of the Fourth Amendment [against an unreasonable search], [the complaining party] must demonstrate that he [or she] personally has an expectation of privacy in the place searched, and that this expectation is reasonable; i.e., one which has 'a source outside of the Fourth Amendment, either by reference to concepts of real or personal property law or to understandings that are recognized and permitted by society.' "[15]

Trespass Addendum. Apart from the modern *Katz* test, the U.S. Supreme Court has in recent years revived an older conception of a Fourth Amendment search and held that a governmental *trespass* into *a constitutionally protected area* [such as a house or vehicle] to find evidence of crime therein, followed by an investigation for such evidence, is *also* a "search" within the meaning of the Fourth Amendment. The rationale for this result is that such a trespass would have been considered a search at the time the Fourth Amendment was adopted. Accordingly, a Fourth Amendment search has occurred if the alleged intrusion satisfies *either* the trespass test or the *modern Katz* test. If the alleged intrusion is a common-law trespass—for example, one akin to the trespassory searches prevalent during the colonial general writs of assistance regime, searches the Framers intended to end—the intrusion is considered a Fourth Amendment "search." But if the intrusion does *not* satisfy this baseline trespass definition, the *Katz* test must be consulted.[16]

---

understood as saying that legitimate presence on the premises is irrelevant to one's expectation of privacy, but it cannot be deemed controlling." 439 U.S. at 141–42, 148.

11. "The Fourth Amendment does not protect all subjective expectations of privacy, but only those that society recognizes as 'legitimate'.... What expectations are legitimate varies, of course, with context ... depending, for example, upon whether the individual asserting the privacy interest is at home, at work, in a car, or in a public park." Vernonia School District 47J v. Acton, 515 U.S. 646, 115 S.Ct, 132 L.Ed.2d 564, 575 (1995).

12. "No single factor determines whether an individual can legitimately claim under the Fourth Amendment that a place should be free of governmental intrusion not authorized by warrant. In assessing the degree to which a search infringes upon individual privacy, the Court has given weight to such factors as the intention of the framers of the Fourth Amendment, the uses to which the individual has put a location, and our societal understanding that certain areas deserve the most scrupulous protection from government invasion." Oliver v. United States, 466 U.S. 170, 104 S.Ct. 1735, 80 L.Ed.2d 214, 223–24 (1984) (internal citations omitted).

13. Rakas v. Illinois, 439 U.S. 128, 143, n. 12, 99 S.Ct. 421, 58 L.Ed.2d 387 (1978). "In my view, that 'right to exclude' [others from the searched premises] often may be a principal determinant in the establishment of a legitimate Fourth Amendment interest." 439 U.S. at 112, 80 L.Ed.2d at 646 (Blackmun, J. concurring).

14. "Legitimation of expectations of privacy by law must have a source outside the Fourth Amendment, either by reference to concepts of real or personal property law or to understandings that are recognized and permitted by society." Rakas v. Illinois, 439 U.S. 128, 144, n. 12, 99 S.Ct. 421, 58 L.Ed.2d 387 (1978).

15. Minnesota v. Carter, 525 U.S. 83, 119 S.Ct. 469, 142 L.Ed.2d 373, 379 (1998), quoting from Rakas v. Illinois, 439 U.S. 128, 143–144, n. 12, 99 S.Ct. 421, 58 L.Ed.2d 387 (1978).

16. United States v. Jones, 565 U.S. ___, 132 S.Ct. 945, 181 L.Ed.2d 911 (2012) (a GPS tracking device placed by government agents on the undercarriage of accused's motor vehicle and its use thereafter to monitor the vehicle's movements on the public streets held to be a Fourth Amendment "search."); Florida v. Jardines, 569 U.S. ___, 133 S.Ct. 1409, 185 L.Ed.2d 495 (2013) (a police entry onto the front porch of accused's home with a drug-sniffing police dog, which dog smelled the front door for the odor of illegal drugs, followed by the dog's "alert" at the door indicating the presence of

This latter test—central to most Fourth Amendment jurisprudence—embraces other types of governmental intrusions, akin to traditional trespassory searches, but falling short thereof, where the intrusion nonetheless invades the core value of privacy in the Fourth Amendment as conceived by the Framers: the security of one's privacy against arbitrary intrusion by government agents.[17]

---

illegal drugs on the premises, held to be an uninvited trespassory intrusion into the curtilage of the home, and therefore a Fourth Amendment "search.").

"We decide whether the attachment of a Global-Positioning-System (GPS) tracking device to monitor an individual's vehicle, and subsequent use of that device to monitor the vehicle's movements on public streets, constitutes a search or seizure under the Fourth Amendment. * * * We hold that the Government's installation of a GPS device on a target's vehicle, and its use of that device to monitor the vehicle's movements, constitutes a 'search.'" United States v. Jones, 181 L.Ed.2d at 916, 918 (2012.)

"We consider whether using a drug sniffing dog on a homeowner's porch to investigate the contents of the home is a 'search' within the meaning of the Fourth Amendment. * * * The government's use of trained police dogs to investigate the home and its immediate surroundings is a 'search' within the meaning of the Fourth Amendment." Florida v. Jardines, 569 U.S. ___, 133 S.Ct. 1409, 185 L.Ed.2d 495, 499, 504 (2013) .

"It is important to be clear about what occurred in this case. The Government physically occupied private property for the purpose of obtaining information. We have no doubt that such a physical intrusion would have been considered a 'search' within the meaning of the Fourth Amendment when it was adopted." United States v. Jones, 181 L.Ed.2d at 918.

"Whatever new methods of investigation may be devised, our task, *at a minimum*, is to decide whether the action would have constituted a 'search' within the original meaning of the Fourth Amendment. Where, as here, the Government obtains information by physically intruding on a constitutionally protected area, such a search has undoubtedly occurred." United States v. Jones, 181 L.Ed.2d at 919, n. 3 (italics in the original).

"Trespass alone does not qualify [as a Fourth Amendment search], but there must be conjoined with that what was present here: an attempt to find something or to obtain information. * * * A trespass on 'houses' or 'effects,' or a Katz invasion of privacy, is not alone a search unless it is done to obtain information; and the obtaining of information is not alone a search unless it is achieved by such trespass or invasion of privacy." United States v. Jones, 181 L.Ed2d at 920, n. 5.

"But, as we have discussed, the Katz reasonable-expectation-of-privacy test has been *added to*, not *substituted for*, the common-law trespassory test." United States v. Jones, 181 L.Ed.2d at 920–21.

The search involved in Jones encompassed two convergent governmental actions: (1) the placement of an operational GPS device on the undercarriage of the respondent's Jeep to obtain evidence therefrom, and (2) the transfer of information from this device detailing the Jeep's movements for the next 28 days to a law enforcement computer, resulting in over 2000 pages of computer printout. Both actions together were necessary to constitute a single Fourth Amendment search. Placing either (1) an inoperable GPS device on the undercarriage of the Jeep or (2) an operable GPS device that law enforcement never used to monitor the Jeep's movements, would constitute an actionable common law trespass of the Jeep, but not one that transferred any information to law enforcement—and thus invaded no privacy interest of the Jeep user which, in turn, constituted no Fourth Amendment search.

"It is clear that the attachment of the GPS device was not in itself a search; if the device had not functioned or if the officers had not used it, no information would have been obtained." United States v. Jones, 565 U.S. ___, 132 S.Ct. 945, 181 L.Ed.2d 911, 927, 928 (2012) (Alito, J. concurring).

"The [Fourth] Amendment establishes a simple baseline, one that for most of our history formed the exclusive basis for its protections: When the Government obtains information by physically intruding on persons houses, papers, or effects, a 'search' within the original meaning of the Fourth Amendment has undoubtedly occurred. By reason of our decision in Katz v. United States ... property rights are not the sole measure of Fourth Amendment violations—but though Katz may add to the baseline, it does not subtract anything from the Amendment's protections when the Government *does* engage in [a] physical intrusion of a constitutionally protected area." Florida v. Jardines, 569 U.S. ___, 133 S.Ct. 1409, 185 L.Ed.2d 495, 500 (2013) (internal citations and quotes omitted).

For a discussion of the old recently-revived trespass test for a Fourth Amendment search, see 1 Wayne LaFave § 2.1 (e) (5th ed. 2012).

17. "The security of one's privacy against arbitrary intrusion by the police—which is at the core of the Fourth Amendment—is basic to a free society. It is therefore implicit in 'the concept of ordered

The U.S. Supreme Court has been led to this expanded *modern* definition largely because of—and to afford constitutional protection for —the twentieth century development of wiretapping and electronic eavesdropping. These intrusions plainly fall short of a traditional common-law search, but nonetheless strike at the core value of privacy in the Fourth Amendment as conceived by the Framers.[18] An invasion of privacy, therefore, is the central concept in defining a Fourth Amendment search—namely, privacy in one's person, house, papers and effects. Indeed, even a trespassory intrusion into a constitutionally protected area represents an invasion of privacy. Both the *Katz* and the trespassory tests are separate definitions of when the government has invaded a person's privacy as conceived by the Framers.[19] Moreover, depending on the circumstances, a given trespassory intrusion into a constitutionally protected area may actually satisfy both tests—although only one test need be met to constitute a Fourth Amendment search.[20]

Properly considered, then, the reasonable expectation of privacy test—like the old recently-revived trespass test—is squarely based on the original understanding of the Framers of the Fourth Amendment. It attempts to capture the fundamental constitutional *value* of the Fourth Amendment, *privacy* as conceived by the Framers, in defining a Fourth Amendment search. Plainly, the Framers and the American colonists of the revolutionary period had a deep sense of privacy that they inherited from their English ancestors—particularly, privacy in their homes—which they conceived in very legalistic terms. They felt that English law protected their homes, their businesses, their vessels, and their private property against general exploratory searches by government officials. When that privacy was not respected, when the British Crown through its customs officers in America 1761–76 insisted on the right to enter people's homes, businesses and other private premises and to search at will for smuggled goods pursuant to general writs of assistance, the American Revolution was born and the Fourth Amendment eventually emerged.[21] The reasonable expectation of privacy test appears to adopt this historical experience in defining a Fourth Amendment search by incorporating the fundamental value of the Amendment as conceived by the Framers—so as to embrace the traditional-type search prevalent during the general writs of assistance regime against which the colonists rebelled, as well as all other equivalent searches accomplished by other means, such as wiretapping and certain other forms of electronic eavesdropping.

---

liberty' and as such enforceable against the States through the Due Process Clause. The knock at the door, whether by day or by night, as a prelude to a search, without authority of law but solely on the authority of the police, did not need the commentary of recent history to be condemned as inconsistent with the conception of human rights enshrined in the history and the basic constitutional documents of English-speaking peoples." Wolf v. Colorado, 338 U.S. 25, 27–28, 69 S.Ct. 1359, 93 L.Ed.2d 1782, 1785–86 (1949), overruled on other grounds, Mapp v. Ohio, 367 U.S. 643, 81 S.Ct. 1684, 6 L.Ed.2d 1081 (1961).

18. "Wolf v. Colorado, 338 U.S. 25, 27–28, 69 S.Ct. 1359, 93 L.Ed.2d 1782, 1785–86 (1949), overruled on other grounds, Mapp v. Ohio, 367 U.S. 643, 81 S.Ct. 1684, 6 L.Ed.2d 1081 (1961).

19. "At bottom, we must assure preservation of that degree of privacy against government that existed when the Fourth Amendment was adopted." United States v. Jones, 565 U.S. ___, 132 S.Ct. 945, 181 L.Ed2d 911, 919 (2012) (internal citation and quotation marks omitted).

20. Florida v. Jardines, 569 U.S. ___, 133 S.Ct. 1409, 185 L.Ed.2d 495, 505 (2013) (Kagan, J. concurring) (police entry onto the front porch of home with a drug-sniffing dog which smells the front door for illegal drug aromas constitutes a Fourth Amendment "search" under *both* the trespass and Katz definitions) ("It is not surprising that in a case involving a home, property concepts and privacy concepts should so align. The law of property 'naturally influence[s]' our 'shared societal expectations' of what places should be free from governmental incursions.") (citations omitted).

21. See generally Chapters 2, 4 and 5 of this work for a discussion of the American historical background of the Fourth Amendment.

The gist of the test, then, as applied by the Court has been a governmental quest for physical and other evidence that is hidden from public view and intended to be kept private, when directed against one's person, house, papers or effects.[22] In this connection, the Court has focused on two questions: (1) what reasonable expectation of privacy does a person enjoy with respect to one's "person[ ], house[ ], papers or effects," and (2) when is that reasonable expectation of privacy officially invaded by the government.

As to the first question, the Court has looked to the relationship that the individual claiming the Fourth Amendment violation has to the person, house, papers or effects, and has, in turn, defined what interests and premises are encompassed thereby. As to the second question, the Court has looked to the type of governmental intrusion involved that is visited on those interests and premises, to determine whether a privacy invasion has been accomplished by this action. We turn now to a consideration of these two components of the reasonable expectation of privacy test—in Sections 3 and 4 below.

Section 3. First Component of a *Katz* Fourth Amendment "Search": Complaining Party Must Have a Reasonable Expectation of Privacy as to Protected Interests[23]

The first component of the modern Fourth Amendment search test is that the complaining party must have a reasonable expectation of privacy as to certain protected interests. At times, the Court has stated this component as a two-fold inquiry: (a) whether the party complaining has manifested a subjective expectation of privacy in the object of the challenged search; and (b) whether society is prepared to recognize this expectation

---

22. The Court's early statement that "a search ordinarily implies a quest [for evidence] by an officer of the law, and a seizure contemplates a forcible dispossession of the owner" [Hale v. Henkel, 201 U.S. 43, 76, 26 S.Ct. 370, 50 L.Ed. 652, 666 (1906)] implicitly assumed that such a search was directed against what the Fourth Amendment describes as one's "person[ ], house[ ], papers [or] effects," and that such evidence was hidden from public view which therefore required a "quest" by "an officer of the law" to discover and seize.

23. What follows is a discussion of the modern *Katz* test for a Fourth Amendment search. As previously noted, however, this is not the *only* test for a Fourth Amendment search. The older recently-revived trespass test must *first* be consulted to determine as a *baseline* whether there has been a trespass by a government official into a constitutionally-protected area, followed by an investigation for evidence. If so, that ends the inquiry as such conduct constitutes a Fourth Amendment search in itself—and the *Katz* test need not be consulted. Only if the conduct involved does *not* satisfy the trespass test is it appropriate to turn to the *Katz* test.

See Section 2, supra, of this chapter at footnote 16 and the accompanying text. For a thorough discussion of the old recently-revived trespass test for a Fourth Amendment search, see 1 Wayne LaFave § 2.1 (e) (5th ed. 2012).

"The [Fourth] Amendment establishes a simple baseline, one that for most of our history formed the exclusive basis for its protections: When the Government obtains information by physically intruding on persons houses, papers, or effects, a 'search' within the original meaning of the Fourth Amendment has undoubtedly occurred. By reason of our decision in Katz v. United States ... property rights are not the sole measure of Fourth Amendment violations—but though Katz may add to the baseline, it does not subtract anything from the Amendment's protections when the Government *does* engage in [a] physical intrusion of a constitutionally protected area." Florida v. Jardines, 569 U.S. ___, 133 S.Ct. 1409, 185 L.Ed.2d 495, 500 (2013) (internal citations and quotes omitted).

as reasonable.[24] The Court, however, has generally emphasized the second or objective portion of this component, to the exclusion of the first subjective portion, on the theory that "constitutional rights are generally not defined by the subjective intent of those asserting those rights."[25] Indeed, the Court has stated that the subjective part of the component is inapplicable where the government induces an individual into believing that he or she has no privacy rights; as, for example, by publicly announcing that henceforth all homes will be subject to warrantless search at the whim of the police—or where an individual is generally ignorant of this country's traditions of freedom and has no idea that one has guaranteed privacy rights.[26] For that reason, the Court rarely examines in detail whether the complaining party actually entertained a subjective expectation of privacy. Indeed, it often assumes this to be true unless the contrary is shown, and concentrates on whether this privacy expectation is reasonable.

In this connection, an expectation of privacy is generally considered reasonable if it is entertained with respect to premises, property and interests expressly protected by the Fourth Amendment—"persons, houses, papers [or] effects"—as to which the complaining party is substantially connected. We will therefore examine reasonable expectations of privacy as to one's (a) "person[ ]" [Section 3a below], (b) "house[ ]" [Section 3b below], and (c) "papers or effects." [Section 3c below].

a. Reasonable expectation of privacy as to one's "person"

(1) Significance of determination as to whether the search of a person has occurred

The Fourth Amendment protects the people against "unreasonable searches" of their "persons." Before determining what this means precisely, it is important to understand the limited significance of this determination. Indeed, in most cases, it has no significance at all. This is so because, typically, the police action that constitutes a Fourth Amendment "search" of a "person"—or other similar police action that falls short of such a search—comes *after* a prior police seizure of that person. For obvious reasons, it is not ordinarily possible for a police officer to obtain evidence from an individual without first seizing the latter's person, whether by temporary detention or arrest. As the Court has stated:

> [T]he obtaining of physical evidence from a person involves, then, a potential Fourth Amendment violation at two different levels [1] the 'seizure' of the 'person'

---

24. "The touchstone of Fourth Amendment analysis is whether a person has a 'constitutionally protected reasonable expectation of privacy.' (citation omitted). *Katz* posits a two-part inquiry: first, has the individual manifested a subjective expectation of privacy in the object of the challenged search? Second, is society willing to recognize that expectation as reasonable?" California v. Ciraolo, 476 U.S. 207, 106 S.Ct. 1809, 90 L.Ed.2d 210, 215 (1986). Smith v. Maryland, 442 U.S. 735, 99 S.Ct. 2577, 61 L.Ed.2d 220 (1979), states that this inquiry "normally" embraces two distinct questions:

"The first is whether the individual, by his conduct, has 'exhibited an actual (subjective) expectation of privacy'—whether, in the words of the *Katz* majority, the individual has shown that 'he seeks to preserve [something] as private.' The second question is whether the individual's subjective expectation of privacy is 'one that society is prepared to recognize as 'reasonable'—whether, in the words of the *Katz* majority, the individual's expectation, viewed objectively, is 'justifiable' under the circumstances."

442 U.S. at 740, 61 L.Ed.2d at 226 (internal citations omitted). See also Bond v. United States, 529 U.S. 334, 120 S.Ct. 1462, 146 L.Ed.2d 365, 370 (2000); United States v. Knotts, 460 U.S. 276, 103 S.Ct. 1081, 75 L.Ed.2d 55, 61 (1983).

25. Hudson v. Palmer, 468 U.S. 517, 104 S.Ct. 3194, 82 L.Ed.2d 393, 402, n. 7 (1984).

26. Smith v. Maryland, 442 U.S. 735, 740, n. 5, 99 S.Ct. 2577, 61 L.Ed.2d 220 (1979).

necessary to bring him into contact with government agents ... and [2] the subsequent search for or seizure of evidence.[27]

In such cases, it is generally irrelevant whether or not the second action, stated above, amounts to a Fourth Amendment search because this has no impact on the admissibility of the evidence secured thereby. If the preceding seizure of the person is deemed "unreasonable," the invalid seizure will generally taint and render inadmissible the subsequent evidence obtained, whether secured by a search or not—as such evidence constitutes the fruit of the preceding illegal seizure under the "fruit of the poisonous" tree doctrine of the *Weeks-Mapp* exclusionary rule.[28] On the other hand, if the preceding seizure of the individual is deemed "reasonable," there will generally be no basis to exclude the evidence subsequently obtained, even assuming it was obtained by a search, provided it was conducted "incident" to the seizure.[29] Consequently, these cases concentrate, as a rule, on whether the preceding Fourth Amendment seizure was a "reasonable" seizure and do not focus on whether the evidence subsequently obtained was secured through a Fourth Amendment search.[30]

There are, however, limited situations where it is critical to determine whether a Fourth Amendment search of the person has occurred. First, there are those cases where the initial governmental intrusion is an alleged Fourth Amendment search of an individual. This may occur when an individual voluntarily comes to the police station, is not arrested or detained in any way, and thereafter reveals certain evidence to the police; or when an individual responds to a grand jury subpoena and thereafter reveals certain evidence to the authorities. In these cases, no Fourth Amendment seizure of the individual's person has occurred, and the question presented is whether the action employed to obtain this evidence constitutes a Fourth Amendment search of the individual's person. If not, the Fourth Amendment would be inapplicable and the evidence admissible. If so, the contrary would be true, and the admissibility of the evidence would generally turn on whether the search was reasonable or unreasonable under the Fourth Amendment.

Secondly, there are those cases where a prior valid Fourth Amendment seizure of a person or property has occurred, but the subsequent alleged search that yields certain evidence cannot be upheld as a "reasonable" search under the circumstances. This may occur during a valid *Terry*-type temporary detention of a person on the street, where the

---

27. United States v. Dionisio, 410 U.S. 1, 8, 93 S.Ct. 764, 769, 35 L.Ed.2d 67 (1973).

28. For a discussion of this doctrine, see Chapter 17, Section 3 of this work. As LaFave has stated: "[I]f an investigation of a person is accomplished by making an illegal seizure of that individual, the evidence obtained is inadmissible as the fruit of the illegal seizure whether or not the post-seizure police action itself qualifies as a search." 1 Wayne LaFave, Search and Seizure § 2.6(a) at 864–865 (5th ed. 2012).

29. For a discussion of searches incident to an arrest, and stop-and-frisk searches, see Chapters 14, Sections 2 and 3 of this work. As LaFave has stated: "[I]f a person has been lawfully arrested, it is really not significant whether certain types of in-custody investigation (e.g., fingerprinting) constitute a Fourth Amendment search; the investigation is lawful in any event because a valid arrest was made." 1 Wayne LaFave, Search and Seizure § 2.6 (a) at 864 (5th ed. 2012).

30. LaFave states:

"In the overwhelming majority of cases in which an objection is raised concerning the obtaining of incriminating evidence from a person, the central issue is whether the antecedent "seizure" of the person was in compliance with the Fourth Amendment. This is because it is not ordinarily possible to obtain such evidence without first making a seizure, and because determination of the seizure issue is likely to govern without regard to whether what happened thereafter was or was not a search".

1 Wayne LaFave, Search and Seizure § 2.6(a) at 864 (5th ed. 2012).

alleged search subsequently conducted is unauthorized under the stop-and-frisk exception to the search warrant requirement rule.[31] It may also occur during a lawful arrest of a person, where the alleged search is not "incident" to the arrest, and is therefore unauthorized under the search-incident-to-arrest exception to the search warrant requirement rule.[32] In these cases, it is critical to determine whether a Fourth Amendment search has occurred following the lawful seizure of the person because, if it has, the search *may* be "unreasonable," as not being authorized by the stop-and-frisk or search-incident-to-a-valid arrest exceptions to the search warrant requirement rule—unless, of course, the search can be upheld under some other exception to the search warrant requirement rule.[33] On the other hand, if *no* Fourth Amendment search has occurred that yielded the evidence in question, the said evidence would be deemed the fruit of the preceding lawful seizure of the person, and therefore would be admissible in evidence.

(2) Nature of the search of a person: examples

Generally speaking, the U.S. Supreme Court, as well as other courts, have implicitly assumed that an individual has a reasonable expectation of privacy with respect to those portions of his or her person that are hidden from public view, including hidden recesses in both one's clothing and body. Any government action that discovers physical objects or other evidence from these hidden recesses has been treated as an invasion of the individual's privacy and therefore a Fourth Amendment search of the person. In accord with this view, the Court has held that the following police actions constitute a Fourth Amendment search of the person: rummaging through an individual's pockets and other inner recesses of one's clothing,[34] patting down an individual's outer clothing so as to discover hidden objects therein,[35] extracting a blood sample from an individual by means of a hyperdermic needle and thereafter testing the blood for alcohol or other chemical content,[36] subjecting a person to a breathalyser test by requiring the production of deep

---

31. For a discussion of the stop-and-frisk exception to the search warrant requirement rule, see Chapter 14, Section 3 of this work.

32. For a discussion of the search-incident-to-a-valid-arrest exception to the search warrant requirement rule, see Chapter 14, Section 2 of this work.

33. For a discussion of the various exceptions to the search warrant requirement rule, see generally Chapter 14 [criminal exceptions] and 15 [civil or administrative exceptions] of this work.

34. Sibron v. New York, 392 U.S. 40, 63, 88 S.Ct. 1889, 20 L.Ed.2d 917 (1968); Beck v. Ohio, 379 U.S. 89, 85 S.Ct. 223, 13 L.Ed.2d 142 (1964).

35. Terry v. Ohio, 392 U.S. 1, 16–17, 88 S.Ct. 1868, 20 L.Ed.2d 889, 903 (1968) ("And it is nothing less than sheer torture of the English language to suggest that a careful exploration of the outer surfaces of a person's clothing all over his or her body in an attempt to find weapons is not a 'search.' Moreover, it is simply fantastic to urge that such a procedure performed in public by a policeman while the citizen stands helpless, perhaps facing a wall with his hands raised, is a 'petty indignity.' It is a serious intrusion upon the sanctity of the person, which may inflict great indignity and arouse strong resentment, and it is not to be undertaken lightly.")

36. Schmerber v. California, 384 U.S. 757, 86 S.Ct. 1826, 16 L.Ed.2d 908, 918 (1966). "We have long recognized that a 'compelled intrusio[n] into the body for blood to be analyzed for alcohol content' must be deemed a Fourth Amendment search. In light of our society's concern for the security of one's person, it is obvious that this physical intrusion, penetrating beneath the skin, infringes an expectation of privacy that society is prepared to recognize as reasonable. The ensuing chemical analysis of the sample to obtain physiological data is further invasion of the tested [person's] privacy interests." Skinner v. Railway Labor Executives Ass'n, 489 U.S. 602, 109 S.Ct. 1402, 103 L.Ed.2d 639, 659 (1989) (internal citations omitted). See Maryland v. King, 569 U.S. ____, 133 S.Ct. 1958, 186 L.Ed.2d 1, 19 (2013). For lower court cases on this issue, see "Searches and Seizures" § 14 West Key No.

lung breath for chemical analysis,[37] the ordered collection and subsequent chemical testing of urine samples from an individual,[38] the taking of a DNA swab of an arrestee and the subsequent analysis of the sample obtained, [39] and taking scrapings from beneath an individual's fingernails.[40] Because compliance with a demand by a government agent that an individual give a urine or breath sample for chemical testing is a Fourth Amendment search of the person, the same result by analogy would surely obtain when an individual complies with a police order to produce whatever the individual has concealed on one's person. Moreover, the Court has assumed that a probe of an individual's body cavities, such as the rectum or vagina, as well as an X-ray of one's body, constitutes a Fourth Amendment search of the person.[41] In each of these cases, however, a search of the person must be confined solely to the actual person of the individual—to one's body and apparel—and does not extend to nearby areas where the individual "constructively" possesses objects therein under personal property law because within easy reach of the individual or otherwise.[42] Nonetheless, the act of seizing such objects may constitute a Fourth Amendment "seizure" of one's "effects."[43]

On the other hand, it is not a Fourth Amendment search of the person for the police or other government agent to take an object from the person of an individual without the individual's consent when the object is held open to public view—although such action clearly constitutes a Fourth Amendment seizure of a paper or effect.[44] This is so

---

37. "Subjecting a person to a breathalyser test, which generally requires the production of alveolar or 'deep lung' breath for chemical analysis ... implicates similar concerns about bodily integrity, and, like the blood-alcohol test we considered in *Schmerber*, should be considered a [Fourth Amendment] search." Skinner v. Railway Labor Executives Ass'n, 489 U.S. 602, 109 S.Ct. 1402, 103 L.Ed.2d 639, 659 (1989). See Maryland v. King, 569 U.S. ____, 133 S.Ct. 1958, 186 L.Ed.2d 1, 19 (2013).

38. "Because it is clear that the collection and testing of urine intrudes upon expectations of privacy that society has long recognized as reasonable, the Federal Courts of Appeal have concluded unanimously, and we agree, that these intrusions must be deemed Fourth Amendment searches." Skinner v. Railway Labor Executives Ass'n, 489 U.S. 602, 109 S.Ct. 1402, 103 L.Ed.2d 639, 660 (1989). "Moreover, urine tests conducted by those [public hospital] staff members were indisputably searches within the meaning of the Fourth Amendment." Ferguson v. City of Charleston, 532 U.S. 67, 121 S.Ct. 1281, 149 L.Ed.2d 205, 215 (2001).

39. "It can be agreed that using a buccal swab on the inner tissues of a person's cheek in order to obtain DNA samples is a [Fourth Amendment] search." Maryland v. King, 569 U.S. ____, 133 S.Ct. 1958, 186 L.Ed.2d 1, 19 (2013) (the taking of a DNA sample and the sample's later analysis treated as Fourth Amendment searches).

40. Cupp v. Murphy, 412 U.S. 291, 93 S.Ct. 2000, 36 L.Ed.2d 900 (1973). See Maryland v. King, 569 U.S. ____, 133 S.Ct. 1958, 186 L.Ed.2d 1, 19 (2013).

41. The Court has not yet decided, however, what standard governs in determining whether such searches are reasonable under the Fourth Amendment. "Because the issues are not presented today we suggest no view on what level of suspicion, if any, is required for nonroutine border searches such as strip, body cavity, or involuntary X-ray searches." United States v. Montoya de Hernandez, 473 U.S. 531, 105 S.Ct. 3304, 87 L.Ed.2d 381, 391, n. 4 (1985). Lower federal courts have treated body cavity probes of this nature, as well as the use of laxatives or emetics to determine what might be concealed in one's stomach, to be Fourth Amendment searches of the person. 5 Wayne LaFave, Search and Seizure § 10.5(e) at 251 (5th ed. 2012).

42. The Court was clearly referring to the concept of constructive possession under personal property law when it stated: "The person in legal possession of a good seized during an illegal search has not necessarily been subject to a Fourth Amendment violation.... [L]egal possession of a seized good is not a proxy for determining whether the owner had a Fourth Amendment interest in it for it does not invariably represent the protected Fourth Amendment interest." United States v. Salvucci, 448 U.S. 83, 91 100 S.Ct. 2547, 65 L.Ed.2d 619, 628–29 (1980).

43. For a discussion of Fourth Amendment "seizures" of "effects," see Chapter 9, Section 3 of this work.

44. See Chapter 9, Section 3 of this work.

because the individual in exposing the object to public view has no reasonable expectation of privacy in the object, and therefore its seizure invades no privacy interest of the individual. Nor is it a Fourth Amendment search, as the Court has held, to require an individual to exhibit personal characteristics that he or she exhibits publicly to the world[45]—such as the timbre of one's voice in a compelled voice exemplar,[46] or the physical appearance of one's handwriting in a compelled handwriting sample.[47] This is so because no privacy interests are implicated by observing or hearing that which an individual exhibits to the public as a matter of everyday life. The Court has also indicated in dicta that the physical characteristics of an individual's fingers are constantly exposed to the public, and that, accordingly, a compelled fingerprint sample involves none of the probing into an individual's private life that marks a Fourth Amendment search of the person.[48] The same might also be said of compelling a person to submit to being photographed or bodily measured, or to appear in court, or to assume a stance, to walk or to make a particular gesture,[49] or, by analogy, to appear in a police line-up—as in each instance the individual is being compelled to reveal that which one openly exhibits to the world.

As previously indicated, however, deeper governmental probes into a person's body to discover hidden properties therein not ordinarily open to public view have been treated as Fourth Amendment searches of the person on the theory that at some point a person has a reasonable expectation of privacy with respect to the inner recesses of the body.[50] In this connection, however, it is uncertain whether the compelled taking of hair samples from a person's body for chemical analysis constitutes a Fourth Amendment search of the person—although the better view appears to be that this constitutes a forcible invasion of one's body integrity and accordingly should be treated as such a search, or at least, as a Fourth Amendment "seizure" of an "effect."[51]

b. Reasonable expectation of privacy as to one's "house": complaining party's substantial connection thereto

The Fourth Amendment protects the people against "unreasonable searches" of their "houses." To come within the ambit of this protection, one must show that the premises in which the evidence was secured constitutes a "house" in which one has a reasonable expectation of privacy because of his or her connection therewith.[52]

---

45. For a discussion of this subject, see 1 Wayne LaFave, Search and Seizure § 2.6(a) (5th ed. 2012).

46. United States v. Dionisio, 410 U.S. 1, 93 S.Ct. 764, 35 L.Ed.2d 67 (1973).

47. United States v. Mara, 410 U.S. 19, 93 S.Ct. 774, 35 L.Ed.2d 99 (1973). For lower court cases on this issue, see "Searches and Seizures" § 14 West Key No.

48. Cupp v. Murphy, 412 U.S. 291, 294–95, 93 S.Ct. 2000, 36 L.Ed.2d 900, 905 (1973). LaFave states that "the lower courts have upheld the fingerprinting of grand jury witnesses without a showing of probable cause," on the apparent theory that such fingerprinting does not constitute a Fourth Amendment search of the person and therefore no probable cause showing was constitutionally required. 1 Wayne LaFave, Search and Seizure § 2.6(a) at 868 (5th ed. 2012).

49. The Court has indicated in dicta that none of the above constitutes a violation of the suspect's Fifth Amendment self-incrimination privilege. Schmerber v. California, 384 U.S. 757, 764, 86 S.Ct. 1826, 16 L.Ed.2d 908 (1966).

50. See Section 3a(2) of this Chapter.

51. See 1 Wayne LaFave, Search and Seizure § 2.6(a) at 869–70 (5th ed. 2012). For a discussion of Fourth Amendment seizures of effects, see Chapter 9, Section 3 of this work.

52. "Fourth Amendment rights are personal, and when a person objects to the search of a place and invokes the exclusionary rule, he or she must have the requisite connection to that place." Minnesota v. Carter, 525 U.S. 83, 119 S.Ct. 469, 142 L.Ed.2d 373, 386 (1998) (Kennedy, J. concurring).

The cases, generally speaking, have held that the Fourth Amendment protects a person's privacy in (1) one's residence, (2) one's commercial premises—that is, in the place where one lives and the place where one works—and (3) one's various other private premises. To be sure, the Fourth Amendment protects people not places, but the degree of protection that the Amendment affords depends, in part, on the person's connection with certain places.[53] We will now consider each of these three types of Fourth Amendment "houses" in subsections (1)–(3) below.

(1) Residential premises: curtilage vs. "open fields"

The law is well settled that the Fourth Amendment protects first and foremost the elemental right of privacy that a person reasonably expects in one's dwelling house, the place where one lives, whether permanently or temporarily. It is in the home, above all else, where a person enjoys the highest reasonable expectation of privacy under the Fourth Amendment. Plainly, the Framers of the Fourth Amendment intended precisely such a result,[54] and the United States Supreme Court has repeatedly so held.[55]

A home, under the Fourth Amendment, includes a variety of private premises in which a person may live, such as a private residential house, a row house or townhouse, an

---

53. Minnesota v. Carter, 525 U.S. 83, 119 S.Ct. 469, 142 L.Ed.2d 373, 379 (1998) ("The Amendment protects persons against unreasonable searches of 'their persons [and] houses' and thus indicates that the Fourth Amendment is a personal right that must be invoked by an individual. (citation with quote omitted). But the extent to which the Fourth Amendment protects people may depend on where those people are."). Katz v. United States, 389 U.S. 347, 361, 88 S.Ct. 507, 19 L.Ed.2d 576, 587–88 (1967) (Harlan, J. concurring) ("As the Court's opinion states, 'the Fourth Amendment protects people, not places.' The question, however, is what protection it affords to those people. Generally, as here, the answer to that question requires reference to a place.").

54. For a discussion of the historical purpose of the Fourth Amendment as it relates to the home, see Chapter 6, Section 2 of this work.

55. "The Fourth Amendment protects the individual's privacy in a variety of settings. In none is this zone of privacy more clearly defined than when bounded by the unambiguous physical dimensions of a individual's home—a zone that finds its roots in clear and specific constitutional terms: 'The right of the people to be secure in their ... houses ... shall not be violated.' That language unequivocally establishes the proposition that '[a]t the very core [of the Fourth Amendment] stands the right of a man to retreat into his own home and there be free from unreasonable governmental intrusion.'" Payton v. New York, 445 U.S. 573, 589–90, 100 S.Ct. 1371, 1381–82, 63 L.Ed.2d 639, 653 (1980), quoting from Silverman v. United States, 365 U.S. 505, 511, 81 S.Ct. 679, 683–84, 5 L.Ed.2d 734 (1961). "'At the very core' of the Fourth Amendment, 'stands the right of a man to retreat into his own home and there be free from unreasonable governmental intrusion.'" Kyllo v. United States, 533 U.S. 27, 121 S.Ct. 2038, 150 L.Ed.2d 94 (2001) (also quoting from Silverman). "At the risk of belaboring the obvious, private residences are places in which an individual normally expects privacy free from governmental interference not authorized by a warrant, and that expectation is plainly one that society is prepared to recognize as justifiable. Our cases have not deviated from this basic Fourth Amendment principle." United States v. Karo, 468 U.S. 705, 104 S.Ct. 3296, 82 L.Ed.2d 530, 541 (1984). "The [Fourth] Amendment reflects the recognition of the Founders that certain enclaves should be free from arbitrary government interference. For example, the Court since the enactment of the Fourth Amendment has stressed 'the overriding respect for the sanctity of the home that has been embedded in our traditions since the origins of the Republic.'" Oliver v. United States, 466 U.S. 170, 104 S.Ct. 1735, 80 L.Ed.2d 214, 224 (1984), quoting from Payton v. New York, 445 U.S. at 601. "The Fourth Amendment embodies this centuries-old principle of respect for the privacy of the home." Wilson v. Layne, 526 U.S. 603, 119 S.Ct. 1692, 143 L.Ed.2d 818, 827 (1999). "[P]hysical entry of the home is the chief evil against which the wording of the Fourth Amendment is directed." United States v. United States District Court 407 U.S. 297, 313, 92 S.Ct. 2125, 32 L.Ed.2d 752 (1972). "When it comes to the Fourth Amendment, the home is the first among equals." Florida v. Jardines, 569 U.S. ___, 133 S.Ct. 1409, 1414, 185 L.Ed.2d 495 (2013).

apartment, or a room in a rooming house.[56] Moreover, a person may have a home away from home, as where one checks in overnight or for a few days stay in a hotel or motel room; for Fourth Amendment purposes, these premises also represent a person's home.[57] Perhaps even make-shift structures erected out of crates, boxes or the like may constitute a person's home for Fourth Amendment purposes—as, for example, shacks or other structures erected by the homeless in metropolitan areas and countryside locations where, unfortunately, many people live by sufferance as squatters. Although technical trespassers, their presence is often condoned by the owner of the property where the structures are located—so that the homeless may entertain a reasonable expectation of privacy in these structures. The same may hold true for an apartment or room where a homeless person or family live by sufferance as squatters in an abandoned building in a blighted urban area. Indeed, one is reminded in this context of William Pitt the Elder's eloquent description of the home as being a man's castle no matter how lowly and pathetic the home may be.[58] On the other hand, a fully mobile motor home located on the public streets is not a home for Fourth Amendment purposes, although it is entitled to Fourth Amendment protection as a motor vehicle (an "effect") with lesser reasonable expectations of privacy;[59] a motor home on blocks in a residential trailer park, however, is undoubtedly entitled to Fourth Amendment protection as a home.[60]

A home, usually a private residential house, often has more living area to it than its physical interior. It may also include an outside living area located near the house and hidden from public view by the house itself, a hedge, a fence or a wall, an area unseen from either the public street or the adjoining property where residents typically enjoy part of their private home life—such as a back porch, a patio, a garden, a pool, or a general yard area where one may relax on lawn chairs, perhaps barbecue and eat an evening meal or otherwise visit with friends and family. This area may also include certain buildings

---

56. Weeks v. United States, 232 U.S. 383, 34 S.Ct. 341, 58 L.Ed. 652 (1914) (owned house); Chapman v. United States, 365 U.S. 610, 81 S.Ct. 776, 5 L.Ed.2d 828 (1961) (rented house); Payton v. New York, 445 U.S. 573, 100 S.Ct. 1371, 63 L.Ed.2d 639 (1980) (apartment); Clinton v. Virginia, 377 U.S. 158, 84 S.Ct. 1186, 12 L.Ed.2d 313 (1964) (apartment); McDonald v. United States, 335 U.S. 451, 69 S.Ct. 191, 93 L.Ed. 153 (1948) (room in rooming house).

57. Hoffa v. United States, 385 U.S. 293, 87 S.Ct. 408, 17 L.Ed.2d 374 (1966) (hotel room); Stoner v. California, 376 U.S. 483, 84 S.Ct. 889, 11 L.Ed.2d 856 (1964 (hotel and motel room); Johnson v. United States, 333 U.S. 10, 68 S.Ct. 367, 92 L.Ed. 436 (1948) (hotel room).

58. William Pitt the Elder, during either the 1763 parliamentary debates on the Cider Act or the 1766 parliamentary debates on the general warrant—historians differ on this—uttered his classic argument:

"The poorest man may, in his cottage, bid defiance to all the forces of the Crown. It may be frail; its roof may shake; the wind may blow through it; the storm may enter; but the King of England may not enter; all his force dares not cross the threshold of the ruined tenement."

N. Lasson at 49–50; W. Cuddihy at 947 n. 151. This is the best-known version of the argument. See Chapter 3, Section 4 of this work.

59. California v. Carney, 471 U.S. 386, 105 S.Ct. 2066, 85 L.Ed.2d 406 (1985).

60. Soldal v. Cook County, 506 U.S. 56, 113 S.Ct.538, 121 L.Ed.2d 450 (1992) (mounted trailer home in trailer park). The same result might also arguably apply to an inoperable car on blocks where, unfortunately, many people live by sufferance in blighted areas of metropolitan areas in this country. The Court, however, has expressly declined to pass on whether "a motor home that is situated in a way or in a place that objectively indicates that it is being used as a residence" should be treated as a home or a motor vehicle for Fourth Amendment purposes. "Among the factors that might be deemed relevant" in resolving this question is "[the motor home's] location, whether the vehicle is readily mobile or, instead, for instance, elevated on blocks, whether the vehicle is licensed, whether it is connected to utilities, and whether it has convenient access to a public road." California v. Carney, 471 U.S. 386, 105 S.Ct. 2066, 85 L.Ed.2d 406, 415, n.3 (1985). See also 3 Wayne LaFave, Search and Seizure §7.2(b) at 738–739 (5th ed. 2012).

associated with living in the home itself, such as a typical garage used for storing the resident's car or other property, a toolshed for tools used to do yard work, home repair and general maintenance, or an outhouse for a home with no indoor plumbing. At common law, this outside, hidden-from-public-view living area and buildings therein constituted part of the curtilage of the home, and such curtilage is today considered an extension of the home itself under the Fourth Amendment.[61]

In addition, the immediate area surrounding the home is considered part of the curtilage—such as the front porch, an adjoining garden, or immediate areas adjacent to the windows in the home. Although some of these areas may be visible from the public street, they are nonetheless tied to the intimacies of the home, are private in nature, and represent part of the home itself.[62] Whether, the entirety of a typical homeowner's yard also falls within the curtilage has not been decided—although arguably at least a portion of it might be considered private in nature, depending of what it is, and therefore part of the home as well.

In determining whether a given outside area constitutes part of the curtilage of the home for Fourth Amendment purposes, the Court has considered certain factors as relevant, although not necessarily decisive, to the inquiry: (1) the physical proximity of the area to the home; (2) whether the area is included within an enclosure surrounding the home; (3) the nature of the uses to which the area is put; and (4) the steps taken by the resident to protect the area from observation by people passing by.[63] These are not talismanic factors, however, and are only useful to the degree to which they bear on the

---

61. "At common law, the curtilage is the area to which extends the intimate activity associated with the 'sanctity of a man's home and the privacies of life'... and therefore has been considered part of the home itself for Fourth Amendment purposes. Thus, Courts have extended Fourth Amendment protection to the curtilage; and they have defined the curtilage, as did the common law, by reference to the factors that determine whether an individual reasonably may expect that an area adjacent to the home will remain private." Oliver v. United States, 466 U.S. 170, 104 S.Ct. 1735, 80 L.Ed.2d 214, 225 (1984); see California v. Ciraolo, 476 U.S. 207, 106 S.Ct. 1809, 90 L.Ed.2d 210 (1986) (fenced-in backyard was part of the curtilage of a home, but the naked-eye observation of the yard from an airplane in public navigable airspace was not a Fourth Amendment search).

62. "But when it comes to the Fourth Amendment, the home is first among equals. At the Amendment's very core stands the right of a man to retreat into his own home and there be free of unreasonable government intrusion. This right would be of little practical value if the State's agents could stand in a home's porch or side garden and trawl for evidence with impunity; the right to retreat would be significantly diminished if the police could enter a man's property and observe his repose outside the front window.

We therefore regard the area immediately surrounding and associated with the home—what our cases call the curtilage—as part of the home for Fourth Amendment purposes....This area around the home is intimately linked to the home, both physically and psychologically, and this is where privacy expectations are most heightened.

....The front porch is the classic example of an area adjacent to the home and to which the activity of home life extends." Florida v. Jardines, 569 U.S. ___, 133 S.Ct. 1409, 1414–1415, 185 L.Ed.2d 495, 501 (2013) (internal citations and quotations omitted).

But cf. United States v. Santana, 427 U.S. 38, 96 S.Ct. 2406, 49 L.Ed.2d 300 (1976) for a contrary ruling which appears to be superceded by *Jardines* based on the latter's revival of the older trespass definition of a Fourth Amendment search to include trespassory entries into constitutionally protected areas. Also see Illinois v. McArthur, 531 U.S. 326, 121 S.Ct. 946, 148 L.Ed.2d 838, 850 (2001) (citing *Santana* in dicta).

63. United States v. Dunn, 480 U.S. 294, 107 S.Ct. 1134, 94 L.Ed.2d 326, 334–35 (1987); also see cases collected at "Searches and Seizures" § 27 West Key No.

central issue of whether the area is so intimately tied to the home that it should be considered a part thereof and thus entitled to Fourth Amendment protection.[64]

By way of contrast, the Fourth Amendment has no application to the "open fields"—that is, to any area that lies outside the curtilage of a home.[65] This includes those portions of hidden-from-public view land located a sufficient enough distance from the home as not to constitute a living area thereof—such as open spaces of land not associated with a home yard,[66] or rural farmland where crops are cultivated.[67] The "open fields" may also include land surrounding a business[68] and need not be "open" or a "field" as those terms are used in common speech; any land not associated with a home curtilage, including a thickly wooded area, is an "open field" for Fourth Amendment purposes.[69]

It therefore follows that it is not a Fourth Amendment search of a "house" for a government agent to enter into the "open fields"—that is, an area outside the curtilage of the home. Still, the act of seizing property while in such an unprotected area constitutes a Fourth Amendment "seizure" of a person's "papers or effects" where it is clear that the property seized was in the actual or constructive possession of, or owned by the person complaining—such as plants growing on a person's land or items of personalty lying thereon.[70] Plainly, the police have no license under the Fourth Amendment to enter upon

---

64. "We do not suggest that combining these factors produces a finely tuned formula that, when mechanistically applied, yields a 'correct' result to all extent-of-curtilage questions. Rather these factors are useful analytical tools only to the extent that, in any given case, they bear upon the centrally relevant consideration—whether the area is so intimately tied to the home itself that it should be placed under the home's 'umbrella' of Fourth Amendment protection." United States v. Dunn, 480 U.S. 294, 107 S.Ct. 1134, 94 L.Ed.2d 326, 335 (1987).

65. "[T]he special protection accorded by the 4th Amendment to the people in their 'persons, house, papers, and effects' is not extended to the open fields. The distinction between the latter and the house is as old as the common law." Hester v. United States, 265 U.S. 57, 59, 44 S.Ct. 445, 68 L.Ed. 898, 900 (1924). "We conclude, from the text of the Fourth Amendment and from the historical and contemporary understanding of its purposes, that an individual has no legitimate expectation that open fields will remain free from warrantless intrusion." Oliver v. United States, 466 U.S. 170, 104 S.Ct. 1735, 80 L.Ed.2d 214, 225–26 (1984). "In applying the *Hester* doctrine over the years, lower courts have applied the open fields characterization to virtually any lands which do not fall within the curtilage." 1 Wayne LaFave, "Search and Seizure," 2.4(a) at 805 (5th ed. 2012). "It is clear, however, that the term 'open fields' may include any unoccupied or undeveloped area outside of the curtilage." Oliver v. United States, 80 L.Ed.2d at 225, n. 11. See "Searches and Seizures" § 27 West Key No. for lower court cases on this issue.

66. Hester v. United States, 265 U.S. 57, 44 S.Ct. 445, 68 L.Ed. 898 (1924) (land adjoining a rural residential house)

67. Oliver v. United States, 466 U.S. 170, 104 S.Ct. 1735, 80 L.Ed.2d 214 (1984) (secluded rural farmland surrounded by fences and no-trespassing signs).

68. Air Pollution Variance Board v. Western Alfalfa Corp., 416 U.S. 861, 94 S. Ct. 2114, 40 L.Ed.2d 607 (1974) (pollution inspection test conducted by state health inspector on land adjoining a business).

69. "It is clear, however, that the term 'open fields' may include any unoccupied or undeveloped area outside of the curtilage. An open field need be neither 'open' nor a 'field' as those terms are used in common speech. For example, ... a thickly wooded area nonetheless may be an open field as that term is used in construing the Fourth Amendment.... Most of the many millions of acres that are 'open fields' are not close to any structure and so not arguably within the curtilage." Oliver v. United States, 466 U.S. 170, 104 S.Ct. 1735, 80 L.Ed.2d 214, 225, n. 11, 226, n.12 (1984). See also 1 Wayne LaFave, Search and Seizure § 2.4(a) (5th ed. 2012) and cases collected.

70. For a discussion of Fourth Amendment "seizures" of "papers and effects," see Chapter 9, Section 3 of this work. "Further, the Fourth Amendment provides ample protection to activities in the open fields that might implicate a person's privacy. An individual who enters a place defined to be 'public' for Fourth Amendment analysis does not lose all claims to privacy and personal security.... For example, the Fourth Amendment's protections against unreasonable arrest or unreasonable seizure

such land and arbitrarily seize anything they see. Some showing of probable cause for the seizure is ordinarily required under the Fourth Amendment.[71]

In addition, buildings and other structures located near a home that are not associated with the private home life of its residents do not fall within the curtilage and are not considered a part of the home for Fourth Amendment purposes—such as a barn, a henhouse or a stable on a farm. These buildings and structures, however, may still constitute a person's "house" under the Fourth Amendment—although clearly not a part of one's home—because they constitute commercial or other similar premises in which one legitimately expects some degree of privacy.[72] These buildings, therefore, may still fall within the ambit of Fourth Amendment protection as a "house" [although not a home] if the person making a Fourth Amendment claim has a reasonable expectation of privacy therein. Also where the structure involved totally fails to qualify as a "house" under the Fourth Amendment—such as a still on a farm—it may nonetheless qualify as an "effect" under the Fourth Amendment if owned by, or in actual or constructive possession of the person making the Fourth Amendment claim thereto. Under such circumstances, a showing of probable cause would be required before the structure could be seized by government agents; presumably, in the case of a still, this showing could ordinarily be made.[73]

A person's home is not divested of its character as a home by the congregation of large numbers of visitors therein—as, for example, where a person hosts a large house party.[74] However, when a person uses one's home as a *commercial* center and invites outsiders in for the purpose of transacting business, legal or illegal, the home has been converted into a business place and is not entitled to Fourth Amendment protection as a home, but only as an commercial business where one has a reasonable expectation of privacy only in those areas that are not open to the public.[75] It follows, then, that private premises that do not qualify as a person's home for Fourth Amendment purposes may nonetheless qualify as a person's business premises under the Fourth Amendment where there is lesser privacy protection than a home.

Clearly, however, a person making a Fourth Amendment claim must show that he or she entertains a reasonable expectation of privacy with respect to the home wherein it is

---

of effects upon the person remain fully applicable." Oliver v. United States, 466 U.S. 170, 104 S.Ct. 1735, 80 L.Ed.2d 214, 225, n. 10 (1984).

71. For a discussion of the reasonableness rules related to the seizure of personal property, see Chapter 12, Section 2 of this work. It should be noted, however, that property placed in a garbage can located on the curb in front of a person's house for public trash collection is considered abandoned by the homeowner outside the curtilage of one's home and is not entitled to Fourth Amendment protection. California v. Greenwood, 486 U.S. 35, 108 S.Ct. 1625, 100 L.Ed.2d 30 (1988).

72. See 1 Wayne LaFave, Search and Seizure § 2.3(d) (5th ed. 2012) and cases collected.

73. For a discussion of what constitutes a Fourth Amendment seizure of personal property, see Chapter 9, Section 3 of this work. For a discussion of the unreasonableness rules that relate to the seizures of personal property, see Chapter 12, Section 2 of this work.

74. "The congregation of a large number of persons in a private home does not transform it into a public place open to the police." Recznik v. City of Lorain, 393 U.S. 166, 89 S.Ct. 342, 21 L.Ed.2d 317, 320 (1968).

75. "But when, as here, the home is converted into a commercial center to which outsiders are invited for purposes of transacting unlawful business, that business is entitled to no greater sanctity than if it were carried on in a store, a garage, or on the street. A government agent, in the same manner as a private person, may accept an invitation to do business for the purposes contemplated by the occupant. Of course, this does not mean that, whenever entry is obtained by invitation and the locus is characterized as a place of business, an agent is authorized to conduct a general search for evidentiary materials." Lewis v. United States, 385 U.S. 206, 87 S.Ct. 424, 17 L.Ed.2d 312, 316 (1966) (undercover government agent invited into defendant's home to buy marijuana; no Fourth Amendment search).

claimed that a governmental search has occurred. This is generally established by showing that such person had a sufficient connection to the home so as to entertain the required reasonable expectation of privacy therein—usually, that such person resides in the home either permanently or temporarily. Accordingly, it has been recognized that a resident home owner, a resident tenant, and a resident family member of the homeowner owner or tenant—all may object (1) to any official illegal entry into the home and any evidence constituting the fruit of such entry, and (2) assuming the initial entry to be lawful, to any physical search conducted on the premises of the home yielding certain evidence, providing the complaining resident in question had an unrestricted right of access to the area searched within the home.[76] Moreover, a person who temporarily resides in the private home of another—such as a short-term or overnight house guest—has the same such Fourth Amendment privacy rights.[77]

Special problems are presented, however, when a person does not permanently or temporarily reside in the home, but is there on the premises for a short period of time at the invitation of the home dweller. In that event, it cannot be said that the person is so connected to the premises that one may reasonably regard same as one's home and have the same robust expectation of privacy therein that the home dweller has. It may, however, still be one's Fourth Amendment "house" for other purposes—business or social—in which one has a lesser reasonable expectation of privacy therein. A person may, at the home dweller's invitation, make another's home one's commercial premises[78] to transact business, so long as something more than a transient business connection such as a pizza delivery is established therein.[79] Also most social guests, who are invited into a home for

---

76. Chapman v. United States, 365 U.S. 610, 81 S.Ct. 776, 5 L.Ed.2d 828 (1961) (tenant of house); Stoner v. California, 376 U.S. 483, 84 S.Ct. 889, 11 L.Ed.2d 856 (1964) (renter of hotel room); McDonald v. United States, 335 U.S. 451, 69 S.Ct. 191, 93 L.Ed. 153 (1948) (renter of room in rooming house); Bumper v. North Carolina, 391 U.S. 543, 88 S.Ct. 1788, 20 L.Ed.2d 797 (1968) (resident grandson of owner of house); Weeks v. United States, 232 U.S. 383, 34 S.Ct. 341, 58 L.Ed. 652 (1914) (owner of house). "We were right to hold in Chapman v. United States ... that the Fourth Amendment protects [a house] tenant against an unreasonable search of his dwelling, even though he is only the leaseholder. And we were right to hold in Bumper v. North Carolina ... that an unreasonable search of a grandmother's house violated her resident grandson's Fourth Amendment rights because the area searched 'was his home.'" Minnesota v. Carter, 525 U.S. 83, 119 S.Ct.469, 142 L.Ed.2d 373, 384 (1998) (Scalia, J. concurring).

77. "To hold that an overnight guest has a legitimate expectation of privacy in his host's home merely recognizes the everyday expectations of privacy that we all share. Staying overnight in another's home is a long-standing social custom that serves functions recognized as valuable by society. We stay in another's' homes when we travel to a strange city for business or pleasure, we visit our parents, or more distant relatives out of town, when we are in between jobs, or homes, or when we house-sit for a friend. We will all be hosts and we will all be guests many times in our lives. From either perspective, we think that society recognizes that a houseguest has a legitimate expectation of privacy in his host's home." Minnesota v. Olson, 495 U.S. 91, 110 S.Ct. 1684, 109 L.Ed.2d 85, 94–95 (1990) (overnight guest); Rakas v. Illinois, 439 U.S. 128, 99 S.Ct. 421, 58 L.Ed.2d 387, 400, 404–05 (1978) approving result in Jones v. United States, 362 U.S. 257, 80 S.Ct. 725 4 L.Ed.2d 697 (1960) (temporary apartment occupant). "The text of the [Fourth] Amendment suggests that its protections extend only to people in 'their' houses. But we have held that in some circumstances a person may have a legitimate expectation of privacy in the house of someone else. In Minnesota v. Olson ... for example, we decided that an overnight guest in a house had the sort of expectation of privacy that the Fourth Amendment protects." Minnesota v. Carter, 525 U.S. 83, 119 S.Ct. 469, 142 L.Ed.2d 373, 379–80 (1998).

78. For a more complete discussion of commercial premises as a Fourth Amendment protected "house," see Section 3b(2) of this Chapter.

79. Minnesota v. Carter, 525 U.S. 83, 119 S.Ct.469, 142 L.Ed.2d 373 (1998) (business invitee in home—who stopped in to cut and bag cocaine for sale, was present there for 2 hours, and had no prior connection with the home—had no reasonable expectation of privacy in home as either as a home or as commercial premises).

conversation or to engage in leisure activities, may make another's home one's "house" as other private premises,[80] and may reasonably expect that one's privacy will not be disturbed by illegal governmental entries therein.[81] On the other hand, a casual visitor who simply drops by a home for one minute to deliver something or say hello and dash off could hardly be said, without more, to have any reasonable expectation of privacy in the home.[82] It is clear, then, that something more must be shown as to such business invitees or social guests than that the person is simply legitimately on the premises with the consent of the home dweller.[83]

(2) Business or commercial premises

The Fourth Amendment also protects the privacy that a person enjoys in one's business premises—that is, in those portions of commercial buildings, offices and other similar places that are not open to the public, wherein a person engages in some type of business or employment activity.[84] "An expectation of privacy in commercial premises, however, is different from, and indeed less than a similar expectation in an individual's home."[85] Nonetheless, it was plainly the judgment of the Framers of the Fourth Amendment that a person should be protected against general exploratory searches by government agents of one's private business premises. Indeed, the American colonists and the leadership of the revolutionary period 1761–76 strongly resisted exploratory searches of their business establishments under the general writs of assistance regime, as being contrary to English law, and sought to restore these legal guarantees of privacy in their businesses by adopting the Fourth Amendment.[86] In accord with this "original understanding," it has been recognized that the term "house" in the Fourth Amendment protects a person's business

---

80. For a more complete discussion of other private premises as a Fourth Amendment protected "house," see Section 3b(3) of this Chapter.

81. Minnesota v. Carter, 525 U.S. 83, 119 S.Ct.469, 142 L.Ed.2d 373 (1998) ("[F]ive members of the Court"—Justice Kennedy concurring, Justice Breyer concurring, and Justice Ginsburg dissenting joined by Justices Stevens and Souter—"would place under the Fourth Amendment shield at least 'almost all social guests.'" 142 L.Ed.2d at 392 n.2 (Ginsburg, J. dissenting)).

82. Rakas v. Illinois, 439 U.S. 128, 142, 99 S.Ct. 421, 58 L.Ed.2d 387, 400 (1978).

83. Rakas v. Illinois, 439 U.S. 128, 141–43, 99 S.Ct. 421, 58 L.Ed.2d 387, 400–01 (1978) ("legitimately-on-the-premises" test for Fourth Amendment protection in private premises expressly rejected).

84. Marshall v. Barlow's Inc., 436 U.S. 307, 98 S.Ct. 1816, 56 L.Ed.2d 305 (1978); See v. City of Seattle, 387 U.S. 541, 87 S.Ct. 1737, 18 L.Ed.2d 943 (1967); G.M. Leasing Corp. v. United States, 429 U.S. 338, 97 S.Ct. 619, 50 L.Ed.2d 530 (1977); Gouled v. United States, 255 U.S. 298, 41 S.Ct. 261, 65 L.Ed. 647 (1921); Mancusi v. DeForte, 392 U.S. 364, 88 S.Ct. 2120, 20 L.Ed.2d 1154 (1968); Silverthorne Lumber Co. v. United States, 251 U.S. 385, 40 S.Ct. 182, 64 L.Ed. 319 (1920); Go-Bart Co. v. United States, 282 U.S. 344, 51 S.Ct. 153, 75 L.Ed. 374 (1931).

85. New York v. Burger, 482 U.S. 691, 700, 107 S.Ct. 2636, 96 L.Ed.2d 601 (1987).

86. See Chapter 2 of this work for a discussion of the general writs of assistance in the American colonies as applied to colonial businesses. Also see Chapter 6 of this work for a discussion of the purposes of the Fourth Amendment, particularly as related to business establishments. "The general warrant was a recurring point of contention in the Colonies immediately preceding the Revolution. The particular offensiveness it engendered was acutely felt by the merchants and businessmen whose premises and products were inspected for compliance with the several parliamentary revenue measures that most irritated the colonists. '[T]he Fourth Amendment's commands grew out of the colonists' experience with the writs of assistance ... [that] granted sweeping power to customs officials and other agents of the King to search at large for smuggled goods'.... Against this background, it is untenable that the ban on warrantless searches was not intended to shield places of business as well as of residence." Marshall v. Barlow's Inc., 436 U.S. 307, 98 S.Ct. 1816, 56 L.Ed.2d 305, 310–11 (1978)

premises provided that two requirements are met. First, the premises searched or portion thereof must be private in nature in the sense that such premises are not open to the public at the time of the search. Second, the premises searched must be directly related to a business or employment activity that the person claiming Fourth Amendment protection carries on therein.

As to the first requirement, it must be shown that the premises searched were closed to the general public at the time of the search. This is so because one may only entertain a reasonable expectation of privacy with respect to premises that are private in nature—premises where one may retreat from the outside world free from the prying eyes of other people. Examples of commercial premises protected by the Fourth Amendment include the following: (a) business premises that are entirely closed to the public, such as warehouses or factories;[87] (b) business premises that are partially closed to the public, such as private work areas, offices or back rooms;[88] and (c) business premises closed to the public during non-business hours, although open to the public during business hours.[89] On the other hand, it has been held that law enforcement officers, even though motivated by a criminal investigative purpose, invade no interest protected by the Fourth Amendment when they enter those portions of business premises that are open to the public at the time of the search.[90] And once on business premises open to the public, these officers may properly make plain sight observations and examine merchandise on the premises in the manner of a normal business customer without conducting a Fourth Amendment search.[91] However, these officers would be clearly prohibited from engaging in a general exploratory search of private areas within these premises, or in arbitrarily seizing property on the premises without probable cause.[92]

---

87. See v. City of Seattle, 387 U.S. 541, 87 S.Ct. 1737, 18 L.Ed.2d 943 (1967) (commercial warehouse). "Not all business or commercial premises are open to the public at large. A factory, for example, may be readily accessible to the employees of the company, but it does not follow from this that police may enter these premises at will." 1 Wayne LaFave, Search and Seizure § 2.4(b) at 823 (5th ed. 2012).

88. Marshall v. Barlow's Inc., 436 U.S. 307, 98 S.Ct. 1816, 56 L.Ed.2d 305 (1978) (work areas of an electrical and plumbing installation business separated from customer service area). "For his actions not to constitute a Fourth Amendment search, the officer must remain in that portion of the [business] premises which is open to the public." 1 Wayne LaFave, Search and Seizure § 2.4(b) at 821 (5th ed. 2012).

89. "The 'implied invitation for customers to come in,' of course, extends only to those times when the [business] premises are, in fact, 'open to the public'; the mere fact that certain [business] premises are open to the public at certain times does not justify entry by the police on other occasions." 1 Wayne LaFave, Search and Seizure § 2.4(b) at 819 (5th ed. 2012).

90. "On this basis, courts have consistently held that police, albeit motivated by an investigative purpose, conducted no [Fourth Amendment] search by merely entering [during business hours] such premises as a bus terminal, auto repair shop, salvage yard, used car lot, dock, real estate office, courier company office, motel, hospital, pool hall, bar, restaurant, furniture store, book store or variety store." 1 Wayne LaFave, Search and Seizure § 2.4(b) at 817–819 (5th ed. 2012) and cases collected.

91. Maryland v. Macon, 472 U.S. 463, 105 S.Ct. 2778, 86 L.Ed.2d 370 1985) (entry by undercover law enforcement officers into adult book store during normal business hours and subsequent examination of books and materials offered for sale to the general public was not a Fourth Amendment search.).

92. "If a police officer has entered [business premises] as would any member of the public, it is not a [Fourth Amendment] search for the officer to conduct himself therein as might be expected of any other person who would enter. Quite clearly, the officer is 'entitled to take note of objects in plain view.' He may also examine merchandise in the fashion that a prospective customer could be expected to do." 1 Wayne LaFave, Search and Seizure § 2.4(b) at 819–820 (5th ed. 2012) and cases collected. "Of course, this does not mean that whenever entry [by a government agent] is obtained by invitation and the locus is characterized as a place of business, an agent is authorized to conduct a general search [of the business] for evidentiary materials." Lewis v. United States, 385 U.S. 206, 87 S.Ct. 424, 17

As to the second requirement, it must be shown that the person making a Fourth Amendment claim engages in some type of business or employment activity on the premises that are searched. This is so because it is the carrying on of such activity on the not-open-to-the-public portion of the business premises searched that entitles a person to entertain a reasonable expectation of privacy therein. Stated differently, this showing makes the business premises in question the person's business "house" under the Fourth Amendment. If a person owns or leases a business, it can generally be said that such person is engaging in a business activity in all areas of the subject premises. As to the non-public portions of such premises, such a person is clearly entitled to Fourth Amendment protection therein—save for those areas exclusively reserved for a business associate or employee.[93] On the other hand, if a person is an employee of a business, he or she is engaging in an employment activity only in those portions of the premises that are set aside for such person's use—either exclusively or jointly with other employees; if such premises are closed to the public, the person is clearly entitled to Fourth Amendment protection therein.[94]

It is an open question whether land surrounding otherwise protected business premises should be considered part of such premises as a "business curtilage" for Fourth Amendment purposes.[95] Surely, however, a business person should be entitled to entertain a reasonable expectation of privacy with respect to such land if the land is used in connection with the business and is otherwise not open to public use or view. As we have seen, a home dweller is accorded Fourth Amendment protection as to the curtilage of one's home, and it would seem that the business person should be accorded similar protection.[96] On the other hand, it is clear that lands, surrounding a business from which the public has not been excluded

---

L.Ed.2d 312, 316 (1966). "But there is no basis for the notion that because a retail store invites the public to enter, it consents to wholesale searches and seizures that do not conform to Fourth Amendment guarantees." Lo-Ji Sales, Inc. v. New York, 442 U.S. 319, 329, 99 S.Ct. 2319, 60 L.Ed.2d 920, 930 (1979) (owner of adult bookstore had Fourth Amendment protection that his books displayed in public area of store would not be arbitrarily seized by police without a warrant).

93. "The businessman, like the occupant of a residence, has a constitutional right to go about his business free from unreasonable official entries into his private commercial property." See v. City of Seattle, 387 U.S. 541, 87 S.Ct. 1737, 18 L.Ed.2d 943 (1967). LaFave states that a person with a property right in private commercial premises has standing to contest a search of such premises. 6 Wayne LaFave, Search and Seizure § 11.3(d) at 227–228 (5th ed. 2012) and cases collected. The same rule obtains where the business owner is a corporation. Silverthorne Lumber Co. v. United States, 251 U.S. 385, 64 L.Ed. 319, 40 S.Ct. 182 (1920).

94. "It has long been settled that one has standing to object to a search of his office, as well as his home." Mancusi v. DeForte, 392 U.S. 364, 88 S.Ct. 2120, 20 L.Ed.2d 1154, 1160 (1968) (union vice-president had standing to contest the search of a large, private, one room union office which he shared with other union officials; union records seized from the office although not in an area reserved for the vice-president). O'Connor v. Ortega, 480 U.S. 709, 107 S.Ct. 1492, 94 L.Ed.2d 714 (1987) (state hospital psychiatrist had a reasonable expectation of privacy in his desk and file cabinets located in his office at the hospital) (one concurring Justice and four dissenting Justices conclude that the psychiatrist had a reasonable expectation of privacy in his entire private office).

95. Dow Chemical Co. v. United States, 476 U.S. 227, n. 7, 106 S.Ct. 1819, 90 L.Ed.2d 226 (1986).

96. "However, 'mechanical operation of the curtilage concept' so as to deprive business lands of any Fourth Amendment protection is inappropriate after *Katz*. The question now is whether the police intruded upon a justified expectation of privacy, and this requires a more careful assessment of how private the particular lands were and how intense the police scrutiny was." 1 Wayne LaFave, Search and Seizure § 2.4(b) at 826–827 (5th ed. 2012) and cases collected at 634–37.

or that is physically too spread out to be used in connection with the business, constitute the "open fields" and are not entitled to Fourth Amendment protection.[97]

(3) *Other private premises*

Even if private premises do not qualify as a person's dwelling house or commercial business, such premises may still constitute a "house" within the meaning of the Fourth Amendment providing the person making the Fourth Amendment claim entertains a reasonable expectation of privacy therein. This catch-all category of "houses" may include, for example, a public telephone booth where a person makes a private telephone call that is electronically intercepted,[98] or, indeed, any building or closed structure as to which the person making a Fourth Amendment claim is otherwise sufficiently connected by property interest, legal possession, or temporary occupation to entertain some reasonable expectation of privacy therein.[99]

It does not include, however, a prison inmate's cell, so that a shakedown search thereof is not governed by the Fourth Amendment.[100] Nor does it include the visitor's room at a jail, so that an electronic interception of a conversation between a visitor and inmate therein is also not governed by the Fourth Amendment.[101] In these two instances, it is thought that any subjective expectation of privacy entertained by the prison inmate or visitor to a jail or prison is not a reasonable one, as it must yield to the obviously pressing security needs of the prison or jail.

c. Reasonable expectation of privacy as to one's "papers or effects": complaining party's substantial connection thereto

(1) *Personal property covered: including auto, vessel and container*

The Fourth Amendment protects the people against "unreasonable searches" of their "papers or effects." The term "effects" means personal property, not real property.[102] The term "papers" includes any printed matter—such as books, records, magazines, documents and the like—as well as first-class mail and other private papers.[103]

---

97. Air Pollution Variance Bd. of Colorado v. Western Alfalfa Corp., 416 U.S. 861, 94 S.Ct. 2114, 40 L.Ed.2d 607 (1974) (pollution inspection test conducted by state health agent on land adjoining a business, from which the public had not been excluded, was the "open fields" and not entitled to Fourth Amendment protection); Dow Chemical Co. v. United States, 476 U.S. 227, 106 S.Ct. 1819, 90 L.Ed.2d 226 (1986) (2000-acre industrial plant complex was the "open fields" and not entitled to Fourth Amendment protection).

98. Katz v. United States, 389 U.S. 347, 88 S.Ct. 507, 19 L.Ed.2d 576 (1967).

99. For cases that have accorded Fourth Amendment protection to persons who temporarily occupy a public toilet stall or a fitting room in clothing stores when surveilled by the police, see 1 Wayne LaFave, Search and Seizure § 2.4(c) (5th ed. 2012). Also for a discussion of when social or business visitors may entertain a reasonable expectation of privacy in another person's home, see Section 3 b(1) of this Chapter.

100. Hudson v. Palmer, 468 U.S. 517, 104 S.Ct. 3194, 82 L.Ed.2d 393 (1984).

101. Lanza v. New York, 370 U.S. 139, 82 S.Ct. 1218, 8 L.Ed.2d 384 (1962).

102. Oliver v. United States, 466 U.S. 170, 104 S.Ct. 1735, 80 L.Ed.2d 214, 223 n. 7 (1984).

103. See, e.g., United States v. Van Leeuwen, 397 U.S. 249, 90 S.Ct. 1029, 25 L.Ed.2d 282 (1970) (first-class mail); In re Jackson, 96 U.S. 727, (6 Otto) 727, 24 L.Ed. 877 (1877) (same); see also Nixon v. Administrator of General Services, 433 U.S. 425, 457–59, 97 S.Ct. 2777, 53 L.Ed.2d 867, 900–901 (1974) (Presidential papers of a purely private nature unconnected with the President's conduct of public duties).

An automobile is an "effect" within the meaning of the Fourth Amendment, but there is a lesser expectation of privacy therein, compared to a home or an office, because of the pervasive governmental regulation of automobiles.[104] Nonetheless, "the word 'automobile' is not a talisman in whose presence the Fourth Amendment fades away and disappears,"[105] as the privacy interests in an automobile are significant.[106] Moreover, the term "automobile" clearly embraces any moving motor vehicle—such as a truck, a camper, a mobile motor home, a van, a taxicab, or a sports utility vehicle.[107] Related thereto, a vessel is considered an "effect" within the meaning of the Fourth Amendment.[108] Indeed, vessels were among the targets of the overreaching general writs of assistance regime that the Fourth Amendment was designed to end by protecting such targets from unreasonable searches.

A traveler's personal luggage is also an "effect" within the meaning of the Fourth Amendment.[109] So is every container that hides its contents from plain view—such as a footlocker, a zippered leather pouch, or even a closed paper bag—as no constitutional distinction can be made between "worthy" and "unworthy" containers.[110]

(2) *Complaining party's substantial connection thereto*

A person claiming a privacy right in these items of personalty, however, must be connected with and treat such items in such a way as to reasonably expect a degree of privacy. In this connection, anyone who lawfully owns or possesses such items of personal property ordinarily has a reasonable expectation of privacy therein. This is so because such a person has a right to exclude others from the property and therefore generally entertains a reasonable expectation of privacy in the interior of such personalty.[111]

Special problems arise, however, where the person complaining does not own or physically possess the protected "effect"—as where such person is a guest passenger in someone else's automobile. Such a guest passenger has no reasonable expectation of

---

104. "It is beyond dispute that a vehicle is an 'effect' as that term is used in the [Fourth] Amendment." United States v. Jones, 565 U.S. ___, 132 S.Ct. 945, 181 L.Ed2d 911, 917–18 (2012); South Dakota v. Opperman, 428 U.S. 364, 367, 96 S.Ct. 3092, 49 L.Ed.2d 1000 (1976); see also Cady v. Dombrowski, 413 U.S. 433, 93 S.Ct. 2523, 37 L.Ed.2d 706 (1973). "The Fourth Amendment does not treat a motorist's car as his castle." Illinois v. Lidster, 540 U.S. 419, 124 S.Ct. 885, 889, 157 L.Ed.2d 843 (2004).

105. Coolidge v. New Hampshire, 403 U.S. 443, 462, 91 S.Ct. 2022, 29 L.Ed.2d 564, 580 (1971).

106. Delaware v. Prouse, 440 U.S. 648, 662–63, 99 S.Ct. 1391, 59 L.Ed.2d 660 (1979).

107. See, e.g., California v. Carney, 471 U.S. 386, 105 S.Ct. 2066, 85 L.Ed.2d 406, 411 (1985) (mobile motor home); Rios v. United States, 364 U.S. 253, 80 S.Ct. 1431, 4 L.Ed.2d 1688 (1960) (taxicab). For a discussion of the search of "automobiles" generally, see Chapter 16, Section 2 of this work.

108. See, e.g., United States v. Villamonte-Marquez, 462 U.S. 579, 103 S.Ct. 2573, 77 L.Ed.2d 22 (1983); United States v. Lee, 274 U.S. 559, 47 S.Ct. 746, 71 L.Ed. 1202 (1927).

109. Bond v. United States, 528 U.S. 334, 120 S.Ct. 1462, 145 L.Ed.2d 365 (2000); see also Arkansas v. Sanders, 442 U.S. 753, 99 S.Ct. 2586, 61 L.Ed.2d 235 (1979).

110. United States v. Ross, 456 U.S. 798, 102 S.Ct. 2157, 72 L.Ed.2d 572, 592 (1982) (zippered leather pouch and closed brown paper bag); United States v. Chadwick, 433 U.S. 1, 97 S.Ct. 2476, 53 L.Ed.2d 538 (1977) (footlocker). For a discussion of the search of containers generally, see Chapter 16, Section 3 of this work.

111. "Legitimate expectations of privacy by law must have a source outside the Fourth Amendment, either by reference to concepts of real or personal property law or to understandings that are recognized and permitted by society. One of the main rights attaching to property is the right to exclude others, and one who owns or lawfully possesses or controls property will in all likelihood have a legitimate expectation of privacy by virtue of this right to exclude." Rakas v. Illinois, 439 U.S. 128, 143 n. 12, 99 S.Ct. 421, 58 L.Ed.2d 387 (1978) (internal citation omitted).

privacy in the automobile and cannot object to a police search of it.[112] The only exception to this result is where the police illegally stop the automobile in the first instance—in which event, the guest passenger and everyone else in the vehicle has been unreasonably seized in violation of their respective Fourth Amendment rights, and all evidence seized from the automobile thereafter would be the fruit of the unreasonable seizure and thus generally excludable at trial under the *Weeks-Mapp* exclusionary rule.[113]

Special problems also arise when the person complaining turns over his or her "papers" or "effects" to a third person for safekeeping. It has been held that a taxpayer—who turns over financial records to an accountant for preparation of the taxpayer's income tax return—has no reasonable expectation of privacy in these records while such records are held by the accountant.[114] Moreover, a bank depositor has no reasonable expectation of privacy in his or her checks, deposit or withdrawal slips held by the depositor's bank.[115] And a criminal defendant who placed his contraband drugs in the purse of an acquaintance to hide them from police was held to have no reasonable expectation of privacy in the purse and could not object to a police search of the purse.[116]

---

112. Rakas v. Illinois, 439 U.S. 128, 99 S.Ct. 421, 58 L.Ed.2d 387 (1978) (police search the glove compartment and beneath the front seat of an automobile, seizing rifle shells and a sawed-off shotgun; guest passenger could not complain of search).

113. "When a police officer makes a traffic stop, the driver of the car is seized within the meaning of the Fourth Amendment. The question in this case is whether the same is true of the passenger. We hold that a passenger is seized as well and so may challenge the constitutionality of the stop." Brendlin v. California, 551 U.S. 249, 127 S.Ct. 2400, 2403, 168 L.Ed.2d 132 (2007).

Moreover, the police seizure of property from the passenger compartment of the automobile generally constitutes a Fourth Amendment *seizure* of property from the possession of every occupant in the automobile. This is so because (a) a Fourth Amendment *seizure* of a person's property occurs when there has been some meaningful governmental interference with the person's possessory interests in the property, whether that possession be legal or illegal [see Chapter 9, Section 3, pp. 126–27 of this work]; and (b) all occupants of an automobile, as a general rule, are in constructive possession of all property in the passenger compartment of the automobile and may be properly arrested for possessing any contraband drugs found therein. [Maryland v. Pringle, 540 U.S. 366, 124 S.Ct. 795, 157 L.Ed.2d 769 (2003)].

In sum :

1. A guest passenger of an automobile can challenge the constitutionality of the *automobile stop* [Brendlin v. California, supra], and if *illegal*, the evidence secured in the automobile subsequent to the stop would be generally inadmissible as the fruit of the poisonous tree.

2. But if the stop is *lawful*, a guest passenger cannot challenge the lawfulness of the *search* of the automobile [Rakas v. Illinois, 439 U.S. 128, 99 S.Ct. 421, 58 L.Ed.2d 387 (1978)].

3. Such a passenger can, however, challenge the lawfulness of the *seizure* of any property taken from the passenger compartment of the automobile. But the only basis for challenging such a seizure is that there was no probable cause to believe that the item seized constituted contraband, evidence of crime, or fruits or instrumentalities of crime. [See Chapter 12, Section 2b(3) at 218–19 of this work].

Also see 6 Wayne LaFave, Search and Seizure § 11.3e at 245–249 (5th ed. 2012) and cases collected.

114. Couch v. United States, 409 U.S. 322, 93 S.Ct. 611, 34 L.Ed.2d 548 (1973) (taxpayer could not challenge an IRS subpoena used to obtain financial records from accountant).

115. United States v. Miller, 425 U.S. 435, 96 S.Ct. 1619, 48 L.Ed.2d 71 (1976) (depositor could not challenge IRS subpoena to obtain depositor's canceled checks, deposit and withdrawal slips from depositor's bank).

116. Rawlings v. Kentucky, 448 U.S. 98, 100 S.Ct. 2556, 65 L.Ed.2d 633 (1980).

Section 4. Second Component of a *Katz* Fourth Amendment "Search": A Government Agent Must Invade the Complaining Party's Reasonable Expectation of Privacy[117]

To constitute a Fourth Amendment "search" under the modern *Katz* test, it is not enough that the person making a Fourth Amendment claim have a reasonable expectation of privacy in particular private premises or property as discussed above. It must also be shown, as a second component, that a governmental agent—by some action—*invaded* the person's reasonable expectation of privacy in such premises or property.

a. Non-consensual and consensual entry onto protected premises or property

In this connection, the nature of the reasonable expectation of privacy entertained by a person often defines the type of governmental action that will invade this expectation. Accordingly, the Court has generally treated any non-consensual, physical entry onto protected premises or property—such as a home or an automobile—as a Fourth Amendment search.[118] Moreover, any physical movement through protected premises for hidden objects or persons after the entry, and any observations made during this process, are usually treated as a Fourth Amendment search.[119] This is so because a person has a reasonable expectation that his or her privacy in such property will not be invaded by such an action.

---

117. What follows is a continuation of the discussion concerning the modern *Katz* test for a Fourth Amendment search As previously noted, however, this is not the *only* test for a Fourth Amendment search. The older recently-revived trespass test must first be consulted to determine as a *baseline* whether there has been a trespass by a government official into a constitutionally-protected area. If so, that ends the inquiry as such conduct constitutes a Fourth Amendment search in itself—and the *Katz* test need not be consulted. Only if the conduct involved does *not* satisfy the trespass test is it appropriate to turn to the *Katz* test.

See Section 2, supra, of this chapter at footnote 16 and the accompanying text. For a thorough discussion of the old recently-revived trespass test for a Fourth Amendment search, see 1 Wayne LaFave, Search and Seizure § 2.1 (e) (5th ed. 2012).

"The [Fourth] Amendment establishes a simple baseline, one that for most of our history formed the exclusive basis for its protections: When the Government obtains information by physically intruding on persons houses, papers, or effects, a 'search' within the original meaning of the Fourth Amendment has undoubtedly occurred. By reason of our decision in Katz v. United States ... property rights are not the sole measure of Fourth Amendment violations—but though Katz may add to the baseline, it does not subtract anything from the Amendment's protections when the Government *does* engage in [a] physical intrusion of a constitutionally protected area." Florida v. Jardines, 569 U.S. ___, 133 S.Ct. 1409, 185 L.Ed.2d 495, 500 (2013) (internal citations and quotes omitted).

118. See, e.g., Johnson v. United States, 333 U.S. 10, 68 S.Ct. 367, 92 L.Ed. 436 (1948) (entry into hotel room); Carroll v. United States, 267 U.S. 132, 45 S.Ct. 280, 69 L.Ed. 543 (1925) (entry into automobile); 1 Wayne LaFave, Search and Seizure § 2.3(b) (5th ed. 2012) (entry into residential premises).

119. See, e.g., Maryland v. Buie, 494 U.S. 325, 110 S.Ct. 1093, 108 L.Ed.2d 276 (1990) ("A protective sweep [of a home for persons who pose a danger to arresting officers therein] is without question a 'search,' as was the patdown in *Terry*."); Segura v. United States, 468 U.S. 796, 104 S.Ct. 3380, 82 L.Ed.2d 599, 606, 608 (1984) (same); See v. City of Seattle, 387 U.S. 541, 87 S.Ct. 1737, 18 L.Ed.2d 943 (1967) (inspection of warehouse for fire code enforcement purposes treated as a Fourth Amendment search); Carroll v. United States, 267 U.S. 132, 45 S.Ct. 280, 69 L.Ed. 543 (1925) (law enforcement

There are special situations, however, where a limited type of non-consensual entry onto private premises has *not* been treated as a Fourth Amendment search. For example, a state welfare statute and administrative rule that require a scheduled visit by a caseworker to a welfare recipient's home as a condition for receiving welfare benefits has been upheld under the Fourth Amendment; this result was reached based on one of several rationales that such a state scheme does not authorize a Fourth Amendment search in the traditional criminal law sense nor does it compel entry upon pain of criminal prosecution, but only upon pain of losing welfare benefits.[120] A contrary result has been reached, however, with respect to statutes that authorize nonconsensual entry onto protected premises or impose a criminal penalty for refusing such entry in order to conduct an inspection of a home for health code or fire code violations, as such inspections are considered Fourth Amendment searches.[121]

Also where the consent to enter protected premises is obtained by the deception or subterfuge of an undercover government agent or informer for the express purpose of buying contraband drugs on the premises, the act of entering the premises and buying the drugs is *not* considered an invasion of the home dweller's reasonable expectation of privacy, and thus is not a Fourth Amendment search, as these acts are within the scope of the obtained consent.[122] The practical basis stated by the Court for this ruling is if such misrepresentations by the agent or informer were constitutionally prohibited, "we would come near to a rule that the use of undercover agents in any manner is virtually unconstitutional per se."[123] Moreover, the act of listening to and later reporting conversations with the home dweller or hotel guest after being invited onto protected premises, albeit through misrepresentations, is not considered an invasion of the home dweller's or hotel guest's reasonable expectation of privacy and is not a Fourth Amendment search.[124] The basis for this ruling is that the home dweller or hotel guest, in revealing matters to an undercover agent or informer, is relying on a misplaced confidence that the agent or informer will not repeat the conversation to the outside world, and not on any reasonable expectation of privacy in the protected premises.[125] Of course, the same result is reached based on similar reasoning where an undercover government agent without any overt misrepresentations enters a business store during regular business hours and examines

---

exploration of interior of an automobile treated as a Fourth Amendment search); Arizona v. Hicks, 480 U.S. 321, 107 S.Ct.1149, 94 L.Ed.2d 347 (1987) (entry into apartment and inspection thereof to investigate shooting therein was a lawful search; but police act of moving stereo equipment around in apartment to discover its serial numbers was a search unrelated to the purposes of the entry and was unlawful).

120. Wyman v. James, 400 U.S. 309, 91 S.Ct. 381, 27 L.Ed.2d 408 (1971). The Court was careful to point out, however, that its holding did not mean that a termination of welfare benefits upon refusal of a home visit would be upheld under the Fourth Amendment under all conceivable circumstances. The Court adverted particularly to the case of unannounced raids of welfare recipient homes, citing Parrish v. Civil Service Comm'n, 66 Cal.2d 260, 425 P.2d 223 (1967); Reich, Midnight Welfare Searches and the Social Security Act, 72 Yale L.J. 1347 (1963), and stated that it would leave such cases for another day. For a critical analysis of the *Wyman* case, see 5 Wayne LaFave, Search and Seizure § 10.3(a) (5th ed. 2012).

121. See v. City of Seattle, 387 U.S. 541, 87 S.Ct. 1737, 18 L.Ed.2d 943 (1967) (fire code inspection of commercial warehouse); Camara v. Municipal Court, 387 U.S. 523, 87 S.Ct 1727, 18 L.Ed.2d 930 (1967) (health inspection of private home).

122. Lewis v. United States, 385 U.S. 206, 87 S.Ct. 424, 17 L.Ed.2d 312 (1966).

123. Lewis v. United States, 385 U.S. at 210.

124. Lewis v. United States, 385 U.S. 206, 87 S.Ct. 424, 17 L.Ed.2d 312 (1966); Hoffa v. United States, 385 U.S. 293, 87 S.Ct. 408, 17 L.Ed.2d 374 (1966).

125. Hoffa v. United States, 385 U.S. at 302.

merchandise that is being offered for sale, such as adult books; the store owner has no reasonable expectation of privacy that undercover police officers will not frequent his place of business, and, accordingly, the act of entering the store and examining the for-sale merchandise does not constitute a Fourth Amendment search.[126] On the other hand, where the government agent or informant exceeds the home dweller's or business owner's invitation to enter and engage in certain activity on the premises and secretly looks through premises to which the agent has not been invited and seizes certain property, the act of looking through such premises for incriminating evidence is considered an invasion of the home dweller or business owner's reasonable expectation of privacy and thus constitutes a Fourth Amendment search.[127]

Finally, there is an implied invitation by custom for any person, including a government agent, to knock on the front door to a home, and to seek permission to talk to anyone therein. This invitation permits the visitor to approach the home through a front path, to knock promptly on the door, to wait briefly to be received, to talk with whomever might answer the door, and finally to leave when the visit is over or if no one answers the knock. There is also an implied invitation for mail carriers and persons delivering packages and flyers to leave their delivery at the front door and promptly leave.[128]

But there is no invitation, for a police officer with a drug-sniffing police dog to enter the front porch of a home and use the dog to smell the front door to detect any illegal drug aromas that might be emanating from the interior; such activity is considered a Fourth Amendment "search." Similarly, there is no invitation for anyone, including the police, to enter the front porch of a home and peer into the front window with a pair of binoculars—as that too is a Fourth Amendment "search."[129]

---

126. Maryland v. Macon, 472 U.S. 463, 105 S.Ct.2778, 86 L.Ed.2d 370 (1985) (adult book store).

127. Lewis v. United States, 385 U.S. at 209, 211, citing Gouled v. United States, 255 U.S. 298, 41 S.Ct. 261, 65 L.Ed. 647 (1921).

128. "We have accordingly recognized that the knocker on the front door is treated as an invitation or license to attempt an entry, justifying ingress into the home by solicitors, hawkers, and peddlers of all kinds. This implicit license typically permits the visitor to approach the home by the front path, knock promptly, wait briefly to be received, and then (absent invitation to linger longer) leave. Complying with that invitation does not require fine-grained legal knowledge; it is generally managed without incident by the Nation's Girl Scouts and trick-or-treaters. Thus, a police officer not armed with a warrant may approach a home and knock, precisely because that is no more than any private citizen might do. Florida v. Jardines, 569 U.S. ___, 133 S.Ct. 1409, 185 L.Ed.2d 495, 502 (internal citations and quotations omitted).

"It is said that members of the public may lawfully proceed along a walkway leading to the front door of a house because custom grants him a license to do so. This rule encompasses categories of visitors whom most homeowners almost certainly wish to allow to approach their front door—friends, relatives, mail carriers, persons making deliveries. But it also reaches categories of visitors who are less universally welcome—'solicitors,' 'hawkers,' 'peddlers,' and the like. * * *

Of course, this license has certain spatial and temporal limits. A visitor must stick to the path that is typically used to approach the front door, such as a paved walkway. A visitor cannot traipse through the garden, meander into the back yard, or take other circuitous detours that veer from the pathway that a visitor would customarily use. * * *

Nor as a general matter, may a visitor come to the front door in the middle of the night without an express invitation. * * *

Similarly, a visitor may not linger at the front door for an extended period. The license is limited to the amount of time it would customarily take to approach the door, pause long enough to see if someone is home, and (if not expressly invited to stay longer), leave." Florida v. Jardines, 569 U.S. ___, 133 S.Ct. 1409, 1421–22, 185 L.Ed.2d 495, 509 (2013) (Alito, J. dissenting) (internal citations and quotations omitted).

129. Florida v. Jardines, 569 U.S. ___, 133 S.Ct. 1409, 185 L.Ed.2d 495, 501 (2013) (held: no implicit invitation of homeowner for police to take a drug-sniffing police dog to the front door of

b. Special governmental actions related to the home and personal property

An "open view" sighting into protected Fourth Amendment premises by a law enforcement agent who is located in a public place [without otherwise violating the complaining party's Fourth Amendment rights] is a classic example of a law enforcement activity that is not considered a Fourth Amendment search; other more intrusive surveillances from this vantage point, however, may constitute a Fourth Amendment search. Also, electronic surveillance techniques used to overhear or see activities within the home may or may not constitute Fourth Amendment searches. And a classic example of a governmental activity that is not a Fourth Amendment search is a "canine sniff" of a suitcase or automobile, in which a trained police dog sniffs the aroma immediately emanating from such property. However, the cases concerning all of these important subjects will be examined in Section 5 of this chapter under the open view doctrine, electronic eavesdropping, and narcotic dog sniffs.

c. Searches of personal property: automobiles, mailed packages and containers

As a general rule, a Fourth Amendment search of an automobile occurs whenever there is a non-consensual governmental entry into the interior of the automobile.[130] Accordingly, a police entry into an automobile to remove papers from the dashboard of the

---

home and smell the front door for drug aromas emanating from the interior; such activity constitutes a Fourth Amendment "search."). Although *Jardines* was decided under the recently-revived trespass test for a Fourth Amendment search, it would seem that in all likelihood the modern *Katz* test for such a search would produce the same result. See Florida v. Jardines, 569 U.S. ___, 133 S.Ct. 1409, 185 L.Ed.2d 495, 505 (2013) (Kagan, J. concurring).

"But introducing a trained police dog to explore the area around the house in the hopes of discovering incriminating information is something else. There is no customary invitation to do that. An invitation to engage in canine forensic investigation assuredly does not inhere in the very act of hanging a [door] knocker. To find a visitor knocking on the door is routine (even if sometimes unwelcome); to spot that same visitor exploring the front path with a metal detector, or marching his bloodhound into the garden before saying hello and asking permission, would inspire most of us to—well, call the police. * * *

The government's use of a trained police dogs to investigate the home and its immediate surroundings is a "search" within the meaning of the Fourth Amendment." Florida v. Jardines, 569 U.S. ___, 133 S.Ct. 1409, 185 L.Ed.2d 495, 502–03, 504 (2013).

"A stranger comes to the front door of your home carrying super-high-powered binoculars. He doesn't knock or say hello. Instead, he stands on the porch and uses the binoculars to peer through your windows, into your home's furthest corners. It doesn't take long (the binoculars are really very fine): In just a couple of minutes, his uncommon behavior allows him to learn details of your life you disclose to no one. Has your 'visitor' trespassed on your property, exceeding the license you have granted to members of the public. Yes, he has. And has he also invaded your 'reasonable expectation of privacy,' by nosing into the intimacies you sensibly sought protected from disclosure? Yes, of course, he has done that too." Florida v. Jardines, 569 U.S. ___, 133 S.Ct. 1409, 185 L.Ed.2d 495, 505 (2013) (Kagan J. concurring) (internal citations omitted).

130. See, e.g., Coolidge v. New Hampshire, 403 U.S. 443, 91 S.Ct. 2022, 29 L.Ed.2d 564 (1971) (search of passenger compartment of auto); United States v. Ortiz, 422 U.S. 891, 95 S.Ct. 2585, 45 L.Ed.2d 623 (1975) (search of auto trunk). But a routine auto safety inspection by governmental officials may not constitute a Fourth Amendment search of an auto. United States v. Ortiz, 422 U.S. at 896 n. 3, 45 L.Ed.2d at 629 n. 3.

automobile to discover the vehicle identification number [VIN] is a Fourth Amendment search.[131] Similarly, the placement by law enforcement agents of an operational GPS device on the undercarriage a motor vehicle and its use thereafter to motor the vehicle's movements in the public streets constitute a Fourth Amendment search.[132] On the other hand, a governmental examination of the *exterior* of an automobile does not constitute a Fourth Amendment search of the vehicle—as the exterior is open to public view and, accordingly, one can have no reasonable expectation of privacy in the outer appearance of a vehicle.[133] Indeed, even the taking of paint scrapings from the exterior of an automobile by police does not constitute a Fourth Amendment search of the automobile[134]—although it may constitute a Fourth Amendment *seizure* of an effect if a paint scraping is considered in itself a piece of personal property.[135] And "open view" sightings of the interior of an automobile by police, even with the use of a flashlight, do not constitute a Fourth Amendment search of an automobile.[136]

Generally, the opening of a mailed package addressed to the complaining party constitutes a Fourth Amendment search of the package when conducted by a law enforcement agent. Indeed, it has been held that law enforcement agents conducted a Fourth Amendment search of an alleged pornographic film taken from a mailed package addressed to the complaining party when the agents viewed such a film on a projector—even though the package was intercepted and turned over to the agents on a "silver platter" by private parties.[137] Moreover, a law enforcement agent's physical manipulation in an exploratory manner of a bus passenger's carry-on canvas bag in an open overhead storage space in the bus has been held to constitute a Fourth Amendment search.[138]

---

131. "The evidence that respondent sought to have suppressed was not the VIN, however, but a gun, the handle of which the officer saw from the interior of the car while reaching for the papers that covered the VIN. While the interior of an automobile is not subject to the same expectations of privacy that exist with respect to one's home, a car's interior is nonetheless subject to Fourth Amendment protection from unreasonable intrusions by the police. We agree with the New York Court of Appeals that the intrusion into that space constituted a [Fourth Amendment] 'search.'" New York v. Class, 475 U.S. 106, 106 S.Ct. 960, 89 L.Ed.2d 81 (1986) (the entry into the auto to discover the partially-obscured VIN was nonetheless reasonable because a VIN is required by federal law to be open to public view from outside the auto).

132. United States v. Jones, 565 U.S. ___, 132 S.Ct. 945, 181 L.Ed.2d 911 (2012). Although *Jones* was decided under the recently-revived trespass test for a Fourth Amendment search, it would seem that in all likelihood the modern *Katz* test for such a search would produce the same result. Compare Florida v. Jardines, 569 U.S. ___, 133 S.Ct. 1409, 185 L.Ed.2d 495, 505 (2013) (Kagan, J. concurring).

133. "The exterior of a car, of course, is thrust into the public eye, and thus to examine it does not constitute a [Fourth Amendment] 'search.'" New York v. Class, 475 U.S. 106, 106 S.Ct. 960, 89 L.Ed.2d 81, 90 (1986). See 1 Wayne LaFave, Search and Seizure § 2.5(b) (5th ed. 2012).

134. "In the present case, nothing from the interior of the car and no personal effects, which the Fourth Amendment has been deemed to protect, were searched or seized or introduced in evidence. With the 'search' limited to the examination of the tire on the wheel and the taking of paint scrapings from the exterior of the vehicle left in the public parking lot, we fail to comprehend what expectation of privacy was infringed. Stated simply, the invasion of privacy, 'if it can be said to exist, is abstract and theoretical.'" Cardwell v. Lewis, 417 U.S. 583, 591–92, 94 S.Ct. 2464, 41 L.Ed.2d 325, 335–36 (1974) (examination of tire treads of auto and taking of paint scrapings from auto were not Fourth Amendment searches) (quoted citation and footnotes omitted).

135. For a discussion of Fourth Amendment seizures of personal property, see Chapter 9, Section 3 of this work.

136. For a discussion of this subject, see Section 5a of this Chapter.

137. Walter v. United States, 447 U.S. 649, 100 S.Ct. 2395, 65 L.Ed.2d 410 (1980) (search held unreasonable because it was conducted without a search warrant).

138. Bond v. United States, 529 U.S. 334, 120 S.Ct. 1462, 146 L.Ed.2d 365 (2000).

On the other hand, it has been held that law enforcement agents do not conduct a Fourth Amendment search merely by examining the contents of a mailed package opened by FedEx employees and turned over to the agents on a "silver platter."[139] Nor is it a Fourth Amendment search for law enforcement agents to re-open a package after arresting the addressee of the package in a "controlled delivery" of same—when U.S. Customs officials had previously conducted a reasonable border search of the package, discovered that the package contained illegal drugs, resealed the package, and had the package delivered to the addressee. The basis for this ruling was that the addressee lost all reasonable expectation of privacy in the package after U.S. Customs had lawfully searched it.[140]

Section 5. Special Search or Seizure Element Problems

a. "Open view" doctrine: "fly-overs" and use of sense-enhancing devices

"What a person knowingly exposes to the public, even in his own home or office, is not a subject of Fourth Amendment protection."[141] This is so because a person has no reasonable expectation of privacy in a home or office or other protected premises with respect to that which is knowingly exposed to the public. Accordingly, any observation by a government agent of such a publicly exposed item, when conducted from outside such protected premises, is generally not considered a Fourth Amendment search.[142] This occurs where a law enforcement officer stands outside a parked automobile on the public street and observes illegal drug evidence located inside the automobile,[143] or where a U.S. Coast Guard officer aboard a vessel observes cases of contraband liquor aboard another nearby vessel,[144] or where a law enforcement agent trespasses on an individual's farmland, stands outside a barn located on the land and observes an illegal drug factory therein through a window.[145] Moreover, the fact that a flashlight or spotlight is used by the law enforcement officer to enhance the officer's observations at night does not change this result.[146] This is known as the "open view doctrine," and should not be confused with the "plain view doctrine."

As will be discussed later, the "plain view doctrine" always "piggybacks" on an otherwise reasonable Fourth Amendment search, in that it is applicable only after a government

139. United States v. Jacobsen, 466 U.S. 109, 104 S.Ct. 1652, 80 L.Ed.2d 85 (1984) (subsequent field testing of the white powder contents of the package to determine whether it was cocaine was also not a Fourth Amendment search).

140. Illinois v. Andreas, 463 U.S. 765, 103 S.Ct. 3319, 77 L.Ed.2d 1003 (1983).

141. Katz v. United States, 389 U.S. 347, 351, 88 S.Ct. 507, 19 L.Ed.2d 576 (1967).

142. "The Fourth Amendment protection of the home has never been extended to require law enforcement officers to shield their eyes when passing by a home on a public thoroughfare. Nor does the mere fact that an individual has taken measures to restrict some views of his activities preclude an officer's observations from a public vantage point where he has a right to be." California v. Ciraolo, 476 U.S. 207, 106 S.Ct. 1809, 90 L.Ed.2d 210, 216 (1986).

143. Texas v. Brown, 460 U.S. 730, 103 S.Ct. 1535, 75 L.Ed.2d 502, 512 (1983); also see cases collected at "Searches and Seizures" § 18 West Key No.

144. United States v. Lee, 274 U.S. 559, 47 S.Ct. 746, 71 L.Ed. 1202 (1927).

145. United States v. Dunn, 480 U.S. 294, 107 S.Ct. 1134, 94 L.Ed.2d 326 (1987).

146. Brown; Lee; Dunn. For lower court cases on this issue, see "Searches and Seizures" §§ 19, 51 West Key Nos.

agent is in the process of conducting a reasonable search and thereafter seizes certain property. Such a seizure is considered reasonable under this doctrine if (a) the property was observed in plain sight during the course of conducting such a reasonable search, and (b) there is probable cause to believe that the property seized constitutes contraband, evidence of crime, or the fruits or instrumentalities of a crime.[147] By contrast, the "open view doctrine" is applicable only if the government agent is outside constitutionally protected premises and from that vantage point observes publicly exposed items located on constitutionally protected premises. Such an observation is not considered a Fourth Amendment search.[148]

Special problems arise, however, where a law enforcement officer makes observations of an individual's home or business from an aircraft flying overhead. It has been held to be an "open view" sighting and not a Fourth Amendment search if the officer makes his observations from the public navigable air space, does not disturb the individual's enjoyment of his property below with undue noise or wind or threat of injury, and employs publicly-available camera equipment. This occurs where such an officer observes through the naked eye incriminating evidence in the curtilage of person's home[149] or in a transparent structure within such a curtilage,[150] or takes aerial photographs of the acreage around a person's business.[151]

On the other hand, a different outcome might well result in each of these cases if highly sophisticated surveillance equipment not generally available to the public is used, such as satellite technology, to see what could not otherwise be seen with the naked eye or with standard camera equipment.[152] Indeed, it has been held that sense-enhancing technological devices, whether used in the air or on the ground, and not generally available to the public—enabling law enforcement agents to obtain information regarding the interior of a home that could not otherwise have been obtained without a physical intrusion therein—constitutes a Fourth Amendment search of the home. An example of such a device is a "thermal imager" that enables law enforcement officers to detect whether high-intensity lamps are being used in the home.[153]

---

147. For a discussion of the "plain view doctrine," see Chapter 12, Section 2c of this work.

148. See generally Ensor v. State, 403 So.2d 349 (Fla. 1981); 1 Wayne LaFave, Search and Seizure § 2.2a (5th ed. 2012); also see cases collected at "Searches and Seizures" §§ 16, 17, 47.1 West Key Nos.

149. California v. Ciraolo, 476 U.S. 207, 106 S.Ct. 1809, 90 L.Ed.2d 210, 216 (1986) (observation made from aircraft 1,000 feet above fenced-in back yard where marijuana plants were growing).

150. Florida v. Riley, 488 U.S. 445, 109 S.Ct. 693, 102 L.Ed.2d 835 (1989) (observation made from helicopter 400 feet above glass greenhouse in back yard; marijuana was growing in greenhouse).

151. Dow Chemical Co. v. United States, 476 U.S. 227, 106 S.Ct. 1819, 90 L.Ed.2d 226 (1986) (EPA aerial mapping of 2,000-acre area surrounding an industrial plant from altitudes of 12,000. 3,00 and 1,200 feet). For lower court cases on the issue of aerial surveillance, see "Searches and Seizures" §§ 20, 56 West Key Nos.

152. Dow Chemical Co. v. United States, 476 U.S. 227, 106 S.Ct. 1819, 90 L.Ed.2d 226, 237 (1986); California v. Ciraolo, 476 U.S. 207, 106 S.Ct. 1809, 90 L.Ed.2d 210, 218, n. 3 (1986).

153. "We think that obtaining by any sense-enhancing technology any information regarding the interior of the home that could not otherwise have been obtained without 'physical intrusion into a constitutionally protected area,' [citation omitted], constitutes a [Fourth Amendment] search—at least where [as here] the technology in question is not in general public use. * * * We have said that the Fourth Amendment draws 'a firm line at the entrance to the house' [citation omitted]. That line, we think, must not only be firm but also bright—which requires clear specification of those methods of surveillance that require a warrant. * * * Where, as here, the Government uses a device that is not in general public use, to explore details of the home that would previously have been unknowable without physical intrusion, the surveillance is a [Fourth Amendment] 'search' and is presumptively unreasonable without a warrant."

Kyllo v. United States, 533 U.S. 27, 121 S.Ct. 2038, 2043, 2046, 150 L.Ed.2d 94 (2001) (warrantless

b. Wiretapping and electronic eavesdropping

A comprehensive treatment of wiretapping and electronic eavesdropping is beyond the scope of this work.[154] Accordingly, only a thumbnail sketch of the broad outlines of Fourth Amendment doctrine will be attempted here.

At first, wiretapping—i.e., electronic interception by law enforcement of a telephone conversation without the consent of either party to the conversation—was not considered a Fourth Amendment search or seizure.[155] Eventually, however, this holding was overruled.[156] It is now well settled that all wiretapping or electronic surveillance in which conversations on the telephone or in a house are intercepted, without the consent of any party to the conversation, is a Fourth Amendment search—and any party to such a conversation, as well as the owner of the house being tapped, may object to the interception of such a conversation.[157]

On the other hand, so-called "third party bugging" of face-to-face or telephone conversations in which one party to the conversation consents to the interception, does not constitute a Fourth Amendment search. This result has been reached on the basis that a person who engages in a conversation with another person takes the risk that the latter person will repeat this conversation to the outside world—and a secret electronic recording of the conversation is nothing more than an accurate account of the conversation that is repeated when played for third parties.[158]

At times, law enforcement agents also engage in other types of electronic investigation in which certain helpful information is obtained, but no conversations are recorded. For example, such agents may install a pen register on a person's telephone line and record solely the telephone numbers dialed from that person's telephone. The Court has held that such a pen register is not a Fourth Amendment search on the ground that a person has no reasonable expectation of privacy in the telephone numbers dialed from one's telephone.[159] Moreover, drug enforcement agents sometimes place an electronic beeper in a container of contraband drugs and thereafter track the movements of such container to a particular person or place after the suspect retrieves it. If the detected movements take place inside protected Fourth Amendment premises, the monitoring is considered a Fourth Amendment search[160]—but not so if the detected movements occur outside protected

---

use of thermal imager, from which it was discovered that home had high-intensity lamps therein, struck down; such information may not be relied on to obtain a search warrant for the home).

154. For a comprehensive treatment of wiretapping and electronic eavesdropping law, see James Garr & Patricia Bellia, The Law of Electronic Surveillance 2 vols. (2012). For a more abbreviated discussion, see 2 John Wesley Hall, Search and Seizure §§ 42.01–42.33 (5th ed. 2013). Also see lower court cases collected at "Criminal Law" § 394.3 West Key No.

155. Olmstead v. United States, 277 U.S. 438, 48 S.Ct. 564, 72 L.Ed. 944 (1928) (classic dissents by Holmes and Brandeis, JJ.).

156. Katz v. United States, 389 U.S. 347, 88 S.Ct. 507, 19 L.Ed.2d 576 (1967) (electronic bug on top of telephone booth held unreasonable Fourth Amendment search as it was conducted without a search warrant).

157. See, e.g., Alderman v. United States, 394 U.S. 165, 89 S.Ct. 961, 22 L.Ed.2d 176 (1969) (owner of "tapped" house need not be a party to the conversation he or she objects to).

158. United States v. White, 401 U.S. 745, 91 S.Ct. 1122, 28 L.Ed.2d 453 (1971); Lopez v. United States, 373 U.S. 427, 83 S.Ct. 1381, 10 L.Ed.2d 462 (1963).

159. Smith v. Maryland, 442 U.S. 735, 99 S.Ct. 2577, 61 L.Ed.2d 220 (1979).

160. United States v. Karo, 468 U.S. 705, 104 S.Ct. 3296, 82 L.Ed.2d 530 (1984) (monitoring was unreasonable because it was conducted without a warrant and the results of same tainted the search warrant for the suspect's house).

premises in public places.[161] By contrast, the trespassory placement by law enforcement agents of an operational GPS device on the undercarriage a person's motor vehicle and its use thereafter to monitor the vehicle's movements on the public streets constitute a Fourth Amendment search.[162]

The Court has not yet considered whether it is a Fourth Amendment search for the government to intercept e-mails, cellular phone calls, Facebook communications, text messages, and pager transmissions. Given the rapidly expanding technology in these and other similar communication devices, the Court has been reluctant to decide these thorny issues until more is known about this technology—as well as the way society views privacy expectations with respect to such devices.[163] When the Court eventually takes up such issues, there may be a need to reconsider older Fourth Amendment privacy formulations that may not be suited to the digital age.[164]

---

161. United States v. Knotts, 460 U.S. 276, 103 S.Ct. 1081, 75 L.Ed.2d 55 (1983) (search warrant for suspect's house based on the public movements of the container upheld). For lower court cases on tracking devices and electronic beepers, see "Searches and Seizures" § 21 West Key No.

162. United States v. Jones, 565 U.S. ___, 132 S.Ct. 945, 181 L.Ed.2d 911 (2012) (decided under the recently-revived trespass test for a Fourth Amendment search).

163. "The Court must proceed with care when considering the whole concept of privacy expectations in communications made on electronic equipment owned by a government employer. The judiciary risks error by elaborating too fully on the Fourth Amendment implications of emerging technology before its role in society has become clear. *** Rapid changes in the dynamics of communication and information transmission are evident not just in the technology itself but in what society accepts a proper behavior. *** Cell phone and text message communications are so pervasive that some persons may consider them to be essential means for self-expression, even self-identification." City of Ontario v. Quon, 560 U.S. 746, 130 S.Ct. 2619, 2629–30, 177 L.Ed.2d 216 (2010) (Court assumes arguendo that a police officer had a reasonable expectation of privacy in text messages that he sent on a pager owned and provided to him by his government employer, and that the latter's audit of such messages constituted a search under the Fourth Amendment).

164. See United States v. Jones, 565 U.S. 546, 132 S.Ct. 945, 181 L.Ed.2d 911, 923, 926–27 (2012) (Sotomayor, J. concurring):

"More fundamentally, it may be necessary to reconsider the premise that an individual has no reasonable expectation of privacy in information voluntarily disclosed to third parties. E.g., Smith, 442 U.S. 742; United States v. Miller, 425 U.S. 435, 443 (1976). This approach is ill suited to the digital age, in which people reveal a great deal of information about themselves to third parties in the course of carrying out mundane tasks. People disclose the phone numbers that they dial or text to their cellular providers; the URLs that they visit and the e-mail addresses with which they correspond to their Internet service providers; and the books, groceries, and medications they purchase to online retailers. Perhaps, as Justice Alito notes, some people may find the 'tradeoff' of privacy for convenience 'worthwhile,' or come to accept this 'diminution of privacy' as 'inevitable,' (citation omitted), and perhaps not. I for one doubt that people will accept without complaint the warrantless disclosure to the Government of a list of every Web site they had visited in the last week, or month, or year. But whatever the societal expectations, they can attain constitutionally protected status only if our Fourth Amendment jurisprudence ceases to treat secrecy as a prerequisite for privacy. I would not assume that all information voluntarily disclosed to some member of the public for a limited purpose is, for that reason alone, disentitled to Fourth Amendment protection. See Smith, 442 U.S. at 749, 99 S.Ct.2577, 61 L.Ed.2d 220 (Marshall, J. dissenting) ("Privacy is not a discrete commodity, possessed absolutely or not at all. Those who disclose certain facts to a bank or phone company for a limited business purpose need not assume that this information will be released to other persons for other purposes"); See also Katz, 389 U.S., at 351–352, 88 S.Ct. 507, 19 L.Ed.2d 576 ('[W]hat [a person] seeks to preserve as private, even in an area accessible to the public, may be constitutionally protected')."

See also Justice Alito's analysis in *Jones* of the brave-new-world digital age and how it may impact on Fourth Amendment protections. United States v. Jones, 565 U.S. 546, 132 S.Ct. 945, 181 L.Ed.2d 911, 923, 932–33 (2012) (Alito, J. concurring).

c. Narcotic "dog sniffs" of luggage, cars or homes

A law enforcement practice has developed where certain police dogs are trained to smell the aroma of various types of illegal drugs—such as marijuana or cocaine—as it emanates from a suitcase or car and to alert on same. Such a "dog sniff," in itself, is not considered a Fourth Amendment search.[165] But any preceding nonconsensual seizure by police of the individual's suitcase or car in order to conduct such a "dog sniff" is a seizure of the person's "effect" within the meaning of the Fourth Amendment. Accordingly, if this seizure is unreasonable in the Fourth Amendment sense, the "dog sniff" is considered the fruit of the preceding unreasonable seizure.[166]

The underlying rationale for this result is that a narcotics "dog sniff" is *sui generis*—namely, the only thing the dog sniff reveals is the odor of contraband drugs emanating from the container or vehicle.[167] Even a false alert by the dog reveals nothing more.[168] And a person has no reasonable expectation of privacy to keep hidden from public view contraband drugs. Accordingly there can be no Fourth Amendment search in such a sniff.[169]

Narcotic "dog sniffs' of the *home*, however, are governed by a different rule—given the highest reasonable expectation of privacy that one enjoys in the home. Where police

---

165. Illinois v. Caballes, 543 U.S. 405, 125 S.Ct. 834, 160 L.Ed.2d 842 (2005) (car); United States v. Place, 462 U.S. 696, 103 S.Ct. 2637, 77 L.Ed.2d 110, 121 (1983) (suitcase); City of Indianapolis v. Edmond, 531 U.S. 32, 121 S.Ct. 447, 148 L.Ed.2d 333, 342–43 (2000) (car). For lower court cases on this issue, see "Searches and Seizures" § 22 West Key No.

166. United States v. Place, 462 U.S. 696, 103 S.Ct. 2637, 77 L.Ed.2d 110 (1983) (unlawful seizure of suitcase at airport tainted subsequent narcotics dog alert on suitcase and rendered invalid a search warrant for the suitcase based on the alert); see City of Indianapolis v. Edmond, 531 U.S. 32, 121 S.Ct. 447, 148 L.Ed.2d 333 (2000) (traffic checkpoint program to discover and interdict contraband narcotics, in which narcotic dogs were used to detect presence of contraband drugs in the cars stopped by the checkpoint, struck down as constituting an unreasonable seizure of the motorists' persons and their cars; narcotics dog sniff procedure arguably tainted by the preceding unreasonable seizure).

167. "In United States v. Place [citation omitted], we treated a canine sniff by a well-trained narcotics detection dog as 'sui generis' because it 'discloses only the presence or absence of narcotics, a contraband item.'" Illinois v. Caballes, 543 U.S. 405, 125 S.Ct. 834, 838, 160 L.Ed.2d 842 (2005) (car). There is some dispute, however, over whether all such dogs are that accurate. See Illinois v. Caballes, 543 U.S. 405, 125 S.Ct. 834, 839–40, 160 L.Ed.2d 842 (2005). (Souter, J. dissenting) and authorities collected. ("The infallible dog, however, is a creature of legal fiction.").

168. Illinois v. Caballes, 543 U.S. 405, 125 S.Ct. 834, 838, 160 L.Ed.2d 842 (2005).

169. "Official conduct that does not 'compromise any legitimate interest in privacy' is not a search subject to the Fourth Amendment. We have held that any interest in possessing contraband cannot be deemed 'legitimate,' and thus governmental conduct that *only* reveals the possession of contraband 'compromises no legitimate privacy interest.' This is because the expectation 'that certain facts will not come to the attention of the authorities' is not the same as an interest in 'privacy that society is prepared to consider as reasonable.'... Accordingly, the use of a well-trained narcotics detection dog — one that does not expose noncontraband items that otherwise would remain hidden from public view—during a lawful traffic stop, generally does not implicate legitimate privacy interests." Illinois v. Caballes, 543 U.S. 405, 125 S.Ct. 834, 837–38, 160 L.Ed.2d 842 (2005) (internal citations omitted) (dog sniff of car conducted during a traffic stop held not a Fourth Amendment search).

As an aside, however, it is arguably an open question whether law enforcement officials can, without reasonable suspicion, use a trained narcotics dog to smell people [or their property] who *have not been seized at all*—such as people as they walk down the public street, or in an airport, or while waiting in their vehicle for a stoplight. But see Illinois v. Caballes, 543 U.S. 405, 125 S.Ct. 834, 839, 160 L.Ed.2d 842 (2005) (Souter, J., dissenting) ("[A]n uncritical adherence to *Place* would render the Fourth Amendment indifferent to suspicionless and indiscriminate sweeps of cars in parking garages and pedestrians on sidewalks; if a sniff is not preceded by a seizure subject to Fourth Amendment notice, it escapes Fourth Amendment review entirely unless it is treated as a search.").

enter the front porch of a person's home with a drug-sniffing police dog, following which the dog sniffs the front door of the home and "alerts" thereon indicating the presence of contraband drug odors emanating therein, a Fourth Amendment "search" has occurred. This is so because such police conduct constitutes an uninvited trespassory intrusion into a constitutionally protected area, the curtilage of the person's home, to investigate the home—which satisfies the property-based definition of such a search.[170]

d. Abandoned property: "dropsy" cases

A person has no reasonable expectation of privacy and no possessory rights in property that the person has abandoned. Consequently, it is neither a Fourth Amendment search nor a Fourth Amendment seizure for a government official to take possession of abandoned property—such as papers left in a waste basket of a person's vacated hotel room,[171] or garbage left for collection on the street in front of a person's home.[172] Another classic example of abandoned property is a suspect's discard of contraband drugs while fleeing from the police.[173] On the other hand, if a person attempts to conceal his property from police inspection by hiding it directly behind him, no abandonment of the property has taken place.[174]

---

170. "We consider whether using a drug-sniffing dog on a homeowner's porch to investigate the contents of the home is a 'search' within the meaning of the Fourth Amendment. * * *

The [Fourth] Amendment establishes a simple baseline, one that for much of our history formed the exclusive basis for its protections. When 'the Government obtains information by physically intruding' on persons, houses, papers or effects, a 'search within the original meaning of the Fourth Amendment' has 'undoubtedly occurred.' By reason of our decision in Katz v. United States ... 'property rights are not the sole measure of Fourth Amendment violations'—but though Katz may add to the baseline, it does not subtract anything from the Amendment's protections 'when the Government *does* engage in [a] physical intrusion of a constitutionally protected area.'

That principle renders this case a straightforward one. The officers were gathering information in an area belonging to Jardines and immediately surrounding his house—in the curtilage of the house, which we have held enjoys protection as part of the home itself. And they gathered that information by physically entering and occupying the area to engage in conduct not explicitly or implicitly permitted by the owner. * * *

The government's use of trained police dogs to investigate the home and its immediate surroundings is a 'search' within the meaning of the Fourth Amendment." Florida v. Jardines, 569 U.S. ___, 133 S.Ct. 1409, 185 L.Ed.2d 495, 500–01 (2013) (internal citations omitted) (decided under the recently-revived trespass test for a Fourth Amendment search).

171. Abel v. United States, 362 U.S. 217, 80 S.Ct. 683, 4 L.Ed.2d 668 (1960).

172. California v. Greenwood, 486 U.S. 35, 108 S.Ct. 1625, 100 L.Ed.2d 30 (1988).

173. California v. Hodari D., 499 U.S. 621, 111 S.Ct. 1547, 113 L.Ed.2d 690 (1991).

174. Smith v. Ohio, 494 U.S. 541, 110 S.Ct.1288, 108 L.Ed.2d 464, 468 (1990) ("[A] citizen who attempts to protect his property from inspection, after throwing it on a car to respond to a police officer's inquiry, clearly has not abandoned that property."). For lower court cases on the issue of abandonment, see "Searches and Seizures" §§ 15, 28 West Key Nos.

Subpart B

The "Unreasonableness Requirement"

Introductory Note

If the threshold "Standing Requirement" for a Fourth Amendment violation is met in a given case, one or more Fourth Amendment searches or seizures have necessarily taken place—that is, there has been a search or seizure of the complaining party's person, house, papers or effects conducted by an agent of the government. In order to constitute a Fourth Amendment violation, however, it is essential that a second Fourth Amendment requirement be met as to at least one of these searches or seizures. This requirement is that the search or seizure in question must be "unreasonable." There is, in turn, a complex set of rules for making this determination—depending on whether we are dealing with a Fourth Amendment *seizure* of a person or property, or a Fourth Amendment *search* of a person or property. We are now at the heart of Fourth Amendment law.

Generally speaking, the courts focus on the *initial* Fourth Amendment intrusion in the case—whether it be a search or a seizure—and determine whether this intrusion is "unreasonable" in the Fourth Amendment sense. If determined to be "unreasonable," the fruits of this search or seizure will generally be tainted and rendered inadmissible in evidence—although not always—under the *Weeks-Mapp* exclusionary rule to be discussed in Chapter 17 of this work.

On the other hand, if determined to be "reasonable," it is then essential to examine the successive searches or seizures in the case, if any, to determine whether these intrusions are also "reasonable" in the Fourth Amendment sense. If all such searches or seizures are "reasonable," the fruits thereof will, of course, be admissible in evidence. But if any one of these intrusions is determined to be "unreasonable," the fruits thereof will generally be tainted and rendered inadmissible in evidence—although not always—under the *Weeks-Mapp* exclusionary rule.

In Chapter 11, we will first examine the general rules and principles of Fourth Amendment unreasonableness applicable to both searches and seizures. In Chapter 12, we will turn to Fourth Amendment *seizures* of persons and property and explore the "unreasonableness" rules that govern these intrusions. Finally in Chapter 13–16, we will examine Fourth Amendment *searches* of private property, and explore the "unreasonableness" rules that govern these intrusions—depending on whether the searches are conducted with or without a warrant.

Chapter 11

General Rules and Principles of Unreasonableness

Section 1. Search Warrant Requirement Rule

In a long line of decisions stretching back three quarters of a century, the U.S. Supreme Court has repeatedly announced a fundamental rule of Fourth Amendment jurisprudence: the search warrant requirement rule. Subject to important exceptions, a search of private premises, particularly a home, must be conducted pursuant to a search warrant issued by a neutral and detached magistrate in compliance with the Warrants Clause of the Fourth Amendment; presumptively, a search of private premises conducted without such a warrant is considered unreasonable, and the burden of proof is on the government to establish an exception to this rule.[1]

1. See, e.g., Agnello v. United States, 269 U.S. 20, 32–33, 46 S.Ct. 4, 70 L.Ed. 145, 149 (1925) ("Save in certain cases as incident to an arrest, there is no sanction in the decisions of the courts, Federal or state, for the search of a private dwelling house without a warrant. Absence of any judicial approval is persuasive authority that it is unlawful.");

United States v. Lefkowitz, 285 U.S. 452, 464, 52 S.Ct. 420, 76 L.Ed. 877, 882 (1932) ("Indeed, the informed and deliberate determinations of magistrates empowered to issue warrants as to what searches and seizures are permissible under the Constitution are to be preferred over the hurried action of officers and others who may happen to make arrests.");

Trupiano v. United States, 334 U.S. 699, 705, 68 S.Ct. 1229, 92 L.Ed. 1663, 1669 (1948) ("It is a cardinal rule that, in seizing goods and articles, law enforcement agents must secure and use a search warrant whenever reasonably practicable.");

McDonald v. United States, 335 U.S. 451, 455, 69 S.Ct. 191, 93 L.Ed. 153, 158 (1948) ("The presence of a search warrant serves a high function. Absent some grave emergency, the Fourth Amendment has interposed a magistrate between the citizen and the police. This was done not to shield criminals nor to make the home a safe haven for illegal activities. It was done so that an objective mind might weigh the need to invade that privacy in order to enforce the law. The right of privacy was deemed too precious to entrust to the discretion of those whose job is the detection of crime and the arrest of criminals. Power is a heady thing; and history shows that the police acting on their own cannot be trusted. We cannot be true to that constitutional requirement and excuse the absence of a warrant without a showing by those who seek exemption from the constitutional mandate that the exigencies of the situation made that course imperative.");

United States v. Jeffers, 342 U.S. 48, 51, 72 S.Ct. 93, 96 L.Ed. 59, 64 (1951) ("Over and again this Court has emphasized that the mandate of the [Fourth] Amendment requires adherence to judicial processes. Only where incident to a valid arrest, or in 'exceptional circumstances' may an exemption lie and then the burden is on those seeking the exemption to show the need for it.") (citations omitted);

Terry v. Ohio, 392 U.S. 1, 20, 88 S.Ct. 1868, 20 L.Ed.2d 889, 905 (1968) ("We do not retreat from our holdings that the police must, whenever practicable, obtain advance judicial approval of searches and seizures through the warrant procedure, or that in most instances failure to comply with the warrant requirement can only be excused by exigent circumstances.") (citations omitted);

Coolidge v. New Hampshire, 403 U.S. 443, 91 S.Ct. 2022, 29 L.Ed.2d 564, 576 (1971) ("Thus the most basic constitutional rule in this area is that 'searches conducted outside the judicial process, without prior approval by judge or magistrate, are per se unreasonable under the Fourth Amendment—subject only to a few specifically established and well-delineated exceptions.' The exceptions are 'jealously and carefully drawn,' and there must be 'a showing by those who seek exception ... that the exigencies of the situation made that course imperative.' 'The burden is on those seeking the exemption to show the need for it.'") (internal citations omitted);

Schneckloth v. Bustamonte, 412 U.S. 218, 93 S.Ct. 2041, 36 L.Ed.2d 854, 858 (1973) ("It is settled under the Fourth and Fourteenth Amendments that a search conducted without a warrant issued upon probable cause is 'per se unreasonable ... subject only to a few specifically established and well-delineated exceptions.'") (citation omitted);

Franks v. Delaware, 438 U.S. 154, 164, 98 S.Ct. 2674, 57 L.Ed.2d 667, 677 (1978) ("The bulwark of Fourth Amendment protection, of course, is the Warrants Clause, requiring that, absent certain exceptions, police obtain a warrant before embarking upon a search.");

Torres v. Puerto Rico, 442 U.S. 465, 471, 99 S.Ct. 2425, 61 L.Ed.2d 1, 8 (1979) ("[A] warrant is normally a prerequisite to a search unless exigent circumstances make compliance with this requirement impossible.");

Arkansas v. Sanders, 442 U.S. 753, 758, 99 S.Ct. 2586, 61 L.Ed.2d 235, 241 (1979) ("[T]his Court has interpreted the [Fourth Amendment] to include the requirement that normally searches of private property be performed pursuant to a search warrant issued in compliance with the Warrants Clause [of the Fourth Amendment]. In the ordinary case, therefore, a search of private property must be both reasonable and pursuant to a properly issued search warrant.") (internal citations omitted);

Steagald v. United States, 451 U.S. 204, 101 S.Ct. 1642, 68 L.Ed.2d 38,45 (1981), quoting from Payton v. New York, 445 U.S. 573, 100 S.Ct. 1371, 63 L.Ed.2d 639, 653 (1980) ("Except in such special situations [exigent circumstances or consent], we have consistently held that the entry into a home to conduct a search or make an arrest is unreasonable under the Fourth Amendment unless done pursuant to a warrant. Thus, we recently observed: 'In terms that apply equally to seizures of property and to seizures of persons, the Fourth Amendment has drawn a firm line at the entrance to the house. Absent exigent circumstances, that threshold may not reasonably be crossed without a warrant.'") (citation omitted);

Robbins v. California, 453 U.S. 420, 423 101 S.Ct. 2841, 69 L.Ed.2d 744, 748–49 (1981) ("This Court has held that a search is per se unreasonable, and thus violates the Fourth Amendment, if the police making the search have not first secured from a neutral magistrate a warrant that satisfies the terms of the Warrant Clause of the Fourth Amendment. Although the Court has identified exceptions to this warrant requirement, the exceptions are 'few,' 'specifically established,' and 'well-delineated.'") (citations omitted);

New York v. Belton, 453 U.S. 454, 457, 101 S.Ct. 2860, 69 L.Ed.2d 768, 773 (1981) ("It is a first principle of Fourth Amendment jurisprudence that the police may not conduct a search unless they first convince a neutral magistrate that there is probable cause to do so. This Court has recognized, however, that 'the exigencies of the situation' may sometimes make exception from the warrant requirement 'imperative.'") (citation omitted);

Welsh v. Wisconsin, 466 U.S. 740, 104 S.Ct. 2091, 80 L.Ed.2d 732, 742 (1984) ("It is not surprising, therefore, that the Court has recognized, 'as a basic principle of Fourth Amendment law,' that searches and seizures inside a home without a warrant are presumptively unreasonable.'") (citation omitted);

United States v. Karo, 468 U.S. 705, 104 S.Ct. 3296, 82 L.Ed.2d 530, 542–43 (1984) ("Warrantless searches are presumptively unreasonable, though the Court has recognized a few limited exceptions to this general rule.");

California v. Carney, 471 U.S. 386, 390–91, 105 S.Ct. 2066, 85 L.Ed.2d 406, (1985) ("This fundamental [Fourth Amendment] right is preserved by a requirement that searches be conducted pursuant to a warrant issued by an independent judicial officer.");

Skinner v. Railway Labor Executives' Ass'n., 489 U.S. 602, 109 S.Ct 1402, 103 L.Ed.2d 639, 661 (1989) ("Except in certain well-defined circumstances, a search or seizure ... is not reasonable unless it is accomplished pursuant to a judicial warrant issued by probable cause.");

National Treasury Employees Union v. Von Raab, 489 U.S. 656, 109 S.Ct. 1384, 103 L.Ed.2d 685 (1989) ("[W]e have often emphasized, and reiterate today, that a search must be supported, as a general matter, by a warrant issued upon probable cause....");

California v. Acevedo, 500 U.S. 565, 111 S.Ct. 1982, 114 L.Ed.2d 619, 634 (1991) ("It remains a

One of the classic formulations of the search warrant requirement rule is stated in *Katz v. United States*:[2]

> Searches conducted without warrants have been held unlawful "notwithstanding facts unquestionably showing probable cause," for the Constitution requires "that

---

'cardinal principle that searches conducted outside the judicial process, without prior approval of judge or magistrate, are per se unreasonable under the Fourth Amendment—subject only to a few specifically established and well-delineated exceptions.'") (citations omitted);

Vernonia School District 47J v. Acton, 515 U.S. 646, 115 S.Ct. 2386, 132 L.Ed.2d 564, 574 (1995) ("Where a search is undertaken by law enforcement to discover evidence of criminal wrongdoing, this Court has said that reasonableness generally requires the obtaining of a judicial warrant.");

Flippo v. West Virginia, 528 U.S. 11, 120 S.Ct. 7, 145 L.Ed.2d 16, 19 (1999) ("A warrantless search by the police is invalid unless it falls within one of the narrow exceptions to the warrant requirement, Katz v. United States,..., none of which the trial court invoked here.");

Maryland v. Dyson, 527 U.S. 465, 119 S.Ct. 2013, 144 L.Ed.2d 442, 445 (1999) ("The Fourth Amendment generally requires police to secure a warrant before conducting a search.");

Brigham City v. Stuart, 547 U.S. 398, 126 S.Ct. 1943, 1947, 164 L.Ed.2d 650 (2006) ("It is a basic principle of Fourth Amendment law that searches and seizures inside a home without a warrant are presumptively unreasonable.") (citation and internal quotation omitted);

Arizona v. Gant, 556 U.S. 322, 129 S.Ct. 1710, 1716, 173 L.Ed.2d 485 (2009) ("Consistent with our precedent, our analysis begins, as it should in every case addressing the reasonableness of a warrantless search, with the basic rule that 'searches conducted outside the judicial process, without prior approval of judge or magistrate, are *per se* unreasonable under the Fourth Amendment—subject only to a few specifically established and well delineated exceptions.' [citation omitted]") ;

Kentucky v. King, 563 U.S. ___, 131 S.Ct. 1849, 1856 179 L.Ed.2d 865(2011) ("Although the text of the Fourth Amendment does not specify when a search warrant must be obtained, this Court has inferred that a warrant must generally be secured. It is a 'basic principle of Fourth Amendment law' we have often said 'that searches and seizures inside a home without a warrant are presumptively unreasonable.' (citations omitted)."

See also United States v. United States District Court, 407 U.S. 297, 92 S.Ct. 2125, 32 L.Ed.2d 752, 765 (1972); Chimel v. California, 395 U.S. 752, 89 S.Ct 2034, 23 L.Ed.2d 685 (1969); Jones v. United States, 357 U.S. 493, 497–98, 78 S.Ct. 1253, 2 L.Ed.2d 1514, 1518–19 (1958); Chapman v. United States, 365 U.S. 610, 613–15, 81 S.Ct. 776, 5 L.Ed.2d 828, 831–32 (1961); Stoner v. California, 376 U.S. 483, 486, 84 S.Ct. 889, 11 L.Ed.2d 856, 859 (1964); Aguilar v. Texas, 378 U.S. 108, 110–11, 84 S.Ct. 1509, 12 L.Ed.2d 723, 726 (1964); United States v. Ventresca, 380 U.S. 102, 106–07, 85 S.Ct. 741, 13 L.Ed.2d 684, 687–88 (1965); Vale v. Louisiana, 399 U.S. 30, 90 S.Ct. 1969, 26 L.Ed.2d 409, 413 (1970); Wyman v. James, 400 U.S. 309, 91 S.Ct. 381, 27 L.Ed.2d 408, 413 (1971); Johnson v. United States, 333 U.S. 10, 13–14, 68 S.Ct. 367, 92 L.Ed. 436, 440 (1948).

See also Chapter 12, Section 2a&b of this work for a discussion of the warrant requirement for the *seizure* of personal property and the exceptions thereto. Illinois v. McArthur, 531 U.S. 326, 121 S.Ct. 946,148 L.Ed.2d 838, 847 (2001), quoting from United States v. Place, 462 U.S. 696, 701, 103 S.Ct. 2637, 77 L.Ed.2d 110, 116–17 (1983). ("In order to enforce that [Fourth Amendment] requirement [of reasonableness], this Court has interpreted the Amendment as establishing rules and presumptions designed to control law enforcement officers that may significantly intrude upon privacy interests. Sometimes those rules require warrants. We have said, for example, that in 'the ordinary case,' seizures of personal property are 'unreasonable within the meaning of the Fourth Amendment,' without more, 'unless ... accomplished pursuant to a judicial warrant,' issued by a neutral magistrate after finding probable cause. We nonetheless have made it clear that there are exceptions to the warrant requirement."

2. 389 U.S. 347, 357, 88 S.Ct. 507, 19 L.Ed.2d 576, 585 (1967) (internal and footnoted citations omitted). This formulation of the rule has been quoted with approval in the following cases: Arizona v. Gant, 556 U.S. 322, 129 S.Ct. 1710, 1716, 173 L.Ed.2d 485 (2006); Minnesota v. Dickerson, 508 U.S. 366, 113 S.Ct. 2130, 124 L.Ed.2d 334, 343–44 (1993); California v. Acevedo, 500 U.S. 565, 111 S.Ct. 1982, 114 L.Ed. 2d 619, 634 (1991); Horton v. California, 496 U.S. 128, 110 S.Ct. 2301, 110 L.Ed. 112, 120 n. 4 (1990); Colorado v. Bannister, 449 U.S. 1, 2, 101 S.Ct. 42, 66 L.Ed.2d 1, 3 (1980); Thompson v. Louisiana, 469 U.S. 17, 105 S.Ct. 409, 83 L.Ed.2d 246, 250 (1984); Mincey v. Arizona, 437 U.S. 385, 390, 98 S.Ct. 2408, 57 L.Ed.2d 290, 298–99 (1978).

> the deliberate, impartial judgment of a judicial officer be interposed between the citizen and the police...." "Over and again this Court has emphasized that the mandate of the [Fourth] Amendment requires adherence to judicial processes," and that searches conducted outside the judicial process, without prior approval by judge or magistrate, are per se unreasonable under the Fourth Amendment—subject only to a few specifically established and well-delineated exceptions.

Another formulation of the rule is stated in *Camara v. Municipal Court*:[3]

> Though there has been general agreement as to the fundamental purpose of the Fourth Amendment, translation of the abstract prohibition against "unreasonable searches and seizures" into workable guidelines for the decision of particular cases is a difficult task which has for many years divided the members of this Court. Nevertheless, one governing principle, justified by history and by current experience, has been consistently followed: except in carefully defined classes of cases, a search of private property without proper consent is unreasonable unless it has been authorized by a valid search warrant.

In accord with this rule, the Court has long held that, subject to certain exceptions, a search of a dwelling house is unreasonable under the Fourth Amendment when conducted without a search warrant, even when there is probable cause to search the house, as this determination should generally be made by a magistrate and not a law enforcement officer.[4] This rule, in turn, applies as well when the purpose of the search is to arrest an individual in a private dwelling—as opposed to seizing an article of property therein.[5] The rule, however, has no application when the arrest is made outside the home, as such an arrest may be made without a warrant.[6] And in dozens of cases decided over the years, the Court

3. 387 U.S. 523, 528–29, 87 S.Ct.1727, 18 L.Ed.2d 930, 935 (1967). This formulation of the rule has been quoted with approval in the following cases: Mancusi v. DeForte, 392 U.S. 364, 88 S.Ct. 2120, 20 L.Ed.2d 1154, 1161 (1968); G.M. Leasing Corp. v. United States, 429 U.S. 338, 97 S.Ct. 619, 50 L.Ed.2d 530, 543 (1977); Michigan v. Tyler, 436 U.S. 499, 506, 98 S.Ct. 1942, 56 L.Ed.2d 486 (1978); Marshall v. Barlow's Inc., 436 U.S. 307, 312, 98 S.Ct. 1816, 56 L.Ed.2d 305, 311 (1978); Massachusetts v. Sheppard, 468 U.S. 981, 104 S.Ct. 3424, 82 L.Ed.2d 737, 743 n.5 (); Groh v. Ramirez, 540 U.S. 551, 124 S.Ct. 1284, 157 L.Ed.2d 1068, 1080 (2004), quoting from Massachusetts v. Sheppard, supra.

4. "Belief, however well-founded, that an article sought is concealed in a dwelling house, furnishes no justification for a search of that place without a warrant." Agnello v. United States, 269 U.S. 20, 33, 46 S.Ct. 4, 70 L.Ed. 145 (1925). "It is settled doctrine that probable cause for belief that certain articles subject to seizure are in a dwelling cannot of itself justify a search without a warrant. (citations omitted). The decisions of this Court have time and again underscored the essential purpose of the Fourth Amendment to shield the citizen from unwarranted intrusions into his privacy. (citations omitted). This purpose is realized by Rule 41 of the Federal Rules of Criminal Procedure, which implements the Fourth Amendment by requiring that an impartial magistrate determine from an affidavit showing probable cause whether information possessed by law-enforcement officers justifies the issuance of a search warrant. Were federal officers free to search without a warrant merely upon probable cause to believe that certain articles are within a home, the provisions of the Fourth Amendment would become empty phrases, and the protection it affords largely nullified." Jones v. United States, 357 U.S. 493, 497–98, 78 S.Ct. 1253, 2 L.Ed.2d 1514, 1518–19 (1958); see also Chapman v. United States, 365 U.S. 610, 613, 81 S.Ct. 776, 5 L.Ed.2d 828, 831 (1961). For a discussion of searches of dwelling houses generally, see Chapter 16, Section 1 of this work.

5. Payton v. New York, 445 U.S. 573, 100 S.Ct. 1371, 63 L.Ed.2d 639 (1980 (entry into defendant's home to arrest defendant; warrant required); Steagald v. United States, 451 U.S. 204, 101 S.Ct. 1642, 68 L.Ed.2d 38 (1981) (entry into defendant's home to arrest a third party; warrant required); see also Kirk v. Louisiana, 536 U.S. 635, 122 S.Ct. 2458, 153 L.Ed.2d 599 (2002).

6. United States v. Watson, 423 U.S. 411, 96 S.Ct. 820, 46 L.Ed.2d 598 (1976).

has struck down searches of dwelling houses and other fixed premises because no search warrant was obtained where no exception to the search warrant requirement rule was applicable.[7]

In addition, the search warrant requirement rule is not confined to homes and other fixed premises. The Court has also struck down searches of containers, such as a footlocker or suitcase, for lack of a search warrant.[8] An identical result has been reached as to the warrantless electronic interception of certain private conversations,[9] as well as the warrantless viewing or warrantless seizure of an alleged obscene film.[10] A search warrant is also generally required to search first class mail.[11]

---

7. See, e.g., Agnello v. United States, 269 U.S. 20, 46 S.Ct.4, 70 L.Ed. 145 (1925) (search of dwelling house); Go-Bart Importing Co. v. United States, 282 U.S. 344, 51 S.Ct. 153, 75 L.Ed. 374 (1931) (search of business office); United States v. Lefkowitz, 285 U.S. 452, 52 S.Ct. 420, 76 L.Ed. 877 (1932)(search of business room); Taylor v. United States, 286 U.S. 1, 52 S.Ct. 466, 76 L.Ed. 951 (1932)(search of garage adjacent to dwelling house); Johnson v. United States, 333 U.S. 10, 68 S.Ct. 367, 92 L.Ed. 436 (1948) (search of hotel room); Trupiano v. United States, 334 U.S. 699, 68 S.Ct.1229, 92 L.Ed. 1663 (1948)(search of barn); McDonald v. United States, 335 U.S. 451, 69 S.Ct.191, 93 L.Ed. 153 (1948) (search of room in rooming house); Jones v. United States, 357 U.S. 493, 78 S.Ct.1253, 2 L.Ed.2d 1514 (1958)(search of dwelling house); Chapman v. United States, 365 U.S. 610, 81 S.Ct. 776, 5 L.Ed.2d 828 (1961)(search of rented dwelling house); Camara v. Municipal Court, 387 U.S. 523, 87 S.Ct. 1727, 18 L.Ed.2d 930 (1967) (search of dwelling house); See v. City of Seattle, 387 U.S. 541, 87 S.Ct. 1737, 18 L.Ed.2d 943 (1967) (search of commercial warehouse); Mancusi v. DeForte, 392 U.S. 364, 88 S.Ct. 2120, 20 L.Ed.2d 1154 (1968) (search of union business office); Vale v. Louisiana, 399 U.S. 30, 90 S.Ct. 1969, 26 L.Ed.2d 409 (1970) (search of dwelling house); Payton v. New York, 445 U.S. 573, 100 S.Ct. 1371, 63 L.Ed.2d 639 (1980) (search of apartment-dwelling house); Steagald v. United States, 451 U.S. 204, 101 S.Ct. 1642, 68 L.Ed.2d 38 (1981) (search of dwelling house); Welsh v. Wisconsin, 466 U.S. 740, 104 S.Ct. 2091, 80 L.Ed.2d 732 (1984) (search of dwelling house); Thompson v. Louisiana, 469 U.S. 17, 105 S.Ct. 409, 83 L.Ed.2d 246 (1984) (search of dwelling house).

"The warrant requirement has been a valued part of our constitutional law for decades, and it has determined the result in scores and scores of cases in courts all over this country." Coolidge v. New Hampshire, 403 U.S. 443, 481, 91 S.Ct. 2022, 29 L.Ed.2d 564, 592 (1971), quoted with approval in United States v. United States District Court, 407 U.S. 297, 315, 92 S.Ct. 2125, 32 L.Ed.2d 752, 765 (1972).

8. United States v. Chadwick, 433 U.S. 1, 7–11, 97 S.Ct. 2476, 53 L.Ed.2d 538, 545–48 (1977), as further explained in United States v. Ross, 456 U.S. 798, 810–11, 102 S.Ct. 2157, 72 L.Ed.2d 572, 585 (1982) (footlocker); Arkansas v. Sanders, 442 U.S. 753, 99 S.Ct. 2586, 61 L.Ed.2d 235 (1979) (suitcase); see also Bond v. United States, 529 U.S. 334, 120 S.Ct. 1462, 146 L.Ed.2d 365 (2000) (federal agent's physical manipulation of bus traveler's carry-on canvas bag held a Fourth Amendment search; no exception, including consent, shown to search warrant requirement rule; "[w]e therefore hold that the agent's physical manipulation of petitioner's bag violated the Fourth Amendment." 146 L.Ed.2d at 370).

9. United States v. United States District Court, 407 U.S. 297, 92 S.Ct. 2125, 32 L.Ed.2d 752 (1972) (electronic interception of private conversations in a home); Alderman v. United States, 394 U.S. 165, 89 S.Ct. 961, 22 L.Ed.2d 176 (1969) (same); Katz v. United States, 389 U.S. 347, 88 S.Ct. 507, 19 L.Ed.2d 576 (1967) (electronic interception of conversation in a public telephone booth).

10. Walter v. United States, 447 U.S. 649, 100 S.Ct. 2395, 65 L.Ed.2d 410 (1980) (film viewed after being turned over to federal agents by a private party); Roaden v. Kentucky, 413 U.S. 496, 93 S.Ct. 2796, 37 L.Ed. 2d 757 (1973) (film seized after state agents viewed film in a public theater).

11. United States v. Van Leeuwen, 397 U.S. 249, 90 S.Ct. 1029, 25 L.Ed.2d 282 (1970) (search upheld of two first class mail packages with a warrant after a 29 hour detention of same pending the issuance of said warrant); In re Jackson, 96 U.S. (6 Otto) 727, 733, 24 L.Ed. 877, 879 (1877) ("The constitutional guaranty of the right of the people to be secure in their papers against unreasonable searches and seizures extends to their papers, thus closed against inspection, wherever they may be. Whilst in the mail, they [letters and sealed packages] can only be opened and examined under like warrant, issued upon similar oath or affirmation, particularly describing the thing to be seized, as is required when papers are subjected to search in one's own household.").

On the other hand, the Court has held that a search warrant is not required for a fully operational automobile on the street because of the latter's extreme mobility and reduced expectation of privacy therein.[12] Where, however, the automobile is not really mobile based on all the circumstances, it has been held that a search of such an automobile, although based on probable cause, was unreasonable for lack of a valid search warrant.[13] Moreover, there are no cases requiring a search warrant for the routine search of a person—although a warrant or court order is required, as a general rule, for serious surgical penetrations of the body to obtain evidence, such as a bullet.[14]

The search warrant requirement rule—which has a long history and has survived both "liberal" and "conservative" Courts in the post-World War II era—is in full accord with the original understanding of the Framers of the Fourth Amendment. This factor no doubt accounts for both the rule's origin and its longevity. As previously shown, one of the major purposes of the Fourth Amendment was to end the abuse of general exploratory searches and seizures wrought by the general writs of assistance regime by constitutionalizing the special writs or special warrants practice of the English common law.[15] Under this practice as understood by the Framers, a search of private premises, particularly a home, required a warrant issued by a magistrate based on proof of wrongdoing and particularly describing the place to be searched and the things to be seized. The search warrant requirement rule fully comports with this original understanding by generally requiring a warrant for such private premises—subject to certain recognized exceptions that the Framers implicitly accepted as part of the English common law, or that are not otherwise inconsistent with the Framer's fundamental vision for the Amendment. A number of these exceptions have been established by the Court over the years, especially in recent years where the purpose of the search has *not* been to discover proof of criminal wrongdoing, but to serve some other aim beyond the normal needs of law enforcement. All of these exceptions will be examined in Chapters 14 and 15 of this work.[16]

---

12. Maryland v. Dyson, 527 U.S. 465, 119 S.Ct. 2013, 144 L.Ed.2d 442 (1999) (warrantless search upheld based on probable cause); Pennsylvania v. Labron, 518 U.S. 938, 116 S.Ct. 2485, 135 L.Ed.2d 1031 (1996) (same). For a discussion of the moving vehicle exception to the search warrant requirement rule, see Chapter 14, Section 4 of this work.

13. Coolidge v. New Hampshire, 403 U.S. 443, 458–64, 91 S.Ct. 2022, 29 L.Ed.2d 564, 578–81 (1971) (Court struck down the search, based on probable cause, of an automobile for lack of a valid search warrant where (a) the automobile was located at the suspect's home; and (b) the suspect, who had been cooperative with police in the past with respect to the murder being investigated, and his wife were removed by police from the scene). "Neither Carroll, supra, nor other cases in this Court require or suggest that in every conceivable circumstance the search of an auto even with probable cause may be made without the extra protection for privacy that a warrant affords." Chambers v. Maroney, 399 U.S. 42, 50, 90 S.Ct. 1975, 26 L.Ed.2d 419, 428 (1970).

14. See, e.g., Winston v. Lee, 470 U.S. 753, 105 S.Ct. 1611, 84 L.Ed.2d 662 (1985) (court order obtained to remove a bullet from defendant's body; order struck down because the proposed surgery was arguably risky and the government's need for the bullet as evidence was not compelling); see also: Schmerber v. California, 384 U.S. 757, 770, 86 S.Ct. 1826, 16 L.Ed.2d 908, 919 (1966) (search warrant requirement rule recognized, but an exigent circumstance exception found for obtaining a blood sample from defendant's body in a DUI case).

15. See Chapter 6, Section 2 of this work.

16. Justices Scalia and Thomas have questioned the viability of the search warrant requirement rule in view of the large number of exceptions thereto. California v. Acevedo, 500 U.S. 565, 111 S.Ct. 1982, 114 L.Ed.2d 619, 635–37 (1991) (Scalia, J. concurring); Groh v. Ramirez, 540 U.S. 551, 124 S.Ct. 1284, 1298, 157 L.Ed.2d 1068 (2004) (Thomas, J. dissenting).

In particular, Justice Scalia has stated that the reasonableness requirement of the Fourth Amendment should "afford[] the protection that the common law afforded" when the Amendment was adopted, which would include "the requirement of a warrant, where the common law required a warrant...." California v. Acevedo, 114 L.Ed.2d at 636 (Scalia, J. concurring). Presumably, this would limit the

The warrant procedure undertaken by a neutral and detached magistrate serves two very important functions that the Framers no doubt felt vital to protect a deeply felt sense of privacy in their homes and businesses. First, the scrutiny by an independent magistrate is intended to eliminate altogether searches not based on probable cause, thus protecting the people from overzealous officers; second, for those searches deemed necessary as based on probable cause, the independent magistrate's oversight is intended to limit the search to a particular place for particular things, thus avoiding the evil of general exploratory searches that the Framers intended to end.[17] Beyond that, when and if a search is ordered, the use of a warrant assures the individual whose property is being searched that an independent magistrate has authorized this search pursuant to established law and has narrowly limited its objectives and scope—thus reducing the perception that the intrusion is merely the random and arbitrary act of a government agent.[18] The classic rationale for the search warrant requirement rule is stated by Justice Jackson in *Johnson v. United States*:[19]

> The point of the Fourth Amendment, which is not often grasped by zealous officers, is not that it denies law enforcement the support of the usual inferences that reasonable men draw from evidence. Its protection consists in requiring that those inferences be drawn by a neutral and detached magistrate instead of being judged by the officer engaged in the often competitive enterprise of ferreting out crime. Any assumption that evidence sufficient to support a magistrate's disinterested determination to issue a search warrant will justify the officers in making a search without a warrant would reduce the Amendment to a nullity and leave the people's homes secure only in the discretion of police officers.

Section 2. General Definition of "Unreasonableness": Balancing Test

The U.S. Supreme Court uses a balancing-test definition of Fourth Amendment unreasonableness when deciding, as a matter of first impression, the reasonableness of a Fourth Amendment intrusion conducted without a warrant. When dealing with such a search, the Court often creates a new exception to the search warrant requirement rule—even dispensing, at times, with both a warrant and any proof of individualized wrongdoing. When dealing with a seizure, especially where it is the initial Fourth Amendment intrusion, a warrant is rarely required and the inquiry is whether to dispense with the probable cause requirement or with any proof of individualized wrongdoing.

Under this test, the Court balances: (1) the nature or degree of the intrusiveness of the governmental invasion into personal privacy or personal security represented by the

---

search warrant requirement rule to private premises such as homes, businesses, vessels, or other houses which required a search warrant for stolen goods at common law [at least as understood by the Founding era Framers]—but would be inapplicable to searches conducted outside such premises, which are currently considered exceptions to the rule.

On the other hand, Justice Thomas has stated that "it is possible that neither the history of the Fourth Amendment nor the common law provides much guidance" in determining whether a search warrant requirement rule is constitutionally required. Groh v. Ramirez, 157 L.Ed.2d at 1088.

17. Coolidge v. New Hampshire, 403 U.S. 443, 467, 91 S.Ct. 2022, 29 L.Ed.2d 564, 583 (1971).

18. Skinner v. Railway Labor Executives' Ass'n., 489 U.S. 602, 109 S.Ct.1402, 103 L.Ed.2d 639, 663 (1989); Illinois v. Gates, 462 U.S. 213, 103 S.Ct. 2317, 76 L.Ed.2d 527, 547 (1983); United States v. Chadwick, 433 U.S. 1, 9, 97 S.Ct. 2476, 53 S.Ct. 538, 547 (1977).

19. 333 U.S. 10, 13–14, 68 S.Ct. 367, 92 L.Ed. 436, 440 (1948).

search or seizure in question, as against (2) the gravity of the governmental interest served by the search or seizure. In striking the appropriate balance, the Court strives, where practicable, to avoid giving government officials the right to conduct searches or seizures at their absolute discretion—(a) by requiring some showing of individualized wrongdoing, or (b) by requiring the use of neutral criteria for conducting the intrusion, or some other like safeguard.[20] In doing so, the Court is attempting to implement one of the central purposes of the Fourth Amendment—namely, to end the abuse of general exploratory searches wrought by the general writs of assistance regime.[21]

Where a warrantless search has a criminal investigative purpose, this balance is usually struck in favor of requiring a search warrant issued in compliance with the Warrant Clause of the Fourth Amendment—except for a few carefully defined exceptions, generally based on some showing of individualized suspicion, that will be examined in Chapter 14 of this work. Where, however, special governmental needs beyond the normal need for law enforcement or other special circumstances are shown, the Court often strikes the balance in favor of dispensing with a warrant—and, at times, dispensing as well with a probable cause requirement, or even any showing of individualized wrongdoing.[22] In doing so, the

---

20. For a thorough discussion of the balancing-of-the-interests approach to Fourth Amendment decision-making, see Chapter 7, Section 3 of this work. "The essential purpose of the proscriptions of the Fourth Amendment is to impose a standard of 'reasonableness' upon the exercise of discretion of government agents, including law enforcement agents, in order to 'safeguard the privacy and security of individuals against arbitrary invasions.' Thus the permissibility of a particular law enforcement practice is judged by balancing its intrusion on the individual's Fourth Amendment interests against its promotion of legitimate governmental interests. Implemented in this manner, the reasonableness standard usually requires, at a minimum, that the facts upon which an intrusion is based be capable of measurement against an 'objective standard,' whether by probable cause or a less stringent test. In those situations in which the balance of interests precludes insistence upon some level of individualized suspicion, other safeguards are generally relied upon to assure that the individual's reasonable expectation of privacy is not 'subject to the discretion of the official in the field.'" Delaware v. Prouse, 440 U.S. 648, 653–54, 99 S.Ct. 1391, 59 L.Ed.2d 660 (1979) (internal citations omitted) (emphasis added).

"The touchstone of our analysis under the Fourth Amendment is always 'the reasonableness in all the circumstances of the particular governmental invasion of a citizen's personal security.' Reasonableness, of course, depends 'on a balance between the public interest and the individual's right to personal security free from arbitrary interference by law officers.'" Pennsylvania v. Mimms, 434 U.S. 106, 98 S.Ct. 330, 54 L.Ed.2d 331, 335–36 (1977) (internal citations omitted) (emphasis added).

21. For a discussion of this historical purpose, see Chapter 6, Section 2 of this work.

22. "For the Fourth Amendment does not proscribe all searches and seizures, but only those that are unreasonable. What is reasonable, of course, 'depends on all the circumstances surrounding the search or seizure and the nature of the search or seizure itself.' Thus, the permissibility of a particular practice 'is judged by balancing its intrusion on the individual's Fourth Amendment interests against its promotion of legitimate governmental interests.' In most criminal cases, we strike the balance in favor of the procedures described by the Warrants Clause of the Fourth Amendment. Except in certain well-defined circumstances, a search or seizure in such a case is not reasonable unless it is accomplished pursuant to a judicial warrant issued upon probable cause. We have recognized exceptions to this rule, however, 'when special needs, beyond the normal need for law enforcement, make the warrant and probable cause requirement impracticable.' When faced with such special needs, we have not hesitated to balance the governmental and privacy interests to assess the practicality of the warrant and probable cause requirements in the particular context." Skinner v. Railway Labor Executives Ass'n, 489 U.S. 602, 109 S.Ct 1402, 103 L.Ed.2d 639, 661 (1989) (internal citations omitted) (drug testing program for railroad employees involved in train accidents upheld).

"While we have long emphasized, and reiterate today, that a search must be supported, as a general matter, by a warrant issued upon probable cause, our decision in *Railway Labor Executives* reaffirms the long-standing principle that neither a warrant nor probable cause, nor, indeed, any measure of individualized suspicion is an indispensable component of reasonableness in every circumstance. As we noted in *Railway Labor Executives*, our cases establish that where a Fourth Amendment intrusion serves special governmental needs, beyond the normal need for law enforcement, it is necessary to

Court creates civil or special needs exceptions to the search warrant requirement rule which will be examined in Chapter 15 of this work.

---

balance the individual's privacy expectations against the Government's interests to determine whether it is impracticable to require a warrant or some level of individualized suspicion in the particular context." National Treasury Employees Union v. Von Raab, 489 U.S. 656, 109 S.Ct. 1384, 103 L.Ed.2d 685, 702 (1989) (internal citations omitted) (drug testing program for U.S. Treasury agents upheld).

"Where a search is undertaken by law enforcement to discover evidence of criminal wrongdoing, this Court has said that reasonableness generally requires the obtaining of a judicial warrant. Warrants cannot be issued, of course, without the showing of probable cause required by the Warrants Clause. But a warrant is not required to establish the reasonableness of all government searches; and when a warrant is not required (and the Warrants Clause not applicable), probable cause is not invariably required either. A search unsupported by probable cause can be constitutional, we have said, 'when special needs, beyond the normal need for law enforcement, make the warrant and probable cause requirements impracticable.'" Vernonia School District 47J v. Acton, 515 U.S. 46, 115 S.Ct.2386, 132 L.Ed.2d 564,574 (1995) (internal citations omitted) (drug testing program for public high school students upheld).

"The Fourth Amendment requires that searches and seizures be reasonable. A search is generally unreasonable in the absence of individualized wrongdoing. While such suspicion is not an 'irreducible' component of reasonableness, we have recognized circumstances where the usual rule does not apply. For example, we have upheld certain regimes of suspicionless searches where the program was designed to serve 'special needs beyond the normal need for law enforcement.'" City of Indianapolis v. Edmond, 531 U.S. 32, 121 S.Ct. 447, 148 L.Ed.2d 333, 340 (2000) (internal citations omitted) (drug interdiction roadblock struck down).

"[W]e generally determine the reasonableness of a search by balancing the nature of the intrusion on the individual's privacy against the promotion of legitimate governmental interests. But we have long held that 'the Fourth Amendment imposes no irreducible requirement of [individualized] suspicion.' '[I]n certain limited circumstances, the Government's need to discover such latent or hidden conditions, or to prevent their development, is sufficiently compelling to justify the intrusion on privacy entailed by conducting such searches without any measure of individualized suspicion.' Therefore in the context of safety and administrative regulations, a search unsupported by probable cause may be reasonable 'when special needs, beyond the normal needs of law enforcement, make the warrant and probable cause requirement impracticable.'" Board of Education of Independent School District No. 92 v. Earls, 536 U.S. 822, 122 S.Ct. 2559, 2564,153 L.Ed.2d 735 (2002).

"The Fourth Amendment's proper function is to constrain, not against all intrusions as such, but against intrusions which are not justified in the circumstances, or which are made in an improper manner. As the text of the Fourth Amendment indicates, the ultimate measure of the constitutionality of a government search is reasonableness. In giving content to the inquiry whether an intrusion is reasonable, the Court has preferred some quantum of individual suspicion as a prerequisite to a constitutional search or seizure. But the Fourth Amendment imposes no irreducible quantum of individualized suspicion.

In some circumstances, such as when faced with special law enforcement needs, diminished expectations of privacy, minimal intrusions, or the like, the Court has found that certain general or individual circumstances may render a warrantless or seizure reasonable. Those circumstances diminish the need for a warrant, either because the public interest is such that neither a warrant or probable cause is required, or because an individual is already on notice, for instance, because of his employment, or the conditions of his release from government custody, that some reasonable police intrusion is to be expected. The need for a warrant is perhaps the least when the search involves no discretion that could be properly limited by the interpolation of a neutral magistrate between the citizen and the law enforcement officer. * * *

Even if a warrant is not required, a search is not beyond Fourth Amendment scrutiny; for it must be reasonable in its scope and manner of execution. Urgent government interests are not a license for indiscriminate police behavior. To say that no warrant is required is merely to acknowledge that rather than employing a per se rule of unreasonableness, we balance the privacy-related and enforcement-related concerns to determine if the intrusion is reasonable. This application of traditional standards of reasonableness requires a court to weigh the promotion of legitimate governmental interests against the degree to which the search intrudes upon individual privacy." Maryland v. King, 569 U.S. ____, 133 S.Ct. 1958, 186 L.Ed.2d 1, 20, 21 (2013) (internal citations and quotations omitted) (DNA swab of the inner cheek of lawfully arrested person during booking process upheld).

Moreover, in determining whether a given search or seizure is reasonable, the Court, with limited exceptions, has looked to objective factors surrounding the incident—not the actual state of mind of the law enforcement officer conducting the search or seizure. The test is whether a reasonably well-trained officer, under the totality of the circumstances, would have conducted the search or seizure in question—not what the officer actually believed or what his or her actual intent or motivations were.[23]

The two limited exceptions recognized to this approach has been where the officer is conducting an inventory search or an administrative inspection search. Neither search may be conducted in "bad faith" for the ulterior purpose of engaging in a general exploratory search for evidence of crime.[24]

Routinely, however, trial courts admit at least some testimony at motion to suppress hearings as to what the arresting or searching officer's actual intent or beliefs were at the time of the incident in question—arguably on the basis that such testimony is admissible as some evidence as to what reasonable officer would have done. The Court, however, has not directly spoken to this issue.

---

23. "An action is 'reasonable' under the Fourth Amendment, regardless of the individual officer's state of mind, 'as long as the circumstances, viewed *objectively,* justify [the] action.' The officer's subjective motivation is irrelevant. It therefore does not matter here—even if their subjective motives could be so neatly unraveled—whether the officers entered the kitchen to arrest respondents and gather evidence against them or to assist the injured and prevent further violence." Brigham City v. Stuart, 547 U.S.398, 126 S.Ct. 1943, 164 L.Ed. 2d 650 (2006) (internal citation omitted) (the exigent circumstances exception to the search warrant requirement rule held applicable so that police could enter a private dwelling without a warrant—regardless of the actual motivation of the officers in question).

"[A]lmost without exception in evaluating alleged violations of the Fourth Amendment[,] the Court has first undertaken an objective assessment of an officer's actions in light of the facts and the circumstances then known to him. * * * [T]he fact that the officer does not have the state of mind which is hypothecated by the reasons which provide legal justification for the officer's action does not invalidate the action taken—as long as the circumstances, viewed objectively, justify that action." Scott v. United States, 436 U.S. 128, 137–38, 98 S.Ct. 1717, 57 L.Ed.2d 1150, 178, 179 (1978)(wiretap properly minimized regardless of the intent of the listening law enforcement agent).

"We have never held outside limited contexts such as an 'inventory search or administrative inspection..., that an officer's motive invalidates objectively justifiable behavior under the Fourth Amendment.' (citations omitted). The reasons for looking to objective factors, rather than subjective intent, are clear. Legal tests based on reasonableness are generally objective, and this Court has long taken the view that 'even-handed law enforcement is best achieved by the application of objective standards of conduct, rather than standards that depend on the subjective state of mind of the officer.'" (citations omitted). Kentucky v. King, 563 U.S. ___, 131 S.Ct. 1849, 1859, 179 L.Ed.2d 865 (2011).

"We think these cases foreclose any argument that the constitutional reasonableness of traffic stops depends on the actual motivations of the individual officers involved. * * * Subjective intentions play no role in ordinary, probable cause analysis." Whren v. United States, 517 U.S. 806, 116 S.Ct. 1769, 1774, 135 L.Ed.2d 89 (1996) (traffic stop upheld for speeding based on probable cause, regardless of officer's alleged ulterior motive to obtain evidence for illegal drugs).

24. "We have never held outside limited contexts such as an 'inventory search or administrative inspection..., that an officer's motive invalidates objectively justifiable behavior under the Fourth Amendment.'" (citations omitted). Kentucky v. King, 563 U.S. ___, 131 S.Ct. 1849, 1859, 179 L.Ed..2d 865 (2011).

See Chapter 14, Section 2a(2) of this work and cases collected for inventory exception to the search warrant requirement rule. Also see Chapter 14, Section 2c(1) of this work and cases collected for the administrative inspection to the search warrant requirement rule.

Section 3. The Evidentiary Standards of Probable Cause and Reasonable Suspicion

In Fourth Amendment jurisprudence, there are two standards of individualized criminal wrongdoing that justify a variety of governmental searches and seizures having a criminal investigative purpose: (1) probable cause, and (2) reasonable suspicion. Both are flexible, non-technical principled standards, not a neat set of readily applied legal rules.[25] The term "probable cause" appears in the Warrants Clause of the Fourth Amendment; the term "reasonable suspicion" began as a legal principle in the landmark 1968 decision of *Terry v. Ohio*.[26]

A "probable cause" showing is required in order for a government official to arrest an individual,[27] to search an automobile under the *Carroll* doctrine,[28] or to effect a full-blown seizure of personal property[29]—or for a magistrate to issue a warrant for search or arrest.[30] A "reasonable suspicion" showing, on the other hand, is a more reduced evidentiary standard, and is required for lesser intrusions into personal privacy or security or where the balance of the competing interests points toward such a result. Such a showing is required when a law enforcement official temporarily detains an individual[31] or personal property[32] for a brief investigative purpose, or conducts a "sweep" of an arrestee's dwelling for dangerous persons after effecting an arrest therein,[33] or searches a public school student's person or purse,[34] or searches a probationer's home,[35] or executes a search warrant in a dwelling without announcing the officer's authority and purpose.[36] At times when the "reasonable suspicion" standard is met, the further investigation permitted thereby may develop additional facts that—in combination with the pre-Fourth Amendment intrusion facts—amount *in toto* to "probable cause" and justify a more intrusive search or seizure.

The term "probable cause"—at least in the ordinary criminal investigative context[37]—has been traditionally defined as a practical, non-technical evidentiary showing of

---

25. "Articulating precisely what 'reasonable suspicion' and 'probable cause' mean is not possible. They are commonsense, nontechnical conceptions that deal with 'the factual and practical considerations of everyday life on which reasonable and prudent men [and women], not legal technicians act.' As such, the standards are not 'readily, or even usefully, reduced to a neat set of legal rules.'" Ornelas v. United States, 517 U.S. 690, 116 S.Ct. 1657, 134 L.Ed.2d 911, 918 (1996) (internal citations omitted).

"Our cases have recognized that the concept of reasonable suspicion is somewhat abstract. But we have deliberately avoided reducing it to a "'neat set of legal rules.'" United States v. Arvizu, 534 U.S. 6, 122 S.Ct. 744, 751, 151 L.Ed.2d 740 (2002) (citation omitted).

26. 392 U.S. 1, 88 S.Ct. 1868, 20 L.Ed.2d 889 (1968)

27. See Chapter 12, Section 1e of this work.

28. See Chapter 14, Section 4a of this work.

29. See Chapter 12, Section 2b(1) of this work.

30. See Chapter 13, Section 2a of this work.

31. See Chapter 12, Section 1a of this work.

32. See Chapter 12, Section 2b(2) of this work.

33. See Chapter 14, Section 2g of this work.

34. See Chapter 15, Section 3c of this work.

35. See Chapter 15, Section 3a of this work.

36. See Chapter 13, Section 4a of this work.

37. For a discussion of the probable cause standard for search warrants issued outside the ordinary criminal investigative context, see Chapter 13, Section 2h of this work.

individualized criminal wrongdoing that amounts to more than reasonable suspicion, but less than proof beyond a reasonable doubt.[38] The term "reasonable suspicion," on the other hand, has been defined as a practical non-technical evidentiary showing of individualized criminal wrongdoing that amounts to less than probable cause and considerably less than a preponderance of the evidence, but more than an inchoate hunch.[39] Obviously, these definitions point in certain general directions, but are hardly self-executing rules.

Under both standards, however, one must be able to point to behavior or other evidence from which a reasonable person might infer *individual* criminal wrongdoing—as opposed to probable cause or reasonable suspicion of criminal wrongdoing pointing toward undetermined persons within a group of people. Moreover, this evaluation must be based on a totality of the circumstances presented to the law enforcement officer on the street; no relevant circumstance can be ignored as inconsequential in itself. Indeed, each circumstance in a series that is innocent individually may constitute probable cause or reasonable suspicion when all circumstances are considered as a whole. And this over-all view of the evidence must be assessed in a practical, non-technical sense from the standpoint of a reasonably well-trained law enforcement officer (a) who is able to make inferences that might elude an untrained person, and (b) who must often make split-second decisions on the street—as opposed to viewing the situation from the standpoint of a detached library scholar. As a result, the Court has been very lenient to law enforcement officers in applying the probable cause and reasonable suspicion standards in the real world—without, at the same time, ceding these decisions entirely to their discretion.[40]

---

38. "In dealing with probable cause, however, as the very name implies, we deal with probabilities. These are not technical; they are the factual and practical considerations of everyday life on which reasonable and prudent men, not legal technicians, act. The standard of proof is accordingly correlative to what must be proved.

'The substance of all the definitions' of probable cause 'is a reasonable ground for belief of guilt.' And this 'means less than evidence which would justify condemnation' or conviction, as Marshall, Ch.J. said for the Court more than a century ago. Since Marshall's time, at any rate, it has come to mean more than bare suspicion: Probable cause exists where 'the facts and circumstances within [the officers'] knowledge, and of which they had reasonably trustworthy information, [are] sufficient in themselves to warrant a man of reasonable caution in the belief that' an offense has been or is being committed.

These long-prevailing standards seek to safeguard citizens from rash and unreasonable interferences with privacy and from unfounded charges of crime. They also seek to give fair leeway for enforcing the law in the community's protection. Because many situations which confront officers in the course of executing their duties are more or less ambiguous, room must be allowed for some mistakes on their part. But the mistakes must be those of reasonable men, acting on facts leading sensibly to their conclusions of probability. The rule of probable cause is a practical, nontechnical conception affording the best compromise that has been found for accommodating these often opposing interests. Requiring more would unduly hamper law enforcement. To allow less would be to leave law-abiding citizens at the mercy of the officers' whim and caprice." Brinegar v. United States, 338 U.S. 160, 69 S.Ct. 1302, 93 L.Ed. 1879, 1890–91 (1949) (emphasis added) (internal citations omitted).

39. "In *Terry*, we held that an officer may, consistent with the Fourth Amendment, conduct a brief, investigatory stop when the officer has a reasonable, articulable suspicion that criminal activity is afoot. While 'reasonable suspicion' is a less demanding standard than probable cause and requires a showing considerably less than preponderance of the evidence, the Fourth Amendment requires at least a minimal level of objective justification for making the stop. The officer must be able to articulate more than an 'inchoate and unparticularized suspicion or 'hunch' of criminal activity.'" Illinois v. Wardlow, 528 U.S. 119, 120 S.Ct. 673, 145 L.Ed.2d 570, 576 (2000) (internal citations omitted).

"Although an officer's reliance on a mere 'hunch' is insufficient to justify a [temporary] stop, the likelihood of criminal activity need not rise to the level required for probable cause, and it falls considerably short of satisfying a preponderance of the evidence standard."United States v. Arvizu, 534 U.S. 266, 122 S.Ct. 744, 751, 151 L.Ed.2d 740 (2002) (citations omitted).

40. For a discussion of how the probable cause and reasonable suspicion standards have been applied in the cases involving arrests and temporary detentions in a way that is highly favorable to

law enforcement, see Chapter 12, Sections 1e and 1l of this work. Also for a similar treatment in the application of the probable cause standard in cases involving search warrants and searches of automobiles, see, respectively, Chapter 13, Section 2a & b and Chapter 14, Section 4d of this work.

Probable cause standard: "The probable cause standard is incapable of precise definition or quantification into percentages because it deals with probabilities and depends on the totality of the circumstances." Maryland v. Pringle, 540 U.S. 366, 124 S.Ct. 795, 800, 157 L.Ed.2d 769 (2003). "This totality of the circumstances approach is far more consistent with our prior treatment of probable cause than is any rigid demand that specific 'tests' be satisfied by every informant's tip. Perhaps the central teaching of our decisions bearing on the probable cause standard is that it is a 'practical, nontechnical conception.' 'In dealing with probable cause, ... as the very name implies, we deal with probabilities. They are not technical; they are the factual and practical considerations on which reasonable and prudent men, not legal technicians, act.' Our observations in United States v. Ortiz ... regarding 'particularized suspicion,' is also applicable to the probable cause standard:

'The process does not deal with hard certainties, but with probabilities. Long before the law of probabilities was articulated as such, practical people formulated certain common-sense conclusions about human behavior; jurors as fact finders are permitted to do the same—and so are law enforcement officers. Finally the evidence thus collected must be seen not in terms of a library analysis by scholars, but as understood by those versed in the field of law enforcement.'

As these comments illustrate, probable cause is a fluid concept—turning on the assessment of probabilities in particular factual contexts—not readily, or even usefully, reduced to a neat set of rules." Illinois v. Gates, 462 U.S. 213, 103 S.Ct. 2317, 76 L.Ed.2d 527, 544 (1983) (internal citations and footnote omitted).

"The test for probable cause is not reducible to 'precise definition or quantification' 'Finely tuned standards such as proof beyond a reasonable doubt or by a preponderance of the evidence..have no place in the [probable-cause] decision.' All we have required is the kind of 'fair probability' on which 'reasonable and prudent [people], not legal technicians, act.'

In evaluating whether the State has met this practical and common sense standard, we have consistently looked to the totality of the circumstances. We have rejected rigid rules, bright-line tests, and mechanistic inquiries in favor of a more flexible, all-things-considered approach." Florida v. Harris, 568 U.S. ____, 133 S.Ct. 1050, 185 L.Ed.2d 61, 67 (2013) (internal citations omitted). "'Under our general Fourth Amendment approach' we 'examin[e] the totality of the circumstances' to determine whether a search is reasonable under the Fourth Amendment." Samson v. California, 547 U.S. 843, 126 S.Ct. 2193, 2197, 165 L.Ed.2d 250 (2006)(internal citation omitted).

Reasonable suspicion standard: "Courts have used a variety of terms to capture the elusive concept of what cause is sufficient to authorize police to stop a person. Terms like 'articulable reasons' and 'founded suspicion' are not self-defining; they fall short of providing clear guidance dispositive of the myriad factual situations that arise. But the essence of all that has been written is that the totality of the circumstances—the whole picture—must be taken into account. Based upon that whole picture, the detaining officers must have a particularized and objective basis for suspecting the particular person stopped of criminal activity.

The idea that an assessment of the whole picture must yield a particularized suspicion contains two elements, each of which must be present before a stop is permissible. *First*, the assessment must be based on all the circumstances. The analysis proceeds with various objective observations, information from police reports, if such are available, and consideration of the modes or patterns of operation of certain kinds of lawbreakers. From these data, a trained officer draws inferences and makes deductions—inferences and deductions which might well elude an untrained person.

The process does not deal with hard certainties, but with probabilities. Long before the law of probabilities was articulated as such, practical people formulated certain common-sense conclusions about human behavior; jurors as fact-finders are permitted to do the same—and so are law enforcement officers. Finally, the evidence thus collected must be seen and weighed not in terms of library analysis by scholars, but as understood by those versed in the field of law enforcement.

The *second* element contained in the idea that an assessment of the whole picture must yield a particularized suspicion is the concept that the process just described must raise a suspicion that a particular individual being stopped is engaged in wrongdoing. Chief Justice Warren speaking for the Court in Terry v. Ohio, supra, said that '[t]his demand for specificity in the information upon which police action is based is the central teaching of this Court's Fourth Amendment jurisprudence.'" United States v. Cortez, 449 U.S. 411, 101 S.Ct. 690, 66 L.Ed.2d 621, 628–29 (1981) (internal citations omitted).

"When discussing how reviewing courts should make reasonable-suspicion determinations, we have said repeatedly that they must look at the 'totality of the circumstances' of each case to see whether the detaining officer has a 'particularized and objective basis' for suspecting legal wrongdoing. This process

Section 4. Other Important Rules and Principles

a. Fruits of search cannot justify a search or seizure

A general exploratory search for evidence of crime is the classic type of unreasonable search that the Fourth Amendment was historically designed to end.[41] Accordingly, it is a bedrock rule of Fourth Amendment law, subject to no exceptions, that a search or seizure cannot be made reasonable by the fruits it produces. On the contrary, the evidentiary basis for a search or seizure conducted for criminal investigative purposes must exist *prior* to the onset of the search or seizure in question.[42] In particular, an arrest cannot be justified by the fruits of the search that follows, and then the search justified as incident to a lawful arrest.[43] As a corollary to this rule, a search that is reasonable in its inception cannot be made *unreasonable* because it fails to uncover the object of the search.[44]

---

allows officers to draw on their own experience and specialized training to make inferences from and deductions about cumulative information available to them that 'might well elude an untrained person.'" United States v. Arvizu, 534 U.S. 266, 122 S.Ct. 744, 750, 151 L.Ed.2d 740 (2002) (citations omitted).

"We have long held that the 'touchstone of the Fourth Amendment is reasonableness.' Reasonableness, in turn, is measured in objective terms by examining the totality of the circumstances. In applying this test, we have consistently eschewed bright-line rules, instead emphasizing the fact-specific nature of the reasonableness inquiry." Ohio v. Robinette, 519 U.S. 33, 117 S.Ct. 417, 136 L.Ed.2d 347, 354 (1996).

Comparison between probable cause and reasonable suspicion standards: "A number of our cases on probable cause have an implicit bearing on the reliable knowledge element of reasonable suspicion, as we have attempted to flesh out the knowledge component by looking to the degree to which the known facts imply prohibited conduct, the specificity of the information received, and the reliability of its source. At the end of the day, however, we have realized that these factors cannot rigidly control, and we have come back to saying that the standards are 'fluid concepts that take their substantive content from the particular contexts' in which they are being assessed.

Perhaps the best that can be said generally about the required knowledge component of probable cause for a law enforcement officer's evidence search is that it raises a 'fair probability' or a 'substantial chance' of discovering evidence of criminal activity. The lesser standard [of reasonable suspicion] for school searches could as readily be described as a moderate chance of finding evidence of wrongdoing." Safford Unified School District v. Redding, 557 U.S. ___ 129 S.Ct. 2633, 2639, 174 L.Ed.2d 354 (2009) (internal citations omitted).

41. For a discussion of this historical purpose, see Chapter 6, Section 2 of this work.

42. "Nor is it material that the search was successful in revealing evidence of a violation of a federal statute. A search prosecuted in violation of the Constitution is not made lawful by what it brings to light." Byars v. United States, 273 U.S. 28, 29, 47 S.Ct. 248, 71 L.Ed. 520, 522 (1927). "We have had frequent occasion to point out that a search is not to be made legal by what it turns up. In law, it is good or bad when it starts and does not change character from its success." United States v. Di Re, 332 U.S. 581, 595, 68 S.Ct. 222, 92 L.Ed. 210, 220 (1948). "Any idea that a search can be justified by what it turns up was long ago rejected in our constitutional jurisprudence." Bumper v. North Carolina, 391 U.S. 543, 88 S.Ct. 1788, 20 L.Ed.2d 797, 802, n.10 (1968) (disapproving a contrary statement by the NC Supreme Court). "Of course, the discoveries of an illegal search cannot be used to validate the probable-cause judgment upon which the legality of the search depends." Whiteley v. Warden of Wyo. State Penitentiary, 401 U.S. 560, 91 S.Ct.1031, 28 L.Ed.2d 306, 312, n. 11 (1971). "The reasonableness of official suspicion [for a *Terry* stop-and-frisk] must be measured by what the officers knew before they conducted their search." Florida v. J.L., 529 U.S. 266, 120 S.Ct. 1375, 1379, 146 L.Ed.2d 254 (2000).

43. "That reasoning, however, 'justify[ing] the arrest by the search and at the same time ... the search by the arrest,' just 'will not do.' As we have had occasion in the past to observe, "'[i]t is axiomatic that an incident search may not precede an arrest and serve as part of its justification.'" Smith v. Ohio, 494 U.S. 541, 110 S.Ct. 1288, 108 L.Ed.2d 464, 467 (1990), quoting from Sibron v. New York, 392 U.S. 40, 63, 88 S.Ct. 1889, 20 L.Ed.2d 917, 934–35 (1968).

"To repeat, an arrest is not justified by what the subsequent search discloses." Henry v. United States, 361 U.S. 98, 80 S.Ct. 168, 4 L.Ed.2d 134, 139 (1959).

44. United States v. Ramirez, 523 U.S. 65, 118 S.Ct. 992, 997 n. 2, 140 L.Ed.2d 191 (1998) ("It is of no consequence that an otherwise lawful entry into a home to arrest a person was unsuccessful in

b. Scope of search rule

It is a mistake to assume that if a search is reasonable at its outset, all search activity that follows will invariably be reasonable also. To the contrary, the scope of a search either with or without a warrant is strictly limited by the circumstances that justified its inception. A search that is reasonable when it begins may become unreasonable if its scope extends beyond that which is necessary to accomplish its objective. Stated differently, where the basis for making a reasonable search empowers the police to look for particular items of property, the search must be confined to those locations where such items may reasonably be found—and to no other places. And if the search exceeds that scope, any seizures of property thereafter are unreasonable under the Fourth Amendment.[45]

---

locating that person because '[i]n determining the existence of probable cause we must concern ourselves only with what the officers had reason to believe at the time of their entry.'") (citation omitted).

45. "If the scope of the search exceeds that permitted by the terms of a validly issued warrant or the character of the relevant exception from the warrant requirement, the subsequent seizure is unconstitutional without more." Horton v. California, 496 U.S. 128, 140, 110 S.Ct. 2301, 110 L.Ed.2d 112, 125 (1990) (emphasis added).

"In Horton v. California [citation omitted], we held '[i]f the scope of the search exceeds that permitted by the terms of a validly issued warrant or the character of the relevant exception to the warrant requirement, the subsequent seizure is unconstitutional without more.' While this does not mean that every police action while inside a home must be explicitly authorized by the text of the warrant, the Fourth Amendment does require that police actions in execution of a warrant be related to the objectives of the authorized intrusion." Wilson v. Layne, 526 U.S. 603, 119 S.Ct. 1692, 143 L.Ed.2d 818, 828 (1999) (internal citation omitted) (emphasis added).

"This Court has held in the past that a search which is reasonable in its inception may violate the Fourth Amendment by virtue of its intolerable intensity and scope. The scope of the search must be 'strictly tied to and justified by' the circumstances which rendered its initiation permissible." Terry v. Ohio, 392 U.S. 1, 88 S.Ct. 1868, 20 L.Ed.2d 889, 904 (1968) (internal citations omitted).

"The Fourth Amendment proceeds as much by limitations upon the scope of governmental action as by imposing preconditions upon its initiation. The entire deterrent purpose of the rule excluding evidence seized in violation of the Fourth Amendment rests on the assumption that 'limitations upon the fruit to be gathered tend to limit the quest itself.' Thus, evidence may not be introduced if it was discovered by means of a seizure and search which were not reasonably related in scope to their justification." Terry v. Ohio, 392 U.S. 1, 28–29, 88 S.Ct. 1868, 20 L.Ed. 2d 889, 910 (1968).

"The Fourth Amendment's prohibition against unreasonable searches and seizures has always been interpreted to prevent a search that is not limited to the particularly described 'place to be searched and the persons or things to be seized,' U.S. Const., Amdt 4, even if the search is made pursuant to a warrant and based on probable cause. The Amendment's protection is not diluted in those situations where it has been determined that legitimate law enforcement interests justify a warrantless search: the search must be limited in scope to that which is justified by the particular purposes served by the exception." Florida v. Royer, 460 U.S. 491, 103 S.Ct. 1319, 75 L.Ed.2d 229, 237–38 (1983).

"The scope of a warrantless search based on probable cause is no narrower—and no broader—than the scope of a search authorized by a warrant supported by probable cause. Only the prior approval of the magistrate is waived; the search otherwise is as the magistrate could authorize." United States v. Ross, 456 U.S. 798, 102 S.Ct. 2157, 72 L.Ed.2d 572, 593 (1982).

"Even if a warrant is not required, a search is not beyond Fourth Amendment scrutiny; for it must be reasonable in its scope and execution. Urgent government interests are not a license for indiscriminate police behavior." Maryland v. King, 569 U.S. ____, 133 S.Ct. 1958, 186 L.Ed.2d 1, 20, 21 (2013).

Judge Charles Moylan of the Maryland Court of Appeals has best illustrated this principle in his frequent lectures to judicial conferences on the Fourth Amendment with the apt aphorism: "You cannot search for an elephant in a matchbox." As further stated by the Court:

> When an official search is properly authorized—whether by consent or by the issuance of a valid warrant—the scope of the search is limited by the terms of its authorization. Consent to search a garage would not implicitly authorize a search of an adjoining house; a warrant to search for a stolen refrigerator would not authorize the opening of a desk drawer. Because 'indiscriminate searches and seizures conducted under the authority of 'general warrants' were the immediate evils that motivated the framing and adoption of the Fourth Amendment,' that Amendment requires that the scope of every authorized search be particularly described. (internal citation omitted).[46]

> Just as probable cause to believe that a stolen lawnmower may be found in a garage will not support a warrant to search an upstairs bedroom, probable cause to believe that undocumented aliens are being transported in a van will not justify a warrantless search of a suitcase. Probable cause to believe that a container placed in a trunk of a taxi contains contraband does not justify a search of the entire cab.[47]

c. Canon of liberal construction

The U.S. Supreme Court has long followed a canon of liberal construction in interpreting the Fourth Amendment against an overly technical reading thereof. In *Boyd v. United States*,[48] the Court rejected an argument that the federal statute under constitutional attack did not authorize a search and seizure but only required a compulsory production of books and papers—and therefore did not come within the literal terms of the Fourth Amendment:

> Though the proceeding in question is divested of many of the aggravating incidents of actual search and seizure, yet, as before said, it contains their substantial purpose. It may be that it is the obnoxious thing in its mildest and least repulsive form; but illegitimate and unconstitutional practices get their first footing in that way, namely: by silent approaches and slight deviations from legal modes of procedure. This can only be obviated by adhering to the rule that *constitutional provisions for the security of person and property should be liberally construed.* A close and literal construction deprives them of half their efficacy and leads to gradual depreciation of the right, as if it consisted more in sound than in substance. It is the duty of the courts to be watchful for the constitutional rights of the citizen, and against any stealthy encroachments thereon. Their motto should be obsta principis [avoid beginnings].[49]

---

46. Walter v. United States 447 U.S. 649, 100 S.Ct. 2395, 65 L.Ed.2d 410, 417–18 (1980).
47. United States v. Ross, 456 U.S. 798, 824, 102 S.Ct. 2157, 72 L.Ed.2d 572, 593 (1982).
48. 116 U.S. 616, 6 S.Ct. 524, 29 L.Ed. 746 (1886).
49. 116 U.S. at 635.

In like fashion, many Supreme Court cases have since relied on the canon of liberal construction to justify a broad reading of Fourth Amendment protections in favor of the individual.[50]

d. "Mere evidence" rule abolished

There was a time when government officials, when conducting an otherwise reasonable search, were prohibited from seizing an individual's incriminating personal property as it constituted "mere evidence" of crime—and were confined solely to the seizure of contraband, fruits and instrumentalities of crime. This result was based on a Fifth Amendment self-incrimination rationale that physical evidence that a person lawfully possessed could not be seized and used as evidence to criminally convict that person.[51]

This view of the self-incrimination privilege, however, eventually was disapproved based on a holding that the privilege protected against only "testimonial compulsion"—that is, being forced to give substantively incriminating written or oral statements of a testimonial nature or the equivalent thereof—and that physical evidence seized from a person did not fall within the privilege.[52] Based on this revised interpretation, the "mere evidence" rule has since been overruled, and government officials while conducting a reasonable search may now seize not only contraband, fruits and instrumentalities of a crime—but also any property that constitutes evidence of a crime, such as clothing worn by the perpetrator of a robbery.[53]

e. Fourth Amendment protects innocent and guilty alike: freedom is indivisible

When courts must decide whether a defense motion to suppress in a criminal case should be granted based on Fourth Amendment grounds, the defendant is placed in a compromising position. Law enforcement officials have seized often very reliable evidence of guilt, and to suppress this evidence is to thwart the truth-seeking function of the court. For this reason, most trial judges are reluctant to grant such motions unless the law clearly requires them to do so. It has therefore been necessary for the Court to remind itself, and all lower federal and state courts, that Fourth Amendment freedom is indivisible—that is, such freedom is enjoyed by both the innocent and the guilty alike. And to "cut corners" to sustain the reasonableness of a search or seizure in order to prevent a guilty person from going free, is to diminish the Fourth Amendment freedom of everyone else in the

---

50. Schneckloth v. Bustamonte, 412 U.S. 218, 228–29, 93 S.Ct. 2041, 36 L.Ed.2d 854 (1973); Coolidge v. New Hampshire, 403 U.S. 443, 454, 91 S.Ct. 2022, 29 L.Ed.2d 564 (1971); Silverman v. United States, 365 U.S. 505, 511, 81 S.Ct. 679, 5 L.Ed.2d 734 (1961); Johnson v. United States, 333 U.S. 10, 17 n. 8, 68 S.Ct. 367, 92 L.Ed. 436 (1948); Sgro v. United States, 287 U.S. 206, 210, 53 S.Ct. 138, 77 L.Ed. 260 (1932); Grau v. United States, 287 U.S. 124, 128, 53 S.Ct. 38, 77 L.Ed. 212 (1932); Go-Bart Importing Co. v. United States, 282 U.S. 344, 357, 51 S.Ct. 153, 75 L.Ed. 374 (1931); Byars v. United States, 273 U.S. 28, 32, 33–34, 47 S.Ct. 248, 71 L.Ed. 520 (1927); Gouled v. United States, 255 U.S. 298, 303–04, 41 S.Ct. 261, 65 L.Ed. 647 (1921); see also Silverthorne Lumber Co. v. United States, 251 U.S. 385, 391–92, 40 S.Ct. 182, 64 L.Ed. 319 (1920).

51. Gouled v. United States, 255 U.S. 298, 41 S.Ct. 261, 65 L.Ed. 647 (1921).

52. Schmerber v. California, 384 U.S. 757, 763–64, 86 S.Ct.1826, 16 L.Ed.2d 908, 916 (1966).

53. Warden, Md. Penitentiary v. Hayden, 387 U.S. 294, 87 S.Ct. 1642, 18 L.Ed.2d 782 (1967).

country.[54] Indeed, "[i]f the illegality of the activity [engaged in by the victim of a search] made constitutional an otherwise unconstitutional search, the Fourth Amendment, reserved for the innocent only, would have little force in regulating police behavior toward either the innocent or the guilty."[55]

Indeed, the "hydraulic pressures" on courts to water down Fourth Amendment freedoms in order to engage in what many regard as a dubious "war on drugs" is of particular concern. As the Court has stated:

> This Court ... is not empowered to suspend constitutional guarantees so that the Government may more effectively wage a "war on drugs." If that war is to be fought, those who fight it must respect the rights of individuals, whether or not those individuals are suspected of having committed a crime.[56]

In this same connection, Justice Brennan has observed, "[i]t is indeed easy to forget, especially in view of current concern over drug trafficking, that the scope of the Fourth Amendment's protection does not turn on whether the activity disclosed is illegal or innocuous," and that "we dismiss this as a 'drug case' only at the peril of our own liberties."[57] Justice Frankfurter has further noted, "[i]t is a fair summary of history to say that the safeguards of liberty have frequently been forged in controversies involving not very nice people."[58] And while a "shabby" character like a drug trafficker may be asserting a Fourth

---

54. "The protection of the 4th Amendment extends to all equally,—to those justly suspected or accused, as well as to the innocent." Agnello v. United States, 269 U.S. 20, 32, 46 S.Ct. 4, 70 L.Ed. 145, 149 (1925).

"This guarantee [the Fourth Amendment] against unreasonable searches and seizures extends to the innocent and guilty alike. " McDonald v. United States, 335 U.S. 451, 69 S.Ct. 191, 93 L.Ed. 153, 157 (1948).

"The 4th Amendment forbids every search that is unreasonable and is construed liberally to safeguard the right of privacy. (citation omitted). Its protection extends to offenders as well as the law-abiding." Lefkowitz v. United States, 285 U.S. 452, 464, 52 S.Ct. 420, 76 L.Ed. 877, 882 (1932).

"The Fourth Amendment was designed to protect both the innocent and the guilty from unreasonable intrusions upon their right of privacy while leaving adequate room for the necessary processes of law enforcement." Trupiano v. United States, 334 U.S. 699,709, 68 S.Ct. 1229, 92 L.Ed. 1663, 1671 (1948).

"[The Fourth Amendment] is general and forbids every search that is unreasonable; it protects all, those suspected or known to be offenders, as well as the innocent...." Go-Bart Importing Co. v. United States, 282 U.S. 344, 357, 51 S.Ct.153, 75 L.Ed. 374, 382 (1931).

"But there is nothing new in the realization that the Constitution sometimes insulates the criminality of the few in order to protect the privacy of us all." Arizona v. Hicks, 480 U.S. 321, 107 S.Ct. 1149, 94 L.Ed.2d 347, 357 (1987).

"Because the strongest advocates of Fourth Amendment rights are frequently criminals, it is easy to forget that our interpretations of such rights apply to the innocent and guilty alike." United States v. Sokolow, 490 U.S. 1, 109 S.Ct. 1581, 104 L.Ed.2d 1, 13 1989) (Marshall, J. dissenting).

"But it is precisely because appeal to the Fourth Amendment is so often made by dubious characters that its infringements call for alert and strenuous resistance. Freedom of speech, of the press, of religion easily summon powerful support against encroachment. The prohibition against unreasonable search and seizure is normally invoked by those accused of crime, and criminals have few friends." Harris v. United States, 331 U.S. 145, 156, 67 S.Ct. 1098, 91 L.Ed. 1399, 1409 (1947) (Frankfurter, J. dissenting)

55. Minnesota v. Carter, 525 U.S. 83, 119 S.Ct. 469, 142 L.Ed.2d 373, 393 (1998) (Ginsberg, J. dissenting).

56. Florida v. Bostick, 501 U.S. 429, 111 S.Ct. 2382, 115 L.Ed.2d 389, 401 (1991); also see Thomas Regnier, *The "Loyal Foot Soldier": Can the Fourth Amendment Survive the Supreme Court's War on Drugs?*, 72 U.Mo.-Kan.City L.Rev. 631 (2004).

57. Florida v. Riley, 488 U.S. 445, 109 S.Ct. 693, 102 L.Ed.2d 835, 850 (1989) (Brennan, J. dissenting).

58. United States v. Rabinowitz, 339 U.S. 56, 69, 70 S.Ct. 430, 94 L.Ed. 653, 662 (1950) (Frankfurter, J. dissenting).

Amendment claim at the bar, the courts "must deal with his case in the context of what are the great themes expressed by the Fourth Amendment."[59] Surely, one of those themes is that all freedom is indivisible, and to violate the Fourth Amendment freedom of the worst among us is to diminish the freedom of us all.

f. Tension between Fourth Amendment claims and law enforcement demands: danger of law enforcement abuse

There is an inevitable tension between Fourth Amendment claims of individual rights and the demands of effective law enforcement. Both interests must be fairly weighed in the balance in determining whether a given search or seizure is reasonable or unreasonable—with a certain preference given to the claim of individual rights in doubtful cases.[60] Indeed, "constitutional provisions for the security of person and property [like the Fourth Amendment] must be liberally construed" because "[a] close and literal construction deprives them of half their efficacy and leads to a gradual depreciation of the right, as if it consisted more in sound than in substance."[61] But in times such as ours where law and order demands often have such strong popular support, courts often feel "hydraulic pressures" to unfairly tip the balance in favor of law enforcement demands. These pressures must be resisted. As stated by the Court,

> The needs of law enforcement stand in constant tension with the Constitution's protections against certain exercises of official power. It is precisely the predictability of these pressures that counsels a resolute loyalty to constitutional safeguards.[62]
>
> Moreover, the mere fact that law enforcement may be made more efficient can never by itself justify disregard of the Fourth Amendment. The investigation of crime would always be simplified if warrants were unnecessary. But the Fourth Amendment reflects the view of those who wrote the Bill of Rights that the privacy of a person's home and property may not be totally sacrificed in the name of maximum simplicity in enforcement of the criminal law.[63]

Beyond that, there is always a certain danger in interpreting the Fourth Amendment that whatever authority the courts cede to law enforcement will be exercised by responsible as well as irresponsible officers who will push their search authority to the limit and beyond. This consideration, too, must be carefully weighed by the courts when assessing the reasonableness of certain law enforcement practices. As Justice Jackson has warned:

> We must remember that the extent of any privilege of search and seizure without a warrant which we sustain, the officers interpret and apply themselves and will

---

59. United States v. Rabinowitz, 339 U.S. 56, 69, 70 S.Ct. 430, 94 L.Ed.2d 653, 662 (1950) (Frankfurter, J. dissenting).

60. See, e.g., Schneckloth v. Bustamonte, 412 U.S. 218, 228–29, 93 S.Ct. 2041, 36 L.Ed.2d 854 (1973); Coolidge v. New Hampshire, 403 U.S. 443, 454, 91 S.Ct. 2022, 29 L.Ed.2d 564 (1971); Silverman v. United States, 365 U.S. 505, 511, 81 S.Ct. 679, 5 L.Ed.2d 734 (1961); Johnson v. United States, 333 U.S. 10, 17 n. 8, 68 S.Ct. 367, 92 L.Ed. 436 (1948); Sgro v. United States, 287 U.S. 206, 210, 53 S.Ct. 138, 77 L.Ed. 260 (1932); Grau v. United States, 287 U.S. 124, 128, 53 S.Ct. 38, 77 L.Ed. 212 (1932); Go-Bart Importing Co. v. United States, 282 U.S. 344, 357, 51 S.Ct. 153, 75 L.Ed. 374 (1931); Byars v. United States, 273 U.S. 28, 32, 33–34, 47 S.Ct. 248, 71 L.Ed. 520 (1927); Gouled v. United States, 255 U.S. 298, 303–04, 41 S.Ct. 261, 65 L.Ed. 647 (1921).

61. Boyd v. United States, 116 U.S. 616, 635, 6 S.Ct. 524, 29 L.Ed.2d 746, 752 (1886).

62. Almeida-Sanchez v. United States, 413 U.S. 266, 93 S.Ct. 2535, 37 L.Ed.2d 596, 603 (1973).

63. Mincey v. Arizona, 437 U.S. 385, 98 S.Ct. 2408, 57 L.Ed.2d 290, 301 (1978).

> push to the limit. * * * [A]n illegal search and seizure usually is a single incident, perpetrated by surprise, conducted in haste, kept purposely beyond the court's supervision and limited only by the judgment and moderation of officers whose own interests are at stake in the search. There is no opportunity for disinterested intervention. The citizen's choice is quietly to submit to whatever the officers undertake or to resist at risk of arrest or immediate violence. And we must remember that the authority which we concede to conduct searches and seizures may be exercised by the most unfit and ruthless officers as well as by the fit and responsible, and resorted to in case of petty misdemeanors as well as in the case of the gravest felonies.[64]

g. Approach to Fourth Amendment issues influences the outcome

"It is true," as Justice Frankfurter has noted, "of journeys in the law that the place you reach depends on the direction you are taking."[65] If a court approaches the Fourth Amendment as a general nuisance that must be overcome in the enforcement of the criminal law, the decision on a Fourth Amendment issue is often inevitable. But if, as it should, a court treats the Fourth Amendment as guaranteeing one of the great rights of a free society, the denial of which led to the American Revolution, the result on the identical issue may be quite different.

> And so how one comes out on a case depends on where one goes in. It makes all the difference in the world whether one approaches the Fourth Amendment as the Court approached it in Boyd v. United States..., in Weeks v. United States..., in Silverthorne Lumber Co. v. United States..., in Gouled v. United States..., or one approaches it as a provision dealing with a formality. It makes all the difference in the world whether one recognizes the central fact about the Fourth Amendment, namely, that it was a safeguard against recurrence of abuses so deeply felt by the Colonies as to be one of the potent causes of the Revolution, or one thinks of it as merely a requirement for a piece of paper.[66]

---

64. Brinegar v. United States, 338 U.S. 160, 69 S.Ct. 1302, 93 L.Ed. 1879, 1894 (1949) (Jackson, J. dissenting).

65. United States v. Rabinowitz, 339 U.S. 56, 69, 70 S.Ct. 430, 94 L.Ed. 653, 662 (1950) (Frankfurter, J. dissenting).

66. United States v. Rabinowitz, 339 U.S. 56, 69, 70 S.Ct. 430, 94 L.Ed. 653, 662 (1950) (Frankfurter, J. dissenting).

Chapter 12

Seizures of Persons and Property

Introduction

The Fourth Amendment provides that "[t]he right of the people to be secure in their persons, houses, papers and effects against unreasonable ... *seizures* shall not be violated." There are certain tests, as well as a considerable body of law, that the United States Supreme Court and other courts have developed in determining whether (a) a given seizure of the *person* or (b) a given seizure of one's *property*, is or is not "unreasonable" in the Fourth Amendment sense. If any such seizure is determined to be unreasonable, it generally means, subject to some exceptions, that the fruits of that unreasonable seizure are not admissible in evidence against the victim of the seizure under the *Weeks-Mapp* exclusionary rule. On other hand, if the subject seizure is determined to be reasonable, it means that the fruits of that reasonable seizure are admissible in evidence under the *Weeks-Mapp* exclusionary rule.[1]

Section 1 of this Chapter will review the unreasonableness rules with respect to a seizure of the *person*, which often is the *initial* Fourth Amendment intrusion in a given case. The analysis here is quite extensive and will occupy most of this chapter. Section 2 of this Chapter will then examine the rules with respect to an unreasonable seizure of one's *property*, which often follows *a preceding* Fourth Amendment intrusion. The analysis here will be relatively brief.

Section 1. Seizure of Persons

a. Two types of seizures of the person: temporary detentions and arrests

There are two types of Fourth Amendment seizures of the person: (1) temporary detentions, and (2) formal arrests or their functional equivalent. All seizures of the person are, as a general rule, treated as arrests or their functional equivalent and must be supported by probable cause. An important exception to this general rule is recognized, however, where the seizure of the person amounts only to a temporary detention. In that event, if the detention has a criminal investigative purpose, it need not be supported by probable cause, and is reasonable if supported by the lesser standard of reasonable suspicion.[2]

---

1. For a detailed discussion of the *Weeks-Mapp* exclusionary rule, see Chapter 17 of this work.

2. "In Dunaway v. New York [citation omitted], the Court reaffirmed the general rule that an official seizure of the person must be supported by probable cause, even if no formal arrest is made.

Temporary detentions may have a criminal investigative purpose, or a civil or special needs purpose that goes beyond the normal need for ordinary criminal law enforcement. The classic example of a temporary criminal detention is a so-called "*Terry* stop" in which police briefly detain a person on the street in order to investigate further a criminal offense involving the detainee.[3] Another example is where the police stop a car for a traffic violation, thereby detaining the driver and passengers,[4] or detain people located on private premises while police execute a search warrant for the premises.[5] Examples of temporary civil or special needs detentions are a DUI traffic checkpoint stop of a car,[6] or a traffic checkpoint stop of a car near the US-Mexican border for the purpose of making citizenship inquiries.[7] As the name necessarily implies, a temporary detention is limited to a relatively brief time and geographical area while the police carry out the purpose of the detention.

A formal arrest, on the other hand, occurs when the police take the person to the police station or jail and formally book the person for a crime, following which official criminal charges may be filed by the prosecuting authorities.[8] There is also a functional equivalent of an arrest where police exceed the limits of a temporary detention, as where police take a person to the police station for questioning or fingerprinting, but without formally booking the person,[9] or take an air traveler to a police interrogation room in an airport for questioning.[10]

---

* * * Although we refused in Dunaway to find an exception that would swallow up the general rule, our opinion recognized that some seizures [of the person] significantly less intrusive than an arrest have withstood scrutiny under the reasonableness standard embodied in the Fourth Amendment. * * *These cases [*Terry v. Ohio* and its progeny] recognize that some seizures [of the person] admittedly covered by the Fourth Amendment constitute such limited intrusions on the personal security of the person detained and are justified by such substantial law enforcement interests that they may be made on less than probable cause, so long as police have an articulable basis for suspecting criminal activity." Michigan v. Summers, 452 U.S. 692, 696, 697, 699,101 S.Ct. 2587, 69 L.Ed.2d 340, 345, 346, 348 (1981).

An overview of the standards of probable cause and reasonable suspicion are discussed at Section 1e of this Chapter.

3. Terry v. Ohio, 392 U.S. 1, 88 S.Ct. 1868, 20 L.Ed.2d 889 (1968).

4. "Temporary detention of individuals during the [police] stop of an automobile, even if only for a brief period and for a limited purpose, constitute a 'seizure' of 'persons' within the meaning of this provision [Fourth Amendment]." Whren v. United States, 116 S.Ct. 1769, 1772 (1996). "There can be no question that the stopping of a vehicle [by police] and the detention of its occupants constitute a 'seizure'[of the person] within the meaning of the Fourth Amendment." Colorado v. Bannister, 449 U.S. 1, 101 S.Ct. 42, 66 L.Ed.2d 1, 4 n.3 (1980); see United States v. Cortez, 449 U.S. 411, 101 S.Ct. 690, 66 L.Ed.2d 621, 628 (1981); "When a police officer makes a traffic stop, the driver of the car is seized within the meaning of the Fourth Amendment. The question in this case is whether the same is true of the passenger. We hold that a passenger is seized as well and so may challenge the constitutionality of the stop." Brendlin v. California, 551 U.S. 249, 127 S.Ct. 2400, 2403, 168 L.Ed.2d 132 (2007).

5. Michigan v. Summers, 452 U.S. 692, 101 S.Ct.2587, 69 L.Ed.2d 340 (1981).

6. Michigan State Police v. Sitz, 496 U.S. 444, 110 S.Ct. 2481, 110 L.Ed.2d 412 (1990).

7. United States v. Martinez-Fuerte, 428 U.S. 543, 96 S.Ct. 3074, 49 L.Ed.2d 1116 (1976).

8. "An arrest is the initial stage of a criminal prosecution. It is intended to vindicate society's interest in having its laws obeyed, and it is inevitably accompanied by future interference with the individual's freedom of movement, whether or not trial or conviction ultimately follows." Terry v. Ohio, 392 U.S. 1, 26, 88 S.Ct. 1868, 20 L.Ed.2d 889, 909 (1968).

9. Dunaway v. New York, 442 U.S. 200, 99 S.Ct.2248, 60 L.Ed.2d 824 (1979) (trip to the police station for questioning); Davis v. Mississippi, 394 U.S. 721, 89 S.Ct. 1394, 22 L.Ed.2d 676 (1969) (trip to police station for fingerprinting and questioning).

10. Florida v. Royer, 460 U.S. 491, 103 S.Ct. 1319, 75 L.Ed.2d 229 (1983) (temporary detention in airport escalated into arrest when defendant taken from airport concourse to police interrogation room at airport).

At times, it is difficult to determine when a temporary *Terry* stop escalates into an arrest or the functional equivalent of same. By definition, however, a *Terry* stop is limited to the purpose of the stop: to freeze the situation so as to allow the police to briefly investigate the reasonable suspicion that provoked the stop.[11] This necessarily imposes certain time and space limitations within which certain permissible investigative techniques may take place. And when the detention strays beyond these limitations, the detention has escalated into the functional equivalent of an arrest.

As for time limitations, police may temporarily detain a defendant in a *Terry* stop for whatever reasonable length of time is necessary to investigate the suspicion that prompted the stop. Clearly, brief questioning of the defendant at the scene of the stop is permissible, limited to the purpose of the stop.[12] And upon making a *Terry* stop of an automobile, police are also authorized to order the driver and all the passengers out of the automobile.[13] Moreover, police may keep their visual, auditory, and smell senses open in this encounter, and—in so doing, but without conducting a Fourth Amendment search—may learn certain information that gives the police probable cause to arrest.[14] During this brief in-

11. "The predicate permitting seizures [of the person] on suspicion short of probable cause is that law enforcement interests warrant a limited intrusion on the personal security of the suspect. The scope of the intrusion permitted will vary to some extent with the particular facts and circumstances of each case. *This much, however, is clear: an investigative detention must be temporary and last no longer than is necessary to effect the purpose of the stop.* Similarly, the investigative methods employed should be the least intrusive means reasonably available to verify or dispel the officer's suspicion in a short period of time. It is the State's burden to demonstrate that the seizure it seeks to justify on the basis of reasonable suspicion was sufficiently limited in scope and duration to satisfy the conditions of the investigative seizure." Florida v. Royer, 460 U.S. 491, 103 S.Ct. 1319, 75 L.Ed.2d 229, 238 (1983) (emphasis added).

"Beginning with Terry v. Ohio..., the Court has recognized that a law enforcement officer's reasonable suspicion that a person may be involved in criminal activity permits the officer to stop the person for a brief time and take additional steps to investigate further. To ensure that the resulting seizure is constitutionally reasonable, a Terry stop must be limited. The officer's actions must be 'justified at its inception, and ... reasonably related in scope to the circumstances which justified the interference in the first place.' For example, the seizure cannot continue for an excessive period of time or resemble a traditional arrest." Hiibel v. Sixth Judicial District Court, 542 U.S. ___, 124 S.Ct. 2451, 2458, 159 L.Ed.2d 292 (2004) (internal citations omitted).

12. "Although not expressly authorized in Terry, United States v. Brignoni-Ponce ... was unequivocal in saying that reasonable suspicion of criminal activity warrants a temporary seizure [of the person] for the purpose of questioning limited to the purposes of the stop. In Brignoni-Ponce, that purpose was to verify or dispel the suspicion that the immigration laws were being violated, a governmental interest that was sufficient to warrant temporary detention for limited questioning. Florida v. Royer, 460 U.S. 491, 103 S.Ct. 1319, 75 L.Ed.2d 229, 237 (1983).

"[W]e hold that when an officer's observations lead him reasonably to suspect that a particular vehicle may contain aliens who are illegally in the country, he may stop the car briefly and investigate the circumstances that provoke the suspicion." United States v. Brignoni-Ponce, 422 U.S. 873, 881, 95 S.Ct. 2574, 45 L.Ed.2d 607, 616–17 (1975).

13. Pennsylvania v. Mimms, 434 U.S. 106, 98 S.Ct. 330, 54 L.Ed.2d 330 (1977) (driver); Maryland v. Wilson, 519 U.S. 408, 117 S.Ct. 882, 131 L.Ed.2d 41 (1997) (passengers). But police may not, without probable cause, conduct a full-blown search of the driver or passengers, their personal property, or the automobile. "In the name of investigating a person who is no more than suspected of criminal activity, police may not carry out a full search of the person, his automobile or other effects." Florida v. Royer, 460 U.S. 491, 103 S.Ct. 1319, 75 L.Ed.2d 229, 237 (1983).

14. See, e.g., United States v. Hensley, 469 U.S. 221, 105 S.Ct. 675, 83 L.Ed.2d 604 (1985) (valid *Terry* stop of motorist by police based on a "wanted flyer" or bulletin issued by another police department; police, after stopping motorist, saw in plain sight the butt of a revolver protruding from under the passenger seat of the stopped automobile, thereby giving police probable cause to arrest the passenger).

vestigatory detention, however, "[i]f the officer does not learn the facts rising to the level of probable cause [to justify an arrest], the individual must be allowed to go on his way."[15] Although there is no outer time limit for the officer to make that determination in a *Terry* stop, such a detention must necessarily be relatively brief—else it will escalate into a *de facto* arrest that will require probable cause to be lawful.[16]

As for space limitations, the detention is clearly proper if it geographically takes place in the immediate vicinity of the stop—although there is no absolute rule to that effect. But, as previously stated, police clearly exceed the limits of a *Terry* stop if, for example, they take the defendant to the police station or its functional equivalent to interrogate the defendant or take the defendant's fingerprints; at that point, a de facto arrest has taken place which requires probable cause to be reasonable.[17] After making a valid *Terry* stop, it is an open question whether police are authorized to take the suspect in a police car for a short distance from the scene of the stop to conduct a "show-up" to see if the victim of or witness to a recent crime can make an identification of the suspect—although, according to LaFave, the better view in the lower federal and state courts is that such a practice is permissible.[18]

---

15. Illinois v. Wardlow 528 U.S. 119, 120 S.Ct. 673, 145 L.Ed.2d 570, 577 (2000).

16. "It is nevertheless clear that a seizure that is lawful at its inception can violate the Fourth Amendment if its manner of execution unreasonably infringes interests protected by the Constitution. A seizure that is justified solely by the interest in issuing a warning [traffic] ticket can become unlawful if it is prolonged beyond the time reasonably required to complete that mission." Illinois v. Caballes, 543 U.S. 405, 125 S.Ct. 834, 837, 160 L.Ed.2d 842 (2005) (internal citation omitted); compare Arizona v. United States, 567 U.S. ___, 132 S.Ct. 2492, 183 L.Ed.2d 351, 378 (2012).

"Obviously, if an investigative stop continues indefinitely, at some point it can no longer be justified as an investigative stop. But our cases impose no rigid time limits on Terry stops.

* * *

In assessing whether a detention is too long in duration to be justified as an investigative stop, we consider it appropriate to examine whether the police diligently pursued a means of investigation that was likely to confirm or dispel their suspicions quickly, during which time it was necessary to detain the defendant. A court making this assessment should take care to consider whether the police are acting in a swiftly developing situation, and in such cases the court should not indulge in unrealistic second-guessing. A creative judge engaged in post-hoc evaluation of the police can almost always imagine some alternative means by which the objectives of the police might have been accomplished. But '[t]he fact that protection of the public might, in the abstract, have been accomplished by 'less intrusive' means does not, in itself, render the search unreasonable.' The question is not simply whether some other alternative was available, but whether the police acted unreasonably in failing to recognize it or to pursue it." United States v. Sharpe, 470 U.S. 675, 105 S.Ct. 1568, 84 L.Ed.2d 605, 615–616 (1985) (a 20-minute delay after a *Terry* stop of a pick-up truck for transporting illegal drugs held reasonable as the defendant caused most of the delay by attempting to escape from the police). See also United States v. Place, 462 U.S. 696, 103 S.Ct. 2637, 77 L.Ed.2d 110 (1983) (90 minute delay for a temporary detention of a suitcase for a narcotics "dog-sniff" held unreasonable). For a discussion of the time and investigative method limits of a *Terry* stop, see 4 Wayne LaFave, Search and Seizure §9.2(f) (5th ed. 2012). Also see cases collected at "Arrest" 63.5(9) West Key No.

17. Dunaway v. New York, 442 U.S. 200, 99 S.Ct. 2248, 60 L.Ed.2d 824 (1979) (police stopped defendant based on reasonable suspicion, took him to police station, and subjected him to custodial interrogation; held: *Terry* stop does not permit this full-blown seizure of the person and is permissible only upon showing of probable cause); Florida v. Royer, 460 U.S. 491, 103 S.Ct. 1319, 75 L.Ed.2d 229 (1983) (same; defendant taken from airport concourse to police interrogation room at airport); Hayes v. Florida, 470 U.S. 811, 105 S.Ct. 1643, 84 L.Ed.2d 705 (1985) (same except defendant taken from his home to police station where he was fingerprinted) (dicta: arguably different result if fingerprinting had taken place in the field, rather than the police station, or had been authorized by a warrant; 84 L.Ed.2d at 710–11).

18. For a discussion of the place limits of a *Terry* stop, see 4 Wayne LaFave, Search and Seizure §9.2 (g) (5th ed. 2012). LaFave approves those cases that have upheld the above-described "show up"

b. Generally no warrant required: exception for arrest in private dwelling

When police make an arrest outside a private dwelling such as on the public streets, no arrest warrant is required under the Fourth Amendment[19]—although police will sometimes obtain one, especially for a fugitive. And no warrant has ever been required for a temporary detention of a suspect on the streets.

But where police make an arrest in a person's dwelling, an arrest warrant is generally required, to enter the dwelling to arrest the home dweller.[20] And if the purpose of the home entry is to arrest a third person, rather than the home dweller, a search warrant is also generally required to enter the dwelling.[21] These results are in full accord with the original understanding of the Framers of the Fourth Amendment which was designed primarily to protect people's privacy in their homes by generally requiring a search warrant to search such premises.[22]

Nonetheless, this general rule for making arrests in dwellings is subject to an exigent circumstances exception—as the rule in itself is applicable only in the absence of consent and exigent circumstances.[23] Accordingly, no warrant is required to enter a dwelling to make an arrest (1) when police are in "hot pursuit" of a fleeing felon and enter a dwelling to arrest the suspect; or (2) when police enter the dwelling to deal with a life-threatening or perilous situation to persons inside or outside the premises or to the police themselves; and (3) when police enter the dwelling to prevent the imminent destruction of evidence of a serious crime.[24]

---

procedure as consistent with a valid *Terry* stop. 4 Wayne LaFave, Search and Seizure § 9.2(g) at 458–463 (5th ed. 2012).

19. United States v. Watson, 423 U.S. 411, 96 S.Ct. 820, 46 L.Ed.2d 598 (1976).

20. Payton v. New York, 445 U.S. 573, 100 S.Ct. 1371, 63 L.Ed.2d 639(1980) (entry into defendant's dwelling to arrest defendant; warrant required); Kirk v. Louisiana, 536 U.S. 635, 122 S.Ct. 2458, 153 L.Ed.2d 599 (2002) (same).

21. Steagald v. United States, 451 U.S. 204, 101 S.Ct. 1642, 68 L.Ed.2d 38 (1981) (entry into defendant's dwelling to arrest third party; search warrant for home required).

22. See Chapter 6, Section 2 of this work.

23. "The issue in this case is whether under the Fourth Amendment, a law enforcement officer may legally search for the subject of an arrest warrant in the home of a third party without first obtaining a search warrant. Concluding that a search warrant must be obtained absent exigent circumstances or consent, we reverse the judgment of the United States Court of Appeals for the Fifth Circuit affirming petitioner's conviction." Steagald v. United States, 451 U.S. 204, 205–06, 101 S.Ct. 1642, 68 L.Ed.2d 38, 41 (1981). "We ... hold that the Fourth Amendment to the United States Constitution, made applicable to the States by the Fourteenth Amendment, prohibits the police from making a warrantless and nonconsensual entry into a suspect's home to make a routine felony arrest. * * * [W]e have no occasion to consider the sort of emergency or dangerous situation, described in our cases as 'exigent circumstances,' that would justify a warrantless entry into a home for the purpose of either search or arrest." Payton v. New York, 445 U.S. 573, 576, 583, 100 S.Ct. 1371, 63 L.Ed.2d 639, 644, 648–49 (1980). Kirk v. Louisiana, 536 U.S. 635, 122 S.Ct. 2458, 153 L.Ed.2d 599 (2002) ("As Payton makes plain, police officers need either a warrant or probable cause plus exigent circumstances to make a lawful arrest into a home." 122 S.Ct. at 2459).

24. For an extensive discussion of the exigent circumstances exception to the search warrant requirement rule for private premises, see Chapter 14, Section 6 of this work. Also, for a detailed consideration of the warrant requirement and its exceptions for arrests made in a dwelling, see 3 Wayne LaFave, Search and Seizure § 6.1 (5th ed. 2012) and cases collected. As an aside, in executing a search or arrest warrant in a dwelling, the Fourth Amendment generally requires that police announce their authority and purpose before they may forcibly enter the dwelling to effect the arrest therein, subject to certain exceptions—which will be discussed later in this work at Chapter 13, Section 4a.

When, however, police enter a dwelling to effect an arrest based on probable cause, but the entry is illegal because the police have no warrant to arrest or search, it does not follow that any evidence seized pursuant thereto is inadmissible in evidence under the *Weeks-Mapp* exclusionary rule. Clearly, any physical evidence obtained or verbal statements made by the victim of the arrest *inside* the dwelling would generally be inadmissible. But any verbal statement made by the victim of the arrest *after* the police have taken him *outside* the home would not be suppressible. At that point, the arrestee is lawfully in custody based on probable cause. The illegality involved in the case is strictly limited to the police action *in* the dwelling, not outside of it.[25]

c. Probable cause justifies custodial arrest for any offense: no limitation for minor offenses or where arrest is unlawful under state law

The Court has held that when there is probable cause to believe that a person has committed a criminal offense—felony or misdemeanor—a law enforcement officer may effect a full custodial arrest without violating the person's Fourth Amendment rights. The fact that the offense in question is punishable by a fine only, and is not a jailable offense, does not change this result.[26] The underlying rationale for this rule is that (1) there is no English or American historical support for a contrary rule prohibiting a full custodial arrest for minor offenses not amounting to a breach of the peace, as indeed, the historical evidence is largely against such a position—and (2) an arrest should be lawful if otherwise supported by probable cause, as a bright-line rule of this nature is much preferable to a case-by-case balancing of the competing interests.[27]

There is, of course, a lurking danger in this rule. The traffic codes in America, for example, are very pervasive and few motorists indeed can avoid violating on occasion some minor provision therein, many of which carry a fine only. Examples include: exceeding the speed limit by one mile per hour, changing lanes without signaling with no traffic in sight, operating one's vehicle in such a manner that the vehicle's front tire slightly touches the highway center line, or forgetting to put on a seat-belt. This necessarily

---

25. New York v. Harris, 495 U.S. 14, 110 S.Ct. 1640, 109 L.Ed.2d 13 (1990) (defendant arrested in his home without a warrant, thereby making arrest illegal while in the house; statement made by defendant in the house inadmissible; statement made by defendant at police station admissible, as defendant was lawfully in custody outside the house; arrest was otherwise based on probable cause; statement was therefore not the fruit of an illegal detention).

26. "The question is whether the Fourth Amendment forbids a warrantless arrest for a minor criminal offense, such as a misdemeanor seatbelt violation punishable only by a fine. We hold that it does not. * * *

"Accordingly, we confirm today what our prior cases have intimated: the standard of probable cause 'applie[s] to all arrests, without the need to 'balance' the interests and circumstances involved in a particular situation.' [citation omitted]. If an officer has probable cause to believe that an individual has committed even a very minor criminal offense in his presence, he may, without violating the Fourth Amendment, arrest the offender." Atwater v. City of Lago Vista, 532 U.S. 927, 121 S.Ct. 1536, 1541, 1557, 19 L.Ed.2d 549 (2001) (Plaintiff in § 1983 action arrested based on probable cause for driving without a seatbelt; held no violation of plaintiff's Fourth Amendment rights; summary judgment properly granted in favor of defendant police).

27. Atwater v. City of Lago Vista, 121 S.Ct. at 1543–57.

means that virtually everyone who drives a car is potentially subject to a full custodial arrest at the discretion of the police—following which the police may have limited authority to search the passenger compartment of the individual's car, and perhaps even have the car towed to a police impoundment lot to inventory the contents of the entire car.[28] Because it is impracticable for the police to arrest every motorist who commits such harmless violations, selective enforcement of the traffic code is necessarily required. Indeed, a culture has developed in America in which a certain amount of minor traffic violations are, in fact, tolerated on a daily basis—to be enforced only in select cases based on the unfettered discretion of law enforcement officers. Given the central purpose of the Fourth Amendment to end the abuse of general exploratory searches conducted in the unfettered discretion of government officials, this may be too much discretionary authority to place in the hands of law enforcement officers.

Still, as previously stated, the Court was convinced (a) that there was no historical support for a contrary rule and thus could not be justified by the original understanding of the Framers, (b) that the practical difficulties of enforcing a contrary case-by-case balancing rule as suggested by Justice O'Connor in dissent would be considerable,[29] and (c) that there was in fact no great problem of the police arresting people in great numbers for fine-only minor offenses.[30]

Moreover, an arrest by a state officer based on probable cause for a minor offense is reasonable under the Fourth Amendment, even though the arrest is otherwise unlawful under state law—as where the state requires a summons, rather than a custodial arrest, for such a minor offense. This is so because the reasonableness of an arrest must be based on Fourth Amendment standards and cannot be rendered unreasonable under this Amendment because state law requires such a result.[31]

---

28. For a discussion of the police right to search a car incident to an arrest of the driver, and to conduct an inventory search of a car following a traffic arrest, see, respectively, Chapter 14, Sections 2f and Chapter 15, Section 2a of this work.

29. Justice O'Connor proposed the following rule: "Instead, I would require that when there is probable cause to believe that a fine-only offense has been committed, the police officer should issue a citation unless the officer is 'able to point to specific and articulable facts which, taken together with rational inferences from those facts, reasonably warrant [the additional] intrusion' of a full custodial arrest." Atwater v. City of Lago Vista, 532 U.S. 927, 121 S.Ct. 1536, 1563–64, 149 L.Ed.2d 549 (2001) (O'Connor, J. dissenting) (internal citation omitted).

30. See Arkansas v. Sullivan, 532 U.S. 769, 121 S.Ct. 1876, 149 L.Ed.2d 994 (2001) (Ginsburg, J. concurring, joined by Stevens, O'Connor and Breyer, JJ.) (expressing the hope that the Court will reconsider *Atwater* if future experience demonstrates "anything like an epidemic of unnecessary minor-offense arrests.").

31. Virginia v. Moore, 553 U.S. 164, 128 S.Ct. 1598, 170 L.Ed. 2d 559 (2008) (arrest by city police officer for misdemeanor of driving with a suspended license based on probable cause held reasonable under the Fourth Amendment—although the arrest was unlawful under state law, as a summons was required for such an offense rather than a custodial arrest) ("We conclude that warrantless arrests for crimes committed in the presence of an arresting officer are reasonable under the Constitution, and that while States are free to regulate such arrests however they desire, state restrictions do not alter Fourth Amendment restrictions.)" 128 S.Ct. at 1607. Similarly, an arrest not based on probable cause is unreasonable under the Fourth Amendment—although the arrest may be lawful under state law, as where state standards on probable cause are more lenient on the police than federal standards. See Ker v. California, 374 U.S. 23, 34, 83 S.Ct. 1623, 10 L.Ed.2d 726 (1963) ("The States are not thereby precluded from developing workable rules governing arrests, searches and seizures to meet 'the practical demands of effective criminal investigation and law enforcement,' provided those rules do not violate the constitutional proscription of unreasonable searches and seizures and the concomitant command that evidence so seized is inadmissible against one who has standing to complain.").

d. Probable cause determination: must be made by a magistrate

The Fourth Amendment requires that a magistrate, not a police officer or a prosecutor, must make the determination of whether "probable cause" exists to make an arrest. This may be done in one of two ways: (1) a magistrate may, *prior to* the arrest, issue an arrest warrant based on an ex parte showing of "probable cause," or (2) a magistrate may, *after* the arrest, make a determination of "probable cause" at a *prompt*, non-adversary hearing.[32] Generally speaking, such a prompt, post-arrest, probable cause determination by a magistrate must take place within 48 hours after arrest.[33] There are, however, two exceptions to this rule.

First, if the delay between arrest and the probable cause determination is *less* than 48 hours, and the *arrested person* can establish that the delay was otherwise unreasonable—i.e., that the delay was for the purpose of gathering evidence to support the arrest, or that the delay was motivated by ill will against the arrested person, or that the delay was for delay's sake—such delay constitutes a violation of the Fourth Amendment, thereby rendering the arrested person's restraint of liberty unreasonable.

Second, if the delay between arrest and probable cause determination is *more* than 48 hours, and the *state* can establish that the delay was due to an emergency or extraordinary circumstances—such delay does not constitute a violation of the Fourth Amendment, and the restraint on the arrested person's liberty is not unreasonable. Delays, however, due to intervening weekends or the time necessary to consolidate the probable cause hearing with other pre-trial proceedings do not qualify as an emergency or extraordinary circumstance.[34]

---

32. "Accordingly, we hold that the Fourth Amendment requires a judicial determination of probable cause as a prerequisite to extended restraint of liberty following arrest. * * * Whatever procedure a State may adopt, it must provide a fair and reliable determination of probable cause as a condition for any significant pretrial restraint of liberty, and this determination must be made by a judicial officer either before or promptly after arrest." Gerstein v. Pugh, 420 U.S. 103, 124–25, 95 S.Ct. 854, 43 L.Ed.2d 54, 71–72 (1975).

33. County of Riverside v. McLaughlin, 500 U.S. 44, 111 S.Ct. 1661, 114 L.Ed.2d 49 (1991).

34. "[W]e believe that a jurisdiction that provides judicial determinations of probable cause within 48 hours of arrest will, as a general matter, comply with the promptness requirement of Gerstein.

"This is not to say that the probable cause determination in a particular case passes constitutional muster simply because it is provided within 48 hours. Such a hearing may nonetheless violate Gerstein if the arrested individual can prove that his or her probable cause determination was delayed unreasonably. Examples of unreasonable delay are delays for the purpose of gathering additional evidence to justify the arrest, a delay motivated by ill will against the arrested individual, or delay for delay's sake. In evaluating whether the delay in a particular case is unreasonable, however, courts must allow a substantial degree of flexibility. Courts cannot ignore the often unavoidable delays in transporting arrested persons from one facility to another, handling late-night bookings where no magistrate is readily available, obtaining the presence of an arresting officer who may be busy processing other suspects or securing the premises of an arrest, or other practical realities.

"Where an arrested individual does not receive a probable cause determination within 48 hours, the calculus changes. In such a case, the arrested individual does not bear the burden of proving an unreasonable delay. Rather, the burden shifts to the government to demonstrate the existence of a bone fide emergency or other extraordinary circumstance. The fact that in a particular case it may take longer than 48 hours to consolidate pretrial proceedings does not qualify as an extraordinary circumstance. Nor, for that matter, do intervening weekends. A jurisdiction that chooses to offer combined proceedings must do so as soon as is reasonably feasible, but in no event later than 48 hours after arrest." County of Riverside v. McLaughlin, 500 U.S. 44, 111 S.Ct. 1661, 114 L.Ed.2d 49, 63 (1991).

It is an open question whether a confession or statement given by a person in police custody after the above time periods have run, but before the required judicial determination of probable cause, is admissible at trial under the *Weeks-Mapp* exclusionary rule.[35] Plainly, however, the suspect is illegally in police custody in violation of his or her Fourth Amendment rights at the time such a confession or statement is given. Indeed, if the suspect applied for a writ of habeas corpus at that point, he or she would *prima facie* be entitled to release. Accordingly, the suspect's confession is arguably the fruit of that illegal detention, so that its admission in evidence would generally be barred under the *Weeks-Mapp* exclusionary rule.[36]

e. Probable cause and reasonable suspicion standards: an overview

The law is settled that an arrest or its functional equivalent must be supported by "probable cause"—a term that is found in the Warrants Clause of the Fourth Amendment.[37] This means that a law enforcement officer must have "probable cause" to believe that a person has committed or is committing a crime before the officer may reasonably "arrest" a person without violating that person's Fourth Amendment rights.[38] "To determine whether an officer had probable cause to arrest an individual, we examine the events leading up to the arrest, and then decide 'whether these historical facts, viewed from the standpoint of an objectively reasonable police officer, amount to' probable cause."[39] The term "probable cause," in turn, has been traditionally defined as a practical, non-technical evidentiary showing of individualized wrongdoing that amounts to *more* than mere suspicion, but *less* than proof beyond a reasonable doubt[40] based on a totality of the circumstances.[41]

The law is also settled that a police officer may temporarily stop a person for a criminal investigative purpose on less than probable cause—namely, based on a reasonable suspicion

35. See Powell v. Nevada, 511 U.S. 79, 114 S.Ct. 1280, 128 L.Ed.2d 1, 8 (1994). Justice Thomas, joined by Chief Justice Rehnquist, filed a dissenting opinion in *Powell* concluding that a *McLaughlin* violation would *not* render a confession inadmissible at trial if obtained after the appropriate time periods had run. 128 L.Ed.2d at 10–12.

36. "Indeed, it has been recognized that the passage of time without an appearance in Court can bring about another Fourth Amendment violation under *Gerstein* and that this will make the confession the fruit of yet another poisonous tree." 6 Wayne LaFave, Search and Seizure § 11.4(b) at 381–382 (5th ed. 2012). For a discussion of *Weeks-Mapp* exclusionary rule in this context, see Chapter 17, Section 3 of this work.

37. "[E]very arrest, and every seizure having the essential attributes of a formal arrest, is unreasonable unless it is supported by probable cause." Michigan v. Summers, 452 U.S. 692, 700, 101 S.Ct. 2587, 69 L.Ed.2d 340, 348 (1981).

38. "Evidence required to establish guilt is not necessary. On the other hand, good faith on the part of the arresting officers is not enough. Probable cause exists if the facts and circumstances known to the officer warrant a prudent man in believing that the offense has been committed. * * * Under our system suspicion is not enough for an officer to lay hands on a citizen. It is better, so the Fourth Amendment teaches, that the guilty sometimes go free than that citizens be subject to easy arrest." Henry v. United States, 361 U.S. 98, 80 S.Ct. 168, 4 L.Ed.2d 134, 139–40 (1959) (internal citations omitted)] (discussion of historical roots of "probable cause).

39. Maryland v. Pringle, 540 U.S. 366, 124 S.Ct. 795, 800, 157 L.Ed.2d 769 (2003), quoting from Ornelas v. United States, 517 U.S. 690, 696, 116 S.Ct. 1657, 134 L.Ed.2d 911 (1996).

40. Brinegar v. United States, 338 U.S. 160, 69 S.Ct. 1302, 93 L.Ed. 1879, 1890–91 (1949). For a general discussion of the evidentiary showing of probable cause, see Chapter 11, Section 3 of this work.

41. Illinois v. Gates, 462 U.S. 213, 103 S.Ct. 2317, 76 L.Ed.2d 527, 543–44 (1983). For a general discussion of the term "probable cause," see Chapter 11, Section 3 of this work.

that the person has committed, is committing or is about to commit a crime, so that the officer may briefly investigate the situation. It all began with the leading case of *Terry v. Ohio.*[42] Although announcing a very narrow stop-and-frisk holding that has since been eroded,[43] the *Terry* Court in its wide-ranging opinion stated that "a police officer may in appropriate circumstances and in an appropriate manner approach a person for purposes of investigating possible criminal behavior even though there is no probable cause to make an arrest,"[44] when based on "specific and articulable facts which, taken together with rational inferences from those facts,"[45] justify a reasonable belief that "criminal activity may be afoot."[46] "And in determining whether the officer acted reasonably in such circumstances, due weight must be given, not to the officer's inchoate and unparticularized suspicion or 'hunch,' but to the specific reasonable inferences which he is entitled to draw from the facts in light of his experience."[47]

In a line of cases decided since then, *Terry* has been oft-cited for the proposition that a police officer may temporarily stop a person based on a reasonable suspicion, grounded in specific and articulable facts, that criminal activity is afoot—i.e., the person has just committed or is committing or is about to commit an offense—so that the officer may further investigate the situation.[48] The rule is largely based on a strong governmental interest in preventing or immediately detecting ongoing criminal activity Moreover, the

---

42. 392 U.S. 1, 88 S.Ct. 1868, 20 L.Ed.2d 889 (1968).

43. At the end of its opinion, the Court announced its narrow holding:

"We merely hold today that where a police officer observes unusual conduct which leads him reasonably to conclude that in light of his experience that criminal activity may be afoot and that the persons with whom he is dealing may be armed and presently dangerous, where in the course of investigating this behavior he identifies himself as a policeman and makes reasonable inquiries, and where nothing in the initial stages of the encounter serves to dispel his reasonable fear for his own or others' safety, he is entitled for the protection of himself and others in the area to conduct a carefully limited search of the outer clothing of such persons in an attempt to discover weapons that might be used to assault him. Such a search is reasonable under the Fourth Amendment, and any weapons seized may properly be introduced in evidence against the person from whom they are taken."

Terry v. Ohio, 392 U.S. 1 at 30–31, 88 S.Ct. 1868, 20 L.Ed.2d at 889.

44. Terry v. Ohio, 392 U.S. at 22, 20 L.Ed.2d at 906–07.

45. Terry v. Ohio, 392 U.S. at 21, 20 L.Ed.2d at 906.

46. Terry v. Ohio, 392 U.S. at 30, 20 L.Ed.2d at 906.

47. Terry v. Ohio, 392 U.S. at 27, 20 L.Ed.2d at 909.

48. "[I]t is clear that not all seizures of the person must be justified by probable cause to arrest for a crime. Prior to Terry v. Ohio, supra, any restraint on the person amounting to a seizure for purposes of the Fourth Amendment was invalid unless justified by probable cause. Terry created a limited exception to this general rule: certain seizures are justifiable under the Fourth Amendment if there is articulable suspicion that a person has committed or is about to commit a crime." Florida v. Royer, 460 U.S. 491, 103 S.Ct. 1319, 75 L.Ed.2d 229, 235–37 (1983). "An investigatory stop is permissible under the Fourth Amendment if supported by reasonable suspicion...." Ornelas v. United States, 517 U.S. 690, 116 S.Ct.1657, 134 L.Ed.2d 911, 918 (1996).

"In Terry v. Ohio ... we held that the police can stop and briefly detain a person for investigative purposes if the officer has reasonable suspicion supported by articulable facts that criminal activity 'may be afoot,' even if the officer lacks probable cause. The officer, of course, must be able to articulate something more than an 'inchoate and unparticularized suspicion or 'hunch.' The Fourth Amendment requires some 'minimal level of objective justification' for making the stop. That level of suspicion is considerably less than proof of wrongdoing by a preponderance of the evidence." United States v. Sokolow, 490 U.S. 1, 109 S.Ct. 1581, 104 L.Ed.2d 1, 10 (1989) (citations omitted).

"The Fourth Amendment prohibits 'unreasonable searches and seizures' by the Government, and its protections extend to brief investigatory stops of persons or vehicles that fall short of a traditional arrest. (citing Terry v. Ohio). Because the 'balance between the public interest and the individual's right to personal security,' tilts in favor of a standard less than probable cause in such cases, the Fourth Amendment is satisfied if the officer's action is supported by reasonable suspicion to believe that same rule applies where there is reasonable suspicion that the detainee has committed a *felony* at some time in the past.[49] Reasonable suspicion, in turn, has been defined as a quantum of proof that is *less* than probable cause and considerably less than a preponderance of the evidence, but *more* than a bare suspicion or an inchoate hunch of criminal activity, based on the totality of the circumstances.[50] Accordingly, a temporary stop for a criminal investigative purpose cannot be made based on bare suspicion or a mere hunch of possible criminal activity.

Under both standards, one must be able to point to behavior or other evidence from which a reasonable person might infer *individual* criminal wrongdoing. Moreover, this evaluation must be based on a totality of the circumstances presented to the law enforcement officer on the street; no relevant circumstance can be ignored as inconsequential in itself.[51]

---

criminal activity 'may be afoot.'" United States v. Arvizu, 534 U.S. 266, 122 S.Ct. 744, 750, 151 L.Ed.2d 740 (2002) (citations omitted).

49. "We need not and do not decide today whether Terry stops to investigate all past crimes, however serious, are permitted. It is enough to say that if police have reasonable suspicion, grounded in specific and articulable facts, that a person they encounter is involved in or wanted in connection with a *completed felony*, then a Terry stop may be made to investigate that suspicion." United States v. Hensley, 469 U.S. 221,105 S.Ct. 675, 83 L.Ed.2d 604, 612 (1985); see also 4 Wayne LaFave, Search and Seizure § 9.2(a) (5th ed. 2012). Arguably, reasonable suspicion that a person has at some time in the past committed a minor offense, such as a fine-only traffic offense, may be insufficient for a temporary *Terry* stop because "[t]he factors in the balance may be somewhat different when a stop to investigate past criminal activity is involved rather than a stop to investigate ongoing criminal conduct."United States v. Hensley, 83 L.Ed.2d at 612.

50. "In *Terry*, we held that an officer may, consistent with the Fourth Amendment, conduct a brief, investigatory stop when the officer has a reasonable, articulable suspicion that criminal activity is afoot. While 'reasonable suspicion' is a less demanding standard than probable cause and requires a showing considerably less than preponderance of the evidence, the Fourth Amendment requires at least a minimal level of objective justification for making the stop. The officer must be able to articulate more than an 'inchoate and unparticularized suspicion or 'hunch' of criminal activity.'" Illinois v. Wardlow, 528 U.S. 119, 120 S.Ct. 673, 145 L.Ed.2d 570, 576 (2000) (internal citations omitted).

"Courts have used a variety of terms to capture the elusive concept of what cause is sufficient to authorize police to stop a person. Terms like 'articulable reasons' and 'founded suspicion' are not self-defining; they fall short of providing clear guidance dispositive of the myriad factual situations that arise. But the essence of all that has been written is that the totality of the circumstances—the whole picture—must be taken into account. Based upon that whole picture, the detaining officers must have a particularized and objective basis for suspecting the particular person stopped of criminal activity."United States v. Cortez, 449 U.S. 411, 101 S.Ct. 690, 66 L.Ed.2d 621, 628–29 (1981).

"When discussing how reviewing courts should make reasonable-suspicion determinations, we have said repeatedly that they must look at the 'totality of the circumstances' of each case to see whether the detaining officer has a 'particularized and objective basis' for suspecting legal wrongdoing. This process allows officers to draw on their own experience and specialized training to make inferences from and deductions about cumulative information available to them that 'might well elude an untrained person.'" United States v. Arvizu, 534 U.S. 266, 122 S.Ct. 744, 750, 151 L.Ed.2d 740 (2002) (citations omitted).

"The Fourth Amendment permits brief investigative stops—such as the traffic stop in this case — when a law enforcement officer has a particularized and objective basis for suspecting a particular person stopped of criminal activity. The reasonable suspicion necessary to justify such a stop is dependent upon both the content of the information possessed by the police and its degree of reliability. The standard takes into account the totality of the circumstances—the whole picture. Although a mere hunch does not create reasonable suspicion, the level of suspicion the standard requires is considerably less that proof of wrongdoing by a preponderance of the evidence, and obviously less than is necessary for probable cause." Navarette v. California, 572 U.S. ___, 134 S.Ct. 1683, 1687, 188 L.Ed.2d 680 (2014) (internal citations and quotation marks omitted).

For a general discussion of the term "reasonable suspicion," see Chapter 11, section 3 of this work.

51. United States v. Arvizu, 534 U.S. 266, 122 S.Ct. 744, 151 L.Ed.2d 740 (2002) (reversing the 9th Circuit Court of Appeals for concluding that seven of the factors involved in the circumstances

Indeed, each circumstance in a series that is innocent individually may constitute probable cause or reasonable suspicion when all circumstances are considered as a whole. And this over-all view of the evidence must be assessed in a practical, non-technical sense from the standpoint of a reasonably well-trained law enforcement officer (a) who is able to make inferences that might elude an untrained person, and (b) who must often make split-second decisions on the street—as opposed to viewing the situation from the standpoint of a detached library scholar.[52]

---

of a temporary stop were not entitled to any consideration, given their otherwise innocent nature when viewed individually; all relevant circumstances must be viewed in totality).

52. Probable cause standard: "This totality of the circumstances approach is far more consistent with our prior treatment of probable cause than is any rigid demand that specific 'tests' be satisfied by every informant's tip. Perhaps the central teaching of our decisions bearing on the probable clause standard is that it is a 'practical, nontechnical conception.' 'In dealing with probable cause, ... as the very name implies, we deal with probabilities. They are not technical; they are the factual and practical considerations on which reasonable and prudent men, not legal technicians, act.' Our observations in United States v. Ortiz ... regarding 'particularized suspicion,' is also applicable to the probable cause standard:

'The process does not deal with hard certainties, but with probabilities. Long before the law of probabilities was articulated as such, practical people formulated certain common-sense conclusions about human behavior; jurors as fact finders are permitted to do the same—and so are law enforcement officers. Finally the evidence thus collected must be seen not in terms of a library analysis by scholars, but as understood by those versed in the field of law enforcement.'

As these comments illustrate, probable cause is a fluid concept—turning on the assessment of probabilities in particular factual contexts—not readily, or even usefully, reduced to a neat set of rules." Illinois v. Gates, 462 U.S. 213, 103 S.Ct. 2317, 76 L.Ed.2d 527, 544 (1983) (internal citations and footnote omitted).

Reasonable suspicion standard: "Courts have used a variety of terms to capture the elusive concept of what cause is sufficient to authorize police to stop a person. Terms like 'articulable reasons' and founded suspicion' are not self-defining; they fall short of providing clear guidance dispositive of the myriad factual situations that arise. But the essence of all that has been written is that the totality of the circumstances—the whole picture—must be taken into account. Based upon that whole picture, the detaining officers must have a particularized and objective basis for suspecting the particular person stopped of criminal activity.

The idea that an assessment of the whole picture must yield a particularized suspicion contains two elements, each of which must be present before a stop is permissible. *First*, the assessment must be based on all the circumstances. The analysis proceeds with various objective observations, information from police reports, if such are available, and consideration of the modes or patterns of operation of certain kinds of lawbreakers. From these data, a trained officer draws inferences and makes deductions—inferences and deductions which might well elude an untrained person.

The process does not deal with hard certainties, but with probabilities. Long before the law of probabilities was articulated as such, practical people formulated certain common-sense conclusions about human behavior; jurors as fact-finders are permitted to do the same—and so are law enforcement officers. Finally, the evidence thus collected must be seen and weighed not in terms of library analysis by scholars, but as understood by those versed in the field of law enforcement.

The *second* element contained in the idea that an assessment of the whole picture must yield a particularized suspicion is the concept that the process just described must raise a suspicion that a particular individual being stopped is engaged in wrongdoing. Chief Justice Warren speaking for the Court in Terry v. Ohio, supra, said that '[t]his demand for specificity in the information upon which police action is based is the central teaching of this Court's Fourth Amendment jurisprudence.'" United States v. Cortez, 449 U.S. 411, 101 S.Ct. 690, 66 L.Ed.2d 621, 628–29 (1981) (internal citations omitted).

"When discussing how reviewing courts should make reasonable-suspicion determinations, we have said repeatedly that they must look at the 'totality of the circumstances' of each case to see whether the detaining officer has a 'particularized and objective basis' for suspecting legal wrongdoing. This process allows officers to draw on their own experience and specialized training to make inferences from and deductions about cumulative information available to them that 'might well elude an untrained person.'" United States v. Arvizu, 534 U.S. 266, 122 S.Ct. 744, 750, 151 L.Ed.2d 740 (2002) (citations omitted).

In applying these admittedly flexible standards, the U.S. Supreme Court—and the lower federal and state courts in the wake thereof—have given law enforcement officials wide-ranging, although not unlimited, authority to make arrests or temporary detentions in fast-moving, emergency encounters on the street and elsewhere while investigating felony offenses—especially crimes of violence, theft and narcotics. The community expects swift police action in investigating such offenses, and by and large, the Court—and the lower federal and state courts—have sustained these intrusions.[53] Only in the rare case, where, to the judicial mind, the law enforcement conduct smacks of police state tactics[54] or where the individual's conduct was relatively innocuous[55] or at worst minimally

---

"We have long held that the 'touchstone of the Fourth Amendment is reasonableness.' Reasonableness, in turn, is measured in objective terms by examining the totality of the circumstances. In applying this test, we have consistently eschewed bright-line rules, instead emphasizing the fact-specific nature of the reasonableness inquiry." Ohio v. Robinette, 519 U.S. 33, 117 S.Ct. 417, 136 L.Ed.2d 347, 354 (1996).

53. For an extensive treatment of the application of the "probable cause" standard for arrests in the U.S. Supreme Court, as well as the lower federal and state courts, see 2 Wayne LaFave, Search and Seizure §§3.1–3.7 at 1–555 (5th ed. 2012). For a similar treatment of the "reasonable suspicion" standard for temporary detentions in the same courts, see 4 Wayne LaFave Search and Seizure §9.1 at 352–369; §9.5 at 643–837 (5th ed. 2012); 1 John Wesley Hall, Search and Seizure §§21.11–21.14 (5th ed. 2013). Also see lower federal and state court cases collected on (a) probable cause for arrest collected at "Arrest" §§63.4 (.5), (1), (2), (3) West Key Nos., and on (b) reasonable suspicion for a temporary detention collected at "Arrest" §§63.5(1), (3.1), (4), (5), (6) West Key Nos.

The following is a representative sampling of felony arrests upheld by the U.S. Supreme Court: Hill v. California, 401 U.S. 797, 91 S.Ct. 1106, 28 L.Ed.2d 484 (1971) (robbery arrest upheld although police were reasonably mistaken that petitioner was the suspect police were seeking); Chambers v. Maroney, 399 U.S. 42, 90 S.Ct. 1975, 26 L.Ed.2d 419 (1970) (robbery arrest of suspects in car upheld); Peters v. New York, 392 U.S. 40, 88 S.Ct. 1889, 20 L.Ed.2d 917 (1968) (attempted burglary arrest in apartment building upheld); Ker v. California, 374 U.S. 23, 83 S.Ct. 1623, 10 L.Ed.2d 726 (1963) (narcotics arrests in apartment upheld).

The following is a representative sampling of temporary detentions upheld by the U.S. Supreme Court: United States v. Arvizu, 534 U.S. 266, 122 S.Ct. 744, 151 L.Ed.2d 740 (2002) (U.S. border patrol stop upheld of suspicious minivan on unpaved road near the U.S. Mexican border that was often used by alien smugglers to avoid a border patrol checkpoint in the area); United States v. Sharpe, 470 U.S. 675, 105 S.Ct. 1568, 84 L.Ed.2d 605 (1985) (temporary detention of suspects for drug trafficking while driving heavily-laden truck and companion car upheld); United States v. Cortez, 449 U.S. 411, 101 S.Ct. 690, 66 L.Ed.2d 621 (1981) (U.S. Border Patrol stop of suspect for alien smuggling while driving a pickup truck near U.S.-Mexican border upheld). Terry v. Ohio, 392 U.S. 1, 88 S.Ct. 1868, 20 L.Ed.2d 889 (1968) (temporary detention of suspects in downtown area during daylight hours based on suspicious conduct that appeared to experienced officer that men were surveying a store for a possible hold-up).

54. For example, a warrantless, functional-equivalent police arrest of a suspect for "investigation" has been consistently struck down where the suspect was picked up on the street without his or her consent and questioned or fingerprinted at the police station. Hayes v. Florida, 470 U.S. 811, 105 S.Ct. 1643, 84 L.Ed.2d 705 (1985) (fingerprinting); Dunaway v. New York, 442 U.S. 200, 99 S.Ct. 2248, 60 L.Ed.2d 824 (1979) (questioning); Davis v. Mississippi, 394 U.S. 721, 89 S.Ct.1394, 22 L.Ed.2d 676 (1969) (fingerprinting). "Nothing is more clear than that the Fourth Amendment was meant to prevent wholesale intrusions upon the personal security of our citizenry, whether these intrusions be deemed 'arrests' or 'investigatory detentions.'" Davis v. Mississippi, 394 U.S. 721, 726–27, 89 S.Ct. 1394, 22 L.Ed.2d 676, 681 (1969).

55. See, e.g., United States v. Brignoni-Ponce, 422 U.S. 873, 95 S.Ct. 2574, 45 L.Ed.2d 607 (1975) (U.S. Border patrol temporary stop of a car on a highway outside San Clemente, California near the U.S.-Mexican border struck down because it was based solely on the fact that the three occupants of the car were of Mexican descent). "Large numbers of native-born and naturalized citizens have the characteristics identified with Mexican ancestry, and even in the border area a relatively small proportion of them are aliens. The likelihood that any given person of Mexican ancestry is an alien is high enough to make Mexican appearance a relevant factor, but standing alone it does not justify stopping all Mexican-Americans to ask if they are aliens." 422 U.S. at 886–87, 45 L.Ed.2d at 619–20.

suspicious[56] or where the information presented to the trial court was vague and incomplete[57]—have the courts struck down such intrusions as not based on probable cause or reasonable suspicion. In particular, if the activity involved is often engaged in by a large number of law-abiding people, the Court has been reluctant to stamp such conduct as worthy of a temporary detention, much less an arrest.[58] Still, if the individual's conduct is susceptible of a reasonable inference of criminal wrongdoing, the fact that it is *also* reasonably susceptible of an inference of innocent behavior is insufficient to render the arrest or stop invalid.[59] All things considered, then, the courts have generally been quite lenient

---

56. See, e.g., Sibron v. New York, 392 U.S. 40, 88 S.Ct. 1889, 20 L.Ed.2d 917 (1968) (no probable cause to arrest suspect or temporarily detain him based solely on the fact that police observed suspect talking to a number of known narcotics addicts over an eight hour period; nothing was passed between the suspect and the addicts, and the content of the conversations was unknown). "The inference that persons who talk to narcotics addicts are engaged in criminal traffic in narcotics is simply not the sort of reasonable inference required to support an intrusion by police upon an individual's personal security." 392 U.S. at 62, 20 L.Ed.2d at 934. Henry v. United States, 361 U.S. 98, 80 S.Ct. 168, 4 L.Ed.2d 134 (1959) (no probable cause to arrest petitioner for theft from an interstate shipment when he was observed by FBI agents with his companion traveling in a car and picking up cartons in an alley in a residential neighborhood; the agents had received information from the employer of the petitioner's companion concerning the companion's implication with interstate shipments, although no accusation of theft from these shipments was ever made). "The rumor about [the companion] is therefore meaningless. * * * So far as the record shows, petitioner had not even been suspected of criminal activity prior to this time. Riding in a car, stopping in an alley, picking up packages, driving away—these are all acts that were outwardly innocent. Their movements in the car had no mark of fleeing men or men acting furtively. The case might be different if the packages had been taken from a terminal or from an interstate trucking platform. But they were not." 361 U.S. at 103, 4 L.Ed.2d at 139.

57. See, e.g., Beck v. Ohio, 379 U.S. 89, 85 S.Ct. 223, 13 L.Ed.2d 142 (1964) (gambling arrest struck down based largely on the paucity of facts presented to sustain the arrest). "When the constitutional validity of an arrest is challenged, it is the function of a court to determine whether the facts available to the officers at the moment of the arrest would 'warrant a man of reasonable caution in the belief' that an offense has been committed. If the court is not informed of the facts upon which the arresting officers acted, it cannot properly discharge that function." 379 U.S. at 96, 13 L.Ed.2d at 148.

58. See, e.g., Brown v. Texas, 443 U.S. 47, 99 S.Ct. 2637, 61 L.Ed.2d 357 (1979) (temporary detention of suspect struck down where police observed suspect walking in opposite direction from another person late at night in an alley located in a neighborhood frequented by drug users). "Officer Vegas testified at appellant's trial that the situation in the alley 'looked suspicious,' but was unable to point to any facts supporting that conclusion. [fn. 2. This situation is to be distinguished from the observations of a trained, experienced police officer who is able to perceive and articulate meaning in given conduct which would be wholly innocent to the untrained observer]. There is no indication in the record that it was unusual for people to be in the alley. The fact that appellant was in a neighborhood frequented by drug users, standing alone, is not a basis for concluding that appellant himself was engaged in criminal conduct. *In short, appellant's activity was no different from the activity of other pedestrians in that neighborhood.*" 443 U.S. at 52, 61 L.Ed.2d at 362 (emphasis added). Reid v. Georgia, 448 U.S. 438, 100 S.Ct. 2752, 65 L.Ed.2d 890 (1980), in which the Court struck down a *Terry* stop by drug agents in the Atlanta airport based on the following facts: (1) defendant arrived on a flight from Ft. Lauderdale which the agent said was a source city for cocaine; (2) defendant arrived early in the morning when the agent said law enforcement activity at the airport is diminished; (3) defendant walked ahead of his companion in the airport concourse, occasionally looked back at the companion, and eventually talked to the companion in the main lobby of the terminal. The Court concluded that first two factors stated above "*describe a very large category of presumably innocent travelers, who would be subject to virtually random seizures were the Court to conclude that as little foundation as there was in this case could justify a seizure.*" 65 L.Ed. 2d at 894 (emphasis added). "Nor can we agree, on this record, that the manner in which the petitioner and his companion walked through the airport reasonably could have led the agent to suspect them of wrongdoing." Id.

59. "Respondent argues that we must rule in his favor because the facts suggested a family in a minivan on a holiday outing. A determination that reasonable suspicion exists, however, need not

with law enforcement officials in applying the standards of probable cause and reasonable suspicion at the street level—without, at the same time, giving law enforcement carte blanche authority to do whatever they think proper.

There is, of course, a certain danger in according law enforcement officials such wide-ranging power—however necessary this may be—because the finger of suspicion is a long one that may very well entangle perfectly law-abiding people in harassing and humiliating encounters with police. There is also the real danger that the victims of such action may often be minorities, the poor and the powerless—the least able to protect themselves against official abuses of power. Certainly, there is a strong governmental interest in enforcing our criminal law so that all are free to walk the streets in relative safety, but not at the expense of police state tactics. Accordingly, the Court has always felt the need to put a limited "bite" in the probable cause and reasonable suspicion standards so that the police do not run amok, no matter how well-intentioned they may be.[60] Indeed, it is settled that subjective good faith on the part of a law enforcement officer does not in itself satisfy the probable cause or reasonable suspicion standards—else "the protections of the Fourth Amendment would evaporate, and the people would be 'secure in their persons, houses, papers or effects,' only in the discretion of the police."[61]

Moreover, the Court has long recognized that an arrest represents a much greater intrusion into one's personal security as opposed to a temporary detention, and accordingly requires a greater threshold of proof to effect. A showing of reasonable suspicion of criminal wrongdoing sufficient for a temporary detention is totally insufficient to effect an arrest.[62] Indeed, the Court has cautioned:

> It is basic that an arrest with or without a warrant must stand on firmer ground than mere suspicion. The quantum of information which constitutes probable cause—evidence that would "warrant a man of reasonable caution in the belief" that a felony has been committed—must be measured by the facts of the particular case. The history of the use, and not infrequent abuse, of the power of arrest cautions that a relaxation of the fundamental requirements of probable cause would "leave law-abiding citizens at the mercy of the officers' whim or caprice."[63]

In short, there are real limits to the otherwise wide-ranging authority of law enforcement officers to police our streets and enforce our criminal law through arrests and temporary detentions. The extent of this considerable authority and the limits thereto will be further explored in the subsections that follow in this Chapter.

---

rule out the possibility of innocent conduct." United States v. Arvizu, 534 U.S. 266, 122 S.Ct. 744, 753, 151 L.Ed.2d 740 (2002).

60. See, e.g., United States v. Brignoni-Ponce, 422 U.S. 873, 888–90, 95 S.Ct. 2574, 45 L.Ed.2d 607, 620–22 (1975) (Douglas, J. concurring). Indeed, one cannot be unmindful of Justice Douglas' ominous warning as the lone dissenter in Terry v. Ohio, 392 U.S. 1, 88 S.Ct. 1868, 20 L.Ed.2d 889 (1968), that the majority's decision "take[s] a long step down the totalitarian path," that "there have been powerful hydraulic pressures throughout our history to water down constitutional guarantees and give the police the upper hand ... [which] pressure has probably never been greater than it is today," that "if the individual is no longer to be sovereign, if the police can pick him up whenever they do not like the cut of his jib, if they can 'seize' and 'search' him in their discretion, we enter a new regime." 392 U.S. at 39, 20 L.Ed.2d at 916.

61. Beck v. Ohio, 379 U.S. 89, 97, 85 S.Ct. 223, 13 L.Ed.2d 142, 148 (1964).

62. See, e.g., Florida v. Royer, 460 U.S. 491, 103 S.Ct. 1319, 75 L.Ed.2d 229 (1983) (temporary stop in airport based on reasonable suspicion upheld, but an arrest based on the same showing struck down).

63. Wong Sun v. United States, 371 U.S. 471, 83 S.Ct. 407, 9 L.Ed.2d 441, 450 (1963).

f. Sources of information: private citizens, police informers and anonymous tipsters

Probable cause and reasonable suspicion may be based in whole or in part on a law enforcement officer's first-hand personal observations or on evidence that would otherwise be admissible at trial. But this is not essential. Probable cause or reasonable suspicion may also be based in whole or in part on hearsay, informer or anonymous tip information or on evidence that would otherwise be inadmissible at trial—so long as it is reasonable under the totality of the circumstances for the officer to effect an arrest or temporary detention based on such evidence. Stated differently, a very practical approach is employed: would a reasonable police officer have responded to the information in question by making an arrest or a *Terry* stop based on the totality of the circumstances.

Private citizens. Often the hearsay information comes from private persons, including crime victims and third party witnesses, who as good citizens report crime to the police. The courts have generally treated such information as inherently reliable unless, in the unusual case, there is something in the underlying circumstances that would cause a reasonable person to doubt the report.[64]

Police informers. At other times, the hearsay information may come from police informers. Here the Court has been somewhat more skeptical because police informers frequently are unsavory characters who have a motive to lie. These informers are sometimes given money by the police in exchange for the information given; they may also have pending criminal cases against them and are seeking leniency for the information they give. Still, the Court has recognized that the use of these often disreputable characters is essential in investigating a variety of criminal offenses, particularly illegal drug offenses. The Court has, accordingly, considered such informer information to be a reliable basis for probable cause or reasonable suspicion—so long as there is some reasonable basis for the police to believe the informer's information, which is ordinarily above and beyond what is required when dealing with the average citizen.

Consequently, the courts have consistently upheld arrests based on a police informant's information provided there is some reasonable basis for crediting the information based on the "totality of the circumstances," including one or more of the following: (a) the detail provided in the report, (b) the informant's asserted basis for his/her information,

64. See 2 Wayne LaFave, Search and Seizure § 3.4 (5th ed. 2012) (cases collected); and 1 John Wesley Hall, Search and Seizure § 621 (5th ed. 2013) (cases collected). See cases collected at "Searches and Seizures" § 38, and "Arrest" § 63.4(7.1), West Key Nos. See also Illinois v. McArthur, 531 U.S. 326, 121 S.Ct. 946, 148 L.Ed.2d 838, 848 (2001) (estranged wife's report that her husband had marijuana in their trailer home after she had emerged therefrom with her personal belongings, while police were standing outside to prevent any potential violence, constituted probable cause to believe the report; constructive seizure of the trailer-home upheld in which the husband was prevented from entering home alone, while police obtained a search warrant for the home); Hiibel v. Sixth Judicial District Court, 542 U.S. 177, 124 S.Ct. 2451, 159 L.Ed.2d 292 (2004) (private citizen informs sheriff's office by phone that he has just seen a man assault a woman in a red and silver GMC truck located at a named location in county; deputy sheriff responds to this location and sees the described truck parked alongside the road with a woman in the truck and a man standing outside the truck; "Here there is no question the initial stop was based on reasonable suspicion, satisfying the Fourth Amendment requirements noted in Brown." 124 S.Ct. at 2457.).

(c) the past proven reliability of the informant, and (d) corroboration of information from other sources.[65] This is shown, for example, where the police have used this informer in the past and the informer's information has always been proven reliable—hence the informer is said to be a reliable informer whom the police have reason to trust.[66] On the other hand, where an informer with no proven record of reliability accuses another of a crime without providing any factual detail, an arrest based thereon has generally been held invalid.[67] These same considerations are also relevant in determining whether to uphold or strike down a temporary detention based on reasonable suspicion—although the strength of the evidence need not be as strong as that needed to constitute probable cause for arrest.[68]

There was a time, however, when the Court required a two-pronged test for corroborating informant information in order to constitute probable cause for any purpose: a veracity prong and a basis-for-knowledge prong. Under the veracity prong, there had to be some showing that the informant was credible or that his or her information was reliable; under the basis-for-knowledge prong, there also had to be some showing as to how the informer came upon the information being disclosed to the police.[69] That strict rule has since been disapproved in favor of a totality-of-the-circumstances approach in which all the surrounding circumstances must be considered in determining whether the informer's information constitutes probable cause; the veracity and basis-for-knowledge prongs are important considerations in this process, but neither are *sine qua non* require-

65. See 2 Wayne LaFave, Search and Seizure § 3.3 at 122–264 (5th ed. 2012); see also cases collected at "Arrest" §§ 63.4(7.1), (8) (9) West Key Nos.

66. See, e.g., Draper v. United States, 358 U.S. 307, 79 S.Ct. 329, 3 L.Ed.2d 327 (1959) (arrest upheld based on (a) police informant's information that suspect was selling narcotics to several addicts and was returning by train from out of town with three ounces of heroin; (b) informant had always given reliable information to police in the past; and (c) informant accurately predicted that suspect would arrive in town by train at a particular time, and accurately described the suspect).

67. Beck v. Ohio, 379 U.S. 89, 85 S.Ct. 223, 13 L.Ed.2d 142 (1964) (gambling arrest held invalid based on (a) undisclosed reports and information from undisclosed persons, and (b) suspect's prior criminal record for illegal gambling); Recznik v. City of Loraine, 393 U.S. 166, 89 S.Ct. 342, 21 L.Ed.2d 317 (1968) (gambling arrest held invalid based on information from unknown "people on the street" that "all sorts of gambling devices" were in suspect's apartment; also police observed a large number of cars parked in the vicinity of suspect's building late at night); Taylor v. Alabama, 457 U.S. 687, 102 S.Ct. 2664, 73 L.Ed.2d 314 (1982) (a robbery arrest held invalid based on a report from a person incarcerated on unrelated charges that "he had heard that [petitioner] was involved in the robbery"); see also Wong Sun v. United States, 371 U.S. 471, 83 S.Ct. 407, 9 L.Ed.2d 441 (1963) (narcotics arrest held invalid based on information received from a person arrested with heroin in his possession, and who not previously been a police informant, that he had bought an ounce of heroin that night from "Blackie Toy," the proprietor of a laundry located at a particular address).

68. "Reasonable suspicion is a less demanding standard than probable cause not only in the sense that reasonable suspicion can be established with information that is different in quantity or content than that required to establish probable cause, but also in the sense that reasonable suspicion can arise from information that is less reliable than that required to show probable cause." Alabama v. White, 496 U.S. 325, 110 S.Ct. 2412, 110 L.Ed.2d 301, 308(1990). See, e.g., Adams v. Williams, 407 U.S. 143, 92 S.Ct. 1921, 32 L.Ed.2d 612 (1972) (an informer's tip that a defendant, seated in a car late at night in a high crime area, was carrying a gun, constituted enough indicia of reliability to justify a *Terry* stop; informer had given the police information in the past, although no showing that the information had proven reliable, and was present at the scene and thus was subject to arrest for giving false information to police if the information proved incorrect.).

69. Aguilar v. Texas, 378 U.S. 108, 84 S.Ct. 1509, 12 L.Ed.2d 723 (1964); Spinelli v. United States, 393 U.S. 410, 89 S.Ct. 584, 21 L.Ed.2d 637 (1969).

ments.[70] The same approach holds true in determining whether the informant's information constitutes reasonable suspicion for a temporary stop.[71]

Anonymous tipsters. On occasion, the hearsay information that a law enforcement officer receives may come from an *anonymous* telephone tipster or an *anonymous* letter. Unlike a tip from a *known* informant who speaks to the police, however, an *anonymous* tip rarely contains much detail, as the person involved is usually guarded in what is said so as to protect his or her anonymity. Consequently, such anonymous tips, by definition, usually fail to demonstrate either (a) the veracity of the tipster, or (b) the basis of the tipster's knowledge.[72]

Of course, in an unusual case, if the tip does demonstrate either of the above, this showing may be enough to constitute reasonable suspicion for a temporary stop, or perhaps even probable cause to arrest—depending on the totality of the circumstances. But absent such a showing, it is settled that, as a general rule, an anonymous tip does not, in itself, provide a sufficient basis for a temporary stop—and *a fortiori* for an arrest. Something more is generally required.[73]

---

70. "We agree ... that an informant's veracity, 'reliability,' and 'basis of knowledge' are all highly relevant in determining the value of his report. We do not agree, however, that these elements should be understood as separate and independent requirements in every case.... Rather, as detailed below, they should be understood simply as closely intertwined issues that may usefully illuminate the common-sense, practical question whether there is 'probable cause' to believe that contraband or evidence is located in a particular place. This totality of the circumstances approach is far more consistent with our prior treatment of probable cause than is any rigid demand that specific 'tests' be satisfied by every informant's tip." Illinois v. Gates, 462 U.S. 213, 103 S.Ct. 2317, 76 L.Ed.2d 527, 543 (1983). "[A] deficiency in one [of these factors] may be compensated for, in determining the over-all reliability of a tip, by a strong showing as to the other [factor], or by some other indicia of reliability. If, for example, a particular informant is known for the unusual reliability of his predictions of certain types of criminal activities in a locality, his failure, in a particular case, to thoroughly set forth the basis of his knowledge surely should not serve as an absolute bar to a finding of probable cause based on his tip.... Conversely, even if we entertain some doubt as to an informant's motives, his explicit and detailed description of alleged wrongdoing, along with a statement that the event was observed first hand, entitles his tip to greater weight than might otherwise be the case." Illinois v. Gates, 76 L.Ed.2d at 545.

71. United States v. Cortez, 449 U.S. 411, 101 S.Ct. 690, 66 L.Ed.2d 621, 628–29 (1981) (totality-of-the-circumstances approach approved)."When discussing how reviewing courts should make reasonable-suspicion determinations, we have said repeatedly that they must look at the 'totality of the circumstances' of each case to see whether the detaining officer has a 'particularized and objective basis' for suspecting legal wrongdoing. This process allows officers to draw on their own experience and specialized training to make inferences from and deductions about the cumulative information available to them 'that 'might well elude an untrained person.'" United States v. Arvizu, 534 U.S. 266, 122 S.Ct. 744, 750–51, 151 L.Ed.2d 740 (2002) (citations omitted). "Informant's tips, like other clues and evidence coming to a policeman on the scene, may vary greatly in their value and reliability. One simple rule will not cover every situation. Some tips completely lacking indicia of reliability, would either warrant no police response or require further investigation before a forcible stop of a suspect would be authorized. But in other situations ... the subtleties of the hearsay rule should not thwart a police response." Adams v. Williams, 407 U.S. 143, 147, 92 S.Ct. 1921, 32 L.Ed.2d 612, 617–18 (1972).

72. Florida v. J.L., 529 U.S. 266, 120 S.Ct. 1375, 1378, 146 L.Ed.2d 254 (2000); Alabama v. White, 496 U.S. 325, 329, 110 S.Ct. 2412, 110 L.Ed.2d 301, 308 (1990).

73. "The opinion in [Illinois v.]Gates recognized that an anonymous tip alone seldom demonstrates the informant's basis of knowledge or veracity inasmuch as ordinary citizens generally do not provide extensive recitations of the basis of their everyday observations and given that the veracity of persons supplying anonymous tips is 'by hypothesis largely unknown and unknowable.' This is not to say that an anonymous tip could never provide the reasonable suspicion necessary for a Terry stop. But the tip in Gates was not an exception to the general rule, and the anonymous tip in this case is like the one in Gates: '[it] provides virtually nothing from which one might conclude that the [the caller] is

The reason for this different treatment of anonymous tipsters, as opposed to known informants, lies in the nature of an anonymous tip. Clearly, such a tipster's anonymity presents a real danger that the tipster may "lie with impunity."[74] Unlike the known informer, the anonymous tipster is unknown and cannot be prosecuted for giving false information to the police if the tip turns out to be a lie. By a simple accusation of crime, such a tipster may set in motion an intrusive arrest, temporary detention or search against a targeted individual. On the other hand, many otherwise truthful tipsters would be reluctant to come forward with information concerning known criminal activity if they had to reveal their identity for fear of reprisals by the suspect or others, or from an understandable desire not to get entangled in the criminal justice system. Accordingly, a cautious totality-of-the-circumstances approach is used by the Court to determine whether an anonymous tip constitutes reasonable suspicion for a temporary stop.[75]

For example, a corroborative showing of reliability is made—sufficient to constitute reasonable suspicion for a temporary stop based on an anonymous tip—if the tipster predicts, in part, the future movements of the suspect. This shows that the tipster has some inside knowledge about the suspect, and that the tipster's accusation of illegal activity is entitled to some credence.[76]

But—subject to an emergency exception to be discussed later—simply because an anonymous tipster gives an accurate description of a person at an accurately described location does not, without more, constitute a sufficient basis to give credence to the tipster's accusation of criminal behavior, and therefore cannot constitute reasonable suspicion for a temporary detention.[77] Otherwise, there would be virtually no limit on

---

either honest or his information reliable; likewise the [tip] gives absolutely no indication of the basis for the [caller's] predictions regarding [defendant's] criminal activities.' By requiring '[s]omething more,' as *Gates* did, we merely apply what we said in Adams [v. Williams]: 'Some tips, completely lacking in reliability, would either warrant no police response or require further investigation before a forcible stop of a suspect would be authorized.'" Alabama v. White, 496 U.S. 325, 110 S.Ct. 2412, 110 L.Ed.2d 301, 308 (1990) (internal citations omitted). See cases collected at "Arrest" §63.4(10) West Key No.

74. Florida v. J.L., 529 U.S. 266, 120 S.Ct. 1375, 1381, 146 L.Ed.2d 254 (2000) (Kennedy, J. concurring).

75. "We have firmly rejected the argument that reasonable cause for an investigative stop can only be based on the officer's personal observation, rather than information supplied by another person. Of course, an anonymous tip alone seldom demonstrates the informant's basis of knowledge or veracity. * * * But under appropriate circumstances, an anonymous tip can demonstrate sufficient indicia of reliability to provide reasonable suspicion to make an investigatory stop." Navarette v. California, 572 U.S. ___, 134 S.Ct. 1683, 1688, 188 L.Ed.2d 680 (2014) (internal citations and quotation marks omitted).

76. Alabama v. White, 496 U.S. 325, 329, 110 S.Ct. 2412, 110 L.Ed.2d 301 (1990) (anonymous telephone tip that defendant possessed cocaine and would be leaving a particular apartment building at a particular time in a particular car and would then go to a particular motel was corroborated by police observation that defendant left the described apartment building at the predicted time, got in the described car and drove toward [but was stopped before she arrived at] the described motel—constituted reasonable suspicion for a temporary *Terry* stop of defendant).

77. "An accurate description of a subject's readily observable location and appearance is of course reliable in this limited sense: It will help police correctly identify the person whom the tipster means to accuse. Such a tip, however, does not show that the tipster has knowledge of concealed criminal activity. The reasonable suspicion here at issue requires that the tip be reliable in its assertion of illegality, not just in its tendency to identify a determinate person." Florida v. J.L., 529 U.S. 266, 120 S.Ct. 1375, 1379, 146 L.Ed.2d 254 (2000) (anonymous telephone tip to police that a described person at a described location is carrying a concealed firearm held insufficient to constitute reasonable suspicion for a temporary investigative stop and frisk; the fact that the description given matches the defendant at the described location does not, without more, constitute a sufficient showing that the

an anonymous tipster's power to cause any person a humiliating temporary detention, so long as the tipster knew how to accurately describe the target and the target's location. This result is not changed by the fact that the anonymous tipster accuses someone of illegal gun possession; there is no "firearm exception" to the reliability analysis required for anonymous tips to justify a temporary detention.[78]

Where, however, in the unusual scenario, the anonymous tipster states the *basis for his knowledge* that a particularly-described suspect at a particular location has just engaged [or is engaging] in criminal activity, such as the tipster's recent eyewitness account of the alleged criminal activity, the calculus weighs significantly in favor of sustaining a temporary Terry stop based on the tip. This is particularly true where the account is given in a 911 emergency call to the police where such calls are typically recorded and can be traced.[79]

An anonymous tip can amount to probable cause to arrest if the corroborative factors are strong enough.[80] But even where such factors do not tip the balance in favor of probable

---

informant's information concerning criminal activity is reliable). Indeed, this case is Alabama v. White, 496 U.S. 325, 110 S.Ct. 2412, 110 L.Ed.2d 301 (1990), but without the predictive behavior.

78. "But an automatic firearms exception to our established reliability analysis would rove too far. Such an exception would enable any person seeking to harass another to set in motion an intrusive, embarrassing police search of a targeted person by placing an anonymous tip falsely reporting the target's unlawful carriage of a gun." Florida v. J.L., 120 S.Ct. 1380.

79. "After a 911 caller reported that a vehicle had run her off the road, a police officer located the vehicle she identified during the call and executed a traffic stop. We hold that the stop complied with the Fourth Amendment because, under the totality of the circumstances, the officer had reasonable suspicion that the driver was intoxicated." Navarette v. California, 572 U.S. ___, 134 S.Ct. 1683, 1686, 188 L.Ed.2d 680 (2014)

In Navarette, an unnamed person made a 911 emergency call to the California Highway Patrol stating that she was a motorist and had just been run off U.S. Highway 1 at mile marker 88 by a silver Ford pickup truck with a particularly described license plate; this information was placed on the Highway Patrol's radio network; 18 minutes later, a Highway Patrol officer spotted this pickup truck on U.S. Highway 1 near mile marker 69 driving south in the direction described in the call; the officer followed the truck for five minutes and noticed nothing unusual; he and another backup officer then pulled the truck over; as the officers approached the truck on foot, they smelled an odor of marijuana coming from the truck; they detained the driver and passenger, searched the truck bed, and seized 30 pounds of marijuana; held: search upheld—the stop of the truck driver, which led to the search, was based on reasonable suspicion.

"By reporting that she had been run off the road by a specific vehicle—a silver Ford F-150 pickup, license plate 8D94925—the caller necessarily claimed eyewitness knowledge of alleged dangerous driving. That basis of knowledge lends significant support to the tip's reliability." 134 S.Ct. at 1689.

"There is also another reason to think that the 911 caller in this case was telling the truth. Police confirmed the truck's location near mile marker 69 (roughly 19 highway miles south of the location reported in the 911 call) at 4:00 p.m. (roughly 18 minutes after the 911 call). That timeline of events suggests that the caller reported the incident soon after she was run off the road. That sort of contemporaneous report has long been treated as especially reliable." 134 S.Ct. at 1689.

"Another indicator of veracity is the caller's use of the 911 emergency system. A 911 call has some features that allow for identifying and tracing callers, and thus provide some safeguards against making false reports with impunity. As this case illustrates, 911 calls can be recorded, which provides victims with an opportunity to identify false tipster's voice and subject him to prosecution. * * * None of this is to suggest that 911 calls are per se reliable. Given the forgoing technological and regulatory developments, however, a reasonable police officer could conclude that a false tipster would think twice before using the system. The caller's use of the 911 system is therefore one of the relevant circumstances that, taken together, justified the officer's reliance on the information reported in the 911 call." 134 S.Ct. at 1989–1690.

80. See Illinois v. Gates, 462 U.S. 213, 103 S.Ct. 2317, 76 L.Ed.2d 527 (1983) (anonymous letter sent to police accusing defendants of drug trafficking and predicting defendant's immediate future travel movements by airplane from Illinois to Florida to obtain illegal drugs, and by car back to Illinois,

cause to arrest, these factors may amount to reasonable suspicion for a temporary detention when combined with the totality of the circumstances in the case.[81]

Nonetheless, there is one important caveat to this entire analysis. It is highly doubtful that *any* showing of reliability or corroboration is required for an anonymous tip if the danger alleged in the tip potentially threatens the lives of countless people—such as a tip that a person has a bomb or a nuclear device in a public place. In that situation, the gravity of the governmental interests involved is enormous and is likely to outweigh any competing privacy interests—sufficient to sustain at least a temporary detention, and perhaps even a search of, say, a briefcase in which the bomb or nuclear device is alleged to be located. The Fourth Amendment is not a suicide pact.[82] The same may be also be true where the anonymous tip concerns criminal activity in a place where there is a diminished expectation of privacy, such as an airport or a school—although, depending on the circumstances, the calculus in that situation might weigh in favor of the individual, absent some extreme danger to lives or property.[83]

g. Arrest or temporary detention based on police "bolo" or radio bulletin

Many times the police officer who actually makes the arrest does so based solely on a physical description of the suspect that comes over the police radio to "be on the lookout" [bolo] for a particular described person who is wanted for a particular offense—based, for example, on an outstanding arrest warrant or information supplied to the police by a third party. Other than this bolo description, the arresting officer usually has no other information about the case. Clearly, the officer may lawfully arrest a person based on this bolo description—provided (a) the bolo itself is based on probable cause [the arrest warrant is valid or the information supplied by a third person amounts to probable cause

---

was corroborated by police investigation that tracked the defendants' activity as predicted; probable cause stated for issuance of search warrant.).

81. "Reasonable suspicion is a less demanding standard than probable cause not only in the sense that reasonable suspicion can be established with information that is different in quantity or content than that required to establish probable cause, but also in the sense that reasonable suspicion can arise from information that is less reliable than that required to show probable cause. * * * Reasonable suspicion, like probable cause, is dependent upon both the content or information possessed by the police and its degree of reliability. Both factors—quantity and quality—are considered in the 'totality of the circumstances'—the whole picture that must be taken into account when evaluating whether there is reasonable suspicion. Thus, if a tip has a relatively low degree of reliability, more information will be required to establish the requisite quantum of suspicion than would be required if the tip were more reliable." Alabama v. White, 496 U.S. 325, 110 S.Ct. 2412, 110 L.Ed.2d 301, 309(1990).

82. Justice Robert Jackson once warned that "[t]here is danger, if the Court does not temper its doctrinaire logic with a little practical wisdom, it will convert the constitutional Bill of Rights into a suicide pact." Terminiello v. Chicago, 337 U.S. 1, 37, 69 S.Ct. 894, 93 L.Ed.2d 1131 (1949) (Jackson, J. dissenting).

83. "The facts of this case do not require us to speculate about the circumstances under which the danger alleged in an anonymous tip might be so great as to justify a search without a showing of reliability. We do not say, for example, that a report of a person carrying a bomb need bear the indicia of reliability we demand of a report of a person carrying a firearm before the police may constitutionally conduct a search. Nor do we hold that public safety officials in quarters where the reasonable expectation of privacy is diminished, such as airports and schools, cannot conduct protective searches on the basis of information insufficient to justify searches elsewhere." Florida v. J.L., 529 U.S. 266,120 S.Ct. 1375, 1380, 146 L.Ed.2d 254 (2000) (internal citations omitted).

to arrest], (b) the description is otherwise sufficiently detailed, and (c) the person arrested matches that description.[84]

Often at a motion-to-suppress hearing, however, there is no proof presented as to the origin or ultimate evidentiary basis of the bolo. Accordingly, the sole issue typically tried is whether the description given in the bolo is sufficient to sustain the arrest. Nonetheless, it would appear that if the bolo was based on an arrest warrant, the absence of proof as to the ultimate evidentiary basis for the arrest warrant would not appear to invalidate the arrest. This is so because the burden of proving that an arrest with a warrant is unreasonable is, by the weight of authority, on the defendant, not the prosecution. On the other hand, if the bolo is not based on an arrest warrant, but instead on information given to the police by a third party, the arrest would appear invalid—as the burden of proof to sustain the validity of a warrantless arrest, by the weight of authority, is on the prosecution, not the defendant.[85]

h. Officer's subjective intent: pretext arrest and stated offense

In applying the probable cause and reasonable suspicion standards, the actual subjective intent or motives of the law enforcement officer effecting the Fourth Amendment intrusion are generally not relevant. The test of probable cause or reasonable suspicion is objective in nature, not subjective.[86] Accordingly, where (a) the police arrest or stop a defendant

---

84. "We do not, of course, question that the ... police were entitled to act on the strength of the radio bulletin. Certainly, police officers called upon to aid other officers in executing arrest warrants are entitled to assume that the officers requesting aid offered the magistrate the information requisite to support an independent determination of probable cause. Where, however, the contrary turns out to be true, an otherwise illegal arrest cannot be insulated from challenge by the decision of the instigating officer to rely on fellow officers to make the arrest." Whitely v. Warden, Wyoming Penitentiary, 401 U.S. 560, 91 S.Ct. 1031, 28 L.Ed.2d 306, 313 (1971) (arrest based on radio bulletin that a particular defendant had an outstanding arrest warrant against him held invalid as the arrest warrant was not based on probable cause).

A police officer may temporarily stop a defendant based on a radio bulletin that the defendant is wanted in another jurisdiction, provided the radio bulletin is based on reasonable suspicion; if not, the stop is unreasonable. "We conclude that, if a flyer or bulletin has been issued on the basis of articulable facts that the wanted person has committed an offense, then reliance on that flyer or bulletin justifies a stop to check identification, to pose questions to the person, or to detain the person briefly while attempting to obtain further information. If the flyer has been issued in the absence of a reasonable suspicion, then a stop in the objective reliance upon it violates the Fourth Amendment." United States v. Hensley, 469 U.S. 221, 105 S.Ct. 675, 83 L.Ed.2d 604, 614 (1985) (citations omitted) (stop upheld based on police testimony that the flyer or bulletin from another police department was issued based on reasonable suspicion).

See generally 2 Wayne LaFave, Search and Seizure § 3.5(b) (5th ed. 2012). But cf. Arizona v. Evans, 514 U.S. 1, 115 S.Ct. 1185, 131 L.Ed.2d 34 (1995) ("good faith" exception to *Weeks-Mapp* exclusionary rule held applicable where police arrest defendant based on a police radio report that defendant had an outstanding arrest warrant against him—although warrant had been quashed where source of error was court clerk's office); Herring v. United States, 555 U.S. 135, 129 S.Ct. 695 (2009) (same holding except source of the error was a police computer, not a court computer, where the error was a negligent but minor, non-recurring police error).

85. For a discussion of the burden of proof rules at a motion-to-suppress hearing, see Chapter 17, Section 6a of this work.

86. "[A]lmost without exception in evaluating alleged violations of the Fourth Amendment, the Court has first undertaken an objective assessment of an officer's actions in light of the facts and circumstances known to him.... [T]he fact that the officer does not have the state of mind which is hypothecated by the reasons which provide the legal justification for the officer's actions does not invalidate the action taken as long as the circumstances, viewed objectively, justify that action." Scott

for a minor offense, such as a traffic violation, and there is probable cause for this arrest or reasonable suspicion for the stop, but (b) the arrest or stop is used as a *pretext* for the police to obtain incriminating evidence of another more serious offense—the arrest or stop is nonetheless reasonable under the Fourth Amendment.[87]

There is, of course, a certain danger in this rule because the traffic codes in America are very pervasive and few people, indeed, can avoid eventually violating some minor provision therein—such as exceeding the speed limit by one mile per hour. This necessarily means that virtually everyone who drives is thereby subject to a temporary police stop at some time at the discretion of the police. But the Court has concluded that there is no principle that would allow it to decide when a law code reached this level of unacceptable expansiveness—nor what standard or what right it would have in selecting provisions in such a code that would merit or not merit enforcement.[88] On the other hand, if police engage in "racial profiling"—that is, in selectively enforcing admitted traffic code violations based on considerations of race—such a practice would violate the affected motorist's rights under the Equal Protection Clause of the Fourteenth Amendment, but not under the Fourth Amendment.[89] Accordingly, a court could prohibit such a practice in a class

---

v. United States, 436 U.S. 128, 137, 138, 98 S.Ct. 1717, 56 L.Ed.2d 168, 177, 178 (1978). "Whether a Fourth Amendment violation has occurred 'turns on an objective assessment of the officer's actions in light of the facts and circumstances confronting him at the time,' and not on the officer's actual state of mind at the time the challenged action was taken." Maryland v. Macon, 472 U.S. 463, 105 S.Ct. 2778, 86 L.Ed.2d 370, 378 (1985) (internal citation omitted). "We think [our prior] cases foreclose any argument that the constitutional reasonableness of traffic stops depend on the actual motivation of the individual officers involved." Whren v. United States, 517 U.S. 806, 116 S.Ct. 1769, 1774, 135 L.Ed.2d 89 (1996) (traffic stop based on probable cause that motorist had committed several civil traffic infractions, including turning without signaling and traveling at an unreasonable speed, is reasonable under the Fourth Amendment; no additional showing need be made that a reasonable police officer as a matter of usual police practice would have made the stop). See also Bond v. United States, 528 U.S. 334, 120 S.Ct. 1462, 146 L.Ed.2d 365, 370, n. 2 (2000).

87. "We think these cases foreclose any argument that the constitutional reasonableness of traffic stops depends on the actual motivations of the individual officers involved. * * * Subjective intentions play no role in ordinary, probable cause Fourth Amendment analysis. * * * For the run-of-the-mine case, which this surely is, we think there is no realistic alternative to the traditional common law rule that probable cause justifies a search or seizure. Here the District Court found that the officers had probable cause to believe that petitioners had violated the traffic code. That rendered the stop reasonable under the Fourth Amendment, the evidence thereby discovered admissible, and the upholding of the convictions by the Court of Appeals correct." Whren v. United States, 517 U.S. 806, 116 S.Ct.1769, 1774, 1777, 135 L.Ed.2d 89 (1996).

In *Whren*, the Court upheld the traffic stop of a defendant by plain-clothes vice officers for speeding and other traffic offenses as based on probable cause, regardless of the officer's alleged ulterior motive to obtain evidence of illegal drugs; open view police observation of cocaine in defendant's hands after the stop justified the seizure of said drugs.

Arkansas v. Sullivan, 532 U.S. 769, 121 S.Ct. 1876, 149 L.Ed.2d 994 (2001) (follows *Whren* and holds that a police officer's subjective motivation in making an arrest based on probable cause for various traffic and other minor offenses as a pretext to search the arrestee's car for narcotics did not render the arrest unreasonable under the Fourth Amendment because subjective intentions of the arresting officer play no role in ordinary, probable cause analysis). see Fernandez v. California, 571 U.S. ___, 134 S.Ct. 1126, 1134–1135,188 L.Ed2d 25 (2014) (an improper police motive cannot invalidate an objectively proper detention or arrest of a joint occupant of premises prior to obtaining a voluntary consent to search the premises from the remaining occupant).

88. Whren v. United States, 517 U.S. 806, 116 S.Ct. 1769, 1777, 135 L.Ed.2d 89 (1996).

89. "We of course agree with petitioners that the Constitution prohibits selective enforcement of the law based on considerations such as race. But the constitutional basis for objecting to intentionally discriminatory application of laws is the Equal Protection Clause, not the Fourth Amendment." Whren v. United States, 517 U.S. 806, 116 S.Ct. 1769, 1774, 135 L.Ed.2d 89 (1996).

action, civil rights declaratory decree/injunctive action, but could not exclude any evidence obtained thereby in a criminal prosecution under the *Weeks-Mapp* exclusionary rule.

Beyond that, if the *objective* facts establish probable cause to arrest for a particular offense, the arrest is lawful under the Fourth Amendment—and is not rendered unlawful because the arresting officer fails to state the proper offense at the time of arrest, but instead relies on another offense for which there is no probable cause to arrest. Moreover, this proper offense need not be "closely related" to, and based on the same conduct as, the offense stated by the arresting officer at the time of arrest.[90] These rules make good sense else "[a]n arrest made by a knowledgeable, veteran officer would be valid [under a given set of facts] whereas an arrest made by a rookie *in precisely the same circumstances* would not."[91] And they are fair to the arrestee as well because a committing magistrate at a non-adversary hearing must determine promptly after a warrantless arrest whether probable cause for the arrest exists based on whatever offense or offenses the government ultimately relies on.[92]

i. Reasonable mistake of fact or law: suspect's ultimate innocence

An arrest or temporary detention may be reasonable under the Fourth Amendment although the justification for the seizure includes a reasonable mistake of fact or law.[93] For example, an arrest has been upheld as based on probable cause where the police arrest a person for violating a statute later declared to be unconstitutional.[94] And a temporary detention has been upheld based on reasonable suspicion where police stop a vehicle for having *one* defective tail light under an ambiguous statute later declared to require *two* inoperable tail lights to trigger its application.[95] The reason for this result is that probable

---

90. "Our cases make clear that an arresting officer's state of mind (except for the facts that he knows) is irrelevant to the existence of probable cause. [citations omitted]. That is, his subjective reason for making the arrest need not be the criminal offense as to which the known facts provide probable cause. * * * The rule that the offense establishing probable cause must be 'closely related' to, and based on the same conduct as, the offense identified by the arresting officer at the time of arrest is inconsistent with this precedent." Devenpeck v. Alford, 543 U.S. 146, 125 S.Ct. 588, 593–94, 160 L.Ed.2d 537 (2004).

91. Devenpeck v. Alford, 125 S.Ct. at 594.

92. See Section 1d of this Chapter and authorities collected.

93. "The Fourth Amendment prohibits 'unreasonable searches or seizures.' Under this standard, a search or seizure may be permissible even though the justification for the action includes a reasonable factual mistake. An officer might, for example, stop a motorist for traveling alone in a high-occupancy vehicle lane, only to discover upon approaching the car that two children are slumped over asleep in the back seat. The driver has not violated the law, but neither has the officer violated the Fourth Amendment.

But what if the officer's mistake is not one of fact but of law? In this case, an officer stopped a vehicle because one of its two brake lights was out, but a court later determined that a single working brake light was all the law required. The question presented is whether such a mistake of law can nonetheless give rise to the reasonable suspicion necessary to uphold the seizure under the Fourth Amendment. We hold that it can. Because the officer's mistake about the brake-light law was reasonable, the stop in this case was lawful under the Fourth Amendment." Heien v. North Carolina, 574 U.S. ___, 134 S.Ct. 1872, ___ L.Ed.2d ___ (2014).

94. Michigan v. DeFillippo, 443 U.S. 31, 99 S.Ct. 2627, 61 L.Ed.2d 343 (1979); see also Chapter 17, Section 5c(3) of this work for a discussion of authority holding that the "good faith" exception to the Fourth Amendment exclusionary rule is applicable where police arrest a person based on a statute latter declared to be unconstitutional.

95. Heien v. North Carolina, 574 U.S. ___, 134 S.Ct. 1872, ___ L.Ed.2d ___ (2014).

cause or reasonable suspicion allows a certain leeway for police to make mistakes in enforcing the law—so long as these mistakes are reasonable under the circumstances of the case.[96]

Suppose, however, there is probable cause to arrest the defendant for a particular crime, but a search of the defendant incident to the arrest reveals no evidence of this crime, but instead evidence of another crime; later, it turns out that the defendant is totally innocent of the crime for which he was arrested. A question arises as to whether this post-arrest information, which reveals that the defendant is innocent of the crime for which he was arrested, renders the arrest unreasonable under the Fourth Amendment. Clearly, it does not.

Under both the probable cause and reasonable suspicion standards, it is irrelevant that further investigation ultimately reveals that the individual involved is entirely innocent of the criminal wrongdoing for which he or she was originally arrested or stopped. The reasonableness of the arrest or temporary detention must be measured by the totality of the circumstances presented at the outset of the intrusion—and is neither hindered nor helped by evidence that turns up after the intrusion.[97]

j. The "drug courier profile"

Over the past several decades, the federal Drug Enforcement Administration has developed a "drug courier profile" describing the various characteristics of people who transport illegal drugs into the United States on commercial airliners from major drug sources outside the country. At times, these drug agents will temporarily detain air travelers in major airports because they allegedly fit this profile. They will ask questions of these travelers, often seeking consent to search the air travelers' luggage. The issue in these cases is whether the evidence of the drug courier profile is enough to constitute reasonable

---

96. "Because many situations which confront officers in the course of executing their duties are more or less ambiguous, room must be allowed for mistakes on their part. But the mistakes must be those of reasonable men, acting on facts leading sensibly to their conclusions of probability." Brinegar v. United States, 338U.S. 160, 69 S.Ct. 1302, 93 L.Ed. 1879, 1891 (1949), cited with approval in Illinois v. Rodriguez, 497 U.S. 177, 110 S.Ct. 2793, 111 L.Ed.2d 148, 159 (1990).

97. Hill v. California, 401 U.S. 797, 91 S.Ct. 1106, 28 L.Ed.2d 484 (1971) (arrest of defendant upheld as based on probable cause information known by police prior to the arrest—even though subsequently it was determined that the police had arrested the wrong man).

"The 'reasonableness' of a particular use of force must be judged from the perspective of a reasonable officer on the scene, rather than the 20/20 vision of hindsight. The Fourth Amendment is not violated by an arrest based on probable cause, even though the wrong person is arrested." Graham v. O'Connor, 490 U.S. 386, 109 S.Ct. 1865, 104 L.Ed.2d 443, 455 (1989).

"It is apparent that in order to satisfy the 'reasonableness' requirement, what is generally true of the many factual determinations that must be regularly made by agents of the government—whether the magistrate issuing the warrant, the police officer executing the warrant, or the police officer conducting a search or seizure under one of the exceptions to the warrant requirement—is not that they always be correct, but that they always be reasonable. As we put it in *Brinegar v. United States* (citation omitted): 'Because many situations which confront officers in the course of executing their duties are more or less ambiguous, room must be allowed for mistakes on their part. But the mistakes must be those of reasonable men, acting on facts leading sensibly to their conclusions of probability.'" Illinois v. Rodriguez, 497 U.S. 177, 110 S.Ct. 2793, 111 L.Ed.2d 148, 159 (1990).

"In allowing such detentions, Terry accepts the risk that officers may stop innocent people. Indeed, the Fourth Amendment accepts that risk in connection with more drastic police action; persons arrested and detained on probable cause to believe that they have committed a crime may turn out to be innocent." Illinois v. Wardlow, 528 U.S. 119, 120 S.Ct. 673, 145 L.Ed.2d 570, 577 (2000).

suspicion for such a temporary detention; clearly, such evidence, without more, cannot constitute probable cause for arrest.[98]

The Court has neither approved the "drug courier profile" as constituting reasonable suspicion for a temporary detention, nor disapproved it as being insufficient for a temporary detention. This is probably because it is a free-floating, flexible profile with no set number of characteristics. Instead, the Court has looked at the behavior of the air traveler on a case-by-case basis and determined whether reasonable suspicion existed for a temporary detention based on the particular facts of each case.

Generally speaking, however, the Court has sustained these drug-courier-profile stops in a variety of factual contexts where the air traveler's behavior seemed highly suspicious as compared with the ordinary air traveler.[99] Only where the behavior of the air traveler seemed innocuous enough, and largely indistinguishable from the run-of-the-mine air traveler, or aroused only a modicum of suspicion, has the Court struck down such detentions as not based on reasonable suspicion.[100]

---

98. For a discussion of the "drug courier profile," see United States v. Mendenhall, 446 U.S. 544, 560–66, 100 S.Ct. 1870, 64 L.Ed.2d 497, 513–17 (1980) (Powell, J. concurring); 4 Wayne LaFave, Search and Seizure § 9.5(f) (5th ed. 2012).

99. In *United States v. Sokolow,* 490 U.S. 1, 109 S.Ct. 1581, 104 L.Ed.2d 1 (1989), the Court upheld a *Terry* stop by drug agents at the Honolulu Airport based on the following factors: (1) defendant bought two round-trip plane tickets to Miami in Honolulu for himself and a female companion, with $2,100 in cash from a large roll of $20 bills; (2) defendant traveled under a name that did not match the name under which his telephone number was listed; (3) defendant stayed in Miami only 48 hours, although the round-trip flight from Honolulu takes 20 hours; (4) defendant looked nervous during the trip; and (5) defendant checked none of his luggage. "Any one of these factors is not in itself proof of any illegal conduct and is quite consistent with innocent travel. But we think taken together they amount to reasonable suspicion." United States v. Sokolow, 104 L.Ed.2d at 11.

In *Florida v. Royer,* 460 U.S. 491, 103 S.Ct. 1319, 75 L.Ed.2d 229 (1983), the Court upheld the initial *Terry* stop of defendant at the Miami International Airport based on the following factors: (1) the defendant was traveling under an assumed name; (2) he paid for his plane ticket in cash with a number of small bills; (3) he put only his name and not his address on his checked luggage;(4) he was very nervous while walking through the airport. "We agree with the State that when the officers discovered that Royer was traveling under an assumed name, this fact, and the facts already known to the officers—paying cash for a one-way ticket, the mode of checking the two bags, and Royer's appearance and conduct in general—were adequate grounds for suspecting Royer of carrying drugs and for temporarily detaining him and his luggage while they attempted to verify or dispel their suspicions in a manner that did not exceed the limits of an investigative detention." Florida v. Royer, 75 L.Ed.2d at 239.

In *Florida v. Rodriguez,* 469 U.S. 1, 105 S.Ct. 308, 83 L.Ed.2d 165 (1984), the Court upheld a *Terry* stop at the Miami International Airport based on the following factors: (1) the defendant and his two companions began speaking furtively with one another when they spotted certain plainclothes officers; (2) one of the companions was overheard saying to the others to "get out of here," (3) both the defendant and one of his companions identified themselves as "Rodriguez," and later this companion changed his story and identified himself as "Blanco," and (4) the defendant attempted to evade the officers by a strange movement in which he pumped his legs up and down rapidly as if he was running in place.

100. In *Reid v. Georgia,* 448 U.S. 438, 100 S.Ct. 2752, 65 L.Ed.2d 890 (1980), the Court struck down a *Terry* stop by drug agents in the Atlanta airport based on the following facts: (1) defendant arrived on a flight from Ft. Lauderdale which the agent said was a source city for cocaine; (2) defendant arrived early in the morning when the agent said law enforcement activity at the airport is diminished; (3) defendant walked ahead of his companion in the airport concourse, occasionally looked back at the companion, and eventually talked to the companion in the main lobby of the terminal. The Court concluded that first two factors stated above "describe a very large category of presumably innocent travelers, who would be subject to virtually random seizures were the Court to conclude that as little foundation as there was in this case could justify a seizure." 65 L.Ed. 2d at 894.

Knowing that there may be some problem with immediately detaining an air traveler based on the "drug courier profile," drug agents often solicit a voluntary encounter with the air traveler and engage the traveler in conversation. This is done in the hope that the air traveler will make certain incriminating or evasive statements, or act in an otherwise highly suspicious manner, during the voluntary encounter. If so, these statements and behavior—plus the "drug courier profile" behavior—may all add up to reasonable suspicion for a later forcible temporary detention. At times, of course, it is not clear when the voluntary encounter ends and the forcible detention begin, but the Court must make this determination in order to decide what pre-detention facts they can consider in determining whether there was reasonable suspicion for the temporary detention.[101]

k. Temporary detention during search warrant execution

Where a search warrant is issued for the search of contraband on private premises, police may temporarily detain the occupants of the premises while a proper search of the premises is conducted.[102] This authority to temporarily detain such occupants is limited to persons on or in the immediate vicinity of the premises being searched—and does not extend to detentions effected outside this geographical area.[103] It is an open question, however, whether such a temporary detention is authorized if the search warrant is *not* for contraband, but for evidence of crime.[104] Presumably, much would depend on the affidavit filed in support of the search warrant, the character of the premises being searched, and the behavior of the individuals on the premises at the time of the search—any one of which or combination thereof might amount to reasonable suspicion for a temporary detention. Where the person detained, however, has no special connection to the premises, such as a patron of a business that is being searched under a warrant, such a person may not be subjected to a pat-down search.[105]

Inherent in this authorization to temporarily detain while a search warrant is being executed is the authority to use reasonable force to effectuate the detention.[106] The use of

---

"Nor can we agree, on this record, that the manner in which the petitioner and his companion walked through the airport reasonably could have led the agent to suspect them of wrongdoing." Id.

101. For a discussion of when a voluntary encounter escalates into a temporary detention, see Chapter 9, Section 2b, supra, of this work.

102. "Thus, for Fourth Amendment purposes, we hold that a warrant to search for contraband founded on probable cause implicitly carries with it the limited authority to detain the occupants of the premises while a proper search is conducted." Michigan v. Summers, 452 U.S. 692, 705, 101 S.Ct. 2587, 69 L.Ed.2d 340, 351 (1981) (occupant was owner of house; police met owner descending the front steps and required him to come in the house while they conducted a search thereof); see Muehler v. Mena, 544 U.S. 93, 125 S.Ct. 1465, 1470, 161 L.Ed. 2d 299 (2005) (search warrant authorized the seizure of deadly weapons used in recent drive-by shooting; occupant was asleep in her bed when the search began) ("Mena's [the occupant's] detention was, under *Summers*, plainly permissible.").

103. Bailey v. United States, 568 U.S. ____, 133 S.Ct. 1031, 185 L.Ed.2d 19 (2013) (stop effected nearly a mile from the premises being searched disapproved as a valid detention during search warrant execution; person detained had left the premises just before search warrant was executed; case remanded to determine whether the detention was a valid Terry stop).

104. "We do not decide the issue whether the same result would be justified if the search warrant merely authorized a search for evidence." Michigan v. Summers, 452 U.S. 692, 705 n. 20, 101 S.Ct. 2587, 69 L.Ed.2d 340 (1981).

105. Ybarra v. Illinois, 444 U.S. 85, 100 S.Ct. 338, 62 L.Ed.2d. 238 (1979) (patrons of a tavern).

106. "Inherent in *Summers*' authorization to detain an occupant of the place to be searched is the authority to use reasonable force to effectuate the detention." Muehler v. Mena, 544 U.S. 93, 125 S.Ct. 1465, 1470, 161 L.Ed. 2d 299 (2005).

handcuffs, however, to detain the occupant is a separate Fourth Amendment intrusion aside from the detention—and therefore requires a separate justification, as where the safety of the officers and occupants require it.[107]

Indeed, when executing a search warrant, the officers may take any reasonable action that is necessary to secure the premises and to ensure their own safety and the efficacy of the search.[108] This authority authorizes the officers to order naked residents found in bed to stand for a brief time while officers secure the premises—although for no longer than is necessary to accomplish this purpose.[109] Accordingly, unreasonable actions in executing a search warrant are prohibited—such as the use of excessive force or restraints that cause unnecessary pain or ones that are imposed for a prolonged and unnecessary period of time.[110]

Excessive force claims of this nature have, to date, arisen solely in the context of civil suits brought against the police for violation of the suspect's Fourth Amendment rights. It is doubtful, however, whether in most cases the *Weeks-Mapp* exclusionary rule would be applicable where police use excessive force to effect an otherwise lawful temporary detention. The excessive force used would not render the detention unlawful and would therefore not generally taint any evidence obtained thereby. On the other hand, if the excessive force used amounted to an unlawful detention in itself—such as an unnecessary handcuffing or forcing a suspect to stand naked for an unreasonable length of time—the entire search might be considered unreasonable and its fruits inadmissible at trial.[111]

Moreover, law enforcement officers are authorized to question any occupant during the detention concerning matters that have nothing to do with the search. This is so because police questioning in itself does not constitute a Fourth Amendment seizure of the individual and therefore does not require a showing of reasonable suspicion.[112] But

---

107. "The imposition of correctly applied handcuffs on Mena [the occupant], who was already lawfully detained during a search of the house, was undoubtedly a separate intrusion in addition to the detention in the converted garage. * * But this was no ordinary search. The governmental interests in not only detaining, but using handcuffs, are at their maximum when, as here, a warrant authorizes a search for weapons and a wanted gang member resides on the premises. In such inherently dangerous situations, the use of handcuffs minimizes the risk to both officers and occupants." Muehler v. Mena, 544 U.S. 93, 125 S.Ct. 1465, 1470–71, 161 L.Ed. 2d 299 (2005) (handcuffing of occupant upheld during search of gang house; one of the gang members resided on the premises; the warrant authorized the seizure of deadly weapons; three other individuals on the premises were also detained and handcuffed).

108. "In executing a search warrant, officers may take reasonable action to secure the premises and to ensure their own safety and the efficacy of the search." Los Angeles County v. Rettele, 550 U.S. 609, 127 S.Ct. 1989, 1992, 167 L.Ed.2d 974 (2007).

109. Los Angeles County v. Rettele, supra (a male and female resident of house found in bed naked forced to stand naked for 1–2 minutes while officers secured premises; held reasonable action, even though house had subsequently been sold to innocent party and nothing incriminating was found).

110. "Unreasonable actions (in executing a search warrant) include the use of excessive force or restraints that cause unnecessary pain or are imposed for a prolonged or unnecessary period of time. * * *

This is not to say, of course, that the deputies were free to force Rettele and Sandler (the residents) to remain motionless and standing for any longer than necessary. We have recognized that 'special circumstances' or possibly a prolonged detention might render a search unreasonable." Los Angeles County v. Rettele, 127 S.Ct. at 1993.

111. Id. Los Angeles County v. Rettele, 127 S.Ct. at 1993

112. Muehler v. Mena, 544 U.S. 93, 125 S.Ct. 1465, 1471–72, 161 L.Ed. 2d 299 (2005) (questioning of occupant's immigration status upheld during otherwise reasonable search of gang house for deadly weapons and evidence of gang membership).

presumably, where the questioning exceeds the time reasonably necessary to conduct the search, the basis for the temporary detention disappears, the detention becomes illegal, and any questioning during this detention would be tainted thereby.[113]

l. Probable cause and reasonable suspicion applications: general factual categories

At the state and lower federal court levels, there are literally thousands of cases deciding whether a given fact pattern does or does not constitute probable cause for arrest or reasonable suspicion for a temporary investigative detention.[114] There are no bright-line rules, however, for determining whether these standards have been met in a given case, as each case must be evaluated based on the totality of the circumstances. Still, there are certain general trends in these cases that allow a practitioner to get a handle on this area of law. Generally speaking, these cases have given the police wide-ranging authority to make intrusive seizures of the person, and yet, at the same time, have set certain limits to that power.

• Dragnet or investigative arrests

Dragnet arrests or arrests for investigation are classic police state tactics prohibited by the Fourth Amendment. Accordingly, the police may not roam the streets, pick up persons they suspect of a crime based on a mere hunch, and take them to the police station or elsewhere for questioning, fingerprinting, or other investigation.[115] Such tactics are the

---

113. See United States v. Place, 462 U.S. 696, 103 S.Ct. 2637, 77 L.Ed.2d 110 (1983) (suitcase held longer than reasonably necessary to conduct a narcotics dog sniff of the suitcase tainted the dog alert on the suitcase and invalidated the search warrant for the suitcase based on the alert); Illinois v. Caballes, 543 U.S. 405, 125 S.Ct. 834, 837, 160 L.Ed.2d 842 (2005) ("It is nevertheless clear that a seizure that is lawful at its inception can violate the Fourth Amendment if its manner of execution unreasonably infringes interests protected by the Constitution. A seizure that is justified solely by the interest in issuing a warning [traffic] ticket can become unlawful if it is prolonged beyond the time reasonably required to complete that mission.") (internal citation omitted).

114. For a detailed analysis of the probable cause standard and how it has been applied in the cases, see 2 Wayne LaFave, Search and Seizure §§ 3.1–3.7 at 1–555 (5th ed. 2012). For a similar treatment of the reasonable suspicion standard in the same courts, see 4 Wayne LaFave, Search and Seizure § 9.1 at 352–369, § 9.5 at 643–837 (5th ed. 2012). Also see lower federal and state court cases on (a) the probable cause standard for arrest collected at "Arrest" §§ 63.4 (.5), (1), (2), (3) West Key Nos.; and on (b) the reasonable suspicion standard for a temporary detention collected at "Arrest" §§ 63.5(1), (3.1), (4), (5) West Key Nos.

115. "Nothing is more clear than that the Fourth Amendment was meant to prevent wholesale intrusions upon the personal security of our citizenry, whether these intrusions be termed 'arrests' or 'investigatory detentions.'" Davis v. Mississippi, 394 U.S. 721, 89 S.Ct. 1394, 22 L.Ed.2d 676, 681(1969) (investigative detention of rape suspect for fingerprinting and questioning struck down; 24 other men also subjected to same detention and questioning).

"The security of one's privacy against arbitrary intrusion by the police—which is at the core of the Fourth Amendment—is basic to a free society. It is therefore implicit in 'the concept of ordered liberty' and as such enforceable against the States through the Due Process Clause. The knock on the door, whether by day or night, as a prelude to a search [or arrest], without authority of law but solely on the authority of the police, did not need the commentary of recent history to be condemned as inconsistent with the conception of human rights enshrined in the history and the basic constitutional documents of English-speaking peoples." Wolf v. Colorado, 338 U.S. 25, 27–28, 69 S.Ct. 1359, 93 L.Ed. 1782, 1785–86 (1949).

"The quantum of information which constitutes probable cause—evidence which would 'warrant a man of reasonable caution in the belief' that a felony has been committed—must be measured by the facts of the particular case. The history of the use, and not infrequent abuse, of the power of arrest cautions that a relaxation of the fundamental requirements of probable cause would 'leave law-quintessential trademarks of a police state and are totally inconsistent with the freedoms guaranteed by the Fourth Amendment.

- **Refusal to answer police questions**

A refusal of a person to answer police questions does not, in itself, constitute a basis for an arrest or temporary detention. Accordingly, a person who is approached by the police without probable cause or reasonable suspicion has a right to refuse to answer such questions and thereafter go about one's business.[116] It is an open question, however, whether this factor can be taken into account as part of the totality of the circumstances in determining whether there is probable cause to arrest or reasonable suspicion for a temporary stop.[117] Nonetheless, it is doubtful that the Court would ever so hold, as no adverse inference from the assertion of one's right to remain silent is generally allowed under our constitutional traditions.

- **Unprovoked flight from the police**

Unprovoked flight from the police, however, is not the same as a simple refusal to answer police questions in which the person thereafter goes about one's business. A flight of this nature tends to indicate a consciousness of guilt, rather than an assertion of the right to remain silent. Although such flight does not in itself constitute probable cause to make an arrest, it is a factor to be considered along with other factors in determining the probable cause issue.[118] Moreover, unprovoked flight from the police in an area known for heavy narcotics trafficking has been held sufficient for a temporary *Terry* stop.[119]

---

abiding citizens at the mercy of the officers' whim or caprice.'" Wong Sun v. United States, 371 U.S. 471, 83 S.Ct. 407, 9 L.Ed.2d 441,450 (1963) (internal citation omitted).

116. "[W]hen an officer, without reasonable suspicion or probable cause, approaches an individual, the individual has a right to ignore the police and go about his business. (citation omitted). And any 'refusal to cooperate, without more, does not furnish the minimal level of justification needed for a detention or seizure.' (citation omitted)." Illinois v. Wardlow, 528 U.S. 119, 120 S.Ct. 673, 145 L.Ed.2d 570, 577 (2000).

"The person approached [by the police], however, need not answer any [police] questions put to him; indeed, he may decline to listen to the questions at all and may go about his business. He may not be detained even momentarily without reasonable objective grounds for doing so; and his refusal to listen or answer does not, without more, furnish those grounds." Florida v. Royer, 460 U.S. 491, 497–98, 103 S.Ct. 1319, 75 L.Ed.2d 229, 236 (1983).

"There is nothing in the Constitution which prevents a policeman from addressing questions to anyone on the street. Absent special circumstances, the person approached may not be detained or frisked but may refuse to cooperate and go on his way. However, given the proper circumstances, such as those in this case, it seems to me that the person may be briefly detained against his will while pertinent questions are directed at him. Of course, the person stopped is not obliged to answer, answers may not be compelled, and refusal to answer furnishes no basis for arrest, although it may alert the officer to the need for continued observation." Terry v. Ohio, 392 U.S. 1, 34, 88 S.Ct. 1868, 20 L.Ed.2d 889, 913 (1968) (White, J. concurring).

117. See 2 Wayne LaFave, Search and Seizure § 3.6(f) at 453–455 (5th ed. 2012). LaFave says "the better view" is that the suspect's refusal to answer police questions may be considered as one factor in the totality of circumstances in determining whether there is probable cause to arrest. Id. at 454.

118. "The flight of a person from the presence of the police is not standing alone sufficient to establish probable cause [to arrest], unless of course the circumstances are such that the flight from the officer itself constitutes a crime. Were it otherwise, 'anyone who does not desire to talk to the police and who either walks or runs away from them would always be subject to legal arrest,'which can hardly 'be countenanced under the Fourth and Fourteenth Amendments.'" 2 Wayne LaFave, Search and Seizure § 3.6(e) at 444 (5th ed. 2012), quoting from United States v. Margeson, 259 F.Supp. 256 (E.D. Pa. 1966).

119. Illinois v. Wardlow, 528 U.S. 119, 120 S.Ct. 673, 145 L.Ed.2d 570 (2000) (temporary stop and weapons frisk upheld; handgun seized).

• Description of perpetrator by crime victim or eye witness

Often police will obtain a description of a criminal perpetrator from a victim or witness to a crime and thereafter arrest or temporarily detain a person whom the police claim matches the description given to them. There are certain factors that the courts consider in determining the lawfulness of such an arrest or temporary detention. Two of the most important factors are: (1) the detail [or lack of detail] of the description of the perpetrator, or of the vehicle in which the perpetrator may have fled; (2) the extent to which the suspect or his or her vehicle does or does not match this description. Also important are: the observed activity or condition of the suspect at the time the suspect is stopped; police knowledge that the suspect has a criminal record, or that the suspect's automobile has been involved in prior criminal activity; the size of the area in which the perpetrator might be found, the number of persons in the area, and the elapsed time from the commission of the crime to the stop of the suspect.[120] In this respect, there is a significant body of authority that the *arrest* of a suspect in the vicinity of a recently committed crime may *not* be made "unless the description of the offender and other relevant circumstances make it more probable than not that [the arrestee] is the offender."[121]

Even though an arrest may not be made based on the above factors, often a temporary detention may be effected based on the same factual showing. Accordingly, a suspect matching some but not all the particulars of the given description, or generally fitting a sketchy description of the perpetrator of a recently committed crime may be sufficient for a temporary stop. This is particularly true when combined with one or more of the following factors: the suspect is seen shortly after the commission of crime in the same general area of the crime or in the same general direction of the perpetrator's flight when combined with few or no people on the street at the time of the stop, furtive activity of the suspect while traveling, or the existence of a prior criminal record of the suspect.[122]

• Association with a person for whom there is probable cause to arrest

If a suspect is in the company of another person for whom there is probable cause to arrest, this association does not, without more, give the police probable cause to arrest the suspect.[123] This is particularly true when the arrest takes place in a quasi-public place, such as a tavern, where many people are present.[124] On the other hand, where the arrest takes place in the small confines of an automobile and there are contraband drugs in the

---

120. 2 Wayne LaFave, Search and Seizure § 3.4(c) (5th ed. 2012), and cases extensively analyzed and collected at 303–330. Also see cases collected at "Arrest" § 63.4(12) West Key No.

121. 4 Wayne LaFave, Search and Seizure § 9.5(h) at 753 (5th ed. 2012).

122. 4 Wayne LaFave, Search and Seizure § 9.5(h) at 750–782 (5th ed. 2012), and cases collected.

123. "But a mere propinquity to others independently suspected of criminal activity does not, without more, give rise to probable cause to search that person. Where the standard is probable cause, a search or a seizure of a person must be supported by probable cause particularized with respect to that person. This requirement cannot be undercut or avoided by simply pointing to the fact that coincidentally there exists probable cause to search or seize another or to search the premises where the person may happen to be." Ybarra v. Illinois, 444 U.S. 85, 100 S.Ct. 338, 62 L.Ed.2d 238, 245 (1979).

"[I]t seems clear beyond question that the mere fact of present association with a person whom the police have grounds to arrest for conduct on some past occasion does not constitute probable cause for the arrest of the associate as well." 2 Wayne LaFave § 3.6(c) at 412 (5th ed. 2012).

124. See Ybarra v. Illinois, 444 U.S. 85, 100 S.Ct. 338, 62 L.Ed.2d 238 (1979) (search warrant for search of public tavern and bartender for possession of controlled substance did not justify detention and search of patron in tavern).

automobile, an arrest of all occupants therein may be proper.[125] Moreover, an association with another [for whom there is probable cause to arrest] may, without more, be a proper basis for a temporary stop.[126]

- **Prior criminal record**

It is clear that a person's prior criminal record does not in itself constitute a basis for making an arrest or a temporary detention.[127] But, it is a factor for the police to take into account in determining whether to effect such actions.

- **Presence in high crime area**

A person's presence in a high crime area does not in itself constitute a basis to arrest a person, but it is a factor to be considered in determining whether there is probable cause to arrest.[128] The same is true of a temporary detention.[129]

- **Presence in public street during late and unusual hours**

An official or unofficial curfew is generally unreasonable for adults—so that one's presence on the public street during late or unusual hours, even in a high crime area, is insufficient to constitute either probable cause to arrest or reasonable suspicion for a temporary stop.[130]

---

125. Compare Maryland v. Pringle, 540 U.S. 366, 124 S.Ct. 795, 157 L.Ed.2d 769 (2003) (arrest of front seat passenger of automobile containing two other occupants upheld; police validly found $763 in rolled up cash in glove compartment and five see-through plastic baggies of cocaine stuffed between back seat arm rest and back seat, following which none of the occupants admitted ownership of the cocaine) with United States v. Di Re, 332 U.S. 581, 68 S.Ct. 222, 92 L.Ed.2d 210 (1948) (arrest of front seat passenger of automobile struck down; police observed another passenger in back seat holding counterfeit gasoline ration coupons, following which this passenger told investigators that he had gotten the coupons from the driver of the automobile).

126. 4 Wayne LaFave, Search and Seizure § 9.5(g) at 734–737 (5th ed. 2012) and cases collected. In United States v. Drayton, 536 U.S. 194, 122 S.Ct. 2105, 2114, 153 L.Ed.2d 242 (2002), the Court in dicta stated that it "may have been the case" that police had reasonable suspicion to detain and frisk one bus passenger after the passenger's traveling companion was lawfully arrested for having contraband drugs on his person, based on the totality of the circumstances.

127. "But those with prior arrests and prior convictions must be allowed to live in the world without the risk of constant harassment, and thus there is no room for an exception to the rule that a brief seizure for investigation may not be based solely upon an individual's past record." 4 Wayne LaFave, Search and Seizure § 9.5(g) at 749 (5th ed. 2012) and cases collected.

128. 2 Wayne LaFave, Search and Seizure § 3.6(g) at 456–461 (5th ed. 2012) and cases collected.

129. "An individual's presence in an area of expected criminal activity, standing alone, is not enough to support a reasonable particularized suspicion that the person is committing a crime. But officers are not required to ignore the relevant characteristics of a location in determining whether the circumstances are sufficiently suspicious to warrant further investigation. Accordingly, we have previously noted the fact that the stop occurred in a 'high crime area' are among the relevant contextual considerations in a Terry analysis." Illinois v. Wardlow, 528 U.S. 119, 120 S.Ct. 673, 145 L.Ed.2d 570 (2000) (internal citation omitted) "In any event, simply being about in a high crime area should not of itself ever be viewed as a sufficient basis for making an investigative stop." 4 Wayne LaFave, Search and Seizure § 9.5(g) at 745–747 (5th ed. 2012) and cases collected.

130. Brown v. Texas, 443 U.S. 47, 99 S.Ct. 2637, 61 L.Ed.2d 357 (1979) (walking late at night in opposite direction from another person in an alley that had a high incidence of illegal drug activity held insufficient for a temporary detention); Levin v. State, 452 So. 2d 652 (Fla. 1984) (walking on public sidewalk at early morning hours in "high class" residential area that had a high burglary rate held insufficient for a temporary detention; adult curfews are unreasonable absent war, natural disaster or riot). "But '[p]resence on the public streets at a late hour * * * does not of itself constitute cause for detention'; there must be other suspicious circumstances." 4 Wayne LaFave, Search and Seizure § 9.5(g) at 742–743 (5th ed. 2012) (internal citation omitted) and cases collected.

But the same may not be true for juveniles.[131] Moreover, reasonable suspicion for a temporary stop is shown where a suspect has large pieces of personal property [i.e., TV sets, typewriters, check-writing machines, computers, suitcases overflowing with clothing] in his possession, at late and unusual hours, in an area with a high burglary/theft rate.[132]

- **Refusal to identify oneself or produce identification papers**

The U.S. Supreme Court has held that (1) a person may not, consistent with the Fourth Amendment, be arrested and convicted for refusal, upon request, to identify himself to a police officer after being stopped by the police [as required by a state statute] where the stop is *unlawful* as not based on reasonable suspicion—and (2) the Fourth Amendment does not allow police [without any reasonable suspicion or perhaps some other reasonable basis] to stop a person solely for an identification check.[133] To date, this country has not instituted an internal passport system routinely required in totalitarian countries—although such proposals have been made in the wake of the September 11, 2001 terrorist attack on the World Trade Center in New York City.

On the other hand, the Court has held that a person may, consistent with the Fourth Amendment, be arrested and convicted for refusal, upon request, to identify himself to a police officer after being stopped by the police [as required by a state statute]—provided (1) the stop is *lawful* as based on reasonable suspicion, and (2) the request for identification is reasonably related to the circumstances that justified the stop.[134]

---

131. See, e.g., Metropolitan Dade County v. Pred, 665 So.2d 252 (Fla. 3d DCA 1995) (Miami-Dade County juvenile curfew ordinance upheld); Note, "Nocturnal Juvenile Curfew Ordinances," 73 Wash.Univ.Law Q. 1711 (1995).

132. 4 Wayne LaFave, Search and Seizure § 9.5(e) at 681–83 (5th ed. 2012) and cases collected.

133. Brown v. Texas, 443 U.S. 47, 99 S.Ct. 2637, 61 L.Ed.2d 357 (1979) (Tex.Crim.Code § 38.02 provided that "(a) person commits an offense if he intentionally refuses to report or gives a false report of his name to a peace officer who has lawfully stopped him and requested the information.").

"The Texas statute under which appellant was stopped and required to identify himself is designed to advance a weighty social objective in large metropolitan centers: prevention of crime. But even assuming that purpose is served to some degree by stopping and demanding identification from an individual without any specific basis for believing he is involved in criminal activity, the guarantees of the Fourth Amendment will not permit it. When such a stop is not based on objective criteria, the risk of arbitrary and abusive police practices exceeds tolerable limits.

The application of Tex. Penal Code Ann. tit. 8, § 38.02 (1974), to detain appellant and require him to identify himself violated the Fourth Amendment because the officers lacked reasonable suspicion to believe appellant had engaged in criminal conduct. Accordingly, appellant may not be punished for refusing to identify himself, and the conviction is reversed." Brown v. Texas, 443 U.S. at 52–53, 61 L.Ed.2d at 363.

134. Hiibel v. Sixth Judicial District Court, 542 U.S. 177, 124 S.Ct. 2451, 2459, 159 L.Ed.2d 292 (2004) (person held validly convicted under a Nevada statute of obstructing a police officer for refusing to give his name to police upon request during a valid *Terry* stop; police were investigating a report that a man had just assaulted a woman in a described truck at a particular location, and upon arrival on the scene, police saw a woman in the described truck and a man standing outside the truck; police detained this man and requested identification, which the man refused).

Nev. Rev. Stat. § 171.123, authorized any peace officer to detain "any person the officer encounters under circumstances which reasonably indicate that the person has committed, is committing or is about to commit a criminal offense," that the officer may detain such person "only to ascertain his identity and the suspicious circumstances surrounding his presence abroad," and that the person so detained "shall identify himself, but may not be compelled to answer any other inquiry of any peace officer." A number of states have stop-and-identify statutes similar to Nevada's statute. For a discussion of these statutes, see Hibel v. Sixth Judicial District Court, 124 S.Ct. at 2456.

"The principles of Terry permit a state to require a suspect to disclose his name in the course of a [valid] Terry stop. * * * A state law requiring a suspect to disclose his name in the course of a valid Terry stop is consistent with Fourth Amendment prohibitions against unreasonable searches and

• Miscellaneous

– Talking and visiting with a number of narcotics addicts on the street is an *insufficient* showing of reasonable suspicion for a temporary stop.[135] But where there is an exchange of a commonly used narcotics package between a suspect and another, particularly when combined with the transfer of cash, an arrest or least a temporary detention is considered reasonable.[136]

– The presence of a person of Mexican ancestry in an automobile near the U.S.-Mexican border is *insufficient* in itself to constitute reasonable suspicion for a temporary stop to determine whether the person is an illegal alien.[137]

– Pacing up and down an excessive number of times [i.e., 24] in front of a store in the downtown area of a large city during the day, while occasionally consulting with nearby companions, has been held a *sufficient* showing of reasonable suspicion for a temporary stop—where an experienced police officer, who observes this behavior, concludes that the men were planning a hold-up of the store.[138]

– A police officer's first-hand observations of a suspect, in a variety of circumstances, may give the police probable cause to arrest where the indications point to possible possession of stolen property or illegal substances. Also a suspect's furtive gestures or response to police questions may give rise to probable cause for arrest.[139]

m. Excessive force in effecting a lawful arrest or temporary detention

The right to make an otherwise lawful arrest or lawful temporary detention necessarily carries with it the right to use a reasonable degree of physical force to effect the arrest or detention. But where the force employed is unreasonable or excessive under the circumstances, the suspect's Fourth Amendment rights have been violated. Of course, whether the degree of force used is reasonable depends on the circumstances of the particular case—including the severity of the crime at issue, whether the suspect poses an immediate threat to the safety of the officers or others, and whether the suspect is actively resisting or evading arrest. And the reasonableness of such force must be judged from the perspective of a reasonable officer on the scene, not by 20/20 hindsight. Police officers on the street must often make split-second judgments—in circumstances that are tense, uncertain, and rapidly evolving—about the amount of force that is necessary

---

seizures * * * Under these principles, an officer may not arrest a person for failure to identify himself if the request for identification is not reasonably related to the circumstances justifying the stop." Hiibel v. Sixth Judicial District Court, 124 S.Ct. at 2459.

135. Sibron v. New York, 392 U.S. 40, 88 S.Ct. 1889, 20 L.Ed.2d 917 (1968).

136. 2 Wayne LaFave, Search and Seizure § 3.6(b) at 396–402 (5th ed. 2012) and cases collected concerning whether a transfer of commonly used narcotics packages constitutes probable cause for an arrest, especially if combined with other suspicious circumstances.

137. United States v. Brignoni-Ponce, 422 U.S. 873, 95 S.Ct. 2574, 45 L.Ed.2d 607 (1975).

138. Terry v. Ohio, 392 U.S. 1, 88 S.Ct. 1868, 20 L.Ed.2d 889 (1968).

139. See generally 2 Wayne LaFave, Search and Seizure § 3.6 (5th ed. 2012), where LaFave canvasses the cases on what type of circumstances constitute [or do not constitute] probable cause to arrest based on a police officer's first hand observations: (a) possible possession of stolen property [pp. 373–379]; (b) possible possession of illegal substances [pp. 379–410]; (c) furtive gestures [pp. 438–448]; (d) response to police questioning of a suspect [pp. 448–456].

in a given situation. Accordingly, the test of whether reasonable force has been used to effect an arrest or temporary detention is whether the officer's actions are objectively reasonable in the facts and circumstances confronting the officer at the scene, without regard to the officer's subjective intent or motivations.[140]

Moreover, when deadly force is used to effect an arrest of a suspect, such force violates the suspect's Fourth Amendment rights only if unreasonable under the circumstances.[141] Accordingly, it was held unreasonable for police to shoot and kill an unarmed suspected felon who was fleeing from the police on foot but otherwise posed no threat to anyone.[142] On the other hand, it was held reasonable for police to ram a fleeing motorist with the pursuing police car, causing the car to crash, rendering the motorist a quadriplegic, in order to stop the motorist's dangerous high-speed police chase from continuing to endanger the lives of innocent bystanders.[143] The same result was reached to end a similar high-speed car chase that endangered innocent lives in the area wherein the police fired 15 shots into the fleeing motorist's car causing the driver to lose control of the car and die in the ensuing crash.[144]

---

140. Graham v. Connor, 490 U.S. 386, 109 S.Ct. 1865, 104 L.Ed.2d 443, 455–56 (1989).

"A claim that law-enforcement officers used excessive force to effect a seizure [of a person] is governed by the Fourth Amendment's' reasonableness' standard. *See Graham v. Connor*, 490 U.S. 386 (1989); *Tennessee v. Garner*, 471 U.S. 1 (1985). In *Graham*, we held that determining objective reasonableness of a particular seizure under the Fourth Amendment 'requires a careful balance of the nature and quality of the intrusion on the individual's Fourth Amendment interests against the countervailing governmental interests at stake.' 490 U.S., at 396 (internal quotation marks omitted). The inquiry requires analyzing the totality of the circumstances. *Ibid.*

We analyze this question from the perspective 'of a reasonable officer on the scene, rather than the 20/20 vision of hindsight.' *Ibid.* We thus 'allo[w] for the fact that police officers are often forced to make split-second judgments—in circumstances that are tense, uncertain, and rapidly evolving—about the amount of force that is necessary in a particular situation.' *Id.*, at 396–397." Plumhoff v. Rickard, 572 U.S. ___, 134 S.Ct. 2012, 2020, 188 L.Ed.2d 1056 (2014).

141. Scott v. Harris, 550 U.S. 372 127 S.Ct. 1769, 1777, 167 L.Ed.2d 686 (2007), interpreting Tennessee v. Garner, 471 U.S. 1, 105 S.Ct. 1694, 85 L.Ed.2d 443 (1985). "It is also conceded, by both sides, that a claim of 'excessive force in the course of making [a] ... seizure of the person ... is properly analyzed under the Fourth Amendment's 'objective reasonableness' standard.'" [citation omitted]. 127 S.Ct. at 1776. "In determining the reasonableness of the manner in which a seizure is effected, '[w]e must balance the nature and quality of the intrusion on the individual's Fourth Amendment interests against the importance of the governmental interests alleged to justify the intrusion.'" [citation omitted]. 127 S.Ct. at 1778.

142. Tennessee v. Garner, 471 U.S. 1, 105 S.Ct. 1694, 85 L.Ed.2d 443, 455–56 (1985), as interpreted in Scott v. Harris, 550 U.S. 372, 127 S.Ct. 1769, 1777, 167 L.Ed.2d 686 (2007).

143. Scott v. Harris, 550 U.S. 372, 127 S.Ct. 1769, 1777, 167 L.Ed.2d 686 (2007). "Instead we lay down a more sensible rule: a police officer's attempt to terminate a dangerous high-speed car chase that threatens the lives of innocent bystanders does not violate the Fourth Amendment, even when it places the fleeing motorist at risk of serious injury or death." 127 S.Ct. at 1779. Justice Ginsburg, in her concurring opinion in Scott, states some of the relevant circumstances for determining whether deadly force for effecting an arrest in this case was reasonable: "Were the lives and well-being of others (motorists, pedestrians, police officers) at risk? Was there a safer way, given the time, place and circumstances, to stop the fleeing vehicle?" 127 S.Ct. at 1779.

144. Plumhoff v. Rickard, 572 U.S. ___, 134 S.Ct. 2012, 188 L.Ed.2d 1056) (2014) ("It stands to reason, that, if police officers are justified in firing at a suspect in order to end a severe threat to public safety, the officers need not stop firing until the threat has ended. * * * This would be a different case if [the police] had initiated a second round of shots after the first round had clearly incapacitated Rickard [the suspect] and had ended any threat of continued flight, or if Rickard had given up. But that is not what happened." 134 S.Ct. at 2022).

As an aside, the passenger in the fleeing car was also killed in *Plumhoff*. But the Court held that the plaintiff [the fleeing motorist's estate] could not rely on the passenger's rights in its argument that

Excessive force claims of this nature have, to date, arisen solely in the context of civil suits brought against the police for violation of the suspect's Fourth Amendment rights. It is doubtful, however, whether in most cases the *Weeks-Mapp* exclusionary rule would be applicable where police use excessive force to effect an otherwise lawful arrest. The excessive force used would not render the arrest unlawful and would therefore not generally taint any evidence obtained from the suspect while under arrest. Only if the excessive force resulted in an enhanced detention, over and above the arrest itself, might the unlawful enhanced restraint render the fruits thereof inadmissible in a criminal trial—such as forcing the arrestee into a secluded location after the arrest was effected and inflicting a severe beating on him.

n. Temporary civil or special needs detention of the person

As previously stated, temporary detentions may have a criminal investigative purpose—or a civil or special needs purpose that goes beyond the normal need for criminal law enforcement. So far in this chapter, we have discussed temporary detentions that have a criminal investigative purpose. Such detentions must be based on reasonable suspicion—and we have explored the various factual contexts in which that reasonable suspicion may or may not be shown. We have also discussed arrests, which must always be based on probable cause, and the various factual contexts in which that showing may or may not be made.

We turn now to a consideration of temporary detentions that have a civil or special needs purpose. These detentions do not require a showing of individualized wrongdoing or reasonable suspicion. Here the Court has engaged in a balancing process to sustain such detentions as a matter of first impression—and have thereafter engaged in a common-law-reasoning process in applying the announced law with respect to that particular detention in future cases. Under this test, the Court balances: (1) the nature or degree of the intrusiveness of the governmental invasion into personal security represented by the seizure in question, as against (2) the gravity of the governmental interest served by the seizure, attempting (3) to avoid giving government officials unfettered discretion to engage in such seizures. Where special governmental needs beyond the normal need for criminal law enforcement are shown, the Court strikes the balance in favor of dispensing with any showing of individualized wrongdoing—probable cause or reasonable suspicion.[145] Otherwise, the detention is disapproved.

---

the force used by the police was unreasonable because Fourth Amendment rights are personal and cannot be vicariously asserted.

"In arguing that too many shots were fired, respondent relies in part on the presence of Kelly Allen in the front seat of the car, but we do not think that this factor changes the calculus. Our cases make clear that Fourth Amendment rights are personal and cannot be vicariously asserted. The question before us is whether petitioners [the police] violated Rickard's [the driver's] Fourth Amendment rights, not Allen's. * * * But Allen's presence in the car cannot enhance Rickard's Fourth Amendment rights. After all, it was Rickard who put Allen in danger by fleeing and refusing to end the chase, and it would be perverse if his disregard for Allen's safety worked to his benefit." 134 S.Ct. at 2022 (internal citations and case quotation marks omitted).

145. "The reasonableness of seizures that are less intrusive than a traditional arrest, depends 'on a balance between the public interest and the individual's right to personal security free from arbitrary interference by law officers.' Consideration of such seizures involves a weighing of the gravity of the public concerns served by the seizure, the degree to which the seizure advances the public interest, and the severity of the interference with individual liberty. A central concern in balancing these competing considerations in a variety of settings has been to assure that an individual's reasonable expectation of privacy is not subject to arbitrary invasions solely at the unfettered discretion of officers

In so doing, the Court has upheld a number of suspicionless civil or special needs detentions of the person utilizing a balancing approach, while striking down others as not meeting the requirements for same.

• Police roadblocks

A police roadblock of motorists based on neutral criteria [i.e., every car or every other car or every third car, etc., is stopped] for a driver's license or car registration check is

---

in the field. To this end, the Fourth Amendment requires that a seizure must be based on specific objective facts indicating that society's legitimate interests require the seizure of the particular individual, or that the seizure must be carried out pursuant to a plan embodying explicit, neutral limitations on the conduct of individual officers." Brown v. Texas, 443 U.S. 47, 50, 99 S.Ct. 2637, 61 L.Ed.2d 357 (1979) (internal citations omitted).

"For the Fourth Amendment does not proscribe all searches and seizures, but only those that are unreasonable. What is reasonable, of course, 'depends on all the circumstances surrounding the search or seizure and the nature of the search or seizure itself.' Thus, the permissibility of a particular practice 'is judged by balancing its intrusion on the individual's Fourth Amendment interests against its promotion of legitimate governmental interests.' In most criminal cases, we strike the balance in favor of the procedures described by the Warrants Clause of the Fourth Amendment. Except in certain well-defined circumstances, a search or seizure in such a case is not reasonable unless it is accomplished pursuant to a judicial warrant issued upon probable cause. We have recognized exceptions to this rule, however, 'when special needs, beyond the normal need for law enforcement, make the warrant and probable cause requirement impracticable.' When faced with such special needs, we have not hesitated to balance the governmental and privacy interests to assess the practicality of the warrant and probable cause requirements in the particular context." Skinner v. Railway Labor Executives' Ass'n, 489 U.S. 602, 109 S.Ct 1402, 103 L.Ed.2d 639, 661 (1989) (internal citations omitted).

"While we have long emphasized, and reiterate today, that a search must be supported, as a general matter, by a warrant issued upon probable cause, our decision in *Railway Labor Executives* reaffirms the long-standing principle that neither a warrant nor probable cause, nor, indeed, any measure of individualized suspicion is an indispensable component of reasonableness in every circumstance. As we noted in *Railway Labor Executives*, our cases establish that where a Fourth Amendment intrusion serves special governmental needs, beyond the normal need for law enforcement, it is necessary to balance the individual's privacy expectations against the Government's interests to determine whether it is impracticable to require a warrant or some level of individualized suspicion in the particular context." National Treasury Employees Union v. Von Raab, 489 U.S. 656, 109 S.Ct. 1384, 103 L.Ed.2d 685, 702 (1989) (internal citations omitted) (emphasis added).

"Where a search is undertaken by law enforcement to discover evidence of criminal wrongdoing, this Court has said that reasonableness generally requires the obtaining of a judicial warrant. Warrants cannot be issued, of course, without the showing of probable cause required by the Warrants Clause. But a warrant is not required to establish the reasonableness of all government searches; and when a warrant is not required (and the Warrants Clause not applicable), probable cause is not invariably required either. A search unsupported by probable cause can be constitutional, we have said, 'when special needs, beyond the normal need for law enforcement, make the warrant and probable cause requirements impracticable.'" Vernonia School District 47J v. Acton, 515 U.S. 646, 115 S.Ct. 2386, 132 L.Ed.2d 564, 574 (1995) (internal citations omitted) (emphasis added).

"The Fourth Amendment requires that searches and seizures be reasonable. A search is generally unreasonable in the absence of individualized wrongdoing. While such suspicion is not an 'irreducible' component of reasonableness, we have recognized circumstances where the usual rule does not apply. For example, we have upheld certain regimes of suspicionless searches where the program was designed to serve 'special needs beyond the normal need for law enforcement.'" City of Indianapolis v. Edmond, 531 U.S. 32, 121 S.Ct. 447, 148 L.Ed.2d 333, 340 (2000) (internal citations omitted) (Court also notes other exceptions: (a) certain administrative-type searches of closely-regulated industries, or of fire-damaged premises to discover the cause of the fire, or of buildings to ensure compliance with city housing codes; and (b) roadblocks to intercept illegal aliens or to remove drunk drivers from the road or to verify motorists' drivers licenses and registration).

reasonable under the Fourth Amendment.[146] But a random police stop of a motorist—apart from a roadblock—for a drivers license or car registration check has been struck down as unreasonable under the Fourth Amendment.[147] Such a stop gives impermissible unfettered discretion to the police to stop whatever motorist the officers choose. A roadblock based on neutral criteria, however, does not suffer from such an infirmity.[148]

Similarly, a drunk driving police roadblock of motorists based on neutral criteria, wherein motorists are briefly stopped and questioned for signs of intoxication, is reasonable under the Fourth Amendment. But a detention beyond such questioning, in which field sobriety tests are required of the motorist, would probably require a showing of reasonable suspicion that the driver is intoxicated.[149] Indeed, during a proper roadblock, police may learn additional facts that give them probable cause to search the vehicle for evidence of crime or to arrest the motorist or passengers, even if the search or arrest is unrelated to the primary purpose of the roadblock.[150]

In each of these cases, a special governmental need was shown beyond the normal needs of criminal law enforcement; namely, the need to promote highway safety. But where that special need is not shown and the *primary* purpose of the roadblock is to detect evidence of ordinary criminal wrongdoing by motorists or passengers, the roadblock is unreasonable under the Fourth Amendment. Accordingly, a police roadblock set up for the *primary* purpose of discovering and interdicting illegal narcotics, in which all cars stopped at the roadblock are circled by a police dog for a narcotics "dog sniff" to detect the presence of narcotics in the auto, has been held unreasonable under the Fourth Amendment.[151] Nonetheless, a police roadblock may be set up for a special emergency purpose—such as a roadblock to thwart a terrorist attack, or to catch a dangerous criminal who is likely to flee via a particular route—as this qualifies as a special governmental need beyond that of ordinary criminal law enforcement.[152]

---

146. Texas v. Brown, 460 U.S. 730, 103 S.Ct. 1535, 75 L.Ed.2d 502, 512 (1983).

147. "Accordingly, we hold that except in those situations in which there is at least articulable and reasonable suspicion that a motorist is unlicensed or that an automobile is not registered, or that either the vehicle or an occupant is otherwise subject to seizure for violation of the law, stopping an automobile and detaining the driver in order to check his [or her] drivers license and the registration of the automobile is unreasonable under the Fourth Amendment. This holding does not preclude the ... States from developing methods for spot checks that involve less intrusion or that do not involve the unconstrained exercise of [police] discretion. Questioning of all oncoming traffic at roadblock-type stops is one possible alternative. We hold only that persons in automobiles on the public roadways may not for that reason alone have their travel and privacy interfered with at the unbridled discretion of the police." Delaware v. Prouse, 440 U.S. 648, 99 S.Ct. 1391, 59 L.Ed.2d 660, 673–74 (1979).

148. For a discussion of roadblocks generally, see 4 Wayne LaFave, Search and Seizure § 9.7(a)(b) (5th ed. 2012).

149. Michigan Dept. of State Police v. Sitz, 496 U.S. 444, 110 S.Ct. 2481, 110 L.Ed.2d 412 (1990) ("Detention of particular motorists for more extensive field sobriety testing may require satisfaction of an individualized suspicion standard." 110 L.Ed.2d at 420).

150. "Our holding also does not impair the ability of police officers to act appropriately upon information that they learn during a checkpoint stop justified by a lawful primary purpose, even where such action may result in the arrest of a motorist for an offense unrelated to that purpose." City of Indianapolis v. Edmund, 531 U.S. 32, 121 S.Ct. 447, 148 L.Ed.2d 333, 347 (2000).

151. City of Indianapolis v. Edmond, 531 U.S. 32, 121 S.Ct. 447, 148 L.Ed.2d 333 (2000). ("Because the primary purpose of the Indianapolis narcotics checkpoint program is to uncover evidence of ordinary criminal wrongdoing, the program contravenes the Fourth Amendment. * * * Without drawing the line at roadblocks designed primarily to serve the general interest in crime control, the Fourth Amendment would do little to prevent such intrusions from becoming a routine part of American life." 148 L.Ed.2d at 343, 344).

152. City of Indianapolis v. Edmond, 531 U.S. 32, 121 S.Ct.447, 148 L.Ed.2d 333, 345 (2000) ("Of course, there are circumstances that may justify a law enforcement checkpoint where the primary

There is, however, an important exception to this analysis. Where the purpose of the roadblock is not to seek self-incriminating information against the stopped motorists or passengers, but instead to solicit their voluntary cooperation in investigating a recent criminal offense, a brief information-seeking roadblock may be reasonable under the Fourth Amendment. Although no special governmental interest is shown here, the law has always permitted police to solicit the voluntary cooperation of the public in investigating crime.[153] But to do this in the case of motorists or passengers, it is necessary to briefly stop the vehicles in which they are located and make the necessary inquiries. This is clearly a minimal, non-threatening invasion of personal liberty that is reasonable under the Fourth Amendment—providing the roadblock in question is purely informational in nature, and is set up at a location and time to advance the governmental interest of detecting the crime being investigated.[154]

• Traffic checkpoint stops near border

The Court has upheld another type of road block that also serves a special governmental need beyond the need for ordinary criminal law enforcement; namely, the need to stem the tide of illegal immigration into the country. Accordingly, the U.S. Border Patrol may, consistent with the Fourth Amendment, stop all vehicles coming through fixed traffic checkpoints *near* the U.S.-Mexican border [but not at the border or its functional equivalent] and direct inquiries concerning the citizenship status of the vehicle's occupants. No reasonable suspicion that the vehicles contain illegal aliens is required to stop cars coming through this checkpoint.[155] But in the absence of probable cause, the Border Patrol has no authority to conduct a search of these vehicles.[156] Nor may the Border Patrol, apart from the traffic checkpoint, conduct roving patrol searches of motor vehicles traveling near the U.S.-Mexican border in the absence of probable cause,[157] or roving patrol, temporary stops of vehicles near the U.S.-Mexican border in the absence of reasonable suspicion.[158]

---

purpose would otherwise, but for some emergency, relate to ordinary crime control. For example, as the Court of Appeals noted, the Fourth Amendment would almost certainly permit an appropriately tailored roadblock to thwart a terrorist attack or to catch a dangerous criminal who is likely to flee by way of a particular route.")

153. "[L]aw enforcement officers do not violate the Fourth Amendment by merely approaching an individual on the street or in another public place, by asking him whether he is willing to answer some questions, [or] by putting questions to him if the person is willing to listen." Florida v. Royer, 460 U.S. 491, 497, 103 S.Ct. 1319, 75 L.Ed.2d 229 (1983).

154. Illinois v. Lidster, 540 U.S. 419, 124 S.Ct. 885, 157 L.Ed.2d 843 (2004) (roadblock set up at location and time of hit-and-run accident that had occurred about week prior thereto to obtain information about the identity of the driver and vehicle involved in the accident; roadblock upheld) ("That does not mean that the [information-seeking] stop is automatically, or even presumptively constitutional. It simply means that we must judge its reasonableness, hence its constitutionality, on the basis of individual circumstances." 124 S.Ct. at 890 [utilizing a balancing test].

155. United States v. Martinez-Fuerte, 428 U.S. 543, 96 S.Ct. 3074, 49 L.Ed.2d 1116 (1976) (Traffic checkpoints were located at San Clemente, California, 66 miles from the border, and Sarila, Texas, 90 miles from the border; cars coming through such checkpoints have not necessarily come from Mexico nor are they necessarily on their way to Mexico, given the side roads off of the highway on which the checkpoints are located). By way of contrast, see Chapter 15, Section 2b of this work for a discussion of routine border searches conducted at the border or its functional equivalent.

156. United States v. Ortiz, 422 U.S. 891, 95 S.Ct. 2585, 45 L.Ed.2d 623 (1975).

157. Almeida-Sanchez v. United States, 413 U.S. 266, 93 S.Ct. 2535, 37 L.Ed.2d 596 (1973).

158. United States v. Brignoni-Ponce, 422 U.S. 873, 95 S.Ct. 2574, 45 L.Ed.2d 607 (1975) (fact that occupants in car are of Mexican ancestry does not constitute reasonable suspicion that they are illegal aliens).

• Random stops of vessels

It is a reasonable seizure of a vessel and its occupants within the meaning of the Fourth Amendment for U.S. Customs officials—without benefit of a roadblock of sorts—to stop and board a vessel *randomly* for inspection of the manifest and vessel documents pursuant to 19 USC § 1581(a), provided the vessel has ready access to the open sea. This result was reached based on the fact that the 19 USC § 1581(a) can be traced back to the First Congress that proposed the Fourth Amendment to the states (an impressive historical pedigree) and (b) the impracticability of setting up a roadblock for vessels that navigate bodies of water.[159]

• Open questions

The civil or special needs detentions discussed above are not, however, a closed list. The Court may very well recognize additional special needs detentions in the future to meet emergency situations that go beyond the normal needs of law enforcement. These yet-to-be-decided detentions may include, for example, temporary detentions to intercept terrorists or serial killers suspected of fleeing via a particular route. There may be others as well. In each case, the Court will no doubt use a balancing approach to determine whether a proposed special needs exception should be accepted or rejected.

Section 2. Seizure of Property: Houses, Papers and Effects

We have now finished discussing "unreasonable seizures" of "persons"; that is, arrests and temporary detentions, both criminal and civil. We now move on to "unreasonable seizures" of "houses, papers or effects." Such property seizures arise in two factual contexts: (a) where a preceding search leads to the property seizure, or (b) where the property seizure is the initial Fourth Amendment intrusion. Both such seizures must be reasonable in the Fourth Amendment sense.

a. Warrant requirement

The U.S. Supreme Court has on occasion stated that the *seizure* of personal or real property—as distinguished from a *search* of same—must generally be conducted with a warrant, subject to recognized exceptions.[160] In this respect, the announced rule is simply

---

159. United States v. Villamonte-Marquez, 462 U.S. 579, 103 S.Ct. 2573, 77 L.Ed.2d 22 (1983).

160. "In order to enforce that [Fourth Amendment] requirement [of reasonableness], this Court has interpreted the Amendment as establishing rules and presumptions designed to control law enforcement officers that may significantly intrude upon privacy interests. Sometimes those rules require warrants. We have said, for example, that in 'the ordinary case' seizures of personal property are 'unreasonable within the meaning of the Fourth Amendment,' without more, 'unless ... accomplished pursuant to a judicial warrant,' issued by a neutral magistrate after finding probable cause. We nonetheless have made it clear that there are exceptions to the warrant requirement." Illinois v. McArthur, 531 U.S. 326, 121 S.Ct. 946, 148 L.Ed.2d 838, 847 (2001) (internal citation omitted) (constructive seizure of house pending the issuance of search warrant for the house, wherein police prevented home dweller from entering house unaccompanied by police, followed by a search of the house with a warrant). "In the ordinary case, the Court has viewed a seizure of personal property as per se unreasonable within the meaning of the Fourth Amendment unless it is accomplished pursuant to a judicial warrant issued upon probable cause and particularly describing the items to be seized." United States v. Place, 462 U.S. 696, 103 S.Ct. 2637, 77 L.Ed.2d 110, 116 (1983) (seizure of suitcase

a corollary of the search warrant requirement rule which requires—subject to recognized exceptions—that a *search* of private premises, particularly the home, must be conducted pursuant to a search warrant issued in compliance with the Warrants Clause of the Fourth Amendment; the property seizures effected during such a search are, of course, authorized when conducted pursuant to the warrant.[161]

But because Fourth Amendment seizures—unlike Fourth Amendment searches—do not usually implicate privacy interests,[162] seizures of property [apart from a search that might require a warrant] rarely require a warrant in themselves, despite the general rule. Indeed, the Court has announced three broad-based exceptions to this warrant requirement for such seizures—plus a standalone "plain view" doctrine—that virtually exempt all property seizures from a warrant requirement [unless the preceding search itself requires a warrant]. Only in rare cases where privacy interests are vitally affected—as, for example, when police actually or constructively seize a home—does the warrant requirement for such *initial* property seizures appear viable.[163]

We turn now to a consideration of the broad-based exceptions to the warrant requirement for seizures of property—as well as the "plain view" doctrine.

b. Exceptions to the warrant requirement for seizures of property

The exceptions to the warrant requirement for the seizure of property have to date all involved *initial* Fourth Amendment intrusions, with no prior Fourth Amendment search.

(1) Seizure of personal or real property pending application for a search warrant

First, no warrant is required for the seizure of personal property for a reasonable time while police obtain a warrant for same—providing there is probable cause to believe that the property holds contraband, fruits or instrumentalities of a crime, or evidence of a crime. The same rule prevails for the constructive seizure of real property, in which police

---

pending the issuance of a search warrant for the suitcase, followed by a search of the suitcase with a warrant).

161. See Chapter 11, Section 1 of this work for a discussion of the search warrant requirement rule. The exceptions to this rule for searches are discussed at Chapters 14 and 15 of this work.

162. "This text [the Fourth Amendment] protects two types of expectations, one involving 'searches,' the other 'seizures.' A 'search' occurs when an expectation of privacy that society is prepared to recognize as reasonable is infringed. A 'seizure' of property occurs where there is some meaningful interference with an individual's possessory interest in property." United States v. Jacobsen, 466 U.S. 109, 113, 104 S.Ct. 1652, 80 L.Ed.2d 85, 94 (1984). "A search compromises the individual interest in privacy; a seizure deprives the individual of dominion over his or her person or property." Horton v. California, 496 U.S. 128, 110 S.Ct. 2301, 110 L.Ed.2d 112, 120 (1990).

163. See, e.g., Soldal v. Cook County, 506 U.S. 56, 113 S.Ct. 538, 121 L.Ed.2d 450 (1992) (police removal of house trailer from its foundations in a mobile home park is a Fourth Amendment seizure of property); Illinois v. McArthur, 531 U.S. 326, 121 S.Ct. 946, 148 L.Ed.2d 838 (2001) (police seal off a home and prevent home dweller to enter home unaccompanied by police while a search warrant is being obtained for home; this warrantless constructive seizure of a home based on probable cause is permissible if based on exigent circumstances; absent such circumstances, such warrantless seizure would be unreasonable).

"seal off" private premises pending a search warrant application, providing an additional requirement of exigent circumstances is shown.[164]

In particular, the Court has upheld the warrantless seizure of a container, such as a footlocker or suitcase, as an initial Fourth Amendment intrusion for a reasonable period of time, while law enforcement officials obtain a warrant for the search of the container, provided probable cause is shown for the search.[165] The same result has been reached where law enforcement officials physically secure a dwelling, preventing the home dweller and others from entering the premises unaccompanied by police, thereby constructively seizing same, for a reasonable period of time while a search warrant is obtained for the search of the dwelling—provided (a) the above probable cause showing is made, and (b) the exigencies of the situation are such that there is probability that the evidence in the house would be destroyed while the warrant is being obtained if the constructive seizure did not take place.[166]

(2) Temporary seizure of property pending further investigation

Second, no warrant is required—if the initial seizure of property is only temporary in nature pending further investigation—where there is reasonable suspicion that the subject property contains the fruits of a crime, the instrumentalities of a crime, or evidence of a crime. In particular, a law enforcement official may temporarily seize an air traveler's luggage at an airport for a narcotics dog-sniff based on the above reasonable suspicion showing—so long as the limits of a temporary detention are not exceeded.[167] Similarly,

---

164. "In various circumstances, this Court has upheld temporary restraints where needed to preserve evidence until police could obtain a warrant. We have found no case in which this Court has held unlawful a temporary seizure [of property] that was supported by probable cause and was designed to prevent the loss of evidence while police diligently obtained a warrant in a reasonable period of time." Illinois v. McArthur, 531 U.S. 326, 121 S.Ct. 946, 148 L.Ed.2d 838, 849 (2001) (internal citations omitted).

165. "Recognizing the generally less intrusive nature of a seizure, the Court has frequently approved warrantless seizures of property, on the basis of probable cause, for the time necessary to secure a warrant, where a warrantless search was either held to be or likely would have been held impermissible." Segura v. United States, 468 U.S. 796, 104 S.Ct. 3380, 82 L.Ed 2d 599, 609–10 (1984) (plurality), citing cases which authorize the seizure of a defendant's footlocker or suitcase based on probable cause while a search warrant for same is being obtained: United States v. Chadwick, 433 U.S. 1, 97 S.Ct. 2476, 53 L.Ed.2d 538 (1977) (seizure of footlocker based on probable cause assumed to be reasonable; Court held that a warrant should have been obtained for same while police held the footlocker); Arkansas v. Sanders, 442 U.S. 753, 99 S.Ct. 2586, 61 L.Ed.2d 235 (1979) (seizure of defendant's suitcase based on probable cause approved; Court held that a warrant should have been obtained for same while police held the suitcase); see also Chambers v. Maroney, 399 U.S. 42, 90 S.Ct. 1975, 26 L.Ed.2d 419 (1970) (seizure of automobile from street based on probable cause is permissible; thereafter, police may search the automobile with or without a warrant).

166. "We hold, therefore, that securing a dwelling, on the basis of probable cause, to prevent the destruction or removal of evidence while a search warrant is being sought is not in itself an unreasonable seizure of either the dwelling or its contents." Segura v. United States, 468 U.S. 796, 104 S.Ct. 3380, 82 L.Ed.2d 599, 612 (1984) (plurality) (police officers entered house and prevented anyone from leaving or touching any property on premises while a search warrant was obtained; constructive seizure upheld).

"Police officers, with probable cause to believe that a man had hidden marijuana in his home, prevented the man from entering the home for two hours while they obtained a search warrant. We must decide whether those officers violated the Fourth Amendment. We conclude that those officers acted reasonably. They did not violate the Amendment's requirements." Illinois v. McArthur, 531 U.S. 326, 121 S.Ct. 946, 148 L.Ed.2d 838, 846 (2001).

167. "In sum, we conclude that when an officer's observations lead him reasonably to believe that a traveler is carrying luggage that contains narcotics, the principles of Terry and its progeny would permit the officer to detain the luggage briefly to investigate the circumstances that aroused his suspicion, provided that the investigative detention is properly limited in scope." United States v.

a temporary detention of en route first class mail based on the above showing is permissible so as to allow a limited investigation of the suspicion that prompted the detention—and if probable cause is developed during this investigation, a reasonable delay is also allowed to obtain a search warrant for the mail.[168]

(3) Seizure of contraband, fruits, instrumentalities and evidence of crime

Third, no warrant is required to seize property discovered with no prior Fourth Amendment intrusion where there is probable cause to believe that the property itself constituted contraband, fruits, instrumentalities or evidence of crime. Accordingly, a person's property discovered by law enforcement officials in a public place may be seized based on the above probable cause showing.[169] Similarly, a container that cannot support a reasonable expectation of privacy as to its contents because there is probable cause that the container

---

Place, 462 U.S. 696, 103 S.Ct. 2637, 77 L.Ed.2d 110, 120 (1983).

In *Place*, federal narcotics agents seized defendant's two carry-on bags as defendant arrived at LaGuardia Airport in NYC from Miami [defendant himself was not detained]—after having been notified by narcotics agents in Miami of (1) defendant's scheduled arrival at LaGuardia, and (2) the Miami agents' reasonable suspicion that defendant was carrying narcotics as a result of an encounter with defendant at the Miami airport. The initial seizure of these two bags was held reasonable as being based on reasonable suspicion. The NYC agents, however, exceeded the time limits of a temporary *Terry* detention of the bags by transporting the bags to Kennedy Airport where a "dog sniff" of the bags took place, all of which took 90 minutes to accomplish from the initial seizure of the bags. NYC agents had ample time to arrange for a "dog sniff" at LaGuardia Airport and thus minimize the intrusion on defendant's Fourth Amendment interests in the bags. Consequently, a search warrant issued for the bags after the dog alerted on the bags was invalid, and the fruits of the search of the bags pursuant to the warrant were inadmissible in evidence against the defendant.

"We note that here the New York agents knew the time of Place's scheduled arrival at LaGuardia, had ample time to arrange for their additional investigation at that location, and thereby could have minimized the intrusion on respondent's Fourth Amendment interests. Thus, although we decline to adopt any outside time limitation for a permissible Terry stop, we have never approved a seizure for the prolonged 90 minute period involved here and cannot do so on the facts presented by this case." United States v. Place, 77 L.Ed.2d at 122.

Also see cases collected at "Searches and Seizures"§ 57 West Key No.

168. United States v. Van Leeuwen, 397 U.S. 249, 90 S.Ct. 1029, 25 L.Ed.2d 282 (1970).

In *Van Leeuwen*, postal authorities detained two packages for a period of 29 hours before obtaining a search warrant for the search of same—following which the authorities resealed the packages and sent them to the defendant who had mailed the same to himself at two different locations. The Court found that (1) there was reasonable suspicion for the detention as to the first package—which within 1 1/2 hours of investigation ripened into probable cause; and (2) there was reasonable suspicion for the detention as to the second package which, due to unavoidable delays, did not ripen into probable cause until 26 hours later. The Court held that holding the packages for 29 hours before obtaining a search warrant as to both packages was reasonable under the circumstances of this case.

As an aside, in In re Jackson, 96 (6 Otto) 727, 24 L.Ed. 877 (1877), the Court held that the Fourth Amendment protects letters and sealed packages from unreasonable searches and generally requires a search warrant based on probable cause in order to search their contents. See 5 Wayne LaFave, Search and Seizure § 10.3(b) (5th ed. 2012).

169. "The court [of appeals] seemingly construes the [Fourth] Amendment to protect only against seizures that are the outcome of a search. But our cases are to the contrary and hold that seizures of property are subject to Fourth Amendment scrutiny even though no search within the meaning of the Amendment has taken place. *More generally, an officer who happens to come across an individual's property in a public area could seize it only if Fourth Amendment standards are satisfied—for example, if the items are evidence of crime or contraband.*" Soldal v. Cook County, 506 U.S. 56,113 S.Ct. 538, 121 L.Ed.2d 450, 463 (1992) (the removal [with the help of police] of a person's house trailer from its foundations at a mobile home park and subsequent transport into the street was a Fourth Amendment seizure of said person's "house" which must satisfy the Amendment's reasonableness requirement. The dismissal of the person's civil rights suit was reversed).

contains contraband and is a common illegal drug container—such as a see-through, zip-lock plastic baggie containing suspect cocaine—may be properly seized without a warrant and its contents tested.[170]

c. The "plain view" doctrine

In contrast to seizures of property conducted as an *initial* Fourth Amendment intrusion discussed above, most seizures of property by law enforcement officials take place during a *prior* Fourth Amendment intrusion. For example, a law enforcement officer may discover items of personal property ("papers or effects") while conducting a Fourth Amendment search of an individual's person, house, or motor vehicle—either with or without a warrant. It is clear that the officer is not privileged to seize any and all property discovered during these searches—even if the prior Fourth Amendment intrusion is reasonable. Something more is required.[171]

(1) Basic requirements

If the search is conducted with a warrant, personal property may be seized if authorized by the warrant. But whether conducted with or without a warrant, the Court in a number of cases has developed the "plain view" doctrine which authorizes an officer to conduct a seizure of personal property during the course of *any* prior Fourth Amendment search if two conditions are met.

First, the item of personal property must be discovered by police during the course of an otherwise *reasonable* Fourth Amendment search or seizure—i.e., a search conducted either with a valid search warrant or under an established exception to the search warrant requirement rule. In this respect, the "plain view" doctrine always "piggybacks" on a prior valid Fourth Amendment intrusion. If, however, the prior intrusion is unreasonable, the plain view seizure of items discovered after said intrusion is considered unreasonable as well.[172]

---

170. "[I]t is well-settled that it is constitutionally reasonable for law enforcement officials to seize 'effects' that cannot support a justifiable expectation of privacy without a warrant based on probable cause to believe that they contain contraband." United States v. Jacobsen, 466 U.S. 109, 104 S.Ct. 1652, 80 L.Ed. 2d 85, 99 (1984). In *Jacobsen*, Fed Ex employees opened a damaged package and discovered four zip lock bags containing a suspect white powder, and turned over same to federal narcotics agents. Court held that the original search by the Fed Ex employees was a private search to which the Fourth Amendment had no application. But when the narcotics agent took possession of the package and the zip lock bags, this was a Fourth Amendment seizure; this was a reasonable seizure, however, as there was probable cause to believe that the white powder was cocaine. The subsequent testing of a trace amount of the powder was a Fourth Amendment seizure, but this was reasonable seizure utilizing a balancing test.

171. "As the Supreme Court has emphasized, the mere fact that some objects are lawfully discovered by an officer within premises does not provide a legal basis for the seizure of those objects. Were it otherwise, it would be possible for police to make wholesale seizures of an untold number of items which would of necessity be observed while the police were lawfully carrying out their arrest or other duties on the premises. Such wholesale seizures would unquestionably violate the Fourth Amendment." 3 Wayne LaFave, Search and Seizure § 6.7(a) at 637 (5th ed. 2012).

172. "[W]e have held that law enforcement officers may seize evidence in plain view, provided that they have not violated the Fourth Amendment in arriving at the spot from which the observation of the evidence is made. See Horton v. California 496 U.S. 128, 136–140, 110 S.Ct. 2301, 110 L.Ed.2d 112 (1990). As we put it in *Horton*, '[i]t is ... an essential predicate to any valid warrantless seizure of incriminating evidence that the officer did not violate the Fourth Amendment in arriving at the place from which the evidence could be plainly seen.' Id. at 136, 110 S.Ct. 2301. So long as this prerequisite is satisfied, however, it does not matter that the officer who makes the observation may

Second, while within the scope of the prior Fourth Amendment intrusion, the police must have *probable cause* to believe that the property to be seized is contraband, fruits or instrumentalities of a crime, or evidence of a crime. Absent such a probable cause showing, the seizure is unreasonable; in particular, reasonable suspicion for a seizure is insufficient.[173] Also, the police may not go beyond the scope of the prior Fourth Amendment intrusion to acquire this probable cause.

The doctrine was first discussed at length in *Coolidge v. New Hampshire,*[174] in which the above two requirements were generally laid down—together with a third requirement that the evidence thus seized must be inadvertently discovered by police. The Court, however, has since eliminated this inadvertence element.[175] Also the *Coolidge* Court articulated the second requirement to the effect that the incriminating nature of the evidence seized must be "immediately apparent" to the police. The Court, however, later altered this to require a showing of "probable cause" to believe that the seized item was incriminating in nature.[176]

As an aside, the *Coolidge* Court saw the "plain view" doctrine as an exception to the search warrant requirement rule. The Court has since revised this view so that the "plain view" doctrine is now seen as a limitation on the power of the police to seize property after a valid Fourth Amendment intrusion—not as an independent authorization to conduct a search without a warrant.[177]

(2) "Plain feel" case

The "plain view" doctrine has been held applicable where the probable cause requirement is met, not by the visual senses, but by the tactile senses; for example, where a police officer, while conducting a valid *Terry* pat-down search, feels an object on the defendant's person that gives the officer probable cause to believe that the said object is a concealed firearm or contraband drugs. Under these circumstances, the officer is privileged both

---

have gone to the spot from which the evidence was seen with the hope of being able to view and seize the evidence. [citation omitted]. Instead, the Fourth Amendment requires only that the steps preceding the seizure be lawful. [citation omitted.]." Kentucky v. King, 563 U.S. ___, 131 S.Ct. 1849, 1858, 179 L.Ed.2d 865 (2011).

173. On the other hand, if only a temporary seizure of property is effected, rather than a full-blown seizure, a reasonable suspicion showing would appear to be sufficient. See discussion of temporary seizures of property under Section 2b(2) of this Chapter.

174. 403 U.S. 443, 91 S.Ct. 2022, 29 L.Ed.2d 564, 581–87 (1971).

175. Horton v. California, 496 U.S. 128, 110 S.Ct. 2301, 110 L.Ed.2d 112 (1990).

176. Arizona v. Hicks, 480 U.S. 321, 107 S.Ct. 1149, 94 L.Ed.2d 347 (1987). In *Hicks*, the police received information that a bullet fired through the floor of defendant's apartment had injured a man in the apartment below. Police validly entered defendant's apartment looking for the shooter, for any other shooting victims, and for weapons, under the exigent circumstances exception to the search warrant requirement rule. They found no one, but did observe new stereo equipment in an otherwise squalid apartment. Police conducted a search outside the scope of the exigent circumstances exception and moved the equipment to get the serial numbers of the equipment, radioed in the numbers, and learned that the equipment had been stolen in a robbery; they then seized the equipment. Prior to this invalid search, the police had no probable cause to believe the stereos were stolen, only reasonable suspicion. Consequently, the seizure could not be justified under the "plain view" doctrine.

177. Texas v. Brown, 460 U.S. 730, 103 S.Ct. 1535, 75 L.Ed.2d 502, 511 (1983); Horton v. California, 496 U.S. 128, 110 S.Ct. 2301, 110 L.Ed.2d 112, 120 (1990). See, e.g., Walter v. United States, 447 U.S. 649, 100 S.Ct. 2395, 65 L.Ed.2d 410 (1980). In *Walter*, private parties turned over to FBI a package which had been misdelivered. The private parties had opened the package and found certain film in boxes, with explicit descriptions and suggestive drawings thereon, indicating the obscene nature of the films. FBI had probable cause to seize the films, but their subsequent viewing of the films without a search warrant was an unreasonable search under the Fourth Amendment.

to conduct a more intrusive search of the defendant's person, and, thereafter to seize the firearm or contraband drugs.[178]

(3) Compare: "open view" doctrine

Under the "open view" doctrine, a law enforcement officer is located outside a constitutionally protected area and, from that vantage point, sees something incriminating within a constitutionally protected area. No prior Fourth Amendment intrusion has generally taken place at the time this observation takes place. For example, a police officer, from a neighbor's yard, is able to see potted marijuana plants in the patio of a suspect's back yard. Or a police officer walks up to a parked car on the public street and looks into the car from a vantage point outside the car. Such observations are not considered Fourth Amendment searches.[179]

By way of contrast, under the "plain view" doctrine, a prior Fourth Amendment intrusion has already taken place when police observe something incriminating. For example, a police officer searches a car and comes across contraband drugs during the search. If (1) the prior Fourth Amendment intrusion of the car is reasonable, and (2) there is probable cause to believe that the suspect items are contraband drugs, the seizure of such items is reasonable under the "plain view" doctrine.[180]

---

178. Minnesota v. Dickerson, 508 U.S. 356, 113 S.Ct. 2130, 124 L.Ed 334 (1993). In *Dickerson,* the seizure, however, was held unreasonable because the officer exceeded the bounds of a valid *Terry* pat-down search for weapons. During the pat-down, the officer felt a soft object that he knew was not a weapon. He then squeezed the object to determine whether it was a bag containing a lump of crack cocaine. He concluded that it was, reached into the suspect's pocket, and seized the bag. Consequently, the "plain view" doctrine was inapplicable to sustain this seizure, as the bag was not discovered during an otherwise reasonable search.

179. For a discussion of the "open view" doctrine, see Chapter 10, Section 5a of this work.

180. See, e.g., Ensor v. State, 403 So.2d 349 (Fla. 1981).

Chapter 13

Searches Conducted with a *Search Warrant*

Section 1. Governed by Warrants Clause of the Fourth Amendment: Presumptively Reasonable

Under the search warrant requirement rule, a search of private premises, particularly a home, must generally be conducted pursuant to a search warrant issued by a neutral and detached magistrate—subject to a number of important exceptions.[1] A search with a warrant, in turn, is governed by the Warrants Clause of the Fourth Amendment: " ... and no warrant shall issue except [1] upon probable cause, supported by oath or affirmation, [2] particularly describing the place to be searched and the persons or things to be seized."

Given this decided preference for search warrants, it is settled that a warrant issued by a neutral and detached magistrate is considered *presumptively* supported by probable cause. Doubtful or marginal cases must be resolved in favor of the magistrate's finding of probable cause, even though such a finding might not be sustainable if the search had been conducted without a warrant.[2] The burden of proof is therefore on the party attacking a search warrant to overcome this presumption and to show that the warrant is *not* supported by probable cause. Indeed, given the Court's strong preference for search warrants generally, the burden of proof on all other issues involving a search with a warrant has traditionally been on the same party—including the facial validity of the warrant and its execution.[3]

---

1. See Chapter 11, Section 1 and cases collected at n. 1 of this work.

2. "Because a search warrant 'provides the detached scrutiny of a neutral magistrate, which is a more reliable safeguard against improper searches than the hurried judgment of a law enforcement officer 'engaged in the often competitive enterprise of ferreting out crime,' we have a expressed a strong preference for warrants and declared that 'in a doubtful or marginal case a search under a warrant may be sustainable where without one it would fail.' Reasonable minds frequently may differ on the question whether a particular affidavit establishes probable cause, and we have thus concluded that the preference for warrants is most appropriately effectuated by according 'great deference' to a magistrate's determination." United States v. Leon, 468 U.S. 897, 104 S.Ct. 3405, 82 L.Ed.2d 677, 692 (1984) (internal citations omitted). "Although in a particular case it may not be easy to determine when an affidavit [for a search warrant] demonstrates the existence of probable cause, the resolution of doubtful or marginal cases should be largely determined by the preference to be accorded to warrants." United States v. Ventresca, 380 U.S. 102, 109, 85 S.Ct. 741, 13 L.Ed.2d 684, 689 (1965). "There is, of course, a presumption of validity with respect to the affidavit supporting the search warrant." Franks v. Delaware, 438 U.S. 154, 98 S.Ct. 2674, 57 L.Ed.2d 667, 682 (1978).

3. For a discussion of which party has the burden of proof at a motion to suppress hearing, see Chapter 17, Section 6a of this work. "With respect to the issue which is usually central in a motion

The Court has stated that the warrant procedure serves two important functions. First, the scrutiny by an independent magistrate is intended to eliminate altogether searches not based on probable cause, thus protecting the people from overzealous law enforcement officers. The flip side to this purpose is that officers have a real incentive to bring *only* substantial search warrant affidavits to magistrates, for fear of having the affidavit rejected if they fail to do so. Second, for those searches deemed necessary as based on probable cause, the magistrate's oversight is intended to limit the search to a particular place for particular things, thus avoiding the evil of general exploratory searches that the Framers intended to end.[4] Beyond that, when and if a search is ordered, the use of a warrant assures the individual whose property is being searched that an independent magistrate has authorized the search pursuant to established law and has narrowly limited its objectives and scope, thus reducing the perception that the intrusion is merely the arbitrary act of a government agent.[5]

Section 2. Probable Cause Requirement

a. Definition of "probable cause": totality of the circumstances approach

The Fourth Amendment provides that no warrant may issue except upon "probable cause." As previously discussed, "probable cause" has been traditionally defined—at least in an ordinary criminal investigative context—as a practical, non-technical evidentiary showing of individualized criminal wrongdoing that amounts to more than mere suspicion, but less than proof beyond a reasonable doubt.[6] Moreover, a totality-of-the-circumstances approach is followed in determining whether there is probable cause to issue a search warrant: that is, the entire factual circumstances, including any hearsay information from private citizens or police informers, must be considered in a given case—as set out in the affidavit and any other sworn proof presented to the magistrate.[7]

There was a time, however, when the Court required a two-pronged test for search warrant affidavits if the affidavit was based on information obtained from a confidential informant. Both a veracity prong and a basis-for-knowledge prong had to be met. Under

to suppress hearing—the reasonableness of the challenged search or seizure—most states follow the rule which is utilized in the federal courts: if the search or seizure was pursuant to a warrant, the defendant has the burden of proof; but if the police acted without a warrant, the burden of proof is on the prosecution." 6 Wayne LaFave, Search and Seizure § 11.2(b) at 50 (5th ed. 2012).

4. Coolidge v. New Hampshire, 403 U.S. 443, 467, 91 S.Ct. 2022, 29 L.Ed.2d 564, 583 (1971).

5. Skinner v. Railway Labor Executives' Ass'n., 489 U.S. 602, 109 S.Ct.1402, 103 L.Ed.2d 639, 663 (1989); Illinois v. Gates, 462 U.S. 213, 103 S.Ct. 2317, 76 L.Ed.2d 527, 547 (1983); United States v. Chadwick, 433 U.S. 1, 9, 97 S.Ct. 2476, 53 L.Ed.2d 538, 547 (1977); Groh v. Martinez, 540 U.S. 551, 124 S.Ct. 1284, 157 L.Ed.2d 1068, 1081 (2004) ("We have long held, moreover, that the purpose of the warrant particularity requirement is not limited to the prevention of general searches.").

6. Brinegar v. United States, 338 U.S. 160, 69 S.Ct. 1302, 93 L.Ed. 1879, 1890–91 (1949). For a general discussion of the "probable cause" standard, see Chapter 11, Section 3 of this work.

7. "The task of the issuing magistrate is simply to make a common-sense decision whether, given all the circumstances set forth in the [search warrant] affidavit before him [or her], including the 'veracity' and 'basis of knowledge' of persons supplying hearsay information, there is a fair probability that contraband or evidence of crime will be found in a particular place. And the duty of the reviewing court is simply to ensure that the magistrate had a 'substantial basis for ... conclud[ing]' that probable cause existed." Illinois v. Gates, 462 U.S. 213, 103 S.Ct. 2317, 76 L.Ed.2d 527, 548 (1983).

the veracity prong, there had to be some showing that the informant was credible or that the information given by the informant was reliable; under the basis-for-knowledge prong, there also had to be some showing as to how the informer came upon the information being disclosed to law enforcement.[8] That strict rule has since been disapproved in favor of a totality-of-the-circumstances approach in which all the surrounding circumstances must be considered in determining whether the informant's information constitutes probable cause; the veracity and basis-for-knowledge prongs are still important considerations in this process, but neither are *sine qua non* requirements.[9]

b. Interpretation of search warrant affidavits: judicial review of magistrate's probable cause determination

Given the decided preference for search warrants and the fact that search warrant affidavits are normally drafted by non-lawyers in the midst and haste of a criminal investigation, the Court has long held that such affidavits must be read by both magistrates and courts in a common sense and realistic fashion—not in a hyper-technical manner in which elaborate specificity is demanded. Indeed, a court's after-the-fact scrutiny of a search warrant affidavit cannot take the form of a *de novo* review, as a magistrate's determination of probable cause must be given great deference. Otherwise law enforcement officials might very well be discouraged from seeking such warrants, and the Court's strong preference for warrants might be defeated. Instead, the standard of review is a deferential one: whether, under the totality of the circumstances, the magistrate had a *substantial basis* for concluding that the search would uncover evidence of criminal wrongdoing.[10] Moreover, the fact that the search pursuant to a warrant uncovers no evidence

8. Aguilar v. Texas, 378 U.S. 108, 84 S.Ct. 1509, 12 L.Ed.2d 723 (1964); Spinelli v. United States, 393 U.S. 410, 89 S.Ct. 584, 21 L.Ed.2d 637 (1969).

9. "We agree ... that an informant's veracity, 'reliability,' and 'basis of knowledge' are all highly relevant in determining the value of his report. We do not agree, however, that these elements should be understood as separate and independent requirements in every case.... Rather, as detailed below, they should be understood simply as closely intertwined issues that may usefully illuminate the common-sense, practical question whether there is 'probable cause' to believe that contraband or evidence is located in a particular place. This totality of the circumstances approach is far more consistent with our prior treatment of probable cause than is any rigid demand that specific "tests" be satisfied by every informant's tip." Illinois v. Gates, 462 U.S. 213, 103 S.Ct. 2317, 76 L.Ed.2d 527, 543 (1983). "[A] deficiency in one [of these factors] may be compensated for, in determining the over-all reliability of a tip, by a strong showing as to the other [factor], or by some other indicia of reliability. If, for example, a particular informant is known for the unusual reliability of his predictions of certain types of criminal activities in a locality, his failure, in a particular case, to thoroughly set forth the basis of his knowledge surely should not serve as an absolute bar to a finding of probable cause based on his tip.... Conversely, even if we entertain some doubts as to an informant's motives, his explicit and detailed description of alleged wrongdoing, along with a statement that the event was observed first hand, entitles his tip to greater weight than might otherwise be the case." Illinois v. Gates, 76 L.Ed.2d at 546. See cases collected at "Searches and Seizures" §§ 115.1, 116, 117, 118, 119 West Key Nos.

10. "If the teachings of the Court's cases are to be followed and the constitutional policy served, affidavits for search warrants ... must be tested and interpreted by magistrates and courts in a common-sense and realistic fashion. They are normally drafted by nonlawyers in the midst and haste of a criminal investigation. Technical requirements of elaborate specificity once exacted under common law pleadings have no proper place in this area. A grudging or negative attitude by reviewing courts will tend to discourage police officers from submitting their evidence to a judicial officer before acting." United States v. Ventresca, 380 U.S. 102, 108, 85 S.Ct. 741, 13 L.Ed.2d 684, 689 (1965).

"Similarly, we have repeatedly said that after-the-fact scrutiny by courts of the sufficiency of a[] [search warrant] affidavit should not take the form of de novo review. A magistrate's 'determination of wrongdoing does not show that there was no probable cause for the warrant as the test of probable cause is based entirely on pre-search evidence presented to the magistrate, not on what the search uncovers.[11]

This means that in the run-of-the-mill case, the magistrate's probable-cause determination should generally be sustained. Indeed, the Court has consistently upheld search warrant affidavits as stating probable cause where the magistrate was presented with at least some underlying circumstances indicating either the presence of criminal activity or incriminating evidence on the premises to be searched.[12] In this respect, the

---

of probable cause should be paid great deference by reviewing courts.' 'A grudging or negative attitude by reviewing courts toward warrants' is inconsistent with the Fourth Amendment's strong preference for searches conducted pursuant to a warrant.' 'Courts should not invalidate warrant[s] by interpreting affidavit[s] in a hyper technical, rather than in a common sense, manner.'

"If affidavits submitted by police officers are subjected to the type of scrutiny some courts have deemed appropriate, police might well resort to warrantless searches, with the hope of relying on consent or some other exception to the warrant clause that might develop at the time of the search. * * * *Reflecting this preference for the warrant process, the traditional standard for review of an issuing magistrate's probable cause determination has been that so long as the magistrate had a 'substantial basis for ... conclud[ing]' that a search would uncover evidence of wrongdoing, the Fourth Amendment requires no more.*" Illinois v. Gates, 462 U.S. 213, 103 S.Ct. 2317, 76 L.Ed.2d 527, 546–47 (1983) (internal citations omitted) (emphasis added).

"'A grudging or negative attitude by reviewing courts toward warrants,' is inconsistent with the desire to encourage use of the warrant process by police officers, and with the recognition that once a warrant has been obtained, intrusion upon interests protected by the Fourth Amendment is less severe than would otherwise be the case. A deferential standard of review is appropriate to further the Fourth Amendment's strong preference for searches conducted pursuant to a warrant." Massachusetts v. Sheppard, 466 U.S. 981, 104 S.Ct. 3424, 82 L.Ed.2d 737 (1984) (internal citations omitted).

"A policeman's [search warrant] affidavit 'should not be judged as an entry in an essay contest,' but rather must be judged by the facts it contains." United States v. Harris, 403 U.S. 573, 579, 91 S.Ct. 2075, 29 L.Ed.2d 723, 731 (1971).

"[W]e do not retreat from the established propositions that only the probability, and not a prima facie showing, of criminal activity is the standard of probable cause; that affidavits of probable cause are tested by much less rigorous standards than those governing the admissibility of evidence at trial; that in judging probable cause magistrates are not to be confined to niggardly limitations or by restrictions on the use of their common sense; and that their determination of probable cause must be paid great deference by reviewing courts." Spinelli v. United States, 393 U.S. 410, 419, 89 S.Ct. 584, 21 L.Ed.2d 637, 645 (1969) (internal citations omitted).

11. "The Fourth Amendment allows warrants to issue on probable cause, a standard well short of absolute certainty. Valid warrants will issue to search the innocent, and people like Rettele and Sadler unfortunately bear the cost." Los Angeles County v. Rettele, 550 U.S. 609, 127 S.Ct. 1989, 1993, 167 L.Ed.2d 974 (2007) (probable cause to search house upheld although upon execution it was discovered that the house had been had been sold to an innocent party). True, but we should always remember that "nothing is easier than to bear other people's calamities with fortitude." W. Somerset Maugham, The Razor's Edge 144 (1944) (Giant Cardinal pocketbook ed. 1963).

12. See, e.g., New York v. P.J. Video, 475 U.S. 868, 106 S.Ct. 1610, 89 L.Ed.2d 871 (1986) (affidavits describing with some particularity the scenes depicted in alleged obscene films); Massachusetts v. Upton, 466 U.S. 727, 104 S.Ct. 2085, 80 L.Ed.2d 721 (1984) (informant information concerning stolen property on premises plus other incriminating facts); Illinois v. Gates, 462 U.S. 213, 103 S.Ct. 2317, 76 L.Ed.2d 527, 543 (1983) (detailed anonymous letter to police accusing person of narcotics trafficking, plus accurately predicted behavior of person); Andresen v. Maryland, 427 U.S. 463, 96 S.Ct. 2737, 49 L.Ed.2d 627 (1976) (complete and thorough affidavits detailing fraudulent activities in sale of land); United States v. Harris, 403 U.S. 573, 91 S.Ct. 2075, 29 L.Ed.2d 723 (1971) (informant statement concerning purchase of illegal liquor on premises plus other incriminating facts); United States v. Ventresca, 380 U.S. 102, 109, 85 S.Ct. 741, 13 L.Ed.2d 684 (1965) (federal agent observations indicating that illegal still was being operated on property); Rugendorf v. United States, 376 U.S. 528, 84 S.Ct. 825, 11 L.Ed.2d 887 (1964) (information supplied by a number of informers that premises to be searched contained proceeds of recent robbery); Jones v. United States, 362 U.S. 257, 80 S.Ct.

Court's decisions here are much like its decisions, and the decisions of other courts, generally sustaining warrantless arrests for felony offenses as based on probable cause.[13]

Still, the deferential standard of review required of a magistrate's probable cause determination, lenient though it is, is not without limits. As will be discussed later, a probable cause finding cannot be based on a search warrant affidavit that (a) merely recites conclusory opinions of criminal wrongdoing, or (b) contains critically false information that was knowingly or recklessly placed there by the affiant, or (c) contains stale information. Moreover, if a search warrant affidavit is sketchy, incomplete or non-incriminating in nature—the reviewing court may conclude that the magistrate did not have a substantial basis for finding probable cause. Great deference must, of course, be paid to the magistrate's determination on this issue, but the magistrate must be given at least some facts upon which to make this determination and cannot act as a rubber stamp for the police.[14]

c. Conclusory search warrant affidavit

It is well-settled that a search warrant affidavit containing merely a conclusory opinion or accusation that criminal wrongdoing has occurred or is occurring on the premises to be searched, but provides none of the underlying circumstances upon which that belief or accusation is based, fails to state probable cause for the issuance of a search warrant.[15]

725, 4 L.Ed.2d 697 (1960); (narcotics informant information plus other corroborating facts); Dombra v. United States, 268 U.S. 435, 45 S.Ct. 546, 69 L.Ed. 1032 (1925) (undercover federal agent purchase of illegal liquor on premises); compare Spinelli v. United States, 393 U.S. 410, 89 S.Ct. 584, 21 L.Ed.2d 637 (1969) (informant information that defendant was operating illegal bookmaking operation from apartment plus other facts held insufficient to state probable cause), result questioned in Illinois v. Gates, 462 U.S. 213, 103 S.Ct. 2317, 76 L.Ed.2d 527, 548 n. 11 (1983). Also see cases collected at "Searches and Seizures" §§ 113.1, 114 West Key Nos.

13. For a discussion of the application of the probable cause standard in warrantless felony arrest cases, see Chapter 12, Section 1e of this work.

14. "Deference to the magistrate, however, is not boundless. * * * [R]eviewing courts will not defer to a warrant based on an affidavit that does not 'provide the magistrate with a substantial basis for determining the existence of probable cause.' 'Sufficient information must be presented to the magistrate to allow that official to determine probable cause; his action cannot be a mere ratification of the bare conclusions of others.' Even if the warrant application was supported by more than a 'bare bones' affidavit, a reviewing court may properly conclude that, notwithstanding the deference that magistrates deserve, the warrant was invalid because the magistrate's probable-cause determination reflected an improper analysis of the totality of the circumstances...." United States v. Leon, 468 U.S. 897, 104 S.Ct. 3405, 82 L.Ed.2d 677, 693–94 (1984) (internal citations omitted).

"This is not to say that probable cause can be made out by affidavits that are merely conclusory, stating only the affiant's or an informer's belief that probable cause exists without detailing any of the 'underlying circumstances' upon which the belief is based. Recital of the circumstances in the affidavit is essential if the magistrate is to perform his detached function and not serve merely as a rubber stamp for the police." United States v. Ventresca, 380 U.S. 102, 108–09, 109, 85 S.Ct. 741, 13 L.Ed.2d 684, 689 (1965).

15. "Our earlier cases illustrate the limits beyond which a magistrate may not venture in issuing a warrant. A sworn statement of an affiant that 'he has cause to suspect and does believe that' liquor illegally brought into the United States is located on certain premises will not do. Nathanson v. United States, 290 U.S. 41, 54 S.Ct. 11, 78 L.Ed. 159 (1933). An affidavit must provide the magistrate with a substantial basis for determining the existence of probable cause, and the wholly conclusory statement in Nathanson failed to meet this requirement. An officer's statement that 'affiants have received reliable information from a credible person and believe' that heroin is stored in a home, is likewise inadequate. Aguilar v. Texas, 378 U.S. 108, 84 S.Ct. 1509, 12 L.Ed.2d 723 (1964). As in *Nathanson*, this is a mere conclusory statement that gives the magistrate virtually no basis at all for making a judgment regarding probable cause. Sufficient information must be presented to the magistrate to allow that official to

This is so because the magistrate is presented with no facts upon which to make a probable cause determination. Accordingly, an affidavit that merely (1) states the affiant's belief that a person possesses contraband property[16] or obscene materials,[17] or (2) states the belief of an informant, denominated as credible, that a person possesses contraband property,[18] or (3) accuses a person of having committed a crime,[19] have all been struck down as being insufficient to constitute probable cause for the issuance of a warrant for search or arrest.

d. False affidavit: knowingly or recklessly made

At times, a search warrant affidavit may contain vitally important information that later proves to be untrue. Nonetheless, so long as the information reasonably appeared accurate and reliable at the time of the warrant's issuance, the fact that the information later proved inaccurate is insufficient to upset a magistrate's finding of probable cause.[20] The underlying rationale for this result is that mistakes and inaccuracies may creep into

---

determine probable cause; his [or her] action cannot be a mere ratification of the bare conclusions of others." Illinois v. Gates, 462 U.S. 213, 103 S.Ct. 2317, 76 L.Ed.2d 527, 548–49 (1983).

"We held in Nathanson v. United States ... that an affidavit [for a warrant] does not state probable cause which merely states the affiant's belief that there is cause to search, without stating facts upon which that belief is based. A fortiori this is true of an affidavit which states only the belief of one not the affiant." Jones v. United States, 362 U.S. 257, 269, 80 S.Ct. 725, 4 L.Ed.2d 697, 707 (1960).

16. Nathanson v. United States, 290 U.S. 41, 54 S.Ct. 11, 78 L.Ed. 159, (1933) (a search warrant affidavit stating that 'he [the affiant] has cause to suspect and does believe that' liquor illegally brought into the United States is located on certain premises, failed to state probable cause for the issuance of a search warrant).

Byars v. United States, 273 U.S. 28, 47 S.Ct. 248, 71 L.Ed. 520 (1927) (search warrant affidavit stating that affiant "has good reason to believe and does believe that the defendant has in his possession" certain illegal liquor, failed to state probable cause for the issuance of a search warrant).

17. Marcus v. Search Warrant, 367 U.S. 717, 731–32, 81 S.Ct. 1708, 6 L.Ed.2d 1127, 1136 (1961) (search warrant affidavit stating a police officer's conclusory opinion that a certain publisher kept for sale "obscene ... publications" at six identified business locations failed to state probable cause for the issuance of a search warrant). Lee Art Theatre, Inc. v. Virginia, 392 U.S. 636, 88 S.Ct. 2103, 20 L.Ed.2d 1313 (1968) (search warrant affidavit of a police officer stating that he had viewed a film and that the film was "obscene" failed to state probable cause for the issuance of a search warrant).

18. Aguilar v. Texas, 378 U.S. 108, 84 S.Ct. 1509,12 L.Ed.2d 723 (1964) (a search warrant affidavit stating that "affiants have received reliable information from a credible person and believe" that heroin is stored in a home, fails to state probable cause for the issuance of a search warrant).

19. Whitely v. Warden, Wyo. State Penitentiary, 401 U.S. 560, 91 S.Ct. 1031, 28 L.Ed.2d 306 (1971) (arrest warrant affidavit stating that on a particular date the two named defendants "did then and there unlawfully break and enter a locked and sealed building" at a particular location, failed to state probable cause for the issuance of an arrest warrant) ("The decisions of this Court concerning Fourth Amendment probable-cause requirements before a warrant for either arrest or search can issue require that the judicial officer issuing such a warrant be supplied with sufficient information to support an independent judgment that probable cause exists for the warrant. * * * Under the cases just cited, [this affidavit] alone could not support the independent judgment of a disinterested magistrate." 401 at 564, 565, 28 L.Ed.2d at 311).

Giordenello v. United States, 357 U.S. 480, 78 S.Ct.1245, 2 L.Ed.2d 1503 (1958) (arrest warrant affidavit stating that the defendant on a particular date and place "did receive, conceal, etc. narcotic drugs, to wit: heroin hydrochloride with knowledge of unlawful importation" in violation of the U.S. Code, failed to state probable cause for the issuance of an arrest warrant).

20. "Warrants need only be supported by 'probable cause,' which demands no more than a proper 'assessment of probabilities in particular factual contexts....' If a magistrate, based on seemingly reliable, but factually inaccurate information, issues a warrant for the search of a house in which a sought-after felon is not present, has never been present, and was never likely to have been present, the owner of that house suffers one of the inconveniences we all expose ourselves to as the cost of

search warrant affidavits, drafted as they often are in the midst and haste of a criminal investigation. Even where the inaccurate information is vital to a determination of probable cause, after-the-fact disclosure of such ought not ordinarily upset search warrants based thereon, because the sworn information appeared reliable at the time to the affiant and the magistrate.

Still, when the Fourth Amendment demands a factual showing sufficient to constitute probable cause for a search warrant, the obvious assumption is that this showing is truthful and made in good faith: that is, that the affiant has not committed perjury or spoken recklessly about matters of which he or she has no knowledge.[21] Indeed, the Fourth Amendment expressly requires that the probable cause showing must be made "on oath or affirmation." Accordingly, it is settled that if vitally-important false information appearing in a search warrant affidavit was placed there by the affiant with knowledge of its falsity, or with reckless disregard as to whether it was true or false, such an affidavit fails to state probable cause for the issuance of a search warrant—provided, of course, there is no other information in the affidavit stating probable cause after the tainted false information has been excluded.[22]

A strict procedure, however, is required for a defendant to challenge a deliberately or recklessly false search warrant affidavit on a motion to suppress. First, the defendant must make a substantial preliminary showing, preferably by affidavit or other similar proof, demonstrating (a) that specifically identified statements in the search warrant affidavit are false, and were knowingly or recklessly placed there by the affiant, and (b) that such false statements were necessary to a finding of probable cause. Second, if such a showing is made, an evidentiary hearing must be held at the defendant's request; if such a showing is not made, the defendant's evidentiary hearing request and motion to suppress must be denied. Third, if an evidentiary hearing is held, the defendant has the burden of establishing the allegations of perjury or reckless disregard by a preponderance of the evidence. Finally, if this burden is met, and there is no probable cause for the issuance of the warrant after the tainted false material is excluded from the affidavit, the defendant's motion to suppress must be granted; otherwise, the motion must be denied.[23]

---

living in a safe society; he does not suffer a violation of the Fourth Amendment." Illinois v. Rodriguez, 497 U.S. 177, 110 S.Ct. 2793, 111 L.Ed.2d 148, 158 (1990) (internal citation omitted).

21. Franks v. Delaware, 438 U.S. 154, 98 S.Ct. 2674, 57 L.Ed.2d 667, 678 (1978).

22. Franks v. Delaware, 438 U.S. 154, 98 S.Ct. 2674, 57 L.Ed 667 (1978). For an extensive discussion of the rule allowing defendants to attack deliberately or recklessly false search warrant affidavits, see 2 Wayne LaFave, Search and Seizure § 4.4 (a)–(d) (5th ed. 2012). Also see cases collected at "Searches and Seizures" § 112 West Key No.

23. "[W]e hold that, where the defendant makes a substantial preliminary showing that a false statement knowingly and intentionally, or with reckless disregard for the truth, was included in the warrant affidavit, and if the allegedly false statement is necessary to a finding of probable cause, the Fourth Amendment requires that a hearing be held at the defendant's request. In the event that at the hearing the allegation of perjury or reckless disregard is established by the defendant by the preponderance of the evidence, and, with the affidavit's false material aside, the affidavit's remaining content is insufficient to establish probable cause, the search warrant must be voided and the fruits of the search excluded to the same extent as if probable cause was lacking on the face of the affidavit. * * *

"In sum, and to repeat what we stated at the beginning of this opinion: There is, of course, a presumption of validity with respect to the affidavit supporting the search warrant. To mandate an evidentiary hearing, the challenger's attack must be more than conclusory and must be supported by more than a mere desire to cross examine. There must be allegations of deliberate falsehood or of reckless disregard of the truth, and those allegations must be accompanied by an offer of proof. They should point out specifically the portion of the warrant affidavit that is claimed to be false; and they should be accompanied by a statement of supporting reasons. Affidavits or sworn or otherwise reliable

The underlying rationale behind this strict procedure—with its rules of pleading, presumption and burden of proof—is to eliminate willy-nilly motions to suppress based on bald allegations of perjury in search warrant affidavits. Plainly, the trial court should not be required to hold an evidentiary hearing involving an alleged false search warrant affidavit unless serious issues of perjury or reckless disregard are raised concerning affidavit information essential to the magistrate's finding of probable cause. And further, a trial court should not be allowed to upset an otherwise valid search warrant affidavit unless the allegations of perjury and reckless disregard have been clearly proven, and the tainted false information was otherwise essential to the magistrate's finding of probable cause.

e. Staleness issue

In determining whether probable cause exists to search private premises, an important consideration is *when* the events described in the search warrant affidavit took place. This is so because the magistrate must determine whether there is probable cause to believe that the premises to be searched *presently* contains contraband or fruits or instrumentalities of a crime, or evidence of a crime—not whether such probable cause existed at sometime in the past. Probable cause to search, which may once have existed at the time of the events described in the affidavit, may eventually grow stale and therefore be insufficient to sustain a *present* finding of probable cause.[24] As an aside, even where the information in the affidavit is not deemed stale at the time the search warrant is issued, the information may nonetheless become stale by the time the search warrant is actually executed if there is undue delay in such execution—thereby invalidating the ensuing search.[25]

Clearly, there is no strict time period after which probable cause that once existed suddenly becomes stale. Each case must stand on its own facts. But two central factors are often considered: (a) the nature of the evidence to be seized or the criminal activity allegedly occurring on the subject premises, and (b) the length of time between the events

---

statements of witnesses should be furnished, or their absence satisfactorily explained. Allegations of negligence or innocent mistake are insufficient. The deliberate falsity or reckless disregard whose impeachment is permitted today is only that of the affiant, not of any nongovernmental informant. Finally, if these requirements are met, and, if when material that is the subject of the alleged falsity or reckless disregard is set to one side, there remains sufficient content in the warrant affidavit to support a finding of probable cause, no hearing is required. On the other hand, if the remaining content is insufficient, the defendant is entitled, under the Fourth and Fourteenth Amendments, to his hearing. Whether he will prevail at that hearing is, of course, another matter." Franks v. Delaware, 438 U.S. 154, 155–56, 171–72, 98 S.Ct. 2674, 57 L.Ed.2d 667, 672, 682 (1978).

24. "[I]t is manifest that the proof [of probable cause] must be of facts so closely related to the time of the issue of the warrant as to justify a finding of probable cause at that time. Whether the proof meets this test must be determined by the circumstances of each case. * * * The statute [implementing Fourth Amendment guarantees] requires [the magistrate] before issuing the warrant to take proof of probable cause. This he must do by examining on oath the complainant and his witness and requiring their affidavits or depositions. The proof supplied must have appropriate relation to the application for the new warrant and must speak as of the time of the issue of that warrant. The [magistrate] has no authority to rely on affidavits which have sole relation to a different time and have not been brought up to date or supplemented so that they can be deemed to disclose grounds existing when the new warrant is issued. The new warrant must rest upon a proper finding and statement by the [magistrate] that probable cause then exists. That determination cannot be left to mere inference or conjecture." Sgro v. United States, 287 U.S. 206, 210–11, 53 S.Ct. 138, 77 L.Ed.2d 260, 263 (1932) (expired warrant re-dated without taking additional proof, struck down as having been issued without any evidentiary showing).

25. For a discussion of this issue, see 2 Wayne LaFave, Search and Seizure § 4.7(a) (5th ed. 2012); 1 John Wesley Hall, Search and Seizure § 6.41 (5th ed. 2013).

described in the affidavit and the issuance of the search warrant and ensuing search. A showing of ongoing established criminal activity on private premises, or of evidence likely to remain thereon for some time, may take a considerable passage of time, perhaps months, before such information becomes stale and insufficient upon which to issue a search warrant. On the other hand, a showing of an isolated act of criminal activity or of evidence likely to be swiftly removed from the premises, may become stale quite quickly, perhaps in a matter of a days or a week—after which it is unlikely that the activity is presently occurring, or the evidence is still located, on the subject premises.[26] In any event, a search warrant affidavit must be read in a common-sense, not a hyper-technical way, according to the standards previously discussed in this chapter.[27]

f. Search of premises in which owner is not a criminal suspect: newspaper searches

It is settled that a search warrant may issue for the search of private premises if there is probable cause to believe that contraband, fruits, instrumentalities, or evidence of crime is located on certain premises, even though the owner or possessor of the premises is not suspected of criminal wrongdoing; a special subpoena duces tecum procedure is not constitutionally required for such third party searches. The underlying rationale for this rule is that a search warrant is not directed at a particular person; it is directed at particular premises and the seizure of particular things. If there is reasonable cause to believe that these things are on these premises, a search warrant may issue; it is totally unnecessary to show that the owner or possessor of the premises is also guilty of criminal wrongdoing. Moreover, a different rule is not required by the First Amendment where the private premises to be searched is a newspaper office. The magistrate, however, should take care to strictly limit the time and scope of the search of a newspaper office, so as not to disrupt the newspaper's operations, and should disallow searches of areas where irrelevant or confidential material may be located.[28]

---

26. United States v. Harris, 403 U.S. 573, 91 S.Ct. 2075, 29 L.Ed.2d 723 (1971) (informant statement that he has been buying illegal whiskey on the premises of a particular residence for a period of two years, and did so within the past two weeks, held not stale information); Andresen v. Maryland, 427 U.S. 463, 96 S.Ct. 2737, 49 L.Ed.2d 627 (1976) (affidavit stating that business records tending to show a real estate fraud in a three-month-old transaction held not stale information, as these records were kept in the ordinary course of business in a law office and real estate office and were likely to be there notwithstanding the three-month delay); see also Berger v. New York, 388 U.S. 41, 87 S.Ct. 1873, 18 L.Ed.2d 1040 (1967) (two-month wiretap extensions based solely on "the public interest" violated the Fourth Amendment). For thorough discussion of the staleness issue, collecting leading federal and state court decisions, see 2 Wayne LaFave, Search and Seizure § 3.7(a) (5th ed. 2012). Also see cases collected at "Searches and Seizures" § 121.1 West Key No.

27. For a discussion of these standards, Section 1b of this Chapter.

28. "Under existing law, valid warrants may be issued to search *any* property, whether or not occupied by a third party, at which there is probable cause to believe that [contraband], fruits, instrumentalities, or evidence of a crime may be found. Nothing on the face of the [Fourth] Amendment suggests that a third party search warrant should not normally issue. * * *

"Search warrants are not directed at persons; they authorize the search of 'place[s]' and the seizure of 'things,' and as a constitutional matter need not even name the person from whom the things will be seized. * * *

"The critical element in a reasonable search is not that the owner of the property is suspected of a crime but that there is reasonable cause to believe that the specific 'things' to be searched for and seized are located on the property to which entry is sought. * * *

"*We do hold, however, that the courts may not, in the name of the Fourth Amendment, forbid the states from issuing warrants to search for evidence simply because the owner or possessor of the place to*

It should be noted, however, that where a third party search of private premises occurs, it is doubtful that anyone other than the third party has the constitutional standing to complain about the search. Without question, the only privacy invaded by the search is that of the third party. The only exception might be an instance in which the evidence seized on the third party's premises is owned or possessed by the person who is eventually charged in the case.[29]

g. Probable cause showing: confined to evidence presented to magistrate

The factual showing by way of affidavit or other sworn proof upon which probable cause for a search warrant rests, must be presented to the magistrate who issues the search warrant—and cannot be supplemented later with additional evidence before the trial judge at a motion to suppress hearing. These additional facts—even if known at the time, but not included in the affidavit—play no part in reviewing the magistrate's determination of probable cause; the probable cause decision must necessarily be confined to the sworn facts submitted to the magistrate, else the Fourth Amendment's warrant protections would be greatly undermined.[30]

---

be searched is not then reasonably suspected of criminal involvement. * * *

"Further, the prior cases do no more than insist that the courts apply the warrant requirements with particular exactitude when First Amendment interests would be endangered by the search. As we see it, no more is required where the warrant requested is for the seizure of criminal evidence reasonably believed to be on the premises occupied by a newspaper. Properly administered, the preconditions for a warrant—probable cause, specificity with respect to the place to be searched and the things to be seized, and overall reasonableness—should afford sufficient protection against the harms that are assertedly threatened by warrants searching newspaper offices.

"There is no reason to believe, for example, that magistrates cannot guard against searches of the type, scope, and intrusiveness that would actually interfere with the timely publication of a newspaper. Nor, if the requirements of specificity and reasonableness are properly applied, policed, and observed, will there be any occasion or opportunity for officers to rummage at large in newspaper files or to intrude into or to deter normal editorial and publication decisions."

Zurcher v. Stanford Daily, 436 U.S. 547, 554–60, 565–66, 98 S.Ct. 1970, 56 L.Ed.2d 525, 534–38, 541–42 (1978) (a search warrant for the search of a college newspaper office directing the seizure of pictures, film, and negatives of a violent clash between police and student demonstrators was upheld, although no one connected with the newspaper was suspected of any crime; a pre-search subpoena duces tecum was not constitutionally required for such search). See 2 Wayne LaFave, Search and Seizure § 4.1 (f)(g) (5th ed. 2012).

29. For a discussion of the Fourth Amendment "Standing Requirement" related to this problem, see Chapter 8, Section 1a; Chapter 9, Section 3; and Chapter 10, Section 3b of this work.

30. "Under the cases of this Court, an otherwise insufficient affidavit [for a warrant] cannot be rehabilitated by testimony concerning information possessed by the affiant when he [or she] sought the warrant but not disclosed to the issuing magistrate. A contrary rule would, of course, render the warrant requirement of the Fourth Amendment meaningless." Whitely v. Warden, Wyo, State Penitentiary, 401 U.S. 560, 91 S.Ct. 1031, 28 L.Ed.2d 306, 311 n. 8 (1971) (internal citation omitted).

"It is elementary that in passing on the validity of a warrant, the reviewing court may consider *only* information brought to the magistrate's attention."Aguilar v. Texas, 378 U.S. 108, 109 n. 1, 84 S.Ct. 1509, 12 L.Ed.2d 723, 725 (1964) (emphasis in original).

"It is, of course, of no consequence that the [federal] agents might have had additional information which could have been given to the [U.S.] Commissioner. 'It is elementary that in passing on the validity of a warrant, the reviewing court may consider *only* information brought to the magistrate's attention.'" Spinelli v. United States, 393 U.S. 410, 413 n.3, 89 S.Ct. 584, 21 L.Ed.2d 637, 642 (1969) (quoting from Aguilar v. Texas).

h. Administrative search warrants

As previously indicated, the standard of probable cause for the issuance of a search warrant in an ordinary criminal investigative context requires a showing of individualized criminal wrongdoing that is less than proof beyond a reasonable doubt, but more that reasonable suspicion.[31] The Court, however, has held that a different probable cause showing is required where the purpose of the governmental search is administrative, rather than normal criminal investigation. Here the Court has tailored the probable cause requirement to meet the administrative purpose involved in the search, often employing a balancing of the relevant governmental and privacy interests to arrive at its result.[32]

(1) Municipal code housing, health or fire inspection warrant

Absent voluntary consent or exigent circumstances, a search warrant is normally required for a governmental inspection of residential, business or other structures to enforce municipal housing, health or fire codes. It is not essential, however, that a probable cause showing be made that the individual structure is in violation of the applicable municipal code—although, of course, this would clearly constitute probable cause for a warrant. It is sufficient if a probable cause showing is made, based on reasonable legislative or administrative standards, that the individual structure falls within a geographical area that reasonably should be periodically inspected for municipal code compliance. The legislative or administrative standards, in turn, necessarily will vary with the municipal code being enforced, but may be based on the passage of a certain time period from the last inspection, the nature of the building being inspected, or the condition of the entire area in which the individual structure is located. Moreover, the warrant when issued must restrict the inspection to only those areas in the structure that are necessary to enforce the municipal code involved. Based on a balancing analysis, the underlying rationale for requiring such a warrant procedure is that the warrant gives assurance to the individual that an independent magistrate [rather than a government agent] has deemed the inspection reasonable, and has specifically limited its scope—while, at the same time, allowing periodic area-wide inspections of structures under established legislative or administrative standards.[33]

---

31. See Section 2a of this Chapter.

32. For lower federal and state court cases collected on administrative search warrants, see "Searches and Seizures" § 129 West Key No.

33. "In summary, we hold that administrative searches of the kind at issue here are significant intrusions upon the interests protected by the Fourth Amendment, that such searches when authorized and conducted without a warrant procedure lack the traditional safeguards which the Fourth Amendment guarantees to the individual....

"[A]ppellant argues not only that code inspection programs must be circumscribed by a warrant procedure, but also that warrants should issue only when the inspector possesses probable cause to believe that a particular dwelling contains violations of the minimum standards prescribed by the code being enforced. We disagree. * * *[W]e think that a number of persuasive factors combine to support the reasonableness of area code inspections. * * *

"Having concluded that the area inspection is a 'reasonable' search of private property, it is obvious that 'probable cause' to issue a warrant to inspect must exist if reasonable legislative or administrative standards for conducting an area inspection are satisfied with respect to a particular dwelling. Such standards, which will vary with the municipal program being enforced, may be based upon the passage of time, the nature of the building (e.g., multi-family apartment house), or the condition of the entire area, but they will not necessarily depend upon specific knowledge of the condition of a particular dwelling. * * *

"Since our holding emphasizes the controlling standard of reasonableness, nothing we say today

(2) OSHA employee health and safety inspection warrant

Similarly, a search warrant is required for an administrative inspection to determine whether the work areas in a place of business are in compliance with federal health and safety regulations protecting employees under the Occupational Safety and Health Act (OSHA)—unless voluntary consent or exigent circumstances are shown. It is not essential, however, that a probable cause showing be made that the business property to be inspected is in violation of the applicable OSHA regulations—although, of course, this would clearly constitute probable cause for a warrant. It is sufficient if a probable cause showing is made that reasonable legislative or administrative standards have been met for conducting an OSHA inspection with respect to a particular business establishment. In particular, probable cause for such a warrant would be made upon a showing that a specific business has been chosen for an inspection on the basis of a general administrative plan for the enforcement of OSHA based on neutral criteria—such as the dispersion of employees in various industries over a specific area, and the desired frequency of inspections in any lesser divisions of this area. Moreover, the warrant when issued must restrict the inspection to only those areas on the business property that are necessary to enforce the OSHA regulations involved, presumably the employee work areas. Based on a balancing analysis, the underlying rationale for requiring such a warrant procedure is that the warrant gives assurance to the individual business owner that an independent magistrate [rather than a government agent] has deemed the inspection reasonable, and has specifically limited its scope—while, at the same time, allowing periodic oftlineinspections of businesses under established legislative or administrative standards.[34]

---

is intended to foreclose prompt inspections, even without a warrant, that the law has traditionally upheld in emergencies. [collecting cases involving the seizure of unwholesome food, a compulsory smallpox vaccination, a health quarantine, or a summary destruction of tubercular cattle]. On the other hand, in the case of the most routine area inspection, there is no compelling urgency to inspect at a particular time or on a particular day. Moreover, most citizens allow inspections of their property without a warrant. Thus, as a practical matter and in light of the Fourth Amendment's requirement that a warrant specify the property to be searched, it seems likely that warrants should normally be sought after entry is refused unless there has been a citizen complaint or there is other satisfactory reason for securing immediate entry."

Camara v. Municipal Court of City and County of San Francisco, 387 U.S. 523, 534, 537–39, 87 S.Ct. 1727, 18 L.Ed.2d 930, 938, 940–42 (1967) (criminal prosecution of apartment leaseholder for refusal to allow warrantless inspection of his apartment for municipal code compliance held prohibited). See 5 Wayne LaFave, Search and Seizure § 10.1c (5th ed. 2012).

"In Camara, we held that the Fourth Amendment bars prosecution of a person who has refused to permit a warrantless code-enforcement inspection of his personal residence. The only question which this case presents is whether Camara applies to similar inspections of commercial structures which are not used as private residences. * * *

"We therefore conclude that administrative entry, without consent, upon portions of commercial premises which are not open to the public may only be compelled through prosecution or physical force within the framework of a warrant procedure. We do not in any way imply that business premises may not reasonably be inspected in many more situations than private homes, nor do we question such accepted regulatory techniques as licensing programs which require inspections prior to operating a business or marketing a product. * * * We hold only that the basic component of a reasonable search under the Fourth Amendment—that it not be enforced without a suitable warrant procedure—is applicable in this context, as in others, to business as well as residential premises."

See v. City of Seattle, 387 U.S. 541, 542, 545–46, 87 S.Ct. 1737, 18 L.Ed.2d 943, 945–46, 947–48 (1967) (criminal conviction of warehouse owner for refusal to permit warrantless municipal fire code inspection of his warehouse reversed).

34. "Whether the Secretary [of Labor] proceeds to secure a warrant or other process, with or without prior notice, his entitlement to inspect will not depend on his demonstrating probable cause

(3) Fire scene inspection warrant

Under the exigent circumstances exception to the search warrant requirement rule, firemen may enter a burning building without a warrant to put out a fire therein and may remain on the scene for a reasonable time after the fire has been extinguished for the purpose of discovering the cause of the fire. But any re-entries onto the premises thereafter to further investigate the cause of the fire, for example several days later, must be made with an fire scene inspection warrant. Such searches serve an administrative purpose of attempting to discover the cause of the fire, as such information is necessary to prevent fires of this nature from occurring in the future—although obviously if the cause of the fire is arson, a criminal prosecution may ensue.[35]

Probable cause for such an administrative warrant, however, requires more than a showing that a fire has occurred on the premises. The need for further inspection to discover the cause of the fire must also be shown, and the proposed inspection must be tailored to minimize the intrusion of privacy necessarily involved. In deciding this issue, certain factors may become relevant: the number of prior warrantless entries on the premises, the lapse of time since the fire, the owner's efforts to secure the premises against intruders, the continued use of the building, and the time and scope of the proposed inspection. Normally, such a warrant will issue in most cases. But the warrant procedure helps assure the property owner that the re-entry is necessary and lawful, and that the ensuing invasion of privacy will be kept to a minimum.[36]

---

to believe that conditions in violation of OSHA exist on the premises. Probable cause in the criminal law sense is not required. For purposes of an administrative search such as this, probable cause justifying the issuance of a warrant may be based not only on specific evidence of an existing violation, but also on a showing that 'reasonable legislative or administrative standards for conducting an ... inspection are satisfied with respect to a particular [establishment].' A warrant showing that a specific business has been chosen for an OSHA search on the basis of a general administrative plan for the enforcement of the Act derived from neutral sources such as, for example, dispersion of employees in various types of industries across a given area, and the desired frequency of searches in any of the lesser divisions of the area, would protect an employer's Fourth Amendment rights. * * *

"A warrant, by contrast, would provide assurances from a neutral officer that the inspection is reasonable under the Constitution, is authorized by statute, and is pursuant to an administrative plan containing specific neutral criteria. Also a warrant would then and there advise the owner of the scope and objects of the search, beyond which limits the inspector is not expected to proceed."

Marshall v. Barlow's Inc., 436 U.S. 307, 320–21, 323, 98 S.Ct. 1816, 56 L.Ed.2d 305, 316, 318 (1978) (internal citation and footnotes omitted) (injunction against enforcement of a warrantless OSHA inspection scheme against a business owner upheld). See 5 Wayne LaFave, Search and Seizure § 10.2(a) (5th ed. 2012).

35. For a discussion of the exigent circumstances exception to the search warrant requirement rule as it relates to fire-fighting, see Chapter 14, Section 6c of this work.

36. "To secure a warrant to investigate the cause of a fire, an official must show more than the bare fact that a fire has occurred. The magistrate's duty is to assure that the proposed search will be reasonable, a determination that requires inquiry into the need for the intrusion on the one hand, and the threat of disruption to the occupant on the other. * * * In the context of investigatory fire searches, which are not programmatic but are responsive to individual events, a more particularized inquiry may be necessary. The number of prior entries, the scope of the search, the time of day when it is proposed to be made, the lapse of time since the fire, the continued use of the building, and the owner's efforts to secure it against intruders might all be relevant factors. Even though a fire victim's privacy must normally yield to the vital objective of ascertaining the cause of the fire, the magistrate can perform the important function of preventing harassment by keeping the invasion to a minimum.* * * Thus, a major function of the warrant is to provide the property owner with sufficient information to assure him of the entry's legality."

Michigan v. Tyler, 436 U.S. 499, 507–08, 98 S.Ct. 1942, 56 L.Ed.2d 486, 497 (1978) (initial warrantless entries into defendant's furniture store to put out a fire on the premises and to investigate

i. Anticipatory search warrants

An anticipatory search warrant is a warrant based on an affidavit showing probable cause that at some future time (but not presently) certain evidence will be located at a specified place—usually subjecting its execution to a future "triggering condition."[37] Such a warrant is constitutional under the Fourth Amendment, providing two conditions are met: (a) there must be probable cause to believe that the "triggering condition" will take place, and (b) there must be probable cause to believe that when the triggering condition occurs, there is a fair probability that certain evidence of crime will be found in a particular place.[38] The triggering condition, however, need not be included in the warrant[39]—although the failure to do so can create certain dangers. For example, an officer who executes the warrant, but did not obtain the warrant, may not be aware of the triggering condition, and may execute the warrant before the triggering condition occurs—thereby rendering the search unreasonable.[40]

Section 3. Particularity Requirements: Place to be Searched and Things to be Seized

The express language of the Warrants Clause of the Fourth Amendment prohibits general warrants: that is, open-ended warrants that do not particularize the place to be searched or things to be seized. This Clause provides that "no warrants shall issue except upon probable cause, supported by oath or affirmation, particularly describing the place to be searched and the things or persons to be seized." As the Court has stated:

> The Warrant Clause of the Fourth Amendment prohibits the issuance of any warrant except one 'particularly describing the place to be searched and the person or things to be seized.' The manifest purpose of this particularity requirement was to prevent general searches. By limiting the authorization to search to the specific areas and things for which there is probable cause to search,

---

the cause of the fire upheld, but re-entries several days later without a warrant to further determine the cause of the fire struck down). See 5 Wayne LaFave, Search and Seizure § 10.4(a)–(d) (5th ed. 2012).

37. United States v. Grubbs, 547 U.S. 90, 126 S.Ct. 1494, 1498, 164 L.Ed.2d 195 (2006). See 2 Wayne LaFave, Search and Seizure § 3.7(c) (5th ed. 2012) for an analysis of the anticipatory search warrant cases.

38. "In other words, for a conditioned anticipatory warrant to comply with the Fourth Amendment's requirement of probable cause, two prerequisites of probability must be satisfied. It must be true not only that *if* the triggering condition occurs 'there is a fair probability that contraband or evidence of crime will be found in a particular place' [citation omitted], but also that there is probable cause to believe the triggering condition *will occur*. The supporting affidavit must provide the magistrate with sufficient information to evaluate both aspects of the probable cause determination." United States v. Grubbs, 547 U.S. 90 126 S.Ct. 1494, 1500, 164 L.Ed.2d 195 (2006) (anticipatory search warrant upheld based on triggering condition of future controlled delivery of child pornography videotape to petitioner's home).

39. United States v. Grubbs, 547 U.S. 90, 126 S.Ct. 1494, 1500–01, 164 L.Ed.2d 195 (2006).

40. United States v. Grubbs, 547 U.S. 90, 126 S.Ct. 1494, 1502, 164 L.Ed.2d 195 (2006) (Souter, J. concurring).

the particularity requirement ensures that the search will be carefully tailored to its justifications, and will not take on the character of the wide-ranging exploratory searches which the Framers intended to prohibit.[41]

a. Place to be searched

A search warrant particularly describes the place to be searched "if the description is such that the officer with a search warrant can with reasonable effort ascertain and identify the place intended."[42] Clearly, a street address in a particular city is sufficient for a house or business, and a street address and apartment number in a stated city is sufficient for an apartment; but any geographical or physical description that leads one with reasonable certainty to the place to be searched complies with the constitutional mandate.[43] Moreover, a reasonable mistake in describing an apartment to be searched in the warrant, causing police to search the incorrect immediately adjoining apartment and to seize certain evidence therein, has been held not to invalidate either the warrant or the ensuing search, providing the police upon discovering the mistake discontinue their search in the incorrect premises.[44]

b. Things to be seized

It is settled that "the requirement that warrants shall particularly describe the things to be seized makes general searches under them impossible and prevents the seizure of one thing under a warrant describing another. As to what is to be taken [under the warrant], nothing is left to the discretion of the officer."[45] Generally speaking, courts have been least demanding in requiring warrant descriptions of contraband property, such as: illegal drugs, illegal gambling items, illegal drug or gambling paraphernalia—so that general descriptions are usually sufficient, although law enforcement officials must describe the contraband as best they can. On the other hand, courts require a more particular de-

---

41. Maryland v. Garrison, 480 U.S. 79, 107 S.Ct. 1013, 94 L.Ed.2d 72, 80 (1987).

42. Steele v. United States, 267 U.S. 498, 45 S.Ct. 414, 69 L.Ed. 757, 760 (1925). See cases collected at "Searches and Seizures" § 126 West Key No.

43. 2 Wayne LaFave, Search and Seizure § 4.5(a)(b) (5th ed. 2012) and cases collected.

44. Maryland v. Garrison, 480 U.S. 79, 107 S.Ct. 1013, 94 L.Ed.2d 72 (1987). In the *Garrison* case, the search warrant described the place to be searched as "the premises known as 2036 Park Avenue third floor apartment" occupied by one "McWebb." The officers who applied for the warrant reasonably and in good faith believed that there was only one third floor apartment at this location—when in fact there were two apartments on this floor: one occupied by McWebb and one occupied by the defendant. After the officers got there, they began searching what they reasonably thought was the only apartment on the third floor, the one supposedly occupied by McWebb, and seized a quantity of heroin, cash and drug paraphernalia. Thereafter, they discovered there were two apartments on the third floor, and that they were in the defendant's apartment, not McWebb's apartment. Whereupon they immediately discontinued their search of the defendant's apartment. The Court held that the warrant was valid and the search and seizure valid because the mistake in question was a reasonable one in describing the apartment in the warrant, and in mistakenly searching defendant's apartment. The Court stated, however, that a different case would be presented if police had known there were two apartments on the third floor, had probable cause to believe that drugs were being sold out of the third floor, but did not know which apartment.

See cases collected at "Searches and Seizures" § 127 West Key No.

45. Marron v. United States, 275 U.S. 192, 48 S.Ct. 74, 72 L.Ed.2d 231, 237 (1927).

scription of property where the item to be seized is alleged to be stolen, so that a general description in the warrant of "stolen" property will not pass constitutional muster.[46] Moreover, "the constitutional requirement that warrants particularly describe the 'things to be seized' is to be accorded the most scrupulous exactitude when the 'things' are books, and the basis for their seizure is the ideas they contain."[47] Beyond that, an open-ended search warrant that leaves blank the items to be seized and is filled in after the search is completed is a general warrant prohibited by the Fourth Amendment.[48]

A search warrant that contains no description of the things to be seized is constitutionally invalid under the Warrants Clause of the Fourth Amendment; the fact that the application or affidavit filed in support of the application contains such a description cannot change this result.[49] Moreover, a search conducted pursuant to such an invalid warrant is considered a warrantless search—and is therefore presumptively unreasonable especially when conducted in the home, and cannot be upheld unless justified by exigent circumstances or some other exception to the search warrant requirement rule.[50] A search warrant can, however, by its express terms incorporate by reference a description of the things to be

---

46. See 2 Wayne LaFave, Search and Seizure § 4.6 (a)–(c) (5th ed. 2012), and cases collected. See also cases collected at "Searches and Seizures" §§ 124, 125, 126, 127 West Key Nos.

47. Stanford v. Texas, 379 U.S. 476, 85 S.Ct. 506, 13 L.Ed.2d 431, 437 (1965) (warrant directing the seizure of books ... concerning the Communist party of Texas" held overbroad); see also Marcus v. Search Warrant, 367 U.S. 717, 81 S.Ct. 1708, 6 L.Ed.2d 1127 (1961) (warrant directing the seizure of "obscene books" held overbroad); 2 Wayne LaFave, Search and Seizure § 4.6(e) (5th ed. 2012).

48. Lo-Ji Sales, Inc. v. New York, 442 U.S. 319, 99 S.Ct. 2319, 60 L.Ed.2d 920 (1979). (open-ended search warrant filled in as books and films were seized by police at adult book store held invalid).

49. Groh v. Ramirez, 540 U.S. 551, 124 S.Ct. 1284, 157 L.Ed.2d 1068 (2004) (warrant described the house to be searched as the things to be seized, an obvious nullity; warrant did not incorporate by reference the supporting application which did contain a description of the things to be seized, nor was the application attached to the warrant; Court rejects argument that the warrant's deficiency was a mere typographical error).

"The warrant was plainly invalid. * * * The fact that the *application* adequately described 'the things to be seized' does not save the *warrant* from its facial invalidity. The Fourth Amendment by its terms requires particularity in the warrant, not in the supporting documents.

* * *

"The warrant did not simply omit a few items from a list of many to be seized, or misdescribe a few of several items. Nor did it make what fairly could be characterized as a mere technical mistake or typographical error. Rather in the space set aside for a description of the items to be seized, the warrant stated that the items consisted of a 'single dwellinghouse residence ... blue in color.' In other words, the warrant did not describe the items to be seized *at all.*" 157 L.Ed.2d at 1078–1079.

50. "In this respect the warrant was so obviously deficient that we must regard the search as warrantless within the meaning of our case law. We are not dealing with formalities. Because the right of a man to retreat into his home and there be free from unreasonable governmental intrusion stands at the very core of the Fourth Amendment, our cases have firmly established the basic principle of Fourth Amendment law that searches and seizures inside a home are presumptively unreasonable. Thus, absent exigent circumstances, a warrantless entry [into the home] to search for weapons or contraband is unconstitutional even when a felony has been committed and there is probable cause to believe that incriminating evidence will be found therein.

We have clearly stated that the presumptive rule against warrantless searches applies with equal force to searches whose only defect is a lack of particularity in the warrant.

* * *

Because petitioner did not have in his possession a warrant particularly describing the things he intended to seize, proceeding with the search was clearly unreasonable under the Fourth Amendment."

Groh v. Ramirez, 540 U.S. 551, 124 S.Ct. 1284, 157 L.Ed.2d 1068, 1079, 1082 (2004) (internal citations and quotation marks omitted).

seized contained in the supporting application or affidavit when such incorporated documents are attached to the warrant.[51]

c. Scope of the search

It is a mistake to assume that if a search warrant is issued ordering the search of particular premises and the seizure of particular evidence, law enforcement officers are privileged to search for that evidence *anywhere* on the described premises that they so desire. On the contrary, such officers are authorized to search *only* those portions of the described premises in which the items to be seized might reasonably be found, and no other places. Indeed, a search under an otherwise valid search warrant into places on the described premises where the items ordered to be seized could *not* reasonably be found renders the search in that location unreasonable under the Fourth Amendment.[52] Stated differently, if a search warrant empowers police to search a house and seize a particularly described stolen refrigerator, police may only search those portions of the house where such an item might reasonably be found; this means that they may not search desk or dresser drawers because a refrigerator could not reasonably be found in such locations. A different result would obtain, however, if the warrant empowered police to seize contraband cocaine, as such an item could reasonably be found in desk or dresser drawers.[53]

---

51. "We do not say that the Fourth Amendment forbids a warrant from cross-referencing other documents. Indeed, most Courts of Appeal have held that a court may construe a warrant with reference to a supporting application or affidavit if the warrant uses appropriate words of incorporation, and if the supporting document accompanies the warrant. But in this case the warrant did not incorporate other documents by reference, nor did either the affidavit or the application (which had been placed under seal) accompany the warrant."

Groh v. Ramirez, 540 U.S. 551, 124 S.Ct. 1284, 157 L.Ed.2d 1068, 1078–79 (2004) (internal citations omitted).

52. "*If the scope of the search exceeds that permitted by the terms of a validly issued warrant* or the character of the relevant exception from the warrant requirement, *the subsequent seizure is unconstitutional without more.*" Horton v. California, 496 U.S. 128, 140, 110 S.Ct. 2301, 110 L.Ed.2d 112, 125 (1990) (emphasis added).

"In Horton v. California [citation omitted], we held '[i]f the scope of the search exceeds that permitted by the terms of a validly issued warrant or the character of the relevant exception to the warrant requirement, the subsequent seizure is unconstitutional without more.' While this does not mean that every police action while inside a home must be explicitly authorized by the text of the warrant, *the Fourth Amendment does require that police actions in execution of a warrant be related to the objectives of the authorized intrusion.*" Wilson v. Layne, 526 U.S. 603, 119 S.Ct. 1692, 143 L.Ed.2d 818, 828 (1999) (internal citation omitted) (emphasis added).

"Just as probable cause to believe that a stolen lawnmower may be found in a garage will not support a warrant to search an upstairs bedroom, probable cause to believe that undocumented aliens are being transported in a van will not justify a warrantless search of a suitcase." United States v. Ross, 456 U.S. 798, 824, 102 S.Ct. 2157, 72 L.Ed.2d 572, 593 (1982).

"The Fourth Amendment's prohibition against unreasonable searches and seizures has always been interpreted to prevent a search that is not limited to the particularly described 'place to be searched and the persons or things to be seized,' U.S. Const., Amdt 4, even if the search is made pursuant to a warrant and based on probable cause." Florida v. Royer, 460 U.S. 491, 103 S.Ct. 1319, 75 L.Ed.2d 229, 237–38 (1983).

"This Court has held in the past that a search which is reasonable in its inception may violate the Fourth Amendment by virtue of its intolerable intensity and scope. The scope of the search must be 'strictly tied to and justified by' the circumstances which rendered its initiation permissible." Terry v. Ohio, 392 U.S. 1, 88 S.Ct. 1868, 20 L.Ed.2d 889, 904 (1968) (internal citations omitted).

See also cases collected at "Searches and Seizures" §§ 147.1, 148 West Key Nos.

53. "When an official search is properly authorized—whether by consent or by the issuance of a valid warrant—the scope of the search is limited by the terms of its authorization. Consent to search

Judge Charles Moylan of the Maryland Court of Appeals has best illustrated this principle in his frequent lectures to judicial conferences on the Fourth Amendment with the apt aphorism: "You cannot search for an elephant in a matchbox."

d. Items subject to seizure

A law enforcement officer conducting a search pursuant to a search warrant is, of course, privileged to seize those items of property that the warrant authorizes the officer to seize—provided the officer is within the proper scope of the search authorized by the warrant, as described above, at the time the seizure is made. But the officer is not limited to seizing only that which is described in the warrant. The officer is also authorized under the "plain view" doctrine to seize any items of property for which there is probable cause, not just reasonable suspicion, to believe that these items constitute contraband, fruits or instrumentalities of a crime, or evidence of a crime—provided that the officer is within the scope of the search authorized by the warrant, as described above, at the time of the seizure.[54]

Section 4. Execution Requirements

a. Forcible entry into a dwelling: knock and announce rule

It is settled that, as a general rule, the Fourth Amendment requires that law enforcement officers must knock on the door and announce their identity and purpose before forcibly entering a dwelling to execute a search or arrest warrant. The underlying rationale for this rule is the high value the Framers of the Fourth Amendment placed on the sanctity of the home, together with their undoubted acceptance of a long-standing common law requirement for government officers to announce, as a general rule, their authority and purpose before forcibly invading a dwelling to perform a legal duty.[55]

---

a garage would not implicitly authorize a search of an adjoining house; *a warrant to search for a stolen refrigerator would not authorize the opening of a desk drawer.* Because 'indiscriminate searches and seizures conducted under the authority of 'general warrants' were the immediate evils that motivated the framing and adoption of the Fourth Amendment,' that Amendment requires that the scope of every authorized search be particularly described." Walter v. United States 447 U.S. 649, 100 S.Ct. 2395, 65 L.Ed.2d 410, 417–18 (1980) (internal citation omitted).

54. For a discussion of the "plain view" doctrine together with cases collected, see Chapter 12, Section 2c of this work.

55. "At the time of the framing [of the Fourth Amendment], the common law of search and seizure recognized a law enforcement officer's authority to break open the doors of a dwelling, but generally indicated that he ought first to announce his presence and authority. In this case, we hold that this common-law principle 'knock and announce' forms a part of the reasonableness inquiry under the Fourth Amendment. * * * "Our own cases have acknowledged that the common-law principle of announcement is 'embedded in Anglo-American law,' but we have never squarely held that this principle is an element of the reasonableness inquiry under the Fourth Amendment. We now so hold. Given the long-standing common-law endorsement of the practice of announcement, we have little doubt that the Framers of the Fourth Amendment thought that the method of an officer's entry into a dwelling was among the factors to be considered in assessing the reasonableness of a search and seizure. Contrary to the decision below, we hold that in some circumstances an officer's unannounced entry into a home might be unreasonable under the Fourth Amendment."

Wilson v. Arkansas, 514 U.S. 927, 115 S.Ct. 1914, 131 L.Ed.2d 976, 979, 982 (1995) (internal citation omitted) (Arkansas Supreme Court decision in state narcotics conviction, that police are

It is important to point out, however, that the Fourth Amendment exclusionary rule does not apply to a violation of the knock-and-announce doctrine; a civil suit, however, may be brought to redress such a violation.[56]

There are, however, important exceptions to this knock-and-announce rule. If law enforcement officers have a reasonable suspicion—and probable cause is not required here—that knocking and announcing their presence would be dangerous or futile, or that it would inhibit the effective investigation of the crime by, for example, allowing the destruction of evidence, they may forcibly enter the dwelling without first announcing their identity and purpose.[57] The underlying rationale for these exceptions is that they strike the proper balance between the legitimate law enforcement concerns and privacy

---

never required to announce their identity and purpose before forcibly entering a dwelling to execute a warrant, is reversed; cause remanded to determine whether the no-knock entry into defendant's dwelling to execute a search warrant was reasonable under the Fourth Amendment).

"In Wilson v. Arkansas [citation omitted], we held that the Fourth Amendment incorporates the common law requirement that police officers entering a dwelling must knock on the door and announce their identity and purpose before attempting forcible entry." Richards v. Wisconsin, 520 U.S. 385, 117 S.Ct. 1416, 137 L.Ed.2d 615, 620 (1997).

"While it is true that a no-knock entry is less intrusive than, for example, a warrantless search, the individual interests implicated by an unannounced, forcible entry should not be unduly minimized. As we observed in Wilson [citation omitted], the common law recognized that individuals should have an opportunity to comply with the law and avoid the destruction of property occasioned by a forcible entry. These interests are not inconsequential.

"Additionally, when police enter a residence without announcing their presence, the residents are not given an opportunity to prepare themselves for such an entry. The State pointed out at oral argument that, in Wisconsin, most search warrants are executed during the late night and early morning hours. The brief interlude between announcement and entry with a warrant may be an opportunity that an individual has to pull on clothes or get out of bed." Richards v. Wisconsin, 520 U.S. 385, 117 S.Ct. 1416, 137 L.Ed.2d 615, 624 n. 5 (1997).

See cases collected at "Searches and Seizures" § 143.1 West Key No.

56. Hudson v. Michigan, 547 U.S. 586, 126 S.Ct. 2159, 165 L.Ed.2d 56 (2006). The Court reached this result because (1) any evidence seized on the premises after such a violation is so attenuated as to dissipate the taint of the original violation, and therefore is not the "fruit of the poisonous tree," and (2) the limited deterrence benefits of applying the exclusionary rule in this context is outweighed by the substantial social costs sustained in such an application, and therefore an exception to the exclusionary rule is shown. 126 S.Ct. at 2163–65, 2165–68. See Justice Kennedy's concurring opinion in *Hudson* emphasizing the importance of vindicating this important doctrine: "It bears repeating that it is a serious matter if law enforcement officers violate the sanctity of the home by ignoring the requisites of lawful entry. Security [in the home] must not be subject to erosion by indifference or contempt." 126 S.Ct. at 2170 (Kennedy, J. concurring).

See also Ch. 17, Sec. 3a & Sec. 5d of this work concerning the Fourth Amendment exclusionary rule—as well as Ch. 17, Sec. 6g of this work for a discussion of civil suits that may be brought to enforce Fourth Amendment rights.

57. "In order to justify a 'no-knock' entry, the police must have a reasonable suspicion that knocking and announcing their presence, under the particular circumstances, would be dangerous or futile, or that it would inhibit the effective investigation of the crime, as, for example, allowing the destruction of evidence." Richards v. Wisconsin, 520 U.S. 385, 117 S.Ct. 1416, 137 L.Ed.2d 615, 624 (1997); see United States v. Banks, 540 U.S. 31, 124 S.Ct. 521, 157 L.Ed.2d 343, 352 (2003).

"In Richards v. Wisconsin [citation omitted], we held that so-called 'no knock' entries are justified when police officers have 'reasonable suspicion' that knocking and announcing their presence before entering would 'be dangerous or futile, or ... inhibit the effective investigation of the crime.' "United States v. Ramirez, 523 U.S. 65, 118 S.Ct. 992, 995, 140 L.Ed.2d 191 (1998).

In accord with U.S. Supreme Court decisions, three emergency exceptions to the knock-and-announce requirement have long been recognized in the lower federal and state courts: (1) where the knock and announce requirements would result in the destruction of the evidence described in the search warrant; (2) where the knock and announce requirements would increase the peril to the executing officers or persons within; and (3) when it is evident from the circumstances that the interests involved; beyond that, these exceptions were generally recognized at common law and therefore were implicitly accepted by the Framers of the Fourth Amendment.[58] And in applying the general rule and exceptions thereto, the Court has proceeded on a case-by-case basis taking into consideration the totality of the circumstances, rather than establishing rigid categories for such searches.[59]

If a reasonable suspicion showing is made to the magistrate establishing a no-knock exception, a no-knock search warrant may be issued[60]—although such a warrant is not essential to a no-knock entry, even where the grounds for such an entry are known at the time of the warrant application.[61] Moreover, the reasonable suspicion showing required

---

authority and purpose of the police is already known to those within the premises. 2 Wayne LaFave, Search and Seizure §§4.8 (d)–(f) (5th ed. 2012).

58. "This [reasonable suspicion] standard [to invoke the exceptions to the knock and announce rule]—as opposed to a probable cause requirement—strikes the appropriate balance between the legitimate law enforcement concerns at issue in the execution of search warrants and the individual privacy interests affected by no-knock entries. This showing is not high, but the police should be required to make it whenever the reasonableness of a no-knock entry is challenged." Richards v. Wisconsin, 520 U.S. 385, 117 S.Ct. 1416, 137 L.Ed.2d 615, 624 (1997).

"This is not to say, of course, that every entry must be preceded by an announcement. The Fourth Amendment's flexible requirement of reasonableness should not be read to mandate a rigid rule of announcement that ignores countervailing law enforcement interests. Even as the petitioner concedes, the common law principle was never stated as an inflexible rule requiring announcement under all circumstances. * * * "We need not attempt a comprehensive catalog of the relevant countervailing factors here. For now, we leave to the lower courts the task of determining the circumstances under which an unannounced entry is reasonable under the Fourth Amendment. We simply hold that although a search or seizure of a dwelling might be constitutionally defective if police officers enter without prior announcement, law enforcement interests may also establish the reasonableness of an unannounced entry." Wilson v. Arkansas, 514 U.S. 927, 115 S.Ct. 1914, 131 L.Ed.2d 976, 982, 984 (1995).

In *Wilson*, the Court canvases the exceptions to the knock and announce requirements at common law and the early American cases without passing on their validity: (1) "courts acknowledged that the presumption in favor of announcement would yield under circumstances presenting a threat of physical violence," (2) "courts held that an officer may dispense with an announcement in cases where a prisoner escapes from him and retreats to his dwelling," and (3) "courts have indicated that unannounced entry may be justified where police officers have reason to believe that evidence would likely be destroyed if advance notice were given." Wilson v. Arkansas, 514 U.S. 927, 115 S.Ct. 1914, 131 L.Ed.2d 976, 983–84 (1995).

59. "Although the notion of reasonable execution must therefore be fleshed out, we have done that case by case largely avoiding categories and protocols for searches. Instead, we have treated reasonableness as a function of the facts so various that no template is likely to produce sounder results than examining the totality of the circumstances in a given case; it is too hard to invent categories without giving short shrift to details that turn out to be important in a given instance, and without inflating marginal ones." United States v. Banks, 540 U.S. 31, 124 S.Ct. 521, 157 L.Ed.2d 343, 352 (2003).

60. "The practice of allowing magistrates to issue no-knock warrants seems entirely reasonable when sufficient cause to do so can be demonstrated ahead of time."Richards v. Wisconsin, 520 U.S. 385, 117 S.Ct. 1416, 137 L.Ed.2d 615, 625 n. 7 (1997); United States v. Ramirez, 523 U.S. 65, 118 S.Ct. 992, 140 L.Ed.2d 191 (1998) (no-knock search warrant upheld).

61. "Nothing in the decisions of this Court, however, indicates that officers requesting a warrant would be constitutionally required to set forth the anticipated means for execution even in those cases where they know beforehand that unannounced or forced entry will be necessary." Dalia v. United States, 441 U.S. 238, 257 n. 19, 99 S.Ct. 1682, 60 L.Ed.2d 177, 192 (1979).

Indeed, there is no Fourth Amendment requirement that a search warrant must set forth the manner in which a warrant must be executed. "Nothing in the language of the Constitution or in this Court's decisions interpreting that language suggests that ... search warrants also must include a specification of the precise manner in which they are to be executed." Dalia v. United States, 441 U.S. 238, 257, 99 S.Ct. 1682, 60 L.Ed.2d 177, 192 (1979) (search warrant ordering the placement of covert to invoke an exception to the knock-and-announce rule does not become higher when law enforcement authorities destroy property as they make their forcible entry into a dwelling.[62] But the destruction of property is a factor in determining whether a search warrant was reasonably executed based on the totality of the circumstances.[63]

It has been held that an exception to the knock and announce rule was shown when a police officer knocked on the defendant's hotel room door armed with a search warrant for illegal drugs, identifying himself as a maintenance man—after which the defendant cracked open the door, saw that one of the officers in the hall was in uniform, and slammed the door shut. The Court concluded that the officers had a reasonable suspicion that the defendant would destroy evidence if given a further opportunity to do so, and consequently were justified in forcibly entering the room to execute the warrant.[64]

It has further been held that an exception to the knock-and-announce rule was shown when federal law enforcement authorities, armed with a no-knock search warrant, forcibly entered the defendant's house to arrest a prison escapee with a violent criminal record for prior prison escapes and who, according to a confidential informer, had access to a stash of weapons at the house. The Court concluded that the law enforcement officials had a reasonable suspicion that knocking and announcing their presence might be dangerous to themselves or others, and consequently were justified in forcibly entering the home to execute the warrant.[65]

On the other hand, it has been held that there is no blanket exception to the knock and announce requirement simply because the executing officers are involved in a felony drug investigation. The underlying rationale for this result is two-fold. First, although

---

electronic eavesdropping device on private premises need not include express authorization to enter such premises to install the device).

62. "Under Richards, a no-knock entry is justified if police have a 'reasonable suspicion' that knocking and announcing would be dangerous, futile, or destructive to the purposes of the investigation. Whether such a 'reasonable suspicion' exists depends in no way on whether police must destroy property in order to enter." United States v. Ramirez, 523 U.S. 65, 118 S.Ct. 992, 996, 140 L.Ed.2d 191 (1998).

Nonetheless, excessive or unnecessary destruction of property in executing a search warrant may be unreasonable under the Fourth Amendment—although it would not affect the admissibility of the evidence seized in the dwelling. "This is not to say that the Fourth Amendment speaks not at all to the manner of executing a search warrant. The general touchstone of reasonableness which governs Fourth Amendment analysis governs the method of execution of the warrant. Excessive or unnecessary destruction of property in the course of a search may violate the Fourth Amendment, even though the entry itself is lawful and the fruits of the search not subject to suppression." United States v. Ramirez, 523 U.S. 65, 118 S.Ct. 992, 996, 140 L.Ed.2d 191 (1998).

63. "Ramirez, for example, cannot be read with the breadth the Government espouses, as 'reflect[ing] a general principle that the need to damage property in order to effectuate an entry to execute a search warrant should not be a part of the analysis of whether the entry itself was reasonable.' At common law, the knock-and-announce rule was traditionally 'justified in part by the belief that announcement generally would avoid 'the destruction or breaking of any house ... by which great damage and inconvenience might ensue.' One point in making an officer knock and announce, then, is to give a person inside a chance to save his door. That is why, in the case with no reason to suspect an immediate risk of frustration or futility in waiting at all, the reasonable wait time may well be longer when police make a forced entry, since they ought to be more certain the occupant has had time to answer the door." United States v. Banks, 540 U.S. 31, 124 S.Ct. 521, 157 L.Ed.2d 343, 355 (2003) (internal citations omitted).

64. Richards v. Wisconsin, 520 U.S. 385, 117 S.Ct. 1416, 137 L.Ed.2d 615 (1997).

65. United States v. Ramirez, 523 U.S. 65, 118 S.Ct. 992, 140 L.Ed.2d 191 (1998) (fact that the escapee was not found in the defendant's house did not change the Court's result; authorities instead discovered defendant, a convicted felon, in possession of a firearm.)

felony drug investigations frequently pose special risks to officer safety and the preservation of evidence, this is not true in all cases. Second, to create an exception for one category of potentially violent crimes, such as felony drug crimes, could logically lead to exceptions for other similar categories of crime, such as armed robbery, thereby undermining the entire knock and announce requirement. It is, accordingly, the duty of a court to evaluate on a case-by-case basis whether the circumstances presented justify dispensing with the knock and announce requirement.[66]

After law enforcement officers have properly announced their identity and purpose while executing a search warrant, a reasonable suspicion showing of exigency or futility—based on a totality of the circumstances—may thereafter develop that allow the officers to forcibly enter the premises. Indeed, the same standards discussed above [exigency or futility] for dispensing with a knock and announce requirement are applicable in determining whether the officers may forcibly enter the premises after they have properly knocked and announced their identity and purpose.[67] Accordingly, it has been held that such an exigency showing was made where (1) law enforcement officers knocked on the door of a small one bedroom apartment and announced their authority and purpose while executing a search warrant for the seizure of disposable contraband drugs (cocaine); (2) the announcement was made in a loud enough voice that officers stationed at the back door of the apartment could hear the announcement; (3) the announcement was made at 2 PM when it may be reasonably assumed that residents are up and about; and (4) the officers waited 15–20 seconds [enough time for anyone therein to get to the bathroom or kitchen and dispose of the cocaine in question] and heard no response from within. Although characterizing the call as "a close one," the Court concluded that there was a reasonable suspicion—based on the totality of the circumstances—that someone inside might be about to destroy the drugs sought, and that the officers properly used a battering ram and forcibly entered the apartment.[68]

---

66. Richards v. Wisconsin, 520 U.S. 385, 117 S.Ct. 1416, 137 L.Ed.2d 615, 620, 632–24 (1997).

67. "[W]e start with a word about standards for requiring or dispensing with a knock and announcement, since the same criteria bear on when the officers [executing a search warrant] could legitimately [and forcibly] enter [private premises] after knocking." United States v. Banks, 540 U.S. 31, 124 S.Ct. 521, 157 L.Ed.2d 343, 351 (2003).

68. United States v. Banks, 540 U.S. 31, 124 S.Ct. 521, 157 L.Ed.2d 343 (2003).

"[T]he issue comes down to whether it was reasonable to suspect imminent loss of evidence after the 10–15 seconds the officers waited prior to forcing their way. Though we agree with Judge Fisher's dissenting opinion that this call is a close one, we think that after waiting 15 to 20 seconds with no response, police could fairly suspect that cocaine would be gone if they waited any longer. Courts of Appeal, indeed, have routinely held similar wait times to be reasonable in drug cases with similar facts including easily disposable evidence (and some courts have found even shorter ones to be reasonable enough)." 157 L.Ed.2d at 353.

This result was not changed by the fact that the apartment dweller was in the shower at the time the officers knocked on the apartment door and claimed he did not hear the officers' knock—and arguably could not, in any event, have responded to the door within 10–15 seconds. This is so because the reasonable suspicion showing must be judged from the perspective of what the officers reasonably suspected prior to the forcible entry, not facts learned by the officers thereafter.

"As for the shower, it is enough to say that the facts known to the police are what count in judging reasonable waiting time, and there is no indication that the police knew that Banks was in the shower and thus unaware of an impending search that he would otherwise have tried to frustrate. And the argument that 15 to 20 seconds was too short for Banks to have come to the door ignores the very risk that justified prompt entry. * * * The significant circumstances include the arrival of the police during the day, when anyone inside would probably have been up and around, and the sufficiency of 15 to 20 seconds for getting to the bathroom or the kitchen to start flushing cocaine down the drain. That is, when circumstances are exigent because a pusher may be near the point of putting his drugs beyond reach, it is imminent disposal, not travel time to the entrance, that governs when the police

It should be noted, however, that the illegal possession of the cocaine sought in this case was a felony, not a minor offense—as the Court expressed no view on what the result might have been if the officers had been seeking evidence of a misdemeanor, rather than a felony.[69] The Court also adverted to the hypothetical case where instead of disposable contraband drugs and a locked front door, the officers had sought a stolen piano—in which event, more wait time might be required before the officers would be justified in using a battering ram to enter the premises.[70]

b. Detention and search of persons on premises

Where a search warrant is issued for the search of contraband on private premises, police may temporarily detain the occupants of the premises while a proper search of the premises is conducted.[71] This authority to temporarily detain such occupants is limited to persons on or in the immediate vicinity of the premises being searched—and does not extend to detentions effected outside this geographical area.[72] It is an open question, however, whether such a temporary detention is authorized if the search warrant is not for contraband, but for evidence of crime.[73] Presumably, much would depend on the affidavit filed in support of the search warrant, the character of the premises being searched, and the behavior of the individuals on the premises at the time of the search, any one of which or combination thereof might amount to reasonable suspicion for a temporary detention. Where the person detained, however, has no special connection to the premises,

---

may reasonably enter. * * * And 15 to 20 seconds does not seem an unrealistic guess about the time someone would need to get in a position to rid his quarters of cocaine." United States v. Banks, 157 L.Ed.2d at 354, 355.

69. "Ramirez and Richards, our cases addressing the role of exigency in assessing the reasonableness of a no knock entry, involved searches by warrant for evidence of a felony, as does this case. In a different context governed by the Fourth Amendment, we have held that the risk of losing evidence of a minor offense is insufficient to make it reasonable to enter a dwelling to make a warrantless arrest. See Welsh v. Wisconsin, 466 U.S. 740, 104 S.Ct. 2091, 80 L.Ed.2d 732 (1984). * * * We intimate nothing here about such warrantless entry cases. Nor do we express a view on the significance of the existence of a warrant in evaluating whether exigency justifies action in knock-and-announce cases when the reason for the search is a minor offense."United States v. Banks, 540 U.S. 31, 124 S.Ct. 521, 157 L.Ed.2d 343, 353 n. 4 (2003).

70. "Suffice it to say that the need to damage property in the course of getting in is a good reason to require more patience than it would be reasonable to expect if the door were open. Police seeking a stolen piano may be able to spend more time to make sure they really need the battering ram." United States v. Banks, 540 U.S. 31, 124 S.Ct. 521, 157 L.Ed.2d 343, 355 (2003).

71. "Thus, for Fourth Amendment purposes, we hold that a warrant to search for contraband founded on probable cause implicitly carries with it the limited authority to detain the occupants of the premises while a proper search is conducted." Michigan v. Summers, 452 U.S. 692, 705, 101 S.Ct. 2587, 69 L.Ed.2d 340, 351 (1981) (police met owner of house descending the front steps and required him to come in the house while they conducted a search therein); Muehler v. Mena, 544 U.S. 93, 125 S.Ct. 1465, 1470, 161 L.Ed. 2d 299 (2005) (search warrant authorized the seizure of deadly weapons used in drive-by shooting; occupant was asleep in her bed when the search began; detention upheld) ("Mena's [the occupant's] detention was, under *Summers*, plainly permissible.").

72. Bailey v. United States, 568 U.S. ____, 133 S.Ct. 1031, 185 L.Ed.2d 19 (2013) (stop effected nearly a mile from the premises being searched disapproved as a valid detention during search warrant execution; person detained had left the premises just before search warrant was executed; case remanded to determine whether the detention was a valid Terry stop).

73. "We do not decide the issue whether the same result would be justified if the search warrant merely authorized a search for evidence." Michigan v. Summers, 452 U.S. 692, 705 n. 20, 101 S.Ct. 2587, 69 L.Ed.2d 340 (1981).

such as a patron of a business premises being searched, such a person may not, on that basis alone, be subjected to a patdown search.[74]

Inherent in the authorization to temporarily detain the occupant of premises while a search warrant is being executed is the authority to use reasonable force to effectuate the detention.[75] The use of handcuffs, however, to detain the occupant is a separate Fourth Amendment intrusion aside from the detention—and therefore requires a separate justification, as where the safety of the officers and occupants require it.[76]

Indeed, when executing a search warrant, the officers may take any reasonable action that is necessary to secure the premises and to ensure their own safety and the efficacy of the search.[77] This authority authorizes the officers to order naked residents found in bed to stand for a brief time while officers secure the premises—although for no longer than is necessary to accomplish this purpose.[78] Accordingly, unreasonable actions in executing a search warrant are prohibited—such as the use of excessive force or restraints that cause unnecessary pain or ones that are imposed for a prolonged and unnecessary period of time.[79]

Moreover, the officers are authorized to question the occupant concerning matters that have nothing to do with the search. This is so because police questioning in itself does not constitute a Fourth Amendment seizure of the individual and therefore does not require a showing of reasonable suspicion.[80] But presumably, where the questioning exceeds the time reasonably necessary to conduct the search, the basis for the temporary

74. Ybarra v. Illinois, 444 U.S. 85, 100 S.Ct. 338, 62 L.Ed.2d 238 (1979) (patrons of a tavern).

75. "Inherent in *Summers*' authorization to detain an occupant of the place to be searched is the authority to use reasonable force to effectuate the detention." Muehler v. Mena, 544 U.S. 93, 125 S.Ct. 1465, 1470, 161 L.Ed. 2d 299 (2005).

76. "The imposition of correctly applied handcuffs on Mena [the occupant], who was already being lawfully detained during a search of the house, was undoubtedly a separate intrusion in addition to the detention in the converted garage. * * But this was no ordinary search. The governmental interests in not only detaining, but using handcuffs, are at their maximum when, as here, a warrant authorizes a search for weapons and a wanted gang member resides on the premises. In such inherently dangerous situations, the use of handcuffs minimizes the risk to both officers and occupants." Muehler v. Mena, 544 U.S. 93, 125 S.Ct. 1465, 1470–71, 161 L.Ed.2d 299 (2005) (handcuffing of occupant upheld during search of gang house; one of the gang members resided on the premises; the warrant authorized the seizure of deadly weapons; three other individuals on the premises were also detained and handcuffed).

77. "In executing a search warrant, officers may take reasonable action to secure the premises and to ensure their own safety and the efficacy of the search." Los Angeles County v. Rettele, 550 U.S. 609, 127 S.Ct. 1989, 1992, 167 L.Ed.2d 974 (2007).

78. Los Angeles County v. Rettele, supra (a male and female resident of house found in bed naked forced to stand naked for 1–2 minutes while officers secured premises; held reasonable action, even though house had subsequently been sold to innocent third party and nothing incriminating was found).

79. "Unreasonable actions (in executing a search warrant) include the use of excessive force or restraints that cause unnecessary pain or are imposed for a prolonged or unnecessary period of time. * * *

This is not to say, of course, that the deputies were free to force Rettele and Sandler (the residents) to remain motionless and standing for any longer than necessary. We have recognized that 'special circumstances' or possibly a prolonged detention might render a search unreasonable." Los Angeles County v. Rettele, 127 S.Ct. at 1993.

80. Muehler v. Mena, 544 U.S. 93, 125 S.Ct. 1465, 1471–72, 161 L.Ed. 2d 299 (2005) (questioning of occupant s immigration status during otherwise reasonable search of gang house for deadly weapons and evidence of gang membership upheld).

detention disappears, the detention becomes illegal, and any questioning during this detention would be tainted thereby.[81]

c. Media or third party ride-along

It is settled that a law enforcement officer who is executing a warrant in a home is not authorized to bring members of the media ["media ride-along"] or other third parties onto the premises during the execution of the warrant when the presence of such parties is not in aid of execution of the warrant; to do so constitutes a violation of the Fourth Amendment rights of the person whose home is searched.[82] On the other hand, where police enter a home under a warrant to search for stolen property, it is permissible to bring third parties onto the premises for the purpose of identifying the stolen property to be seized—as such parties are clearly in aid of execution of the warrant.[83] A home dweller is entitled to recover damages and other relief in a *Bivens* or § 1983 civil rights lawsuit against police for an illegal "media ride-along" as described above.[84]

It is doubtful, however, whether the *Weeks-Mapp* exclusionary rule would apply to any evidence seized by the police during an illegal "media ride-along" search because the police are clearly in the home lawfully pursuant to the warrant; only the media representatives are unlawfully on the premises. On the other hand, evidence seized in the home by unauthorized media representatives during such a search might be suppressible under the *Weeks-Mapp* exclusionary rule as they are on the premises illegally with the permission of the police, and therefore are arguably agents of the government.[85] Still, the inevitable discovery rule limitation to the exclusionary rule could arguably be applicable in a given

---

81. Illinois v. Caballes, 543 U.S. 405, 125 S.Ct. 834, 837, 160 L.Ed.2d 842 (2005) ("It is nevertheless clear that a seizure that is lawful at its inception can violate the Fourth Amendment if its manner of execution unreasonably infringes interests protected by the Constitution. A seizure that is justified solely by the interest in issuing a warning [traffic] ticket can become unlawful if it is prolonged beyond the time reasonably required to complete that mission."). (internal citation omitted); compare United States v. Place, 462 U.S. 696, 103 S.Ct. 2637, 77 L.Ed.2d 110 (1983) (suitcase held longer than reasonably necessary to conduct a narcotics dog sniff of a suitcase tainted the dog alert on the suitcase and invalidated the search warrant for the suitcase based on the alert).

82. "We hold that it is violation of the Fourth Amendment for police to bring members of the media or other third parties into a home during the execution of a warrant when the presence of the third parties in the home was not in aid of the execution of the warrant." Wilson v. Layne, 526 U.S. 603, 119 S.Ct. 1692, 143 L.Ed.2d 818, 830 (1999).

83. "Where the police enter a home under the authority of a warrant to search for stolen property, the presence of third parties for the purpose of identifying the stolen property has long been approved by this Court and our common law tradition." Wilson v. Layne, 526 U.S. 603, 119 S.Ct. 1692, 143 L.Ed.2d 818, 828 (1999).

84. Wilson v. Layne, 526 U.S. 603, 119 S.Ct. 1692, 143 L.Ed.2d 818 (1999). As an aside, the Court in *Wilson* also held that the police were immune from a *Bivens* or a § 1983 civil suit because it was not "clearly established" at the time of the search that the "media ride-along" practice was constitutionally impermissible. But this immunity holding does not apply to future "media ride-alongs" now that it is "clearly established" that they violate the Fourth Amendment.

For a discussion of the *Bivens* § 1983 civil rights suit as an enforcement for violations of Fourth Amendment rights, see Chapter 17, Section 6g of this work.

85. In this context, LaFave notes that "the police would seem hard-pressed to claim that explorations by the media within the premises are not attributable to official action, given that the media's presence was brought about by the police. The exclusionary rule thus might very well apply in the assumed circumstances, subject of course to the possible exception of the inevitable discovery doctrine if the media representatives have done no more than the warrant obligated the police to do." 3 Wayne LaFave, Search and Seizure § 6.1(a) at 367 (5th ed. 2012).

case—if the government could show that the police would have inevitably discovered the evidence seized by the media representatives, even if the media had not been present.[86] All of these questions have yet to be decided by the Court.[87]

Section 5. Neutral and Detached Magistrate

It is settled that under the Fourth Amendment a search warrant can only be issued by a neutral and detached magistrate, traditionally connected with the court, rather than by someone connected with law enforcement.[88] The magistrate need not be a judge or a lawyer, although many are, but must be (1) neutral and detached from law enforcement, and (2) capable of determining the issue of probable cause.[89] Accordingly, law enforcement

---

For a discussion of the governmental element of the constitutional Standing Requirement for a Fourth Amendment violation, see Chapter 8, Section 2 of this work.

86. For a discussion of the inevitable discovery rule limitation to the *Weeks-Mapp* exclusionary rule, see Chapter 17, Section 3c of this work.

87. "Even though such ["media ride-along"] actions might violate the Fourth Amendment, if the police are lawfully present, the violation of the Fourth Amendment is the presence of the media and not the presence of the police. We have no occasion here to decide whether the exclusionary rule would apply to any evidence discovered or developed by the media representatives." Wilson v. Layne, 526 U.S. 603, 119 S.Ct. 1692, 143 L.Ed.2d 818, 830 n. 2 (1999).

88. "The point of the Fourth Amendment, which often is not grasped by zealous officers, is not that it denies law enforcement the support of the usual inferences which reasonable men draw from evidence. Its protection consists in requiring that those inferences be drawn by a neutral and detached magistrate instead of being judged by the officer engaged in the often competitive enterprise of ferreting out crime." Johnson v. United States, 333 U.S. 10, 13–14, 68 S.Ct. 367, 92 L.Ed. 436 (1948).

"The Fourth Amendment requires that search warrants be issued only 'upon probable cause, supported by Oath or affirmation, particularly describing the place to be searched and the persons or things to be seized.' Finding these words to be 'precise and clear,' this Court has interpreted them to require [that] warrants must be issued by neutral and detached magistrates." Dalia v. United States, 441 U.S. 238, 99 S.Ct. 1682, 60 L.Ed.2d 177, 191 (1979).

"To implement the Fourth Amendment's protection against unfounded invasions of liberty and privacy, the Court has required that the existence of probable cause be decided by a neutral and detached magistrate whenever possible." Gerstein v. Pugh, 420 U.S. 103, 95 S.Ct. 854, 43 L.Ed.2d 54, 64 (1975).

"No search warrant is valid if the procedure for the issuance of the warrant is inadequate to ensure the sort of neutral contemplation by a magistrate of the grounds for the search and its proposed scope, which lies at the heart of the Fourth Amendment." Sibron v. New York, 392 U.S. 40, 59, 88 S.Ct. 1889, 20 L.Ed.2d 917, 933 (1968).

89. "An examination of the Court's decisions reveals that the terms 'magistrate' and 'judicial officer' have been used interchangeably. Little attempt has been made to define either term, to distinguish the one from the other, or to advance one as the definitive Fourth Amendment requirement. We find no commandment in either term, however, that all warrant authority must reside exclusively in a lawyer or judge. Such a requirement would have been incongruous when even within the federal system warrants were until recently widely issued by nonlawyers.

"To attempt to extract further significance from the above terminology would be both unnecessary and futile. The substance of the Constitution's warrant requirements does not turn on the labeling of the issuing party. The warrant traditionally has represented an independent assurance that a search and arrest will not proceed without probable cause to believe that a crime has been committed and the person or place named in the warrant is involved in the crime. *Thus, an issuing magistrate must meet two tests. He must be neutral and detached, and he must be capable of determining whether probable cause exists for the requested arrest or search. This Court has long insisted that inferences of probable cause be drawn by 'a neutral and detached magistrate instead of being judged by the officer engaged in the often competitive enterprise of ferreting out crime.'* * * * "What we do reject today is any per se invalidation of a state or local warrant system on the ground that the issuing magistrate is not a lawyer or judge.

personnel, such as the U.S. Attorney General, a State Attorney General, or a prosecuting attorney, cannot serve as a neutral and detached magistrate and issue search or arrest warrants.[90] On the other hand, a non-lawyer municipal court clerk connected with the court may issue warrants.[91]

Moreover, a magistrate is not neutral and detached if he or she has a financial stake in issuing warrants; accordingly, a magistrate who is paid for every search warrant issued, but not paid when a warrant is declined, is not neutral and detached and may not constitutionally issue warrants.[92] And an otherwise qualified magistrate fatally compromises the neutrality required of a magistrate by joining the search party to help execute the search warrant when issued—and, in so doing, invalidates the subject warrant.[93] It is permissible, however, for a magistrate to view a suspect obscene film in a theater as a ordinary paying patron with law enforcement personnel, and thereafter to issue a search warrant on the theater premises for the seizure of the film just viewed.[94]

Communities may have sound reasons for delegating the responsibility of issuing warrants to competent personnel other than judges or lawyers." Shadwick v. City of Tampa, 407 U.S. 345, 349–50, 352, 92 S.Ct. 2119, 32 L.Ed.2d 783, 788, 790 (1972) (emphasis added) (internal citations and footnote omitted) (a non-lawyer, non-judge, municipal court clerk attached to the court may serve as a committing magistrate). See cases collected at "Searches and Seizures" § 104 West Key No.

90. United States v. United States District Court, 407 U.S. 297, 92 S.Ct. 2125, 32 L.Ed.2d 752 (1972) (U.S. Attorney General disapproved as a committing magistrate to issue electronic surveillance warrants); Coolidge v. New Hampshire, 403 U.S. 443, 91 S.Ct. 2022, 29 L.Ed.2d 564 (1971) (state attorney general disapproved as a magistrate to issue a search warrant); Gerstein v. Pugh, 420 U.S. 103, 95 S.Ct. 854, 43 L.Ed.2d 54 (1975) (prosecuting attorney disapproved as a magistrate to make a required post-arrest determination of probable cause after a warrantless arrest); Mancusi v. DeForte, 392 U.S. 364, 370–71, 88 S.Ct. 2120, 20 L.Ed.2d 1154, 1161(1968) (prosecuting attorney disapproved as a magistrate to issue a search warrant). See 2 Wayne LaFave, Search and Seizure § 4.2(a) (5th ed. 2012).

91. Shadwick v. City of Tampa, 407 U.S. 345, 92 S.Ct. 2119, 32 L.Ed.2d 783 (1972) (Court declines to decide whether a magistrate may be lodged *outside* the judicial branch of government). See 2 Wayne LaFave, Search and Seizure § 4.2 (c) (5th ed. 2012).

92. Connally v. Georgia, 429 U.S. 245, 97 S.Ct. 546, 50 L.Ed.2d 444 (1977) (JP paid $5.00 fee for every search warrant issued; no fee if search warrant declined). See 2 Wayne LaFave, Search and Seizure § 4.2(b) (5th ed. 2012).

93. Lo-Ji Sales, Inc. v. New York, 442 U.S. 319, 99 S.Ct. 2319, 60 L.Ed.2d 920 (1979) (search warrant voided). See 2 Wayne LaFave, Search and Seizure § 4.2 (d) (5th ed. 2012).

94. Heller v. New York, 413 U.S. 483, 93 S.Ct. 2789, 37 L.Ed.2d 745 (1973), as explained in Lo-Ji Sales v. New York, 442 U.S. 319, 327, 99 S.Ct. 2319, 60 L.Ed.2d 920, 929 (1979).

Chapter 14

Warrantless Searches and *Criminal* Exceptions to the Search Warrant Requirement Rule

Section 1. An Overview of Exceptions to the Search Warrant Requirement Rule

As previously discussed, a search conducted without a search warrant is per se unreasonable under the Fourth Amendment, subject to certain important exceptions.[1] Accordingly, to determine whether a given *warrantless* search is reasonable in the Fourth Amendment sense, all relevant exceptions to the search warrant requirement rule must be examined. If one of the exceptions is applicable, the search is considered reasonable, even if other exceptions may be inapplicable; if no such exception is applicable, however, the search is considered unreasonable.[2]

Although the Court has never expressly so stated, it seems clear from its decisions that there are two general types of exceptions to the search warrant requirement rule: (1) criminal exceptions, and (2) civil or special needs exceptions. The criminal exceptions all serve a compelling investigative purpose in ordinary criminal law enforcement cases in which the societal costs of obtaining a warrant are deemed to outweigh the reasons for resorting to a warrant.[3] The civil or special needs exceptions, on the other hand, serve a

---

1. See, e.g., Katz v. United States, 389 U.S. 347, 357, 88 S.Ct. 507, 19 L.Ed.2d 576, 585 (1967); Coolidge v. New Hampshire, 403 U.S. 443, 91 S.Ct. 2022, 29 L.Ed.2d 564, 576 (1971); see also Chapter 11, Section 1 of this work. As an aside, the existence of probable cause to search a dwelling is *not* an exception to this search warrant requirement rule. "It is settled doctrine that probable cause for belief that certain articles subject to seizure are in a dwelling cannot of itself justify a search without a warrant." Jones v. United States, 357 U.S. 493, 497–98, 78 S.Ct. 1253, 2 L.Ed. 2d 1514, 1518 (1958).

2. See, e.g., Vale v. Louisiana, 399 U.S. 30, 33–35, 90 S.Ct. 1969, 26 L.Ed.2d 409, 413–14 (1970) (exceptions found inapplicable, and search held unreasonable); Coolidge v. New Hampshire, 403 U.S. 443, 453–73, 91 S.Ct. 2022, 29 L.Ed.2d 564, 575–87 (1971) (same).

3. "Nonetheless, there are some exceptions to the warrant requirement. These have been established where it was concluded that the public interest required some flexibility in the application of the general rule that a valid warrant is a prerequisite for a search. Thus a few 'jealously and carefully drawn' exceptions provide for those cases where the societal costs of obtaining a warrant, such as danger to law officers or the risk of loss of evidence, outweigh the reasons for prior recourse to a neutral magistrate. But because each exception to the warrant requirement impinges to some extent on the protective purpose of the Fourth Amendment, the few situations in which a search may be conducted in the absence of a warrant have been carefully delineated and 'the burden is on those seeking the exemption to show the need for it.'" Arkansas v. Sanders, 442 U.S. 753, 759–60, 99 S.Ct.

compelling public purpose that the warrant procedure, and at times the probable cause or individualized suspicion requirement, is deemed ill-suited to accomplish based on a balancing of competing governmental and privacy concerns.[4] In particular, where special governmental needs beyond the normal need for criminal law enforcement are shown, the Court generally strikes the balance in favor of dispensing with a warrant—and, at times, dispensing as well with a probable cause requirement, or even any showing of individualized wrongdoing.[5] At other times, however, the Court reaches the same result by

---

2586, 61 L.Ed.2d 235, 242 (1979) (internal citations omitted).

"It is true that there have been some exceptions to the warrant requirement. But those exceptions are few in number and carefully delineated; in general, they serve the legitimate needs of law enforcement officers to protect their own well-being and preserve evidence from destruction." United States v. United States District Court, 407 U.S. 297, 318, 92 S.Ct. 2125, 32 L.Ed.2d 752, 767 (1972).

"Our cases hold that procedure by way of a warrant is preferred, although in a wide range of diverse situations we have recognized flexible, common sense exceptions to this requirement." Texas v. Brown, 460 U.S. 730, 735, 103 S.Ct. 1535, 75 L.Ed.2d 502, 509 (1983).

4. For a representative statement of the balancing approach, see Delaware v. Prouse, 440 U.S. 648, 653–55, 99 S.Ct. 1391, 59 L.Ed.2d 660 (1979); and Brown v. Texas, 443 U.S. 47, 50–51, 99 S.Ct. 2637, 61 L.Ed.2d 357 (1979). For other statements of the balancing approach, see: O'Connor v. Ortega, 480 U.S. 709, 107 S.Ct. 1492, 94 L.Ed.2d 714, 724 (1987); Tennessee v. Garner, 471 U.S. 1, 105 S.Ct. 1694, 85 L.Ed.2d 1, 7 (1985); United States v. Montoya de Hernandez, 473 U.S. 531, 105 S.Ct. 3304, 87 L.Ed.2d 381, 388 (1985); New Jersey v. T.L.O., 469 U.S. 325, 105 S.Ct. 733, 83 L.Ed.2d 720, 731–32 (1985); United States v. Place, 462 U.S. 696, 103 S.Ct. 2637, 77 L.Ed.2d 110, 118 (1983); United States v. Villamonte-Marquez, 462 U.S. 579, 103 S.Ct. 2573, 77 L.Ed.2d 22, 30 (1983); Bell v. Wolfish, 441 U.S. 520, 559, 99 S.Ct. 1861, 60 L.Ed.2d 447 (1979); Pennsylvania v. Mimms, 434 U.S. 106, 109, 98 S.Ct.330, 54 L.Ed.2d 331 (1977); United States v. Martinez-Fuerte, 428 U.S. 543, 554–55, 96 S.Ct. 3074, 49 L.Ed.2d 1116 (1976); Terry v. Ohio, 392 U.S. 1, 20–21, 88 S.Ct. 1868, 20 L.Ed.2d 889 (1968); Camara v. Municipal Court, 387 U.S. 523, 536–37, 87 S.Ct. 1727, 18 L.Ed.2d 930 (1967).

5. "Although we usually require that a search be undertaken only pursuant to a warrant (and thus supported by probable cause, as the Constitution says warrants must be (citation omitted)), we have permitted exceptions when 'special needs, beyond the normal need for law enforcement, make the warrant and probable cause requirement impracticable.'(citation omitted)." Griffin v. Wisconsin, 483 U.S. 868, 107 S.Ct. 3164, 97 L.Ed.2d 709, 717 (1987) (search of probationer's home by probation officers upheld).

"For the Fourth Amendment does not proscribe all searches and seizures, but only those that are unreasonable. What is reasonable, of course, 'depends on all the circumstances surrounding the search or seizure and the nature of the search or seizure itself.' Thus, the permissibility of a particular practice 'is judged by balancing its intrusion on the individual's Fourth Amendment interests against its promotion of legitimate governmental interests.' In most criminal cases, we strike the balance in favor of the procedures described by the Warrants Clause of the Fourth Amendment. Except in certain well-defined circumstances, a search or seizure in such a case is not reasonable unless it is accomplished pursuant to a judicial warrant issued upon probable cause. *We have recognized exceptions to this rule, however, 'when special needs, beyond the normal need for law enforcement, make the warrant and probable cause requirement impracticable.' When faced with such special needs, we have not hesitated to balance the governmental and privacy interests to assess the practicality of the warrant and probable cause requirements in the particular context.*" Skinner v. Railway Labor Executives' Ass'n, 489 U.S. 602, 109 S.Ct 1402, 103 L.Ed.2d 639, 661 (1989) (internal citations omitted) (emphasis added) (drug testing program for train employees involved in train accidents upheld).

"While we have long emphasized, and reiterate today, that a search must be supported, as a general matter, by a warrant issued upon probable cause, our decision in *Railway Labor Executives* reaffirms the long-standing principle that neither a warrant nor probable cause, nor, indeed, any measure of individualized suspicion is an indispensable component of reasonableness in every circumstance. As we noted in *Railway Labor Executives*, our cases establish that *where a Fourth Amendment intrusion serves special governmental needs, beyond the normal need for law enforcement, it is necessary to balance the individual's privacy expectations against the Government's interests to determine whether it is impracticable to require a warrant or some level of individualized suspicion in the particular context.*" National Treasury Employees Union v. Von Raab, 489 U.S. 656, 109 S.Ct. 1384, 103 L.Ed.2d 685, 702 (1989) (internal citations omitted) (emphasis added) (drug testing program for Treasury agents employing the standard balancing process for determining Fourth Amendment reasonableness without requiring a showing of special governmental needs.[6] In this entire balancing process, the Court creates, at times, special needs exceptions to the search warrant requirement rule, and at other times straight civil exceptions *sans* any showing of special governmental needs. Moreover, the physical scope of a search authorized by a given exception is strictly limited to that which is required to carry out the purpose of the exception.[7]

As previously stated, all relevant exceptions must generally be examined to determine whether a given warrantless search is reasonable or unreasonable under the Fourth Amendment. Merely because one exception is inapplicable does not necessarily mean that the search is unreasonable, as another exception may be applicable. Only where no relevant exception is applicable can it be said that a warrantless search is unreasonable under the Fourth Amendment.[8]

There is an important limitation, however, to this general proposition. Some exceptions necessarily involve or presuppose a prior seizure of an individual's person or property before the search in question takes place; if this seizure is unreasonable under the Fourth Amendment, any evidence secured as the fruit of this seizure would generally be inadmissible in evidence under the *Weeks-Mapp* exclusionary rule. And that may include the fruits of the search that immediately follows the prior unreasonable seizure.

---

involved in drug enforcement upheld).

"Where a search is undertaken by law enforcement to discover evidence of criminal wrongdoing, this Court has said that reasonableness generally requires the obtaining of a judicial warrant. Warrants cannot be issued, of course, without the showing of probable cause required by the Warrants Clause. But a warrant is not required to establish the reasonableness of all government searches; and when a warrant is not required (and the Warrants Clause not applicable), probable cause is not invariably required either. *A search unsupported by probable cause can be constitutional, we have said, 'when special needs, beyond the normal need for law enforcement, make the warrant and probable cause requirements impracticable.'*" Vernonia School District 47J v. Acton, 515 U.S. 646, 115 S.Ct. 2386, 132 L.Ed.2d 564, 574 (1995) (citations omitted) (emphasis added) (drug testing program for public high school athletes upheld).

"The Fourth Amendment requires that searches and seizures be reasonable. A search is generally unreasonable in the absence of individualized wrongdoing. While such suspicion is not an 'irreducible' component of reasonableness, we have recognized circumstances where the usual rule does not apply. For example, *we have upheld certain regimes of suspicionless searches where the program was designed to serve 'special needs beyond the normal need for law enforcement.'*" City of Indianapolis v. Edmond, 531 U.S. 32, 121 S.Ct. 447, 148 L.Ed.2d 333, 340 (2000) (internal citations omitted) (emphasis added) (traffic roadblock to interdict drug traffic struck down).

6. Samson v. California, 547 U.S. 843, 126 S.Ct. 2193, 2200 n. 3, 165 L.Ed.2d 250 (2006) (general balancing definition of reasonableness used to hold that a warrantless, suspicionless search of a parolee did not violate the parolee's Fourth Amendment rights; special governmental needs showing not required.).

7. "But a warrantless search must be 'strictly circumscribed by the exigencies which justify its initiation.'" Mincey v. Arizona 437 U.S. 385, 393, 98 S.Ct. 2408, 57 L.Ed.2d 290, 300 (1978), quoting from Terry v. Ohio, 392 U.S. 1, 25–26, 88 S.Ct. 1868, 20 L.Ed.2d 889 (1968); see Horton v. California, 496 U.S. 128, 110 S.Ct. 2301,110 L.Ed.2d 112, 125 (1990). "Moreover, we have limited the scope of each exception [to the search warrant requirement rule] to that which is necessary to accommodate the identified needs of society." Arkansas v. Sanders, 442 U.S. 753, 760, 99 S.Ct. 2586, 61 L.Ed.2d 235, 242 (1979).

8. See, e.g., Flippo v. West Virginia, 528 U.S. 11, 120 S.Ct. 7, 145 L.Ed.2d 16, 19–20 (1999) (warrantless search of home based on a non-existent "murder scene" exception to the warrant requirement disapproved; cause remanded without prejudice for state to invoke any applicable exception to the warrant requirement, including consent, to sustain the search) ("A warrantless search by the police is invalid unless it falls within one of the exceptions to the warrant requirement ... none of which the trial court invoked here.").

The criminal exceptions will be examined in this chapter and include search incident to a lawful arrest, stop and frisk, moving-vehicle *Carroll* doctrine, consent, and exigent circumstances. The civil or special needs exceptions, on the other hand, will be examined in Chapter 15.

Section 2. Search Incident to a Lawful Arrest

a. The wingspan rule

After over half a century of flux and uncertainty,[9] the law is now settled that after making a lawful arrest, a law enforcement officer is authorized to search (1) the arrestee's person, and (2) the physical area into which the arrestee may physically reach to grab a weapon or evidentiary item; this is the so-called wingspan rule announced in the leading case of *Chimel v. California*.[10] The scope of police authority to search incident to a lawful arrest undoubtedly extends to containers possessed by the arrestee at the time of arrest.[11] On the other hand, a search beyond this physical scope cannot be justified as a search incident to a lawful arrest, with some exceptions to be discussed below. Of course, a

---

9. For a discussion of the zig-zag progression of U.S. Supreme Court decisions from 1914–1969, announcing various rules on the physical scope of a search incident to a lawful arrest that eventually led to the rule we have today, see 3 Wayne LaFave, Search and Seizure § 6.3(b) at 458–461 (5th ed. 2012).

10. "When an arrest is made, it is reasonable for the arresting officer to search the person arrested in order to remove any weapons that the latter might seek to use in order to resist arrest or effect his escape. Otherwise, the officer's safety might well be endangered, and the arrest itself frustrated. In addition, it is entirely reasonable for the arresting officer to search for and seize any evidence on the arrestee's person in order to prevent its concealment or destruction. And the area into which an arrestee might reach to grab a weapon or evidentiary items must, of course, be governed by a like rule. A gun on a table or in a drawer in front of one who is arrested can be as dangerous to the arresting officer as one concealed in the clothing of the person arrested. There is ample justification, therefore, for a search of the arrestee's person and the area 'within his immediate control'—construing that phrase to mean the area within which he might gain possession of a weapon or destructible evidence.

There is no comparable justification, however, for routinely searching any room other than that in which an arrest occurs—or, for that matter, for searching through all the desk drawers or other closed or concealed areas in that room itself. Such searches, in the absence of well-recognized exceptions, may be made only under the authority of a search warrant." Chimel v. California, 395 U.S. 752, 89 S.Ct. 2034, 23 L.Ed.2d 685, 694 (1969), overruling United States v. Rabinowitz, 339 U.S. 56, 70 S.Ct. 430, 94 L.Ed. 653 (1950), and Harris v. United States, 331 U.S. 145, 67 S.Ct. 1098, 91 L.Ed. 1399 (1947); see also Riley v. California, 574 U.S. ___, 134, S.Ct. 2473, 2483, 189 L.Ed.2d 430 (2014), reaffirming Chimel's wingspan rule by quoting with approval the first paragraph of the above quoted passage.).

In *Chimel*, the Court held that the search of the defendant's entire three-bedroom house—including the attic, garage and small workshop—was not incident to the defendant's lawful arrest effected at the front door of the house.

For lower federal and state court cases on the scope of a search incident to an arrest, see "Searches and Seizures" § 52, "Arrest" §§ 71.1 (4.1), (5), (8) West Key Nos.

11. California v. Acevedo, 500 U.S. 565, 111 S.Ct. 1982, 114 L.Ed 2d 619, 631 (1991) ("And the police often will be able to search containers without a warrant ... as a search incident to a lawful arrest.... Under Belton, the same probable cause to believe that a container holds drugs will allow the police to arrest the person transporting the container and search it.").

search that is not incident to an otherwise lawful arrest may nonetheless be justified based on some other applicable exception to the search warrant requirement rule.

As just alluded to, in order for this exception to apply, the arrest itself must be lawful. Indeed, an illegal arrest is an independent Fourth Amendment violation as it is an unreasonable seizure of the person, and will generally taint and render inadmissible the fruits of such a seizure under the *Weeks-Mapp* exclusionary rule.[12] If that be the case, no other exceptions to the search warrant requirement rule need be examined, because the fruits of the search that follows the illegal arrest would, on that account alone, be generally barred from evidence.

b. Rationale for exception

The rationale for this exception seems obvious enough. It would be entirely impracticable to require a search warrant in order to conduct a search incident to an otherwise lawful arrest. There is a real danger that before a search warrant could be obtained, the arrestee might injure or kill the arresting officer with a concealed weapon, make an escape with such a weapon, or destroy evidence. There is, accordingly, a pressing need to immediately conduct a warrantless search incident to the arrest in order to disarm the suspect and to preserve evidence for later use at trial.[13] "Indeed, the label 'exception' is a bit of a misnomer in this context, as warrantless searches incident to arrest occur with far greater frequency than searches with a warrant."[14]

Beyond that, the Framers of the Fourth Amendment clearly had no intention of requiring search warrants for searches incident to an arrest as defined by *Chimel*. As previously noted, the Framers intended to end the abuse of general exploratory searches and seizures wrought by the general writs of assistance regime [1761–76] by constitutionalizing the special warrants or special writs practice of the English common law that generally required a search warrant to conduct a search of private premises.[15] Clearly, there was no thought that a search of an arrestee incident to an arrest, so necessary to disarm the suspect and preserve evidence, required a search warrant.

---

12. For a discussion of (1) unreasonable seizures of the person, see Chapter 12, Section 1 of this work; and (2) the evidentiary consequences thereof under the *Weeks-Mapp* exclusionary rule, see Chapter 17, Section 3 of this work.

13. "In [United States v. Robinson, 414 U.S. 218, 234, 94 S.Ct. 467, 38 L.Ed.2d 427(1973)], we noted the two historical rationales for the 'search incident' exception: (1) the need to disarm the suspect in order to take him into custody, and (2) the need to preserve evidence for later use at trial." Knowles v. Iowa, 525 U.S. 113, 119 S.Ct. 484, 142 L.Ed.2d 492, 498 (1998).

"Among the exceptions to the warrant requirement is a search incident to a lawful arrest. [citation omitted]. The exception derives from interests of officer safety and evidence preservation that are typically implicated in arrest situations. [citation omitted].

In *Chimel*, we held that a search incident to arrest may only include the arrestee's person and the area 'within his immediate control—construing that phrase to mean the area from within which he might gain possession of a weapon of a weapon or destructible evidence. That limitation, which continues to define the boundaries of the exception, ensures that the scope of a search incident to arrest is commensurate with its purposes of protecting officers and safeguarding any evidence of the offense of arrest that an arrestee might conceal or destroy." Arizona v. Gant, 556 U.S. 322, 129 S.Ct. 1710, 1716, 173 L.Ed.2d 485 (2009).

14. Riley v. California, 573 U.S. ___ 134 S.Ct. 2473, 2482, 189 L.Ed.2d 430 (2014).

15. See Chapter 6, Section 2 of this work.

c. Search of person: purpose of search irrelevant

A search of the person of a lawfully-arrested individual—as opposed to the wingspan area into which the arrestee might reach—has a long-standing common law acceptance and is deemed a reasonable search, quite apart from being an exception to the search warrant requirement rule. Consequently, even if the arresting officer is not searching for weapons or evidence of crime following a custodial arrest, a search of the arrestee's person is nonetheless considered reasonable in the Fourth Amendment sense.[16] Of course, most of the time law enforcement officers search a lawfully arrested suspect to safeguard evidence and to ensure their own safety; such a search is a reasonable search as it is incident to a lawful arrest.[17] Law enforcement agents, however, may not conduct a warrantless search of a cell phone pursuant to this exception, where they have seized the phone from the arrestee's person at the point of arrest.[18]

---

16. "The authority to search the person incident to a full custodial arrest, while based on the need to disarm and to discover evidence, does not depend on what a court may later decide was the probability in a particular arrest situation that weapons or evidence would in fact be found upon the *person* of the suspect. A custodial arrest of a suspect based on probable cause is a reasonable intrusion under the Fourth Amendment; that intrusion being lawful, a search incident to an arrest requires no additional justification. It is the fact of the lawful arrest which establishes the authority to search, and *we hold that in the case of a lawful custodial arrest a full search of the person is not only an exception to the warrant requirement of the Fourth Amendment, but is also a reasonable search under that Amendment.*" United States v. Robinson, 414 U.S. 218, 94 S.Ct. 467, 38 L.Ed. 427, 440–41 (1973) (emphasis added). But see Riley v. California, 574 U.S. ___, 134, S.Ct. 2473, 2483–2485, 189 L.Ed.2d 430 (2014), which reaffirms this rule, allows police to seize a cell phone from the person of an arrestee after a lawful arrest, but, absent exigent circumstances, requires police to get a search warrant to search the digital data on the phone.

In *Robinson*, the Court held that it was reasonable under the Fourth Amendment for police to search the person of a defendant who was arrested for operating a motor vehicle after revocation of defendant's drivers license—even though the arresting officer had no subjective fear of the defendant, did not suspect that defendant was armed, and was not searching for fruits and instrumentalities of the offense for which defendant was arrested.

See Gustafson v. Florida, 414 U.S. 260, 94 S.Ct. 488, 38 L.Ed.2d 456 (1973) (search of defendant's person after lawful arrest for driving without a valid driver's license held reasonable under authority of *Robinson*).

"Also uncontested is the right on the part of the Government, always recognized under English and American law, to search the person of the accused when lawfully arrested. The validity of the search of a person incident to a lawful arrest has been regarded as settled from its first annunciation, and has remained virtually unchallenged. Even in that context, the Court has been clear that individual suspicion is not necessary, because the constitutionality of a search incident to arrest does not depend on whether there is any indication that the person arrested possesses weapons or evidence. The fact of a lawful arrest, standing alone, authorizes a search." Maryland v. King, 569 U.S. ____, 133 S.Ct. 1958, 186 L.Ed.2d 1, 21–22 (2013) (internal quotation marks and citations omitted).

17. "When officers have probable cause to believe that a person has committed a crime in their presence, the Fourth Amendment permits them to search the suspect in order to safeguard evidence and ensure their own safety." Virginia v. Moore, 553 U.S. 164, 128 S.Ct. 1598, 1608, 170 L.Ed.2d 559 (2008).

18. Riley v. California, 574 U.S. ___, 134 S.Ct. 2473, 189 L.Ed.2d 430 (2014) (warrantless search by police of a modern cell phone—of the "smart phone" and "flip phone" variety—seized from the person of a suspect in two companion cases following an arrest of each suspect held unreasonable under the Fourth Amendment as (a) not conducted with a search warrant, and (b) not otherwise justified under the search incident to a lawful arrest exception to the search warrant requirement rule).

"We therefore decline to extend *Robinson* to searches of data on cell phones, and hold instead that officers must generally secure a warrant before conducting such a search. " 134 S.Ct. at 2485.

d. Search may precede arrest

In a routine arrest, a search incident to that arrest usually takes place after the arrest has been physically effected. But this is not essential to invoke the exception. A search incident to a lawful arrest may actually precede the physical arrest—providing the arrest is based on probable cause developed prior to the search, and is not based on the fruits of the search.[19] This rule, of course, makes good sense, else form would triumph over substance. Surely, it makes no difference whether the arrest is *formally* effected prior to or after the incidental search—so long as there is probable cause for the arrest quite apart from what is discovered during the search.

e. Release of suspect after search

It is rare that police will release a suspect after a search incident to the arrest has been conducted, and incriminating evidence seized. But it may happen. The evidence that is uncovered in such a search, although subject to seizure under the "plain view" doctrine, may nonetheless require some type of scientific or chemical analysis. Police may feel that the totality of the evidence in the case developed both before and after the arrest, although amounting to probable cause, may not be enough to convict. Accordingly, they may temporarily release the suspect and have the seized evidence tested, following which they may re-arrest the suspect if the tests prove incriminating. Under these unusual circumstances, such a search would seem clearly reasonable as it was conducted incident to the preceding arrest based on probable cause, notwithstanding a subsequent police decision to temporarily release the suspect. Indeed, such a search has been upheld where the suspect was not formally arrested but only temporarily detained, where the detention was based on probable cause as required for an arrest.[20]

---

19. Rawlings v. Kentucky, 448 U.S. 98, 100 S.Ct. 2556, 65 L.Ed.2d 633 (1980) (search of suspect's person held incident to arrest effected after the search was conducted, where probable cause to arrest existed prior to the search). "Of course, the fruits of a search may not be used to justify an arrest to which it is incident, but this means only that probable cause to arrest must precede the search. If the prosecution shows probable cause to arrest prior to a search of a man's person, it has met its total burden. There is no case in which a defendant may validly say, 'Although the officer had a right to arrest me at the moment when he seized and searched my person, the search is invalid because he did not arrest me until afterwards.'" Peters v. New York, 392 U.S. 40, 77, 88 S.Ct. 1889, 20 L.Ed.2d 917, 943 (1968) (Harlan, J. concurring). This analysis is fully supported by case law throughout the country. See, e.g., Justice Roger Traynor's decision in People v. Simon, 45 Cal.2d 645, 290 P.2d 531 (1955); 3 Wayne LaFave, Search and Seizure § 5.4(a) (5th ed. 2012) and cases collected.

"It is axiomatic that an incident search may not precede an arrest and serve as part of its justification." Sibron v. New York, 392 U.S. 40, 63, 88 S.Ct. 1889, 20 L.Ed.2d 917, 934–35 (1968); Smith v. Ohio, 494 U.S. 541, 110 S.Ct. 1288, 108 L.Ed.2d 464 (1990) (probable cause to arrest cannot be based on the fruits of the arrest).

20. Cupp v. Murphy, 412 U.S. 291, 295, 93 S.Ct. 2000, 36 L.Ed.2d 900, 905 (1973) (defendant voluntarily came to police station alone in response to a police request; police were investigating the strangulation death of defendant's wife; while there, police noticed a dark spot that resembled blood on the defendant's finger; police requested permission to take a sample of scrapings from beneath defendant's fingernails; defendant refused; police detained defendant without formally arresting him, took the aforesaid scrapings, and released the defendant; the scrapings were later tested and turned out to contain traces of skin and blood cells, as well as fabric from the victim's nightgown; *held*: the search and seizure of the fingernail scrapings was "constitutionally permissible under the principles of Chimel v. California."). See 3 Wayne LaFave, Search and Seizure § 5.4(b) at 253–257 (5th ed. 2012).

f. Arrest of automobile driver or passenger

Notwithstanding the *Chimel* wingspan rule, the Court has adopted a limited exception thereto—confined to a search incident to the arrest of a driver or passenger in a motor vehicle. Accordingly, when a law enforcement officer makes an arrest of a motor vehicle occupant, the officer is authorized to conduct a search of the vehicle's passenger compartment and any container therein [but not the trunk] only where:

(1) the arrestee is unsecured and within reaching distance of the passenger compartment at the time of the arrest, or

(2) it is reasonable to believe that evidence relevant to the crime of arrest might be found in the passenger compartment.[21]

The Court has noted that the first situation will rarely arise because law enforcement officers are almost always able to promptly effect an arrest without the arrestee having access to the subject vehicle. But if unable to do so safely during which the potential arrestee is unsecured and has ready access to the vehicle, the officers are allowed to search the passenger compartment in the course of the struggle in order to protect themselves from weapons therein and for evidence preservation.[22] This search will necessarily go beyond the physical wingspan of the arrestee.

---

21. "Accordingly, we ... hold that the *Chimel* rationale authorizes police to search a vehicle incident to a recent occupant's arrest only when the arrestee is unsecured and within the reaching distance of the passenger compartment.

Although it does not follow from *Chimel*, we also conclude that circumstances unique to the vehicle context justifies a search incident to a lawful arrest when it is 'reasonable to believe evidence relevant to the crime of arrest might be found in the vehicle.' * * *

Police may search a vehicle incident to a recent occupant's arrest only if the arrestee is within reaching distance of the passenger compartment at the time of the search or it is reasonable to believe the vehicle contains evidence of the offense of arrest."Arizona v. Gant, 556 U.S. 322, 129 S.Ct. 1710, 1719, 1723, 173 L.Ed.2d 485 (2009) (search of motor vehicle held not incident to traffic arrest of driver for driving with a suspended license; driver was handcuffed and placed in the back of police patrol car at time of arrest); see also Riley v. California, 574 U.S. ___, 134, S.Ct. 2473, 2484, 189 L.Ed.2d 430 (2014), which reaffirms this rule.

"As result, the Court [in Gant] adopted a new, two-part rule under which an automobile search incident to a recent occupant's arrest is constitutional (1) if the arrestee is within reaching distance of the vehicle during the search, or (2) if the police have reason to believe that the vehicle contains evidence relevant to the crime of arrest." Davis v. United States, 564 U.S. ____, 131 S.Ct. 2419, 2425, 180 L.Ed.2d 285 (2011) (internal citation marks omitted).

The current exception also leaves undisturbed the Court's prior rulings that under this exception (a) *containers* in the vehicle's passenger compartment may also be searched, but (b) the vehicle's *trunk* may not be searched. New York v. Belton, 453 U.S. 454, 101 S.Ct. 2860, 69 L.Ed.2d 768, 775 (1981). Indeed, the Gant Court expressly stated that under its second holding, as stated above , "the offense of arrest will [often] supply a basis for searching the *passenger compartment* of an arrestee's vehicle *and any containers therein.*" Arizona v. Gant, 556 U.S. 322, 129 S.Ct. 1710, 1719, 173 L.Ed.2d 485 (2009) (emphasis and brackets added). Moreover, the entire Gant decision was centered on searches of the passenger compartment of a motor vehicle, not the vehicle's trunk—which clearly cannot be searched under the search-incident-to-arrest exception.

For an extensive analysis of the *Gant* decision and the issues that may still be unresolved, see 3 Wayne LaFave, Search and Seizure §§7.1(c) (d) at 697–720 (5th ed. 2012).

22. "Because officers have many means of ensuring the safe arrest of vehicle occupants, it will be the rare case in which an officer is unable to fully effectuate an arrest so that a real possibility of access to the arrestee's vehicle remains. [citation omitted]. But in such a case a search incident to arrest is reasonable under the Fourth Amendment." Arizona v. Gant, 556 U.S. 322, 129 S.Ct. 1710 n. 4, 173 L.Ed.2d 485 (2009). Moreover, Justice Alito agrees in his dissenting opinion (joined by C.J. Roberts, and Kennedy and Breyer, JJ.): "First, in the great majority of cases, an officer making an arrest is able

The Court has further noted that the second situation arises only where the arrest is for an offense that one can reasonably expect to find evidence thereof in the vehicle. This necessarily excludes minor traffic violations—like speeding or a defective tail light—which rarely, if ever, involve physical evidence. But the exception can apply to arrests for certain felonies or serious misdemeanors—both of which may encompass physical evidence one might expect to find in the vehicle.[23] This search can go beyond the physical wingspan of the arrestee and extend to the entire passenger compartment of the vehicle, including containers therein. Indeed, the arrestee may be safely secured in a patrol car at the time of the search.

This exception represents a limited retreat from earlier more expansive U.S. Supreme Court rulings that allowed *as a bright line rule* an automatic police search of a motor vehicle's passenger compartment following an arrest of the driver or passenger of the vehicle. As previously noted, such a search is now allowed only in limited situations that are tethered more to the original justification for searches incident to arrest.[24]

If this exception is inapplicable, a search of the arrestee's vehicle is unreasonable under the Fourth Amendment—unless the police obtain a search warrant for the vehicle or show that another exception to the search warrant requirement applies.[25]

g. The "protective sweep" rule

There is yet another exception to the *Chimel* wingspan rule. When arresting a person on private premises, law enforcement officers are automatically allowed to look in closets and other spaces *immediately adjoining* the place in the premises where the arrest takes place, even though the areas searched may be technically beyond the wingspan of the

---

to handcuff the arrestee and remove him to a secure place before conducting a search incident to the arrest." 129 S.Ct. at 1730.

23. "In many cases, as when a recent occupant is arrested for a traffic violation, there will be no reasonable basis to believe the vehicle contains relevant evidence. [citations omitted]. But in others, including *Belton* and *Thornton*, the offense of arrest will supply a basis for searching the passenger compartment of an arrestee's vehicle and any containers therein." Arizona v. Gant, 556 U.S. 322, 129 S.Ct. 1710, 1719, 173 L.Ed.2d 485 (2009).

24. New York v. Belton, 453 U.S. 454, 101 S.Ct. 2860, 69 L.Ed.2d 768, 775 (1981) ("Accordingly, we hold that when a policeman has made a lawful custodial arrest of the occupant of an automobile, he may, as a contemporaneous incident of that arrest, search the passenger compartment of that automobile."); see Thornton v. United States, 541 U.S. 615, 124 S.Ct. 2127, 158 L.Ed.2d 905 (2004) (following Belton).

As previously noted, the Court has since backed off Belton's broad rule (1): "Accordingly, we hold that *Belton* does not authorize a vehicle search after the arrestee has been secured and cannot access the interior of the vehicle." Except for one situation: (2) "[W]e also conclude that circumstances unique to the automobile context justify a search incident to arrest when it is reasonable to believe that evidence of the offense of arrest might be found in the vehicle." Arizona v. Gant, 556 U.S. 322, 129 S.Ct. 1710, 1714, 173 L.Ed.2d 485 (2009).

The second portion of the above holding was apparently tacked on to get Justice Scalia's vote and secure a majority of Justices for the Court's opinion. Indeed, this point had previously been suggested by Justice Scalia's concurring opinion in Thornton, 124 S.Ct. at 2127, which was expressly referenced and followed by the *Gant* Court in its opinion. Id.

25. "Police may search a vehicle incident to a recent occupant's arrest only if the arrestee is within reaching distance of the passenger compartment at the time of the search or it is reasonable to believe the vehicle contains evidence of the offense of arrest. When these justifications are absent, a search of an arrestee's vehicle will be unreasonable unless police obtain a warrant or show that another exception to the warrant requirement applies."Arizona v. Gant, 556 U.S. 322, 129 S.Ct. 1710, 1723–24, 173 L.Ed.2d 485 (2009).

arrestee. Like a search incident to the arrest of a motorist, there is a need for a bright-line rule so as to protect the safety of the arresting officer.[26]

Beyond that, police may also briefly "sweep" the entire premises if there is a reasonable suspicion that there are other persons on the premises who may pose a danger to those at the arrest scene. This protective sweep must be limited to a cursory inspection of those spaces on the premises where a person may be found, and does not authorize a general exploratory search of the *entire* premises. For that reason, an inspection of jewelry cases and bathroom medicine cabinets in the home would not be authorized because a person could not hide in such spaces.[27]

h. Search must be contemporaneous with the arrest

It has long been held, even prior to *Chimel*, that a search incident to a lawful arrest must be contemporaneous in time and place with the arrest; a search conducted at another time or place removed from the arrest is generally not considered incident to the arrest.[28] Thus, a search of a defendant's dwelling has been held not incident to an arrest of the defendant made at another part of town,[29] or made several blocks away on the street,[30] or made a short distance outside the house,[31] or made several blocks away in another person's house,[32] or made two days later in a different city.[33]

There are, however, a few wrinkles to this "contemporaneous requirement." Clothing and other evidence taken by police from an arrestee, while the latter is in custody at a local jail after being arrested on the street, is considered incident to a prior arrest on the street. "[S]earches and seizures that could be made on the spot at the time of the arrest

---

26. " We also hold that as an incident to the arrest the officers could, as a precautionary matter and without probable cause or reasonable suspicion, look in closets and other spaces immediately adjoining the place of arrest from which an attack could immediately be launched." Maryland v. Buie, 494 U.S. 325, 110 S.Ct. 1093, 108 L.Ed.2d 276, 286 (1990).

27. "Beyond that, however, we hold that there must be articulable facts which, taken together with rational inferences from those facts, would warrant a reasonably prudent officer in believing that the area to be swept harbors an individual posing a danger to those at the arrest scene. * * * We should emphasize that such a protective sweep, aimed at protecting the officers, if justified by the circumstances, is nevertheless not a full search of the premises, but may extend only to a cursory inspection of those spaces where a person may be found. The sweep takes no longer than is necessary to dispel the reasonable suspicion of danger and in any event no longer than it takes to complete the arrest and depart the premises." Maryland v. Buie, 494 U.S. 325, 110 S.Ct. 1093, 108 L.Ed.2d 276, 286–287 (1990). For lower federal and state case on protective sweep searches, see "Searches and Seizures" § 71 West Key No.

28. "The rule allowing contemporaneous searches is justified, for example, by the need to seize weapons and other things which might be used to assault an officer or effect an escape, as well as the need to prevent the destruction of evidence of the crime—things which could easily happen where the weapon or evidence is on the accused's person or under his immediate control. But these justifications are absent where a search is remote in time or place from the arrest. Once an accused is under arrest and in custody, then a search made at another place, without a warrant, is simply not incident to the arrest." Preston v. United States, 376 U.S. 364, 367, 84 S.Ct. 881, 11 L.Ed.2d 777, 780–781 (1964).

29. Weeks v. United States, 232 U.S. 383, 34 S.Ct. 341, 58 L.Ed. 652 (1914).

30. James v. Louisiana, 382 U.S. 36, 86 S.Ct. 151, 15 L.Ed.2d 30 (1965) (hotel room).

31. Vale v. Louisiana, 399 U.S. 30, 90 S.Ct. 1969, 26 L.Ed.2d 409 (1970).

32. Agnello v. United States, 269 U.S. 20, 46 S.Ct. 4, 70 L.Ed. 145 (1925).

33. Stoner v. California, 376 U.S. 483, 84 S.Ct. 889, 11 L.Ed.2d 856 (1964).

may legally be conducted when the accused arrives at the place of detention."[34] This rule is more a matter of administrative convenience than anything else—as a more thorough search of an arrestee may not be possible, following a patdown search for weapons, until the arrestee has been taken to jail. Moreover, when, as sometimes happens, a police officer lawfully arrests a suspect and requests identification, the officer, as an incident of a lawful arrest, is authorized to accompany the suspect into the latter's residence, where the suspect says his identification is located, to obtain the identification. It is clearly reasonable for a police officer, as a matter of routine, to monitor the movements of such an arrested person by entering the residence, rather than let the person enter the premises alone and possibly escape. A search of the arrestee's dwelling, of course, is not authorized, but if the officer sees contraband or evidence of crime in plain view while in the dwelling, the officer is privileged to seize such evidence under the "plain view" doctrine.[35]

i. Seizure of alleged obscene film

The warrantless seizure of an alleged obscene film following an arrest raises certain First Amendment concerns. Consequently, the seizure of such a film, following an arrest of a person for the public exhibition of such a film in a commercial theater, has been held unreasonable under the Fourth Amendment because it was accomplished without a warrant and without a prior judicial determination that the film was obscene.[36] A film of this nature can only be seized pursuant to a search warrant in which there has been a judicial determination that the film is obscene.[37]

j. "Plain view" seizure of evidence

During an otherwise proper search incident to arrest as thus defined, law enforcement officers will sometimes discover certain physical objects. If there is probable cause to believe that these objects are contraband, fruits or instrumentalities of a crime, or evidence of a crime, the officers are privileged to seize such objects under the "plain view" doctrine—whether such objects are related or unrelated to the offense for which the suspect was arrested.[38]

---

34. United States v. Edwards, 415 U.S. 800, 94 S.Ct. 1234, 39 L.Ed.2d 771, 775 (1974); see also Illinois v. Lafayette, 462 U.S. 640, 103 S.Ct. 2605, 77 L.Ed.2d 65 (1983) (same result based on the civil inventory exception to the search warrant requirement rule; see Chapter 15, Section 2a(4) of this work).

35. Washington v. Chrisman, 455 U.S. 1, 102 S.Ct. 812, 70 L.Ed.2d 778 (1982) (police officer observed marijuana and a marijuana pipe while in defendant's dormitory room and lawfully seized same under the "plain view" doctrine; proper for officer to go in the defendant's room following a lawful arrest of defendant to obtain defendant's identification, even though the defendant asked the officer to remain outside the room). For a discussion of the "plain view" doctrine, see Chapter 12, Section 2c of this work.

36. Roaden v. Kentucky, 413 U.S. 496, 93 S.Ct. 2796, 37 L.Ed.2d 757 (1973) (the local sheriff and prosecutor purchased tickets to a drive-in theater, watched the film which was being commercially shown there, following which the sheriff proceeded to the projectionist booth, arrested the defendant [manager of the theater] for exhibiting an obscene film, and seized the film incident to the arrest; held: seizure of the film was unreasonable).

37. For a discussion of the rules governing the search and seizure of materials presumptively protected by the First Amendment, such as books and films, see Chapter 16, Section 6 of this work.

38. For a discussion of the "plain view" doctrine, see Chapter 12, Section 2c of this work

Section 3. "Stop and Frisk" Search

a. General rule

In the landmark case of *Terry v. Ohio*,[39] the Court held that a law enforcement officer, after making a valid temporary detention of a person based on reasonable suspicion, is allowed to conduct a patdown search of the outer clothing of the detainee for weapons, provided there is a showing of articulable suspicion that the detainee is armed and dangerous.[40] The purpose of this limited patdown search is not to discover evidence of crime, but to allow the officer to pursue his or her investigation without fear of being violently assaulted.[41] As a consequence, a full-blown search of the person, in which an officer reaches into the pants pockets and other hidden recesses of the detainee's clothing, is not justified by this exception because such an extensive search is unnecessary to determine if the detainee is armed.[42]

---

39. 392 U.S. 1, 88 S.Ct. 1868, 20 L.Ed.2d 889, 911(1968).

40. "We merely hold today that [a] where a police officer observes unusual conduct which leads him reasonably to conclude that criminal activity may be afoot and the persons with whom he is dealing are armed and dangerous, [b] where in the course of investigating this behavior he identifies himself as a policeman and makes reasonable inquiries, and [c] where nothing in the initial stages of the encounter serves to dispel his reasonable fear for his own or others' safety, he is authorized for the protection of himself and others in the area to conduct a carefully limited search of the outer clothing of such persons in an attempt to discover weapons which might be used to assault him. Such a search is a reasonable search under the Fourth Amendment, and any weapons seized may properly be introduced against the person from whom they are taken." Terry v. Ohio, 392 U.S. 1, 88 S.Ct. 1868, 20 L.Ed.2d 889, 911(1968) (bracketed letters added).

In *Terry*, an experienced police officer observed defendant and a companion one afternoon walking back and forth peering into the front of a store about 12 times in downtown Cleveland, Ohio, following which they would confer with one another and later with a third person. Based on his police experience, the officer had reasonable suspicion that these men were casing the store for a robbery and were armed and dangerous. He approached defendant and two companions, identified himself, asked their names; when they mumbled something in response, the officer immediately frisked them, feeling a gun under defendant's outer clothing. The Court upheld the initial stop and frisk; the Court also upheld the seizure of the gun.

"In a pathmarking decision, Terry v. Ohio [numerical citation omitted], the Court considered whether an investigatory stop (temporary detention) and frisk (patdown for weapons) may be conducted without violating the Fourth Amendment's ban on unreasonable searches and seizures. The Court upheld 'stop and frisk' as constitutionally permissible if two conditions are met. First, the investigatory stop must be lawful. That requirement is met in an on-the-street encounter, *Terry* determined, when the police officer reasonably suspects that the person apprehended is committing or has committed a criminal offense. Second, to proceed from a stop to a frisk, the police officer must reasonably suspect that the person stopped is armed and dangerous." Arizona v. Johnson, 555 U.S. 323, 129 S.Ct. 781, 784 172 L.Ed.2d 694 (2009).

41. "The purpose of this limited [Terry] search is not to discover evidence of crime, but to allow the officer to pursue his investigation without fear of violence, and thus the frisk for weapons might be equally necessary and reasonable, whether or not carrying a concealed weapon violated any applicable state law. So long as the officer is entitled to make a forcible stop, and has reason to believe that the suspect is armed and dangerous, he may conduct a weapons search limited in scope to its protective purpose." Adams v. Williams, 407 U.S. 143, 92 S.Ct. 1921, 32 L.Ed.2d 612, 617 (1972).

42. In *Sibron v. New York*, 392 U.S. 40, 88 S.Ct. 1889, 20 L.Ed.2d 917 (1968), the Court struck down a full-blown search of a detainee when a police officer reached into detainee's pocket to determine whether the detainee had narcotics therein, and pulled out several glassine envelopes containing heroin, while effecting a temporary *Terry* stop.

"In this case, with no attempt at an initial limited exploration for arms, Patrolman Martin thrust his hand into Sibron's pocket and took from him envelopes of heroin. His testimony shows that he

If, while conducting a valid patdown search for weapons, the officer feels a hidden object that gives one probable cause to believe that the detainee is carrying a concealed weapon, (a) the acquisition of this knowledge is considered valid under the "plain view" doctrine, sometimes referred to as the "plain feel" extension of this doctrine, which relies on both tactile as well as visual inspection while conducting an otherwise reasonable search;[43] and (b) based on this knowledge, the officer is privileged (i) to reach into the hidden recesses of the detainee's clothing, thereby conducting a full-blown search of the detainee, based on the search-incident-to-a-valid arrest exception discussed in the previous section of this chapter, and (ii) to seize any concealed weapon [or contraband, fruits or instrumentalities of crime, or evidence of crime] in the detainee's pocket under the "plain view" doctrine.[44]

But—and here things get technical—if during the initial patdown search for weapons, the officer acquires no knowledge to give one probable cause to believe that the detainee has a weapon, the search at that point must cease. If, nonetheless, the search illegally continues, and the officer manipulates with one's fingers the hidden object on the detainee's person to determine if it is contraband drugs, the extended search is invalid under the *Terry* stop-and-frisk exception, as it is conducted outside the scope of this search warrant exception—thereby tainting any searches or seizures that follow, and rendering the fruits thereof generally inadmissible under the *Weeks-Mapp* exclusionary rule.[45]

Although most valid *Terry* stops for felony offenses justify an automatic patdown search of the detainee for weapons, it does not follow that every valid *Terry* stop justifies such an intrusion. To conduct a patdown search, there must also be a showing of reasonable suspicion that the detainee is armed and dangerous—which requirement is met where the detention itself is for an offense in which the offender would likely be armed.[46] But

---

was looking for narcotics, and he found them. The search was not reasonably limited in scope to the accomplishment of the only goal which might conceivably have justified its inception—the protection of the officer by disarming a potentially dangerous man. Such a search violates the guarantee of the Fourth Amendment which protects the sanctity of the person against unreasonable intrusions on the part of all government agents." Sibron v. New York, 392 U.S. at 65–66, 88 S.Ct. 1889, 20 L.Ed.2d at 936 (1968).

43. "If a police officer lawfully pats down a suspect's outer clothing and feels an object whose contour or mass makes its identity immediately apparent, there has been no invasion of the suspect's privacy beyond that already authorized by the officer's search for weapons; if the object is contraband, its warrantless seizure would be justified by the same practical considerations that inhere in the plain view context."Minnesota v. Dickerson, 508 U.S. 366,113 S.Ct. 2130, 124 L.Ed.2d 334, 345 (1993).

44. Terry v. Ohio, 392 U.S. 1, 88 S.Ct. 1868, 20 L.Ed.2d 889,911(1968) (patdown search of detainee revealed contour of a gun, thereby giving police probable cause to arrest detainee, to conduct full-blown search of detainee's person, and to seize a gun found during such search); see Chapter 12, Section 2c of this work for a discussion of the "plain view" doctrine.

45. Minnesota v. Dickerson, 508 U.S. 366, 113 S.Ct. 2130, 124 L.Ed.2d 334, 348–49 (1993) (search held invalid as conducted outside scope of valid stop-and-frisk search). "If the protective search goes beyond what is necessary to determine if the suspect is armed, it is no longer valid under Terry and its fruits will be suppressed." 124 L.Ed.2d at 344.

46. "Where a [Terry] stop is reasonable, however, the right to frisk must be immediate and automatic if the reason for the stop is, as here, an articulable suspicion of a crime of violence. Just as a full search incident to a lawful arrest requires no additional justification, a limited frisk incident to a lawful stop must often be rapid and routine. There is no reason why an officer, rightly but forcibly confronting a person suspected of a serious crime, should have to ask one question and take the risk that the answer might be a bullet." Terry v. Ohio, 392 U.S. 1, 33, 88 S.Ct. 1868, 20 L.Ed.2d 889, 913 (1968) (Harlan, J. concurring).

"Lower courts have been inclined to view the right to frisk as being 'automatic' whenever the suspect has been stopped upon suspicion that he has committed, was committing, or was about to commit a type of crime for which the offender would likely be armed, whether the weapon would be used to actually commit the crime, to escape if the scheme went awry, or for protection against the where neither the basis for the detention itself nor other surrounding circumstances present a reasonable suspicion that the detainee is armed and dangerous, as in a routine traffic stop where the officer issues a ticket to the motorist—police are not privileged to conduct a patdown search of the detainee.[47] During a lawful traffic stop, however, the police may question the driver or any passenger concerning any criminal offense [even if unrelated to the stop] and need not have reasonable suspicion that such person is involved in said criminal offense—so long as the questioning does not measurably extend the duration of the traffic stop.[48]

As an aside, in order for this exception to apply, the temporary detention itself must be lawful. Indeed, an illegal temporary detention is an independent Fourth Amendment violation as it is an unreasonable seizure of the person—and will generally taint and render inadmissible the fruits of such a seizure under the *Weeks-Mapp* exclusionary rule.[49] If that be the case, no other exceptions to the search warrant requirement rule need be

---

victim or others involved. This includes such suspected offenses as robbery, burglary, rape, assault with weapons, homicide, and dealing in large quantities of narcotics. In such circumstances, then, 'the officer's reasonable belief may derive as much from his experience in similar cases as from his precise knowledge of the dangerous propensities of the suspect at hand.'" 4 Wayne LaFave, Search and Seizure § 9.6(a) at 853–855 (5th ed. 2012) (footnotes and citations omitted).

47. Ybarra v. Illinois, 444 U.S. 85, 100 S.Ct. 338, 62 L.Ed.2d 238 (1979) (being present as a patron on the premises of a tavern while a search warrant was being executed therein for contraband drugs did not, without more, constitute a basis for conducting a patdown search of the patron); see also Sibron v. New York, 392 U.S. 40, 88 S.Ct. 1889, 20 L.Ed.2d 917 (1968) (detainee, who was seen over a number of hours conversing with known narcotics addicts on the street, could not be searched by police, as there was no showing that the detainee was armed and dangerous).

"Accordingly, we hold that, in a traffic-stop setting, the first *Terry* condition—a lawful investigatory stop—is met whenever it is lawful for police to detain an automobile and its occupants pending inquiry into a vehicular violation. The police need not have, in addition, cause to believe that any occupant of the vehicle is involved in criminal activity. To justify a patdown of the driver or a passenger, however, just as in the case of a pedestrian reasonably suspected of criminal activity, the police must harbor reasonable suspicion that the person subjected to the frisk is armed and dangerous."Arizona v. Johnson, 555 U.S. 323, 129 S.Ct. 781, 784, 172 L.Ed.2d 694 (2009).

"But for other types of crimes, such as trafficking in small quantities of narcotics, possession of marijuana, illegal possession of liquor, prostitution, bookmaking, shoplifting, underage drinking, driving under the influence and lesser traffic offenses, minor assault without weapons, or vagrancy, as well as when the stop is for a legitimate noncriminal reason, there must be, as Justice Harlan noted in *Terry* 'other circumstances present [to justify a patdown search].'" 4 Wayne LaFave, Search and Seizure § 9.6(a) at 855–857 (5th ed. 2012) (footnotes and citations omitted). For illustrative examples of such "other circumstances," see LaFave, supra, at pp. 857–63 and cases collected.

48. "A lawful roadside stop begins when a vehicle is pulled over for investigation of a traffic violation. The temporary seizure of the driver and passengers ordinarily continues, and remains reasonable, for the duration of the stop. Normally, the stop ends when the police have no further need to control the scene, and inform the driver and passengers they are free to leave. [citation omitted]. An officer's inquiries into matters unrelated to the justification for the traffic stop, this Court has made clear, does not convert the encounter into something other than a lawful seizure, so long as those inquiries do not measurably extend the duration of the stop." Arizona v. Johnson, 555 U.S. 323, 129 S.Ct. 781, 788, 172 L.Ed.2d 694 (2009) (police questioning of passenger during a lawful traffic stop concerning criminal gang activity, where there was no reasonable suspicion of same, did not render the passenger's detention unlawful, and thus invalidate the later patdown search of the passenger; on remand, however, state appellate court could determine whether the patdown was nonetheless unlawful if there was no reasonable suspicion that the passenger was armed and dangerous).

49. For a discussion of (1) unreasonable seizures of the person, see Chapter 12, Section 1, of this work; and (2) the evidentiary consequences thereof under the *Weeks-Mapp* exclusionary rule, see Chapter 17, Section 3 of this work.

examined, because the fruits of the search that follows the illegal detention would on that account alone be generally barred from evidence.

b. Rationale for exception

Like a search incident to an arrest, a stop and frisk search could not, as a practical matter, be carried out with a search warrant. Before a search warrant could be obtained, the detainee would obviously have an opportunity to assault the detaining officer with a hidden weapon; a warrantless frisk must therefore immediately follow the stop, else the officer's safety would be placed at risk.[50] Plainly, this result is fully consistent with the intent of the Framers of the Fourth Amendment, who clearly had no purpose whatever to regulate such searches with a search warrant.

c. Automobile weapons search

There is, however, a special rule for the search of an automobile driver or passenger who has been temporarily detained. After a valid *Terry* stop of such an occupant, the police may search the passenger compartment [but not the trunk] of the automobile for weapons for their own self-protection and safety—provided there is reasonable suspicion that "the suspect is dangerous and ... may gain immediate control of weapons" that threaten the investigating officers; if weapons or contraband drugs are found during this search, the same may be seized under the "plain view" doctrine. There is, however, no *automatic* right to search an automobile during a valid temporary stop of the driver or other occupant—as indeed only a full custodial arrest may justify such a search, which, in itself, is limited in nature and is not automatic.[51]

---

50. "We do not retreat from our holdings that the police must, whenever practicable, obtain advance judicial approval of searches and seizures through the warrant procedure or that in most instances failure to comply with the warrant procedure can only be excused by exigent circumstances. But we deal with an entire rubric of police conduct—necessarily swift action predicated upon on-the-spot observations of an officer on the beat—which historically has not been, and as a practical matter could not be, subjected to the warrant procedure." Terry v. Ohio, 392 U.S. 1, 88 S.Ct. 1868, 20 L.Ed.2d 889, 905 (1968).

"The purpose of this limited [patdown] search is not to discover evidence of crime, but to allow the officer to pursue his investigation without fear of violence, and thus the frisk for weapons might be equally necessary and reasonable, whether or not carrying a concealed weapon violated any applicable state law." Adams v. Williams, 407 U.S. 143, 146, 92 S.Ct. 1921, 32 L.Ed.2d 612, 617 (1972).

51. "In Terry v. Ohio ... we upheld the validity of a protective search for weapons in the absence of probable cause to arrest because it is unreasonable to deny a police officer the right 'to neutralize the threat of physical harm,' when he possesses an articulable suspicion that an individual is armed and dangerous. We did not, however, expressly address whether such a protective search for weapons could extend to an area beyond the person in the absence of probable cause to arrest. In the present case, respondent David Long was convicted for possession of marijuana found by police in the passenger compartment and trunk of the automobile that he was driving. The police searched the passenger compartment because they had reason to believe that vehicle contained weapons dangerous to the officers. We hold that the protective search of the passenger compartment was reasonable under the principles articulated in Terry and other decisions of this Court. * * * These principles compel our conclusion that the search of the passenger compartment of an automobile, limited to those areas in which a weapon may be placed or hidden, is permissible if the police officer possesses a reasonable belief based on 'specific and articulable facts which, taken together with rational inferences from those facts, reasonably warrant' the officers in believing that the suspect is dangerous and the suspect may gain immediate control of weapons. [fn. 14].We stress that our decision does not mean that police may conduct automobile searches whenever they conduct an investigative stop, *although the 'bright*

Beyond that, there is no justification for conducting such a passenger compartment search in a routine traffic stop of a non-dangerous motorist to whom police issue a traffic ticket, but do not take into custody.[52] Moreover, after a valid *Terry* stop of a car, police may, without more, order the driver and occupants out of the car to complete the police investigation.[53]

Section 4. Moving Vehicle Exception: *Carroll* Doctrine

a. General rule

In the landmark case of *Carroll v. United States*,[54] the Court held that law enforcement officers may conduct a warrantless search of a moving vehicle, such as an automobile, if there is probable cause to believe that the vehicle contains (a) contraband, (b) fruits or instrumentalities of a crime, and, under a later ruling, (c) evidence of crime.[55] Two re-

---

line' we drew in Belton clearly authorizes such a search whenever officers effect a custodial arrest.] * * * If, while conducting a legitimate Terry search of the interior of the automobile, the officer should, as here, discover contraband other than weapons, he clearly cannot be required to ignore the contraband, and the Fourth Amendment does not require its suppression in such circumstances." Michigan v. Long, 463 U.S. 1032, 103 S.Ct. 3469, 77 L.Ed.2d 1201, 1210, 1220, n. 14 (1983) (citations omitted).

Belton, however, [as mentioned in the above italicized portion of the *Long* opinion] has since been modified to disallow automatic searches of the passenger compartment of autos after a lawful arrest of any occupant in the auto. "Accordingly, we ... hold that the *Chimel* rationale authorizes police to search a vehicle incident to a recent occupant's arrest only when the arrestee is unsecured and within the reaching distance of the passenger compartment.

"Although it does not follow from *Chimel*, we also conclude that circumstances unique to the vehicle context justifies a search incident to a lawful arrest when it is 'reasonable to believe evidence relevant to the crime of arrest might be found in the vehicle.' * * *

"Police may search a vehicle incident to a recent occupant's arrest only if the arrestee is within reaching distance of the passenger compartment at the time of the search or it is reasonable to believe the vehicle contains evidence of the offense of arrest."Arizona v. Gant, 556 U.S. 322, 129 S.Ct. 1710, 1719, 1723, 173 L.Ed.2d 485 (2009) (search of motor vehicle held not incident to traffic arrest of driver for driving with a suspended license; driver was handcuffed and placed in the back of police patrol car at time of arrest). See Section 2f of this Chapter for a discussion of the *Gant* decision and its retreat from the expansive *Belton* holding.

In *Long*, police stopped defendant who was driving his car at an excessive speed around midnight in a rural area and swerved into a ditch. Defendant appeared to be under the influence of something when police talked to defendant who was outside the car, as defendant did not respond to police questions. Defendant was about to re-enter his car, when police spotted a large hunting knife in the interior of the car. Police immediately patted defendant down, went into the interior of the car, looked under the arm rest, and found a pouch containing marijuana. The Court upheld this search on the basis that the police had a reasonable suspicion that the car contained weapons immediately dangerous to the officers, and that the marijuana was properly seized during the course of this search.

For lower federal and state court cases on this issue, see "Searches and Seizures" § 68 West Key No. See also Chapter 12, Section 2c of this work for a discussion of the "plain view" doctrine.

52. Knowles v. Iowa, 525 U.S. 113, 119 S.Ct. 484, 142 L.Ed.2d 492 (1998) (search of automobile "incident to a traffic citation" struck down).

53. Pennsylvania v. Mimms, 434 U.S. 106, 98 S.Ct. 330, 54 L.Ed.2d 331 (1977) (driver); Maryland v. Wilson, 137 L.Ed.2d 41 (1997) (passengers).

54. 267 U.S. 132, 45 S.Ct. 280, 69 L.Ed. 543 (1925). Remarkably, a Florida statute was shortly thereafter enacted adopting the entire *Carroll* opinion as the law of Florida on automobile searches. § 933.19, Fla. Stat.

55. Warden Md. Penitentiary v. Hayden, 387 U.S. 294, 87 S.Ct. 1642, 18 L.Ed.2d 782 (1967); see Chapter 11, Section 4d of this work.

quirements must be met for this exception to apply: (1) the moving vehicle must be mobile, i.e., operational, capable of being moved from the jurisdiction; and (2) there must be probable cause to believe that the vehicle contains contraband, evidence of crime or fruits or instrumentalities of a crime. It is unnecessary, however, to show that it was, in fact, impracticable to obtain a warrant for such a vehicle; no special exigency or emergency situation need be shown, as the vehicle's mobility itself supplies the exigency.[56] Where, however, a vehicle is not readily mobile at the time the police confront it, a subsequent search thereof, although based on probable cause, is unreasonable for lack of a valid search warrant—as, for example, where the vehicle is located at the suspect's home, and the suspect is otherwise in police custody with no one left at the home to remove the vehicle from the jurisdiction.[57]

As an aside, this exception necessarily presupposes that the police are in lawful possession of the moving vehicle that they search. Indeed, an illegal seizure of the moving vehicle is an independent Fourth Amendment violation, as it is an unreasonable seizure of a Fourth Amendment "effect." This may happen, for example, if police illegally stop a person who is driving a moving vehicle, in which event police have unreasonably seized both the person of the driver, and the moving vehicle. Such an unreasonable seizure will generally taint and render inadmissible the fruits thereof under the *Weeks-Mapp* exclusionary rule.[58] If that be the case, no other exceptions to the search warrant requirement rule need be examined, because the fruits of the search that follows the illegal seizure of the moving vehicle would on that account alone be barred from evidence.

b. Moving vehicles covered

Although most of the cases under the *Carroll* doctrine involve automobiles and at times refer to this exception as the "automobile" exception, the doctrine is applicable to any self-propelled vehicle—including a truck, a boat, an airplane and the like.[59] To be a

---

56. "The Fourth Amendment generally requires police to secure a warrant before conducting a search. As we recognized 75 years ago in Carroll v. United States..., there is an exception to this requirement for searches of vehicles. And under our established precedent the 'automobile exception' has no separate exigency requirement."Maryland v. Dyson, 527 U. S. 465, 119 S.Ct. 2013, 144 L.Ed.2d 442 (1999) (citations omitted) (search of automobile based on probable cause upheld, although it was arguably practicable for police to have obtained a warrant for the auto). "If a car is readily mobile and probable cause exists to believe it contains contraband, the Fourth Amendment thus permits police to search the vehicle without more." Pennsylvania v. Labron, 518 U.S. 938, 116 S.Ct. 2485, 135 L.Ed.2d 1031 (1996) (same holding as *Dyson*).

57. Coolidge v. New Hampshire, 403 U.S. 443, 458–64, 91 S.Ct. 2022, 29 L.Ed.2d 564, 576–581(1971) (Court struck down the search of an automobile, based on probable cause, for lack of a valid search warrant where (a) the automobile was located at the suspect's home; and (b) both the suspect [who had been cooperative with police in the past with respect to the murder being investigated] and his wife were removed by police from the scene—so that there was no one left with access to the auto; under these circumstances, especially where police had the suspect under surveillance for weeks, the Court concluded that a valid warrant was required for the search of the auto). "Neither Carroll, supra, nor other cases in this Court require or suggest that in every conceivable circumstance the search of an auto even with probable cause may be made without the extra protection for privacy that a warrant affords." Chambers v. Maroney, 399 U.S. 42, 50, 90 S.Ct. 1975, 26 L.Ed.2d 419, 428 (1970).

58. For a discussion of (1) unreasonable seizures of the person, see Chapter 12, Section 1, of this work; and (2) the evidentiary consequences thereof under the *Weeks-Mapp* exclusionary rule, see Chapter 17, Section 3 of this work.

59. See, e.g., United States v. Lee, 274 U.S. 559, 47 S.Ct. 746, 71 L.Ed. 1202 (1927); (warrantless search of a motorboat at sea based on probable cause upheld); 3 Wayne LaFave, Search and Seizure §7.2 at 721 n.2 (5th ed. 2012) and cases collected; "Searches and Seizures" §59 West Key No.

moving vehicle, the vehicle in question must be mobile or operational—that is, capable of being moved from place to place. Accordingly, a motorized mobile home operating on the public streets is covered by this exception, and is not entitled to Fourth Amendment protection as a home.[60]

c. Rationale for exception

The primary rationale for this exception is the moving vehicle's mobility which, by its very nature, makes it generally impracticable for police to obtain a warrant. As stated by the *Carroll* Court, "it is not practicable to secure a warrant because the vehicle can quickly be moved out of the locality or jurisdiction in which the warrant must be sought."[61]

There is also a second rationale for the rule: the reduced expectation of privacy in automobiles and other motor vehicles, as compared to a home or office. Due to the pervasive governmental regulation of such vehicles, the motoring public may reasonably expect to be stopped and their vehicle examined without a warrant for scheduled inspections, or for various equipment violations, or for improper operation of the vehicle, or if license plates or inspection stickers have expired. Accordingly, one's reasonable expectation of privacy in an automobile or like vehicle is clearly diminished as a result of this pervasive regulation, and warrants are ill-suited to carry out the purpose of such regulation.[62]

---

60. California v. Carney, 471 U.S. 386, 105 S.Ct. 2066, 85 L.Ed.2d 406 (1985).

61. Carroll v. United States, 267 U.S. 132, 153, 45 S.Ct. 280, 69 L.Ed. 543 (1925).

62. "However, although ready mobility alone was perhaps the original justification for the vehicle exception, our later cases have made clear that ready mobility is the not the only reason for the exception. The reasons for the vehicle exception, we have said are two-fold. 'Beside the element of mobility, less rigorous warrant requirements govern because the expectation of privacy in one's automobile is significantly less than that relating to one's home or office.' * * *

These reduced expectations of privacy derive ... from the pervasive regulation of vehicles capable of traveling on the public highways. As we explained in South Dakota v. Opperman..., an inventory search case:

Automobiles, unlike homes, are subjected to pervasive and continuing regulation and controls, including periodic inspection and licensing requirements. As an everyday occurrence, police stop and examine vehicles when license plates or inspection stickers have expired, or if other violations, such as exhaust fumes or excessive noise, are noted, or if headlights or other safety equipment are not in working order.

The public is fully aware that it is accorded less privacy in its automobile because of this compelling need for regulation. * * * In short, the pervasive schemes of regulation, which necessarily lead to reduced expectations of privacy, and the exigencies attendant to ready mobility justify searches without prior recourse to the authority of a magistrate so long as the overriding standard of probable cause is met."California v. Carney, 471 U.S. 386, 105 S.Ct. 2066, 85 L.Ed.2d 406, 413–14 (1985) (internal citations omitted).

"Our first cases establishing the automobile exception to the Fourth Amendment's warrant requirement were based on the automobile's 'ready mobility,' an exigency sufficient to excuse failure to obtain a search warrant once probable cause to conduct the search is clear. (citations omitted). More recent cases provide a further justification: the individual's reduced expectation of privacy in an automobile, owing to its pervasive regulation. (citation omitted). If a car is readily mobile and probable cause exists to believe it contains contraband, the Fourth Amendment permits police to search the vehicle without more. (citation omitted)." Pennsylvania v. Labron, 518 U.S. 938, 116 S.Ct. 2485, 135 L.Ed.2d 1031, 1035–36 (1996).

"There is still another distinguishing factor [underlying the *Carroll* doctrine]. 'The search of an automobile is far less intrusive on the rights protected by the Fourth Amendment than the search of one's person or of a building.' (citation omitted). One has a lesser expectation of privacy in a motor vehicle because its function is transportation and it seldom serves as one's residence or as the repository of personal effects. A car has little capacity for escaping public scrutiny. It travels public thoroughfares

d. Probable cause showings

The term "probable cause" has been traditionally defined as a practical, non-technical evidentiary showing of individualized wrongdoing that amounts to more than reasonable suspicion, but less than proof beyond a reasonable doubt.[63] In applying this highly flexible standard under the *Carroll* doctrine, the U.S. Supreme Court has given law enforcement officials wide-ranging, although not unlimited, authority to search moving vehicles without a warrant in fast-moving emergency encounters on the street while investigating felony offenses—especially crimes of violence, theft, narcotics,[64] and, at an earlier time in our history, contraband liquor.[65]

---

where its occupants and its contents are in plain view." Cardwell v. Lewis, 417 U.S. 583, 590, 94 S.Ct. 2464, 41 L.Ed.2d 325, 335 (1974).

63. Brinegar v. United States, 338 U.S. 160, 69 S.Ct. 1302, 93 L.Ed. 1879, 1890–91 (1949).

64. See, e.g., Chambers v. Maroney, 399 U.S. 42, 46–47, 90 S.Ct. 1975, 26 L.Ed.2d 419, 425–26 (1970) (police had probable cause to search an auto without a warrant when (a) they stopped an auto, on the public streets, that matched the witness' description of the getaway car (a green compact station wagon containing four men) in a service station robbery committed less than an hour before; (b) the auto contained four men, one wearing a green sweater, with a trench coat in the auto; and (c) the witnesses described one of the robbers as wearing a green sweater and the other as wearing a trench coat).

United States v. Johns, 469 U.S. 478, 105 S.Ct. 881, 83 L.Ed.2d 890 (1985) (US customs officials had probable cause to search two pickup trucks without a warrant when they (a) followed these trucks to a remote airstrip 50 miles from the US-Mexican border; (b) saw two airplanes land on the airstrip on two separate occasions during which one truck drove up to the airplane; and (c) approached the trucks, smelled an odor of marijuana coming from the trucks, and saw in open view in the back of the pickup trucks packages wrapped in dark green plastic and sealed with tape, packages that the agents knew from their prior experience are commonly used to smuggled marijuana; seizure of marijuana from these packages upheld).

Colorado v. Bannister, 449 U.S. 1, 101 S.Ct. 42, 66 L.Ed.2d 1 (1980) (police had probable cause to search auto without a warrant when they (a) lawfully stopped the auto on the public streets for speeding, (b) saw in open view while standing outside the auto(i) that the driver and his companion matched the description given in a radio dispatch report of persons suspected of stealing motor vehicle parts, and (ii) that certain auto lug nuts and wrenches were scattered throughout the auto; seizure of the lugnuts and wrenches upheld).

California v. Carney, 471 U.S. 386, 105 S.Ct. 2066, 85 L.Ed.2d 406 (1985) (state drug enforcement agents had probable cause to search mobile motor home in public parking lot when they (a)observed defendant and a companion enter defendant's mobile motor home on the streets where they remained for slightly over an hour, (b) questioned the companion when he left the motor home, and (c) the companion stated that he received marijuana from defendant in exchange for sexual favors, which corroborated information from another source that the motor home was being used to exchange marijuana for sex; seizure of marijuana from the motor home upheld).

New York v. Class, 475 U.S. 106, 106 S.Ct. 960, 89 L.Ed.2d 81 (1986) (police had probable cause to search auto without a warrant when they (a) lawfully stopped the auto on the public street for speeding and driving with a cracked windshield, and (b) saw the butt of a gun protruding from underneath the driver's seat in open view, while properly reaching into the auto to move papers from the dashboard to see the auto VIN no.; seizure of gun upheld).

The cases in the lower federal courts and state courts follow a similar pattern on this issue. "Searches and Seizures" § 62 West Key No.

65. See, e.g., Carroll v. United States, 267 U.S. 132, 45 S.Ct. 280, 69 L.Ed. 543 (1925) (federal alcohol agents had probable cause to search an auto without a warrant when they (a) saw the defendant driving an auto on a highway between Detroit and Grand Rapids, Michigan, a regular route for introducing illegal liquor into the U.S. from Canada; (b) recognized the defendant as a man with whom the agents in an undercover capacity had negotiated to buy illegal liquor about three months before, but which sale never materialized; (c) recognized the auto as the same auto the defendant was driving in the earlier aborted liquor sale; and (d) stopped the auto, searched it and seized 68 bottles

Only in a limited range of cases where, to the judicial mind, the law enforcement conduct smacks of police state tactics, or the individual's conduct is relatively innocuous or only slightly suspicious, has the Court been inclined to strike down such intrusions as not based on probable cause. Although admittedly the extent of the police power is great in this area, this by no means declares a field day for law enforcement officials to search moving vehicles on the street virtually at their discretion.[66] Indeed, to sanction such arbitrary conduct in the name of effective law enforcement would be contrary to one of the primary purposes of the Fourth Amendment—namely, to end the abuse of general exploratory searches by government officials, as wrought by the general writs of assistance regime 1761–76.[67]

e. Place for search of vehicle

If there is probable cause to search a moving vehicle located on the public streets, police may search the vehicle there, or may tow the vehicle to a more secure location,

---

of contraband liquor).

Brinegar v. United States, 338 U.S. 160, 165–171, 69 S.Ct. 1302, 93 L.Ed. 1879, 1885–88 (1949) (follows *Carroll* as being indistinguishable on the facts) (federal alcohol agents had probable cause to search an auto without a warrant when they (a) saw the defendant driving the auto which appeared to be heavily loaded; (b) the agent recognized the defendant (i) as a man the agent had arrested for transporting illegal liquor five months earlier, (ii) as a man the agent had seen loading liquor into a truck on two occasions in the area in the preceding six months, (c) saw the defendant proceeding on a highway that was a transport route for liquor from a "wet" state (Missouri) to a "dry" state (Okla.); (d) followed the defendant who thereupon sped up his auto and attempted to evade the agent in a high-speed chase; and (e) finally stopped the auto, searched it and seized 13 cases of contraband liquor).

Scher v. United States, 305 U.S. 251, 59 S.Ct.174, 83 L.Ed. 151 (1938) (federal alcohol agents had probable cause to search an auto without a warrant when they (a) received information from an informant that at a particular time and place a Dodge auto with described license plates would transport contraband whiskey from a specified dwelling; (b) went to the described location and saw the described auto; (c) heard, from their vantage point, what seemed to be heavy paper packages passing over wood near the auto, and auto doors slamming; (d) followed the auto driven by the defendant to an open garage of a defendant's residence; (e) got out of their car, confronted the defendant, identified themselves, and stated that they had information that the auto contained bootleg liquor, to which the defendant replied that it was "just a little for a party"; and (f) opened the trunk of the auto and seized 88 bottles of contraband liquor).

Husty v. United States, 282 U.S. 694, 51 S.Ct. 240, 75 L.Ed. 629 (1931) (federal alcohol agents had probable cause to search an auto when they (a) received information from an informant, who had given them reliable information in the past, that defendant had contraband liquor in two described autos at a particular location; (b) were familiar with the defendant as he had two prior convictions for violations of the Prohibition Act; (c) went to the location described by the informant and saw one of the described autos parked on the public street; (d) observed the defendant and companions enter the auto and drive off; and (e) stopped the auto, searched it and seized 18 cases of contraband whiskey).

See also: United States v. Lee, 274 U.S. 559, 47 S.Ct. 746, 71 L.Ed. 1202 (1927) (U.S. Coast Guard officer in patrol boat shined a searchlight on a motorboat at sea and observed numerous cases of contraband liquor on the deck of the motorboat, thereby giving the officer probable cause to board the motorboat and seize the liquor.

66. "[T]he Carroll doctrine does not declare a field day for the police in searching automobiles. Automobile or no automobile, there must be probable cause for the search." Almeida-Sanchez v. United States, 413 U.S. 266, 269, 93 S.Ct. 2535, 37 L.Ed.2d 596, 600–01 (1973) (operating an automobile near the U.S.-Mexican border insufficient basis for roving border patrol to search the auto for illegal aliens); Ortiz v. United States, 422 U.S. 891, 95 S.Ct. 2585, 45 L.Ed.2d 623 (1975) (traveling by automobile through a border patrol traffic checkpoint near the U.S.-Mexican border insufficient basis to search the auto for illegal aliens).

67. See Chapter 6, Section 2 of this work.

such as a police station, and search the vehicle there; in either event, a search warrant need not be obtained.[68] If the vehicle is towed to the more secure location, the search need not take place immediately and may be accomplished at a later time, although the search cannot be postponed indefinitely.[69] Moreover, a moving vehicle may be seized from a public place if police have probable cause to believe that the vehicle is forfeitable contraband under a state or federal statute—for example, if the vehicle is being used to deliver illegal drugs—and thereafter the automobile may be inventoried at another more secure location.[70] Finally, law enforcement agents, in pursuit of an automobile that the agents have probable cause to search, may follow the auto to an open garage at a private residence and search the auto there, although not the garage itself.[71]

f. Scope of vehicle search: containers and passengers

Where there is probable cause to believe that a moving vehicle contains contraband or fruits or instrumentalities of a crime or evidence of crime, all areas within the vehicle may be searched, so long as the object of the search may reasonably be found in those areas—including all containers therein.[72] This rule extends to containers that belong not only to the driver, but to all passengers in the motor vehicle—such as a purse left on a

---

68. Chambers v. Maroney, 399 U.S. 42, 90 S.Ct. 1975, 26 L.Ed.2d 419 (1970); Florida v. Meyers, 466 U.S. 380, 104 S.Ct. 1852, 80 L.Ed.2d 381 (1984). "[I]t is axiomatic that 'searches conducted outside the judicial process, without prior approval by judge or magistrate, are per se unreasonable under the Fourth Amendment—subject only to a few specifically well-established and well-delineated exceptions.' One of these exceptions recognized at least since Carroll v. United States ... exists when an automobile or other vehicle is stopped and the police have probable cause to believe it contains evidence of crime. Carroll upheld the legality of a search that was conducted immediately after the stop. Since Carroll, warrantless searches have been found permissible even when the car was searched and after being seized and moved to the police station. In each of these latter cases, the search was constitutionally permissible because an immediate on-the-scene search would have been permissible." Colorado v. Bannister, 449 U.S. 1, 101 S.Ct. 42, 66 L.Ed.2d 1, 3–4 (1980).

69. United States v. Johns, 469 U.S. 478, 105 S.Ct. 881, 83 L.Ed.2d 890, 896–99 (1985) (3-day delay in search of packages taken from pickup trucks towed to DEA headquarters upheld).

70. Florida v. White, 526 U.S. 559, 119 S.Ct. 1555, 143 L.Ed.2d 748 (1999) (car seized from parking lot at defendant's place of employment after the defendant was arrested there; police had previously seen the defendant using car to deliver cocaine; later inventory search of car found crack cocaine in car ashtray; held: reasonable seizure of the car, thereby sustaining the later search, based on principles of *Carroll* and founding era statutes).

71. Scher v. United States, 305 U.S. 251, 59 S.Ct.174, 83 L.Ed. 151 (1938)

72. United States v. Ross, 456 U.S. 798, 102 S.Ct. 2157, 72 L.Ed.2d 572 (1982) [overruling Robbins v. California, 453 U.S. 420, 101 S.Ct. 2841, 69 L.Ed.2d 744 (1981)] (probable cause that defendant was selling narcotics out of the trunk of his car and had narcotics in the car justified a warrantless search of paper bag and zippered leather pouch found in trunk of car); Michigan v. Thomas, 458 U.S. 259, 102 S.Ct. 3079, 73 L.Ed.2d 750 (1982) (probable cause that car contained marijuana justified search of the air vents under the car dashboard, as marijuana might be hidden there; revolver discovered in air vents properly seized).

"We hold that the scope of the warrantless search authorized by that exception [the *Carroll* moving vehicle exception] is no broader and no narrower than a magistrate could legitimately authorize by warrant. If probable cause justifies the search of a lawfully stopped vehicle, it justifies the search of every part of the vehicle and its contents that may conceal the object of the search." United States v. Ross, 456 U.S. 798, 102 S.Ct. 2157, 72 L.Ed.2d 572, 594 (1982).

"Just as probable cause to believe that a stolen lawnmower may be found in a garage will not support a warrant to search an upstairs bedroom, probable cause to believe that undocumented aliens are being transported in a van will not justify a warrantless search of a suitcase. Probable cause to believe that a container placed in the trunk of a taxi contains contraband does not justify a search of the entire cab." United States v. Ross, 456 U.S. 798, 824, 102 S.Ct. 2157, 72 L.Ed.2d 572, 593 (1982).

car seat.[73] On the other hand, where there is probable cause to believe that only a container located in a motor vehicle has contraband or evidence of crime therein [but no probable cause to believe that the rest of the vehicle contains contraband or evidence of crime], the container [but not the entire vehicle] may be searched without a warrant.[74] Also, this exception does not, without more, confer a right on law enforcement officers to search the person of a passenger in the automobile.[75]

g. "Plain view" seizure of evidence

During an otherwise proper *Carroll* moving vehicle search as thus defined, law enforcement officers are privileged to seize any physical evidence under the "plain view" doctrine if there is probable cause to believe that this evidence constitutes contraband, fruits or instrumentalities of a crime, or evidence of a crime—whether such objects are related or unrelated to the probable cause that justified the search in the first instance.[76]

Section 5. Consent Search

a. General rule of voluntariness

Under the consent exception to the search warrant requirement rule, law enforcement officers may search private premises and other protected property or an individual's person without a warrant—provided the individual whose property or person is searched, freely

---

For lower federal and state court cases on this point of law, see "Searches and Seizures" § 65 West Key No.

73. "We hold that police officers with probable cause to search a car may inspect passengers' belongings found in the car that are capable of concealing the object of the search." Wyoming v. Houghton, 119 S.Ct. 1297, 1304 (1999) (police, with probable cause to search car for illegal drugs, could search passenger's purse left on front seat of car).

74. "The Court in *Ross* put it this way: 'The scope of a warrantless search of a vehicle ... is not determined by the nature of the container in which the contraband is secreted. Rather it is defined by the object of the search and the places in which there is probable cause to believe it may be found.' It went on to note: 'Probable cause to believe that a container placed in the trunk of a taxi contains contraband or evidence does not justify a search of the entire cab.' We reaffirm that principle. In the case before us, the police had probable cause to believe that the paper bag in the automobile trunk contained marijuana. That probable cause now allows a warrantless search of the paper bag. The facts in the record reveal that the police did not have probable cause to believe that contraband was hidden in any other part of the automobile and a search of the entire vehicle would have been without probable cause and unreasonable under the Fourth Amendment." California v. Acevedo, 500 U.S. 565, 111 S.Ct. 1982, 114 L.Ed.2d 619, 634 (1991)

Acevedo overruled the results reached and rationale of *United States v. Chadwick*, 433 U.S. 1, 97 S.Ct 2476, 61 L.Ed.2d 538 (1977) (footlocker in trunk of car searched; probable cause that footlocker contained marijuana; search held invalid because conducted without a warrant); and Arkansas v. Sanders, 442 U.S. 753, 99 S.Ct. 2586, 61 L.Ed.2d 235 (1979) (same result for search of suitcase in taxicab). Under *Acevedo*, the footlocker in *Chadwick* and the suitcase in *Sanders* could be searched without a warrant, but not the entire vehicle.

75. United States v. Di Re, 332 U.S. 581, 583–87, 68 S.Ct. 222, 92 L.Ed. 210, 214–16 (1948). "United States v. Di Re ... held that probable cause to search a car did not justify a body search of a passenger." Wyoming v. Houghton, 526 U.S. 295, 119 S.Ct. 1297, 1302, 143 L.Ed.2d 408 (1999).

76. See Chapter 12, Section 2c of this work for a discussion of the "plain view" doctrine.

and voluntarily consents to the search, and is not coerced, either expressly or impliedly, into giving such consent.[77] The prosecution has the burden to show by a preponderance of the evidence that the consent was freely and voluntarily given.[78]

A voluntary consent search is an important tool in the arsenal of law enforcement officers, and is often used in investigating crime where no probable cause for a given search otherwise exists.[79] Moreover, an individual as a good citizen may very well want to cooperate with the police by consenting to a search of one's premises, so as to dispel any unfounded suspicions and to help the police apprehend a third party. To require a search warrant in these circumstances would be completely unreasonable.[80]

---

77. "It is well settled under the Fourth and Fourteenth Amendments that a search conducted without a warrant issued upon probable cause is 'per se unreasonable ... subject only to a few specifically established and well-delineated exceptions.' It is equally well-settled that one of the specifically established exceptions to the requirements of both a warrant and probable cause is a search that is conducted pursuant to consent. * * *

But the Fourth and Fourteenth Amendments require that a consent [to search] not be coerced, by explicit or implicit means, by implied threat or covert force.* * *

We hold only that when the subject of a search is not in custody and the State attempts to justify a search on the basis of his consent, the Fourth and Fourteenth Amendments require that it demonstrate that consent was in fact voluntarily given and not the result of duress or coercion, express or implied." Schneckloth v. Bustamonte, 412 U.S. 218, 93 S.Ct. 2041, 36 L.Ed.2d 858, 863, 875 (1973) (defendant's consent for police to search his car held voluntary); see United States v. Watson, 423 U.S. 411, 96 S.Ct. 820, 46 L.Ed.2d 598, 609 (1976) (rule of *Schneckloth* extended to a defendant in police custody; consent search of car upheld).

78. "When a prosecutor seeks to rely on consent to justify the lawfulness of a search, he [or she] has the burden of proving that the consent was, in fact, freely and voluntarily given." Bumper v. North Carolina, 391 U.S. 543, 88 S.Ct. 1788, 20 L.Ed.2d 797, 802 (1968). "In any event, the controlling burden of proof at suppression hearings [on the consent issue] should impose no greater burden than proof by a preponderance of the evidence." United States v. Matlock, 415 U.S. 164, 94 S.Ct. 988, 39 L.Ed.2d 242, 253, n. 14 (1974).

79. "In situations where the police have some evidence of illicit activity, but lack probable cause to arrest or search, a search authorized by valid consent may be the only means of obtaining important and reliable evidence."

"Consent searches are part of the standard investigatory techniques of law enforcement agencies. They normally occur on a highway, or in a person's home or office, and under informal and unstructured conditions. The circumstances that prompt the initial request to search may develop quickly or be a logical extension of investigative police questioning." Schneckloth v. Bustamonte, 412 U.S. 218, 227, 231–32, 93 S.Ct. 2041, 36 L.Ed.2d 854, 863, 865 (1973).

"The so-called consent search is frequently relied upon by police as a means of investigating suspected criminal conduct." 4 Wayne LaFave, Search and Seizure § 8.1 at 2 (5th ed. 2012).

80. "It would be unreasonable—indeed, absurd—to require police officers to obtain a warrant when the sole owner or occupant of a house or apartment voluntarily consents to a search. The owner of a home has a right to allow others to enter and examine the premises, and there is no reason why the owner should not be permitted to extend the same privilege to police officers if that is the owner's choice. Where the owner believes that he or she is under suspicion, the owner may want the police to search the premises so that their suspicions are dispelled. This may be particularly important where the owner has a strong interest in the apprehension of the perpetrator of a crime and believes that the suspicions of the police are deflecting the course of their investigation. The owner may want the police to search even when they lack probable cause, and if a warrant were always required, this could not be done. And even if the police could establish probable cause, requiring a warrant despite the owner's consent would needlessly inconvenience everyone involved—not only the officers and the magistrate but also the occupant of the premises, who would generally either be compelled or would feel a need to stay until the search was completed." Fernandez v. California, 571 U.S. ___, 134 S.Ct. 1126, 1132, 188 L.Ed2d 25 (2014).

Voluntariness, in turn, is a question of fact to be determined based on the totality of the circumstances of the case,[81] which means that the same factors that go into determining whether a confession is voluntary are equally applicable in a consent search case.[82] Accordingly, the following factors are important in determining whether a consent to search was given voluntarily: the accused's youth, lack of education, or low intelligence; the lack of any advice to the accused of his or her constitutional rights; the length of the detention; the repeated and prolonged nature of the questioning; and the use of physical punishment such as deprivation of food or sleep.[83] Law enforcement officers, however, are not required to give *Miranda*-like advice that the suspect has a right to refuse to give such consent—before asking the suspect for a consent to search, although this is a factor to be considered in determining whether the consent is voluntary based on the totality of the circumstances.[84] Nor are such officials required to advise a suspect that the suspect is free to go, if not in custody, before obtaining a consent to search.[85]

b. Application of general rule

Ordinarily, absent unusual circumstances, a verbal consent given by a person to search private premises or property upon a simple request by the police is routinely upheld by the courts as voluntarily given.[86] Indeed, most consents to search are given promptly and voluntarily on the street, and are not the product of custodial or even extended police

---

81. "[T]he question whether a consent to search was in fact 'voluntary' or was the product of duress or coercion, express or implied, is a question of fact to be determined from the totality of all the circumstances." Schneckloth v. Bustamonte, 412 U.S. 218, 227, 93 S.Ct. 2041, 36 L.Ed.2d 854, 862–863 (1973). "The Fourth Amendment test for a valid consent to search is that the consent be voluntary, and '[v]oluntariness is a question of fact to be determined from all the circumstances.'" Ohio v. Robinette, 519 U.S. 33, 117 S.Ct. 417, 136 L.Ed.2d 347, 355 (1996) (citation omitted).

82. Schneckloth v. Bustamonte, 412 U.S. 218, 223–227, 93 S.Ct. 2041, 36 L.Ed.2d 854, 860–862 (1973).

83. Schneckloth v. Bustamonte, 412 U.S. 218, 223–227, 229, 248, 93 S.Ct. 2041, 36 L.Ed.2d 854, 860–862, 864, 875 (1973). For an extensive discussion of the factors that bear upon the voluntariness of a consent search, see 4 Wayne LaFave, Search and Seizure § 8.2 at 65–187 (5th ed. 2012).

84. "Voluntariness is a question of fact to be determined under all the circumstances, and while the subject's knowledge of a right to refuse [consent] is a factor to be taken into account, the prosecution is not required to demonstrate such knowledge as a prerequisite to establishing voluntary consent." Schneckloth v. Bustamonte, 412 U.S. 218, 248–49, 93 S.Ct. 2041, 36 L.Ed.2d 854, 875 (1973) (defendant's consent for police to search his car after a traffic stop held voluntary, although police did not advise defendant that he had a right to refuse such consent); United States v. Drayton, 536 U.S. 194, 122 S.Ct. 2105, 153 L.Ed.2d 242 (2002) (defendant's consent to search his person while aboard as a passenger on an interstate commercial bus held voluntary, although police did not advise defendant of his right to refuse such consent).

85. Ohio v. Robinette, 519 U.S. 33, 117 S.Ct. 417, 136 L.Ed.2d 347 (1996) (consent upheld to search a detained motorist's automobile).

86. See, e.g., United States v. Watson, 423 U.S. 411, 424–25, 96 S.Ct. 820, 46 L.Ed.2d 598, 609 (1976) ("There was no overt act or threat of force against Watson proved or claimed. There were no promises made to him and no indication of more subtle forms of coercion that might flaw his judgment. He had been arrested and was in custody, but his consent was given while on the public street, not in the confines of the police station.") (consent given to U.S. Border Patrol to search pickup truck held voluntarily given, absent any evidence of coercion).

For lower federal and state court cases on the voluntariness of consents to search as well as words or conduct expressing consent or mere acquiescence to authority, see "Searches and Seizures" §§ 172, 179.1, 180, 181 West Key Nos.

questioning. Moreover, the fact that the person consenting to the search is in police custody at the time consent is given does not in itself make the consent involuntary.[87] But a consent to search is generally considered involuntary when given while the suspect is *unlawfully* in police custody, as the consent is generally tainted by the prior unreasonable seizure of the suspect's person.[88]

Beyond that, a submission to a police claim of lawful authority to conduct a given search does not constitute a voluntary consent to search.[89] Accordingly, a consent to search is generally considered involuntary, and the search unreasonable, when given in response (a) to a police announcement that the officers have come to search the suspect's premises,[90] or (b) to a police demand for entry onto private premises;[91] or (c) to a police assertion that they have a search warrant for the search of the suspect's premises, and the warrant later turns out to be invalid or nonexistent.[92] In each of these situations, the consent given

87. United States v. Watson, 423 U.S. 411, 96 S.Ct. 820, 46 L.Ed.2d 598, 609 (1976); see 4 Wayne LaFave, Search and Seizure § 8.2 at 65–187 (5th ed. 2012) for a comprehensive discussion of the relevant factors in determining whether a given consent to search has been freely and voluntarily given.

88. Florida v. Royer, 460 U.S. 491, 103 S.Ct. 1319, 75 L.Ed.2d 229, 242–43 (1983) (consent to search suitcase held tainted and involuntary after defendant was subjected to a functional arrest in police interrogation room at airport based on no probable cause; Court concluded that the consent was "tainted by the illegality and was ineffective to justify the search." 75 L.Ed.2d at 243). See cases collected at "Searches and Seizures" § 184 West Key No.

"Similarly, officers may seek consent-based encounters *if they are lawfully present in the place where the consensual encounter occurs.* If consent is freely given, it makes no difference that an officer may have approached the person with the hope or expectation of obtaining consent." Kentucky v. King, 563 U.S. ___, 131 S.Ct. 1849, 1858, 179 L.Ed.2d 865 (2011) (internal citations omitted) (italics added).

89. "Conversely, if under all the circumstances it has appeared that the consent was not given voluntarily—that it was coerced by threats or force, or granted only in a submission to a claim of lawful authority—then we have found the consent invalid and the search unreasonable." Schneckloth v. Bustamonte, 412 U.S. 218, 233, 93 S.Ct. 2041, 36 L.Ed.2d 854, 866 (1973). "[W]here the validity of a search rests on consent, the State has the burden of proving that the necessary consent was obtained and that it was freely and voluntarily given, a burden that is not satisfied by showing a mere submission to a claim of authority." Florida v. Royer, 460 U.S. 491, 497, 103 S.Ct. 1319, 75 L.Ed.2d 229, 236 (1983).

90. Amos v. United States, 255 U.S. 313, 41 S.Ct. 266, 65 L.Ed. 654 (1921) (consent held coerced when federal agents told defendant's wife that they had come to search the premises, and she opened the door to let the agents in).

91. Johnson v. United States, 333 U.S. 10, 68 S.Ct. 367, 92 L.Ed. 436 (1948) (police officer smelled opium coming from defendant's hotel room; officer knocked on door, identified himself as a police officer and said he wanted to talk to her; defendant opened the door and let the officer in). "Entry to defendant's living quarters, which was the beginning of the search, was demanded under color of office. It was granted in submission to authority rather than as an understanding and intentional waiver of a constitutional right." 92 L.Ed. at 440.

92. "The issue thus presented is whether a search can be justified as lawful when that 'consent' has been given after the official conducting the search has asserted that he possesses a warrant. We hold that there can be no consent under such circumstances. * * * This burden [of the state to show voluntary consent to search] cannot be discharged by showing no more than acquiescence to a claim of lawful authority. A search conducted in reliance upon a warrant cannot later be justified on the basis of consent if it turns out that the warrant was invalid. The result can be no different when it turns out that the State did not even attempt to rely on the validity of the warrant or fails to show that there was, in fact, any warrant at all." Bumper v. North Carolina, 391 U.S. 543, 88 S.Ct. 1788, 20 L.Ed.2d 797, 803–04 (1968). (third party consent of defendant's grandmother to search house where defendant and grandmother lived was held involuntary; police announced, "I have a search warrant to search your house," and the grandmother responded, "Go ahead;" at the motion to suppress hearing, state did not rely on the warrant to justify the search).

constitutes an acquiescence to a preceding assertion of police authority—and is generally considered coerced.[93] On the other hand, if the police announcement in each of these situations is entirely supportable—and police otherwise have a legal right to enter the premises because they have a valid search warrant or are operating under an applicable exception to the search warrant requirement rule other than consent—the search is considered reasonable based on the warrant or the relevant warrant exception, but not under the consent exception.[94]

c. Third-party consent

It is settled that a joint occupant of private premises or property may give the police voluntary consent to search such premises or property—as against the absent, nonconsenting co-occupant.[95] Even where the ostensible joint occupant is later determined *not* to be a joint occupant, the search may nonetheless be upheld as based on voluntary consent if the asserted joint occupant had *apparent* authority to given such consent—

Lo-Ji Sales, Inc. v. New York, 442 U.S. 319, 99 S.Ct. 2319, 60 L.Ed.2d 920, 930 (1979) (adult book store clerk cooperates with police after being placed under arrest at store and told that police have a search warrant which turns out to be invalid; held: involuntary consent).

93. See cases collected at "Searches and Seizures" § 182 West Key No. But see 4 Wayne LaFave, Search and Seizure § 8.2(a) at 74–75 (5th ed. 2012) for a discussion of whether additional circumstances in the case might make the consent voluntary, notwithstanding a prior unsupportable police claim of a lawful authority to search.

94. United States v. Biswell, 406 U.S. 311, 92 S.Ct. 1593, 32 L.Ed.2d 87 (1972) (federal treasury agent conducted a proper administrative inspection without a warrant of a locked storeroom in a pawnshop pursuant to the federal Gun Control Act of 1968; the search was expressly *not* upheld based on consent when the pawnshop owner agreed to the search after the agent asserted a right to inspect the storeroom without a warrant pursuant to the said Act, and showed a copy of the Act to the pawnshop owner). "Respondent's submission to lawful authority and his decision to step aside and permit the inspection rather than force a criminal prosecution is analogous to a householder's acquiescence in a search pursuant to a warrant when the alternative is a possible criminal prosecution for refusing entry or a forcible entry. In neither case does the lawfulness of the search depend upon consent; in both, there is lawful authority independent of the will of the householder who might, other things being equal, prefer no search at all." 32 L.Ed.2d at 91–92.

95. "It has been assumed by the parties and the courts below that the voluntary consent of any joint occupant of a residence to search the premises jointly occupied is valid against the co-occupant, permitting evidence discovered in the search to be used against him at a criminal trial. * * * [M]ore recent authority here clearly indicates that the consent of one who possesses common authority over the premises or effects is valid as against the absent, nonconsenting person with whom that authority is shared. * * * These cases at least make clear that when the prosecution seeks to justify a warrantless search by proof of voluntary consent, it is not limited to proof that consent was given by the defendant, but may show permission from a third party who possessed common authority over or other sufficient relationship to the premises or effects sought to be inspected. * * * Common authority, is, of course, not to be implied from the mere property interest a third party has in the premises. The authority which justifies the third-party consent does not rest upon the law of property, with its attendant historical and legal refinements, but rests rather on mutual use of the property by persons generally having joint access or control for most purposes, so that it is reasonable to recognize that any of the co-habitants has the right to permit the inspection in his own right and that the others have assumed the risk that one of their number might permit the common area to be searched." United States v. Matlock, 415 U.S. 164, 94 S.Ct. 988, 39 L.Ed.2d 242, 248, 249, 250, n. 7 (1974) (internal citations omitted). For an extensive discussion of the subject of third party consent, 4 Wayne LaFave, Search and Seizure §§ 8.3–8.6 (5th ed. 2012). Also see cases collected at "Searches and Seizures" § 177 West Key No.

that is, if based on all the circumstances, the law enforcement officers reasonably believed at the time of the search that such person was, in fact, a joint occupant of the premises.[96]

Certain people, however, do not as a matter of law possess joint control over another's premises and cannot give consent to search such premises. For example, a landlord of a rented house generally has no authority to consent to a police search of his tenant's house.[97] Similarly, a hotel clerk generally has no authority to consent to the police search of a guest's room.[98] On the other hand, when a man and woman are living together, either as man and wife or outside of matrimony, either may consent to a police search of the premises where they live.[99] And a person in possession of a container, such as a duffel bag, that has been entrusted to him or her by the owner may consent to a search of the container.[100]

On the other hand, a warrantless search by law enforcement officers of private premises shared by two occupants—where one occupant consents to the search, but a co-occupant expressly objects to the search and is *physically-present* on the premises—cannot be justified under the consent exception to the search warrant requirement rule and, therefore, without more, is unreasonable under the Fourth Amendment as to the non-consenting co-occupant.[101] But where one occupant objects to the search but is *lawfully* detained or

---

96. Illinois v. Rodriguez, 497 U.S. 177, 110 S.Ct. 2793, 111 L.Ed.2d 148 1990).

"To the Fourth Amendment rule ordinarily prohibiting the warrantless entry of a person's house as unreasonable *per se*, one 'jealously and carefully drawn' exception recognizes the validity of searches with the voluntary consent of an individual possessing authority. That person might be the householder against whom evidence is sought, or a fellow occupant who shares common authority over property, when the suspect is absent, and the exception for consent extends even to entries and searches with the permission of a co-occupant whom the police reasonably, but erroneously, believe to possess shared authority as an occupant. [citation omitted]." Georgia v. Randolph, 547 U.S. 103, 126 S.Ct. 1515, 1520, 164 L.Ed.2d 208 (2006) (internal citations omitted).

97. Chapman v. United States, 365 U.S. 610, 81 S.Ct.776, 5 L.Ed.2d 828 (1961). Also see cases collected at "Searches and Seizures" § 175 West Key No. "A person on the scene who identifies himself, say, as a landlord or hotel manager calls up no customary understanding of authority to admit guests without the consent of the current occupant. A tenant in the ordinary course does not take rented premises subject to any formal or informal agreement that the landlord may let visitors into the dwelling, and a hotel guest customarily has no reason to expect the manager to allow anyone but his own employees into the room. In these circumstances, neither state-law property rights, nor common contractual arrangements, nor any other source points to a common understanding of authority to admit third parties generally without the consent of a person occupying the premises." Georgia v. Randolph, 547 U.S. 103, 126 S.Ct. 1515, 1522, 164 L.Ed.2d 208 (2006) (internal citations omitted).

98. Stoner v. California, 376 U.S. 483, 84 S.Ct. 889, 11 L.Ed.2d 856 (1964). Also see cases collected at "Searches and Seizures" § 176 West Key No.

99. United States v. Matlock, 415 U.S. 164, 94 S.Ct. 988, 39 L.Ed.2d 242, 248–49 (1974) (girl friend may give consent to search of room where she and her boy friend live); see also Illinois v. Rodriguez, 497 U.S. 177, 110 S.Ct. 2793, 111 L.Ed.2d 148 (1990) (same result where it reasonably appeared to police that girl friend was living on premises, even though she was not). For cases involving consents to search given by family members, see "Search and Seizure" § 178 West Key No.

100. Frazier v. Cupp, 394 U.S. 731, 89 S.Ct. 1420, 22 L.Ed.2d 684 (1969).

101. "The Fourth Amendment recognizes a valid warrantless entry and search of premises when police obtain the voluntary consent of an occupant who shares, or is reasonably believed to share, authority over the area in common with a co-occupant who later objects to the use of the evidence so obtained. [citations omitted]. The question here is whether such an evidentiary seizure is likewise lawful with the permission of one occupant when the other, who later seeks to suppress the evidence, is present at the scene and expressly refuses to consent. We hold that, in the circumstances here at issue, a physically present co-occupant's stated refusal to permit entry prevails, rendering the warrantless search unreasonable and invalid as to him." * * * "We therefore hold that a warrantless search of a shared dwelling for evidence over the express refusal of consent by a physically present resident cannot be justified as reasonable as to him on the basis of consent given by the other resident." Georgia v. Randolph, 547 U.S. 103, 126 S.Ct. 1515, 1518–19, 1526, 164 L.Ed.2d 208 (2006) (search of marital

arrested and removed from the scene, the remaining occupant may later give consent to a police search of the premises—although such consent would be insufficient if the initial removal of the objecting occupant were not otherwise reasonable.[102]

---

home with consent of wife, but over the express objection of husband held a violation of husband's Fourth Amendment rights).

The Court notes, however, that a different result would obtain if the *exigent circumstances exception* to the search warrant requirement rule is shown. See Sec. 6, infra, of this chapter. For example, where the circumstances show that it is reasonably necessary to protect a resident from domestic violence, "it would be silly to suggest that the police would commit a tort by entering, say, to give a complaining tenant the opportunity to collect belongings and get out safely, or to determine whether violence (or threat of violence) has just occurred or is about to (or is soon to), however much a spouse or other co-tenant objected." 126 S.Ct. at 1525. "Sometimes, of course, the very exchange of information like this in front of the objecting inhabitant may render consent irrelevant by creating an exigency that justifies immediate action on the police's part: if the objecting tenant cannot be incapacitated from destroying easily disposable evidence during the time required to get a warrant. [citations omitted], a fairly perceived need to act on the spot to preserve evidence may justify entry and search under the exigent circumstances exception to the warrant requirement." 126 S.Ct. at 1524, n.6. But the state does not argue that the exigent circumstances exception was applicable in this case. 126 S.Ct. at 1528.

The Court also notes that "[t]he co-tenant acting on his own initiative may be able to deliver evidence to the police [citation omitted], and can tell the police what he knows, for use before a magistrate in getting a warrant." 126 S.Ct. 1524.

102. Fernandez v. California, 571 U.S. ___, 134 S.Ct. 1126, 188 L.Ed.2d 25 (2014) (police investigate a possible gang-related attack on a man in the street; they are led by the assault victim to an apartment where one of the attackers might be located; police hear sounds of screaming and fighting inside the apartment; police knock on the door and a woman crying and carrying a baby appears; she shows signs of having been beaten up; police tell the woman to step outside the apartment as they want to do a sweep of the premises; petitioner appears and says: "You don't have any right to come in here; I know my rights"; police physically remove petitioner from the apartment and place him under arrest; one hour later, police return to the apartment and obtain consent from the woman living there to search the apartment; in the apartment, police find and seize gang paraphernalia, a butterfly knife, ammunition and a sawed-off shotgun; held the search was reasonable under the Fourth Amendment as it was conducted with valid consent).

"Our cases firmly establish that police officers may search jointly occupied premises if one of the occupants consents. In Georgia v. Randolph..., we recognized a narrow exception to this rule, holding that the consent of one occupant is insufficient when another occupant is present and objects to the search. In this case, we consider whether Randolph applies if the objecting person is absent when another consents. Our opinion in Randolph took great pains to emphasize that its holding was limited to situations in which the objecting occupant is physically present. We therefore refuse to extend Randolph to the very different situation in this case, where consent was provided by an abused woman after her male partner had been removed from the apartment they shared." Fernandez v. California. 134 S.Ct. at 1129–1130 (internal citations omitted).

"We therefore hold that an occupant who is absent due to a lawful detention or arrest stands in the same shoes as an occupant who is absent for any other reason." Fernandez v. California. 134 S.Ct. at 1134.

"In Randolph, the Court suggested in dictum that consent by one occupant might not be sufficient if 'there is evidence that the police have removed the potentially objecting tenant from the entrance for the sake of avoiding a possible objection.' 547 U.S. at 121. We do not believe the statement should be read to suggest that improper motive may invalidate objectively justified removal. Hence it does not govern here.

The Randolph dictum is best understood not to require an inquiry into the subjective intent of officers who detain or arrest a potential objector but instead to refer to situations in which the removal of the potential objector is not objectively reasonable." Fernandez v. California. 134 S.Ct. at1134–1135.

Moreover, a young child living in a home with his parents may have the power to admit police to the common areas of the home, but would have no authority to consent to a police search of his parents' bedroom.[103]

d. Scope of consent search

In measuring the scope of a suspect's consent to search certain premises or property, the test is one of objective reasonableness: what would a reasonable person have understood by the exchange between the police and the consenting party as to what physical area the police could search?[104] Where a suspect gives a voluntary general consent to search his or her automobile, law enforcement officers may search the interior of the automobile and all unlocked containers therein, provided the evidence police say they are looking for can reasonably be found in these areas—but apparently may not search locked containers such as a locked briefcase without express consent to do so.[105] Moreover, the consenting party may expressly limit the areas on the premises that the police may search.[106]

e. "Plain view" seizure of evidence

During an otherwise voluntary consent search, law enforcement officers are privileged to seize any physical evidence under the "plain view" doctrine if there is probable cause to believe that this evidence constitutes contraband, fruits or instrumentalities of a crime, or evidence of a crime—whether such objects are related or unrelated to the evidence that the officers were looking for.[107]

---

103. "[A] child of eight might well be considered to have the power to consent to the police crossing the threshold into that part of the house where any caller, such as a pollster or salesman, might well be admitted, but no one would reasonably expect such a child to be in a position to authorize anyone to rummage through his parents' bedroom." Georgia v. Randolph, 547 U.S. 103, 126 S.Ct. 1515, 1522, 164 L.Ed.2d 208 (2006) [internal quotation from the LaFave treatise omitted].

104. "The standard for measuring the scope of a suspect's consent [to search] under the Fourth Amendment is that of objective reasonableness—what would the typical reasonable person have understood by the exchange between the officer and the suspect? The question before us, then is whether it is reasonable to consider a suspect's general consent to search his car to include consent to examine a paper bag lying on the floor of the car. We think it does." Florida v. Jimeno, 500 U.S. 248, 111 S.Ct. 1801, 114 L.Ed.2d 297, 302–03 (1991).

105. In Florida v. Jimeno, 500 U.S. 248, 111 S.Ct. 1801, 114 L.Ed.2d 297 (1991), the Court distinguishes State v. Wells, 539 So.2d 464 (Fla. 1989), relied on by the Florida Supreme Court in affirming the suppression order under review. "There the Supreme Court of Florida held that consent to search the trunk of a car did not include authorization to pry open a locked briefcase found inside the trunk. It is very likely unreasonable to think that a suspect, by consenting to the search of his trunk, has agreed to the breaking open of a locked briefcase within the trunk, but it is otherwise with respect to a closed paper bag." 114 L.Ed.2d at 304.

In *Jimeno*, the police officer told the defendant that the officer believed the defendant was carrying narcotics; the defendant gave a voluntary general consent for police to search defendant's car, placing no restrictions on the consent. The Court held that it was proper for the police to look in a closed paper bag lying on the floor of the car.

106. "A suspect may of course limit as he chooses the scope of the search to which he consents." Florida v. Jimeno, 500 U.S. 248, 111 S.Ct. 1801, 114 L.Ed.2d 297, 304 (1991). For a discussion of the scope of a consent search, see 4 Wayne LaFave, Search and Seizure § 8.1(c) (5th ed. 2012). Also see cases collected at "Searches and Seizures" § 186 West Key No.

107. See Chapter 12, Section 2c of this work for a discussion of the "plain view" doctrine.

Section 6. Exigent Circumstances Search

a. General rule

The Court has recognized an exigent circumstances exception to the search warrant requirement rule, in which police are confronted with a serious emergency requiring an intrusion into protected Fourth Amendment premises where there is no time to obtain a search warrant to deal with the emergency. Under this fairly loose, fact-specific exception, police are authorized to make a warrantless, nonconsensual entry onto private premises [or otherwise invade protected Fourth Amendment interests] in order to deal with certain emergency situations. The compelling public necessity for such an exception is frequently obvious, although how one applies it in given cases may be debatable.

Although the Court has not articulated an exhaustive list of the emergencies involved in this exception, the exception has to date revolved around three general scenarios with possible variations on each: (1) police in "hot pursuit" of a fleeing felon enter private premises to arrest the suspect; (2) police or firemen enter private premises to deal with a situation that is life-threatening or perilous to persons inside or outside the premises or to these officials themselves; and (3) police enter private premises to prevent the imminent destruction of evidence of a serious crime. In each case, there is no time to obtain a warrant; immediate action is required to deal with the emergency. Each of these general scenarios, however, are fact-specific. In determining whether this exception applies, the Court necessarily looks to the totality of the circumstances presented by each case.[108]

---

108. "Accordingly, the warrant requirement is subject to certain reasonable exceptions....One well-recognized exception applies 'when the exigencies of the situation' make the needs of law enforcement so compelling that [a] warrantless search is objectively reasonable under the Fourth Amendment....

"This Court has identified several exigencies that may justify a warrantless search of a home. Under the 'emergency aid exception, for example, [1] 'officers may enter a home without a warrant to render emergency assistance to an injured occupant or to protect an occupant from immediate injury.' [2] Police may enter premises without a warrant when they are in immediate pursuit of a fleeing subject. [3]And—what is relevant here—the need 'to prevent the immediate destruction of evidence' has long been recognized as a sufficient justification for a warrantless search. [internal citations omitted; bracketed numbers added]." Kentucky v. King, 563 U.S. ___, 131 S.Ct. 1849, 1856, 179 L.Ed.2d 865 (2011) (internal citations and quotation marks omitted) (bracketed numbers added).

"We have held, for example, that law enforcement officers may make a warrantless entry onto private property to fight a fire and investigate its cause, to prevent the imminent destruction of evidence [citation omitted], or to engage in 'hot pursuit' of a fleeing suspect. [citation omitted]. * * * One exigency obviating the requirement of a warrant is the need to assist persons who are seriously injured or threatened with such injury .... Accordingly, law enforcement officers may enter a home without a warrant to render emergency assistance to an injured occupant or to protect an occupant from imminent injury." Brigham City v. Stuart, 547 U.S. 398, 126 S.Ct. 1943, 1947, 164 L.Ed.2d 650 (2006) (internal citations omitted).

"As noted, the warrant requirement is subject to exceptions. One well-recognized exception, and the one at issue in this case, applies when the exigencies of the situation make the needs of law enforcement so compelling that a warrantless search is objectively reasonable under the Fourth Amendment..A variety of circumstances may give rise to an exigency sufficient to justify a warrantless search, including law enforcement's need to provide emergency assistance to an occupant of a home, engage in a 'hot pursuit' of a fleeing suspect, or enter a building to put out a fire and investigate its cause. As relevant here, we have also recognized that in some circumstances law enforcement officers may conduct a search without a warrant to prevent the imminent destruction of evidence. While these contexts do not necessarily involve equivalent dangers, in each a warrantless search is potentially reasonable because there is a compelling need for official action and no time to secure a warrant.

Of course, if this exception is inapplicable because the police entry into private premises or private property is deemed unreasonable under the Fourth Amendment, the ensuing search will be unreasonable and its fruits will generally be inadmissible under the *Weeks-Mapp* exclusionary rule. If that be the case, no other exceptions to the search warrant requirement rule need be examined, because the fruits of the search that follow the illegal entry would on that account alone be generally barred from evidence under the *Weeks-Mapp* exclusionary rule.[109] Of course, the house entry may, in unusual circumstances, be reasonable notwithstanding the absence of exigent circumstances—as, for example, if the householder voluntarily consents to the entry.[110]

b. Hot pursuit of a fleeing felon

Law enforcement officers are privileged to enter a home without a warrant when in immediate pursuit of a person whom they have probable cause to arrest for a felony, and who has just entered the house to escape apprehension.[111] The rule is generally inapplicable, however, where only a minor offense is involved, such as a civil traffic infraction.[112] But

---

"To determine whether a law enforcement officer faced an emergency that justified acting without a warrant, this Court looks to the totality of the circumstances. We apply this finely tuned approach to Fourth Amendment reasonableness in this context because the police action at issue lacks the traditional justification that a warrant provides. Absent that established justification, the fact-specific nature of the reasonableness inquiry demands that we evaluate each case of alleged exigency based on its own facts and circumstances." Missouri v. McNeely, 569 _____, 133 S.Ct. 1552, 185 LEd..2d 696, 704–05 (2013) (internal citations and quotation marks omitted).

"The Minnesota Supreme Court applied essentially the correct standard in determining whether exigent circumstances existed. The court observed that 'a warrantless intrusion may be justified by hot pursuit of a fleeing felon, or imminent destruction of evidence, or the need to prevent a suspect's escape, or the risk of danger to the police or to other persons inside or outside the dwelling. The court also apparently thought that in the absence of hot pursuit there must at least be probable cause to believe that one or more of the other factors justifying the entry were present and that in assessing the danger, the gravity of the crime and the likelihood that the suspect is armed and dangerous should be considered." Minnesota v. Olson, 495 U.S. 91, 110 S.Ct. 1684, 109 L.Ed.2d 85, 95–96 (1990) (emphasis added).

The Court has also stated that a warrantless search of private premises to deal with an emergency public health situation is constitutionally permissible—such as the seizure of unwholesome food, a compulsory small pox vaccination, a health quarantine, or the summary destruction of tubercular cattle. Camara v. Municipal Court, 387 U.S. 523, 539, 87 S.Ct. 1727, 18 L.Ed.2d 930, 941 (1967).

For lower federal and state court cases on the exigent circumstances exception, see "Searches and Seizures" §§42.1, 43, 44, 45 West Key Nos.

109. See Chapter 17, Section 3 of this work for a discussion of the fruit of the poisonous tree doctrine.

110. See, e.g., Flippo v. West Virginia, 528 U.S. 11, 120 S.Ct. 7, 145 L.Ed.2d 16, 20 (1999) (remand to determine if consent search exception to warrant requirement was applicable, where exigent circumstances exception was inapplicable). For a discussion of consent searches, see the preceding section of this chapter.

111. Warden Md. Penitentiary v. Hayden, 387 U.S. 294, 87 S.Ct. 1642, 18 L.Ed.2d 782 (1967) (armed robbery of business by suspect who fled on foot; witnesses in a car followed suspect until he entered house; police arrived within minutes and entered house; warrantless entry upheld).

United States v. Santana, 427 U.S. 38, 96 S.Ct. 2406, 49 L.Ed.2d 300 (1976) (police pursue an illegal drug sale suspect into her home; drug sale to undercover officer had just taken place a short distance away and seller was arrested; police then traveled by car to nearby residence to arrest suspect who was the drug source for the sale; suspect was standing in front doorway of her house when police arrived and shouted "police;" suspect retreated into her house; warrantless entry upheld).

For lower federal and state court cases on the issue of hot pursuit, see "Searches and Seizures" §§43, 44, 45 West Key Nos.

112. "Our hesitation in finding exigent circumstances, especially when warrantless arrests in the home are at issue, is especially appropriate when the underlying offense for which there is probable

absent a showing of hot pursuit or some immediate danger to persons in the house or to the police, to be discussed in the next subsection, the Court has held that a non-consensual entry to effect a felony arrest in the home must be authorized by a valid search or arrest warrant.[113] Moreover, where the officers are not in immediate pursuit of the suspect, but the suspect is simply traced in the fullness of time to a particular house in which no one therein is in immediate danger, the exception is inapplicable.[114]

c. Life-threatening or perilous situations

Law enforcement officers may also enter private premises, such as a home, and make a warrantless search of the premises if there is probable cause to believe that a life-threatening or perilous situation exists on the premises, in which someone may be in need of immediate aid; this rule applies even though the officers' *subjective* intent in entering the premises may have been to make an arrest of persons therein—so long as the *objective* facts justified the entry to protect life and limb.[115]

---

cause to arrest is relatively minor. Before agents of the government may invade the sanctity of the home, the burden is on the government to demonstrate exigent circumstances that overcome the presumption of unreasonableness that attaches to all warrantless home entries. When the government's interest is only to arrest for a minor offense, that presumption of unreasonableness is difficult to rebut, and the government usually should be allowed to make such arrests only with a warrant issued upon probable cause by a neutral and detached magistrate." "[A]pplication of the exigent-circumstances exception in the context of a home entry should rarely be sanctioned when there is probable cause to believe that only a minor offense, such as the kind involved in this case, has been committed.") Welsh v. Wisconsin, 466 U.S. 740, 104 S.Ct 2091, 80 L.Ed.2d 732, 743, 745 (1984) (drunk driving suspect abandoned his car at scene of one-car accident and walked a short distance to his nearby home; witnesses called the police and directed them to defendant's home; police entered the home and arrested the defendant at night less than an hour after the accident; in Wisconsin, the drunk driving offense was a civil traffic offense only; warrantless entry struck down; no hot pursuit; suspect was no danger to anyone, having left his car at the scene of the accident; no real emergency existed to ascertain defendant's blood alcohol level for this non-jailable offense).

113. Payton v. New York, 445 U.S. 573, 100 S.Ct. 1371, 63 L.Ed.2d 639 (1980); Steagald v. United States, 451 U.S. 204, 101 S.Ct. 1642, 68 L.Ed.2d 38 (1981). "Our decision in Payton, allowing home arrests [without a warrant] upon a showing of probable cause and exigent circumstances, was also expressly limited to felony arrests." Welsh v. Wisconsin, 466 U.S. 740, 104 S.Ct 2091, 80 L.Ed.2d 732, 743 at n. 11 (1984). For a discussion of the Payton-Stegald rule requiring a warrant to effect an arrest in the home, see Chapter 12, Section 1b of this work.

114. Minnesota v. Olson, 495 U.S. 91, 110 S.Ct. 1684, 109 L.Ed.2d 85 (1990) (police traced a robbery suspect to a house, although not in immediate pursuit of the suspect, entered the house, and arrested the defendant therein; there was no danger to anyone in the house; the Court defers to the Minnesota Supreme Court's conclusion that a warrant should have been obtained prior to police entering the house; exigent circumstances exception not applicable).

115. "One exigency obviating the requirement of a warrant is the need to assist persons who are seriously injured or threatened with such injury.... [citations omitted]. Accordingly, law enforcement officers may enter a home without a warrant to render emergency assistance to an injured occupant or to protect an occupant from imminent injury. [citations omitted]. * * *

"An action is 'reasonable' under the Fourth Amendment, regardless of the individual officer's state of mind 'as long as the circumstances viewed *objectively* justify [the] action.' [citations omitted]. The officer's subjective motivation is irrelevant. [citations omitted]. It therefore does not matter here—even if their subjective motives could be so neatly unraveled—whether the officers entered the kitchen to arrest the respondents and gather evidence against them or to assist the injured and prevent further violence." Brigham City v. Stuart, 547 U.S. 398, 126 S.Ct. 1943, 1947, 1948, 164 L.Ed.2d 650 (2006) (police properly entered home without a warrant to break up a brawl they could see was taking place therein; this result is not changed by the fact that the officers' subjective intent in entering the premises may have been to make an arrest and gather evidence to support the arrest).

See also: "A reasonable police officer could read these [U.S. Supreme Court] decisions to mean

Moreover, when officers enter premises where a homicide may have been committed, the officers may sweep the premises for homicide victims, the potential killer, and weapons—and may seize any evidence of crime in "plain view" while engaged in such a sweep. Any search thereafter, however, must be conducted with a search warrant, as there is no "murder scene" exception to the search warrant requirement rule—and if no warrant is obtained, the search is considered unreasonable and the fruits thereof are generally inadmissible in evidence under the *Weeks-Mapp* exclusionary rule.[116]

---

that the Fourth Amendment permits an officer to enter a residence if the officer has a reasonable basis for concluding that there is an imminent threat of violence." Ryburn v. Huff, 565 U.S. ___, 132 S.Ct. 987, 181 L.Ed.2d 966, 970 (2012) (qualified immunity shielded from civil rights suit defendant police officers who entered homeowner's residence investigating a threatened mass shooting at a public school after student's mother rushed into house when asked by police whether there were any guns in the house).

"Therefore although searches and seizures inside a home without a warrant are presumptively unreasonable, that presumption can be overcome. For example, the exigencies of the situation [may] make the needs of law enforcement so compelling that the warrantless search is objectively reasonable.

"*Brigham City* identified on such exigency: the need to assist persons who are seriously injured or threatened with such injury. Thus, law enforcement officers may enter a home without a warrant to render emergency assistance to protect an occupant from imminent injury. This emergency aid exception does not depend on the officers' subjective intent or the seriousness of any crime they are investigating when the emergency arises. It requires only an objectively reasonable basis for believing that a person within [the house] is in need of immediate aid." Michigan v. Fisher, 558 U.S. 45, 130 S.Ct. 546, 175 L.Ed.2d 410 (2009) (internal case quotations and citations omitted) (Brigham decision followed on its facts) (police properly entered home without a warrant where man whom police could see through a window was in a rage throwing items around in the house with blood on his hand—so as to render aid to the man or any person he might be hurling things at; three windows in house were broken with glass still on ground outside; truck in driveway was smashed up with blood on the hood and on clothes inside truck; blood was on one of the doors to the house).

116. "Numerous state and federal cases have recognized that the Fourth Amendment does not bar police officers from making warrantless entries and searches when they reasonably believe that a person within is in need of immediate aid. Similarly, when the police come upon the scene of a homicide they may make a prompt warrantless search of the area to see if there are other victims or if the killer is still on the premises. 'The need to protect or preserve life or avoid serious injury is justification for what would be otherwise illegal absent the emergency.' And the police may seize any evidence that is in plain view during the course of their legitimate emergency." Mincey v. Arizona, 437 U.S. 385, 98 S.Ct. 2408, 57 L.Ed. 290, 300 (1978) (internal citation omitted). Also see 3 Wayne LaFave, Search and Seizure § 6.5 (d)(e) (5th ed. 2012), and cases collected at "Searches and Seizures" § 42.1 West Key No.

Mincey involves a classic "drug bust" gone bad, a scene from an action movie. An undercover narcotics police officer arranged to buy narcotics from defendant in the latter's apartment and had left to get the money to complete the transaction. When the officer returned, he had nine plainclothes policemen with him. The officers forced their way into the apartment and a shootout took place between the police officers and the people in the apartment. Several people were severely wounded, including the defendant; the undercover officer was killed. After the shooting, police went through the apartment to find out who had been shot and then summoned medical assistance. Ten minutes later, homicide detectives were on the scene; they conducted an intensive four-day search of the apartment. The Court held that this four-day search was outside the scope of the exigent circumstances exception to the search warrant requirement rule; police needed a search warrant to conduct such an intensive search. *Specifically, the Court rejected a "murder scene" exception to the search warrant requirement rule.*

Although the Court in Mincey sends the case back to sort out which of the above police searches in the apartment might qualify under the exigent circumstances exception and expresses no view thereon, it would seem that the initial police sweep was reasonable under the exigent circumstances exception, but that all the warrantless searches thereafter were outside the scope of this exception. If so, any evidence of crime seen and seized during this initial sweep would be a reasonable seizure under the "plain view" doctrine; anything else seized in the subsequent searches would be unreasonable as

Firemen may enter a burning building without a warrant to put out a fire therein, and may seize any evidence of an arson in plain view while engaged in their fire-fighting activity.[117] The firemen may also remain on the scene for a reasonable time after the fire has been extinguished for the purpose of discovering the cause of the fire. But generally any re-entries onto the premises thereafter [for example, several days later] must be made with an administrative-type warrant—and, as a rule, any warrantless re-entries are considered unreasonable and the fruits thereof inadmissible in evidence under the *Weeks-Mapp* exclusionary rule.[118] On the other hand, a warrant is unnecessary for such post-

---

not within the purview of the same doctrine.

"We noted [in *Mincey v. Arizona*] that police may make warrantless entries onto premises if they reasonably believe a person is in need of immediate aid and may make prompt searches of a homicide scene for possible other victims or a killer on the premises, (citation omitted), but we rejected any general 'murder scene exception' as 'inconsistent with the Fourth and Fourteenth Amendments ... The warrantless search of Mincey's apartment was not constitutionally permissible simply because a homicide had recently occurred there.'" Flippo v. West Virginia, 528 U.S. 11, 120 S.Ct. 7, 145 L.Ed.2d 16, 20 (1999) (citation omitted).

In *Thompson v. Louisiana*, 469 U.S. 17, 105 S.Ct. 409, 83 L.Ed.2d 246 (1984), the Court applied *Mincey* to strike down another "murder scene" search of a house. In that case, the defendant's daughter called the police and reported that the defendant had just telephoned to say that she had just shot her husband and had taken a quantity of pills in a suicide attempt, and then, changing her mind, had called the daughter for help. Police arrived at defendant's house, entered apparently without consent, discovered the husband dead of a gunshot wound in a bedroom and the defendant in another bedroom unconscious due to a drug overdose, and inspected the other rooms in the house to find no other victims. They then called the ambulance for the defendant. [So far, it would seem that the police entry and search was within the exigent circumstances exception, but the plot thickens]. Thirty-five minutes after the defendant was transported to the hospital, two homicide investigators from the sheriff's office conducted a thorough two-hour search in the house for evidence of crime. They found three items during this search: (a) a gun inside a chest of drawers in the same room as the dead body, (b) a torn-up note in the waste basket of the adjoining bathroom and (c) an alleged suicide note found folded up inside a Xmas card on the top of the chest of drawers. The Court held that this general exploratory search for evidence was outside the scope of the exigent circumstances exception, and that the warrantless seizure of evidence during this search was unreasonable under the 4th Amendment. The homicide investigators needed a warrant to continue their investigations at the defendant's house.

In *Flippo v. West Virginia*, 528 U.S. 11, 120 S.Ct. 7, 145 L.Ed.2d 16 (1999), the Court applied *Mincey* to disapprove a "murder scene" exception to the search warrant requirement rule used by state courts to uphold a 16-hour search of a rented cabin in a state park—following defendant's 911 call to police that he and his wife had been attacked by an intruder. The case was remanded to determine whether the search was conducted with defendant's consent or whether some other exception to the search warrant requirement rule might apply. The Court held that the subject search could not be upheld under the emergency or exigent circumstances exception to the search warrant requirement rule.

117. "Our decisions have recognized that a warrantless entry by criminal law enforcement officials may be legal when there is a compelling need for official action and no time to secure a warrant. *** A burning building clearly presents an exigency of sufficient proportions to render a warrantless entry 'reasonable.' Indeed, it would defy reason to suppose that firemen must secure a warrant or consent before entering a burning structure to put out the blaze. And once in the building for this purpose, firefighters may seize evidence of arson in plain view." Michigan v. Tyler, 436 U.S. 499, 98 S.Ct. 1942, 56 L.Ed.2d 486, 498 (1978).

118. "For these reasons, officials need no warrant to remain in a building for a reasonable time to investigate the cause of a blaze after it has been extinguished. And if the warrantless entry to put out the fire and determine its cause is constitutional, the warrantless seizure of evidence while inspecting the premises for these purposes is also constitutional." Michigan v. Tyler, 436 U.S. 499, 98 S.Ct. 1942, 56 L.Ed.2d 486, 499 (1978).

In *Tyler*, the Court held that (a) the initial warrantless entry into the defendant's leased furniture store to put out a fire therein shortly after midnight, (b) the firemen's activity on the premises to put the fire out and thereafter investigate the cause of the fire until 4 AM, and (c) subsequent warrantless re-entry by the same firemen at 9AM during daylight hours to continue their investigation—were fire entries if the fire has so gutted the building that no person could entertain a reasonable expectation of privacy therein.[119]

d. Destruction or removal of evidence[120]

Finally, the Court has recognized an exception to the search warrant requirement rule where a non-consensual entry onto private premises is necessary to prevent the immediate destruction of evidence of a crime—provided there is a reasonable basis for believing that such evidence is in the process of being destroyed on the premises. Moreover, this rule applies even where the police precipitate the destruction of such evidence by knocking on the door to such premises and announcing that they are police—as this action does not constitute a violation of the Fourth Amendment or a threat to do so. This exception, however, is inapplicable where the police precipitate this destruction of evidence by violating the Fourth Amendment or threatening to do so—as, is the case, where police threaten to forcibly enter the premises unless admitted when they, in fact, have no reasonable basis for doing so.[121]

---

all reasonable under the exigent circumstances exception. Various items of evidence and pictures were taken during these inspections—all reasonably obtained under the "plain view" doctrine. The defendant was charged and convicted of a conspiracy to burn his leased furniture store.

However, the subsequent warrantless re-entry by firemen onto the defendant's premises several days later and further warrantless re-entries on a number of occasions within the next three weeks for the purpose of gathering evidence of arson—were all held unreasonable in

Tyler as being outside the scope of the exigent circumstances exception; the firemen needed an administrative-type warrant to continue their investigations at the building. Evidence obtained during these re-entries was not admissible under the "plain view" doctrine.

See Michigan v. Clifford 464 U.S. 287, 104 S.Ct. 641, 78 L.Ed.2d 477 (1984) (post-fire search of arson defendant's home at 1:30 PM, 6 ? hours after firemen had extinguished the fire therein [including a search of the basement and later the rest of the house], was held unreasonable because it was conducted without a warrant) (plurality opinion; result concurred in by five Justices).

See also 5 Wayne LaFave, Search and Seizure § 10.4 (5th ed. 2012); Chapter 13, Section 2h of this work for a discussion of administrative search warrants; Chapter 12, Section 2c of this work for a discussion of the "plain view" doctrine; and Chapter 17, Section 3 of this work for a discussion of the fruit of the poisonous tree doctrine.

119. "Some fires may be so devastating that no reasonable privacy interests remain in the ash and ruins, regardless of the owner's subjective expectations." Michigan v. Clifford, 464 U.S. 287, 104 S.Ct. 641, 78 L.Ed.2d 477, 483 (1984) (plurality opinion).

120. For a discussion of related exceptions to the general rule requiring a warrant for the *seizure* [as opposed to a search] of personal or real property [i.e., seizures pending application for a search warrant, and seizures pending further investigation], see Chapter 12, Section 2b(1)(2) of this work.

121. "It is well established that 'exigent circumstances', including the need to prevent the destruction of evidence, permit police officers to conduct an otherwise permissible search [on private premises] without first obtaining a warrant." Kentucky v. King, 563 U.S. ___, 131 S.Ct. 1849, 1853–54, 179 L.Ed.2d 865 (2011).

"Accordingly, the warrant requirement is subject to certain reasonable exceptions. One well-recognized exception applies 'when the exigencies of the situation' make the needs of law enforcement so compelling that [a] warrantless search is objectively reasonable under the Fourth Amendment. (citations omitted).

"This Court has identified several exigencies that may justify a warrantless search of a home. Under the 'emergency aid exception, for example, [1] 'officers may enter a home without a warrant to render emergency assistance to an injured occupant or to protect an occupant from immediate injury.' [2] Police may enter premises without a warrant when they are in immediate pursuit of a fleeing subject. *[3]And—what is relevant here—the need 'to prevent the immediate destruction of evidence' has long been recognized as a sufficient justification for a warrantless search.* [internal citations omitted; bracketed numbers added]." Kentucky v. King, 563 U.S. ___, 131 S.Ct. 1849, 1856, 179 L.Ed.2d 865 (2011)

The Court has held, however, that police entry into a home to make an arrest for a nonjailable drunk driving traffic offense so as to prevent the destruction of evidence [namely, the home dweller's blood alcohol level] was not justified under the exigent circumstances exception to the search warrant requirement rule.[122] Moreover, the Court has struck down a warrantless entry onto business premises by IRS agents to levy on corporate assets in satisfaction of a tax deficiency. The exigent circumstances exception to the warrant requirement was inapplicable because the agents had at least a day to obtain a search warrant for the defendant's office, and the evidence therein was otherwise in no danger of disappearing.[123]

e. Other searches

The exigent circumstances exception to the search warrant requirement rule is not confined to entries and searches of homes and business premises. The Court has also indicated that this exception is applicable to intrusions into the human body to prevent the destruction of certain internal chemical evidence, and to searches of luggage to disarm a bomb or weapon that is dangerous to others.[124]

(italics added).

"Where, as here, the police did not create the exigency by engaging or threatening to engage in conduct that violates the Fourth Amendment, warrantless entry to prevent the destruction of evidence is reasonable and is thus allowed." Kentucky v. King, 563 U.S. ___, 131 S.Ct. 1849, 1858, 179 L.Ed.2d 865 (2011) (police knock loudly on apartment door and loudly announce "police" [resulting in noises in apartment that police thought illegal drugs were being destroyed] did not in itself render inapplicable the exigent circumstances exception to the search warrant requirement rule; case remanded to determine whether these noises constituted a reasonable basis for the police belief that such drugs were being destroyed).

"For these reasons, we conclude that the exigent circumstances rule applies when police do not gain entry to premises by means of actual or threatened violation of the Fourth Amendment." Kentucky v. King, 563 U.S. ___, 131 S.Ct. 1849, 1862, 179 L.Ed.2d 865 (2011).

"There is a strong argument to be made that, at least in most circumstances, the exigent circumstances rule should not apply where the police, without a warrant or any legally sound basis for a warrantless entry, threaten that they will enter without permission unless admitted. In this case, however, no such actual threat was made, and therefore we have no need to reach that question." Kentucky v. King, 563 U.S. ___, 131 S.Ct. 1849, 1858, n. 4, 179 L.Ed.2d 865 (2011).

On the other hand, the Court has struck down warrantless nonconsensual home entries where no showing was made that evidence of crime was in danger of being destroyed or removed. Johnson v. United States, 333 U.S. 10, 68 S.Ct. 367, 92 L.Ed. 436, 441 (1948) ("No evidence or contraband was threatened with removal or destruction ..."); United States v. Jeffers, 342 U.S. 48, 72 S.Ct. 93, 96 L.Ed. 59, 64 (1951) ("[N]or was there an arrest or imminent destruction, removal, or concealment of the property intended to be seized."); McDonald v. United States, 335 U.S. 451, 69 S.Ct. 191, 93 L.Ed. 153, 158 (1948) "Nor was the property in the process of destruction ..."); Vale v. Louisiana, 399 U.S. 30, 90 S.Ct. 1969, 26 L.Ed.2d 409, 414 (1970) ("The goods ultimately seized were not in the process of destruction." "We decline to hold that an arrest on the street can provide its own 'exigent circumstances' so as to justify a warrantless search of the arrestee's house.").

122. Welsh v. Wisconsin, 466 U.S. 740, 104 S.Ct. 2091, 80 L.Ed.2d 732, 743 (1984) ("Our hesitation in finding exigent circumstances, especially when warrantless arrests in the home are at issue, is especially appropriate when the underlying offense for which there is probable cause to arrest is relatively minor. Before agents of the government may invade the sanctity of the home, the burden is on the government to demonstrate exigent circumstances that overcome the presumption of unreasonableness that attaches to all warrantless home entries.").

123. G.M. Leasing Corp. v. United States, 429 U.S. 338, 97 S.Ct. 619, 50 L.Ed.2d 530, 549 (1977). For a discussion of this aspect of the exigent circumstances exception, see 3 Wayne LaFave, Search and Seizure § 6.5(b) (5th ed. 2012). Also see cases collected at "Searches and Seizures" §§ 42.1, 45 West Key Nos.

124. In striking down the warrantless search of a footlocker in *United States v. Chadwick*, 433 U.S. 1, 97 S.Ct. 2476, 53 L.Ed.2d 538, 551 n.9 (1977), the Court stated that "if officers have reason to

The Court has held, however, that there is no *automatic* exigent circumstances exception for a nonconsensual blood test of a motorist lawfully arrested for drunk driving. The natural alcohol elimination rate in the bloodstream for a given drunk driver arrestee represents a *gradual* destruction of evidence and therefore an important factor in determining whether this exception applies. But it is not a *decisive* factor as the issue must be determined case-by-case based on the totality of the circumstances. The question presented in each case is whether there was reasonably sufficient time for law enforcement officers to obtain a warrant authorizing a blood draw from the arrestee without significantly undermining the efficacy of the blood test. If so, a warrant must be obtained; if not, a warrantless blood draw is justified under the exigent circumstances exception.[125]

f. "Plain view" seizure of evidence

During a valid exigent circumstances search of a home or other private premises, law enforcement officers are privileged to seize any physical evidence under the "plain view" doctrine if there is probable cause to believe that this evidence constitutes contraband, fruits or instrumentalities of a crime, or evidence of a crime, so long as the search is

---

believe that luggage contains some immediately dangerous instrumentality, such as explosives, it would be foolhardy to transport it to the station house without opening the luggage and disarming the weapon."

The Court made a similar comment in striking down the warrantless search of a suitcase in *Arkansas v. Sanders,* 442 U.S. 753, 99 S.Ct. 2586, 61 L.Ed.2d 235, 245 n. 11 (1979): "There may be cases in which the special exigencies of the situation would justify the warrantless search of a suitcase. Cady v. Dombrowski, 413 U.S. 433, 93 S.Ct. 2523, 37 L.Ed.2d 706 (1973) (police had reason to suspect automobile trunk contained a weapon). Generally, however, such exigencies will depend upon the probable contents of the luggage and the suspect's access to those contents."

In *Winston v. Lee,* 470 U.S. 753, 105 S.Ct. 1611, 84 L.Ed.2d 662 (1985), the Court affirmed a federal court injunction against the surgical removal of a bullet lodged in a robbery suspect's chest, primarily because of the danger to the suspect's life in such surgery and the lack of a compelling need by the state for the bullet as evidence, given the other evidence of guilt against the suspect.

125. Missouri v. McNeely, 569 U.S. ____, 133 S.Ct. 1552, 185 L..Ed.2d 696. (2013) (Court rejects state's proposed *per se* rule authorizing a warrantless blood test in all drunk driving cases; Court does not determine whether a warrantless blood test was justified under the particular facts of this case—as state did not advance this argument).

"The question presented here is whether the natural metabolization of alcohol in the bloodstream presents a *per se* exigency that justifies an exception to the Fourth Amendment's warrant requirement for nonconsensual bloodtesting in all drunk driving cases. We conclude it does not, and we hold, consistent with general Fourth Amendment principles, that exigency in this context must be determined case by case based on the totality of the circumstances. * * * We hold that in drunk driving investigations, the natural dissipation of alcohol in the bloodstream does not constitute an exigency in every case sufficient to justify conducting a blood test without a warrant." 185 L.Ed2d. at 702. "In those drunk-driving investigations where police officers can reasonably obtain a warrant before a blood sample can be drawn without significantly undermining the efficacy of the search, the Fourth Amendment mandates that they do so." Id. at 185 L.Ed.2d at 696.

There are typical delays that can occur in drunk driving arrests that may impact on whether there was sufficient time to secure a warrant for a blood draw—such as delays associated with an accompanied accident investigation and a possible trip to the emergency room. Equally significant to this issue is the proliferation of available procedures in many jurisdictions for law enforcement officers to secure a warrant rapidly by telephone, radio or other electronic transmission. For a discussion of these and related issues, see Chief Justice Roberts' separate opinion [concurring in part, and dissenting in part] in Missouri v. McNeely, 569 U.S. ____, 133 S.Ct. 1552, 185 L..Ed.2d 696, 716 (2013), as well as the Court's opinion itself of which a portion is joined by only a plurality of the justices at Section IIC.

within the scope of the exception.[126] But any search on such premises that is not confined to the purpose of the exigent circumstances entry is considered unreasonable, if not otherwise justified by some other search warrant exception.[127]

126. See Chapter 12, Section 2c of this work for a discussion of the "plain view" doctrine.

127. In Arizona v. Hicks, 480 U.S. 321, 107 S.Ct. 1149, 94 L.Ed.2d 347 (1987), the Court accepted the holding of the Arizona courts that a police entry into an apartment to look for gunmen, victims and weapons was justified under the exigent circumstances exception to the search warrant requirement rule, after police received information that a person in this apartment had fired a shot through the floor of the apartment and actually injured a person in the apartment below. However, the Court held that the police seizure of stereo equipment inside the apartment did not fall within the purview of the "plain view" doctrine because the police did not have probable cause to believe that the equipment was stolen. Indeed, the police went outside the scope of the exigent circumstances exception when they moved the stereo equipment to get the serial numbers of the equipment in question; this was a Fourth Amendment search not justified by the subject exception.

Chapter 15

Warrantless Searches and *Civil or Special Needs* Exceptions to the Search Warrant Requirement Rule

Section 1. Introduction

As discussed in the prior chapter, a search conducted without a search warrant is per se unreasonable under the Fourth Amendment, subject to certain important exceptions.[1] These exceptions are generally divided into (1) criminal exceptions, and (2) civil or special needs exceptions. The criminal exceptions all serve a compelling investigative purpose in ordinary criminal law enforcement cases in which the societal costs of obtaining a warrant are deemed to outweigh the reasons for resorting to a warrant. These exceptions are examined in the preceding chapter.

The civil or special needs exceptions, on the other hand, have a compelling public purpose that the warrant procedure, and at times the probable cause or individualized suspicion requirement, is deemed ill suited to accomplish based on a balancing of competing governmental and privacy concerns. Essentially, under this approach, the Court balances two factors: (1) the degree of intrusion into individual privacy or personal security represented by the search or seizure in question, as against (2) the promotion of legitimate governmental interests served by such intrusion. In striking the appropriate balance, the Court strives, where practicable, to avoid giving government officials the right to conduct searches or seizures at their absolute discretion—(a) by requiring some showing of individualized wrongdoing, or (b) by requiring the use of neutral criteria[2] for conducting the intrusion, or some other like safeguard—so that, upon either showing, there is an assurance that the invasion of individual privacy or personal security is not based on the arbitrary discretion of the government official conducting the search or seizure.[3] In

1. See, e.g., Katz v. United States, 389 U.S. 347, 357, 88 S.Ct. 507, 19 L.Ed.2d 576, 585 (1967); Coolidge v. New Hampshire, 403 U.S. 443, 91 S.Ct. 2022, 29 L.Ed.2d 564, 576 (1971); see also Chapter 11, Section 1 of this work.

2. "Neutral criteria" consists of standards unconnected with criminal wrongdoing that guide law enforcement discretion in making certain civil or administrative seizures of persons, such as roadblock stops of motor vehicles [i.e., stopping every vehicle or every other vehicle for a drivers license or DUI check]. See Chapter 12, Section 1n of this work.

3. For a representative statement of the balancing approach, see Delaware v. Prouse, 440 U.S. 648, 653–55, 99 S.Ct. 1391, 59 L.Ed.2d 660 (1979); and Brown v. Texas, 443 U.S. 47, 50–51, 99 S.Ct. 2637, 61 L.Ed.2d 357 (1979). For other statements of the balancing approach, see: O'Connor v. Ortega, 480 U.S. 709, 107 S.Ct. 1492, 94 L.Ed.2d 714, 724 (1987); Tennessee v. Garner, 471 U.S. 1, 105 S.Ct.

particular, where special governmental needs beyond the normal need for criminal law enforcement are shown, the Court generally strikes the balance in favor of dispensing with a warrant—and, at times, dispensing as well with a probable cause requirement, or even any showing of individualized wrongdoing.[4] At times, however, the Court reaches

---

1694, 85 L.Ed.2d 1, 7 (1985); United States v. Montoya de Hernandez, 473 U.S. 531, 105 S.Ct. 3304, 87 L.Ed.2d 381, 388 (1985); New Jersey v. T.L.O., 469 U.S. 325, 105 S.Ct. 733, 83 L.Ed.2d 720, 731–32 (1985); United States v. Place, 462 U.S. 696, 103 S.Ct. 2637, 77 L.Ed.2d 110, 118 (1983); United States v. Villamonte-Marquez, 462 U.S. 579, 103 S.Ct. 2573, 77 L.Ed.2d 22, 30 (1983); Bell v. Wolfish, 441 U.S. 520, 559, 99 S.Ct. 1861, 60 L.Ed.2d 447 (1979); Pennsylvania v. Mimms, 434 U.S. 106, 109, 98 S.Ct. 330, 54 L.Ed.2d 331 (1977); United States v. Martinez-Fuerte, 428 U.S. 543, 554–55, 96 S.Ct. 3074, 49 L.Ed.2d 1116 (1976); Terry v. Ohio, 392 U.S. 1, 20–21, 88 S.Ct. 1868, 20 L.Ed.2d 889 (1968); Camara v. Municipal Court, 387 U.S. 523, 536–37, 87 S.Ct. 1727, 18 L.Ed.2d 930 (1967).

4. "Although we usually require that a search be undertaken only pursuant to a warrant (and thus supported by probable cause, as the Constitution says warrants must be (citation omitted), we have permitted exceptions when 'special needs, beyond the normal need for law enforcement, make the warrant and probable cause requirement impracticable.'(citation omitted)." Griffin v. Wisconsin, 483 U.S. 868, 107 S.Ct. 3164, 97 L.Ed.2d 709, 717 (1987) (search of probationer's home by probation officers upheld).

"For the Fourth Amendment does not proscribe all searches and seizures, but only those that are unreasonable. What is reasonable, of course, 'depends on all the circumstances surrounding the search or seizure and the nature of the search or seizure itself.' Thus, the permissibility of a particular practice 'is judged by balancing its intrusion on the individual's Fourth Amendment interests against its promotion of legitimate governmental interests.' In most criminal cases, we strike the balance in favor of the procedures described by the Warrants Clause of the Fourth Amendment. Except in certain well-defined circumstances, a search or seizure in such a case is not reasonable unless it is accomplished pursuant to a judicial warrant issued upon probable cause. *We have recognized exceptions to this rule, however, 'when special needs, beyond the normal need for law enforcement, make the warrant and probable cause requirement impracticable.' When faced with such special needs, we have not hesitated to balance the governmental and privacy interests to assess the practicality of the warrant and probable cause requirements in the particular context.*" Skinner v. Railway Labor Executives Ass'n, 489 U.S. 602, 109 S.Ct 1402, 103 L.Ed.2d 639, 661 (1989) (internal citations omitted) (emphasis added) (drug testing program for train employees involved in train accidents upheld).

"While we have long emphasized, and reiterate today, that a search must be supported, as a general matter, by a warrant issued upon probable cause, our decision in *Railway Labor Executives* reaffirms the long-standing principle that neither a warrant nor probable cause, nor, indeed, any measure of individualized suspicion is an indispensable component of reasonableness in every circumstance. As we noted in *Railway Labor Executives*, our cases establish that *where a Fourth Amendment intrusion serves special governmental needs, beyond the normal need for law enforcement, it is necessary to balance the individual's privacy expectations against the Government's interests to determine whether it is impracticable to require a warrant or some level of individualized suspicion in the particular context.*" National Treasury Employees Union v. Von Raab, 489 U.S. 656, 109 S.Ct. 1384, 103 L.Ed.2d 685, 702 (1989) (internal citations omitted) (emphasis added) (drug testing program for Treasury agents involved in drug interdiction upheld).

"Where a search is undertaken by law enforcement to discover evidence of criminal wrongdoing, this Court has said that reasonableness generally requires the obtaining of a judicial warrant. Warrants cannot be issued, of course, without the showing of probable cause required by the Warrants Clause. But a warrant is not required to establish the reasonableness of all government searches; and when a warrant is not required (and the Warrants Clause not applicable), probable cause is not invariably required either. *A search unsupported by probable cause can be constitutional, we have said, 'when special needs, beyond the normal need for law enforcement, make the warrant and probable cause requirements impracticable.'*" Vernonia School District 47J v. Acton, 515 U.S. 646, 115 S.Ct. 2386, 132 L.Ed.2d 564,574 (1995) (citations omitted) (emphasis added) (drug testing program for public schoolchildren who engage in school athletic programs upheld).

"The Fourth Amendment requires that searches and seizures be reasonable. A search is generally unreasonable in the absence of individualized wrongdoing. While such suspicion is not an 'irreducible' component of reasonableness, we have recognized circumstances where the usual rule does not apply. For example, *we have upheld certain regimes of suspicionless searches where the program was designed* the same result by employing the standard balancing process for determining Fourth Amendment reasonableness without requiring a showing of special governmental needs.[5] In this entire balancing process, the Court creates, at times, special needs exceptions to the search warrant requirement rule, and at other times straight civil exceptions *sans* any showing of special governmental needs. To date, they include as primary exceptions: an inventory search, a border search, and an administrative inspection search—and as secondary exceptions: a probationer's home search, a public school student search, a prison inmate or pre-trial detainee search, a public employee search, a drug testing search, and an airport or public building electronic search. These exceptions will be discussed in this chapter.[6]

The underlying basis for such exceptions seems perfectly consistent with the primary purpose of the Fourth Amendment: namely, to end the practice of general exploratory searches for evidence of crime as was practiced by the general writs of assistance regime 1761–76.[7] Where the primary aim of a search is *not* to discover evidence of crime in ordinary criminal investigations, as was true with the writs-of-assistance searches, but to serve other important governmental interests—the search cannot be condemned as a classical type of search that the Fourth Amendment was designed to end.

The physical scope of a search authorized by a given special needs exception is strictly limited to that which is required to carry out the purpose of the exception.[8] But if during the course of such a strictly limited search, an item is discovered that constitutes contraband, or instrumentalities or fruits of a crime, or evidence of a crime, such items may be seized under the "plain view" doctrine.[9]

In those civil or special needs exceptions where neither probable cause nor reasonable suspicion is required, the police officer's motivation in conducting the search may be

---

to serve 'special needs beyond the normal need for law enforcement.'" City of Indianapolis v. Edmond, 531 U.S. 32, 121 S.Ct. 447, 148 L.Ed.2d 333, 340 (2000) (internal citations omitted) (emphasis added) (traffic roadblock to interdict drug trafficking struck down).

"[W]e generally determine the reasonableness of a search by balancing the nature of the intrusion on the individual's privacy against the promotion of legitimate governmental interests. But we have long held that the Fourth Amendment imposes no irreducible requirement of [individualized] suspicion.' '[I]n certain limited circumstances, the Government's need to discover such latent or hidden conditions, or to prevent their development, is sufficiently compelling to justify the intrusion on privacy entailed by conducting such searches without any measure of individualized suspicion.' Therefore in the context of safety and administrative regulations, a search unsupported by probable cause may be reasonable 'when special needs, beyond the normal needs of law enforcement, make the warrant and probable cause requirement impracticable.'" Board of Education of Independent School District No. 92 v. Earls, 536 U.S. 822, 122 S.Ct. 2559, 2564, 153 L.Ed.2d 735 (2002) (internal citations and quotations omitted) (drug testing program for public schoolchildren engaged in competitive extracurricular school activities upheld).

5. Samson v. California, 547 U.S. 843, 126 S.Ct. 2193, 2200 n. 3, 2201 n. 4, 165 L.Ed.2d 250 (2006) (general balancing definition of reasonableness used to hold that a warrantless, suspicionless search of a parolee did not violate the parolee's Fourth Amendment rights; special governmental needs showing not required.).

6. For a discussion of civil or special needs *detentions of the person*, see Chapter 12, Section 1n of this work.

7. For a discussion of this historical purpose, see Chapter 6, Section 2 of this work.

8. "But a warrantless search must be 'strictly circumscribed by the exigencies which justify its initiation.'" Mincey v. Arizona 437 U.S. 385, 393, 98 S.Ct. 2408, 57 L.Ed.2d 290, 300 (1978), quoting from Terry v. Ohio, 392 U.S. 1, 25–26, 88 S.Ct. 1868, 20 L.Ed.2d 889 (1968); see Horton v. California, 496 U.S. 128, 110 S.Ct. 2301,110 L.Ed.2d 112, 125 (1990). "Moreover, we have limited the scope of each exception [to the search warrant requirement rule] to that which is necessary to accommodate the identified needs of society." Arkansas v. Sanders, 442 U.S. 753, 760, 99 S.Ct. 2586, 61 L.Ed.2d 235, 242 (1979).

9. See Chapter 12 Section 2c of this work for a discussion of "plain view" doctrine.

highly relevant, although totally irrelevant in determining whether an arrest or temporary detention is reasonable.[10] In particular, if the officer uses the inventory search or the administrative inspection search in bad faith as a subterfuge to engage in a general exploratory search for evidence of crime, the subject exception is generally considered inapplicable and the search unreasonable.[11] By the same reasoning, other civil or special needs exceptions that do away with a showing of individualized criminal wrongdoing cannot, as a general rule, be used by law enforcement officers as a pretext for engaging in a general exploratory search for evidence of crime—else the exception may be perverted and the primary purpose of the Fourth Amendment defeated.[12]

The exceptions to the search warrant requirement rule discussed in this chapter are not, however, a closed list. The Court may very well carve out additional civil or special needs exceptions in the future based on a balance of competing governmental and privacy concerns described above. In particular, special needs exceptions that serve a purpose beyond the usual needs of ordinary criminal law enforcement may be recognized—such as searches to intercept bombs, biological or germ warfare material, poison gas, or nuclear devices left in public places by terrorists, or searches to apprehend an escaping terrorist or serial killer suspected of fleeing via a particular route.[13] The Fourth Amendment is not a national suicide pact, and under the balancing test for reasonableness, is flexible enough to accommodate such searches without subverting the underlying purpose of the Fourth Amendment or its basic values.[14] These basic values are nonetheless very important in the balancing process—given our long-standing democratic commitment to uphold fundamental constitutional principles especially in times of crisis, turmoil, and confusion.[15]

---

10. See, e.g., Chapter 12, Section 1h of this work for a discussion of the point that an officer's subjective intent or motivation is irrelevant in determining whether there is probable cause to arrest or reasonable suspicion to conduct a temporary stop.

11. See, e.g., discussion of relevant cases in City of Indianapolis v. Edmond, 531 U.S. 32, 121 S.Ct. 447, 148 L.Ed.2d 333, 346 (2000), and Whren v. United States, 517 U.S. 806, 116 S.Ct. 1769, 1773, 135 L.Ed.2d 89 (1996). As an aside, if *programmatically*, the primary purpose of a police roadblock is to detect ordinary criminal wrongdoing, rather than serve other special needs beyond the normal needs of law enforcement, the seizure of persons in vehicles stopped by the roadblock is unreasonable. City of Indianapolis v. Edmund, supra (drug interdiction roadblock held unreasonable).

"[W]e have held in the context of programmatic searches conducted without individual suspicion—such as checkpoints to combat drunk driving or drug trafficking—that 'an inquiry into *programmatic purpose* is sometimes appropriate. [citations omitted]. But this inquiry is directed at ensuring that the purpose behind the program is not 'ultimately indistinguishable from the general interest in crime control.' [citation omitted]. It has nothing to do with discerning what is in the mind of the individual officer conducting the search." Brigham City v. Stuart, 547 U.S. 398, 126 S.Ct. 1943, 1948, 164 L.Ed.2d 650 (2006).

12. "*With the exception of some special needs and administrative search cases*, 'we have been unwilling to entertain Fourth Amendment challenges based on the actual motivations of the individual officers.'" United States v. Knights, 534 U.S. 12, 122 S.Ct. 587, 151 L.Ed.2d 497 (2001) (citations omitted) (emphasis added).

13. Compare City of Indianapolis v. Edmond, 531 U.S. 32, 121 S.Ct. 447, 143 L.Ed.2d 333, 345 (2000) ("[T]he Fourth Amendment would almost certainly permit an appropriately tailored roadblock to thwart a terrorist attack or to catch a dangerous criminal who is likely to flee by way of a particular route.").

14. Justice Robert Jackson once warned that "[t]here is danger, if the Court does not temper its doctrinaire logic with a little practical wisdom, it will convert the constitutional Bill of Rights into a suicide pact." Terminiello v. Chicago, 337 U.S. 1, 37, 69 S.Ct. 894, 93 L.Ed.2d 1131 (1949) (Jackson, J. dissenting).

15. "[T]he measure of a country's greatness is its ability to retain compassion in time of crisis. No nation in recorded history has a greater tradition of revering justice and fair treatment for all its citizens

Section 2. Primary Civil or Special Needs Exceptions

a. Inventory search

(1) General rule: vehicles

It is settled that police may, pursuant to established police procedures, impound and inventory the contents of a motor vehicle, whenever police lawfully impound such a vehicle; no warrant or probable cause is required for such an inventory. The purpose of such an inventory is to protect the police against subsequent claims by the owner that police lost or stole property in the car; to protect the owner's property while in police custody; and to protect the police from any danger from the vehicle's contents.[16] The rationale for this exception is that a warrant and a showing of probable cause is impracticable and ill-suited to achieve these important objectives.[17] The contents of containers in the motor vehicle may also be inventoried provided it is done according to standard police procedures,[18] but not if the police have no such standard procedure.[19]

(2) Initial vehicle impoundment

As previously noted, the initial impoundment of the vehicle must be lawful, i.e., based on standard police procedures, for the inventory exception to apply. This may occur where police discover an abandoned vehicle on the street,[20] or lawfully arrest the driver where the driver's vehicle would otherwise be left in some peril on the street,[21] or lawfully seize a vehicle for later forfeiture proceedings.[22] In this respect, it is essential that the inventory search be a bona fide inventory according to standard police criteria and procedures, not a subterfuge for a general exploratory search for evidence of crime.[23] In enforcing this

---

in times of turmoil, confusion and tension than ours. This is a country that stands tallest in troubled times, a country that clings to fundamental principles, cherishes its constitutional heritage, and rejects simple solutions that compromise the values of our democratic system." Furman v. Georgia, 408 U.S. 238, 370, 92 S.Ct. 2726, 33 L.Ed.2d 346, 424 (1972) (Justice Thurgood Marshall concurring).

16. South Dakota v. Opperman, 428 U.S. 364, 96 S.Ct. 3092, 49 L.Ed.2d 1000 (1976); Colorado v. Bertine, 479 U.S. 367, 107 S.Ct. 738, 93 L.Ed.2d 739 96 S.Ct. 3092, 49 L.Ed.2d 1000 (1987); see also 3 Wayne LaFave, Search and Seizure § 7.4(a) (5th ed. 2012) and cases collected. For a criticism of this exception that also collects the relevant cases, see 2 John Wesley Hall, Search and Seizure §§ 40.1–40.25–31.25 (5th ed. 2013). Also see cases collected at "Searches and Seizures" § 66 West Key No.

17. "[I]nventory searches are now a well-defined exception to the warrant requirement of the Fourth Amendment. The policies behind the warrant requirement are not implicated in an inventory search; nor is the related concept of probable cause." Colorado v. Bertine, 479 U.S. 367, 374, 107 S.Ct. 738, 93 L.Ed.2d 739, 745 (1987).

18. Colorado v. Bertine, 479 U.S. 367, 374, 107 S.Ct. 738, 93 L.Ed.2d 739 (1987) (closed backpack opened and contents inventoried; search upheld).

19. Florida v. Wells, 495 U.S. 1, 110 S.Ct.1632, 109 L.Ed.2d 1 (1990) (locked suitcase forced open and contents inventoried; search struck down).

20. South Dakota v. Opperman, 428 U.S. 364, 96 S.Ct. 3092, 49 L.Ed.2d 1000 (1976).

21. Colorado v. Bertine, 479 U.S. 367, 374, 107 S.Ct. 738, 93 L.Ed.2d 739 (1987); Florida v.Wells, 495 U.S. 1, 110 S.Ct.1632, 109 L.Ed.2d 1 (1990).

22. Cooper v. California, 386 U.S. 58, 87 S.Ct. 788, 17 L.Ed.2d 730 (1967).

23. "Our view that standardized criteria or established routine must regulate the opening of containers found during inventory searches is based on the principle that *an inventory search must not be a ruse for a general rummaging in order to discover evidence. The individual police officer must not be allowed so much latitude that inventory searches are turned into a 'purposeful and general means of discovering evidence of crime.'*" Florida v. Wells, 495 U.S. 1, 110 S.Ct.1632, 109 L.Ed.2d 1, 6 (1990)

rule, there are two critical factors to consider: (1) whether the police have standardized procedures for impounding and inventorying motor vehicles, and (2) whether the police followed these procedures.[24]

It is unnecessary for the police to offer the driver an opportunity to make arrangements for the disposal of the vehicle short of impoundment when the driver is arrested.[25] But if the driver does make such arrangements on his own—as, for example, by consenting to have a passenger with a drivers license be responsible for the vehicle—and the police nonetheless impound vehicle and inventory it, the impoundment and inventory would appear to be conducted in bad faith motivated by a police desire to conduct a general exploratory search for evidence of crime, which is not permissible. Of course, if the driver has been unlawfully taken into custody in the first instance, this would necessarily make the subsequent impoundment of the vehicle entirely unreasonable.

(3) Scope of vehicle inventory

An inventory of a motor vehicle may be unreasonable because of its intolerable intensity and scope. It is doubtful, for example, that the police can remove vehicle parts or go into inaccessible areas—such as air vents or engine and carburetor crevices under the hood of the vehicle—because these are not places where people store their belongings, and therefore it is unnecessary to look in such places to conduct an inventory of personal property within the vehicle. By way of contrast, if police have probable cause under the *Carroll* doctrine to search the vehicle for contraband drugs, it seems clear that police could reasonably search these hidden areas in the vehicle where drugs could very well be hidden. But not so for an inventory search.[26]

(4) Other inventory searches

The inventory exception is not limited to impounded motor vehicles. It also applies to a standardized inventory of an arrestee's possessions prior to police booking and jailing the arrestee.[27]

(internal citation omitted) (emphasis added).

"We conclude that ... reasonable police procedures administered in good faith satisfy the Fourth Amendment, even though courts might as a matter of hindsight be able to devise equally reasonable rules requiring a different procedure. * * * Our decisions have always adhered to the requirement that inventories be conducted according to standard criteria. * * * Nothing ... prohibits the exercise of police discretion [in deciding whether to impound or park and lock the car after arresting the driver] *so long as that discretion is exercised according to standard criteria and on the basis of something other than suspicion of evidence of criminal activity.*" Colorado v. Bertine, 479 U.S. 367, 374, 107 S.Ct. 738, 93 L.Ed.2d 739, 747 n. 6, 748 (1987) (emphasis added).

See 3 Wayne LaFave, Search and Seizure § 7.5(e) (5th ed. 2012) for a discussion of subterfuge inventories conducted to discover evidence of crime.

24. Although not constitutionally required, the prosecution, as a matter of better practice, would be well advised to have these procedures put in writing in a police manual or similar official directive so that the standardized nature of the practice is not open to any doubt. This is particularly true because the inventory exception is at times susceptible of being used as a general exploratory search for evidence of crime—which factor may cast doubt, at the trial level, on the credibility of a law enforcement officer's uncorroborated testimony that the search procedure followed in a particular case was in accord with standardized police inventory practice. See John Wesley Hall, Search and Seizure 40.08–40.09 (5th ed. 2013).

25. Colorado v. Bertine, 479 U.S. 367, 374, 107 S.Ct. 738, 93 L.Ed.2d 739 (1987).

26. 3 Wayne LaFave, Search and Seizure § 7.4(a) at 854–855 (5th ed. 2012); 2 John Wesley Hall, Search and Seizure § 40.20 (5th ed. 2013).

27. "The question here is whether, consistent with the Fourth Amendment, it is reasonable for police to search the personal effects of a person under lawful arrest as part of the routine administrative

b. Border search

(1) General rule

It is settled that U.S. Customs officials may, without a warrant, conduct a "routine" border search of all travelers as they enter into the United States from abroad. A border search of this nature is a search of the traveler's person, suitcases, vehicle, vessel or other personal belongings; no probable cause or reasonable suspicion is required for such a search.[28] By definition, border searches must take place at the international border of the United States or its functional equivalent.[29] A traveler from the continental United States

---

procedure at a police station house incident to booking and jailing the suspect. * * *

[W]e hold that it is not 'unreasonable' for police, as part of the routine procedure incident to incarcerating an arrested person, to search any container or article in his possession in accordance with established inventory procedures." Illinois v. LaFayette, 462 U.S. 640, 103 S.Ct. 2605, 77 L.Ed. 65, 69, 73 (1983) (inventory of contents of arrestee's shoulder bag in which contraband drugs were discovered and seized). For lower federal and state court cases collected on this issue, see "Searches and Seizures" § 58 West Key No.

28. "Travelers may be so stopped in crossing an international boundary because of national self-protection reasonably requiring one entering the country to identify himself as entitled to come in, and his belongings as effects which may be lawfully brought in." Carroll v. United States, 267 U.S. 132, 45 S.Ct. 280, 69 L.Ed.2d 543, 551–52 (1925).

"The Government's interest in preventing the entry of unwanted persons and effects is at its zenith at the international border. Time and again, we have stated that 'searches made at the border, pursuant to the longstanding right of the sovereign to protect itself by stopping and examining persons and property crossing into this country, are reasonable simply by virtue of the fact that they occur at the border.' Congress, since the beginning of our Government, 'has granted the Executive plenary authority to conduct routine searches and seizures at the border, without probable cause or a warrant, in order to regulate the collection of duties and to prevent the introduction of contraband into this country.' The modern statute that authorized the search in this case, 46 Stat. 747, 19 U.S.C. § 1581(a), [is] derived from a statute passed by the First Congress..., and reflects the 'impressive historical pedigree' of the Government's power and interest. It is axiomatic that the United States, as sovereign, has the inherent authority to protect, and a paramount interest in protecting, its territorial integrity." United States v. Flores-Montano, 540 U.S. 149, 124 S.Ct. 1582, 1585–86, 158 L.Ed.2d 311 (2004) (internal citations omitted) (search of the gas tank of incoming traveler's automobile at a port of entry in Southern California upheld: no reasonable suspicion required).

"That searches made at the border, pursuant to the longstanding right of the sovereign to protect itself by stopping and examining persons and property crossing into this country, are reasonable simply by virtue of the fact that they occur at the border, should by now, require no extended demonstration.* * * Border searches, then, from the adoption of the Fourth Amendment have been considered to be 'reasonable' by the single fact that the person or item in question had entered into our country from the outside. There has never been any additional requirement that the reasonableness of a border search depended on the existence of probable cause. This longstanding recognition that searches at our borders without probable cause and without a warrant are nonetheless 'reasonable' has a history as old as the Fourth Amendment itself. We reaffirm it here." United States v. Ramsey, 431 U.S. 606, 97 S.Ct. 1972, 52 L.Ed.2d 617, 626, 628 (1977).

In *Ramsey*, a US Customs official in NYC opened eight suspect bulky envelopes which had been mailed from Thailand to the defendants in the District of Columbia. The official discovered heroin in these envelopes. The envelopes were then re-sealed and delivered under surveillance to the defendants. The defendants were then arrested after taking possession of the heroin. The Court held that the warrantless search of the envelopes by US Customs was a reasonable border search.

See 5 Wayne LaFave, Search and Seizure § 10.5(a) (5th ed. 2012); 2 John Wesley Hall, Search and Seizure Ch. 35 (5th ed. 2013).

29. "[Border searches] may in certain circumstances take place, not only at the border itself, but at its functional equivalents as well. For example, searches at an established station near the border, at a point marking the confluence of two or more roads that extend from the border, might be functional equivalents of border searches. For another example, a search of the passengers and cargo

to a United States territory such as Puerto Rico, however, has not crossed an international border into the United States and may not be subjected to a border search.[30]

(2) Detention of and more intensive search of traveler

Any detention of a traveler entering the United States, beyond the time necessary to conduct a routine customs search at the border, must be based on reasonable suspicion.[31] But a delay necessary to conduct a routine border search requires no such showing.[32]

An intensive, non-routine search of the incoming traveler's person at the border [such as a strip search, a body cavity search, or an X-ray search] may also require some showing of reasonable suspicion. But the Court has never squarely decided this issue.[33] Lower federal and state court cases, however, have required a showing of reasonable suspicion to conduct a strip search.[34] The cases have struggled for a standard to conduct a body cavity search, but currently require a showing of reasonable suspicion.[35]

On the other hand, an intensive search of an incoming traveler's vehicle—such as searching the vehicle's gas tank after disassembling it and later replacing it—does not require a showing of reasonable suspicion. The only possible limitation to such a search is that it must not be carried out in an abusive manner—such as severely damaging the vehicle.[36]

---

of an airplane arriving at a St. Louis airport after a non-stop flight from Mexico City would clearly be the functional equivalent of a border search." Almeida-Sanchez v. United States, 413 U.S. 266, 93 S.Ct. 2535, 37 L.Ed.2d 596, 602 (1973) (roving patrol search of car 20 miles from US-Mexican border held not a border search).

30. Torres v. Puerto Rico, 442 U.S. 465, 99 S.Ct. 2425, 61 L.Ed.2d 1 (1979) (Puerto Rican statute authorizing such a search struck down).

31. United States v. Montoya de Hernandez, 473 U.S. 531, 105 S.Ct. 3304, 87 L.Ed.2d 381 (1985) (16-hour detention of air traveler, who had flown in from Colombia to the LA International Airport, upheld based on reasonable suspicion that the traveler was smuggling narcotics in her alimentary canal—i.e., that she had ingested narcotics through the mouth and presumably would expel them later from her system by defecation).

"We hold that the detention of a traveler at the border, beyond the scope of a routine customs search and inspection, is justified at its inception if customs agents, considering all the facts surrounding the traveler and her trip, reasonably suspect that the traveler is smuggling contraband in her alimentary canal." United States v. Montoya De Hernandez, 87 L.Ed.2d at 391.

32. United States v. Flores-Montano, 540 U.S. 149, 124 S.Ct. 1582, 158 L.Ed.2d 311 (2004) (one-hour delay at border while customs officials disassembled, searched and reassembled the gas tank to traveler's automobile was a normal delay: no reasonable suspicion required) ("We think it clear that one to two-hour delays at international borders are to be expected." 124 S.Ct. at 1587, n. 3).

33. "[W]e suggest no view on what level of suspicion, if any, is required for non-routine border searches such as strip, body cavity or involuntary X-ray searches." United States v. Montoya de Hernandez, 473 U.S. 531, 105 S.Ct. 3304, 87 L.Ed.2d 381, 391, n.8. (1985).

34. 5 Wayne LaFave, Search and Seizure § 10.5(c) (5th ed. 2012).

35. 5 Wayne LaFave, Search and Seizure § 10.5(e) (5th ed. 2012).

36. "For the reasons stated, we conclude that the Government's authority to conduct suspicionless inspections at the border includes the authority to remove, disassemble, and reassemble the vehicle's fuel tank. While it may be true that some searches of property are so destructive as to require a different result, this is not one of them." United States v. Flores-Montano, 540 U.S. 149, 124 S.Ct. 1582, 1587, 158 L.Ed.2d 311 (2004) (fuel tank search of traveler's automobile upheld: vehicle not damaged).

For cases that have held that drilling into a vehicle to conduct a border search requires a showing of reasonable suspicion, see: United States v. Rivas, 157 F.3d 364 (5th Cir. 1998); United States v. Robles, 45 F.3d 1 (1st Cir. 1995); United States v. Carreon, 872 F.2d 1436 (10th Cir. 1989). The Court, however, has expressly declined to pass on the reasonableness of such drilling searches: "We again leave open the question whether, and under what circumstances, a border search might be deemed 'unreasonable' because of the particularly offensive manner it is carried out." United States v. Flores-Montano, 124 S.Ct. at 1586–57, n. 2 (quoting from previous case, quotation marks omitted).

(3) Related detentions and searches near the border

There are some detentions and searches by federal officials near the border [but not at the border or its functional equivalent] that are related to, but are not the same as border searches. Permanent traffic checkpoints near the border may be established in which federal officials are allowed to stop motor vehicles and make brief inquiries of the occupants concerning their citizenship status. No reasonable suspicion is required for such stops and inquiries.[37] However, federal officials may not search these vehicles unless they have probable cause to do so.[38] Nor may a motor vehicle be stopped near the border [not at an established traffic checkpoint] for inquiries concerning the occupant's citizenship unless based on reasonable suspicion; being of Mexican descent does not constitute reasonable suspicion that the person is an illegal alien.[39] Moreover, roving patrols near the border cannot conduct border searches of automobiles; there must be probable cause to conduct such searches.[40]

c. Administrative inspection search

(1) General rule

Commercial enterprises are often subject to various legislative schemes that require periodic warrantless inspections of the business by government officials for various purposes. Although the Fourth Amendment clearly protects commercial businesses from unreasonable search and seizure, the Court has held that these legislative inspection schemes do not violate the Fourth Amendment where: (1) the business involved in a "closely regulated industry" that is affected with the public interest, and (2) the statutory scheme meets certain criteria: (a) there must be a substantial governmental interest that informs the regulatory scheme pursuant to which the inspection is made; (b) the warrantless inspection must be necessary to further the regulatory scheme; and (c) the statutory inspection program must provide a constitutionally adequate substitute for a warrant in that (i) it must advise the business owner that the inspection is made pursuant to law and has a defined scope, and (ii) it must limit the discretion of the inspecting officials. Moreover, the inspection that is accomplished in a given case must be in compliance with the relevant statute and cannot be in violation thereof, else the search is unreasonable under the Fourth Amendment. Finally, the fact that a particular inspection scheme involving a "closely regulated industry" has penal sanctions does not in itself render the scheme a violation of the Fourth Amendment under this exception—so long as the searching officer does not use the scheme as a pretext to gather evidence of penal law violations.[41]

---

37. United States v. Martinez-Fuerte, 428 U.S. 543, 96 S.Ct. 3074, 49 L.Ed.2d 1116 (1976).
38. United States v. Ortiz, 422 U.S. 891, 95 S.Ct. 2585, 45 L.Ed.2d 623 (1975).
39. United States v. Brignoni-Ponce, 422 U.S. 873, 95 S.Ct. 2574, 45 L.Ed.2d 607 (1975).
40. Almeida-Sanchez v. United States, 413 U.S. 266, 93 S.Ct. 2535, 37 L.Ed.2d 596 (1973).
41. For an excellent summary of the law in this area, see New York v. Burger, 482 U.S. 691, 107 S.Ct. 2636, 96 L.Ed.2d 601, 612–14, 620–23 & n. 27 (1987); also see 5 Wayne LaFave, Search and Seizure § 10.2 (5th ed. 2012). For a discussion of the pretext point, see City of Indianapolis v. Edmond, 531 U.S. 32, 121 S.Ct. 447, 148 L.Ed.2d 333, 346 (2000), and Whren v. United States, 517 U.S. 806, 116 S.Ct. 1769, 1773, 135 L.Ed.2d 89 (1996).

(2) Statutory inspection programs of particular businesses

The Court has upheld statutory inspection programs for the following "closely regulated" industries: the liquor industry,[42] the firearms industry,[43] the coal mining industry,[44] and the automobile junkyard industry.[45] Subsequently, the Court has characterized these decisions as having created an exception to the Fourth Amendment warrant and probable cause requirements because a "special need" beyond the need of ordinary criminal law enforcement is presented by such inspection programs.[46]

On the other hand, the Court has struck down warrantless statutory inspection schemes in the following areas and has required administrative search warrants[47] for such inspections: OSHA job safety health inspections for all businesses in interstate commerce,[48] and health and fire code inspections of homes and businesses.[49] In a related area, the Court has interpreted federal tax collection statutes in light of Fourth Amendment principles so as *not* to authorize a warrantless entry onto private premises to levy on a taxpayer's property in payment for tax deficiencies; the Fourth Amendment requires a warrant for such an entry.[50]

(3) Other related administrative inspections

The Court has also upheld other administrative-type inspections, such as: a scheduled home visit by a welfare worker as a condition for receiving welfare benefits,[51] marine safety and documents inspection of a vessel after a random stop of the vessel in waters with ready access to the open sea,[52] and a drivers license and car registration inspection at traffic roadblocks.[53]

Section 3. Secondary Civil or Special Needs Exceptions

a. Probationer and parolee search[54]

The Court has held that a warrantless search of a probationer's home by a probation officer satisfied the demands of the Fourth Amendment and was a reasonable search within the meaning of that Amendment—because it was carried out pursuant to a state

42. Colonnade Catering Co. v. United States, 397 U.S. 78, 90 S.Ct.774, 25 L.Ed.2d 60 (1970) (forcible entry into liquor storeroom not authorized by the statute and therefore unreasonable under Fourth Amendment).

43. United States v. Biswell, 406 U.S. 311, 92 S.Ct. 1593, 32 L.Ed.2d 87 (1972).

44. Donovan v. Dewey, 452 U.S. 594, 101 S.Ct. 2534, 69 L.Ed.2d 262 (1981).

45. New York v. Burger, 482 U.S. 691, 107 S.Ct. 2636, 96 L.Ed.2d 601 (1987).

46. Griffin v. Wisconsin, 483 U.S. 868, 107 S.Ct. 3164, 97 L.Ed.2d 709, 717 (1987).

47. For a discussion of administrative search warrants, see Chapter 13, Section 2h of this work.

48. Marshall v. Barlow's, Inc., 436 U.S. 307, 98 S.Ct. 1816, 56 L.Ed.2d 305 (1978).

49. Camara v. Municipal Court, 387 U.S. 523, 87 S.Ct. 1727, 18 L.Ed.2d 930 (1967); See v. City of Seattle, 387 U.S. 541, 87 S.Ct. 1737, 18 L.Ed.2d 943 (1967).

50. G.M. Leasing Corp. v. United States., 429 U.S. 338, 97 S.Ct. 619, 50 L.Ed.2d 530, 546–47 (1977).

51. Wyman v. James, 400 U.S. 309, 91 S.Ct. 381, 27 L.Ed.2d 408 (1971).

52. United States v. Villamonte-Marquez, 462 U.S. 579, 103 S.Ct. 2573, 77 L.Ed.2d 22 (1983).

53. Delaware v. Prouse, 440 U.S. 648, 99 S.Ct. 1391, 59 L.Ed.2d 660 (1979 (dicta).

54. For a thorough discussion of probationer and parolee searches, see 5 Wayne LaFave, Search and Seizure § 10.10 at 516 et. seq. (5th ed. 2012).

probation regulation which itself satisfied the Fourth Amendment's reasonableness requirement. This regulation authorized a warrantless search by a probation officer of a probationer's home, in order to properly supervise the probationer, based, in effect, on a showing of reasonable suspicion that the home contained contraband. Using for the first time a "special needs" analysis, the Court concluded that neither a warrant nor a showing of probable cause was required for the search of a probationer's home because both would unduly restrict the state's supervision of a person on probation. A "special need," apart from ordinary criminal law enforcement, was presented by the state's operation of its probationary system.[55]

But a search of a probationer's home based on reasonable suspicion need not be confined to a probation officer search designed to enforce probationary conditions. Using a balancing analysis, the Court has subsequently upheld a police search of a probationer's residence while investigating a criminal offense based on reasonable suspicion—where the probationer was subject to a probation condition requiring that the probationer consent to warrantless and suspicionless searches of one's home, person or property by either the probation officer or the police.[56] Beyond that, the Court has expressly declined to decide whether a probationer's acceptance of the above-stated probationary condition constitutes a voluntary consent to such a search,[57] or whether this condition so diminished or eliminated the probationer's reasonable expectation of privacy that no showing of individualized suspicion is required for the search of a probationer's residence.[58]

---

55. Griffin v. Wisconsin, 483 U.S. 868, 107 S.Ct. 3164, 97 L.Ed.2d 709 (1987). In *Griffin,* a probation officer received information from a police detective that there were or might be guns in the defendant probationer's home; this information was sufficient under the state regulation for the probation officer to search the defendant's home; a gun was found in defendant's home; held reasonable search.

"In Griffin v. Wisconsin, the Supreme Court upheld a warrantless search [based] on reasonable suspicion of a probationer's home conducted pursuant to an administrative regulation applicable to all probationers...." 5 Wayne LaFave, Search and Seizure § 10.10(c) at 539 (5th ed. 2012).

56. "We hold that the balance of these considerations requires no more than reasonable suspicion to conduct a search of this probationer's house. The degree of individualized suspicion required of a search is a determination of when there is a sufficiently high probability that criminal conduct is occurring to make the intrusion on the individual's privacy interest reasonable. Although the Fourth Amendment ordinarily requires the degree of probability embodied in the term 'probable cause,' a lesser degree satisfies the Constitution when the balance of governmental and private interests makes such a standard reasonable. Those interests warrant a lesser probable cause standard here. *When an officer has reasonable suspicion that a probationer subject to a search condition is engaged in criminal activity, there is enough likelihood that criminal conduct is occurring that an intrusion on the probationer's significantly diminished privacy interests is reasonable.*

The same circumstances that lead us to conclude that reasonable suspicion is constitutionally sufficient also render a warrant requirement unnecessary."United States v. Knights, 354 U.S. 112, 122 S.Ct. 587, 592–93, 151 L.Ed.2d 497 (2001) (internal citations omitted) (emphasis added) (reasonable suspicion that probationer had arson materials in his apartment justified a warrantless search of his apartment by investigating police, where probationer was subject to a probation condition that he "submit his person, property, place of residence, vehicle, personal effects to search at anytime, with or without a search warrant, warrant of arrest or reasonable cause by any probation officer or law enforcement officer.").

57. "We need not decide today whether Knight's acceptance of the [probation] search condition constituted consent in the *Schneckloth* sense of a complete waiver of his Fourth Amendment rights ..."United States v. Knights, 354 U.S. 112, 122 S.Ct. 587, 591, 151 L.Ed.2d 497 (2001).

58. "We do not decide whether the probation condition so diminished or completely eliminated, Knight's reasonable expectation of privacy (or constituted consent ...) that a search by a law enforcement officer without any individualized suspicion would have satisfied the reasonableness requirement of the Fourth Amendment. The terms of the probation condition permit such a search, but we need not address the constitutionality of a suspicionless search because the search in this case was supported

It does not follow, however, that "an opinion upholding the constitutionality of a particular search implicitly holds unconstitutional any search that is not like it."[59] Accordingly, the Court has, in fact, done away with any constitutional requirement of reasonable suspicion for a *parolee* search—a result that seems equally applicable to a *probationary* search. Namely, the Court has held that a suspicionless search of a parolee by a police officer under a state statute that authorized such a search did not violate the parolee's Fourth Amendment rights.[60] The only limitation to this holding is that under the applicable state law, the parolee search cannot be "arbitrary, capricious or harassing"—a limitation that resembles a due process restriction and therefore an arguable requirement of the Fourth Amendment as well.[61] As in probationary searches, the Court expressly declined to decide whether the parolee's acceptance of a parole condition that authorized such a suspicionless search constituted a voluntary consent to such a search.[62]

b. Prison inmate or pre-trial detainee search

A prison inmate has no reasonable expectation of privacy in his or her prison cell; random shakedown searches of a prison inmate's cell are therefore not prohibited by the Fourth Amendment, as the Amendment is inapplicable to such searches.[63] It is also not a violation of a prison inmate's Fourth Amendment rights for prison authorities to intercept mail sent by an inmate to a third party.[64]

---

by reasonable suspicion." United States v. Knights, 354 U.S. 112, 122 S.Ct. 587, 592 n. 6, 151 L.Ed.2d 497 (2001).

59. United States v. Knights, 534 U.S. 112, 122 S.Ct. 587, 590, 151 L.Ed.2d 497 (2001).

60. "California law provides that every prisoner eligible for release on state parole 'shall agree in writing to be subject to search or seizure by a parole officer or other peace officer at any time of the day or night, with or without a search warrant and with or without cause.' [citation omitted]. We granted certiorari to decide whether a suspicionless search, conducted under the authority of this statute, violates the Constitution. We hold that it does not." * * * "Thus, we conclude that the Fourth Amendment does not prohibit a police officer from conducting a suspicionless search of a parolee." Samson v. California, 547 U.S. 843, 126 S.Ct. 2193, 2196, 2202, 165 L.Ed.2d 250 (2006) (suspicionless search of parolee's person on the street by police officer upheld; the officer knew petitioner was on parole).

61. "The concern that California's suspicionless search system gives officers unbridled discretion to conduct searches, thereby inflicting dignitary harms that arouse strong resentment in parolees and undermine their ability to reintegrate into productive society, is belied by California's prohibition on 'arbitrary, capricious or harassing' searches." Samson v. California, 547 U.S. 843, 126 S.Ct. 2193, 2202, 165 L.Ed.2d 250 (2006). As the Court notes, a search by a police officer of a person not known to the officer to be on parole has been held unreasonable under California law.126 S.Ct. at 2202 n.5. "It would necessarily be arbitrary, capricious and harassing to conduct a suspicionless search of someone without knowledge of the status that renders that person, in the State's judgment, susceptible to such an invasion." 126 S.Ct. at 2208 n. 7 (Stevens, J. dissenting).

62. "Because we find that the search at issue is reasonable under our general Fourth Amendment approach, we need not reach the issue whether 'acceptance of the search condition constituted consent in the *Schneckloth* ... sense of a complete waiver of his Fourth Amendment rights.'" Samson v. California, 547 U.S. 843, 126 S.Ct. 2193, 2199 n. 3, 165 L.Ed.2d 250 (2006) (internal citation omitted). See Justice Stevens rejection of the consent theory in this context as "sophistry." 126 S.Ct. at 2206 n. 4 (Stevens, J. dissenting).

63. Hudson v. Palmer, 468 U.S. 517,104 S.Ct. 3194 82 L.Ed.2d 393 (1984).

64. Stroud v. United States, 251 U.S. 15, 40 S.Ct. 50,64 L.Ed. 103 (1919). In *Stroud*, the "Bird Man of Alcatraz," Robert Stroud, was convicted of the murder of a prison guard at Leavenworth Federal Penitentiary. Stroud voluntarily wrote certain letters apparently of an incriminating nature and submitted them for mailing; based on standard prison procedures, these letters were read by the prison authorities before being sent out, as a means of maintaining prison discipline. Upon reading these letters, the prison authorities turned them over to the federal district attorney; the letters were

Indeed, the Court has upheld, against a Fourth Amendment claim, the intensive strip-search procedures of two pre-trial detention centers in which all arrestees admitted to the *general population of the jail* were required for jail safety and health reasons (a) to disrobe and shower under the close visual observation of jail officials, and (b) to manipulate their body parts upon demand—so that the officials could look for contraband, weapons, scars, marks, gang membership tattoos, wounds, lice and diseases. These procedures were applicable to all such arrestees admitted to the general jail population—regardless of the circumstances of the arrest, the nature of the suspected offense, or the arrestee's demeanor or criminal history.[65]

---

introduced in evidence at Stroud's trial. The Court held that Stroud's Fourth Amendment rights were not violated by this search.

65. Florence v. Board of Chosen Freeholders, 566 U.S. ___, 132 S.Ct. 1510, 182 L.Ed.2d 566 (2012) (petitioner was arrested pursuant to a warrant for non-payment of a fine on a minor offense; it was later found that the fine had subsequently been paid but the warrant not withdrawn; held: no exemption required for minor offense arrestees).

"This case presents the question of what rules, or limitations, the Constitution imposes on searches of arrested persons who are held in jail while their cases are being processed * * * In addressing this type of constitutional claim, courts must defer to the judgment of correctional officials unless the record contains substantial evidence showing their policies are an unnecessary or unjustified response to the problems of jail security. That necessary showing has not been made in this case." 182 L.Ed.2d at 572.

"The question here is whether undoubted security imperatives involved in jail supervision override the assertion that some detainees must be *exempt* from the more invasive search procedures at issue absent reasonable suspicion of a concealed weapon or other contraband. The Court has held that deference must be given to the officials in charge of the jail unless there is 'substantial evidence' demonstrating their response to the situation is exaggerated. [citation omitted]. Petitioner has not met this standard, and the record provides full justifications for the procedures used." 182 L.Ed.2d at 577.

The Court, however, left open a number of questions: (1) whether strip-search procedures would be necessary if the arrestee was held without assignment to the general jail population; (2) whether strip-search procedures would be justified where the person was arrested for a minor offense and could have been held in available facilities apart from the general jail population; (3) whether strip-search procedures would be justified if they involved the touching of arrestees by jail officials

(1) "This case does not require the Court to rule on the types of searches that would be reasonable in instances where, for example, a detainee will be held without assignment to the general population and without substantial contact with other detainees." 182 L.Ed.2d at 582.

(2) "The circumstances before this Court, however, do not present the opportunity to consider a narrow exemption of the sort Justice Alito describes [citation omitted] which might restrict whether an arrestee whose detention has not yet been reviewed by a magistrate or other judicial officer, and who can be held in available facilities removed from the general population, may be subjected to the types of procedures at issue here." Id.

(3) "There may also be legitimate concerns about the invasiveness of searches that involve the touching of detainees. These issues, however, are not implicated on the facts of this case, however, and it unnecessary to consider them." 182 L.Ed.2d at 583.

"It is important to note, however, that the Court does not hold that it is *always* reasonable to conduct a full strip search of an arrestee whose detention has not been reviewed by a judicial officer and who could be held in available facilities apart from the general population. Most of those arrested for minor offenses are not dangerous, and most are released from custody prior to or at the time of their initial appearance before a magistrate. In some cases, the charges are dropped. In others, arrestees are released either on their own recognizance or on minimal bail. In the end, few are sentenced to incarceration. For these persons, admission to the general jail population, with the concomitant humiliation of a strip search, may not be reasonable." Florence v. Board of Chosen Freeholders, 566 U.S. ___, 132 S.Ct. 1510, 182 L.Ed.2d 566, 584 (2012) (Alito, J. concurring). Compare Atwater v. City of Lago Vista, 532 U.S. 318, 121 S.Ct. 1569, 149 L.Ed.2d 549 (2001) (person arrested for non-jailable seat belt violation was held in separate cell and not admitted to general population).

See also Florence v. Board of Chosen Freeholders, 566 U.S. ___, 132 S.Ct. 1510, 182 L.Ed.2d 566, 583 (2012) (Roberts, C.J. concurring) ("As with Justice Alito, however, it is important to me that the

A federal custodial institution's search rules for pre-trial detainees have been upheld by the Court as not constituting an unreasonable search of the detainees in violation of the detainees' Fourth Amendment rights. The first rule precluded the detainee from being present when a shakedown search of the detainee's cell was conducted by institution officials. The second rule required the detainee to submit to a strip search and a visual examination of body cavities after every contact visit between the detainee and someone from outside the institution. No probable cause was required for the strip search or the body cavity visual inspection.[66]

Body cavity inspections, however, do involve substantial invasions of the detainee's privacy and must be carried out in a reasonable, not an abusive manner.[67] This would appear to preclude random body cavity searches conducted at the whim of prison officials.[68] Moreover, intentional harassment by jail officials of even the most hardened criminals cannot be tolerated in a civilized society.[69]

c. Public school student search

(1) General rule

In *New Jersey v T.L.O.*,[70] the Court, using a balancing approach, held that a warrantless search of a public school student's purse by school authorities may be conducted upon a showing of reasonable suspicion to believe that the search will turn up evidence that the student has violated or is violating the law or school rules;[71] the ensuing search must be reasonably related in scope to accomplishing the purpose of the search, and must not be excessively intrusive in view of the student's sex and age and the nature of the violation.[72]

Court does not foreclose the possibility of an exception to the rule it announces. * * * The Court is nonetheless wise to leave open the possibility of exceptions, to ensure that we 'not embarrass the future.'") (citation omitted).

66. A balancing test of Fourth Amendment reasonableness was employed to reach this result. Bell v. Wolfish, 441 U.S. 520, 99 S.Ct.1861, 60 L.Ed.2d 447, 480–82 (1979).

67. Bell v. Wolfish, 441 U.S. 520, 99 S.Ct. 1861, 60 L.Ed.2d 447, 480 (1979).

68. For a thorough discussion of searches directed at prisoners, see 5 Wayne LaFave, Search and Seizure § 10.9 (5th ed. 2012).

69. Florence v. Board of Chosen Freeholders, 566 U.S. ___, 132 S.Ct. 1510, 182 L.Ed.2d 566, 582 (2012), citing Hudson v. Palmer, 468 U.S. 517, 528, 104 S.Ct. 3194, 82 L.Ed.2d 393 (1984).

70. 469 U.S. 325, 105 S.Ct. 733, 83 L.Ed.2d 720 (1985).

71. "When the object of a school search is the enforcement of a school rule, a valid search assumes, of course, the rule's legitimacy. The Court said plainly in New Jersey v. T.L.O. [citation omitted] that standards of conduct for schools are for school administrators to determine without second-guessing by courts lacking the experience to appreciate what may be needed. Except in patently arbitrary instances, Fourth Amendment analysis takes the rule as a given, as it should obviously do in this case." Safford Unified School District v. Redding, 557 U.S. 364,129 S.Ct. 2633, 174 L.Ed.2d 354 (2009) (school rule prohibiting possession of all prescription or over-the-counter drugs without prior school permission held obviously proper).

72. "Under ordinary circumstances, a search of a [public school] student by a teacher or other school official will be 'justified at its inception' when there are reasonable grounds for suspecting that the search will turn up evidence that the student has violated or is violating either the law or the rules of the school. Such a search will be permissible in its scope when the measures adopted are reasonably related to the objectives of the search and are not excessively intrusive in light of the age and sex of the student and the nature of the infraction." New Jersey v. T.L.O., 469 U.S. 325, 105 S.Ct. 733, 83 L.Ed.2d 720, 734–35 (1985).

In *T.L.O.*, a teacher discovered the juvenile smoking in the girl's bathroom in violation of school rules. The juvenile was taken to the principal's office where she denied to the vice-principal that she had ever smoked before. The Court held that this showing gave the vice-principal reasonable suspicion

In particular, the Court concluded that a public school student while on school property has a reasonable expectation of privacy with respect to the student's person and other containers the student may bring to school—such as a purse, wallet, or gym bag—in which items of a non-contraband, personal nature may be stored.[73] Ordinarily, such

---

to search the purse which the juvenile was carrying. This search revealed a pack of cigarettes which the vice-principal seized; it also revealed a package of rolling paper which the school official recognized as paper used to roll marijuana cigarettes. The vice principal then conducted a more thorough search of the purse and discovered marijuana, a substantial amount of $1.00 bills, a list of students that owed the juvenile money, and two letters indicating that the juvenile was selling marijuana to students. The Court held that the second search was based on reasonable suspicion, namely the marijuana rolling paper discovered in the first search.

"'We have thus applied a standard of reasonable suspicion to determine the legality of a [public] school administrator's search of a student and have held that a school search 'will be permissible in its scope when the measures adopted are reasonably related to the objectives of the search and not excessively intrusive in light of the age and sex of the student and the nature of the infraction.'" Safford Unified School District v. Redding, 557 U.S. 364, 129 S.Ct. 2633, 174 L.Ed.2d 354 (2009) (quoting from New Jersey v. T.L.O.).

In Redding, a strip search of a 13-year-old female public school student was held a violation of her Fourth Amendment rights because the scope of the search was too intensive. There was reasonable suspicion to believe that the student had brought prescription and over-the-counter drugs to school in violation of school rules. But because there was no reason to suspect that these drugs posed a danger to the school or that they were concealed in her underwear, the strip search was held unreasonable under the Fourth Amendment..129 S.Ct. 2633 (2009) (but the school official who ordered the search was held entitled to qualified immunity from liability in this civil rights lawsuit because the Fourth Amendment right asserted in factual context of case was not clearly established at the time of the search).

"The issue here is whether a 13-year-old student's Fourth Amendment right was violated when she was subjected to a search of her bra and underpants by [public] school officials acting on reasonable suspicion that she had brought forbidden prescription and over-the-counter drugs to school. Because there was no reason to suspect the drugs presented a danger or were concealed in her underwear, we hold that the search did violate the Constitution, but because there is reason to question the clarity with which the right was established, the official who ordered the unconstitutional search is entitled to qualified immunity from liability." 129 S.Ct. at 2637–2638 [S.Ct.].

"Here the content of the suspicion failed to match the degree of the intrusion. Wilson [the school official] knew beforehand that the pills were prescription-strength ibuprofen and over-the-counter naproxen, common pain relievers equivalent to two Advil, or one Aleve. He must have been aware of the nature and limited threat of the specific drugs he was searching for, and while just about anything can be taken in quantities that will do real harm, Wilson had no reason to suspect that large quantities of the drugs were being passed around, or that individual students were receiving great numbers of pills.

Nor could Wilson have suspected that Savana [the public school student] was hiding common painkillers in her underwear. * * * But where the categorically extreme intrusiveness of a search down to the body of an adolescent require some justification in suspected facts, general possibilities fall short; a reasonable search that extensive calls for suspicion that will pay off. * * *

In sum, what was missing from the suspected facts that pointed to Savana was any indication of danger to the students from the power of the drugs or their quantity, or any reason to suppose that Savana was carrying pills in her underwear. We think the combination of these deficiencies was fatal to finding the search reasonable." 129 S.Ct. at 2642–43.

73. "We have recognized that even a limited search of the person is a substantial invasion of privacy. We have also recognized that searches of closed items of personal luggage are intrusions on protected privacy interests for 'the Fourth Amendment provides protection to the owner of every container that conceals its contents from plain view.' A search of a child's person or other bag carried on her [or his] person, no less than a similar search carried out on an adult, is undoubtedly a severe violation of subjective expectations of privacy. * * * Nor does the State's suggestion that children have no legitimate need to bring personal property into the schools seem well anchored in reality. Students at a minimum must bring to school not only the supplies needed for their studies, but also keys, money, and the necessaries of personal hygiene and grooming. In addition, students may carry on their persons or in purses or wallets such nondisruptive yet highly personal items as photographs, letters, and diaries. Finally students may have perfectly legitimate reasons to carry with them a variety of legitimate non-

privacy may not be invaded by public school authorities except upon the aforesaid showing of reasonable suspicion.[74]

Subsequently, the Court has characterized this decision as having created an exception to the Fourth Amendment warrant and probable cause requirements because warrantless searches of public school students on school grounds by school authorities present a "special need" beyond the need for ordinary criminal law enforcement.[75]

(2) Open questions

The Court, however, expressly declined to decide whether a public school student has a reasonable expectation of privacy in lockers, desks, or other school property provided for the storage of school supplies—or to express any opinion on the standards (if any) governing searches of such areas by school officials or by other public authorities acting at the request of school officials.[76] The Court also noted that the individualized suspicion standard might be relaxed for public school students in other appropriate but undefined circumstances [i.e., a school drug testing program], and reserved the question whether the Fourth Amendment exclusionary rule should be applied to unreasonable searches of public school students.[77] Moreover, the Court declined to express an opinion as to what the standard should be if the public student search by school officials was done with or at the behest of law enforcement agencies.[78] Finally, the Court has subsequently indicated that schools are places where public school students generally enjoy a diminished expectation of privacy.[79]

d. Public employee search

In *O'Connor v. Ortega*,[80] the Court held that a public employer may conduct a warrantless search of a public employee's office based on reasonable suspicion that the search will turn up evidence that the employee is guilty of work-related misconduct, or that the search is otherwise necessary for a noninvestigatory work-related purpose, such as to retrieve a file. The Court also noted that the individualized suspicion standard might be relaxed in the appropriate circumstances. The ensuing search is reasonable in scope if it

---

contraband items, and there is no reason to conclude that they have necessarily waived all rights to privacy in such items by bringing them onto the school grounds." New Jersey v. T.L.O., 469 U.S. 325, 105 733, 83 L.Ed.2d 720, 732, 733 (1985) (citations omitted).

74. As an aside, a program of suspicionless drug testing of student athletes, as well as students who participate in competitive extracurricular activities, in a public school setting has been upheld by the Court. See Section 3e(2) of this chapter.

75. Griffin v. Wisconsin, 483 U.S. 868, 107 S.Ct. 3164, 97 L.Ed.2d 709, 717 (1987).

76. New Jersey v. T.L.O., 469 U.S. 325, 105 S.Ct. 733, 83 L.Ed.2d 720, 732, n.5 (1985). LaFave states that public students may enjoy a reasonable although diminished expectation of privacy in their school lockers. 5 Wayne LaFave, Search and Seizure § 10.11(b) at 619 (5th ed. 2012).

77. New Jersey v. T.L.O., 469 U.S. 325, 105 S.Ct. 733, 83 L.Ed.2d 720, 729 n. 3 & 735 n. 8 (1985). For a thorough discussion of public school student searches, see 5 Wayne LaFave, Search and Seizure § 10.11 (5th ed. 2012). As an aside, the search and seizure exclusionary rule has consistently been applied by the state courts to unreasonable public student searches in juvenile delinquency proceedings; LaFave agrees with this line of cases. 1 Wayne LaFave, Search and Seizure § 1.7(b) (5th ed. 2012).

78. New Jersey v. T.L.O., 469 U.S. 325, 105 S.Ct. 733, 83 L.Ed.2d 720, 735 n. 7 (1985). "Lower [federal and state] courts, however, have held or suggested that the usual probable cause test obtains if the police are involved in the search in any significant way." 5 Wayne LaFave, Search and Seizure § 10.11 (b) at 626–627 (5th ed. 2012).

79. Florida v. J.L., 529 U.S. 266,120 S.Ct. 1375, 1380, 146 L.Ed.2d 254 (2000).

80. 480 U.S. 709, 107 S.Ct. 1492, 94 L.Ed.2d 714 (1987).

is confined to those areas where the object of the search might be found.[81] Subsequently, the Court has characterized this decision as having created an exception to the Fourth Amendment warrant and probable cause requirements because warrantless, work-related

81. "We hold, therefore, that public employer intrusions on the constitutionally protected privacy interests of government employees for noninvestigatory, work-related purposes, as well as work-related misconduct, should be judged by the standard of reasonableness under all the circumstances. * * * Ordinarily, a search of an employee's office by a supervisor will be 'justified at its inception' when there are reasonable grounds for suspecting that the search will turn up evidence that the employee is guilty of work-related misconduct, or that the search is necessary for a noninvestigatory work-related purpose such as to retrieve a file. * * * [W]e need not decide whether individualized suspicion is an *essential* element of the standard of reasonableness that we adopt today. The search will be permissible in its scope when 'the measures adopted are reasonably related to the objectives of the search and not excessively intrusive in light of ... the nature of the [misconduct].'" (citations omitted). O'Connor v. Ortega, 480 U.S. 709, 107 S.Ct. 1492, 94 L.Ed.2d 714, 728–29 (1987) (state hospital officials search the office, desk and file cabinets of state-employed psychiatrist based on evidence of work-related misconduct; civil rights suit brought by psychiatrist; Court holds that summary judgment for either party was inappropriate, and sends the case back for trial). See 5 Wayne LaFave, Search and Seizure § 10.3(d) (5th ed. 2012).

"Although as a general matter, warrantless searches are *per se* unreasonable under the Fourth Amendment, there are a few specifically established and well-delineated exceptions to that general rule. The Court has held that the special needs of the workplace justify one such exception. [O'Connor v. Ortega cite omitted].

Under the approach of the O'Connor plurality, when conducted for a noninvestigatory, work-related purpose or for the investigatio[n] of work-related misconduct, a government employer's warrantless search is reasonable if it is justified at its inception, and if the measures adopted are reasonably related to the objectives of the search and not excessively intrusive in light of the circumstances giving rise to the search." City of Ontario v. Quon, 560 U.S. 746, 130 S.Ct. 2619, 2630, 177 L.Ed2d 216 (2010) (internal citations and quotation marks omitted).

In Quon the Court, using the O'Connor standard, held that a city employer's audit of text messages sent by respondent police officer on a pager [owned by the city and issued to the officer] was a reasonable search under the Fourth Amendment based on the governmental employee exception to the search warrant requirement rule—assuming arguendo that the police officer had a reasonable expectation of privacy in such messages, and that the city's audit of these messages was a search within the meaning of the Fourth Amendment. The search was (a) reasonable at its inception because it was conducted for a non-investigative, work-related purpose [i.e., to determine whether the character limit for its pagers under the city's contract with the wireless company that provided such pagers was too low to meet the city's needs] as respondent police officer was continually going over the monthly contract limit; and (b) the scope of the audit was reasonably related to achieving this goal [i.e., city got transcripts from the wireless company for two months where respondent had exceeded the monthly character limit to see if the messages were work-related]. Accordingly, respondent's Fourth Amendment lawsuit against the city required, as the trial court found, a judgment for the city.

The Quon Court also recited another part of the O'Connor standard concerning the "operational realities" of the workplace: "[B]ecause some government offices may be so open to fellow employees that no expectation of privacy is reasonable, a court must consider the operational realities of the workplace in order to determine whether an employee's Fourth Amendment rights are implicated. On this view, the question whether an employee has a reasonable expectation of privacy must be addressed on a case-by-case basis." City of Ontario v. Quon, 130 S.Ct. at 2628 (internal citations and quotation marks omitted). The Court further noted that these "operational realities" "could diminish an employee's privacy expectations, and this diminution could be taken into consideration into when assessing the reasonableness of a workplace search." Id.

The Quon Court also upheld the pager audit in question based on Justice Scalia's standard stated in his concurring opinion in O'Connor. Under this standard, the offices of governmental employees are covered under the Fourth Amendment as a general matter without any inquiry into the "operational" realities" of the workplace, and that such searches should be upheld where conducted to retrieve work-related materials or to investigate violations of workplace rules—searches of the sort that are regarded as reasonable and normal in the private-employer context. Id. Aside from rejecting the "operational realities" approach, the Scalia standard is arguably much the same as the O'Connor standard. Tellingly, searches by public employers of their employees' desks and offices present a "special need" beyond the need for ordinary criminal law enforcement.[82]

e. Drug testing search

(1) General principle

Using the balancing test for Fourth Amendment reasonableness, the Court has upheld four warrantless, nonconsensual drug-testing programs that require no showing of individualized suspicion, and have struck down two other such programs. Running through each of these cases is one central principle. If the primary purpose of the drug testing program is to serve a "special need" of government above and beyond the normal governmental need for ordinary criminal law enforcement, the program does not, generally speaking, violate the Fourth Amendment rights of the persons tested under the program. But if the primary purpose of the program is to serve normal law enforcement demands, the program violates the Fourth Amendment rights of the persons so tested.

(2) Programs upheld

Accordingly, the Court has upheld Federal Railroad Administration safety regulations mandating that railroads administer blood and urine tests to railroad employees involved in certain railroad accidents and authorizing the same tests for railroad employees who violate certain government safety rules.[83] The primary purpose of this program was to prevent a serious problem of train accidents, some of which had been caused in the past by railroad employees under the influence of drugs—a purpose that served a "special need" of government above and beyond the normal demands of criminal law enforcement.

The Court has also upheld a U.S. Customs Service drug-testing program mandating urine tests of its employees who seek transfer or promotion to positions that directly involve the interdiction of illegal drugs into the country or that require the employee to carry a firearm.[84] The primary purpose of the program was to prevent drug users from ever occupying such sensitive law enforcement positions. Once again, this served a "special need" of government above and beyond the normal demands of criminal law enforcement.

And the Court has upheld two drug-testing programs for public schoolchildren, noting the diminished expectation of privacy enjoyed by such children under the Fourth Amendment. One such program was adopted by an Oregon public school district in which all students who participated in school athletic programs were subjected to random urinalysis testing in which urine samples were given students while fully clothed [male students at a urinal, and female students in an enclosed toilet stall while a school monitor listened outside the booth for the sounds of urination].[85] The primary purpose of this

---

however, the Court declines to decide which of these two standards states Fourth Amendment law—although courts will probably continue to apply the O' Connor standard until instructed otherwise.

82. Griffin v. Wisconsin, 483 U.S. 868, 107 S.Ct. 3164, 97 L.Ed.2d 709, 717 (1987).

83. Skinner v. Railway Labor Executives Ass'n, 489 U.S. 602, 109 S.Ct. 1402, 108 L.Ed.2 639 (1989).

84. National Treasury Employees Union v. Von Raab, 489 U.S. 656, 109 S.Ct. 1384, 103 L.Ed.2d 685 (1989).

85. Vernonia School District 47J v. Acton, 515 U.S. 646, 115 S.Ct. 2386, 132 L.Ed.2d 564 (1995). Under this program, all athletes were tested at the beginning of the season. Thereafter on a weekly basis the names of all athletes were placed in a pool from which 10% were blindly drawn for testing

program was to prevent drug use by athletes—who were otherwise susceptible to injury and to inflicting injury if not drug-free—and to thereby discourage drug use by the entire student body as the athletes were often student role models. The results of the testing were kept confidential, were not turned over to law enforcement authorities, and the only consequence visited upon the student who failed the test was that he or she was barred from participating in school athletics. This program thus served a "special need" of government apart from the normal governmental demand for criminal law enforcement.

Another such program upheld was adopted by an Oklahoma public school district in which all students who participated in competitive extracurricular activities [i.e., athletics, band, choir, cheerleading] were subjected to random urinalysis in much the same manner as the Oregon program, except that all male students were allowed to give their urine samples in enclosed toilet stalls.[86] The primary purpose of the program was to prevent and deter drug use among public schoolchildren where such drug use was otherwise a problem in the schools involved. As in the Oregon program, the only consequence visited upon a student who failed such a random test was a limited one: expulsion from all extracurricular school activities; no law enforcement or academic consequence was imposed. This program thus served a "special need" of government apart from the normal governmental demand for ordinary criminal law enforcement.

(3) Programs struck down

The Court, however, has struck down a Georgia statute requiring that all candidates for state office, in order to qualify for a place on the state ballot, present a certificate from a state-approved laboratory stating that the candidate submitted to a urinalysis drug test within 30 days prior to qualifying and that the tests were negative.[87] The basis for this result was that the program did not serve a "special need" of government apart from the normal governmental need for ordinary criminal law enforcement, because no serious problem of drug use among elected officials in Georgia was demonstrated, and that the program was not well-designed, in any event, to prevent such drug use.

And the Court has struck down a cocaine drug-testing program administered by a public hospital and designed with the help of local police, in which pregnant women receiving care at the hospital were given urine tests to determine cocaine use and were placed in a substance abuse clinic if tested positive, following which they were turned over to the police for criminal prosecution if they again tested positive for cocaine in future urine tests or missed an appointment with a drug counselor.[88] The primary purpose of this program was to use the threat of arrest and criminal prosecution in order to force the women into drug treatment, and thus did not serve a "special need" of government apart from the normal governmental need for criminal law enforcement.

---

that week. Both the athlete and the athlete's parents were required to sign a consent form for such testing as a precondition for participating in the school athletic program.

86. Board of Education of Independent School District No. 92 v. Earls, 536 U.S. 822, 122 S.Ct. 2559, 153 L.Ed.2d 735 (2002).

87. Chandler v. Miller, 520 U.S. 305, 117 S.Ct. 1295, 137 L.Ed.2d 513 (1997).

88. Ferguson v. City of Charleston, 532 U.S. 67, 121 S.Ct. 1281, 149 L.Ed.2d 205 (2001) (case remanded to determine whether plaintiffs voluntarily consented to the drug-testing program).

f. Airport or public building electronic search

The Court in dicta has approved the practice—now adopted in airports as air travelers board commercial flights and as the public enters many public buildings—of subjecting such people to electronic searches of their persons and personal belongings at permanent checkpoints to detect the presence of weapons and bombs, so as to thwart the danger of aircraft highjackings and terrorist attacks.[89] If the electronic search indicates that the individual has something metal either on the individual's person or in a container the individual is carrying, a further search of the person or container, limited to determining the source of the metal, is clearly reasonable.[90]

Plainly, the gravity of the governmental interests served by such airport and public building searches greatly outweigh the privacy interests at stake. This is especially true given our experience with the extreme danger posed by terrorists in our midst, such as the aircraft highjacking attacks on the Pentagon and New York City's World Trade Center that led to death of thousands of people on September 11, 2001. Although privacy interests should be respected wherever practicable in carrying out such searches, the Fourth Amendment is not a national suicide pact requiring that we disregard important security concerns and leave vulnerable the lives of countless people.[91] At the very least, limited electronic searches, followed by more intrusive searches if the proper evidentiary showing is made, are therefore entirely reasonable in the Fourth Amendment sense to guard against these extreme dangers.[92]

Beyond that, a full search of checked baggage as air travelers board commercial air flights—quite apart from a preceding electronic search—may occasionally be carried out by some airlines for some commercial air flights. These searches, although amounting to a greater intrusion into personal privacy than an electronic search, would nonetheless appear entirely reasonable under the Fourth Amendment, given the gravity of the governmental interests thereby served by this action.

g. Search of Presidential papers and related materials

The Court has held that a federal statute—requiring the Administrator of General Services to take control of all of former President Richard Nixon's presidential papers,

---

89. See, e.g., Chandler v. Miller, 520 U.S. 305, 117 S.Ct. 1295, 137 L.Ed.2d 513, 529 (1997); National Treasury Employees Union v. Von Raab, 489 U.S. 656, 109 S.Ct. 1384, 103 L.Ed.2d 685, 708 n. 3 (1989).

90. See 5 Wayne LaFave, Search and Seizure, §§ 10.6, 10.7(a) (5th ed. 2012), and 2 John Wesley Hall, Search and Seizure §§ 41.09–41.13 (5th ed. 2013) for a thorough discussion of these types of searches, collecting relevant cases.

91. Justice Robert Jackson once warned that "[t]here is danger, if the Court does not temper its doctrinaire logic with a little practical wisdom, it will convert the constitutional Bill of Rights into a suicide pact." Terminiello v. Chicago, 337 U.S. 1, 37, 69 S.Ct. 894, 93 L.Ed.2d 1131 (1949) (Jackson, J. dissenting). On the other hand, Justice Thurgood Marshall has stated that "[n]o nation in the recorded history of man has a greater tradition of revering justice and fair treatment for all its citizens in times of turmoil, confusion and tension than ours," that "[t]his is a country that stands tallest in troubled times, a country that clings to fundamental principles, cherishes its constitutional heritage, and rejects simple solutions that compromise the values that lie at the roots of our democratic system." Furman v. Georgia, 408 U.S. 238, 370, 92 S.Ct. 2726, 33 L.Ed.2d 346, 424 (1972) (Marshall, J. concurring).

92. For lower federal and state court cases on airport boarding searches, see "Searches and Seizures" § 72 West Key No.

tape recordings and other materials for screening by the federal government archivists—was facially constitutional against a variety of constitutional attacks. Under the statute and regulations promulgated thereunder, the archivists were directed to conduct a comprehensive screening of these materials and thereafter retain all materials related to the "Watergate affair" for public and prosecutorial access; those of a purely personal or private nature were to be returned to President Nixon.

As to the Fourth Amendment claim, the Court first concluded that a Fourth Amendment search was authorized by the statute only with respect to President Nixon's private papers and materials unrelated to his Presidential duties, but not with respect to the public materials. The Court further concluded that this statutorily authorized, warrantless search was reasonable within the meaning of the Fourth Amendment because of (1) the extremely small amount of materials that were purely private, (2) the virtual impossibility of segregating this small quantity of private materials prior to conducting comprehensive screening of all the materials, (3) the unblemished record of the government archivists for discretion so as not to publicly reveal the content of the returned private materials, and (4) the important public interest served by preservation of the public materials related to the "Watergate affair."[93]

This holding is obviously very fact-specific. But it does demonstrate that the purely private papers and materials of a President or other public official are entitled to Fourth Amendment protection. Clearly, they cannot be seized and searched without a warrant, absent a showing of reasonableness—which necessarily requires the Court to balance the relevant interests involved.

h. Routine booking procedure search: DNA sample

When a person is lawfully arrested and taken to jail or other holding facility to be formally booked, the Court has upheld certain types of ensuing searches during the routine administrative booking process as reasonable under the Fourth Amendment. As already discussed, the arrestee's person and accompanying containers may be searched by jail or holding officials when booking the arrestee—and any items seized may be inventoried as part of a reasonable inventory search.[94]

Accordingly, where a person has been arrested for a serious offense [such as a crime of violence or attempted violence] based on probable cause, a scientifically approved DNA sample may be taken from the arrestee, and the sample obtained may be later analyzed, as part of a routine booking procedure. Although this action by government officials constitutes a search, it is a reasonable search within the meaning of the Fourth Amendment. This is so because such a search is relatively non-intrusive in nature, is comparable to well-established photographing and fingerprinting procedures during booking, and is a reasonable means of identifying the arrestee.[95]

---

93. Nixon v. Administrator of General Services, 433 U.S. 425, 457–59, 97 S.Ct. 2777, 53 L.Ed.2d 867, 900–901 (1974).

94. See Section 2a(4) of this chapter, citing Illinois v. LaFayette, 462 U.S. 640, 103 S.Ct. 2605, 77 L.Ed.2d 65, 69, 73 (1983). As an aside, if the arrestee is later admitted into the general jail population, additional more intrusive searches of the arrestee have also been upheld. See Section 3b of this section for a discussion of the cases in this area.

95. "Upon these considerations, the Court concludes that DNA identification of arrestees is a reasonable search that can be considered part of a routine booking procedure. When officers make an arrest based on probable cause to hold for a serious offense and they bring the suspect to the station to be detained in custody, taking and analyzing a cheek swab of the arrestee's DNA is, like fingerprinting

Section 4. Rejected Exceptions

Often using a balancing approach, the U.S. Supreme Court has rejected exceptions to the search warrant requirement rule for the following types of searches:

- a warrantless search of private premises by IRS agents to enforce the tax laws by levying on taxpayer property for tax deficiencies;[96]
- a warrantless housing code or fire code inspection of a home or business;[97]
- a warrantless OSHA inspection of a business;[98]
- a warrantless search of private premises to investigate the cause of a prior fire on the premises;[99]
- a warrantless electronic eavesdropping search by federal government agents in "domestic security cases;"[100]
- a warrantless search of private premises on which a homicide or serious criminal assault has just occurred (no "murder scene exception");[101]

---

and photographing, a legitimate police booking procedure under the Fourth Amendment." Maryland v. King, 569 U.S. ____, 133 S.Ct. 1958, 186 L.Ed.2d 1, 32 (2013) (italics added) (DNA swab of defendant's inner cheek for skin cells after defendant was lawfully arrested for assault with a shot gun, and a later lab analysis of the sample obtained, upheld under the Fourth Amendment).

"The legitimate government interest served by the Maryland DNA Collection Act is one that is well established: the need for law enforcement officers in a safe and accurate way to process and identify the persons and possessions they must take into custody." Maryland v. King, 569 U.S. ____, 133 S.Ct. 1958, 186 L.Ed.2d 1, 21 (2013).

"In sum, there can be little reason to question the legitimate interest of the government in knowing for an absolute certainty the identity of the person arrested, in knowing whether he is wanted elsewhere, and in ensuring his identification in the event he flees prosecution. To that end, courts have confirmed that the Fourth Amendment allows police to take certain routine administrative steps incident to arrest—i.e., booking, photographing, and fingerprinting. DNA identification of arrestees, of the type approved by the Maryland statute here at issue, is no more than an extension of methods of identification long used in dealing with persons under arrest. In the balance of reasonableness required by the Fourth Amendment, therefore, the Court must give great weight both to the significant government interest at stake in the identification of arrestees and to the unmatched potential of DNA identification to serve that interest." Maryland v. King, 569 U.S. ____, 133 S.Ct. 1958, 186 L.Ed.2d 1, 29 (2013) (internal quotations and citations omitted).

"By comparison to this substantial government interest and the uniqueness of DNA identification, the intrusion of a cheek swab to obtain a DNA sample is a minimal one. * * * A gentle rub along the inside of the cheek does not break the skin, and involves virtually no risk, trauma or pain. A crucial factor in analyzing the magnitude of the intrusion is the extent to which the procedure may threaten the safety or health of the individual, and nothing suggests that a bucal swab poses any physical danger whatever. A brief intrusion of an arrestee's person is subject to the Fourth Amendment, but a swab of this nature does not increase the indignity already attendant to normal arrests." Maryland v. King, 569 U.S. ____, 133 S.Ct. 1958, 186 L.Ed.2d 1, 29, 30–31 (2013) (internal quotations and citations omitted).

96. G.M. Leasing Corp. v. United States, 429 U.S. 338, 97 S.Ct. 619, 50 L.Ed.2d 530, 544–46 (1977).

97. Camara v. Municipal Court, 387 U.S. 523, 528–34, 87 S.Ct. 1727, 18 L.Ed.2d 930, 935–38 (1967); See v. City of Seattle, 387 U.S. 541, 87 S.Ct. 1737, 18 L.Ed.2d 943 (1967).

98. Marshall v. Barlow's Inc., 436 U.S. 307, 98 S.Ct. 1816, 56 L.Ed.2d 305 (1978).

99. Michigan v. Tyler, 436 U.S. 499, 506–09, 98 S.Ct. 1942, 56 L.Ed.2d 486, 496–98 (1978).

100. United States v. United States District Court, 407 U.S. 297, 92 S.Ct. 2125, 32 L.Ed.2d 752 (1972).

101. Mincey v. Arizona, 437 U.S. 385, 98 S.Ct. 2408, 57 L.Ed.2d 290 (1978).

- a warrantless "intermediate border" search by Puerto Rican authorities of all travelers and their baggage entering Puerto Rico from the United States;[102]
- a warrantless search of private premises pursuant to a subpoena duces tecum issued by a prosecuting attorney.[103]

102. Torres v. Puerto Rico, 442 U.S. 465, 99 S.Ct. 2425, 61 L.Ed.2d 1 (1979).
103. Mancusi v. DeForte, 392 U.S. 364, 370–71, 88 S.Ct. 2120, 20 L.Ed.2d 1154, 1161(1968).

Chapter 16

Special Unreasonableness Requirement Problems

The "Unreasonableness Requirement" for a Fourth Amendment violation presents special problems that require separate analysis. This is so because such problems are either so sprawling in nature, cross-cutting many doctrinal rules and principles, so as to invite considerable confusion, or are otherwise so unique or unusual that they deserve special attention. We turn now to a consideration of these problems.

Section 1. Searches of Homes

a. Premises protected: person's connection thereto

The law is settled that the Fourth Amendment protects first and foremost the elemental right of privacy that a person reasonably expects in one's dwelling, the place where one lives. It is in the home, above all else, where a person enjoys the highest reasonable expectation of privacy under the Fourth Amendment. Plainly, the Framers of the Fourth Amendment intended precisely such a result,[1] and the United States Supreme Court has repeatedly so held.[2]

---

1. For a discussion of the historical purpose of the Fourth Amendment as it relates to the home, see Chapter 6, Section 2, supra, of this work.

2. "The Fourth Amendment protects the individual's privacy in a variety of settings. In none is this zone of privacy more clearly defined than when bounded by the unambiguous physical dimensions of a individual's home—a zone that finds its roots in clear and specific constitutional terms. 'The right of the people to be secure in their ... houses ... shall not be violated.' That language unequivocally establishes the proposition that '[a]t the very core [of the Fourth Amendment] stands the right of a man to retreat into his own home and there be free from unreasonable governmental intrusion.'" Payton v. New York, 445 U.S. 573, 589–90, 100 S.Ct. 1371, 1381–82, 63 L.Ed.2d 639, 653 (1980), quoting from Silverman v. United States, 365 U.S. 505, 511, 81 S.Ct. 679, 683–84, 5 L.Ed.2d 734 (1961). "'At the very core' of the Fourth Amendment, 'stands the right of a man to retreat into his own home and there be free from unreasonable governmental intrusion.'" Kyllo v. United States, 533 U.S. 27, 121 S.Ct. 2038, 2041, 150 L.Ed.2d 94 (2001) (also quoting from Silverman). "At the risk of belaboring the obvious, private residences are places in which an individual normally expects privacy free from governmental interference not authorized by a warrant, and that expectation is plainly one that society is prepared to recognize as justifiable. Our cases have not deviated from this basic Fourth Amendment principle." United States v. Karo, 468 U.S. 705, 104 S.Ct. 3296, 82 L.Ed.2d 530, 541 (1984). "The [Fourth] Amendment reflects the recognition of the Founders that certain enclaves should be free from arbitrary government interference. For example, the Court since the enactment of the Fourth Amendment has stressed 'the overriding respect for the sanctity of the home that has been embedded in our traditions since the origins of the Republic.'" Oliver v. United States, 466 U.S. 170, 104 S.Ct. 1735, 80 L.Ed.2d 214, 224 (1984), quoting from Payton v. New York, 445 U.S. at 601.

A home under the Fourth Amendment, however, includes a variety of private premises in which a person may live, such as a private residential house, a row house or townhouse, an apartment, a room in a rooming house, and a hotel or motel room. With respect to a single family home, not only is the interior of the house protected, but also the "curtilage" of the home,[3] which includes two types of outdoor home areas. The first is any outside living area that is shielded from public view, such as a backyard patio enclosed by a wall or bushes. The second is the immediate area surrounding the home—such as the front porch, an adjoining garden, or areas adjacent to the windows in the home. Although some of these latter areas may be visible from the public street, they are nonetheless tied to the intimacies of the home, are private in nature, and represent part of the home itself.[4] To assert Fourth Amendment protection in a home, one must live therein—either permanently or temporarily; this includes an overnight visitor in the home.[5]

b. Nature of search

Generally speaking, a government agent conducts a Fourth Amendment search of a home by making a non-consensual physical entry therein. It is *not*, however, a Fourth

---

"The Fourth Amendment embodies this centuries-old principle of respect for the privacy of the home." Wilson v. Layne, 526 U.S. 603, 119 S.Ct. 1692, 143 L.Ed.2d 818, 827 (1999). "[P]hysical entry of the home is the chief evil against which the wording of the Fourth Amendment is directed." United States v. United States District Court 407 U.S. 297, 313, 92 S.Ct. 2125, 32 L.Ed.2d 752 (1972). "The Fourth Amendment protects '[t]he right of the people to be secure in their ... houses,' and it is beyond dispute that the home is entitled to special protection as the center of the private lives of our people. Security of the home must be guarded by the law in a world where privacy is diminished by enhanced surveillance and sophisticated communication systems." Minnesota v. Carter, 525 U.S. 83, 119 S.Ct. 469, 142 L.Ed.2d 373, 386 (1998) (Kennedy, J. concurring).

3. "At common law, the curtilage is the area to which extends the intimate activity associated with the 'sanctity of a man's home and the privacies of life'... and therefore has been considered part of the home itself for Fourth Amendment purposes. Thus, Courts have extended Fourth Amendment protection to the curtilage; and they have defined the curtilage, as did the common law, by reference to the factors that determine whether an individual reasonably may expect that an area adjacent to the home will remain private." Oliver v. United States, 466 U.S. 170, 104 S.Ct. 1735, 80 L.Ed.2d 214, 225 (1984); see California v. Ciraolo, 476 U.S. 207, 106 S.Ct. 1809, 90 L.Ed.2d 210 (1986) (fenced-in backyard was part of the curtilage of a home, but the naked-eye observation of the yard from an airplane in public navigable airspace was not a Fourth Amendment search).

4. "When it comes to the Fourth Amendment, the home is the first among equals. At the Amendment's core stands 'the right of a man to retreat into his own home and there be free of unreasonable governmental intrusion.' This right would be of little practical value if the State's agents could stand in a home's porch or side garden and trawl for evidence with impunity; the right to retreat would be significantly diminished if the police could enter a man's property and observe his repose outside the front window.

We therefore regard the area "immediately surrounding and associated with the home"—what our cases call the curtilage—as "part of the home for Fourth Amendment purposes".... .This area around the home is intimately linked to the home, both physically and psychologically," and is where "privacy expectations are most heightened.

.... The front porch is the classic example of an area adjacent to the home and "to which the activity of home life extends." Florida v. Jardines, 569 U.S. ___, 133 S.Ct. 1409, 185 L.Ed.2d 495, 501 (2013) (internal citations omitted).

But see United States v. Santana, 427 U.S. 38, 96 S.Ct. 2406, 49 L.Ed.2d 300 (1976) for a contrary ruling which appears to be superceded by *Jardines* based on latter's revival of the older trespass definition of a Fourth Amendment search to include trespassory entries into constitutionally protected areas. Also see Illinois v. McArthur, 531 U.S. 326, 121 S.Ct. 946, 148 L.Ed.2d 838, 850 (2001) (citing *Santana* in dicta).

5. For a full discussion of all of the issues raised in the foregoing paragraph, collecting the relevant cases, see Chapter 10, Section 3(b)(1) of this work.

Amendment search for an undercover government agent to enter a person's home by deception or subterfuge and buy contraband drugs from the home dweller—or to testify later as to what the home dweller said during this visit. Also it is not a Fourth Amendment search of a home for a law enforcement officer to view a person's home from the public street or the public navigable air space in an airplane. On the other hand, obtaining by sense-enhancing technology information regarding the interior of a home that could not otherwise be obtained without physical intrusion into the home constitutes a Fourth Amendment search of the home—at least where the technology in question is not in general use, such as a thermal-imaging device that can determine whether high-intensity lamps are present in the home.[6]

c. Search warrant requirement

In an unbroken line of decisions stretching back nearly a century, the U.S. Supreme Court has repeatedly announced a fundamental rule of Fourth Amendment jurisprudence: the search warrant requirement rule. Subject to important exceptions, a search of private premises—particularly a home—must be conducted pursuant to a search warrant issued by a neutral and detached magistrate in compliance with the Warrants Clause of the Fourth Amendment; presumptively, a search of private premises conducted without such a warrant is considered unreasonable, and the burden of proof is on the government to establish an exception to this rule.[7] As a corollary to this rule, where police make an arrest in a person's dwelling, an arrest warrant is generally required in order to enter the dwelling to arrest the home dweller.[8] And if the purpose of the home entry is to arrest a third person, rather than the home dweller, a search warrant is generally required to enter the dwelling to effect the arrest.[9] In many cases decided over the years, the Court has consistently struck down searches of dwelling houses because no search warrant was obtained and no exception to the search warrant requirement rule was applicable.[10]

---

6. For a full discussion of the issues raised in this paragraph, collecting the relevant cases, see Chapter 10, Sections 4a & 5a of this work.

7. See Chapter 11, Section 1, supra, and cases collected at footnote 1.

8. Payton v. New York, 445 U.S. 573, 100 S.Ct. 1371, 63 L.Ed.2d 639 (1980) (entry into defendant's dwelling to arrest defendant; warrant required).

9. Steagald v. United States, 451 U.S. 204, 101 S.Ct. 1642, 68 L.Ed.2d 38 (1981) (entry into defendant's dwelling to arrest third party; search warrant for home required).

10. See, e.g., Agnello v. United States, 269 U.S. 20, 46 S.Ct. 4, 70 L.Ed. 145 (1925) (search of dwelling house); Taylor v. United States, 286 U.S. 1, 52 S.Ct. 466, 76 L.Ed. 951 (1932) (search of garage adjacent to dwelling house); Johnson v. United States, 333 U.S. 10, 68 S.Ct. 367, 92 L.Ed. 436 (1948) (search of hotel room); Trupiano v. United States, 334 U.S. 699, 68 S.Ct.1229, 92 L.Ed. 1663 (1948) (search of barn); McDonald v. United States, 335 U.S. 451, 69 S.Ct.191, 93 L.Ed. 153 (1948) (search of room in rooming house); Jones v. United States, 357 U.S. 493, 78 S.Ct.1253, 2 L.Ed.2d 1514 (1958) (search of dwelling house); Chapman v. United States, 365 U.S. 610, 81 S.Ct. 776, 5 L.Ed.2d 828 (1961) (search of rented dwelling house); Camara v. Municipal Court, 387 U.S. 523, 87 S.Ct. 1727, 18 L.Ed.2d 930 (1967) (search of dwelling house); Mancusi v. DeForte, 392 U.S. 364, 88 S.Ct. 2120, 20 L.Ed.2d 1154 (1968) (search of union business office); Vale v. Louisiana, 399 U.S. 30, 90 S.Ct. 1969, 26 L.Ed.2d 409 (1970) (search of dwelling house); Payton v. New York, 445 U.S. 573, 100 S.Ct. 1371, 63 L.Ed.2d 639 (1980) (search of apartment and dwelling house); Steagald v. United States, 451 U.S. 204, 101 S.Ct. 1642, 68 L.Ed.2d 38 (1981) (search of dwelling house); Welsh v. Wisconsin, 466 U.S. 740, 104 S.Ct. 2091, 80 L.Ed.2d 732 (1984) (search of dwelling house); Thompson v. Louisiana, 469 U.S. 17, 105 S.Ct. 409, 83 L.Ed.2d 246 (1984) (search of dwelling house).

"The warrant requirement has been a valued part of our constitutional law for decades, and it has determined the result in scores and scores of cases in courts all over this country." Coolidge v. New Hampshire, 403 U.S. 443, 481, 91 S.Ct. 2022, 29 L.Ed.2d 564, 592 (1971), quoted with approval in

In the event, however, that police obtain a search warrant for the search of a home, the warrant must be based on probable cause, must particularly describe the place to be searched and the things to be seized, must be properly executed, and must be issued by a neutral and detached magistrate.[11] There is a presumption in favor of the validity of a search warrant, at least on the issue of probable cause; the burden of proof is therefore on the defendant to show that the search warrant is invalid on the probable cause issue[12] and perhaps on the facial validity of the warrant, its execution, and other related issues as well.[13]

d. Applicable exceptions to search warrant requirement rule

There are three possible exceptions to the search warrant requirement rule that are applicable to the warrantless search of a home.

(1) Exigent circumstances[14]

The Court has recognized an exigent circumstances exception to the search warrant requirement rule—in which police are confronted with a serious emergency of some type, requiring an intrusion into protected Fourth Amendment interests, when there is no time to obtain a search warrant to deal with the emergency. Under this fairly loose, fact-specific exception, police are authorized to make a warrantless, nonconsensual entry onto private premises [including a home] in order to deal with certain emergency situations.

Although the Court has not articulated an exhaustive list of the emergencies involved in this exception, the exception has to date revolved around three general scenarios with possible variations on each: (1) police in "hot pursuit" of a fleeing felon enter private premises to arrest the suspect; (2) police or firemen enter private premises to deal with a situation that is life-threatening or perilous to persons inside or outside the premises or to the police themselves; and (3) police enter private premises to prevent the imminent destruction of evidence of a serious crime. In each case, there is no time for the police to obtain a warrant; immediate action is required to deal with the emergency.[15]

United States v. United States District Court, 407 U.S. 297, 315, 92 S.Ct. 2125, 32 L.Ed.2d 752, 765 (1972).

11. For a full discussion of these subjects, collecting the relevant cases, see Chapter 13, Sections 2–5 of this work.

12. "There is, of course, a presumption of validity with respect to the affidavit supporting the search warrant." Franks v. Delaware, 438 U.S. 154, 98 S.Ct. 2674, 57 L.Ed.2d 667, 682 (1978). "Although in a particular case it may not be easy to determine when an affidavit [for a search warrant] demonstrates the existence of probable cause, the resolution of doubtful or marginal cases should be largely determined by the preference to be accorded to warrants." United States v. Ventresca, 380 U.S. 102, 109, 85 S.Ct. 741, 13 L.Ed.2d 684, 689 (1965).

13. See 6 Wayne LaFave, Search and Seizure § 11.2(b) at 50 (5th ed. 2012).

14. For a full discussion of the exigent circumstances exception to the search warrant requirement rule, collecting relevant cases, see Chapter 14, Section 6 of this work.

15. "Accordingly, the warrant requirement is subject to certain reasonable exceptions. One well-recognized exception applies 'when the exigencies of the situation' make the needs of law enforcement so compelling that [a] warrantless search is objectively reasonable under the Fourth Amendment.

This Court has identified several exigencies that may justify a warrantless search of a home. Under the 'emergency aid exception, for example, [1] 'officers may enter a home without a warrant to render emergency assistance to an injured occupant or to protect an occupant from immediate injury.' [2] Police may enter premises without a warrant when they are in immediate pursuit of a fleeing subject. [3] And—what is relevant here—the need 'to prevent the immediate destruction of evidence' has long been recognized as a sufficient justification for a warrantless search. [internal citations omitted; bracketed numbers added]." Kentucky v. King, 563 U.S. ___, 131 S.Ct. 1849, 1856, 179 L.Ed.2d 865 (2011).

(2) Consent search[16]

Under the consent exception to the search warrant requirement rule, law enforcement officers may search a home without a warrant—provided the home dweller freely and voluntarily consents thereto and is not coerced, either expressly or impliedly, into giving such consent.[17] Even where the ostensible home dweller is later determined *not* to live there, the search may nonetheless be upheld as based on the otherwise voluntary consent of such person—if the asserted home dweller had the *apparent* authority to given such consent: that is, if based on all the circumstances, the law enforcement officers reasonably believed at the time of the search that such person did, in fact, live on the premises.[18] On the other hand, a warrantless search by law enforcement officers of private premises shared by two occupants—where one occupant consents to the search, but *a physically present* co-occupant expressly objects to the search—cannot be justified under the consent exception to the search warrant requirement rule and, therefore, without more, is unreasonable under the Fourth Amendment as to the non-consenting co-occupant.[19] The prosecution has the burden to show by a preponderance of the evidence that the consent was freely and voluntarily given.[20]

A submission to an unsupportable police claim of lawful authority to conduct a search of a home, however, does not constitute a voluntary consent to search.[21] Accordingly, a

---

"We have held, for example, that law enforcement officers may make a warrantless entry onto private property to fight a fire and investigate its cause, to prevent the imminent destruction of evidence, or to engage in 'hot pursuit' of a fleeing suspect. * * * One exigency obviating the requirement of a warrant is the need to assist persons who are seriously injured or threatened with such injury. Accordingly, law enforcement officers may enter a home without a warrant to render emergency assistance to an injured occupant or to protect an occupant from imminent injury." Brigham City v. Stuart, 547 U.S. 398, 126 S.Ct. 1943, 1947, 164 L.Ed.2d 650 (2006) (internal citations omitted).

16. For a full discussion of the consent exception to the search warrant requirement rule, collecting relevant cases, see Chapter 14, Section 5 of this work.

17. "It is well settled under the Fourth and Fourteenth Amendments that a search conducted without a warrant issued upon probable cause is 'per se unreasonable ... subject only to a few specifically established and well-delineated exceptions.' (citations omitted). It is equally well settled that one of the specifically established exceptions to the requirements of both a warrant and probable cause is a search that is conducted pursuant to consent. (citations omitted). * * * But the Fourth and Fourteenth Amendments require that a consent [to search] not be coerced, by explicit or implicit means, by implied threat or covert force. * * * We hold only that when the subject of a search is not in custody and the State attempts to justify a search on the basis of his consent, the Fourth and Fourteenth Amendments require that it demonstrate that consent was in fact voluntarily given and not the result of duress or coercion, express or implied." Schneckloth v. Bustamonte, 412 U.S. 218, 93 S.Ct. 2041, 36 L.Ed.2d 854, 858, 863, 875 (1973) (defendant's consent for police to search his car held voluntary); see United States v. Watson, 423 U.S. 411, 96 S.Ct. 820, 46 L.Ed.2d 598, 609 (1976) (rule of *Schneckloth* extended to a defendant in police custody; consent search of car upheld).

18. Illinois v. Rodriguez, 497 U.S. 177, 110 S.Ct. 2793, 111 L.Ed.2d 148 (1990).

19. Georgia v. Randolph, 547 U.S. 103, 126 S.Ct. 1515, 1518–19, 1526, 164 L.Ed.2d 208 (2006).

20. "When a prosecutor seeks to rely on consent to justify the lawfulness of a search, he [or she] has the burden of proving that the consent was, in fact, freely and voluntarily given." Bumper v. North Carolina, 391 U.S. 543, 88 S.Ct. 1788, 20 L.Ed.2d 797, 802 (1968). "In any event, the controlling burden of proof at suppression hearings [on the consent issue] should impose no greater burden than proof by a preponderance of the evidence." United States v. Matlock, 415 U.S. 164, 94 S.Ct. 988, 39 L.Ed.2d 242, 253, n. 14 (1974).

21. "Conversely, if under all the circumstances it has appeared that the consent was not given voluntarily—that it was coerced by threats or force, or granted only in submission to a claim of lawful authority—then we have found the consent invalid and the search unreasonable." Schneckloth v. Bustamonte, 412 U.S. 218, 233, 93 S.Ct. 2041, 36 L.Ed.2d 854, 866 (1973). "[W]here the validity of

consent to search a home is generally considered involuntary, and the search unreasonable, when given in response (a) to a police announcement that the officers have come to search the suspect's premises, when they otherwise have no legal right to do so;[22] or (b) to a police demand for entry onto private premises, when the officers otherwise have no legal authority to make such an entry;[23] or (c) to a police assertion that they have a search warrant for the search of the suspect's premises, and the warrant later turns out to be invalid or nonexistent.[24] In each of these situations, the consent given constitutes an acquiescence to a preceding assertion of unlawful police authority—and is generally considered tainted.[25]

(3) *Search incident to a lawful arrest: the "protective sweep" rule*[26]

When lawfully arresting a person at his or her home, law enforcement officers are automatically allowed to look in closets and other spaces immediately adjoining the place in the premises where the arrest takes place—even though the areas searched may be technically beyond the physical reach of the arrestee. Beyond that, police may also briefly "sweep" the entire home if there is a reasonable suspicion that there are other persons on the premises who may pose a danger to those at the arrest scene. This protective sweep

---

a search rests on consent, the State has the burden of proving that the necessary consent was obtained and that it was freely and voluntarily given, a burden that is not satisfied by showing a mere submission to a claim of authority." Florida v. Royer, 460 U.S. 491, 497, 103 S.Ct. 1319, 75 L.Ed.2d 229, 236 (1983).

22. Amos v. United States, 255 U.S. 313, 41 S.Ct. 266, 65 L.Ed. 654 (1921) (consent held coerced when federal agents told defendant's wife that they had come to search the premises, and she opened the door to let the agents in). Of course, if, in fact, the police have the authority to conduct the search in question, the search is valid by virtue of that authority—although the defendant may acquiesce in the officer's assertion of authority at the time of the search. United States v. Biswell, 406 U.S. 311, 92 S.Ct. 1593, 32 L.Ed.2d 87, 91–92 (1972) (search upheld as a valid administrative inspection of a pawnshop under the federal gun control act; defendant acquiesced in the inspection in the face of the federal agent's assertion of authority to make the inspection).

23. Johnson v. United States, 333 U.S. 10, 68 S.Ct. 367, 92 L.Ed. 436 (1948) (police officer smelled opium coming from defendant's hotel room; officer knocked on door, identified himself as a police officer and said he wanted to talk to her; defendant opened the door and let the officer in). "Entry to defendant's living quarters, which was the beginning of the search, was demanded under color of office. It was granted in submission to authority rather than as an understanding and intentional waiver of a constitutional right." 92 L.Ed. at 440.

24. "The issue thus presented is whether a search can be justified as lawful when that 'consent' has been given after the official conducting the search has asserted that he possesses a warrant. We hold that there can be no consent under such circumstances. * * * This burden [of the state to show a voluntary consent to search] cannot be discharged by showing no more than acquiescence to a claim of lawful authority. A search conducted in reliance upon a warrant cannot later be justified on the basis of consent if it turns out that the warrant was invalid. The result can be no different when it turns out that the State did not even attempt to rely on the validity of the warrant or fails to show that there was, in fact, any warrant at all." Bumper v. North Carolina, 391 U.S. 543, 88 S.Ct. 1788, 20 L.Ed.2d 797, 803–04 (1968) (third party consent of defendant's grandmother to search house where defendant and grandmother lived was held involuntary; police announced, "I have a search warrant to search your house," and the grandmother responded, "Go ahead;" at the motion to suppress hearing, state did not rely on the warrant to justify the search). Lo-Ji Sales, Inc. v. New York, 442 U.S. 319, 99 S.Ct. 2319, 60 L.Ed.2d 920, 930 (1979) (After being placed under arrest at store and told that police have a search warrant which turns out to be invalid, adult book store clerk cooperates with police in locating certain films that were seized ; held: involuntary consent).

25. But see 4 Wayne LaFave, Search and Seizure § 8.2(a) at 74–75 (5th ed. 2012) for a discussion of whether additional circumstances in the case might make the consent voluntary, notwithstanding a prior unsupportable police claim of a lawful authority to search.

26. For a complete discussion of the search-incident-to-a-lawful-arrest exception to the search warrant requirement rule, see Chapter 14, Section 2 of this work.

must be limited to a cursory inspection of those spaces on the premises where a person may be found, and does not authorize a general exploratory search of the premises. For that reason, for example, an inspection of jewel cases and bathroom medicine cabinets in the home would not be authorized because a person could not hide in such spaces.[27]

e. Inapplicable exceptions to search warrant requirement rule

(1) Probable cause

The Court has long held that a probable cause belief by police that a dwelling house contains evidence otherwise subject to seizure—such as contraband, fruits or instrumentalities of a crime, or evidence of a crime—does not constitute a basis to search the house without a search warrant. Such a probable cause determination must be made by a magistrate and not a law enforcement officer.[28]

(2) Administrative inspection

The Court has struck down a warrantless statutory inspection scheme for health code inspections of homes and has required administrative warrants for same—unless the homeowner voluntarily consents to the inspection.[29]

f. Scope of search

Assuming the police have lawfully entered a home either with or without a warrant, it does not follow that the police may search anywhere in the home that they desire. To the contrary, the scope of a search either with or without a warrant is strictly limited by

---

27. "Beyond that, however, we hold that there must be articulable facts which, taken together with rational inferences from those facts, would warrant a reasonably prudent officer in believing that the area to be swept harbors an individual posing a danger to those at the arrest scene. * * * We should emphasize that such a protective sweep, aimed at protecting the officers, if justified by the circumstances, is nevertheless not a full search of the premises, but may extend only to a cursory inspection of those spaces where a person may be found. The sweep takes no longer than is necessary to dispel the reasonable suspicion of danger and in any event no longer than it takes to complete the arrest and depart the premises." Maryland v. Buie, 494 U.S. 325, 110 S.Ct. 1093, 108 L.Ed.2d 276, 286–287 (1990).

28. "Belief, however well-founded, that an article sought is concealed in a dwelling house, furnishes no justification for a search of that place without a warrant." Agnello v. United States, 269 U.S. 20, 33, 46 S.Ct. 4, 70 L.Ed. 145 (1925). "It is settled doctrine that probable cause for belief that certain articles subject to seizure are in a dwelling cannot of itself justify a search without a warrant. (citations omitted). The decisions of this Court have time and again underscored the essential purpose of the Fourth Amendment to shield the citizen from unwarranted intrusions into his privacy. (citations omitted). This purpose is realized by Rule 41 of the Federal Rules of Criminal Procedure, which implements the Fourth Amendment by requiring that an impartial magistrate determine from an affidavit showing probable cause whether information possessed by law-enforcement officers justifies the issuance of a search warrant. Were federal officers free to search without a warrant merely upon probable cause to believe that certain articles are within a home, the provisions of the Fourth Amendment would become empty phrases, and the protection it affords largely nullified." Jones v. United States, 357 U.S. 493, 497–98, 78 S.Ct. 1253, 2 L.Ed.2d 1514, 1518–19 (1958); see also Chapman v. United States, 365 U.S. 610, 613, 81 S.Ct. 776, 5 L.Ed.2d 828, 831 (1961).

29. Camara v. Municipal Court, 387 U.S. 523, 87 S.Ct. 1727, 18 L.Ed.2d 930 (1967); compare See v. City of Seattle, 387 U.S. 541, 87 S.Ct. 1737, 18 L.Ed.2d 943 (1967) (fire code inspection of commercial warehouse requires search warrant absent consent). For a discussion of administrative search warrants, see Chapter 13, Section 2h of this work.

the circumstances that justified its inception. A search that is reasonable when it begins may become unreasonable if its scope extends beyond that which is necessary to accomplish its objective. Stated differently, where the basis for making a search of a home empowers the police to look for particular items of property, the search must be confined to those locations where such items may reasonably be found—and to no other places.[30]

As stated by the Court:

> When an official search is properly authorized—whether by consent or by the issuance of a valid warrant—the scope of the search is limited by the terms of its authorization. Consent to search a garage would not implicitly authorize a search of an adjoining house; a warrant to search for a stolen refrigerator would not authorize the opening of a desk drawer. Because 'indiscriminate searches and seizures conducted under the authority of 'general warrants' were the immediate evils that motivated the framing and adoption of the Fourth Amendment,' that Amendment requires that the scope of every authorized search be particularly described. (internal citation omitted).[31]
>
> "Just as probable cause to believe that a stolen lawnmower may be found in a garage will not support a warrant to search an upstairs bedroom, probable cause to believe that undocumented aliens are being transported in a van will not justify a warrantless search of a suitcase. Probable cause to believe that a container placed in a trunk of a taxi contains contraband does not justify a search of the entire cab."[32]

g. Seizure of evidence within the dwelling house

Assuming, however, that the police lawfully enter a home, either with or without a warrant, and discover evidence within the proper scope of their search authority, it does not follow that the police are automatically privileged to seize such evidence. In order to seize any property within the home, the police officer must either: (1) be authorized to

---

30. "This Court has held in the past that a search which is reasonable in its inception may violate the Fourth Amendment by virtue of its intolerable intensity and scope. The scope of the search must be 'strictly tied to and justified by' the circumstances which rendered its initiation permissible." Terry v. Ohio, 392 U.S. 1, 88 S.Ct. 1868, 20 L.Ed.2d 889, 904 (1968) (internal citations omitted).

"The Fourth Amendment proceeds as much by limitations upon the scope of governmental action as by imposing preconditions upon its initiation. The entire deterrent purpose of the rule excluding evidence seized in violation of the Fourth Amendment rests on the assumption that 'limitations upon the fruit to be gathered tend to limit the quest itself.' Thus, evidence may not be introduced if it was discovered by means of a seizure and search which were not reasonably related in scope to their justification." Terry v. Ohio, 20 L.Ed. 2d at 910 (internal citation omitted).

"The Fourth Amendment's prohibition against unreasonable searches and seizures has always been interpreted to prevent a search that is not limited to the particularly described 'place to be searched and the persons or things to be seized,' U.S. Const., Amdt 4, even if the search is made pursuant to a warrant and based on probable cause. The Amendment's protection is not diluted in those situations where it has been determined that legitimate law enforcement interests justify a warrantless search: the search must be limited in scope to that which is justified by the particular purposes served by the exception." Florida v. Royer, 460 U.S. 491, 103 S.Ct. 1319, 75 L.Ed.2d 229, 237–38 (1983).

"The scope of a warrantless search based on probable cause is no narrower—and no broader—than the scope of a search authorized by a warrant supported by probable cause. Only the prior approval of the magistrate is waived; the search otherwise is as the magistrate could authorize." United States v. Ross, 456 U.S. 798, 102 S.Ct. 2157, 72 L.Ed.2d 572, 593 (1982).

31. Walter v. United States 447 U.S. 649, 100 S.Ct. 2395, 65 L.Ed.2d 410, 417–18 (1980).

32. United States v. Ross, 456 U.S. 798, 824, 102 S.Ct. 2157, 72 L.Ed.2d 572, 593 (1982).

make the seizure under the search warrant that the officer has;[33] or (2) have probable cause to believe that the property seized is contraband, fruits or instrumentalities of a crime, or evidence of a crime.[34]

Section 2. Automobile Searches

Although an automobile is fully protected as an "effect" under the Fourth Amendment, there is a lesser expectation of privacy therein, compared to a home or an office, primarily because of the pervasive governmental regulation of automobiles.[35] Nonetheless, "the word 'automobile' is not a talisman in whose presence the Fourth Amendment fades away and disappears,"[36] as the privacy interests in an automobile are significant.[37]

Special problems are presented, however, when police conduct a warrantless search of an automobile that is being operated on the street—an occurrence that happens with some frequency in this country. In the usual automobile search, three Fourth Amendment intrusions are involved: (1) the police *stop* the automobile while it is being operated on the public streets, (2) the police then *search* the automobile, and (3) in the ensuing search, the police *seize* items of property discovered in the automobile. Each of these intrusions must be analyzed separately.[38]

a. Stop of the automobile

In the usual "police stop" of the automobile, the police typically turn on the siren and flashing lights on their patrol car, directing a motorist to pull over, following which the motorist complies. When the vehicle comes to a stop, a Fourth Amendment submission-to-authority seizure of the person of the driver and all passengers in the vehicle has been accomplished.[39]

---

33. For a discussion of the Fourth Amendment requirement that a search warrant must particularly describe the property to be seized, and that the executing officer is authorized to seize that property, see Chapter 13, Section 3b of this work.

34. For a discussion of the application of the "plain view" doctrine in this context, collecting relevant cases, see Chapter 12, Section 2c of this work.

35. South Dakota v. Opperman, 428 U.S. 364, 367, 96 S.Ct. 3092, 49 L.Ed.2d 1000 (1976); see also Cady v. Dombrowski, 413 U.S. 433, 93 S.Ct. 2523, 37 L.Ed.2d 706 (1973).

36. Coolidge v. New Hampshire, 403 U.S. 443, 462, 91 S.Ct. 2022, 29 L.Ed.2d 564, 580 (1971).

37. Delaware v. Prouse, 440 U.S. 648, 662–63, 99 S.Ct. 1391, 59 L.Ed.2d 660 (1979).

38. For a thorough discussion of the rules governing the search and seizure of vehicles generally, see 3 Wayne LaFave, Search and Seizure §§7.1–7.5 (5th ed. 2012).

39. See Chapter 9, Section 2b of this work for a discussion of Fourth Amendment submission-to-authority seizures of the person. "When a police officer makes a traffic stop, the driver of the car is seized within the meaning of the Fourth Amendment. The question in this case is whether the same is true of the passenger. We hold that a passenger is seized as well and so may challenge the constitutionality of the stop." Brendlin v. California, 551 U.S. 249, 127 S.Ct. 2400, 2403, 168 L.Ed.2d 132 (2007); "Temporary detentions of individuals during the [police] stop of an automobile, even if only for a brief period and for a limited purpose, constitute a 'seizure' of 'persons' within the meaning of the Fourth Amendment." Whren v. United States, 517 U.S. 806, 116 S.Ct. 1769, 1772, 135 L.Ed.2d 89 (1996) (police direct an auto on the public streets to pull over and the driver complies; held Fourth Amendment seizure of the person). "There can be no question that the stopping of a vehicle [by police] and the detention of its occupants constitute a 'seizure' within the meaning of the Fourth Amendment." Colorado v. Bannister, 449 U.S. 1, 101 S.Ct. 42, 66 L.Ed.2d 1, 4 at n. 3 (1980) (same).

On the other hand, if the driver does *not* comply with the police directive to pull over and attempts to flee, *no* Fourth Amendment seizure of the person has taken place. Any evidence thrown out of the vehicle during a later police pursuit of the vehicle constitutes abandoned property; accordingly, the police retrieval of this property from the street does not constitute a Fourth Amendment search or seizure of the property.[40] But if the police catch up with the vehicle and physically force the vehicle to stop, the driver and all passengers in the vehicle have been subjected at that point to a Fourth Amendment *physical* seizure of the person.[41]

Whether the above-described seizure of the person is a *submission-to-authority* seizure or a *physical* seizure, the central question is whether this seizure is reasonable or unreasonable in the Fourth Amendment sense. Such a seizure is reasonable if based on probable cause to believe that the driver or a passenger has committed or is committing a criminal offense—or reasonable suspicion to believe the same thing, if only a temporary detention follows rather than an arrest. If the seizure is for a traffic violation witnessed by the police, the seizure is reasonable—and the police officer's subjective motivations for effecting the seizure are irrelevant.[42] But if the seizure is *not* based on probable cause or reasonable suspicion, the driver and passengers in the automobile have been unreasonably seized within the meaning of the Fourth Amendment—which unreasonable seizure will generally taint and render inadmissible any evidence obtained by police in a subsequent search of the automobile under the *Weeks-Mapp* exclusionary rule.

b. Search of the automobile

Assuming, however, that the seizure of persons in the automobile is based on probable cause or reasonable suspicion, the next question is whether the police may then search the automobile without a search warrant. The short answer is "yes"—provided the prosecution establishes that one of six possible exceptions to the search warrant requirement rule is applicable in the case. Before examining these exceptions, four caveats are in order.

(1) Important caveats

- If no search warrant exception is applicable, the search of the automobile is unreasonable.[43]
- The guest passengers in the automobile have no standing to object to the police search of the automobile,[44] although they have standing to object to the preceding seizure of their persons based on the police stop of the automobile [and if such seizure is unreasonable, the ensuing police seizure of items in the automobile

---

40. California v. Hodari D., 499 U.S. 621, 111 S.Ct. 1547, 113 L.Ed.2d 690, 697 (1991) (evidence discarded by defendant while in flight from police held admissible in evidence); County of Sacramento v. Lewis, 523 U.S. 833, 118 S.Ct. 1708, 140 L.Ed.2d 1043, 1056 n. 7 (1998).

41. See Chapter 9, Section 2a of this work for a discussion of Fourth Amendment physical seizures of the person.

42. Whren v. United States, 517 U.S. 806, 116 S.Ct.1769, 1774, 1777, 135 L.Ed.2d 89 (1996).

43. Coolidge v. New Hampshire, 403 U.S. 443, 462, 91 S.Ct. 2022, 29 L.Ed.2d 564, 580 (1971).

44. Rakas v. Illinois, 439 U.S. 128, 99 S.Ct. 421, 58 L.Ed.2d 387 (1978) (police search the glove compartment and beneath the front seat of an automobile, seizing rifle shells and a sawed-off shotgun; guest passenger could not complain of search).

during a subsequent search would be tainted and generally rendered inadmissible in evidence].[45]

- When the police lawfully stop an automobile, anything they later see by looking in the automobile while standing outside the vehicle [even while using a flashlight] does *not* constitute a Fourth Amendment search of the automobile. Anything seen from this vantage point may give the police probable cause to search the automobile.[46] [Of course, if the automobile is illegally stopped, this "open view" observation would be tainted, and any evidence obtained in a subsequent police search of the automobile would generally be rendered inadmissible].
- The scope of the search is limited by the purpose of the exception. A search conducted outside the scope of the exception means that the exception is inapplicable, and that, generally speaking, the search is unreasonable and its fruits inadmissible.[47]

(2) Applicable exceptions to search warrant requirement rule

There are six possible search warrant exceptions for the warrantless search of an automobile. If any one exception is applicable, the search is reasonable: if none are applicable, the search is unreasonable. All relevant exceptions must therefore be examined.

• Search incident to a lawful arrest[48]

When a law enforcement officer makes an arrest of a motor vehicle occupant, the officer is authorized to conduct a search of the vehicle's passenger compartment and any container therein [but not the trunk] only where:

(1) the arrestee is unsecured and within reaching distance of the passenger compartment at the time of the arrest, or

(2) it is reasonable to believe that evidence relevant to the crime of arrest might be found in the passenger compartment.[49]

---

45. "When a police officer makes a traffic stop, the driver of the car is seized within the meaning of the Fourth Amendment. The question in this case is whether the same is true of the passenger. We hold that a passenger is seized as well and so may challenge the constitutionality of the stop." Brendlin v. California, 551 U.S. 249, 127 S.Ct. 2400, 2403, 168 L.Ed.2d 132 (2007); see 6 Wayne LaFave, Search and Seizure § 11.3(e) at 243–249 (5th ed. 2012) and cases collected.

46. Texas v. Brown, 460 U.S. 730, 103 S.Ct. 1535, 75 L.Ed.2d 502 (1983).

47. "Just as probable cause to believe that a stolen lawnmower may be found in a garage will not support a warrant to search an upstairs bedroom, probable cause to believe that undocumented aliens are being transported in a van will not justify a warrantless search of a suitcase. Probable cause to believe that a container placed in a trunk of a taxi contains contraband does not justify a search of the entire cab." United States v. Ross, 456 U.S. 798, 824, 102 S.Ct. 2157, 72 L.Ed.2d 572, 593 (1982). See Chapter 11, Section 4b of this work.

48. This exception is examined at Chapter 14, Section 2 of this work.

49. Arizona v. Gant, 556 U.S. 322, 129 S.Ct. 1710, 1719, 1723, 173 L.Ed.2d 485 (2009). "As result, the Court [in Gant] adopted a new, two-part rule under which an automobile search incident to a recent occupant's arrest is constitutional (1) if the arrestee is within reaching distance of the vehicle during the search, or (2) if the police have reason to believe that the vehicle contains evidence relevant to the crime of arrest." Davis v. United States, 564 U.S. ___, 131 S.Ct. 2419, 2425, 180 L.Ed.2d 285 (2011) (internal citation and quotation marks omitted).

The first situation rarely arises because law enforcement officers almost always promptly effect an arrest upon deciding to do so.[50] The second situation necessarily excludes minor traffic violations—like speeding or a defective tail light—which rarely, if ever, involve physical evidence that might be found in the vehicle.[51]

As an aside, however, if the police give the driver a traffic ticket and do *not* arrest the driver or any of the passengers, the police may *not* search the automobile under this exception—although arguably some other exception to the search warrant requirement rule might be applicable.[52]

• "Stop and frisk" search[53]

If during a lawful temporary detention of the driver or passenger of an automobile, the police may search the passenger compartment [but not the trunk] of the automobile for weapons for their own self-protection and safety—provided there is reasonable suspicion that "the suspect is dangerous and ... may gain immediate control of weapons" that threaten the investigating officers. If weapons or contraband drugs are found during such a reasonable search, the same may be seized under the "plain view" doctrine. There is, however, no *automatic* right to search an automobile during a valid temporary stop of the driver or other occupant, as indeed only a full custodial arrest may justify such a search—which, in itself, is limited in nature as explained in the preceding subsection.[54]

• *Carroll* "moving vehicle" search[55]

Police may search an automobile [including the trunk] based on probable cause to believe that the automobile contains contraband, or the fruits or instrumentalities of a crime, or evidence of a crime.[56] The search may take place on the street—or at a police impoundment lot or other similar location after the automobile has been towed.[57] Containers within the automobile may be searched if the object of the search may be located in such containers—including a container that belongs to an automobile passenger.[58] But if the sole probable cause to search the automobile is that a container in the automobile has the aforesaid incriminating items, only the container may be searched—and not the rest of the automobile.[59]

---

50. Arizona v. Gant, 556 U.S. 322, 129 S.Ct. 1710, 1719, 173 L.Ed.2d 485 (2009).

51. Arizona v. Gant, 556 U.S.322, 129 S.Ct. 1710, 1719, 173 L.Ed.2d 485 (2009).

52. Knowles v. Iowa, 525 U.S. 113, 119 S.Ct. 484, 142 L.Ed.2d 492 (1998) (police under state law could have lawfully arrested defendant for speeding, but instead issued a traffic citation and then searched defendant's car, finding marijuana; held unreasonable search).

53. This exception is examined at Chapter 14, Section 3 of this work.

54. Michigan v. Long, 463 U.S. 1032, 103 S.Ct. 3469, 77 L.Ed.2d 1201, 1210, 1220, n. 14 (1983).

55. This exception is examined at Chapter 14, Section 4 of this work.

56. Carroll v. United States, 267 U.S. 132, 45 S.Ct. 280, 69 L.Ed. 543 (1925); Chambers v. Maroney, 399 U.S. 42, 90 S.Ct. 1975, 26 L.Ed.2d 419 (1970); Florida v. Meyers, 466 U.S. 380, 104 S.Ct. 1852, 80 L.Ed.2d 381 (1984).

57. Colorado v. Bannister, 449 U.S. 1, 101 S.Ct. 42, 66 L.Ed.2d 1, 3–4 (1980); Chambers v. Maroney, 399 U.S. 42, 90 S.Ct. 1975, 26 L.Ed.2d 419 (1970).

58. United States v. Ross, 456 U.S. 798, 102 S.Ct. 2157, 72 L.Ed.2d 572, 594 (1982) (search of containers in automobile upheld); Wyoming v. Houghton, 526 U.S. 295, 119 S.Ct. 1297, 1304 143 L.Ed.2d 408 (1999) (police, who had probable cause to search car for illegal drugs, could search passenger's purse left on front seat of car).

59. California v. Acevedo, 500 U.S. 565, 111 S.Ct. 1982, 114 L.Ed.2d 619, 634 (1991).

• Consent search[60]

A person may consent to a police search of his or her automobile, but the consent must be freely and voluntarily given.[61] The state has the burden of establishing such consent by a preponderance of the evidence.[62] The driver need not be advised that he or she has a right to refuse consent—although this is a factor to be considered in determining whether the consent is voluntary based on the totality of the circumstances.[63] A consent given to search is generally considered involuntary if the defendant is *illegally* in custody at the time the consent is given,[64] or if the police assert prior thereto that they have a right to search the automobile.[65] But if the person is *lawfully* in police custody at the time consent is given, the fact of the custody itself does not render the consent involuntary.[66]

If a general consent is given to search an automobile, usually the entire automobile [including the trunk] and unlocked containers therein may be searched, providing the object of the search may be found in such places, but locked containers in the automobile may not be searched.[67] And a person may always limit the scope of the search to which he or she consents.[68]

• Inventory search[69]

When police lawfully seize an automobile, they may inventory the contents of the entire automobile when otherwise authorized by standard police procedures. The purpose of such an inventory is (1) to protect the police against subsequent claims by the owner that police lost or stole property in the car, (2) to protect the owner's property while in police custody, and (3) to protect the police from any danger from the vehicle's contents.[70] The initial impoundment of the automobile must be lawful based on standard police procedures. This may occur when police lawfully arrest the driver if the car would otherwise be left in some peril on the street. The contents of containers in the vehicle may also be inventoried provided the inventory is done according to standard police procedures, but not if the police have no such standard procedure.[71] The inventory must be a bona fide

---

60. This exception is examined at Chapter 14, Section 5.
61. Schneckloth v. Bustamonte, 412 U.S. 218, 93 S.Ct. 2041, 36 L.Ed.2d 854, 863, 879 (1973) (defendant's consent for police to search his car held voluntary).
62. Bumper v. North Carolina, 391 U.S. 543, 88 S.Ct. 1788, 20 L.Ed.2d 797, 802 (1968). United States v. Matlock, 415 U.S. 164, 94 S.Ct. 988, 39 L.Ed.2d 242, 253, n. 14 (1974).
63. Schneckloth v. Bustamonte, 412 U.S. 218, 248–49, 93 S.Ct. 2041, 36 L.Ed.2d 854, 875 (1973).
64. See, e.g., Florida v. Royer, 460 U.S. 491, 103 S.Ct. 1319, 75 L.Ed.2d 229, 242–43 (1983) (consent to search suitcase held tainted and involuntary after defendant was subjected to a functional arrest in police interrogation room at airport based on no probable cause; Court concluded that the consent was "tainted by the illegality and was ineffective to justify the search." 75 L.Ed.2d at 243).
65. Schneckloth v. Bustamonte, 412 U.S. 218,233, 93 S.Ct. 2041, 36 L.Ed.2d 854, 866 (1973); Florida v. Royer, 460 U.S. 491, 497, 103 S.Ct. 1319, 75 L.Ed.2d 229, 236 (1983).
66. United States v. Watson, 423 U.S. 411, 96 S.Ct. 820, 46 L.Ed.2d 598, 609 (1976).
67. Florida v. Jimeno, 500 U.S. 248, 111 S.Ct. 1801, 114 L.Ed.2d 297, 302–03, 304 (1991).
68. Florida v. Jimeno, 500 U.S. 248, 111 S.Ct. 1801, 114 L.Ed.2d 297, 304 (1991).
69. This exception is examined at Chapter 15, Section 2a of this work.
70. South Dakota v. Opperman, 428 U.S. 364, 96 S.Ct. 3092, 49 L.Ed.2d 1000 (1976); Colorado v. Bertine, 479 U.S. 367, 374, 107 S.Ct. 738, 93 L.Ed.2d 739 (1987).
71. Colorado v. Bertine, 479 U.S. 367, 107 S.Ct. 738, 93 L.Ed.2d 739 (1987); Florida v. Wells, 495 U.S. 1, 110 S.Ct. 1632, 109 L.Ed.2d 1 (1990) (locked suitcase forced open and contents inventoried; inventory struck down).

inventory according to standard police criteria and procedures, not a subterfuge for a general exploratory search of the vehicle for evidence of crime.[72]

- **Exigent circumstances search**[73]

If there is probable cause to believe that an emergency situation exists that requires a search of the automobile—i.e., in hot pursuit of a fleeing felon into the vehicle, the imminent destruction of evidence in the vehicle, or the present risk of danger to the police or others inside caused by something dangerous in the vehicle such as an explosive device—the automobile may be entered and searched for the purposes mentioned.[74]

c. Seizure of evidence in the automobile

If a warrantless search of an automobile is reasonable [because it fits within one of the above exceptions to the Fourth Amendment search warrant requirement rule], it does not follow that the police are privileged to seize anything they discover in the automobile during the course of the search.[75] Accordingly, the U.S. Supreme Court in a number of cases has developed the "plain view" doctrine that authorizes an officer to seize items of personal property during the course of such a search only if two conditions are met:

> First, the item of personal property must be discovered by police during the course of an otherwise reasonable Fourth Amendment search of the automobile. If discovered *outside* the scope of such a search, the ensuing seizure is unreasonable.
>
> Second, the police must have probable cause to believe that the seized property is contraband, fruits or instrumentalities of a crime, or evidence of a crime. Absent such probable cause the seizure is unreasonable; in particular, reasonable suspicion for such a full-blown seizure is insufficient. But if police effect only a temporary seizure of the property, a reasonable suspicion showing is sufficient.[76]

Section 3. Container Searches and Seizures

Special problems arise when police search or seize what the Court has generically denominated as a "container."[77]

---

72. See, e.g., Florida v. Wells, 495 U.S. 1, 110 S.Ct. 1632, 109 L.Ed.2d 1, 6 (1990). City of Indianapolis v. Edmund, 531 U.S. 32, 121 S.Ct. 447, 148 L.Ed.2d 333, 346 (2000); Whren v. United States, 517 U.S. 806, 116 S.Ct. 1769, 1773, 135 L.Ed.2d 89 (1996).

73. This exception is examined at Chapter 14, Section 6 of this work.

74. See generally Kentucky v. King, 563 U.S. ___, 131 S.Ct. 1849, 1856, 179 L.Ed.2d 865 (2011).

75. 3 Wayne LaFave, Search and Seizure § 6.7(a) at 637 (5th ed. 2012).

76. The "plain view" doctrine is examined at Chapter 12, Section 2c of this work. See, e.g., Coolidge v. New Hampshire, 403 U.S. 443, 91 S.Ct. 2022, 29 L.Ed.2d 564, 581–87 (1971); Texas v. Brown, 460 U.S. 730, 103 S.Ct. 1535, 75 L.Ed.2d 502, 511 (1983); Arizona v. Hicks, 480 U.S. 321, 107 S.Ct. 1149, 94 L.Ed.2d 347 (1987); Horton v. California, 496 U.S. 128, 110 S.Ct. 2301, 110 L.Ed.2d 112 (1990).

77. For a thorough discussion of the rules governing the search of containers, see 3 Wayne LaFave, Search and Seizure § 5.5 (5th ed. 2012). See also 2 John Wesley Hall, Search and Seizure Ch. 39 (5th ed. 2013).

a. Searches

(1) *Nature of containers protected*

It is settled that a person has a reasonable expectation of privacy in a container that he or she owns or possesses—such as a footlocker, a suitcase, a briefcase, a portfolio, a duffel bag, a paper bag, or any other receptacle in which a person's private property may be carried or stored. Indeed, there is no constitutional distinction made between "worthy" or "unworthy" containers; all are entitled to constitutional protection. This surely makes sense as people have every right to expect some privacy when they place their belongings in containers of this nature—designed, as they are, to safe keep the owner's possessions and to shield them from public view. Indeed, people frequently put some of their most intimate property and private papers in such containers, especially when they travel; plainly, society recognizes as reasonable a person's subjective expectation of privacy in the interior of such containers, no matter how fancy or humble the container may be. Accordingly, a governmental inspection of such a container constitutes a "search" within the meaning of the Fourth Amendment.[78]

There is, however, no reasonable expectation of privacy in a container if the contents thereof can be inferred from its outer appearance—or if the container is transparent or open so that its contents are visible from the outside.[79] This is so because one cannot

---

78. United States v. Ross, 456 U.S. 798, 102 S.Ct. 2157, 72 L.Ed.2d 572 (1982) (paper bag and zippered pouch) approving, in part, Robbins v. California, 453 U.S. 420, 101 S.Ct. 2841, 69 L.Ed.2d 744, 750–51 (1981) (opaque plastic bags); United States v. Chadwick, 433 U.S. 1, 13, 97 S.Ct. 2476, 53 L.Ed.2d 538, 549 (1977) (footlocker); Arkansas v. Sanders, 442 U.S. 753, 762 n. 9, 99 S.Ct. 2586, 61 L.Ed.2d 235, 244 (1979) (suitcase); Bond v. United States, 529 U.S. 334, 120 S.Ct. 1462, 146 L.Ed.2d 365 (2000) (bus traveler's carry-on canvas bag).

"One point on which the Court was in virtually unanimous agreement in *Robbins* was that a constitutional distinction between 'worthy' and 'unworthy' containers would be improper. Even though such a distinction perhaps could evolve in a series of cases in which paper bags, locked trunks, lunch buckets and orange crates were placed on one side of the line or the other, the central purpose of the Fourth Amendment forecloses such a distinction. For just as the most frail cottage in the kingdom is absolutely entitled to the same guarantees of privacy as the most majestic mansion, so also may a traveler who carries a toothbrush and a few articles of clothing in a paper bag or knotted scarf claim an equal right to conceal his possessions from official inspection as the sophisticated executive with the locked attache case.

As Justice Stewart stated in Robbins, *the Fourth Amendment provides protection to the owner of every container that conceals its contents from plain view.*" United States v. Ross, 456 U.S. at 822, 72 L.Ed.2d at 592 (footnotes omitted).

79. "Not all containers and packages found by police during a search will deserve full Fourth Amendment protection. [1] Thus, some containers (for example a kit of burglar tools or a gun case) by their very nature cannot support any reasonable expectation of privacy because their contents can be inferred from their outer appearance. [2] Similarly, in some cases the contents of a package will be open to 'plain view,' thereby obviating the need for a warrant." Arkansas v. Sanders, 442 U.S. 753, 764 n. 13, 99 S.Ct. 2586, 61 L.Ed.2d 235, 245 (1979) (numerical brackets added).

The first type of case mentioned above, is "little more than another variation of the 'plain view' [doctrine], since, if the distinctive configuration of a container proclaims its contents, the contents cannot fairly be said to have been removed from a searching officer's view. The same would be true, of course, if the container were transparent, or otherwise clearly revealed its contents." The second type of case mentioned above "obviously refers to items in a container that is not closed." "In short ... unless the container is such that its contents are said to be in plain view, those contents are fully protected by the Fourth Amendment." Robbins v. California, 453 U.S. 420, 427, 101 S.Ct. 2841, 69 L.Ed.2d 744, 751 (1981).

entertain a reasonable expectation of privacy as to items that are open to public view. Accordingly, a container and its contents may be subject to seizure without a warrant—if the viewing of the container is otherwise lawful, and there is probable cause to believe that such contents constitute contraband, or the fruits or instrumentalities of a crime, or evidence of crime.[80] Should, for example, a law enforcement officer lawfully view an opaque balloon commonly used to package heroin, or a transparent plastic baggie containing cocaine, such items may clearly be seized and their contents removed without a warrant.[81]

Beyond that, there is no reasonable expectation in a sealed container placed in the mail, after it has been lawfully intercepted and searched by government officials—so that when such a container is resealed and delivered to the addressee by undercover law enforcement officers in a "controlled" delivery, the subsequent re-opening of the container by such officers without a warrant after having arrested the addressee at the point of delivery, is not a Fourth Amendment search of the container. Once a container has been lawfully searched by government officials, there can hardly be a reasonable expectation of privacy in its contents, as the government is now well aware of same. It therefore makes little sense to require a warrant [or an exception to the warrant requirement rule] for the second search of the container, as this intrusion is not governed by the Fourth Amendment.[82]

(2) Search warrant requirement rule

It is well-settled that a governmental search of private property conducted without a search warrant is per se unreasonable under the Fourth Amendment—subject to certain well-established exceptions that the government has the burden of proof to establish.[83] Although this rule is primarily applicable to fixed premises, such as a home or business, it has also been applied to containers.[84] Accordingly, a search of a container must, as a general rule, be conducted with a search warrant, subject to certain exceptions.

(3) Applicable exceptions to the search warrant requirement rule

There are five possible exceptions to the search warrant requirement rule that may apply to a warrantless search of a container in a given case. All relevant exceptions must therefore be examined to determine if such a search is reasonable under the Fourth Amendment. If one of these exceptions is applicable, the search is reasonable—even if the other exceptions are inapplicable. If none of the exceptions are applicable, however, the search is unreasonable.

---

80. For a discussion of the unreasonableness rules concerning the seizure of personal property, see Chapter 12, Section 2 of this work.

81. Texas v. Brown, 460 U.S. 730, 742–43, 103 S.Ct. 1535, 75 L.Ed.2d 502, 514 (1983) (police seizure of opaque, green knotted balloon commonly used to package narcotics upheld under the "plain view" doctrine); Texas v. Brown, 460 U.S. at 750–51, 75 L.Ed.2d at 519–20 (Stevens, J. concurring); 3 Wayne LaFave, Search and Seizure § 5.5(f) (5th ed. 2012).

82. Illinois v. Andreas, 463 U.S. 765, 103 S.Ct. 3319, 77 L.Ed.2d 1003 (1983).

83. See Chapter 11, Section 1 of this work and the long line of cases collected at fn. 1.

84. United States v. Chadwick, 433 U.S. 1, 7–11, 97 S.Ct. 2476, 53 L.Ed.2d 538, 545–48 (1977), as further explained in United States v. Ross, 456 U.S. 798, 810–11, 102 S.Ct. 2157, 72 L.Ed.2d 572, 585 (1982) (footlocker); Arkansas v. Sanders, 442 U.S. 753, 757–761, 99 S.Ct. 2586, 61 L.Ed.2d 235, 240–243 (1979) (suitcase); see also Bond v. United States, 529 U.S. 334, 120 S.Ct. 1462, 146 L.Ed.2d 365 (2000) (federal agent's physical manipulation of bus traveler's carry-on canvas bag held a Fourth Amendment search; no exception to search warrant requirement rule as urged by the Government; "[w]e therefore hold that the agent's physical manipulation of petitioner's bag violated the Fourth Amendment." 146 L.Ed.2d at 370).

But there is one important caveat to keep in mind. If the search in question is *preceded* by an unreasonable seizure of the complaining party's person [such as an illegal arrest or illegal temporary detention],[85] or an unreasonable seizure of that person's property [such as an automobile], it is—with rare exceptions—unnecessary to examine *any* exceptions to the search warrant requirement rule. Such a seizure will almost always taint and generally render inadmissible the fruits thereof under the *Weeks-Mapp* exclusionary rule—including the fruits of a container search conducted immediately after such an unreasonable seizure of the person or the person's property.[86]

The possible applicable exceptions to the search warrant requirement rule for a warrantless container search are as follows.

• Search incident to a lawful arrest: container in automobile or on person[87]

After making a lawful custodial arrest of an occupant of an automobile, a law enforcement officer may search, incident to the arrest, the *passenger compartment* of the automobile, but not the trunk (a) if the occupant is within reaching distance of the vehicle during the search, or (b) if the police have probable cause to believe that the vehicle contains evidence relevant to the crime of arrest. In the process thereof, the officer may search any *containers* found in the automobile passenger compartment.[88] There appears to be no principled reason why police cannot also search any containers in the arrestee's *physical possession* at the point of arrest. But law enforcement agents may not conduct a warrantless search of a cell phone, pursuant to this exception, where they have seized the phone from the arrestee at the point of arrest.[89]

---

85. For a discussion of illegal arrests and illegal detentions of the person, see Chapter 12, Section 1 of this work.

86. For a discussion of the fruit of the poisonous tree doctrine, see Chapter 17, Section 3 of this work.

87. This exception is examined at Chapter 14, Section 2 of this work.

88. Arizona v. Gant, 556 U.S. 322, 129 S.Ct. 1710, 1719, 1723, 173 L.Ed.2d 485 (2009) (search of motor vehicle held not incident to traffic arrest of driver for driving with a suspended license; driver was handcuffed and placed in the back of police patrol car at time of arrest).

"As result, the Court [in Gant] adopted a new, two-part rule under which an automobile search incident to a recent occupant's arrest is constitutional (1) if the arrestee is within reaching distance of the vehicle during the search, or (2) if the police have reason to believe that the vehicle contains evidence relevant to the crime of arrest." Davis v. United States, 564 U.S. ____, 131 S.Ct. 2419, 2425, 180 L.Ed.2d 285 (2011) (internal citation and quotation marks omitted).

"The current exception also leaves undisturbed the Court's prior rulings that under this exception (a) *containers* in the vehicle's passenger compartment may also be searched, but (b) the vehicle's *trunk* may not be searched. New York v. Belton, 453 U.S. 454, 101 S.Ct. 2860, 69 L.Ed.2d 768, 775 (1981). Indeed, the Gant Court expressly stated that under its second holding, as stated above , "the offense of arrest will [often] supply a basis for searching the *passenger compartment* of an arrestee's vehicle *and any containers therein*." Arizona v. Gant, 556 U.S. 322, 129 S.Ct. 1710, 1719, 173 L.Ed.2d 485 (2009) (emphasis and brackets added).

89. Riley v. California, 574 U.S. ___, 134 S.Ct. 2473, 186 L.Ed.2d 430 (2014) (warrantless search by police of a modern "smart phone" and a modern "flip phone" seized from the person of a suspect in two companion cases following an arrest of each suspect; held unreasonable under the Fourth Amendment as (a) not conducted with a search warrant, and (b) not otherwise justified under the search incident to a lawful arrest exception to the search warrant requirement rule).

"We therefore decline to extend *Robinson* to searches of data on cell phones, and hold instead that officers must generally secure a warrant before conducting such a search. * * * Our holding, of course, is not that the information on a cell phone is immune from search; it is instead that a warrant is generally required before such a search, even when a cell phone is seized incident to arrest. * * Our

• Moving vehicle exception: *Carroll* doctrine[90]

Where there is probable cause to believe that a moving vehicle [such as an automobile] contains contraband, fruits or instrumentalities of a crime, or evidence of crime, all areas within the vehicle may be searched, including all containers therein—so long as the object of the search may reasonably be found in those areas.[91] Accordingly, if there is probable cause to believe that illegal drugs may be in an automobile at any location therein, police may search all containers therein, as drugs can be concealed in a container. But if there is probable cause to believe that the automobile contains a stolen refrigerator, police may not search a briefcase or luggage found therein because a refrigerator cannot be concealed in such a container.[92] Moreover, if there is probable cause to search a container in an automobile, the police may enter the automobile and search the container without a warrant.[93]

• Exigent circumstances[94]

The Court, in dicta, has indicated that police may conduct a warrantless search of a container—where there is a reasonable basis to believe that the container harbors a weapon or bomb that presents an immediate danger to others.[95]

---

answer to the question of what police must do before searching a cell phone incident to an arrest is simple—get a warrant." 134 S.Ct. at, 2485, 2493, 2495.

90. This exception is examined at Chapter 14, Section 4 of this work.

91. United States v. Ross, 456 U.S. 798, 102 S.Ct. 2157, 72 L.Ed.2d 572 (1982) [overruling Robbins v. California, 453 U.S. 420, 101 S.Ct. 2841, 69 L.Ed.2d 744 (1981)] (probable cause that defendant was selling narcotics out of the trunk of his car and had narcotics in the car justified a warrantless search of paper bag and zippered leather pouch found in trunk of car); Michigan v. Thomas, 458 U.S. 259, 102 S.Ct. 3079, 73 L.Ed.2d 750 (1982) (probable cause that car contained marijuana justified search of the air vents under the car dashboard, as marijuana might be hidden there; revolver discovered in air vents properly seized).

"We hold that the scope of the warrantless search authorized by that exception [the *Carroll* moving vehicle exception] is no broader and no narrower than a magistrate could legitimately authorize by warrant. If probable cause justifies the search of a lawfully stopped vehicle, it justifies the search of every part of the vehicle and its contents that may conceal the object of the search." United States v. Ross, 456 U.S. 798, 102 S.Ct. 2157, 72 L.Ed.2d 572, 594 (1982).

"Just as probable cause to believe that a stolen lawnmower may be found in a garage will not support a warrant to search an upstairs bedroom, probable cause to believe that undocumented aliens are being transported in a van will not justify a warrantless search of a suitcase. Probable cause to believe that a container placed in a trunk of a taxi contains contraband does not justify a search of the entire cab." United States v. Ross, 456 U.S. 798, 824, 102 S.Ct. 2157, 72 L.Ed.2d 572, 593 (1982).

92. For a discussion of the reasonableness rules on the scope of an otherwise reasonable search, see Chapter 11, Section 4b of this work.

93. California v. Acevedo, 500 U.S. 565, 111 S.Ct. 1982, 114 L.Ed.2d 619, 634 (1991) overruled the results reached and rationale of United States v. Chadwick, 443 U.S. 1, 99 S.Ct 2476, 53 L.Ed.2d 538 (1977) (footlocker in trunk of car searched; probable cause that footlocker contained marijuana; search held invalid because conducted without a warrant); and Arkansas v. Sanders, 442 U.S. 753, 99 S.Ct. 2586, 61 L.Ed.2d 235 (1979) (same result for search of suitcase in taxicab). Under Acevedo, the footlocker in Chadwick and the suitcase in Sanders could be searched without a warrant, but not the entire vehicle. Chadwick and Sanders remain viable, however, outside the automobile context—so that search of a suitcase generally requires a search warrant, for example, the suitcase of an air traveler. See United States v. Place, 462 U.S. 696, 103 S.Ct. 2637, 77 L.Ed. 110 (1983) (search warrant for search of air traveler's suitcase tainted by illegal seizure of suitcase in which a narcotics dog alerted on suitcase).

94. This exception is examined at Chapter 14, Section 6 of this work.

95. In striking down the warrantless search of a footlocker in United States v. Chadwick, 443 U.S. 1, 97 S.Ct. 2476, 53 L.Ed.2d 538, 551 n.9 (1977), the Court stated that "if officers have reason to believe that luggage contains some immediately dangerous instrumentality, such as explosives, it

• Consent search[96]

Where a person gives a voluntary general consent to search his or her automobile, law enforcement officers may search the interior of the automobile and all *unlocked* containers therein, provided the evidence the police say they are looking for can reasonably be found in these areas—but apparently they may not search *locked* containers, such as a locked briefcase.[97] Moreover, the consenting party may expressly limit the areas on the premises that the police may search.[98] In measuring the scope of the person's consent to search, the test is that of objective reasonableness: what would a reasonable person have understood by the exchange between the police and the consenting party as to what physical area the police could search?[99]

• Border search[100]

A warrantless search by U.S. Customs officials of luggage and other containers brought into the country by a traveler at the border or its functional equivalent[101] is the quintessential type of search allowed by the border exception.

---

would be foolhardy to transport it to the station house without opening the luggage and disarming the weapon."

The Court made a similar comment in striking down the warrantless search of a suitcase in Arkansas v. Sanders, 442 U.S. 753, 99 S.Ct. 2586, 61 L.Ed.2d 235, 245 n. 11 (1979): "There may be cases in which the special exigencies of the situation would justify the warrantless search of a suitcase. Cady v. Dombrowski, 413 U.S. 433, 93 S.Ct. 2523, 37 L.Ed.2d 706 (1973) (police had reason to suspect automobile trunk contained a weapon). Generally, however, such exigencies will depend upon the probable contents of the luggage and the suspect's access to those contents."

96. This exception is examined at Chapter 14, Section 5 of this work.

97. In Florida v. Jimeno, 500 U.S. 248, 111 S.Ct. 1801, 114 L.Ed.2d 297 (1991), the Court distinguishes State v. Wells, 539 So.2d 464 (Fla. 1989), relied on by the Florida Supreme Court in affirming the suppression order under review. "There the Supreme Court of Florida held that consent to search the trunk of a car did not include authorization to pry open a locked briefcase found inside the trunk. It is very likely unreasonable to think that a suspect, by consenting to the search of his trunk, has agreed to the breaking open of a locked briefcase within the trunk, but it is otherwise with respect to a closed paper bag." 114 L.Ed.2d at 304.

In *Jimeno*, the police officer told the defendant that the officer believed the defendant was carrying narcotics; the defendant gave a voluntary general consent for police to search defendant's car, placing no restrictions on the consent. The Court held that it was proper for the police to look in a closed paper bag lying on the floor of the car.

98. "A suspect may of course delimit as he chooses the scope of the search to which he consents." Florida v. Jimeno, 500 U.S. 248, 111 S.Ct. 1801, 114 L.Ed.2d 297, 304 (1991). For a discussion of the scope of a consent search, see 4 Wayne LaFave, Search and Seizure § 8.1(c) (5th ed. 2012).

99. "The standard for measuring the scope of a suspect's consent [to search] under the Fourth Amendment is that of objective reasonableness—what would the typical reasonable person have understood by the exchange between the officer and the suspect? The question before us, then, is whether it is reasonable to consider a suspect's general consent to search his car to include consent to examine a paper bag lying on the floor of the car. We think it does." Florida v. Jimeno, 500 U.S. 248, 111 S.Ct. 1801, 114 L.Ed.2d 297, 302–03 (1991).

100. This exception is examined at Chapter 15, Section 2b of this work.

101. "[Border searches] may in certain circumstances take place, not only at the border itself, but at its *functional equivalents* as well. For example, searches at an established station near the border, at a point marking the confluence of two or more roads that extend from the border, might be functional equivalents of border searches. For another example, a search of the passengers and cargo of an airplane arriving at a St. Louis airport after a non-stop flight from Mexico City would clearly be the functional equivalent of a border search." Almeida-Sanchez v. United States, 413 U.S. 266, 93 S.Ct. 2535, 37 L.Ed.2d 596, 602 (1973) (roving patrol search of car 20 miles from US-Mexican border held not a border search) (emphasis added).

- **Inventory search**[102]

In an otherwise valid inventory search of a motor vehicle, the contents of containers therein may be inventoried provided it is done according to standard police procedure,[103] but apparently not if the police have no such standard procedure.[104] Moreover, the inventory exception is not limited to impounded motor vehicles. It also applies to a standardized inventory of an arrestee's possessions prior to police booking and jailing the arrestee.[105]

b. Seizures[106]

It is clear that a "container" is an item of personal property—and thus is a protected "effect" within the meaning of the Fourth Amendment.[107] In turn, "[a] [Fourth Amendment] seizure of [such] property occurs when there has been some meaningful interference [by a government agent] with an individual's possessory interests in [such] property."[108]

The Court has upheld the warrantless seizure of a container, as an initial Fourth Amendment intrusion, for a reasonable period of time while law enforcement officials obtain a warrant for the search of the container—provided there is probable cause to believe that the container holds contraband, fruits or instrumentalities of a crime, or evidence of a crime.[109] Beyond that, if the initial seizure of the container is only temporary in nature

---

102. This exception is examined at Chapter 15, Section 2a of this work.

103. Colorado v. Bertine, 479 U.S. 367, 374, 107 S.Ct. 738, 93 L.Ed.2d 739 (1987) (closed backpack opened and contents inventoried)

104. Florida v. Wells, 495 U.S. 1, 110 S.Ct.1632, 109 L.Ed.2d 1 (1990) (locked suitcase forced open and contents inventoried).

105. "The question here is whether, consistent with the Fourth Amendment, it is reasonable for police to search the personal effects of a person under lawful arrest as part of the routine administrative procedure at a police station house incident to booking and jailing the suspect. * * *

[W]e hold that it is not 'unreasonable' for police, as part of the routine procedure incident to incarcerating an arrested person, to search any container or article in his possession in accordance with established inventory procedures." Illinois v. LaFayette, 462 U.S. 640, 103 S.Ct. 2605, 77 L.Ed. 65, 69, 73 (1983) (contents of arrestee's shoulder bag inventoried at jail; contraband drug discovered in bag and seized).

106. For a discussion of the unreasonableness rules governing the seizure of personal property, see Chapter 12, section 2 of this work.

107. "The framers [of the Fourth Amendment] would have understood the term 'effects' to be limited to personal property, rather than real property." Oliver v. United States, 466 U.S. 170, 104 S.Ct. 1735, 80 L.Ed.2d 223 n. 7 (1984)."A traveler's luggage is clearly an 'effect' protected by the [Fourth] Amendment." Bond v. United States, 529 U.S. 334, 120 S.Ct. 1462, 145 L.Ed.2d 365, 369 (2000); Ross v. United States, 456 U.S. 798, 102 S.Ct. 2157, 72 L.Ed.2d 572, 592 (1982) (zippered leather pouch and closed brown paper bag protected by Fourth Amendment); United States v. Chadwick, 433 U.S. 1, 97 S.Ct. 2476, 53 L.Ed.2d 538 (1977) (footlocker protected by the Fourth Amendment).

108. United States v. Jacobsen, 466 U.S. 109, 113, 104 S.Ct. 1652, 80 L.Ed.2d 85, 94 (1984).

109. "Recognizing the generally less intrusive nature of a seizure, the Court has frequently approved warrantless seizures of property, on the basis of probable cause, for the time necessary to secure a warrant, where a warrantless search was either held to be or likely would have been held impermissible." Segura v. United States, 468 U.S. 796, 104 S.Ct. 3380, 82 L.Ed 2d 599, 609–10 (1984) (plurality), citing cases which authorize the seizure of a defendant's footlocker or suitcase based on probable cause while a search warrant for same is being obtained: United States v. Chadwick, 433 U.S. 1, 97 S.Ct. 2476, 53 L.Ed.2d 538 (1977) (seizure of footlocker based on probable cause assumed to be reasonable; Court held that a warrant should have been obtained for same while police held the footlocker); Arkansas v. Sanders, 442 U.S. 753, 99 S.Ct. 2586, 61 L.Ed.2d 235 (1979) (seizure of defendant's suitcase based on probable cause approved; Court held that a warrant should have been obtained for same while police held the suitcase); see also Chambers v. Maroney, 399 U.S. 42, 90 S.Ct. 1975, 26 L.Ed.2d

pending further investigation, a lesser showing of reasonable suspicion, rather than probable cause, is required that the container conceals contraband, the fruits of a crime, the instrumentalities of a crime, or evidence of a crime—so long as the temporal and physical limits of a temporary detention are not exceeded.[110]

Section 4. Subpoena Duces Tecum

a. Constructive search and seizure

A grand jury, a prosecuting attorney, an administrative agency or a legislative committee at times may issue a subpoena duces tecum or similar order directing a person to produce certain books and records for the demanding agency's inspection in connection with a particular investigation. Although the *issuance and service* of such a subpoena, standing alone, does *not* invade any protected Fourth Amendment interest of the subpoenaed person,[111] the actual production of the books and records by the subpoenaed person in compliance with this process constitutes a constructive Fourth Amendment search and seizure—and accordingly the subpoena must satisfy Fourth Amendment standards of reasonableness.[112]

---

419 (1970) (seizure of automobile from street based on probable cause is permissible; thereafter, police may obtain a warrant for the search of same or search automobile without a warrant);

110. "In sum, we conclude that when an officer's observations lead him reasonably to believe that a traveler is carrying luggage that contains narcotics, the principles of *Terry* and its progeny would permit the officer to detain the luggage briefly to investigate the circumstances that aroused his suspicion, provided that the investigative detention is properly limited in scope." United States v. Place, 462 U.S. 696, 103 S.Ct. 2637, 77 L.Ed.2d 110, 120 (1983).

In *Place*, federal narcotics agents seized defendant's two carry-on bags as defendant arrived at LaGuardia Airport in NYC from Miami [defendant himself was not detained], after having been notified by narcotics agents in Miami of (1) defendant's scheduled arrival at LaGuardia, and (2) the Miami agent's reasonable suspicion that defendant was carrying narcotics, as a result of an encounter with defendant at the Miami airport. The initial seizure of these two bags was held reasonable as being based on reasonable suspicion. The NYC agents, however, exceeded the time limits of a temporary *Terry* detention of the bags by transporting the bags to Kennedy Airport where a "dog sniff" of the bags took place, all of which took 90 minutes from the initial seizure of the bags. NYC agents had ample time to arrange for a "dog sniff" at LaGuardia Airport and thus minimize the intrusion on defendant's Fourth Amendment interests in the bags. Consequently, a search warrant issued for the bags after the dog alerted on the bags was invalid, and the fruits of the search of the bags pursuant to the warrant were inadmissible in evidence against the defendant.

"We note that here the New York agents knew the time of Place's scheduled arrival at LaGuardia, had ample time to arrange for their additional investigation at that location, and thereby could have minimized the intrusion on respondent's Fourth Amendment interests. Thus, although we decline to adopt any outside time limitation for a permissible Terry stop, we have never approved a seizure for the prolonged 90 minute period involved here and cannot do so on the facts presented by this case." United States v. Place, 77 L.Ed.2d at 122.

111. Wheeldin v. Wheeler, 373 U.S. 647, 649–650, 83 S.Ct.1441, 10 L.Ed.2d 605, 610 (1963) (service of an unresponded-to U.S. House Un-American Activities Committee subpoena *held* not a Fourth Amendment search or seizure; complaint for damages based on such service properly dismissed).

112. "We are of the opinion that an order for the production of books and papers may constitute an unreasonable search and seizure within the Fourth Amendment. While a search ordinarily implies a quest for evidence by an officer of the law, and a seizure contemplates a forcible dispossession of the owner, still, as was held in the *Boyd* case, the substance of the offense is the compulsory production of private papers, whether under a search warrant or a *subpoena duces tecum*, against which a person,

b. General reasonableness standards

There are three minimal standards of reasonableness that a subpoena duces tecum or similar such order must satisfy—and whether such standards have been met in a given case may be litigated in court on a motion to quash the subpoena before any compliance therewith:

> First, the inquiry must be one that the demanding agency is authorized by law to make;
>
> Second, the materials subpoenaed must be relevant to this inquiry; and
>
> Third, the subpoena must adequately specify the documents to be produced, and cannot be too indefinite, overly broad or unduly burdensome for the subpoenaed person to comply with.[113]

As to the first requirement, it is unnecessary that a specific charge or complaint of violation of law be pending in order for the demanding agency's investigation to be

---

be he individual or corporation, is entitled to protection." Hale v. Henkel, 201 U.S. 43, 76, 26 S.Ct. 370, 50 L.Ed. 652, 666 (1906); Oklahoma Press Publishing Co. v. Walling, 327 U.S. 186, 195, 202, 66 S.Ct. 494, 90 L.Ed. 614, 622, 625 (1946) (subpoena duces tecum presents no question of "actual search and seizure" but does involve a "'figurative' or 'constructive' search").

Of course, if the officer serving the subpoena conducts a search of private premises to obtain the materials subpoenaed [rather than allowing the subpoenaed person to produce such materials to the demanding agency as required by the subpoena], the search is unreasonable under the Fourth Amendment unless otherwise justified by an exception to the general rule requiring search warrants—as a subpoena does not and constitutionally cannot authorize a search by a government official of such premises. Mancusi v. DeForte, 392 U.S. 364, 88 S.Ct. 2120, 20 L.Ed.2d 1154 (1968) (search of union office pursuant to a subpoena duces tecum issued by a prosecuting attorney held unreasonable).

113. "Without attempt to summarize or accurately distinguish all of the cases, the fair distillation, in so far as they apply merely to the production of corporate records and response to a subpoena or order authorized by law and safeguarded by judicial sanction, seems to be that ... the Fourth [Amendment], if applicable, at the most guards against abuse only by way of too much indefiniteness or breadth in the things required to be 'particularly described,' if also the inquiry is one the demanding agency is authorized by law to make and the materials specified are relevant. The gist of the protection is in the requirement, expressed in terms, that the disclosure sought shall not be unreasonable." Oklahoma Press Publishing Co. v. Walling, 327 U.S. 186, 208, 66 S.Ct. 494, 90 L.Ed. 614, 629 (1946).

"Of course a governmental investigation into corporate matters [through an administrative subpoena or order] may be of such a sweeping nature and so unrelated to the matter properly under inquiry as to exceed the investigatory power. But it is sufficient if the inquiry is within the authority of the agency, the demand is not too indefinite and the information sought is reasonably relevant." United States v. Morton Salt Co., 338 U.S. 632, 652, 70 S.Ct. 357, 94 L.Ed. 401, 416 (1950) (internal citation omitted).

"It is now settled that, when an administrative agency subpoenas corporate books or records, the Fourth Amendment requires that the subpoena be sufficiently limited in scope, relevant in purpose, and specific in directive so that compliance will not be unduly burdensome. The agency has the right to conduct all reasonable inspections of such documents which are contemplated by the statute, but it must delimit the confines of a search by designating the needed documents in a formal subpoena. In addition, while the demand to inspect may be issued by the agency, in the form of an administrative subpoena, it may not be made and enforced by the inspector in the field, and the subpoenaed party may obtain judicial review of the reasonableness of the demand prior to suffering penalties for refusing to comply." See v. City of Seattle, 387 U.S. 541, 544–45, 87 S.Ct. 1737, 18 L.Ed.2d 943, 947 (1967).

For an excellent review of these three standards, collecting all relevant cases, see 2 Wayne LaFave, Search and Seizure § 4.13 (5th ed. 2013). Also see 2 John Wesley Hall, Search and Seizure §§ 49.01–49.21 (5th ed. 2013), as well as cases collected at "Searches and Seizures" § 75 West Key No.

authorized by law; it is sufficient that the purpose of the investigation is authorized by appropriate statute or other lawful authority.[114] As to the second requirement, it would appear that the materials subpoenaed are presumed relevant to the demanding agency's investigation, unless there is *no reasonable possibility* that this is the case.[115] As to the third requirement, the documents to be produced must be relatively specific given the nature of the investigation, and otherwise adequate, but not excessive for the purposes of the demanding agency's inquiry[116]—a requirement, according to LaFave, that is the most litigated of the three requirements.[117]

In a long line of cases, the U.S. Supreme Court has applied these requirements with some leniency in favor of the demanding agency, and has generally upheld subpoenas duces tecum issued by a grand jury or administrative agency.[118] In two cases, however,

114. "It is not necessary, as in the case of a warrant, that a specific charge or complaint of violation of law be pending or that the order be made pursuant to one. It is enough that the investigation be made for a lawfully authorized purpose, within the power of Congress to command. This has been ruled most often perhaps in relation to grand jury investigations, but also frequently in respect to general or statistical investigations authorized by Congress." Oklahoma Press Co. v. Walling, 327 U.S. 186, 209, 66 S.Ct. 494, 90 L.Ed.2d 614, 630 (1946).

115. "[W]here, as here, a grand jury subpoena is challenged on relevancy grounds, the motion to quash must be denied unless the [trial court] determines that there is no reasonable possibility that the category of materials that the Government seeks will produce information relevant to the general subject of the grand jury's investigation." United States v. R. Enterprises, Inc., 498 U.S. 292, 301, 111 S.Ct. 722, 112 L.Ed.2d 795, 807 (1991) (decided under Rule 17(c) of the Federal Rules of Criminal Procedure).

116. "Beyond this[,] the [Fourth Amendment] requirement of reasonableness, including particularity in 'describing the place to be searched, and the persons or things to be seized,' also literally applicable to warrants, comes down to [a] specification [in the subpoena] of the documents to be produced [that is] adequate, but not excessive for the purposes of the relevant inquiry." Oklahoma Press Co. v. Walling, 327 U.S. 186, 209, 66 S.Ct. 494, 90 L.Ed.2d 614, 630 (1946) (bracketed material added).

117. 2 Wayne LaFave, Search and Seizure § 4.13(d) at 1075 (5th ed. 2012).

118. Consolidated Rendering Co. v. Vermont, 207 U.S. 541, 28 S.Ct. 178, 52 L.Ed. 327 (1908) (grand jury subpoena directing the production of (a) books, papers related to any dealings or business between the corporation subpoenaed and the cattle commissioners of the state of Vermont related to a complaint of selling diseased meat between January 1, 1904 and the date of the subpoena in October 1906, and (b) checks and vouchers described by date and amount; held documents subpoenaed described with sufficient particularity); Hammond Packing Co. v. Arkansas, 212 U.S, 322, 29 S.Ct. 370, 53 L.Ed. 530 (1909) (court order directing corporation to produce any books, papers and documents in the corporation relating to the merits of a civil action instituted by the State of Arkansas to revoke the corporation's permit to do business in Arkansas because of certain alleged price-fixing activities, but with the proviso that the corporation shall not be required to produce these papers at any one time if it would interfere with the operation of the corporation's business; held: subpoena did not violate the corporation's Fourth Amendment rights); Wilson v. United States, 221 U.S. 361, 31 S.Ct. 538, 55 L.Ed. 771 (1911) (grand jury subpoena directing a corporate president to produce "letter-press copy books" of the corporation "containing copies of letters and telegrams" signed by the corporate president during the months of May and June 1909 pertaining to an alleged violation of federal law; held: the subpoena was suitably specific and properly limited in scope, no violation of the Fourth Amendment); Brown v. United States, 276 U.S. 134, 48 S.Ct. 288, 72 L.Ed. 500 (1928) (grand jury subpoena duces tecum directed an unincorporated association to produce all letters or telegrams or copies of same passing between the association and its predecessor and their officers, agents and members between January 1, 1922 and June 15, 1925 related to certain enumerated pricing activities then under investigation arising from the sale of certain goods; held: the subpoena specifies a reasonable period of time and reasonably particularizes the items to be produced); United States v. White, 322 U.S. 694, 64 S.Ct. 1248, 88 L.Ed. 1542 (1944) (grand jury subpoena directing a union to produce certain records may not be resisted on self-incrimination grounds; neither the Fourth nor the Fifth Amendment confers a self-incrimination privilege on a union, as the privilege only protects individuals); Oklahoma Press Publishing Co. v. Walling, 327 U.S. 186, 66 S.Ct. 494, 90 L.Ed. 614 (1946) (subpoena duces tecum

the Court has struck down overly-broad subpoenas on the ground that the third requirement of specificity was not met.[119]

Section 5. Surgical Intrusions into the Body

a. Fourth Amendment search: antecedent seizure of person

At times, government agents will order a non-consensual surgical intrusion into a person's body in an effort to extract evidence of crime.[120] To date, the Court has confronted

---

issued by an administrator of the U.S. Labor Dept., Wage and Hour Division, directing various newspaper publishing companies to produce specified records to determine whether these companies were violating the Fair Labor Standards Act; held: subpoena met all three Fourth Amendment requirements and is constitutionally valid); United States v. Morton Salt Co., 338 U.S. 632, 70 S.Ct. 357, 94 L.Ed. 401 (1950) (Federal Trade Commission order requiring corporation to file reports on how it complied with a court decree enforcing an FTC cease-and-desist order concerning corporate pricing policies; held: the order did not violate Fourth Amendment requirements); McPhaul v. United States, 364 U.S. 372, 81 S.Ct. 138, 5 L.Ed.2d 136 (1960) (House Un-American Activities Committee subpoena duces tecum commanding a person to appear before the committee and produce "all records, correspondence and memoranda pertaining to the organization of, the affiliation with other organizations and all monies received or expended by the Civil Rights Congress [an alleged subversive organization]"; held: subpoena required the production of relevant and sufficiently specific documents).

119. "Applying the test of reasonableness to the present case, we think the subpoena duces tecum is far too sweeping in its terms to be regarded as reasonable. It does not require the production of a single contract, or of contracts with a particular corporation, or a limited number of documents, but all understandings, contracts, or correspondence between MacAndrews & Forbes Company, and no less than six different companies, as well as all reports made and accounts rendered by such companies from the date of the organization of the MacAndrews & Forbes Company, as well as all letters received from that company since its organization from more than a dozen different companies, situated in seven different states in the Union.

If the writ had required the production of all the books, papers and documents found in the office of MacAndrews and Forbes Company, it would scarcely be more universal in its operation or more completely put a stop to the business of that company. Indeed it is difficult to say how its business could be carried on after it had been denuded of this mass of material, which is not shown to be necessary in the prosecution of this case, and is clearly in violation of the general principle of law with regard to the particularity required in the description of documents necessary to a search warrant or a subpoena." Hale v. Henkel, 201 U.S. 43, 76–77, 26 S.Ct. 370, 50 L.Ed. 652, 666 (1906) (grand jury subpoena duces tecum directed to the authorized agent of MacAndrews & Forbes Co.).

"[I]n the case of the American Tobacco Company, the [mandamus order prayed for] exhibition during business hours, when the commission's agent requests it, of all letters and telegrams received by the company from, or sent by it to, all of its jobber customers, between January 1, 1921, to December 31, 1921, inclusive. In the case of the P. Lorillard Company the same requirement is made, and also all letters, telegrams, or reports from or to its salesmen, or from or to all tobacco jobbers' or wholesale grocers' associations, all contracts or arrangements with such associations, and correspondence and agreements with a list of corporations named. * * * "Anyone who respects the spirit as well as the letter of the 4th Amendment would be loath to believe that Congress [under the FTC Act] intended to authorize one of its subordinate agencies to sweep all our traditions into the fire, and to direct fishing exhibitions into private papers on the possibility that they may disclose evidence of crime. We do not discuss the question whether it could do so if it tried, as nothing short of the most explicit language would induce us to attribute to Congress that intent. The interruption of business, the possible revelation of trade secrets, and the expense that compliance with the commission's wholesale demand would cause, are the least of our considerations. It is contrary to the first principles of justice to allow a search through all the respondents' records in the hope that something will turn up." Federal Trade Commission v. American Tobacco Co., 264 U.S. 298, 305–06, 44 S.Ct. 336, 68 L.Ed. 696, 700–01 (1924) (opinion by Holmes, J.).

120. For an analysis of the cases on this subject, see 2 Wayne LaFave, Search and Seizure § 4.1(e) (5th ed. 2012).

two such surgical intrusions: (1) the taking of a blood sample, and (2) a surgical operation with a general anesthetic to extract a lodged bullet. It is undisputed that such an intrusion constitutes a Fourth Amendment search of the person—and that generally, as an antecedent, a Fourth Amendment seizure of the person is required in order to conduct the intrusion.[121] As to the latter, it is equally undisputed that there must be probable cause for the antecedent seizure of the person before any surgical intrusion of the arrestee's body can take place.[122]

b. Warrant requirement and standards of reasonableness

Absent an emergency, a surgical intrusion into a person's body by a government agent must be done by a warrant or court order upon a showing that the procedure is reasonable based on all the circumstances. Only where it is shown that the evidence sought to be discovered is in reasonable danger of disappearing may such a warrant or court order be dispensed with.[123] The Court has not yet decided whether a proposed surgical operation requires an *adversary* hearing before same may be ordered by a court; ordinarily, warrants may issue at an ex parte hearing, but the rule may be different where the proposed surgery is a major, rather than a minor procedure.

But whether conducted with or without a warrant or court order, a surgical intrusion into a person's body for evidence of crime is a major invasion of one's reasonable expectation of privacy, and must therefore satisfy Fourth Amendment reasonableness standards. This showing of reasonableness, however, is not made merely upon proof that there is probable cause to arrest the individual in question, and that the proposed intrusion would be likely to produce evidence of crime.[124] Something more must also be shown. As stated by the Court:

> The reasonableness of surgical intrusions beneath the skin depends on a case-by-case approach, in which the individual's interest in privacy and security are weighed against the community's need for evidence in conducting the procedure. In a given case, the question whether the community's need for evidence outweighs the substantial privacy interest at stake is a delicate one admitting of few categorical answers.[125]

---

121. Schmerber v. California, 384 U.S. 757, 768, 86 S.Ct. 1826, 16 L.Ed.2d 908, 918 (1966).

122. Schmerber v. California, 384 U.S. at 768–69, 16 L.Ed.2d at 918–19 (1966) (probable cause shown to arrest defendant for drunk driving; blood sample taken after arrest).

123. "Search warrants are ordinarily required for searches of dwellings, and, absent an emergency, no less could be required where intrusions into the human body are concerned." Schmerber v. California, 384 U.S. 757, 770, 86 S.Ct. 1826, 16 L.Ed.2d 908, 919 (1966) (warrant unnecessary to take blood sample of arrestee in drunk driving case, upon exigent showing that the level of alcohol in blood was in danger of disappearing before a warrant could be obtained).

Such a result, however, depends on the totality of the circumstances in each case—as was true in *Schmerber*. Although *gradual* dissipation of alcohol in the bloodstream of a drunk driver is an important factor in determining whether a warrantless blood draw may be taken from such a driver, there is *no per se* exigent circumstances exception to the warrant requirement that applies in all drunk driving cases. If, in fact, "police officers can reasonably obtain a warrant before a blood sample can be drawn without significantly undermining the efficacy of the search, the Fourth Amendment mandates that they do so." Missouri v. McNeely, 569 _____, 133 S.Ct. 1552, 185 LEd..2d 696, 707 (2013).

124. "A compelled surgical intrusion into an individual's body for evidence, however, implicates expectations of privacy and security of such magnitude that the intrusion may be 'unreasonable' even if likely to produce evidence of crime." Winston v. Lee, 470 U.S. 753, 105 S.Ct. 1611, 84 L.Ed.2d 662, 668 (1985) (the government "plainly had probable cause to conduct the search," 84 L.Ed.2d at 670, but the proposed surgery was nonetheless held unreasonable under the Fourth Amendment).

125. Winston v. Lee, 470 U.S. 753, 105 S.Ct. 1611, 84 L.Ed.2d 662, 669 (1985).

There are two privacy factors that must be considered in this balancing process. First, a crucial factor is the extent to which the surgical procedure may threaten the life or health of the individual; a surgical intrusion of this nature may be unreasonable if it endangers the life or safety of the individual. Second, another important factor is the *extent* of the intrusion upon the individual's dignitary interests in personal privacy and bodily integrity. These two privacy factors must be weighed against the government's interest in fairly and accurately determining the guilt or innocence of the individual.[126]

c. Application of Fourth Amendment standards

In *Schmerber v. California*,[127] the Court upheld the nonconsensual taking of a blood sample without a warrant from a person who was arrested for drunk driving. The Court concluded that the arrest was based on probable cause, and that the presence of a warrant was excused because of the emergency showing that the alcohol in the defendant's bloodstream would rapidly be absorbed by the body before a warrant could be obtained. The Court also looked to the delay that took place in transporting the suspect to the hospital to treat his injuries sustained in an accompanying auto accident.[128] As to the privacy factors discussed above, the Court further concluded that the blood sample extraction was a perfectly safe, commonplace medical procedure performed in a reasonable manner by a physician in a hospital, involving virtually no risk, trauma or pain—and that implicitly the extent of the intrusion upon individual dignitary interests was minimal. On the other hand, the blood sample itself was highly probative evidence of the amount of alcohol in the defendant's bloodstream. The Court, however, warned as follows:

---

126. "A crucial factor in analyzing the magnitude of the [surgical] intrusion ... is the extent to which the procedure may threaten the health or safety of the individual. * * * Notwithstanding the existence of probable cause, a search for evidence of crime may be unjustifiable if it endangers the life or health of the suspect.

Another factor is the extent of intrusion upon the individual's dignitary interests in personal privacy and bodily integrity. * * * Weighed against these individual interests is the community's interest in fairly and accurately determining guilt or innocence. This interest is of course of great importance." Winston v. Lee, 470 U.S. 753, 105 S.Ct. 1611, 84 L.Ed.2d 662. 669–70 (1985).

127. 384 U.S. 757, 86 S.Ct. 1826, 16 L.Ed.2d 908 (1966).

128. In Missouri v. McNeely, 569 _____, 133 S.Ct. 1552, 185 LEd..2d 696, 707 (2013), the Court read Schmerber as decided on its particular facts and refused to adopt a *per se* rule that the natural dissipation of alcohol in the bloodstream created a *per se* exigency that dispenses with a warrant for a blood draw in all drunk driving cases—although noting this factor was most important to its result in Schmerber.

"The question presented here is whether the natural metabolization of alcohol in the bloodstream presents a *per se* exigency that justifies an exception to the Fourth Amendment's warrant requirement for nonconsensual bloodtesting in all drunk driving cases. We conclude it does not, and we hold, consistent with general Fourth Amendment principles, that exigency in this context must be determined case by case based on the totality of the circumstances. * * * We hold that in drunk driving investigations, the natural dissipation of alcohol in the bloodstream does not constitute an exigency in every case sufficient to justify conducting a blood test without a warrant."185 L.2d at 702, 715.

"In finding the warrantless blood test reasonable in *Schmerber*, we considered all the facts and circumstances of the particular case and carefully based our holding on those specific facts." 185 L.2d at 706.

"Regardless of the exact [alcohol] elimination rate, it is sufficient for our purposes to note that because an individual's alcohol level gradually declines soon after he stops drinking, a significant delay in testing will negatively affect the probative value of the results. This fact was crucial to our holding in *Schmerber*...." 185 L.2d at 707. Nonetheless, "[i]n those drunk-driving investigations where police officers can reasonably obtain a warrant before a blood sample can be drawn *without significantly undermining the efficacy of the search*, the Fourth Amendment mandates that they do so." 185 L.2d at 707 (emphasis added).

> That today we hold that the Constitution does not forbid the State's minor intrusion into an individual's body under stringently limited conditions in no way indicates that it permits more substantial intrusions, or intrusions under other conditions.[129]

In accord with this warning, the Court in *Winston v. Lee*[130] approved a court injunction against a proposed nonconsensual surgical operation to extract a bullet lodged in the chest of a defendant charged with attempted armed robbery. Although there was probable cause for the defendant's arrest, the Court concluded that the two privacy factors involved in the balancing process outweighed the government's need for the bullet as evidence at the defendant's trial. In particular, the Court noted that the medical risk for the proposed surgery, although not extremely severe, was a subject of considerable dispute among the physicians who testified below, and that the proposed surgery into the defendant's chest, under general anesthesia, was a severe intrusion into personal privacy and bodily integrity. On the other hand, the government failed to show a compelling need for the bullet as evidence at trial because it had other substantial evidence of guilt against the defendant aside from the bullet.

Section 6. Search and Seizure of Materials Presumptively Protected by the First Amendment

On occasion, a government agent will conduct a search and seizure of expressive materials, such as books and films, on the basis that the materials are allegedly obscene, and charge the owner or possessor with violating the obscenity laws. Because these materials are presumptively protected by the First Amendment, special rules under both the First and the Fourth Amendments govern the search and seizure of such material.[131]

a. Warrant requirement

A police officer who arrests a person for exhibiting an allegedly obscene film in a commercial theater is not authorized to seize the film as an incident of that arrest; a search warrant is required for such a seizure. The rationale for this rule is that a warrantless seizure of this sort constitutes a form of prior restraint generally prohibited by the First Amendment. The First and Fourth Amendments require that a magistrate, rather than a police officer, must make a pre-seizure, probable cause determination that the film is

---

129. Schmerber v. California, 384 U.S. 757, 772, 86 S.Ct. 1826, 16 L.Ed.2d 908, 920 (1966).

130. 470 U.S. 753, 105 S.Ct. 1611, 84 L.Ed.2d 662 (1985).

131. "The First Amendment imposes special constraints on searches and seizures of presumptively protected material, and requires that the Fourth Amendment be applied with 'scrupulous exactitude' in such circumstances. Consequently, the Court has imposed particularized rules applicable to searches for and seizures of allegedly obscene films, books, and papers." Maryland v. Macon, 472 U.S. 463, 105 S.Ct. 2778, 86 L.Ed.2d 370, 376 (1985) (internal citations omitted).

"Thus, while the general rule under the Fourth Amendment is that any and all contraband, instrumentalities, and evidence of crimes may be seized on probable cause (and even without a warrant in various circumstances), it is otherwise when materials presumptively protected by the First Amendment are involved. It is '[t]he risk of prior restraint, which is the underlying basis for the special Fourth Amendment protections accorded searches for and seizures of First Amendment materials' that motivates this rule." Fort Wayne Books, Inc. v. Indiana, 489 U.S. 46, 109 S.Ct. 916, 103 L.Ed.2d 34, 51 (1989) (internal citations omitted).

obscene and issue a search warrant based thereon before the film may be seized.[132] Because both films and books are presumptively protected by the First Amendment, it would appear the same rule applies when police arrest a person for selling allegedly obscene books in a commercial book store, and then seize the books without a warrant.

b. Probable cause showing for warrant

"[A]n application for a warrant ordering the seizure of materials presumptively protected by the First Amendment [is] evaluated by the same [flexible] standard of probable cause used to review warrant applications generally."[133] Accordingly, such an application need not include the alleged obscene material for the magistrate to review; a supporting affidavit is sufficient for the issuance of the warrant if the affidavit describes the material in question with sufficient particularity to demonstrate probable cause that the material is obscene.[134] Beyond that, there is no constitutional prohibition for a magistrate to go to a commercial theater with police, view a public performance of the film as a paying patron, and thereafter issue a search warrant for the police to seize the film upon a probable cause finding of obscenity.[135]

A search warrant for the seizure of allegedly obscene materials cannot be issued based on a sworn conclusory opinion of a police officer that the published material sought to be seized is obscene. This is so because a magistrate, not a police officer, must determine whether there is probable cause that the publications in question are obscene.[136]

---

132. "In each case [previously decided by the Court], the material seized fell arguably within First Amendment protection, and the taking brought to an abrupt halt an orderly and presumptively legitimate distribution or exhibition. Seizing a film then being presented to the general public presents essentially the same restraint on expression as the seizure of all the books in a bookstore. Such precipitate action by a police officer without the authority of a constitutionally sufficient warrant, is plainly a form of prior restraint and is, in those circumstances, unreasonable under Fourth Amendment standards. The seizure is unreasonable, not simply because it would have been easy to secure a warrant, but rather because prior restraint of the right of expression, whether by books or film, calls for a higher hurdle in the evaluation of reasonableness." Roaden v. Kentucky, 413 U.S. 496, 504, 93 S.Ct. 2796, 37 L.Ed. 2d 757, 764 (1973) (police seizure of an alleged obscene film publicly shown in a commercial theater struck down for failure to obtain a search warrant; the warrantless seizure could not be justified as being incident to an arrest of the theater manager on the premises).

"Similarly, where seizure is sought of allegedly obscene material, the judgment of the arresting officer alone is insufficient to justify issuance of a search warrant, or seizure without a warrant incident to arrest." Zurcher v. Stanford Daily, 436 U.S. 547, 565, 98 S.Ct. 1970, 56 L.Ed.2d 525, 541 (1978).

See also Near v. Minnesota, 283 U.S. 697, 51 S.Ct. 625, 75 L.Ed. 1357 (1931) (leading case generally prohibiting the prior restraint of materials presumptively protected by the First Amendment).

133. New York v. P.J. Video, Inc., 475 U.S. 868, 106 S.Ct. 1610, 89 L.Ed.2d 871, 880 (1986).

134. New York v. P.J. Video, Inc., 475 U.S. 868, 106 S.Ct. 1610, 89 L.Ed.2d 871 (1986) (search warrant affidavits describing with some particularity the scenes depicted in films upheld as demonstrating probable cause that the films were obscene). For a discussion of the probable cause standard generally, see Chapter 11, Section 3, supra, of this work. And for a discussion of the probable cause standard as applied to search warrants, see Chapter 13, Section 2, supra, of this work.

135. See Heller v. New York, 413 U.S. 483, 93 S.Ct. 2789, 37 L.Ed.2d 745 (1973) (judge accompanied by police viewed a public performance of a film in a theater, and thereafter signed a warrant for the seizure of the film upon a finding that the film was obscene).

136. Marcus v. Search Warrant, 367 U.S. 717, 731–32, 81 S.Ct. 1708, 6 L.Ed.2d 1127, 1136 (1961) (six search warrants, based on a police officer's conclusory opinion that a publisher kept for sale at

c. Adversary hearing vs. ex parte hearing

The First and Fourth Amendments require a *pre-seizure adversary* hearing "designed to focus searchingly on the question of obscenity"[137] before a magistrate may issue an order for the seizure of allegedly obscene books or films being sold or shown to the public—where *all* available copies of such material are seized so as to block their further distribution or exhibition; the fact that a *post-seizure* adversary hearing is afforded on the obscenity issue does not change this result. The underlying rationale for this rule is that otherwise a form of prior restraint, generally prohibited by the First Amendment, would be authorized in which expressive materials could be preliminarily blocked from circulation and distribution.[138]

The First and Fourth Amendments, however, do not require a pre-seizure adversary hearing where only a *single* copy of a particular book, magazine or film is seized under a search warrant for the purpose of preserving such material as evidence at a subsequent criminal proceeding—leaving other copies of the material behind on the premises. In that event, the individual can continue to sell or exhibit this expressive material, pending an adversary hearing on the obscenity issue, and no prior restraint of the material has taken place. Accordingly, a search warrant for the seizure of the above-described material may issue after an *ex parte* hearing normally conducted in search warrant cases—provided

---

six business locations "obscene ... publications," struck down).

"The procedure under which the warrant issued solely upon the conclusory assertions of the police officer without any inquiry by the [magistrate] into the factual basis of the officer's conclusions was not a procedure 'designed to focus searchingly on the question of obscenity,' and therefore fell short of constitutional requirements." Lee Art Theatre, Inc. v. Virginia, 392 U.S. 636, 637, 88 S.Ct. 2103, 20 L.Ed.2d 1313, 1315 (1968) (internal citation omitted) (search warrant for seizure of allegedly obscene film struck down as it was based on a conclusory affidavit by a police officer that the film was obscene).

137. Marcus v. Search Warrant, 367 U.S. 717, 731–32, 81 S.Ct. 1708, 6 L.Ed.2d 1127, 1136 (1961).

138. Marcus v. Search Warrant, 367 U.S. 717, 81 S.Ct. 1708, 6 L.Ed.2d 1127 (1961) (large scale confiscation of alleged obscene books, magazines and photographs seized from newsstands under purported authority of search warrants issued in pre-seizure ex parte hearing, pending a post-seizure adversary hearing, struck down); Fort Wayne Books, Inc. v. Indiana, 489 U.S. 46, 109 S.Ct. 916, 103 L.Ed.2d 34 (1989) (same result involving a RICO seizure order issued at pre-seizure ex parte hearing that shut down adult book stores, pending a post-seizure adversary hearing).

"In a line of cases dating back to Marcus v. Search Warrant..., this Court has repeatedly held that rigorous procedural safeguards must be employed before expressive materials can be seized as 'obscene.' In Marcus, and again in A Quantity of Books v. Kansas..., the Court invalidated large-scale confiscations of books and films, where numerous copies of selected books were seized without a prior adversarial hearing on their obscenity. In those cases, and the ones that immediately came after them, the Court established that pre-trial seizures of expressive materials could only be undertaken pursuant to a 'procedure 'designed to focus searchingly on the question of obscenity.' "

"We refined that approach further in our subsequent decisions. Most importantly, in Heller v. New York..., the Court noted that 'seizing films to destroy them or to block their distribution or exhibition is a very different matter from seizing a single copy of a film for the bona fide purpose of preserving it as evidence in a criminal proceeding.' As a result, we concluded that until there was a 'judicial determination of the obscenity issue in an adversary proceeding,' exhibition of a film could not be restrained by seizing all the available copies of it. The same is obviously true for books or other expressive materials." Fort Wayne Books, Inc. v. Indiana, 489 U.S. 46, 109 S.Ct. 916, 103 L.Ed.2d 34, 51 (1989) (internal citations omitted).

a prompt post-seizure judicial determination at an adversary hearing is afforded to ultimately determine the obscenity question.[139]

On the other hand, as previously stated, expressive material such as a book or film may not be taken out of circulation so that no items of same remain—either preliminarily or permanently—until there has been a judicial determination that this material is obscene after an adversary hearing.[140]

d. Search warrant particularity: books and films to be seized

"[T]he constitutional requirement [of the Fourth Amendment] that warrants particularly describe the 'things to be seized' is to be accorded the most scrupulous exactitude when the 'things' are books, and the basis for their seizure is the ideas they contain."[141] Accordingly, a search warrant ordering the seizure of all "books ... concerning the Communist Party of Texas"[142] or the seizure of "obscene books"[143] constitutes a general warrant prohibited by the Fourth Amendment. The Court has not stated, however, what particular description of expressive materials would pass constitutional muster—but clearly describing the books to be seized by title or by detailed physical description would be sufficient.[144]

This rule related to books would appear to apply also to films and other First Amendment protected materials. These materials also must be described with similar exactness.[145]

---

139. "But seizing films to destroy them or block their distribution is a very different matter from seizing a single copy of a film for the bona fide purpose of preserving it as evidence in a criminal proceeding, particularly where, as here, there is no showing or pre-trial claim that the seizure of the copy prevented continuing exhibition of the film. If such a seizure is pursuant to a warrant, issued after a determination of probable cause by a neutral magistrate, and following the seizure, a prompt judicial determination of the obscenity issue in an adversary proceeding is available at the request of any interested party, the seizure is constitutionally permissible. In addition, on a showing to the trial court that other copies of the film are not available to the exhibitor, the court should permit the seized film to be copied so that showing can be continued pending a judicial determination of the obscenity issue in an adversary hearing. Otherwise the film must be returned.

"With these safeguards, we do not perceive that an adversary hearing *prior* to a seizure by lawful warrant would materially increase First Amendment protection." Heller v. New York, 413 U.S. 483, 492–93, 93 S.Ct. 2789, 37 L.Ed.2d 745, 754–55 (1973) (adversary hearing not required for issuance of search warrant for seizure of film where no showing was made that this was the theater's only copy of the film, and prompt post-seizure determination in an adversary hearing on the obscenity issue is afforded at the request of either party).

140. "While a single copy of a book or film may be seized and retained for evidentiary purposes based on a finding of probable cause, the publication may not be taken out of circulation completely until there has been a determination of obscenity after an adversary hearing." Fort Wayne Books, Inc. v. Indiana, 489 U.S. 46, 109 S.Ct. 916, 103 L.Ed.2d 34, 51 (1989). See also 2 Wayne LaFave, Search and Seizure § 4.1(d) (5th ed. 2012).

141. Stanford v. Texas, 379 U.S. 476, 485, 85 S.Ct. 506, 13 L.Ed.2d 431, 437 (1965).

142. Stanford v. Texas, 379 U.S. 476, 85 S.Ct. 506, 13 L.Ed.2d 431 (1965).

143. Marcus v. Search Warrant, 367 U.S. 717, 81 S.Ct. 1708, 6 L.Ed.2d 1127 (1961).

144. See 2 Wayne LaFave, Search and Seizure § 4.6(e) at 811–812 (5th ed. 2012).

145. "Where the materials sought to be seized may be protected by the First Amendment, the requirements of the Fourth Amendment must be applied with 'scrupulous exactitude.' * * * Where presumptively protected [First Amendment] materials are sought to be seized, the warrant requirement

e. Neutral and detached magistrate

It is a Fourth Amendment requirement that a search warrant must be issued by a neutral and detached magistrate.[146] A judge, however, who issues a search warrant for the seizure of obscene material and thereafter joins the police in executing the search warrant is not a neutral and detached magistrate, and the search warrant involved is invalid.[147] It is permissible, however, for the magistrate to view an alleged obscene film in a theater as an ordinary paying patron, and thereafter to issue a search warrant on the theater premises for the seizure of the film just viewed.[148]

f. Undercover officer activities in adult book store

An undercover law enforcement officer may enter an adult book store during business hours, examine the materials offered for sale therein, and purchase those materials as an ordinary paying patron. The officer's entry into the store and subsequent examination of the materials offered for sale therein does *not* constitute a Fourth Amendment search of the owner's bookstore; and the officer's subsequent purchase of the materials offered for sale does not constitute a Fourth Amendment seizure of book store owner's materials.[149] But if instead of buying the material, the undercover officer takes the material from the owner's possession without paying for it, a Fourth Amendment seizure of bookstore owner's material clearly has taken place.[150]

Section 7. Searches Based on Drug-Sniffing Dog Alert

A law enforcement practice has developed in recent years where certain police dogs are trained to smell the aroma of various types of illegal drugs—such as marijuana or cocaine—as odor emanates from motor vehicles or containers that police lawfully come upon, and to alert on same. This "dog sniff" is not considered a Fourth Amendment search and need not be based on probable cause or reasonable suspicion; nor need it be conducted with a search warrant.[151]

---

should be administered to leave as little as possible to the discretion or whim of the officer in the field." Zurcher v. Stanford Daily, 436 U.S. 547, 564, 98 S.Ct. 1970, 56 L.Ed.2d 525, 541 (1978).

146. For a discussion of this requirement, see Chapter 13, Section 5 of this work.

147. Lo-Ji Sales, Inc. v. New York, 442 U.S. 319, 99 S.Ct. 2319, 60 L.Ed.2d 920 (1979) (search warrant voided).

148. Heller v. New York, 413 U.S. 483, 93 S.Ct. 2789, 37 L.Ed.2d 745 (1973), as discussed in Lo-Ji Sales, Inc. v. New York, 60 L.Ed.2d at 929.

149. Maryland v. Macon, 472 U.S. 463, 105 S.Ct. 2778, 86 L.Ed.2d 370, 376–77 (1985).

150. Lo-Ji Sales, Inc. v. New York, 442 U.S. 319, 99 S.Ct. 2319, 60 L.Ed.2d 920, 930 (1979) ("But there is no basis for the notion that because a retail store invites the public to enter, it consents to wholesale searches and seizures [of materials therein] that do not conform to Fourth Amendment guarantees.").

151. United States v. Place, 462 U.S. 696, 103 S.Ct. 2637, 77 L.Ed.2d 110, 121 (1983) (suitcase); City of Indianapolis v. Edmond, 531 U.S. 32, 121 S.Ct. 447, 148 L.Ed.2d 333, 342–43 (2000) (car). For lower court cases on this issue, see "Searches and Seizures" § 22 West Key No.

As an aside, however, it is an open question whether law enforcement officials can, without reasonable suspicion, use a trained narcotics dog to smell people [or their property] who *have not been seized at all*—such as people as they walk down the public street, or disembarking from an airplane in an airport, or while waiting in their vehicle for a stoplight. But see Illinois v. Caballes, 543 U.S. 405, 125 S.Ct.

If the dog "alerts" on a motor vehicle during a lawful traffic stop indicating that it has detected an illegal drug aroma, police have probable cause to search the vehicle under the Carroll moving vehicle exception to the search warrant requirement rule—provided it is shown that the dog has been properly trained to detect the odor of illegal drugs, although this showing need not involve an exhaustive set of records.[152] Similarly, if the dog alerts on a suitcase or other container that police have lawfully come upon, probable cause for the search is also shown—but a search warrant is generally required to search the suitcase, given the heightened privacy expectations in such a container.[153]

It should be noted, however, that any preceding nonconsensual seizure by police of the individual's moving vehicle or container in order to conduct such a "dog sniff" is a *seizure* of the person's "effect" within the meaning of the Fourth Amendment. Accordingly, if this seizure is *unreasonable* in the Fourth Amendment sense, the "dog sniff" is considered the fruit of the preceding unreasonable seizure—and any subsequent search based on the sniff is tainted, making the fruits thereof inadmissible in evidence under the Weeks-Mapp exclusionary rule.[154]

834, 839, 160 L.Ed.2d 842 (2005) (Souter, J., dissenting) ("[A]n uncritical adherence to *Place* would render the Fourth Amendment indifferent to suspicionless and indiscriminate sweeps of cars in parking garages and pedestrians on sidewalks; if a sniff is not preceded by a seizure subject to Fourth Amendment notice, it escapes Fourth Amendment review entirely unless it is treated as a search.").

152. "In this case, we consider how a court should determine if the 'alert' of a drug-detection dog during a traffic stop provides probable cause to search a vehicle. The Florida Supreme Court held that the State must in every case present an exhaustive set of records, including a log of the dog's performance in the field, to establish the dog's reliability. We think that demand inconsistent with the 'flexible standard' of probable cause. * * *

"[E]vidence of a dog's satisfactory performance in a certification or training program can itself provide sufficient reason to trust his alert. If a bona fide organization has certified a dog after testing his reliability in a controlled setting, a court can presume (subject to any conflicting evidence offered) that the dog's alert provides probable cause to search. The same is true, even in the absence of formal certification, if the dog has recently and successfully completed a training program that evaluated his proficiency in locating drugs. * * *

"A defendant, however, must have an opportunity to challenge such evidence of a dog's reliability, whether by cross-examining the testifying officer or by introducing his own fact or expert witnesses. The defendant, for example, may contest the adequacy of a certification or training program, perhaps asserting that its standards are too lax or its methods faulty. So too, the defendant may examine how the dog (or handler) performed in the assessments made in those settings. Indeed, evidence of the dog's (or handler's) performance in the field, although susceptible to the kind of misinterpretation we have discussed, may sometimes be relevant, as the Solicitor General acknowledged at oral argument." Florida v. Harris, 568 U.S. ____, 133 S.Ct. 1050, 185 L.Ed.2d 61, 65, 69 (2013) (probable cause to search defendant's truck held established—based on a trained drug-sniffing dog's "alert" on the truck; the dog had [a] successfully completed two extensive police training programs in drug detection for dogs, together with a 40 hour drug detection refresher course, and [b] received a one year certification in drug detection from a reputable private company, although this certificate had expired at the time of the sniff in this case).

153. United States v. Chadwick, 433 U.S. 1, 7–11, 97 S.Ct. 2476, 53 L.Ed.2d 538, 545–48 (1977), as further explained in United States v. Ross, 456 U.S. 798, 810–11, 102 S.Ct. 2157, 72 L.Ed.2d 572, 585 (1982) (footlocker); Arkansas v. Sanders, 442 U.S. 753, 757–761, 99 S.Ct. 2586, 61 L.Ed.2d 235, 240–243 (1979) (suitcase); Bond v. United States, 529 U.S. 334, 120 S.Ct. 1462, 146 L.Ed.2d 365 (2000) (federal agent's physical manipulation of bus traveler's carry-on canvas bag held a Fourth Amendment search; no exception to search warrant requirement rule as urged by the Government; "[w]e therefore hold that the agent's physical manipulation of petitioner's bag violated the Fourth Amendment." 146 L.Ed.2d at 370); compare United States v. Place, 462 U.S. 696, 103 S.Ct. 2637, 77 L.Ed.2d 110, 121 (1983) (search warrant sought for the search of a suitcase at airport after drug-sniffing dog alerted thereon).

154. United States v. Place, 462 U.S. 696, 103 S.Ct. 2637, 77 L.Ed.2d 110 (1983) (unlawful seizure of suitcase at airport tainted subsequent narcotics dog alert on suitcase and rendered invalid a search

Narcotic "dog sniffs' of the *home* are governed by a different rule than are motor vehicles or containers—given the highest reasonable expectation of privacy that one enjoys in the home. Where police enter the front porch of a person's home with a drug-sniffing police dog, following which the dog sniffs the front door of the home and "alerts" thereon indicating the presence of contraband drug odors emanating therein, a Fourth Amendment "search" has occurred.[155] To conduct such a "dog sniff" search of a home, the search must be reasonable in the Fourth Amendment sense—which generally means it must be conducted with a search warrant, unless an exception to the search warrant requirement rule is applicable.[156]

Section 8. Cell Phone Searches

A search warrant is generally required in order for law enforcement officials to search the digital contents of a modern cell phone—absent an exception to the search warrant requirement rule. The search incident to a lawful arrest exception, however, is inapplicable to such a search. Law enforcement agents may not conduct a warrantless search of a cell phone pursuant to this exception, where they have seized the phone from the arrestee at the point of arrest.[157]

---

warrant for the suitcase based on the alert); see City of Indianapolis v. Edmond, 531 U.S. 32, 121 S.Ct. 447, 148 L.Ed.2d 333 (2000) (traffic checkpoint program to discover and interdict contraband narcotics, in which narcotic dogs were used to detect presence of contraband drugs in the cars stopped by the checkpoint, struck down as constituting an unreasonable seizure of the motorists' persons and their cars; narcotics dog sniff procedure arguably tainted by the preceding unreasonable seizure).

155. "We consider whether using a drug-sniffing dog on a homeowner's porch to investigate the contents of the home is a 'search' within the meaning of the Fourth Amendment. * * *

"The [Fourth] Amendment establishes a simple baseline, one that for much of our history formed the exclusive basis for its protections. When the Government obtains information by physically intruding on persons, houses, papers or effects, a search within the original meaning of the Fourth Amendment has undoubtedly occurred. By reason of our decision in Katz v. United States ... property rights are not the sole measure of Fourth Amendment violations—but though Katz may add to the baseline, it does not subtract anything from the Amendment's protections when the Government *does* engage in [a] physical intrusion of a constitutionally protected area.

"That principle renders this case a straightforward one. The officers were gathering information in an area belonging to Jardines and immediately surrounding his house—in the curtilage of the house, which we have held enjoys protection as part of the home itself. And they gathered that information by physically entering and occupying the area to engage in conduct not explicitly or implicitly permitted by the owner. * * *

"The government's use of trained police dogs to investigate the home and its immediate surroundings is a 'search' within the meaning of the Fourth Amendment." Florida v. Jardines, 569 U.S. ___, 133 S.Ct. 1409, 185 L.Ed.2d 495, 499, 500–01, 504 (2013) (internal citations and quotation marks omitted).

156. See the discussion of searches of the home at Section 1 of this Chapter.

157. Riley v. California, 574 U.S. ___, 134 S.Ct. 2473, 189 L.Ed.2d 430 (2014) (warrantless search by police of a modern "smart phone" and a modern "flip phone" seized from the person of a suspect in two separate cases following an arrest of each suspect; held unreasonable under the Fourth Amendment as (a) not conducted with a search warrant, and (b) not otherwise justified under the search incident to a lawful arrest exception to the search warrant requirement rule).

"We therefore decline to extend *Robinson* to searches of data on cell phones, and hold instead that officers must generally secure a warrant before conducting such a search. * * * Our holding, of course, is not that the information on a cell phone is immune from search; it is instead that a warrant is generally required before such a search, even when a cell phone is seized incident to arrest. * * Our answer to the question of what police must do before searching a cell phone incident to an arrest is simple—get a warrant." 134 S.Ct. at, 2485, 2493, 2495.

The reason for this result is that the modern cell phone—both the "smart phone" and "flip phone" variety—is in fact a minicomputer with an immense storage capacity which typically contains a vast amount of private information and items which heretofore could only be found in a private home or business.[158] It is light years away from a small container—like a cigarette package, a billfold, a purse, a paper bag, or a briefcase—that the police may search without a warrant incident to a lawful arrest of one who has such a container on his or her person.[159] Nonetheless, the exigent circumstances exception to the search warrant requirement rule may be applicable in a given case, depending on the facts and circumstances, which could authorize such a search without a warrant.[160]

For a general discussion of the search incident to a lawful arrest exception to the search warrant requirement rule, see Chapter 14, Section 2 of this work.

158. "Cell phones differ in both a quantitative and qualitative sense from other objects that might be kept on an arrestee's person. The term 'cell phone' is itself misleading shorthand; many of these devices are in fact minicomputers that also happen to have the capacity to be used as a telephone. They could just as easily be called cameras, video players, rolodexes, calendars, tape recorders, libraries, albums, televisions, maps or newspapers. * * *

The current top-selling smart phone has a standard capacity of 16 gigabytes and is available with up to 64 gigabytes). Sixteen gigabytes translates to millions of pages of text, thousands of pictures, or hundreds of videos. Cell phones couple that capacity with the ability to store many different types of information: Even the most basic phones that sell for less than $20 might hold photographs, picture messages, text messages, Internet browsing history, a calendar, a thousand entry phone book, and so on. * * *

The storage capacity of cell phones has several interrelated consequences for privacy. First, a cell phone collects in one place many distinct types of information—an address, a note, a prescription, a bank statement, a video—that reveal much more in combination than any isolated record. Second, a cell phone's capacity allows even just one type of information to convey far more than previously possible. The sum of an individual's private life can be reconstructed through a thousand photographs labeled with dates, locations, and descriptions; the same cannot be said of a photograph or two of a loved one tucked into a wallet. Third, the data on a cell phone can date back to the purchase of the phone, or even earlier. A person might carry in his pocket a slip of paper reminding him to call Mr. Jones; he would not carry a record of all his communications with Mr. Jones for the past several months, as would routinely be kept on a phone. * * *

Indeed, a cell phone search would typically expose to the government far more than the most exhaustive search of a house." Riley v. California, 574 U.S. ___, 134 S.Ct. 2489, 2491, 114 L.Ed.2d 430 (2014) (internal citations omitted).

159. "The United States asserts that a search of all data stored on a cell phone [after arrest] is 'materially indistinguishable' from searches of all sorts of physical items. That is like saying a ride on horseback is materially indistinguishable from a flight to the moon. Both are ways of getting from point A to point B, but little else justifies lumping them together. Modern cell phones, as a category, implicate privacy concerns far beyond those implicated by the search of a cigarette pack, a wallet or a purse." Riley v. California, 574 U.S. ___, 134 S.Ct. 2473, 2488–2489, 189 L.Ed.2d 430 (2014) (bracketed material added) (internal citation omitted).

See California v. Acevedo, 500 U.S. 565, 111 S.Ct. 1982, 114 L.Ed 2d 619, 631 (1991) ("And the police often will be able to search containers without a warrant ... as a search incident to a lawful arrest.... Under Belton, the same probable cause to believe that a container holds drugs will allow the police to arrest the person transporting the container and search it.").

160. See Chapter 14, Section 6 of this work for a discussion of the exigent circumstances exception to the search warrant requirement rule.

"Moreover, even though the search incident to a lawful arrest exception does not apply to cell phones, other case-specific exceptions may still justify a warrantless search of a particular phone. One well-recognized exception applies when the exigencies of the situation make the needs of law enforcement so compelling that a warrantless search is objectively reasonable under the Fourth Amendment. Such exigencies could include the need to prevent the imminent destruction of evidence in individual cases, to pursue a fleeing suspect, and to assist persons who are seriously injured or are threatened with imminent injury. * * *

In light of the availability of the exigent circumstances exception, there is no reason to believe that law enforcement officers will not be able to address some of the more extreme hypotheticals that have been suggested: a suspect texting an accomplice who, it is feared, is preparing to detonate a bomb, or a child abductor who may have information about the child's location in the cell phone. The defendants here recognize—indeed, they stress—that such fact specific threats may justify a warrantless search of cell phone data."

[footnote 2 material]: "In Wurie's case [below], for example, the dissenting first Circuit judge argued that exigent circumstances could have justified a search of Wurie's phone. See F.3d 1, 17 (2013) (opinion of Howard, J. dissenting) (discussing the repeated calls from 'my house,' the suspected location of the drug stash. But the majority concluded that the Government had not made an exigent circumstances argument. See *id.*, at 1. The Government acknowledges the same in this Court." Riley v. California, 574 U.S. ___, 134 S.Ct. 2473, 2494, 2494 & fn 2, 189 L.Ed.2d _430 (2014) (certain internal citations omitted).

"To the extent that law enforcement still has specific concerns about the potential loss of evidence in specific cases, there are more targeted ways to address these concerns. If the police are truly confronted with a' now or never' situation—for example, circumstances suggesting that a defendant's phone will be the target of an imminent remote-wipe attempt—they may be able to rely on exigent circumstances to search the phone immediately. Or, if officers happen to seize a phone in an unlocked state, they may be able to disable the automatic-lock feature in order to prevent the phone from locking and encrypting data. Such a preventive measure could be analyzed under the principles set forth in our decision in *McArthur*, 531 U.S. 326, which approved officers' reasonable steps to secure a scene to preserve evidence while they awaited a warrant." 134 S.Ct. at 2487–2488 (some internal citations omitted).

Subpart C

Enforcement of the Fourth Amendment

Introductory Note

If both the "Standing" and "Unreasonableness" requirements for a Fourth Amendment violation have been met, the next question to consider is whether sanctions should be imposed for the violation—the chief sanction being the *Weeks-Mapp* exclusionary rule adopted by the U.S. Supreme Court.

It is well settled that this exclusionary rule is not automatically applicable in all proceedings for all Fourth Amendment violations. Indeed, "[w]hether the exclusionary rule's remedy is appropriate in a particular case has long been regarded as an issue separate from whether the Fourth Amendment rights of the party seeking to invoke the rule were violated by police conduct."[1] Although the rule *generally* excludes all evidence obtained from the victim of an unreasonable search or seizure at the victim's federal or state criminal trial, there are some important limitations and exceptions; moreover, the rule has only once been applied by the Court outside the criminal trial context.

We turn now to a more detailed consideration of the exclusionary rule. As an aside, we will later briefly examine the sanction of a civil suit as an additional means of enforcing Fourth Amendment guarantees.

1. Illinois v. Gates, 462 U.S. 213, 223, 103 S.Ct. 2317, 76 L.Ed.2d 527 (1983); see Arizona v. Evans, 514 U.S. 1, 115 S.Ct. 1185, 131 L.Ed.2d 34, 44 (1995); United States v. Leon, 468 U.S. 897, 104 S.Ct. 3405, 82 L.Ed.2d 677, 688 (1984).

Chapter 17

Historical Development, Nature and Purpose, and Substantive Law of the Exclusionary Rule

Section 1. Historical Development

As previously shown, the Framers of the Fourth Amendment clearly intended to create a legal guarantee of constitutional rights to be enforced by the federal courts—and did not intend these rights to be merely a set of high-minded admonitions for government officials to aspire to in their discretion.[2] Nonetheless, it took over a century for the U.S. Supreme Court to adopt an exclusionary rule to enforce Fourth Amendment freedoms in federal criminal prosecutions. This long delay was in large part due to the lack of any substantial federal criminal code for most of the nineteenth century, and thus the relative absence of federal criminal prosecutions where the issue might have been raised on a defense motion to suppress.

By way of contrast, the issue of an exclusionary rule did arise during the nineteenth century in the state courts where the criminal laws in the country were chiefly enforced. Defendants in state criminal prosecutions sought to exclude illegally seized evidence under the state constitutional search and seizure guarantees. Before 1914, twenty-six states considered whether to adopt an exclusionary rule for such evidence and rejected it, while only one state [Iowa] accepted it.[3]

This result was largely the product of a long-held understanding that a law enforcement officer who engaged in illegal conduct, such as an unreasonable search and seizure, was acting purely as a private person outside the scope of his official authority, and not as an agent of the state. The officer could be sued for his private illegal acts, but not the state—as was the case with the many law suits successfully brought against the King's messengers who executed the lawless general warrants in England during the American colonial period.[4] It therefore made no sense to punish the state for the officer's lawless conduct by excluding the fruits of such private action in a criminal prosecution. Gradually, however, this un-

2. See Chapter 6, Section 3 of this work.

3. See Appendix Tables A & B and cases collected, Wolf v. Colorado, 338 U.S. 25, 33–34, 69 S.Ct. 1359, 93 L.Ed.2d 1782 (1949).

4. For a detailed discussion of the general warrants controversy in England (1762–1770) and the impact it had on the eventual passage of the Fourth Amendment in America, see Chapter 3 of this work.

derstanding changed; government officers who engaged in lawless behavior in connection with their official duties were eventually considered agents of the state. This development set the stage for the appearance and later expansion of the Fourth Amendment exclusionary rule in the twentieth century, both in the federal and state courts.[5]

a. *Weeks v. United States*

By 1914, federal criminal laws had expanded enormously; federal criminal prosecutions were no longer a rarity; and the understanding had arrived that federal agents acting lawlessly were nonetheless still agents of the federal government. Accordingly, in that year the U.S. Supreme Court in *Weeks v. United States*[6] held that the Fourth Amendment applied to the federal government, and that to enforce that guarantee any evidence secured by *federal* officials in violation of the Fourth Amendment was inadmissible in a *federal* criminal trial against the victim of the unreasonable search or seizure. But the Court also held that the Fourth Amendment did not apply to the *states*, and that accordingly any evidence—secured by *state* officials [under circumstances which if conducted by federal officials would constitute a violation of the Fourth Amendment] and then handed over on a "silver platter" to federal officials—was admissible in a federal criminal trial against the victim of the search or seizure. The latter holding came to be known as the "silver platter doctrine."

In *Weeks*, the Court dealt with an unreasonable search conducted by federal officials in clear violation of the Fourth Amendment. The case began when a local police officer in Kansas City, Missouri arrested the defendant at the city railroad station. Other officers in the same department then went to the defendant's house across town, searched it, seized certain property, and turned it over to a U.S. Marshal. Later in the day, local police officers returned with the U.S. Marshal to the defendant's house and together they searched the house a second time and seized additional property. *Both searches were conducted without a search warrant and without a shred of legal authority.*

The defendant was indicted and convicted in a federal court for using the U.S. mails to sell chances in a lottery. The defendant petitioned the court for the return of all the property seized from his house in these two searches, and objected at trial when the government sought to introduce a portion of the seized property. The basis for this petition and objection was that the property had been obtained in violation of the defendant's Fourth Amendment rights. The trial court ordered the return of all property that the government did not intend to use as evidence at trial, and denied the motion as to the balance of the property seized. The trial court also overruled the defendant's objection to the government's offer of evidence at trial.

The U.S. Supreme Court reversed the conviction on the ground that the property seized in the second federal-state-conducted search of the defendant's home was obtained in violation of the defendant's Fourth Amendment rights and was erroneously admitted in evidence, adopting for the first time an exclusionary rule for federal criminal trials. The evidence seized by the local police in the first search, however, was not subject to exclusion because the Fourth Amendment did not apply to state officials, and accordingly could be handed over on a "silver platter" to federal officials for use at a federal criminal trial.

---

5. For a comprehensive discussion of this legal development, see Thomas Y. Davies, "Recovering the Original Fourth Amendment," 98 Mich.L.Rev. 547, 660–67 (Dec. 1999).

6. 232 U.S. 383, 34 S.Ct. 341, 58 L.Ed.2d 652 (1914).

State courts were thereafter free to accept or reject the *Weeks* exclusionary rule as a means of enforcing their respective state constitutional guarantees on search and seizure [all of which were in substance the same as the Fourth Amendment]. Accordingly, between 1914 and 1949, a minority of states [16] elected to adopt such an exclusionary rule—while a majority [31] rejected it.[7]

b. *Wolf v. Colorado*

The second holding of *Weeks,* however, gradually came under attack in the ensuing years as the constitutional battle for making the Bill of Rights enforceable against the states under the Fourteenth Amendment began gathering momentum. As part of this debate, it was urged that both the Fourth Amendment and the *Weeks* exclusionary rule should be applied to the states. In *Wolf v. Colorado,*[8] the Court faced the issue and rendered a mixed verdict. The Court held that the right of privacy—the core of the Fourth Amendment—did apply to the states under the Due Process Clause of the Fourteenth Amendment, thus overruling a contrary holding in *Weeks.* But the Court further held that the *Weeks* exclusionary rule was not a rule of constitutional law and did not apply to the states under the Due Process Clause of the Fourteenth Amendment—a result that proved to have a very short shelf life.

c. *Elkins v. United States*

Because the Fourth Amendment, in essence, now applied to the states under *Wolf,* it became increasingly clear that state officials should not be allowed to seize evidence in violation of the Fourth Amendment, and then turn it over on a "silver platter" to federal authorities for use against the search victim in a federal criminal trial—as the *Weeks* Court had held under the "silver platter" doctrine. Not surprisingly, then, the U.S. Supreme Court, eleven years later, overruled this doctrine and held in *Elkins v. United States*[9] that evidence obtained by state officials in violation of the Fourth Amendment was inadmissible in a federal criminal trial against the victim of the illegal search or seizure—even though the evidence may have been turned over on a "silver platter" to federal officials with no prior federal participation. By that time, a slight majority of the states [26] had adopted an exclusionary rule in whole or in part to enforce their state constitutional guarantees on search and seizure—a considerable increase over the number of such exclusionary states [16] at the time of *Wolf.*[10]

d. *Mapp v. Ohio*

After *Elkins,* the only remaining courtroom open to the admission of evidence seized in violation of the Fourth Amendment was in a state court, and it became obvious that there was no principled reason for this result. Accordingly, the next year, the U.S. Supreme Court in *Mapp v. Ohio*[11] completed the cycle it had begun in *Weeks* and held that any evidence

---

7. See Appendix Tables D–I and cases collected, Wolf v. Colorado, 338 U.S. 25, 35–38, 69 S.Ct. 1359, 93 L.Ed. 1782 (1949).

8. 338 U.S. 25, 69 S.Ct. 1359, 93 L.Ed. 1782 (1949).

9. 364 U.S. 206, 80 S.Ct. 1437, 4 L.Ed.2d 1669 (1960).

10. See Appendix Tables I–II and cases collected in *Elkins v. United States,* supra.

11. 367 U.S. 643, 81 S.Ct. 1684, 6 L.Ed.2d 1081 (1961).

obtained in violation of the Fourth Amendment could not be admitted in a state court against the victim of the unreasonable search or seizure. In particular, the Court held that the *Weeks* exclusionary rule was enforceable against the states under the Due Process Clause of the Fourteenth Amendment—thus overruling the contrary holding of *Wolf.*

As in *Weeks*, the Court in *Mapp* was faced with a clear violation of the Fourth Amendment. In that case, *local police officers forcibly entered the defendant's house without a search warrant, and without a shred of legal authority searched the house and seized certain alleged obscene materials.*

The Court simply could not countenance such a blatantly unreasonable search or seizure by allowing such evidence to convict the defendant—and thus, the *Weeks* exclusionary rule was extended to the states. As a result, it became established constitutional law from that day forward that any evidence seized by federal or state officials in violation of the Fourth Amendment was inadmissible in a federal or state criminal trial against the victim of the illegal search or seizure—subject to certain important limitations and exceptions.[12]

Section 2. The Nature and Purpose of the Exclusionary Rule

It is settled that the *Weeks-Mapp* exclusionary rule is a judicially created remedy adopted by the U.S. Supreme Court to enforce Fourth Amendment guarantees.[13] The rule is not expressly provided for in the Fourth Amendment, but is considered a necessary requirement in order to enforce its provisions, else the Amendment would be reduced to a mere "form of words."[14]

In this respect, the exclusionary rule, along with the limitations and exceptions thereto that the Court has carved out over the years, is entirely consistent with the original understanding of the Framers of the Fourth Amendment. As previously discussed, the Bill of Rights, including the Fourth Amendment, was not intended by its Framers to be a set of high-minded admonitions for government officials to aspire to in their discretion. Nor was this charter of freedom meant to be a series of rights that Congress at its option could implement by passing appropriate enforcement measures. To the contrary, the Framers intended the federal courts to enforce the Bill of Rights as a legal guarantee.[15] The *Weeks-Mapp* exclusionary rule, with its limitations and exceptions, is the primary remedy that the Court has fashioned to give the Fourth Amendment the force of law.

The exclusionary rule is a prudential doctrine created by the Court to compel respect for the Fourth Amendment; [16] it is also, in part, a rule of constitutional law, as it has been held enforceable against the states under the Due Process Clause of the Fourteenth Amend-

---

12. For a summary of the historical development of the *Weeks-Mapp* exclusionary rule, see United States v. Janis, 428 U.S. 433, 443–47, 96 S.Ct. 3021, 49 L.Ed.2d 1046, 1054–57 (1976).

13. United States v. Leon, 468 U.S. 897, 906, 104 S.Ct. 3405, 82 L.Ed.2d 677, 687 (1984); United States v. Callandra, 414 U.S. 338, 348, 94 S.Ct. 613, 38 L.Ed.2d 561, 571 (1974); Stone v. Powell, 428 U.S. 465, 482, 96 S.Ct. 3037, 49 L.Ed.2d 1067, 1081 (1976).

14. Mapp v. Ohio, 367 U.S. 643, 648, 81 S.Ct. 1684, 6 L.Ed.2d 1081 (1961).

15. For a discussion of this historical purpose of the Fourth Amendment, see Chapter 6, Section 3 of this work.

16. Davis v. United States, 564 U.S. ___ 131 S.Ct. 2419, 2426, 180 L.Ed.2d 285 (2011); Pennsylvania Bd. of Probation and Parole v. Scott, 524 U.S. 357, 363, 118 S.Ct. 2014, 141 L.Ed.2d 344 (1998).

ment.[17] It is not, however, a constitutional right of the individual who invokes it.[18] To the contrary, the use in a given proceeding of evidence illegally seized from such an individual does not itself violate the Fourth Amendment. Indeed, the Fourth Amendment violation is complete upon the actual commission of the unreasonable search or seizure, and the subsequent exclusion of the fruits thereof cannot cure that violation.[19]

Instead the *Weeks-Mapp* exclusionary rule was adopted to protect the general public, not the individual who invokes the rule. Its primary purpose is to deter law enforcement officials from committing *future* violations of the Fourth Amendment against innocent people by removing the incentive for such officials to disregard it.[20] The U.S. Supreme Court has classically expressed this rationale in *Elkins v. United States:*[21]

> The rule is calculated to prevent, not repair. Its purpose is to deter—to compel respect for the constitutional guaranty in the only effective available way—by removing the incentive to disregard it.[22]

Or as Justice Jackson has expressed it:

> Only occasional and more flagrant abuses come to the attention of the courts, and then only those where the search yields incriminating evidence and the defendant is at least sufficiently compromised to be indicted. If the officers raid a home, an office, or stop and search an automobile but find nothing incriminating, this invasion of personal liberty of the innocent often finds no practical redress. There may be, and I am convinced there are, many unlawful searches of homes and automobiles of innocent people which turn up nothing incriminating, in which no arrest is made, about which the courts do nothing, and about which we never hear.
>
> Courts can protect the innocent against such invasion only indirectly and through the medium of excluding evidence against those who are frequently guilty.[23]

The *Weeks-Mapp* exclusionary rule, however, exacts a serious societal cost because it excludes probative evidence that impedes the truth-seeking function of a court proceeding. Accordingly, it has been held applicable in a given proceeding or situation only after the Court—in a case of first impression—conducts a balancing analysis in which the deterrent benefits of the rule are considered to outweigh its societal costs, so that the rule can, in

17. Mapp v. Ohio, 367 U.S. 643, 648, 81 S.Ct. 1684, 6 L.Ed.2d 1081 (1961), overruling a contrary holding in Wolf v. Colorado, 338 U.S. 25, 69 S.Ct. 1359, 93 L.Ed. 1782 (1949).

18. Davis v. United States, 564 U.S. ___ 131 S.Ct. 2419, 2426, 180 L.Ed.2d 285 (2011); Herring v. United States, 555 U.S. 135, 129 S.Ct. 695, 700, 172 L.Ed.2d 496 (2009).

19. Pennsylvania Board of Probation and Parole v. Scott, 524 U.S. 357, 118 S.Ct. 2014, 141 L.Ed.2d 344, 351 (1998); United States v. Leon, 468 U.S. 897, 906, 104 S.Ct. 3405, 82 L.Ed.2d 677, 687 (1984); United States v. Callandra, 414 U.S. 338, 348, 94 S.Ct. 613, 38 L.Ed.2d 561, 571 (1974); Stone v. Powell, 428 U.S. 465, 482, 96 S.Ct. 3037, 49 L.Ed.2d 1067, 1081 (1976).

20. Davis v. United States, 564 U.S. ___, 131 S.Ct. 2419, 2426, 180 L.Ed.2d 285 (2011); Arizona v. Evans, 514 U.S. 1, 115 S.Ct. 1185, 131 L.Ed.2d 34, 43–44 (1995); United States v. Callandra, 414 U.S. 338, 348, 94 S.Ct. 613, 38 L.Ed.2d 561, 571 (1974); Stone v. Powell, 428 U.S. 465, 482, 96 S.Ct. 3037, 49 L.Ed.2d 1067, 1083 (1976); United States v. Janis, 428 U.S. 433, 446, 96 S.Ct. 3021, 49 S.Ct. 1046, 1056 (1976); Terry v. Ohio, 392 U.S. 1, 88 S.Ct. 1868, 20 L.Ed.2d 889, 900–01 (1968).

21. 364 U.S. 206, 217, 80 S.Ct. 1437, 4 L.Ed.2d 1669, 1677 (1960).

22. This formulation of the deterrence rationale has been quoted with approval by the Court many times. See, e.g., United States v. Callandra, 414 U.S. 338, 94 S.Ct. 613, 38 L.Ed.2d 561, 571 (1974); Brown v. Illinois, 422 U.S. 590, 599, 95 S.Ct. 2254, 45 L.Ed.2d 416, 424 (1975).

23. Brinegar v. United States, 338 U.S. 160, 181, 69 S.Ct. 1302, 93 L.Ed. 1879 (1949) (Jackson, J. dissenting), quoted with approval in Elkins v. Maryland, 364 U.S. 206, 217–18, 80 S.Ct.1437, 4 L.Ed.2d 1669 (1960).

fact, accomplish its deterrent purpose.[24] It is not automatically applicable in all proceedings and in all situations. It finds its most consistent application, however, in criminal trials where the fruits of the unreasonable search or seizure are sought to be used against a criminal defendant who is the victim of such search or seizure.[25] But even here, the Court has recognized some important exceptions thereto—principally to impeach a testifying criminal defendant,[26] for "knock and announce" violations prior to executing a search warrant,[27] or where the violation is shown to have been committed in objective "good faith" without any culpability by the government official involved.[28]

This dominant deterrent purpose is not based on conclusive empirical data that the exclusionary rule does, in fact, deter illegal searches and seizures, as the studies conducted on this issue have generally been considered problematical by the Court.[29] It is instead based on fundamental notions of common sense and practical observation. It has seemed only logical to the Court that law enforcement officials would be encouraged to commit illegal searches and seizures if they knew they could use the fruits thereof to criminally convict their victims, and conversely that they would be deterred if they knew they could not benefit from this wrongdoing.[30] Moreover, the exclusionary rule has also been thought to encourage the law enforcement community as a whole to inculcate Fourth Amendment ideals into its value system, a result that appears to have borne fruit through appropriate and wide spread search and seizure training programs for officers.[31] In this connection, the Court has had no trouble in balancing this common sense deterrent effect of the rule as against the rule's societal costs in determining whether to extend the exclusionary rule

---

24. Hudson v. Michigan, 547 U.S. 586, 126 S.Ct. 2159, 2163, 165 L.Ed.2d 56 (2006);

Pennsylvania Board of Probation and Parole v. Scott, 524 U.S. 357, 118 S.Ct. 2014, 141 L.Ed.2d 344, 351 (1998); Arizona v. Evans, 514 U.S. 1, 115 S.Ct. 1185, 131 L.Ed.2d 34, 43–44 (1995); United States v. Leon, 468 U.S. 897, 906, 104 S.Ct. 3405, 82 L.Ed.2d 677, 687 (1984); United States v. Callandra, 414 U.S. 338, 348, 94 S.Ct. 613, 38 L.Ed.2d 561, 571 (1974); Stone v. Powell, 428 U.S. 465, 482, 96 S.Ct. 3037, 49 L.Ed.2d 1067, 1081 (1976).

Moreover, the flagrancy of the Fourth Amendment violation weighs in favor of applying the exclusionary rule so as to deter such serious misconduct—while less egregious violations weigh against such application. "The extent to which the exclusionary rule is justified by these deterrence principles varies with the culpability of the law enforcement conduct. As we said in Leon, 'an assessment of the flagrancy of the police misconduct constitutes an important step in the calculus' of applying the exclusionary rule. [citation omitted]." Herring v. United States, 555 U.S. 135 129 S.Ct. 695, 701, 172 L.Ed.2d 496(2009).

25. Pennsylvania Board of Probation and Parole v. Scott, 524 U.S. 357, 118 S.Ct. 2014, 141 L.Ed.2d 344, 351 (1998).

26. For a discussion of the impeachment exception to the exclusionary rule, see Section 5a of this Chapter.

27. Hudson v. Michigan, 547 U.S. 586, 126 S.Ct. 2159, 2165–68, 165 L.Ed.2d 56 (2006).

28. For a discussion of the "good faith" exception to the exclusionary rule, see Section 5c of this Chapter.

29. "Since as a practical matter it is never easy to prove a negative, it is hardly likely that conclusive factual data could ever be assembled [to establish the deterrent effect of the exclusionary rule]." Elkins v. United States, 364 U.S. 206, 218, 80 S.Ct. 1437, 4 L.Ed.2d 1669 (1960). See also United States v. Janis, 428 U.S. 433, 449–53, 96 S.Ct. 3021, 49 L.Ed.2d 1046, 1058–60 (1976) concluding that empirical studies to date on the deterrent effect of the exclusionary rule were flawed.

30. See, e.g., Wolf v. Colorado, 338 U.S. 25, 44, 69 S.Ct. 1359, 93 L.Ed. 1782, 1794 (1949) (Murphy, J. dissenting) ("The conclusion is inescapable that but one remedy exists to deter violations of the [Fourth Amendment] search and seizure clause. That is the rule which excludes illegally obtained evidence. Only by exclusion can we impress on the zealous prosecutor that violations of the Constitution will do him no good. And only when that point is driven home can the prosecutor be expected to emphasize the importance of observing constitutional demands in his instructions to the police.").

31. Stone v. Powell, 428 U.S. 465, 492, 96 S.Ct. 3037, 49 L.Ed.2d 1067, 1086–87 (1976).

outside the criminal trial context, or whether to adopt an objective "good faith" exception to the rule in a particular case.[32] And from a pragmatic point of view, it has never appeared to the Court that federal or state law enforcement agencies have had any substantial problems living with the exclusionary rule, or with the Fourth Amendment, and still effectively enforcing our criminal law.[33]

In recent years, however, the Court has become less impressed with the exclusionary rule as the *only* effective remedy to deter Fourth Amendment violations. The Court has noted that a strong federal civil suit now exists, with attorney fee provisions, that can be brought against federal and state law enforcement officers who violate a person's "clearly established" Fourth Amendment rights [34]—something which did not exist when the *Weeks* and *Mapp* cases were decided. This development, along with the emergence of increasing police professionalism in officer training programs and strengthened internal disciplinary programs, has impressed the Court as also having a deterrent effect on Fourth Amendment violations.[35]

These considerations have influenced the Court in moving in the direction of further limiting the exclusionary rule's impact—as, for example in staying the effect of the rule for evidence secured from private premises following a knock and announce violation in executing a search warrant.[36] As the Court has stated:

> We cannot assume that exclusion in this context is necessary deterrence because we found that it was necessary in different contexts and long ago. That would be forcing the public today to pay for sins and inadequacies that existed almost half a century ago.[37]

Indeed, the exclusionary rule's deterrent effect is only operative when law enforcement officers discover incriminating evidence which may later be excluded in court when a criminal prosecution is brought. On the other hand, a lawsuit based on a Fourth Amendment violation is available where no incriminating evidence is found and no criminal prosecution ensues—thereby operating as a deterrent in such cases. As a result, the Court has long adopted these two remedies as particularly suited to enforce Fourth Amendment guarantees in their appropriate realms.

As an aside, however, it is extremely doubtful that the civil remedy could ever supplant the exclusionary rule where incriminating evidence is found—as a defendant in such a case would be highly compromised in the eyes of any potential civil jury and would have little hope of bringing a successful action to deter such behavior. This is particularly true if the defendant has a criminal record and would otherwise be extremely unsympathetic to a civil jury. Accordingly, the Court has always retained the exclusionary rule as the appropriate remedy to deter Fourth Amendment violations in cases where incriminating evidence is discovered and a criminal prosecution brought.

---

32. See Section 4b of this Chapter for a discussion of the Court's rejection, using a balancing analysis, of the exclusionary rule outside the criminal trial context.

33. See, e.g., Elkins v. United States, 364 U.S. 206, 218, 80 S.Ct. 1437, 4 L.Ed.2d 1669 (1960). For studies that demonstrate that the *Weeks-Mapp* exclusionary rule has had a minimal impact on the criminal prosecution and conviction rate, see Leonard Levy, "The Exclusionary Rule," Criminal Justice and the Supreme Court 148–50 (1990).

34. For a discussion of the federal civil rights remedy as a means of enforcing Fourth Amendment rights, see Section 6 g, infra, of this chapter.

35. For a discussion of this development reflecting the above views, see Hudson v. Michigan, 547 U.S. 586, 126 S.Ct..2159, 2167–2168, 165 L.Ed.2d 56 (2006).

36. Hudson v. Michigan, 547 U.S. 586, 126 S.Ct. 2159, 165 L.Ed.2d 56 (2006).

37. Hudson v. Michigan, 547 U.S. 586, 126 S.Ct. 2159, 2167, 165 L.Ed.2d 56 (2006).

Beyond that, there is a compelling but often-unstated fundamental principle of fairness that underlies the *Weeks-Mapp* exclusionary rule and serves as a weighty justification for at least the core portion of the rule. This principle, borrowed from a common law maxim, is that the government should not benefit from its own wrongdoing.[38] Although this principle is not absolute and may give way in the presence of other competing principles, it is surely a powerful consideration against abolishing the exclusionary rule entirely. It simply defies all notions of equity for the government to come into court with the fruits of an illegal search and seizure and *in all cases* shove it down the throat of the victim thereof by using these ill-gotten gains to criminally convict such victim—particularly where the government acts in deliberate or reckless defiance of an individual's well-established Fourth Amendment rights.

Justice Holmes classically expressed this revulsion when the Court (a) struck down a subpoena issued against a corporate defendant based on the fruits of a prior outrageously lawless search of the defendant's business, and (b) reversed the corporate defendant's contempt conviction for refusing to obey such a fruit-of-the-poisonous-tree subpoena:

> The proposition could not be presented more nakedly. It is that although of course its [prior] seizure [of papers] was an outrage which the government now regrets, it may study the papers before it returns them, copy them, and then use the knowledge it has gained to call upon the owners in a more regular form [through a subpoena] to produce them; that the protection of the Constitution covers the physical possession, but not any of the advantages that the government can gain over the object of its pursuit by doing the forbidden act.... In our opinion such is not the law. It reduces the Fourth Amendment to a mere form of words.... The essence of a provision forbidding the acquisition of evidence in a certain way is that not merely evidence so acquired shall not be used before the court, but that it shall not be used at all.[39]

Justice Brandeis has also classically expressed this distaste for government lawlessness:

> Our government is the potent, the omnipresent teacher. For good or evil, it teaches the whole people by its example. Crime becomes contagious. If the government becomes a lawbreaker, it breeds contempt for the law; it invites every man to become a law unto himself; it invites anarchy. To declare that in the administration of the criminal law the end justifies the means—to declare that the government may commit crimes in order to secure the conviction of a private criminal—would bring terrible retribution. Against that pernicious doctrine, this court should resolutely set its face.[40]

This fundamental principle of fairness has also found expression in U.S. Supreme Court cases to the effect that the courts, as "an imperative of judicial integrity," ought not countenance lawless government conduct by admitting the fruits of an unreasonable search or seizure as evidence in proceedings before them, at least not on a routine basis.[41]

---

38. Zap v. United States, 328 U.S. 624, 66 S.Ct. 1277, 90 L.Ed.2d 1477, 1482–83 (1946) ("[T]he evidence so obtained is suppressed on the theory that the government may not profit from its own wrongdoing.").

39. Silverthorne Lumber Co. v. United States, 251 U.S. 385, 391–92, 40 S.Ct. 182, 64 L.Ed. 319, 321 (1920).

40. Olmstead v. United States, 277 U.S. 438, 485, 48 S.Ct. 564, 72 L.Ed. 944, 960 (1928) (Brandeis, J. dissenting).

41. See, e.g., Terry v. Ohio, 392 U.S. 1, 88 S.Ct.1868, 20 L.Ed 2d 889, 901 (1968); Elkins v. United States, 364 U.S. 206, 80 L.Ed.2d 1437, 4 L.Ed.2d 1669,1680–81 (1960).

Although this rationale has "limited force" and has not been accepted as the dominant purpose of the *Weeks-Mapp* exclusionary rule because of the limitations and exceptions to the exclusionary rule that the Court has carved out over the years, it survives today as a corollary to the fundamental fairness principle that underlies the core of the exclusionary rule.[42]

There is, of course, a countervailing principle of fairness that militates against the exclusionary rule. This fairness principle was classically expressed in the 1920s by then-Judge Benjamin Cardozo that the criminal should not be allowed to go free—as the exclusionary rule sometimes permits, by suppressing evidence of guilt—merely because the constable has blundered by unwittingly violating the criminal's Fourth Amendment rights.[43] But that principle has since been largely accommodated by the Court by recognizing in certain discrete circumstances a "good faith" exception to the exclusionary rule, where the constable has unknowingly violated the defendant's Fourth Amendment rights by making an objectively reasonable mistake of law or fact, or an otherwise isolated non-recurring negligent mistake.[44]

Where, however, the police violate an individual's well-established Fourth Amendment rights either intentionally or recklessly or with gross negligence, it has simply rankled the Court to admit the fruits of such a violation against the victim of this outrage. The leading exclusionary rule cases, *Weeks* and *Mapp,* are good examples of where law enforcement officers acted without the slightest justification for their actions in plain violation of the defendant's Fourth Amendment rights. The Court simply could not abide such conduct and adopted an exclusionary rule for the fruits of such a search.

Indeed, the *Weeks* Court stated in exasperation that the Fourth Amendment "might as well be stricken from the Constitution" if the fruits of such a patent violation were routinely admitted in evidence against the victim of such a violation.[45] And the Court in *Mapp* added that "[n]othing can destroy a government more quickly than its failure to observe its own laws, or worse, its disregard of the charter of its own existence."[46] Indeed, the abuses that gave rise to the exclusionary rule [in Weeks, Silverthorne and Mapp] featured intentional —or at least reckless— law enforcement misconduct that was patently unconstitutional.[47]

This lawless result that attends the absence of an exclusionary rule has never been better illustrated than in the person of Justice Roger Traynor of the California Supreme Court. In 1942, when states were still free to accept or reject an exclusionary rule, Justice Traynor authored the opinion for the court that rejected such a rule for California.[48] But thirteen years later in 1955, Traynor authored the opinion for the same court that overruled this decision and adopted an exclusionary rule for that state.[49] Justice Traynor later explained the reason for this remarkable shift in position:

> My misgivings about its admissibility [illegally seized evidence] grew as I observed time after time it was being offered and admitted as a routine procedure. It

42. Stone v. Powell, 428 U.S. 465, 485, 96 S.Ct. 3037, 49 L.Ed.2d 3037, 1082–83 (1976).

43. People v. Defore, 242 N.Y. 13, 21, 150 N.E. 585, 587 (1926) ("The criminal is to go free because the constable has blundered."); see also Bivens v. Six Unknown Named Agents of Federal Bureau of Narcotics, 403 U.S. 388, 415, 91 S.Ct. 1999, 29 L.Ed.2d 619, 635 (1971) (Burger, C.J. dissenting).

44. For a discussion of the "good faith" exception to the exclusionary rule, including the underlying balancing principle thereof, see section 5c of this Chapter.

45. Weeks v. United States, 232 U.S. 383, 394, 34 S.Ct. 341, 58 L.Ed. 652 (1914).

46. Mapp v. Ohio, 367 U.S. 643, 659, 81 S.Ct. 1684, 6 L.Ed.2d 1081, 1092 (1961).

47. Herring v. United States, 555 U.S. 135, 129 S.Ct. 695, 702, 172 L.Ed.2d 496 (2009).

48. People v. Gonzalez, 20 Cal.2d 165, 124 P.2d 44 (1942).

49. People v. Cahan, 44 Cal.2d 434, 282 P.2d 905 (1955).

> became impossible to ignore the corollary that illegal searches and seizures were also a routine procedure subject to no effective deterrent; else how could illegally obtained evidence come into court with such regularity? It was one thing to condone an occasional constable's blunder, to accept his illegally obtained evidence so that the guilty would not go free. It was quite another to condone a steady course of illegal police procedures that deliberately and flagrantly violated the Constitution of the United States as well as the state constitution.[50]

In accord with this long historical development, it is clear that the exclusionary rule is applicable to deter Fourth Amendment violations *only* where the offending law enforcement officer or officers act with some degree of culpability—as was true, for example, of the officers who lawlessly searched the defendant's home in the decisions that created the rule in *Weeks* and *Mapp*. Indeed, this has long been the very core of the exclusionary rule and by definition represents its essential nature and purpose. The Court is currently in the process of fleshing out what that culpability consists of in its steady expansion of the "good faith" exception to the exclusionary rule.[51] In so doing, however, "the continued operation of the exclusionary rule, as settled and defined by [Supreme Court] precedents, is not in doubt."[52]

Section 3. Fruit of the Poisonous Tree Doctrine

a. General rule

Subject to certain exceptions, the *Weeks-Mapp* exclusionary rule bars the introduction at a criminal trial of all evidence that constitutes the "fruit" of the unreasonable search or seizure in question when offered against the victim of such a search or seizure.[53] This so-called "fruit of the poisonous tree" doctrine may be broken down into two parts.

First, the doctrine presumptively bars all evidence that would not have come to light "but for" the subject unreasonable search or seizure. This is known as the actual causation test and excludes any variety of evidence that was obtained during the actual commission of the unreasonable search or seizure—as well as virtually any evidence that the government was later led to as a result of knowledge learned during the unreasonable search or seizure.

Second, there is an important outer limitation to this sweeping actual causation rule. It is admittedly rather vague. But it acts as an important safety valve against applying the exclusionary rule to evidence that, to the judicial mind, seems extremely removed from the search and seizure in question, and thus beyond the deterrent purpose of the rule.

---

50. Roger Traynor, "Mapp v. Ohio at Large in the Fifty States," 1962 Duke L.J. 319, 321–22 (1962).

51. For a discussion of the "good faith" exception to the exclusionary rule, see Section 5c of this chapter.

52. Hudson v. Michigan, 547 U.S. 586, 126 S.Ct. 2159, 2170, 165 L.Ed.2d 56 (2006) (Kennedy, J. concurring) (bracketed material added).

"The Constitution protects property owners ... by interposing, *ex ante*, the 'deliberate, impartial judgment of a judicial officer ... between the citizen and the police' [citation omitted], and by providing, *ex post*, a right to suppress evidence improperly obtained and a cause of action for damages." United States v. Grubbs, 547 U.S. 90, 126 S.Ct. 1494, 1501, 164 L.Ed.2d 195 (2006).

53. For a comprehensive discussion of the fruit of the poisonous tree doctrine, collecting relevant federal and state cases, see 6 Wayne LaFave, Search and Seizure § 11.4 (5th ed. 2012). Also see cases collected at "Criminal Law" § 394.1(3) West Key No.

This limitation is that the evidence so obtained must not be so attenuated by intervening events or otherwise, so as to dissipate the taint of the prior unreasonable search or seizure. This is known as the "dissipation of taint" limitation.

The oft-stated formulation of the entire doctrine is stated in *Wong Sun v. United States*:[54]

> We need not hold that all evidence is the "fruit of the poisonous tree" simply because it would not have come to light but for the illegal actions of the police. Rather the more apt question is "whether, granting the establishment of the primary illegality, the evidence to which instant objection is made has been come at by exploitation of that illegality or by means sufficiently distinguishable to be purged of the primary taint." (citation omitted).

Stated in perhaps more concrete terms:

> The exclusionary rule prohibits introduction into evidence of tangible materials seized during an unlawful search. Beyond that, the exclusionary rule also prohibits the introduction of derivative evidence, both tangible and testimonial, that is the product of the primary evidence or that is otherwise acquired as a result of the unlawful search, up to the point at which the connection with the unlawful search becomes "so attenuated as to dissipate the taint."[55]

b. Examples of derivative fruits of an unreasonable search or seizure

(1) Generally

Under the fruit of the poisonous tree doctrine, any physical evidence seized by law enforcement officers during an illegal search, any testimony as to what the officers observed during the course of an illegal search or seizure, and any photographs taken of the illegally seized evidence are all inadmissible in evidence.[56] This result is not changed by the fact that the tangible property seized during an unreasonable search of a house is, in fact, owned by a third party and not the home dweller; this property too is subject to suppression upon motion of the home dweller.[57] A criminal defendant, however, is not entitled to the *return* of illegally seized evidence where the evidence is contraband, such as illegal drugs.[58]

(2) Electronically intercepted statements, fingerprints, dog-sniff alert

Beyond that, there are certain other less-than-obvious items of evidence that are also suppressible under the exclusionary rule as the derivative fruits of an illegal search or seizure. Oral statements electronically intercepted and recorded as a result of an unreasonable Fourth Amendment search and seizure are inadmissible in evidence.[59] Fingerprints taken

---

54. 371 U.S. 471, 487–88, 83 S.Ct. 407, 9 L.Ed.2d 441 (1963).

55. Murray v. United States, 487 U.S. 533, 108 S.Ct. 2529, 101 L.Ed.2d 472, 480 (1988) (citation omitted).

56. Wong Sun v. United States, 371 U.S. 471, 83 S.Ct. 407, 9 L.Ed.2d 441, 454 (1963); 6 Wayne LaFave, Search and Seizure § 11.4 at 322, n. 1 (5th ed. 2012).

57. Alderman v. United States, 394 U.S. 165, 176–77, 89 S.Ct. 961, 22 L.Ed.2d 176 (1969).

58. INS v. Lopez-Mendoza, 468 U.S. 1032, 104 S.Ct. 3479, 82 L.Ed.2d 778, 790–91 (1984) and cases collected.

59. Katz v. United States, 389 U.S. 347, 88 S.Ct. 507, 19 L.Ed.2d 576 (1967) (defendant's intercepted conversation in illegally bugged telephone booth); Alderman v. United States, 394 U.S. 165, 89 S.Ct. 961, 22 L.Ed.2d 176 (1969) (illegal electronic surveillance of defendant's business of all conversations

from a defendant while illegally under arrest or illegally detained are subject to suppression, even though the act of taking the fingerprints is not in itself a Fourth Amendment search of the defendant's person.[60] Similarly, a "dog-sniff alert" by a trained police dog on an illegally seized suitcase cannot be used to obtain a search warrant for the suitcase because the alert is the product of the illegal seizure of the suitcase, even though the "dog sniff" itself does not constitute a Fourth Amendment search of the suitcase.[61]

(3) Lineup and in-court identification; discovery of witness

An identification of a defendant in a police lineup is suppressible if the defendant is illegally under arrest or is illegally detained at the time of the lineup, even though the actual lineup identification of the defendant is not in itself a Fourth Amendment search of the defendant's person.[62] This result is changed, however, where prior to the lineup the illegally arrested defendant is brought before a committing magistrate who advises the defendant of his rights and sets bail—on the theory that the defendant thereafter is in custody based on the magistrate's commitment, not on the illegal arrest.[63] Also a crime victim's identification of such a defendant in court is not generally considered the fruit of the defendant's illegal arrest and ordinarily is admissible in evidence—on the theory that such an identification, coming much later after the arrest, is the product of the witness's recollection of the criminal perpetrator during the crime, and thus fails the "but for" actual causation test.[64] Moreover, the testimony of a witness who is discovered as a result of knowledge learned during an illegal search or seizure is not generally subject to suppression.[65]

(4) Statements made to the police

The Court has held that written and oral statements made by a defendant to the police during custodial interrogation while illegally detained, whether by arrest or temporary detention, are generally inadmissible in evidence under the exclusionary rule.[66] The only exception to this rule is where intervening events between the arrest and the confession, or other factors, dissipate the taint of the illegal detention. In this connection, the Court considers as relevant factors the temporal proximity of the arrest and the statement, the presence of intervening circumstances, and the purpose and flagrancy of the official misconduct. The fact that *Miranda* warnings are given to the defendant prior to such statements and that the statements are otherwise voluntary does not in itself dissipate this taint, although it is a factor to be considered by the court in determining the issue. The prosecution bears the burden of proving that the confession or statement is admissible.[67]

---

therein); Silverman v. United States, 365 U.S. 505, 81 S.Ct. 679, 5 L.Ed.2d 734 (1961) (defendant's intercepted conversations in row house through illegal spike mike driven into party wall).

60. Hayes v. Florida, 470 U.S. 811, 105 S.Ct.1643, 84 L.Ed.2d 705 (1985); Davis v. Mississippi, 394 U.S. 721, 89 S.Ct.1394, 22 L.Ed.2d 676 (1969).

61. United States v. Place, 462 U.S. 696, 103 S.Ct. 2637, 77 L.Ed.2d 110 (1983) (search warrant for illegally seized suitcase based a narcotics dog sniff alert voided).

62. United States v. Crews, 445 U.S. 463, 100 S.Ct. 1244, 63 L.Ed.2d 537 (1980).

63. Johnson v. Louisiana, 406 U.S. 356, 92 S.Ct. 1620, 32 L.Ed.2d 152, 161 (1972).

64. United States v. Crews, 445 U.S. 463, 100 S.Ct. 1244, 63 L.Ed.2d 537 (1980).

65. United States v. Ceccolini, 435 U.S. 268, 98 S.Ct. 1054, 55 L.Ed.2d 268 (1978) (no per se rule of exclusion; cost/benefit analysis used for application of exclusionary rule).

66. Florida v. Royer, 460 U.S. 491, 103 S.Ct. 1319, 75 L.Ed.2d 229, 238 (1983) ("[S]tatements [to the police] given [by a suspect] during a period of illegal detention are inadmissible even though voluntarily given if they are the product of the illegal detention and not the result of an independent act of free will.").

67. "[W]ell-established precedent requires suppression of [a defendant's] confession [obtained during an illegal arrest or detention] unless that confession was 'an act of free will [sufficient] to purge

(5) *Contrary examples*

• "Knock-and-announce" violation. Any evidence secured on private premises pursuant to a valid search warrant after law enforcement officers have forcibly entered the premises in violation of the "knock and announce" doctrine[68] is considered so attenuated as to dissipate the taint of the original "knock and announce" violation. This is so because, the "interest[s] protected" by the "knock-and-announce" requirement is not "served by suppression of the evidence obtained."[69] Accordingly, the "fruit of the poisonous tree" doctrine—and therefore, the Fourth Amendment exclusionary rule—is inapplicable to such evidence.[70]

---

the primary taint of the unlawful invasion.' Demonstrating that purgation is, of course, a function of circumstantial evidence with the burden of persuasion on the state. Relevant considerations include observance of Miranda, '[t]he temporal proximity of the arrest and the confession, the presence of intervening circumstances, and particularly, the purpose and flagrancy of the official misconduct.'" Kaupp v. Texas, 538 U.S. 626, 123 S.Ct. 1843, 1847, 155 L.Ed.2d 814 (2003) (internal citations omitted). For a general discussion of the application of the exclusionary rule to a defendant's confessions or statements to the police, see Taylor v. Alabama, 457 U.S. 687, 102 S.Ct. 2664, 73 L.Ed.2d 314, 319 (1979).

In the following cases, the Court held that the defendant's statements obtained through police interrogation constituted the fruit of the defendant's prior illegal arrest, although *Miranda* warnings were given to the defendant. Brown v. Illinois, 422 U.S. 590, 95 S.Ct. 2254, 45 L.Ed.2d 416 (1975) (illegal arrest for police questioning; statement obtained two hours later); Dunaway v. New York, 442 U.S. 200, 99 S.Ct. 2248, 60 L.Ed.2d 824 (1979) (arrest for investigation; oral statement obtained one hour later; reduced to writing a day later); Taylor v. Alabama, supra (arrest without probable cause based on vague tip; statement obtained six hours later; defendant visited by girl friend and male companion before statement); Kaupp v. Texas 538 U.S. 626, 123 S.Ct. 1843, 155 L.Ed.2d 814 (2003) (arrest without probable cause for police questioning in a murder investigation; confession obtained at police station shortly after arrest following 10–15 minutes of questioning; no intervening circumstances). And in another case, the Court held a statement obtained from a defendant illegally detained by police was inadmissible where no warnings of rights were given. Wong Sun v. United States, 371 U.S. 471, 83 S.Ct. 407, 9 L.Ed.2d 441 (1963) (defendant Toy illegally arrested in his bedroom; statement immediately obtained by police in bedroom).

On the other hand, in the following cases, the Court held that the defendant's statements to the police were not the fruit of the defendant's prior illegal arrest. Wong Sun v. United States, supra (defendant Wong Sun was illegally arrested; he was then arraigned in court and released on his own recognizance; several days later he voluntarily came to police station, was interrogated, and confessed); Rawlings v. Kentucky, 448 U.S. 98, 100 S.Ct. 2556, 65 L.Ed.2d 633 (1980) (defendant and his companions illegally held in house while search warrant was being obtained; after warrant arrived, *Miranda* warnings are given; police ordered defendant's companion to empty her purse; she does so and tells defendant to take what was his; defendant admits to owning certain drugs in purse); Harris v. New York, 495 U.S. 14, 110 S.Ct. 1640, 109 L.Ed.2d 13 (1990) (defendant arrested in his home without a warrant, thereby making arrest illegal while in the house; see Chapter 12, Section 1b, supra, of this work; statement made by defendant in the house inadmissible; statement made by defendant at police station admissible, as defendant was lawfully in custody outside the house; arrest was otherwise based on probable cause; statement was therefore not the fruit of an illegal detention).

68. See Ch. 13, Sec. 4 of this work for a discussion of the "knock-and-announce" requirements which law enforcement must follow when executing a search warrant.

69. "Attenuation can occur, of course, when the causal connection is remote. [citation omitted]. Attenuation also occurs when, even given a direct connection, the interest protected by the constitutional guarantee that has been violated would not be served by suppression of the evidence obtained." Hudson v. Michigan, 547 U.S. 586, 126 S.Ct 2159, 2164, 165 L.Ed.2d 56 (2006).

70. "One of those interests [protected by the "knock-and-announce" rule] is the protection of human life and limb, because an unannounced entry may provoke violence in supposed self defense by the surprised resident. Another interest is the protection of property. Breaking a house (as the old cases put it) absent an announcement would penalize someone who did not know of the process, of which if he had notice, it is to be presumed that he would obey it. The knock-and-announce rule

• Warrantless arrest in a person's home. Any evidence secured *outside* a person's home [such as a person's statement to the police]—following an illegal arrest in the home based on probable cause but without a required search or arrest warrant[71]—is not considered the "fruit of the poisonous tree" because (a) such a person is lawfully in custody based on probable cause once he is removed from the home, and (b) the purpose of the warrant requirement would not be served by suppressing such a statement. Accordingly, the "fruit of the poisonous tree" doctrine—and therefore, the Fourth Amendment exclusionary rule—is inapplicable to such evidence.[72]

On the other hand, any evidence secured *inside* the home from such a person [such as a person's statement to the police] following such an illegal arrest is considered the "fruit of the poisonous tree" because (a) the person is unlawfully in custody without a warrant while inside his home, and (b) the purpose of the warrant requirement is served by suppressing such evidence. Accordingly, the "fruit of the poisonous tree" doctrine—and therefore, the Fourth Amendment exclusionary rule—is applicable to such evidence.[73]

c. Refinements: independent source doctrine and inevitable discovery rule

It is settled that if the evidence sought to be suppressed was derived from a source *independent* of the illegal search or seizure, the exclusionary rule is inapplicable. This is so because the illegal search or seizure was not an *actual cause* of the discovery of the subject evidence. This is known as the independent source doctrine, and is nothing more than

---

gives individuals the opportunity to comply with the law and to avoid the destruction of property occasioned by a forcible entry. And thirdly, the knock-and-announce rule protects those elements of privacy and dignity that can be destroyed by a sudden entrance. * * *

What the knock-and-announce rule has never protected, however, is one's interest in preventing the government from seeing or taking evidence described in a warrant. Since the interests that were violated in this case have nothing to do with the seizure of evidence, the exclusionary rule is inapplicable." Hudson v. Michigan, 547 U.S. 586, 126 S.Ct 2159, 2165, 165 L.Ed.2d 56 (2006) [internal citations and quotations omitted]. See also Ch. 17, Sec. 5d of this supplement in which the Court also carves out an exception to the Fourth Amendment exclusionary rule for knock-and-announce violations.

71. A routine arrest in a person's home without a search or arrest warrant and without consent or exigent circumstances is unreasonable under the Fourth Amendment. Payton v. New York, 445 U.S. 573, 100 S.Ct. 1371, 63 L.Ed.2d 639 (1980); see also Steagald v. United States, 451 U.S. 204, 101 S.Ct. 1642, 68 L.Ed..2d 38 (1981). See discussion of this subject at Ch. 12, Sec. 1b of this work.

72. "We hold that, where the police have probable cause to arrest a suspect, the [Fourth Amendment] exclusionary rule does not bar the State's use of a statement made by the defendant outside of his home, even though the statement is taken after [a routine felony] arrest [of the defendant] made in the home [without a warrant] in violation of [the rule stated] in Payton [v. New York]." Harris v. New York, 495 U.S. 14, 110 S.Ct. 1640, 109 L.Ed.2d 13, 22 (1990).

"We do hold that the station house statement in this case was admissible because [at that time], Harris was in legal custody ... and because the statement, while the product of an arrest and being in custody, was not the fruit of the fact that the arrest was made in the house rather than someplace else. To put the matter another way, suppressing the statement taken outside the house would not serve the purpose of the [Payton] rule that made Harris' in-house arrest illegal." Harris v. New York, 495 U.S. 14, 110 S.Ct. 1640, 109 L.Ed.2d 13, 21–22 (1990).

73. "The warrant requirement for an arrest in the home is imposed to protect the home, and anything incriminating the police gathered from arresting Harris in his home, rather than elsewhere, has been excluded, as it should have been; the purpose of the rule has thereby been vindicated." Harris v. New York, 495 U.S. 14, 110 S.Ct. 1640, 109 L.Ed.2d 13, 22 (1990).

a variation on the "but for" actual causation test of the fruit of the poisonous tree doctrine previously discussed.[74] To invoke the doctrine, it must be shown that the fruits of the initial illegal search or seizure (1) formed no basis for the *decision* to conduct the subsequent lawful search that led to the items ultimately seized, and (2) formed no *evidentiary basis* for this subsequent search as well.[75]

This doctrine has particular application where law enforcement officers illegally enter private premises, illegally detain the occupants therein, and wait until other officers arrive later and lawfully search the premises either with or without a search warrant. Any evidence seized is obviously derived from the second lawful search, not the prior illegal entry and detention.[76] The same result also obtains where the initial wave of officers illegally make plain sight observations of contraband or evidence of crime while on the premises, but conduct no seizures of same, so long as these observations form no basis for the entry and search by the second wave of officers.[77] In either case, the evidence seized from the premises was actually obtained by the lawful actions of the second wave of officers, not the prior illegal actions of the first wave of officers—and consequently such evidence is not barred by the exclusionary rule.

The inevitable discovery rule is a variation of the independent source doctrine. But under the inevitable discovery rule [to use the above example], the first wave of officers who engage in illegal activity *actually seize* the evidence sought to be suppressed. Nonetheless, the evidence seized is admissible because it would have been, ultimately and inevitably, discovered lawfully by the second wave of officers—even if there had there been no illegal activity by the first wave. The underlying rationale for this result seems obvious enough. The exclusionary rule should place the government back in the position it would have been in if it had *not* engaged in the subject illegality, i.e., without the fruits of its illegal conduct—but surely not in a *worse* position. Which would be the case in this scenario if the subject evidence were excluded, notwithstanding its inevitable later

---

74. Silverthorne Lumber Co. v. United States, 251 U.S. 385, 40 S.Ct. 182, 64 L.Ed. 319 (1920); 6 Wayne LaFave, Search and Seizure § 11.4(a) at 334–338 (5th ed. 2012).

75. The Court in Murray v. New York, 487 U.S. 533, 108 S.Ct. 2529, 101 L.Ed.2d 472 (1988), held that where there is an initial illegal police entry onto premises followed by the issuance of a search warrant that leads to the seizure of evidence on the same premises, the government, under the independent source doctrine, has "the onerous burden of convincing a trial court that no information gained from the illegal entry affected either [1] the law enforcement officers' decision to seek a warrant or [2] the magistrate's decision to grant it." * * * "The ultimate question, therefore, is whether the search pursuant to warrant was in fact a genuinely independent source of the information and tangible evidence [ultimately obtained]. This would *not* have been the case if [1] the agents' *decision* to seek the warrant was prompted by what they had seen during the initial entry, or [2] if information obtained during that entry was presented to the Magistrate and affected his decision to issue the warrant." 108 L.Ed.2d at 482, 483–84 (1988) (emphasis and brackets added).

In *Murray*, federal agents illegally entered a warehouse, observed bales of marijuana therein, immediately withdrew when they found no one there, and thereafter kept the warehouse under surveillance while others of their number obtained a search warrant for the warehouse. The agents' affidavit in support of the warrant did not mention the prior illegal entry, but otherwise stated probable cause for the warrant based on information obtained prior to the illegal entry. The warrant was then executed and the bales of marijuana in the warehouse were seized. The trial court denied the defendant's motion to suppress, and the Court of Appeals affirmed based on the independent source doctrine.

The Supreme Court, however, reversed with directions for the trial court to determine "whether the warrant-authorized search of the warehouse was an independent source of the challenged evidence in the sense we have described." 108 L.Ed.2d at 484.

76. Segura v. United States, 468 U.S. 796, 104 S.Ct. 3380, 82 L.Ed.2d 599 (1984).

77. Murray v. United States, 487 U.S. 533, 108 S.Ct. 2529, 101 L.Ed.2d 472 (1988).

lawful discovery. Thus, the evidence comes in under this variation of the independent source doctrine.[78]

The U.S. Supreme Court has formulated the inevitable discovery rule as follows:

> If the prosecution can establish by a preponderance of the evidence that the information [sought to be suppressed] ultimately and inevitably would have been discovered by lawful means ... the deterrence rationale [for the exclusionary rule] has so little basis that the evidence should be received.[79]

The central terms of the rule are "ultimately and inevitably would have been discovered." These are not terms of speculation. They are terms of certainty. In context, they mean that the subject evidence—in order to be admissible under the inevitable discovery rule—was *bound* to have been discovered *after* the completion of the illegal search, through later lawful methods which were perfectly predictable under the circumstances. Ordinarily, this requires the prosecution to establish that certain investigative procedures were already in place around the time of the illegal search [or were bound to be put in place shortly thereafter] which would have clearly led to the evidence sought to be suppressed.[80] And the prosecution has the burden of establishing this ultimate and inevitable event by "a preponderance of the evidence."

This burden is clearly satisfied in the above-stated example where the second wave of officers obtain an otherwise valid search warrant for the search of the premises in question at or around the time of the prior illegal search by the first wave of officers. Or where the seized evidence is a dead body in a murder investigation unlawfully discovered in a rural area as a result of an illegal confession obtained from the defendant—when a simultaneous search party was in the immediate vicinity at the time of the discovery of the body and would have found it shortly thereafter.[81] Or where a well-established police procedure of inventorying lawfully-impounded automobiles would have discovered incriminating evidence in a vehicle which initially had been searched unlawfully by police—after the vehicle was lawfully seized.[82]

On the other hand, the government does not get a "do-over" under the inevitable discovery rule. After law enforcement officers have conducted an otherwise unreasonable search or seizure, they cannot start over under this doctrine and show that they *could have* lawfully discovered the subject evidence through a different method had they chosen to do so. For example, where the police conduct an unlawful search of a home without

---

78. Nix v. Williams, 467 U.S. 431, 104 S.Ct. 2501, 81 L.Ed.2d 377, 388 (1984) (bracketed material added); 6 Wayne LaFave, Search and Seizure § 11.4(a) at 338–350 (5th ed. 2012); "Criminal Law" § 394.1(3) West Key No. and cases collected.

79. Nix v. Williams, 467 U.S. 431, 104 S.Ct. 2501, 81 L.Ed.2d 377, 387–88 (1984).

80. "To establish [the inevitable discovery rule] to exclusion, the government must show that 'certain proper and predictable investigative procedures would have been utilized' [even if no illegal search or seizure had occurred] and 'that those procedures would have inevitably resulted in the discovery of the evidence'" sought to be suppressed. Thomas K. Clancy, The Fourth Amendment: Its History and Interpretation. 644 (2008), quoting from Stokes v. State, 423 A.2d 552, 555 (Md. 1980) (bracketed material added).

81. Nix v. Williams, 467 U.S. 431, 104 S.Ct. 2501, 81 L.Ed.2d 377 (1984).

82. 6 Wayne LaFave, Search and Seizure § 11.4(a) at 339–340 (5th ed. 2012), citing Clough v. State, 92 Nev. 602, 555 P.2d 840 (1976) (court assumes auto was unlawfully searched following lawful drunk driving arrest and lawful impoundment of auto; inevitable discovery rule applies as auto would have been lawfully inventoried thereafter).

a legally-required search warrant, but want to start over and show that they could have gotten such a warrant had they chosen to apply for one. The inevitable discovery rule is inapplicable to such a case as the search involved is a classic unreasonable search under the Fourth Amendment whose fruits have long been held inadmissible against the victim of the search. Once an unreasonable search has been conducted, its fruits are generally inadmissible at trial, and later police efforts to start over and proceed in a lawful manner to discover the same evidence cannot sanitize the original illegality.[83]

---

83. Jones v. United States, 357 U.S. 493, 497–98, 78 S.Ct. 1253, 2 L.Ed.2d 1514, 1518–1519 (1958) ("It is settled doctrine that probable cause for belief that certain articles subject to seizure are in a dwelling cannot of itself justify a search without a warrant ... Were federal officers free to search without a warrant merely upon probable cause to believe that certain articles were within a home, the provisions of the Fourth Amendment would become empty phrases, and the protection it affords largely nullified.") (search of home struck down as it was conducted without a legally-required search warrant; fact that a search could have been obtained for the home held irrelevant); Mancusi v. DeForte, 392 U.S. 364, 372 n. 12, 88 S.Ct. 2120, 20 L.Ed.2d 1154, 1162 (1968) ("It is, of course, immaterial that the State might have been able to obtain the same papers [sought to be suppressed] by means that did not violate the Fourth Amendment." citing to Silverthorne Lumber Co.); Silverthorne Lumber Co. v. United States, 251 U.S. 385, 40 S.Ct. 182, 64 L.Ed. 319, 322 (1920) ("[T]he rights ... against unreasonable search and seizure are to be protected even if the same result might have been achieved in a lawful way.").

"Searches conducted without warrants have been held unlawful notwithstanding facts unquestionably showing probable cause, for the Constitution requires that the deliberate, impartial judgment of a judicial officer be interposed between the citizen and the police. Over and again this Court has emphasized that the mandate of the [Fourth] Amendment requires adherence to judicial processes, and that searches conducted outside the judicial process, without prior approval by judge or magistrate, are per se unreasonable under the Fourth Amendment—subject only to a few specifically established and well-delineated exceptions." Katz v. United States, 389 U.S. 347, 357, 88 S.Ct. 507, 19 L.Ed.2d 576, 585 (1967) (internal and footnoted citations and quotation marks omitted).

The above formulation has been quoted with approval in the following cases: Minnesota v. Dickerson, 508 U.S. 366, 113 S.Ct. 2130, 124 L.Ed.2d 334, 343–44 (1993); California v. Acevedo, 500 U.S. 565, 111 S.Ct. 1982, 114 L.Ed. 2d 619, 634 (1991); Horton v. California, 496 U.S. 128, 110 S.Ct. 2301, 110 L.Ed. 112, 120 n. 4 (1990); Colorado v. Bannister, 449 U.S. 1, 2, 101 S.Ct. 42, 66 L.Ed.2d 1, 3 (1980); Thompson v. Louisiana, 469 U.S. 17, 105 S.Ct. 409, 83 L.Ed.2d 246, 250 (1984); Mincey v. Arizona, 437 U.S. 385, 390, 98 S.Ct. 2408, 57 L.Ed.2d 290, 298–99 (1978).

"The point of the Fourth Amendment, which often is not grasped by zealous officers, is not that it denies law enforcement the usual inferences which reasonable men draw from evidence. Its protection consists that those inferences be drawn by a neutral and detached magistrate instead of being judged by the officer engaged in the often competitive enterprise of ferreting out crime. Any assumption that evidence sufficient to support a magistrate's disinterested determination to issue a search warrant will justify the officer in making a search without a warrant would reduce the Amendment to a nullity and leave the people's homes secure only in the discretion of police officers." Johnson v. United States, 333 U.S. 10, 68 S.Ct. 367, 92 S.Ct. 436, 440 (1948) (warrantless search of hotel room held violation of 4th Amendment, although police had probable cause to search the room and could have obtained a search warrant, but declined to do so; fruits of the search held inadmissible).

"That [inevitable discovery] rule does not refer to discovery that would have taken place if the police behavior in question had (contrary to fact) been lawful. The doctrine does not treat as critical what *hypothetically could* have happened had the police acted lawfully in the first place. * * * The government cannot, for example, avoid suppression of evidence seized without a warrant (or pursuant to a defective warrant) simply by showing that it could have obtained a valid warrant had it sought one." Hudson v. Michigan, 547 U.S. 586, 126 S.Ct. 2159, 2178, 165 L.Ed.2d 56 (2006) (Breyer, J. dissenting). "[I]t is essential that courts not lose sight of the fact that mechanical application of the inevitable discovery doctrine will encourage unconstitutional shortcuts. If the doctrine were applied when such a shortcut was intentionally taken, the effect would be to read out of the Fourth Amendment the requirement that other more elaborate and protective procedures be followed. This is particularly apparent when the shortcut was a bypassing of the Fourth Amendment warrant requirement ..." "In

Section 4. Applicability of Exclusionary Rule to Given Proceedings

a. General rule: criminal trials and forfeiture proceedings

The U.S. Supreme Court has applied the exclusionary rule almost exclusively to federal and state criminal trials.[84] Indeed, the only court proceeding outside the criminal trial context that the exclusionary rule has been applied to is a civil forfeiture proceeding which is quasi-criminal in nature. In this proceeding, the government seeks the forfeiture of a person's non-contraband, personal property because it was used in the commission of a crime. Although the property sought to be forfeited is not suppressible even if illegally seized, any other illegally seized evidence from the respondent offered at the forfeiture proceeding is suppressible. For example, where the government seeks to forfeit a person's automobile because it was allegedly used to violate the liquor laws, the automobile itself would not be suppressible, but any contraband liquor illegally seized from the automobile is inadmissible in evidence in the civil forfeiture proceeding.[85]

b. Proceedings other than criminal trials: exclusionary rule rejected

Other than quasi-criminal forfeiture proceedings, the Court has consistently refused to extend the exclusionary rule to proceedings outside the criminal trial context on the ground that the societal costs for imposing the rule in such proceedings outweighed whatever deterrent benefit the rule might have in that context.

(1) Grand jury proceedings

Illegally seized evidence obtained in violation of a person's Fourth Amendment rights is admissible before the grand jury that is considering an indictment against such person. Moreover, a person subpoenaed as a witness before the grand jury cannot refuse to answer questions asked of such person on the ground that the question is based on evidence seized in violation of the witness's Fourth Amendment rights. An indictment based in whole or in part on such illegally seized evidence is not subject to dismissal.[86]

(2) Civil proceedings

Where state law enforcement agents illegally seize evidence in violation of a taxpayer's Fourth Amendment rights and turn it over on a "silver platter" to federal agents, who had no participation in the illegal search or seizure, such evidence has been held admissible in an IRS civil tax proceeding against the taxpayer.[87] The Court, however, has left open

---

short, the argument that if we hadn't done it wrong, we would have done it right is far from compelling." 6 Wayne LaFave, Search and Seizure § 11.4(a) at 343, 347 (5th ed. 2012) (internal quotations omitted).

84. Pennsylvania Board of Probation and Parole v. Scott, 524 U.S. 357, 118 S.Ct. 2014, 141 L.Ed.2d 344, 351 (1998) ("[W]e have repeatedly declined to extend the exclusionary rule to proceedings other than criminal trials.").

85. One 1958 Plymouth Sedan v. Pennsylvania, 380 U.S. 693, 85 S.Ct. 1246, 14 L.Ed.2d 170 (1965).

86. United States v. Calandra, 414 U.S. 338, 94 S.Ct. 613, 38 L.Ed.2d 561 (1974).

87. United States v. Janis, 428 U.S. 433, 96 S.Ct. 3021, 49 L.Ed.2d 1046 (1976).

the question whether this result might be different if there had been federal participation in the illegal search[88]—or if the civil proceeding had been brought by the sovereign of the offending law enforcement officer who conducted the illegal search.[89] Nonetheless, the Court has stated that the exclusionary rule does not generally apply to a civil proceeding, federal or state, except forfeiture proceedings which are really quasi-criminal in nature.[90]

(3) Deportation proceedings

The exclusionary rule is inapplicable to a deportation hearing, so that credible evidence illegally obtained from an alien in violation of the alien's Fourth Amendment rights is admissible at the alien's deportation hearing.[91] This result, however, is different if the Fourth Amendment violation is so egregious that it violates notions of fundamental fairness and undermines the probative value of the evidence obtained.[92]

(4) Parole revocation proceedings

The exclusionary rule does not bar the introduction at a parole revocation hearing of evidence seized in violation of the parolee's Fourth Amendment rights.[93] Presumably, the same rule would apply to a probation revocation hearing as well as other similar conditional release revocation proceedings.[94]

(5) Federal habeas corpus proceedings

Although the exclusionary rule is applicable to a state criminal trial and to appellate proceedings thereafter, it is not applicable to a collateral attack, federal habeas corpus proceeding—so long as the defendant has been afforded a full and fair opportunity to litigate the Fourth Amendment claim in the state courts.[95] Such an opportunity is not afforded, however, where the defendant is not given effective assistance of counsel in the state courts. In that event, the defendant may litigate the Fourth Amendment claim in a federal habeas corpus proceeding.[96]

6) Miscellaneous criminal and related proceedings

Although the Court has applied the exclusionary rule to a juvenile delinquency proceeding without comment and state courts have routinely done the same,[97] the Court has never squarely decided the issue.[98] The Court has also not decided whether the exclusionary rule should be applied to a preliminary hearing, a bail hearing, a sentencing hearing or an extradition hearing.[99]

---

88. United States v. Janis, 428 U.S. 433, 96 S.Ct. 3021, 49 L.Ed.2d 1046, 1061 n. 31 (1976).
89. United States v. Janis, 428 U.S. 433, 96 S.Ct. 3021, 49 L.Ed.2d 1046, 1061 (1976).
90. United States v. Janis, 428 U.S. 433, 96 S.Ct. 3021, 49 L.Ed.2d 1046, 1057 (1976).
91. INS v. Lopez-Mendoza, 468 U.S. 1032, 104 S.Ct. 3479, 82 L.Ed.2d 778 (1984).
92. INS v. Lopez-Mendoza, 468 U.S. 1032, 104 S.Ct. 3479, 82 L.Ed.2d 778, 793 n. 5 (1984).
93. Pennsylvania Board of Probation and Parole v. Scott, 524 U.S. 357, 118 S.Ct. 2014, 141 L.Ed.2d 344 (1998).
94. 1 Wayne LaFave, Search and Seizure § 1.6(g) (5th ed. 2012).
95. Stone v. Powell, 428 U.S. 465, 96 S.Ct. 3037, 49 L.Ed.2d 1067, 1080 (1976).
96. Kimmelman v. Morrison, 477 U.S. 365, 106 S.Ct. 2574, 91 L.Ed.2d 305 (1986).
97. See, e.g., Florida v. J.L., 529 U.S. 266, 120 S.Ct. 1375, 146 L.Ed.2d 254 (2000); 1 Wayne LaFave, Search and Seizure § 1.7(b) at 320 (5th ed. 2012).
98. New Jersey v. T.L.O., 469 U.S. 325, 105 S.Ct. 733, 83 L.Ed.2d 720, 729 n. 3 (1985).
99. See 1 Wayne LaFave, Search and Seizure § 1.6(d)–(f) (5th ed. 2012) for a collection of state and lower federal court cases on this subject.

c. New proceedings and exceptions

The Court employs a cost/benefit balancing analysis in determining whether to apply the exclusionary rule to a new proceeding or to create a new exception to the exclusionary rule. The likely social benefits in deterring future illegal searches or seizures is weighed against its substantial social cost.[100]

Section 5. Exceptions to the Exclusionary Rule at Criminal Trials

Even in the criminal trial context, the Court has adopted four important exceptions to the exclusionary rule.

a. Impeachment of defendant's trial testimony

A defendant's trial testimony, whether elicited on direct or cross examination, may be impeached by the prosecution with evidence seized in violation of the defendant's Fourth Amendment rights.[101] The only exception to this rule is where the prosecution has elicited testimony from the defendant through *improper* cross examination questions, such as questions outside the scope of the direct examination. In that instance, the prosecution cannot use evidence obtained in violation of the defendant's Fourth Amendment rights to impeach such improperly elicited testimony.[102] As an aside, the prosecution may not impeach a *defense witness'* trial testimony with evidence seized in violation of the defendant's Fourth Amendment rights.[103]

b. Defendant's body or identity

The defendant's body or identity is not suppressible under the exclusionary rule even if the defendant has been illegally arrested.[104] Moreover, a trial court is not deprived of jurisdiction over the defendant's person because the defendant was illegally arrested.[105] Nor can a criminal conviction be voided because the defendant was illegally brought into the court's jurisdiction for trial.[106]

---

100. See, e.g., INS v. Lopez-Mendoza, 468 U.S. 1032, 104 S.Ct. 3479, 82 L.Ed.2d 778, 786 (1984). Also see Chapter 7, Section 3c of this work.

101. United States v. Havens, 446 U.S. 620, 100 S.Ct. 1912, 64 L.Ed.2d 559 (1980) (cross examination); Walder v. United States, 347 U.S. 62, 74 S.Ct. 354, 98 L.Ed. 503 (1954) (direct examination).

102. Agnello v. United States, 269 U.S. 20, 46 S.Ct. 4, 70 L.Ed. 145 (1925).

103. James v. Illinois, 493 U.S. 307, 110 S.Ct. 648, 107 L.Ed.2d 676 (1990).

104. INS v. Lopez-Mendoza, 468 U.S. 1032, 104 S.Ct. 3479, 82 L.Ed.2d 778, 786 (1984); United States v. Crews, 445 U.S. 463, 100 S.Ct. 1244, 63 L.Ed.2d 537, 547–48 (1980).

105. United States v. Alvarez-Machain, 504 U.S. 655, 112 S.Ct. 2188, 119 L.Ed.2d 441 (1992); Frisbie v. Collins, 342 U.S. 519, 72 S.Ct. 509, 96 L.Ed. 541 (1952); Ker v. Illinois, 119 U.S. 436, 7 S.Ct. 225, 30 L.Ed. 421 (1886).

106. Gerstein v. Pugh, 420 U.S. 103, 95 S.Ct. 854, 43 L.Ed.2d 54, 68 (1975).

c. The "good faith" exception

(1) Balancing test

By far, the most important and complex exception to the exclusionary rule in the criminal trial context is the "good faith" exception. This exception has been applied in certain discrete factual situations which will be discussed shortly. In the process of applying the exception, however, the Court has developed a balancing test to determine whether the exclusionary rule or the good faith exception is applicable in a given case.

That test, briefly stated, is that the exclusionary rule is inapplicable and the good faith exception applies

(a) when law enforcement officials act with a reasonable good faith but mistaken belief that their conduct is lawful and does not violate the Fourth Amendment, or

(b) when their conduct constitutes only an isolated, non-recurring negligent violation of Fourth Amendment rights

In either of these two events, the deterrent benefits of the rule is outweighed by the heavy costs of imposing the rule, as, in the Court's view, the law enforcement officer in question has not acted with any degree of culpability.

On the other hand, where the law enforcement conduct constitutes a (a) deliberate, (b) reckless, (c) grossly negligent, or(d) recurring or systemic disregard of Fourth Amendment rights, the exclusionary rule is applicable and the good faith exception is inapplicable—as, in each of these four events, the deterrent benefits of the rule outweighs the costs of imposing the rule, as the offending law enforcement officer has acted with some degree of culpability that needs to be deterred.[107]

Stated differently, the exclusionary rule should only be applied where a government agent has with some culpability violated a person's Fourth Amendment rights, not when the agent, based on otherwise proper training, has made a reasonable good faith mistake of fact or law that his or her actions were perfectly lawful—or has made merely an isolated, non-culpable negligent mistake of fact or law. Indeed, to apply the rule in cases of this nature may very well breed disrespect for the law by turning the criminal trial into a game where violations of little-understood rules or minor mistakes of fact or law may allow a law breaker, sometimes a heinous one, to escape any punishment: the criminal ought not

107. "To trigger the exclusionary rule, police conduct must be sufficiently deliberate that exclusion can meaningfully deter it, and sufficiently culpable that such deterrence is worth the price paid by the justice system. As laid out in our cases, the exclusionary rule serves to deter deliberate, reckless, or grossly negligent conduct, or in some circumstances recurring or systemic negligence." Herring v. United States, 555 U.S. 135, 129 S.Ct. 695, 702, 172 L.Ed.2d 496 (2009).

"The basic insight of the [good faith] *Leon* line of cases is that deterrence benefits of exclusion 'var[y] with the culpability of the law enforcement conduct' at issue. When the police exhibit 'deliberate,' 'reckless,' or 'grossly negligent' disregard for Fourth Amendment rights, the deterrent value of exclusion is strong and tends to outweigh the resulting costs. But when the police act with an objectively 'reasonable good-faith belief' that their conduct is lawful, or when their conduct involves only simple 'isolated' negligence, the 'deterrence rationale loses much of its force' and exclusion cannot 'pay its way.'

The Court has over time applied this good-faith exception over a range of cases."

Davis v. United States, 564 U.S. 135, 131 S.Ct. 2419, 2427–28, 180 L.Ed.2d 285(2011) (internal citations omitted) (emphasis added).

go free because the constable has *reasonably* blundered or has acted in an otherwise *non-culpable* manner.[108]

Of course, as Fourth Amendment rules become more established and otherwise mistaken or negligent police practices are identified, a reasonable or negligent good faith mistake of law or fact—depending on the type of mistake—may no longer be regarded as reasonable or non-culpable in the future. In that event, the deterrence rationale may be perfectly applicable as the law enforcement community, with the benefit of further experience, is now equipped with further knowledge of law and facts and may not be able to repeat the same violation of Fourth Amendment rights without suffering the exclusionary remedy. This correction is arguably apt else the good faith exception might otherwise be applicable to patently culpable police behavior.

Given this concern, the Court in future cases will no doubt flesh out what it means by "isolated negligent" violations of the Fourth Amendment, which stay the operation of the exclusionary rule—as opposed to "intentional," "grossly negligent," "reckless" and "recurring or systemic" violations of the Fourth Amendment, which trigger the exclusionary rule. Plainly, this will require some fine line-drawing if the exclusionary rule is to remain a viable deterrent against lawless police conduct—else as Justice Breyer has warned, "the good faith exception will swallow the exclusionary rule."[109]

We turn now to the discrete factual situations where the Court has applied the "good faith" exception to the exclusionary rule.

(2) The Leon *search warrant rule*

The Court has held that the exclusionary rule is inapplicable to evidence obtained by law enforcement officers acting in objective reasonable reliance on a search warrant issued by a neutral and detached magistrate, but ultimately found to be invalid. The test for invoking this exception, however, is not the *subjective* good faith of the officers involved. The test is whether these officers acted in *objective reasonable reliance* on the search warrant they use to obtain the evidence sought to be suppressed. This means that their good faith belief that they had a valid warrant to conduct the search must have a reasonable objective basis.[110]

---

108. Stone v. Powell, 428 U.S. 465, 491, 96 S.Ct. 3037, 49 L.Ed.2d 1067, 1086 (1976) ("[I]f applied indiscriminately, it [the exclusionary rule] may very well have the opposite effect of generating disrespect for the law and administration of justice.").

Also see: Arkansas v. Sanders, 442 U.S. 753, 757, 99 S.Ct. 2586, 61 L.Ed.2d 235, 240 (1979) ("Although the general principles applicable to claims of Fourth Amendment violations are well settled, litigation over requests for suppression of highly relevant evidence continues to occupy much of the attention of our courts at all levels of the state and federal judiciary. Courts and law enforcement officials often find it difficult to discern the proper application of these principles to individual cases, because the circumstances giving rise to suppression requests can vary almost infinitely. Moreover, an apparently small difference in the factual situation frequently is viewed as a controlling difference in determining Fourth Amendment requests.").

109. Davis v. United States, 564 U.S. ___, 131 S.Ct. at 2439, 180 L.Ed.2d 285 (2011) (Breyer, J. dissenting).

110. United States v. Leon, 468 U.S. 897, 104 S.Ct. 3405, 82 L.Ed.2d 677, 684, 696 n. 20 (1984); Massachusetts v. Sheppard, 468 U.S. 981, 104 S.Ct. 3424, 82 L.Ed.2d 737, 743 (1984); "*Leon* itself, for example, held that the exclusionary rule does not apply when police conduct a search in 'objectively reasonable reliance' on a warrant later held invalid. The error in such a case rests with the issuing magistrate, not the police officer, and '[punish[ing] the errors of judges' is not the office of the exclusionary rule." Davis v. United States, 564 U.S. ___, 131 S.Ct. 2419, 2428, 180 L. Ed.2d 285 (2011) (internal citations omitted). See cases collected at "Criminal Law" § 394.4(5.1),(6), (7), (8) West Key Nos.

This exception necessarily assumes that the officers properly executed the subject search warrant and searched only those places and for those objects that it was reasonable to believe were covered by the warrant.[111] Moreover, the term "officers" in the exception refers not only to the officers who executed the warrant, but also the officers who obtained the warrant or who supplied the information for the warrant; all must act with objective reasonableness in obtaining and executing the warrant.[112]

In explaining its announced rule, however, the *Leon* Court indicated four (4) circumstances in which it would *not* be objectively reasonable for the officer to believe that the warrant was properly issued.

The first and most important circumstance is where the search warrant affidavit fails to state probable cause and a reasonably well-trained officer would have known this, as in the case of a bare-bones, conclusory affidavit.[113] Indeed, given the extremely relaxed standard for determining whether probable cause exists to issue a search warrant under *Illinois v. Gates,*[114] a search warrant affidavit that failed this lenient standard might not be—depending on the case—the type of affidavit that a reasonably well-trained police officer would believe stated probable cause.[115] Nonetheless, the threshold for establishing this exception remains a high one. This is so because in the ordinary case a lay law enforcement officer cannot be expected to question the magistrate's decision to issue the warrant, as it is the magistrate's responsibility to pass on the probable cause issue in the case—not the officer.[116]

---

111. United States v. Leon, 468 U.S. 897, 104 S.Ct. 3405, 82 L.Ed.2d 677, 695 n. 19 (1984). "This means that *Leon* cannot be invoked in the prosecution's favor on such issues as whether the warrant was executed in a timely fashion, whether entry without prior notice of authority and purpose to execute the warrant was permissible (when not authorized by the warrant itself), whether certain persons were properly detained and searched incident to execution of the warrant, whether the scope and intensity and duration of the warrant execution were excessive, and whether certain items not named in the warrant were properly seized." 1 Wayne LaFave, Search and Seizure § 1.3(f) at 90–91 (5th ed. 2012).

But cf. Hudson v. Michigan, 547 U.S. 586, 126 S.Ct. 2159, 2165–68, 165 L.Ed.2d 56 (2006), in which the Court held that a knock and announce violation in executing a search warrant is in itself an independent exception to the exclusionary rule. See Section 5d of this chapter for a discussion of this exception.

112. United States v. Leon, 468 U.S. 897, 104 S.Ct. 3405, 82 L.Ed.2d 677, 698 n. 24 (1984).

113. United States v. Leon, 468 U.S. 897, 104 S.Ct. 3405, 82 L.Ed.2d 677, 699 (1984); see, e.g., Nathanson v. United States, 290 U.S. 41, 54 S.Ct. 11, 78 L.Ed. 159 (1933) (affiant states that "he has cause to suspect and does suspect that certain merchandise [smuggled liquor on which import duties have not been paid] is now deposited within the premises of [defendant] being described as a 2-story framed building located at [address]."); Aguilar v. Texas, 378 U.S. 108, 84 S.Ct. 1509, 12 L.Ed.2d 723 (1964) (affidavit states: "affiants have received information from a credible person that heroin, marijuana, barbiturates and other narcotics are being kept at the above-described premises for the purpose of sale and use contrary to the provisions of the law."). Also see Chapter 13, Section 2c of this work for a discussion of conclusory search warrant affidavits.

114. 462 U.S. 213, 103 S.Ct. 2317, 76 L.Ed.2d 527 (1983); see Chapter 13, Section 2a of this work for a discussion of the *Gates* case.

115. 1 Wayne LaFave, Search and Seizure § 1.3(f) at 112–116 (5th ed. 2012); see "Criminal Law" § 394.4(6) West Key No. for cases dealing with whether a variety of defective search warrant affidavits qualify for the *Leon* good faith exception.

116. "Where the alleged Fourth Amendment violation involves a search or seizure pursuant to a warrant, the fact that a neutral magistrate has issued a warrant is the clearest indication that the officers acted in an objectively reasonable manner or, as we have sometimes put it, in 'objective good faith.' (citation omitted). Nonetheless, under our precedents, the fact that a neutral magistrate has issued a warrant authorizing the allegedly unconstitutional search or seizure does not end the inquiry into objective reasonableness. Rather we have recognized an exception allowing suit when 'it is obvious that no reasonably competent officer would have concluded that a warrant should issue.' (citation

The second circumstance is where the warrant is facially so defective in failing to describe the place to be searched or the things to be seized that a reasonably well-trained police officer would have been aware of this—as, for example, when the warrant contains no description whatever of the things to be seized.[117] Nonetheless, the threshold for establishing this circumstance is a high one as well. A lay police officer cannot ordinarily be expected to question the magistrate's decision to issue the warrant with the required constitutional descriptions, as it is the magistrate's responsibility to pass on the facial validity of the warrant—not the officer.[118]

The third circumstance is where the search warrant affidavit contains false information that the officer either knew was false or should have known was false except for his or her reckless disregard of the truth.[119] The final circumstance is where the magistrate who issued the warrant wholly abandoned his or her judicial role, as where the magistrate helps the police execute the warrant.[120]

Beyond that, *Leon* would also appear to be inapplicable when the evidence upon which the search warrant was issued was itself obtained in violation of the defendant's Fourth Amendment rights. This is so because a magistrate is never asked to pass on whether the evidence presented by the police for a warrant was itself lawfully obtained—and thus if such a warrant is issued, the police have no reason to entertain a "good faith" belief that their pre-warrant evidence-gathering activity was lawful. The issue then becomes whether this pre-warrant evidence obtained in violation of the Fourth Amendment [which taints the subsequently-obtained search warrant] was itself secured by law enforcement officers sufficient to trigger the "good faith" or some other exception to the exclusionary rule.[121]

---

omitted). The 'shield of immunity' otherwise conferred by the warrant (citation omitted) will be lost, for example, where the warrant was 'based on an affidavit so lacking in indicia of probable cause as to render official belief in its existence entirely unreasonable.' (citation omitted).

"Our precedents make clear, however, that the threshold for establishing this exception is a high one, and it should be. As we explained in *Leon*, '[i]n the ordinary case, an officer cannot be expected to question the magistrate's probable cause determination' because 'it is the magistrate's responsibility to determine whether the officer's allegations establish probable cause and, if so, to issue a warrant comporting in form with the requirements of the Fourth Amendment.' (citation omitted)." Messerschmidt v. Millender, 565 U.S. ___, 132 S.Ct. 1235, 182 L.Ed.2d 47, 58–59 (2012).

Although *Messerschmidt* involves a qualified immunity defense against a civil suit brought to redress the alleged violation of Fourth Amendment rights, the same standard of objective reasonableness applicable to such a defense applies as well to the *Leon* "good faith" exception to the exclusionary rule. Messerschmidt v. Millender, 565 U.S. ___, 132 S.Ct. 1235, 182 L.Ed.2d 47, 58 n. 1(2012).

117. United States v. Leon, 468 U.S. 897, 104 S.Ct. 3405, 82 L.Ed.2d 677, 699 (1984). See: Groh v. Ramirez, 540 U.S. 551, 124 S.Ct. 1284, 157 L.Ed.2d 1068 (2004) (officer who executed a search warrant that contained *no description* of the things to be seized could not rely on an objective "good faith" qualified immunity defense under *Leon* in a *Bivens* civil suit brought against the officer).

118. See Messerschmidt v. Millender, 565 U.S. ___, 132 S.Ct. 1235, 182 L.Ed.2d 47, 58–59 (2012).

119. United States v. Leon, 468 U.S. 897, 104 S.Ct. 3405, 82 L.Ed.2d 677, 699 (1984); see Franks v. Delaware, 438 U.S. 154, 98 S.Ct. 2674, 57 L.Ed.2d 667 (1978). LaFave states that this circumstance "constitutes a rather small qualification to *Leon*, for defendants have rarely been successful in overcoming the problems of proof which attend a *Franks* attack upon a warrant." 1 Wayne LaFave, Search and Seizure § 1.3(f) at 92 (5th ed. 2012). For a discussion of when a false affidavit may not constitute a basis for a search warrant issued thereon, see Chapter 13, Section 2d of this work.

120. United States v. Leon, 468 U.S. 897, 107 S.Ct. 1160, 82 L.Ed.2d 677, 699 (1984); see Lo-Ji Sales, Inc. v. New York, 442 U.S. 319, 99 S.Ct. 2319, 60 L.Ed.2d 920 (1979); also see 1 Wayne LaFave, Search and Seizure § 1.3(f) at 93–96 (5th ed. 2012).

121. See generally 1 Wayne LaFave, Search and Seizure § 1.3(f) at 96–99 (5th ed. 2012).

(3) *Arrest or search based on a legislative enactment later declared unconstitutional*

The Court has also held that the exclusionary rule is inapplicable to evidence obtained by officers acting in objective reasonable reliance upon a statute or ordinance that specifically authorizes the officer to conduct a search or make an arrest which leads to a search—where the statute or ordinance is declared unconstitutional by a court *after* the search or arrest. This exception, however, is inapplicable if a reasonably well-trained officer would have known that the statute or ordinance was obviously unconstitutional—plainly, a high threshold of proof in order to establish, as passing on the constitutionality of such enactments is clearly a judicial function, not a police function.[122]

(4) *Arrest based on court-generated computer error*

The Court has held that the exclusionary rule is inapplicable to evidence obtained by officers incident to an arrest based on a police computer record indicating the existence of an outstanding arrest warrant—which record is later determined to be in error as the warrant had previously been quashed—where (a) the source of the error is *a court employee* who failed to notify the police that the warrant had been quashed, and (b) the police rely on this court-generated computer error in making an arrest.[123]

(5) *Arrest based on a negligent police computer error*

The Court has further held that the exclusionary rule does not apply to the fruits of an illegal arrest based on a negligent *police computer* error—one which was isolated and non-recurring in nature—that an outstanding arrest warrant existed against the arrestee, when the subject warrant had in fact been previously recalled.[124] The rationale for this

---

122. Illinois v. Krull, 480 U.S. 340, 107 S.Ct. 1160, 94 L.Ed.2d 364 (1987) (holding applies to legislative enactments authorizing arrest or search); also see the pre-*Leon* case of Michigan v. DeFillippo, 443 U.S. 31, 99 S.Ct. 2627, 61 L.Ed.2d 343 (1979) (arrest for violating a statute later declared unconstitutional—upheld as based on probable cause). "*Illinois v. Krull* [citation omitted], extended the good faith exception to searches conducted in reasonable reliance on subsequently invalidated statutes. *Id. At 349–350,* 107 S.Ct. 1160 ('legislators, like judicial officers, are not the focus of the rule')." Davis v. United States, 564 U.S. ___, 131 S.Ct. 2419, 2428, 180 L. Ed.2d 265 (2011).

123. Arizona v. Evans, 514 U.S. 1, 115 S.Ct. 1185, 131 L.Ed.2d 34 (1995). "*In Arizona v. Evans, supra,* the Court applied the good-faith exception in a case where the police reasonably relied on erroneous information concerning an arrest warrant in a database maintained by judicial employees." Davis v. United States, 564 U.S. ___, 131 S.Ct. 2419, 2428, 180 L. Ed.2d 265 (2011).

124. Herring v. United States 555 U.S. 135, 129 S.Ct. 695, 172 L.Ed.2d 496 (2009).

"The Fourth Amendment forbids 'unreasonable searches and seizures,' and this usually requires the police to have probable cause or a warrant before making an arrest. What if an officer reasonably believes that there is an outstanding arrest warrant, but that belief turns out to be wrong because of a negligent bookkeeping error by another police employee ? The parties here agree that the ensuing arrest is still a violation of the Fourth Amendment, but dispute whether contraband found during a search incident to that arrest must be excluded in a later prosecution.

"Our cases establish that such suppression is not an automatic consequence of a Fourth Amendment violation. Instead, the question turns on the culpability of the police and the potential of exclusion to deter wrongful police conduct. Here the error was the result of isolated negligence attenuated from the arrest. We hold that in these circumstances the jury should not be barred from considering all the evidence." Herring v. United States, 129 S.Ct. at 698.

In Herring, a county police officer arrested a man [Herring] after being informed by the police clerk of an adjoining county that the man had an outstanding arrest warrant in that county for failure to appear on a felony charge. The officer conducted a search incident to the arrest and seized a pistol result was that the exclusionary rule does not apply to negligent isolated police errors of this nature, but only to deliberate, *grossly* negligent, or reckless police conduct—as well as recurring or systemic police negligence.[125]

It is arguable, however [depending on the circumstances of the case], that the law enforcement agency responsible for the computer mistake may not be able to rely on such a factual mistake in the future after such a computer error has now been identified—as the agency may thereafter have to "clean up its act" and see to it that mistakes of this nature where innocent people are wrongly arrested do not continue to occur. If the police fail to take such corrective action, their conduct might be called "grossly negligent" and the exclusionary applicable. Moreover, the requirement of "recurring or endemic police negligence" in the operation of its computer system may only refer to when a litigant as *an initial matter* identifies the glitch in the system—not later when the glitch has already been brought to police attention. The Court, however, has not spoken to any of these issues.

(6) Search based on binding appellate precedent later overruled

The Court has held that the exclusionary rule is inapplicable to a search conducted in objectively reasonable reliance on a binding appellate precedent that validates the search, which decision was later overruled by the U.S. Supreme Court after the search was conducted.[126] The rationale for this decision is that the police could in no way be deterred by

---

from the man's person and illegal drugs from the car the man was driving. Shortly thereafter, however, the aforesaid police clerk discovered that the subject warrant had been recalled five months previously and immediately so informed the officer's department.

Normally, when a warrant is recalled in the adjoining police department, that fact is conveyed to the clerk who enters same in the police computer and the physical copy of the warrant is disposed of. In this case, however, the warrant was destroyed, but for whatever reason the recall of the warrant was never entered in the police computer database—so that the warrant information was erroneously still in the police computer.

Herring was indicted in federal court for illegally possessing the above gun and drugs. His motion to suppress same was denied by the trial court and Herring was convicted. The court of appeals and the U.S. Supreme Court affirmed.

See 1 Wayne LaFave, Search and Seizure § 1.6(i), at 284–313 (5th ed. 2012), for an extensive analysis and critique of the *Herring* decision.

125. "To trigger the exclusionary rule, police conduct must be sufficiently deliberate that exclusion can meaningfully deter it, and sufficiently culpable that such deterrence is worth the price paid by the justice system. As laid out in our cases, the exclusionary rule serves to deter deliberate, reckless, or grossly negligent conduct, or in some circumstances recurring or systemic negligence. The error in this case does not rise to that level. * * *

"In light of our repeated holdings that the deterrent effect of suppression must be substantial and outweigh any harm to the judicial system [citation omitted], we conclude that when police mistakes are the result of negligence such as that described here, rather than systemic error or reckless disregard of constitutional requirements, any marginal deterrence does not 'pay its way.' [citation omitted]. In such a case, the criminal should not 'go free because the constable has blundered.' [citation omitted]." Herring v. United States, 129 S.Ct. at 702, 704.

126. Davis v. United States , 564 U.S. ___ 131 S.Ct. 2419, 180 L.Ed.2d 285 (2011).

"The question here is whether to apply this [exclusionary] sanction when the police conduct a search in compliance with binding precedent that is later overruled. Because suppression would do nothing to deter police misconduct in these circumstances, and it because it would come at a high cost to both truth and public safety, we hold that searches conducted in objectively reasonable reliance on binding appellate precedent are not subject to the exclusionary rule. * * *

"The basic insight of the [good faith] *Leon* line of cases is that deterrence benefits of exclusion 'var[y] with the culpability of the law enforcement conduct' at issue. When the police exhibit 'deliberate,' 'reckless,' or 'grossly negligent' disregard for Fourth Amendment rights, the deterrent value of exclusion is strong and tends to outweigh the resulting costs. But when the police act with an objectively 'reasonable good-faith belief' that their conduct is lawful, or when their conduct involves only simple applying the exclusionary rule to this otherwise non-culpable conduct—as their action was in strict compliance with what the law was at the time of the search.[127]

There may be, however, one limitation to this ruling. This exception may not apply to the litigant who secures an overruling decision of the U.S. Supreme Court—even though this decision was rendered after the search under attack was conducted. This limitation may be necessary so as not to discourage litigants from seeking the U.S. Supreme Court to overrule one of its decisions and invalidate the search the litigant was subjected to.[128]

'isolated' negligence, the 'deterrence rationale loses much of its force' and exclusion cannot 'pay its way.'

"The Court has over time applied this good-faith exception over a range of cases."

Davis v. United States, 564 U.S. ___ 131 S.Ct. 2419, 2427–28, 180 L.Ed.2d 285 (2011).

In Davis, local police conducted a routine traffic stop of the Petitioner who was driving a car and later arrested him for DUI. Police also arrested an occupant in the car for giving a false name to the police. Both were handcuffed and placed in the back of separate patrol cars. Police then searched the passenger compartment of Petitioner's car and seized a revolver from inside the Petitioner's jacket. This search was conducted in full compliance with an 11th Circuit precedent [United States v. Gonzalez, 71 F.3d 819, 824–27 (11th Cir. 1996)] which interpreted New York v. Belton, 453 U.S. 454, 458–59, 101 L.Ed.2d 768 (1981), to allow law enforcement officials to search, as here, the passenger compartment of an auto after arresting an occupant of the auto, even though the occupant was handcuffed and was secured away from the car at the time of the search.

After the search was conducted, however, the U.S. Supreme Court overruled Belton in another case [Arizona v. Gant, 556 U.S. 322, 129 S.Ct. 1710, 173 L.Ed.2d 485 (2009)], thereby overruling Gonzalez as well. In the instant case, the U.S. Supreme Court held that Gant applied retroactively to the present case, but that the exclusionary rule was inapplicable under the good faith exception to the exclusionary rule. Davis v. United States, 564 U.S. ___ 131 S.Ct. 2419, 2424 2426–27, 180 L.Ed.2d 285 (2011) (internal citations omitted).

See 1 Wayne LaFave, Search and Seizure § 1.3(h) at 139–146 (5th ed. 2012), for an extensive analysis and critique of the Davis decision, concluding, "And thus Davis (which even appears to expand the breadth of Herring) shares with that decision a most troubling aspect: it looks like a recipe for the total abandonment of the Fourth Amendment exclusionary rule." Id. at 146.

127. "The search incident to Davis' arrest in this case followed the Eleventh Circuit's *Gonzalez* precedent to the letter. Although the search turned out to be unconstitutional under *Gant*, all agree that the officers' conduct with the then-binding Circuit law was not culpable in any way.

"Under our exclusionary rule precedent, this acknowledged absence of police culpability dooms Davis's claim. Police practices trigger the harsh sanction of exclusion only when they are deliberate enough to yield 'meaningful deterrence, and culpable enough to be worth to be 'worth the price paid by the judicial system.' The conduct of the officers here was neither of these things." Davis v. United States, 564 U.S. ___ 131 S.Ct. 2419, 2428,180 L.Ed.2d 285(2011) (internal citations omitted).

As an aside, Justice Sotomayor in her concurring opinion in Davis v. United States, 564 U.S. ___, 131 2419, 2435, 180 L.Ed.2d 285 (2011), points out that this case "does not present the markedly different question whether the exclusionary rule applies when the law governing the constitutionality of the search is unsettled."

Arguably, the conduct of a law enforcement officer might be characterized as "grossly negligent" [thus triggering the exclusionary rule] if the officer, faced with unclear legal authority, nonetheless proceeds with an otherwise unauthorized or questionable search or seizure. Surely, the incentive in cases of this nature should be for the officer to err in favor of respecting, rather than disregarding constitutional rights—and this consideration would argue in favor of imposing the exclusionary rule here. Compare United States v. Johnson, 457 U.S. 537, 561, 102 S.Ct. 2579, 73 L.Ed.2d 202 (1982).

128. "Davis argues that the Fourth Amendment precedents of *this* Court will be effectively insulated from challenge under a good exception for reliance on appellate precedent. * * *

"At most, Davis' argument might suggest that—to prevent Fourth Amendment law from becoming ossified—the petitioner in a case that results in the overruling of one of this Court's precedents should be given the victory by permitting the suppression of evidence in that one case. Such a result would undoubtedly be a windfall to this one random litigant. But the exclusionary rule is 'not a personal constitutional right'. It is a 'judicially created' sanction specifically designed as a 'windfall' to deter

d. Knock and announce violation

We come now to the fourth and final exception to the exclusionary rule in the context of a criminal trial. Evidence secured from private premises pursuant to a valid search warrant after law enforcement officers forcibly have entered the premises in violation of the "knock and announce" doctrine[129] is admissible in evidence as an exception to the Fourth Amendment exclusionary rule.[130] The Court engaged in a balancing process to reach this holding, concluding that the social costs of applying the exclusionary rule to "knock and announce" violations outweighed whatever deterrence benefits might be gained from such an application. In particular, the Court was impressed with the deterrence benefits that already exist from (a) civil suits, and (b) the increasing professionalism of police forces—benefits that were not present to the extent they were at the time Mapp v. Ohio was decided in 1961.[131]

Section 6. Miscellaneous Procedural and Appellate Considerations: Alternative Civil Remedy

a. Motion to suppress: evidentiary hearing and burden of proof

It is settled that the court, not a jury, must determine whether evidence allegedly seized in violation of a defendant's Fourth Amendment rights is admissible in evidence at a criminal trial.[132] In the federal courts and most state jurisdictions, the usual procedural method by which this issue is raised is a pre-trial motion to suppress filed by the defendant seeking the suppression of any evidence obtained by government agents in violation of the defendant's Fourth Amendment rights. A pre-trial evidentiary hearing is then held by the court in which evidence is received, and the court decides the disputed issues of fact and law.[133]

---

future Fourth Amendment violations. The good faith exception is a judicially created exception to this judicially created rule. *Therefore in a future case, we could, if necessary, recognize a limited exception to the good-faith exception for a defendant who obtains a judgment over-ruling one of our Fourth Amendment precedents*." Davis v. United States, 564 U.S. ___ 131 S.Ct. 2419, 2433–34, 180 L.Ed.2d 285 (2011) (internal citations omitted) (emphasis added).

129. See Ch. 13, Sec. 4 for a discussion of the "knock-and-announce" requirements which law enforcement must follow when executing a search warrant.

130. Hudson v. Michigan, 547 U.S. 586, 126 S.Ct. 2159, 2165–68, 165 L.Ed.2d 56 (2006). "In sum, the social costs of applying the exclusionary rule to knock-and-announce violations are considerable; the incentives to such violations are minimal to begin with, and the extant deterrence against them are substantial—incomparably greater than the factors deterring warrantless entries when Mapp was decided. Resort to the massive remedy of suppressing evidence of guilt is unjustified." 126 S.Ct. at 2168.

The Court also concluded, as an alternative holding, that evidence secured on private premises pursuant to a valid search warrant following a "knock and announce" violation is so attenuated as to dissipate the taint of such violation, and is therefore not barred from evidence by the "fruit of the poisonous tree" doctrine. See Ch. 17, Sec. 3b(5) of this supplement.

131. Hudson v. Michigan, 547 U.S. 586, 126 S.Ct. 2159, 2167–68, 165 L.Ed. 56 (2006).

132. Steele v. United States, 267 U.S. 505, 45 S.Ct. 417, 69 L.Ed. 761, 764 (1925).

133. 6 Wayne LaFave, Search and Seizure § 11.2(a)(b) (5th ed. 2012); Fed.R.Crim.P. 12 (b)(3)(C) 41 (fh; see cases collected at "Criminal Law" § 394.6(1)(2)(3)(4)(5) West Key Nos.

At the hearing on the motion to suppress, the rules of evidence normally applicable in criminal trials are relaxed—so that hearsay evidence is generally admissible, although the evidentiary rules of privilege appear applicable.[134] On the other hand, where the evidence sought to be suppressed was seized pursuant to a search warrant, the probable cause for the issuance of the warrant must have been presented to the magistrate who issued the warrant, and cannot be supplemented by testimony adduced at the motion-to-suppress hearing.[135] If the defendant testifies at this hearing, this testimony is inadmissible at trial as substantive evidence of guilt,[136] although it might arguably be admissible to impeach the defendant as a witness at trial.[137]

At the hearing on the motion to suppress, it is important to determine which party has the burden of proof—i.e., the burden of going forward with the evidence and the burden of persuasion—to establish that the "Standing" and "Unreasonableness" requirements for a Fourth Amendment violation have been met.[138] If the party with the burden of proof in both senses fails to present any evidence, or presents evidence that leaves the trial court in doubt, the result must necessarily be an adverse ruling against that party.[139] The Court's decisions to date weigh heavily in favor of placing that burden on the defendant, but with some important limitations.

As to the "Standing Requirement," the Court seems to have placed the burden of proof squarely on the defendant.[140] But if the "Standing Requirement" goes unchallenged by the

---

134. United States v. Matlock, 415 U.S. 164, 94 S.Ct. 988, 39 L.Ed.2d 242, 250–52 (1974); "Criminal Law" § 394.6(4) West Key No.

135. Spinelli v. United States, 393 U.S. 410, 89 S.Ct. 584, 21 L.Ed.2d 637, 642 n. 3 (1969); Whitely v. Warden of Wyo., State Penitentiary, 401 U.S. 560, 91 S.Ct. 1031, 28 L.Ed.2d 306, 311 n. 8 (1971).

136. Simmons v. United States, 390 U.S. 377, 88 S.Ct. 967, 19 L.Ed.2d 1247 (1968).

137. Compare Harris v. New York, 401 U.S. 222, 91 S.Ct. 643, 28 L.Ed.2 1 (1971) (a *Miranda*-barred confession may nonetheless be used to impeach a defendant who testifies at trial). But cf. 6 Wayne LaFave, Search and Seizure § 11.2(d) at 83–87 (5th ed. 2012), which suggests that *Harris* may be inapplicable to a defendant's motion-to-suppress testimony in view of New Jersey v. Portash, 440 U.S. 450, 99 S.Ct. 1292, 59 L.Ed.2d 501 (1979) (defendant's grand jury testimony given under a grant of immunity could not be used to impeach the defendant's trial testimony).

138. For a thorough discussion of the burden-of-proof rules on motions to suppress in cases at the federal and state level, see 6 Wayne LaFave, Search and Seizure § 11.2(b) (5th ed. 2012); 2 John Wesley Hall, Search and Seizure § 60.45 (5th ed. 2012). The "Standing Requirement" and "Unreasonableness Requirement" for a Fourth Amendment violation are discussed at Chapters 8–10 and 11–16, respectively, of this work. Also see "Criminal Law" § 394.5(4), and "Searches and Seizures"§§ 192.1, 193, 194, West Key Nos. for more cases on this issue.

139. 6 Wayne LaFave, Search and Seizure § 11.2(b) at 49 (5th ed. 2012)

140. Jones v. United States, 362 U.S. 257, 261, 80 S.Ct. 725, 4 L.Ed.2d 697, 702 (1960) ("Ordinarily, then, it is entirely proper to require of one who seeks to challenge the legality of a search as a basis for suppression of relevant evidence that he allege, and that if the allegation be disputed that he establish, that he himself was the victim of the invasion of privacy."); Rakas v. Illinois, 439 U.S. 128, 130, fn.1, 99 S.Ct. 421, 58 L.Ed.2d 387 (1978) ("The proponent of a motion to suppress has the burden of establishing that his own Fourth Amendment rights were violated.") Rawlings v. Kentucky, 448 U.S. 98, 104, 100 S.Ct. 2556, 65 L.Ed.2d 633, 641 (1980) ("Petitioner [the defendant], of course, bears the burden of proving not only that the search of Cox's [a third party] purse was illegal, but also that he had a legitimate expectation of privacy in that purse."); see also Florida v. Riley, 488 U.S. 445, 109 S.Ct. 693, 102 L.Ed.2d 835, 843 (1989) (plurality) (police surveillance of a greenhouse in defendant's residential backyard, using a helicopter hovering 400 feet above the greenhouse, did not constitute an invasion of defendant's reasonable expectation of privacy in the greenhouse or home and therefore was not a Fourth Amendment search; "there is [no] intimation here that the helicopter interfered with [defendant]'s normal use of the greenhouse or of the parts of the curtilage," and "[a]s far as the record reveals, no intimate details connected with the use of the home or curtilage were observed."); Florida v. Riley, 102 L.Ed.2d at 845 (O'Connor, J. concurring) ("In my view, the defendant must bear the burden of proving that his expectation of privacy was a reasonable one, and thus a

prosecution at the trial level and is raised for the first time on appeal, an appellate court cannot sustain a denial of a motion to suppress for failure of the defendant to establish this requirement, but must remand for an evidentiary hearing on that issue.[141]

As to the "Unreasonableness Requirement," the Court also seems to have squarely placed the burden of proof on the defendant.[142] But this defense burden appears *prima facie* satisfied upon a showing that the search or seizure was carried out without a warrant, because presumptively a search conducted without a search warrant is considered per se unreasonable,[143] and a warrantless seizure of property is subject to a similar rule.[144] At that point, the burden shifts to the prosecution to establish that the warrantless search or seizure was nonetheless reasonable[145]—i.e., (1) that the warrantless search fits within one of the exceptions to the general rule requiring that searches must be conducted with

---

'search' within the meaning of the Fourth Amendment); "On this basis, it might be said that the prevailing rule that the defendant has the burden [of proof] with respect to standing is sound, for the matter of standing usually concerns the defendant's interest in an expectation of privacy concerning the place searched or the objects seized, about which the defendant will be the most knowledgeable." 6 Wayne LaFave, Search and Seizure § 11.2(b) at 62–63 54th ed. 2012).

141. Combs v. United States, 408 U.S. 224, 92 S.Ct. 2284, 33 L.Ed.2d 308 (1972).

142. Rawlings v. Kentucky, 448 U.S. 98, 104, 100 S.Ct. 2556, 65 L.Ed.2d 633, 641 (1980) ("Petitioner [the defendant], of course, bears the burden of proving not only that the search of Cox's [a third party] purse was illegal, but also that he had a legitimate expectation of privacy in that purse."); Rakas v. Illinois, 439 U.S. 128, 130, fn.1, 99 S.Ct. 421, 58 L.Ed.2d 387 (1978) ("The proponent of a motion to suppress has the burden of establishing that his own Fourth Amendment rights were violated.").

143. "Searches conducted without warrants have been held unlawful 'notwithstanding facts unquestionably showing probable cause,' for the Constitution requires 'that the deliberate impartial, judgment of a judicial officer be interposed between the citizen and the police ...' 'Over and again this Court has emphasized that the mandate of the [Fourth] Amendment requires adherence to judicial processes,' and that searches conducted outside the judicial process, without prior approval by judge or magistrate, are per se unreasonable under the Fourth Amendment—subject only to a few specifically established and well-delineated exceptions." Katz v. United States, 389 U.S. 347, 357, 88 S.Ct. 507, 19 L.Ed.2d 576, 585 (1967) (internal and footnoted citations omitted). This formulation has been quoted with approval in Mincey v. Arizona, 437 U.S. 385, 390, 98 S.Ct. 2408, 57 L.Ed.2d 290, 298–99 (1978); Colorado v. Bannister, 449 U.S. 1, 2, 101 S.Ct. 42, 66 L.Ed.2d 1, 3 (1980); Thompson v. Louisiana, 469 U.S. 17, 105 S.Ct. 409, 83 L.Ed.2d 246, 250 (1984); Minnesota v. Dickerson, 508 U.S. 366, 113 S.Ct. 2130, 124 L.Ed.2d 334, 343–44 (1993).

144. "In order to enforce that [Fourth Amendment] requirement [of reasonableness], this Court has interpreted the Amendment as establishing rules and presumptions designed to control law enforcement officers that may significantly intrude upon privacy interests. Sometimes those rules require warrants. We have said, for example, that in 'the ordinary case' seizures of personal property are 'unreasonable within the meaning of the Fourth Amendment,' without more, 'unless ... accomplished pursuant to a judicial warrant,' issued by a neutral magistrate after finding probable cause. We nonetheless have made it clear that there are exceptions to the warrant requirement." Illinois v. McArthur, 531 U.S. 326, 121 S.Ct. 946, 148 L.Ed.2d 838, 847 (2001) "In the ordinary case, the Court has viewed a seizure of personal property as per se unreasonable within the meaning of the Fourth Amendment unless it is accomplished pursuant to a judicial warrant issued upon probable cause and particularly describing the items to be seized." United States v. Place, 462 U.S. 696, 103 S.Ct. 2637, 77 L.Ed.2d 110, 116 (1983).

145. For a discussion of the warrant requirement rules that presumptively require warrants for searches, and place the burden of proof on the prosecution to establish an exception thereto in a given case, see Chapter 11, Section 1of this work; also see Chapter 12, Section 2a of this work for a similar requirement relating to the warrantless seizure of property.

"With respect to the issue which is usually central in a motion to suppress hearing—the reasonableness of the challenged search or seizure—most states follow the rule which is utilized in the federal courts: if the search or seizure was pursuant to a warrant, the defendant has the burden of proof; but if the police acted without a warrant the burden of proof is on the prosecution." 6 Wayne LaFave, Search and Seizure§ 11.2(b) at 50 (5th ed. 2012).

a warrant,[146] or (2) that the warrantless seizure of property fits within one of the exceptions to the general rule requiring that seizures of property must be conducted with a warrant,[147] or (3) that a warrantless seizure of a person was based on probable cause or reasonable suspicion.[148]

On the other hand, if a *search* is conducted with a search warrant, there is a presumption in favor of the validity of the warrant, at least on the issue of probable cause;[149] the burden of proof is therefore clearly on the defendant to show that the search warrant is invalid for lack of probable cause. The defendant may also have the same burden of proof as to facial validity of the warrant, its execution, and other related issues.[150] By analogy, the same approach would seem to hold true where a *seizure* of a person or property is conducted with a warrant; such seizures also appear presumptively reasonable, and the defendant has the burden of showing otherwise.[151]

The party with the burden of proof on a motion-to-suppress hearing must satisfy its burden by a preponderance of the evidence, but is subject to no higher standard.[152]

b. Preservation of error doctrine

In order for the U.S. Supreme Court or any appellate court to review a Fourth Amendment question, it is essential that the issues involved be properly raised in the courts below by both the defendant and the prosecution in a criminal case. This doctrine, generally speaking, requires that an appropriate objection be made to the evidence sought to be suppressed, and that the basic Fourth Amendment arguments for and against such suppressed evidence also be raised, else the appellate court will generally not entertain the Fourth Amendment point on the merits. Ordinarily, the *defendant* properly preserves a Fourth Amendment issue for appellate review by: (a) filing a pre-trial motion to suppress based on Fourth Amendment grounds and litigating the issue in a pre-trial evidentiary hearing in which the basic arguments urged on appeal are urged in the trial court; (b)

---

146. For a detailed discussion of the criminal and civil or administrative exceptions to the search warrant requirement rule, see Chapters 14 and 15 of this work.

147. For a discussion of the exceptions to the rule that seizures must be conducted with a warrant, see Chapter 12, Section 2b of this work.

148. For a discussion of the reasonableness of warrantless seizures of the person, see Chapter 12, Section 1 of this work.

149. "There is, of course, a presumption of validity with respect to the affidavit supporting the search warrant." Franks v. Delaware, 438 U.S. 154, 98 S.Ct. 2674, 57 L.Ed.2d 667, 682 (1978). "Although in a particular case it may not be easy to determine when an affidavit [for a search warrant] demonstrates the existence of probable cause, the resolution of doubtful or marginal cases should be largely determined by the preference to be accorded to warrants." United States v. Ventresca, 380 U.S. 102, 109, 85 S.Ct. 741, 13 L.Ed.2d 684, 689 (1965).

150. "[A] search with a warrant has a stronger claim to justification on later, judicial review than a search without one." Illinois v. McArthur, 531 U.S. 326, 121 S.Ct. 946, 148 L.Ed.2d 838 (2001) (Souter, J. concurring), citing 5 Wayne LaFave, Search and Seizure § 11.2(b) at 38 (3d ed. 1996) [now 6 LaFave, Search and Seizure § 11.2(b) at 50 (5th ed. 2012)]. ("[M]ost states follow the rule which is utilized in the federal courts: if the search or seizure was pursuant to a warrant, the defendant has the burden of proof; but if the police acted without a warrant the burden of proof is on the prosecution.").

151. See 6 Wayne LaFave, Search and Seizure § 11.2(b) at 50 (5th ed. 2012).

152. "In any event, the controlling burden of proof at suppression hearings should impose no greater burden than proof by a preponderance of the evidence." United States v. Matlock, 415 U.S. 164, 177, fn. 14, 94 S.Ct. 988, 39 L.Ed.2d 242, 253 (1974).

renewing the motion with a proper objection when the alleged illegal evidence is offered in evidence at trial, and (c) raising the same motion-to-suppress issues again on appeal.[153]

Occasionally, the Supreme Court will relax this preservation requirement where the Court is convinced that the issue was otherwise properly litigated below—(1) as where the issue is raised by the defendant at trial in the state court on a motion for directed verdict, provided there was no strategic trial reason why the defendant declined to contemporaneously object to the alleged illegal evidence at trial,[154] or (2) where the state appellate court, in fact, decides the Fourth Amendment issue on appeal, although the issue may not have been preserved at trial.[155] Where, however, either the defendant or the prosecution fails to make an argument on the merits in the courts below, and raises it for the first time before the U.S. Supreme Court, the Court ordinarily will refuse to consider the argument on the merits.[156] Moreover, non-jurisdictional defects of this nature must be raised by the respondent in the brief in opposition to the petition for certiorari, and cannot be raised for the first time in respondent's brief on the merits, else the point is waived.[157]

---

153. For a discussion of the subject of a defendant's waiver of Fourth Amendment issues for appellate review, see 6 Wayne LaFave, Search and Seizure § 11.1(a)(b) (5th ed. 2012).

154. Henry v. Mississippi, 379 U.S. 443, 85 S.Ct. 564, 13 L.Ed.2d 408, 413–14 (1965).

155. Chambers v. Maroney, 399 U.S. 42, 90 S.Ct. 1975, 26 L.Ed.2d 419, 425 n. 5 (1970); Franks v. Delaware 438 U.S. 154, 98 S.Ct. 2674, 57 L.Ed.2d 667, 675–76 (1978).

156. Giordenello v. United States, 357 U.S. 480, 78 S.Ct. 1245, 2 L.Ed.2d 1503,1510–11 (1958) (Court declines to entertain Government's argument that the defendant's arrest pursuant to an arrest warrant was lawful, apart from the warrant, as being based on probable cause—when government did not make that argument at trial); Brown v. United States, 411 U.S. 223, 93 S.Ct. 1565, 36 L.Ed.2d 208, 214 n. 4 (1973) (Court refuses to entertain defendant's "standing" argument based on defendant's alleged property interest and constructive possession in the property seized—when defendant did not made this argument in the courts below or in the certiorari petition to the Court); Hayes v. Florida, 470 U.S. 811, 105 S.Ct. 1643, 84 L.Ed.2d 705, 709 n. 1 (1985) (Court refuses to entertain state's argument that the inevitable discovery rule was applicable here—when this argument was never made or passed on in the state courts below); Illinois v. Gates, 462 U.S. 213, 103 S.Ct. 2317, 76 L.Ed.2d 527, 535 (1983) (Court declines to consider state's argument that the good faith exception to the exclusionary rule is applicable to this case—when this argument was never made or passed on in the state courts below); Arizona v. Hicks, 480 U.S. 321, 107 S.Ct. 1149, 94 L.Ed.2d 347, 357 (1987) (same). Ker v. California, 374 U.S. 23, 83 S.Ct. 1623, 10 L.Ed.2d 726, 744 (1963) (Court refuses to entertain defendant's contention at oral argument that the search of his car violated his Fourth Amendment rights—when he did not raise this issue in the state courts and the issue was not passed on by the state courts, nor was the issue raised by the defendant in his certiorari petition to the Court or brief in support thereof). Whitely v. Warden, Wyo. Penitentiary, 401 U.S. 560, 91 S.Ct.1031, 28 L.Ed.2d 306, 314 (1971) (Court rejects state's procedural argument that the case should be sent back to the state courts to develop facts showing that the magistrate issuing the arrest warrant had other information, besides the sworn complaint, upon which to issue the arrest warrant—where the state had relied on the record below in the state courts and never claimed that the record was incomplete); Illinois v. McArthur, 531 U.S. 326, 121 S.Ct. 946, 148 L.Ed.2d 838, 850 (2001) (Court refuses to entertain defendant's argument that police proceeded without probable cause in barring him from entering his residence while a search warrant for the residence was being obtained, as defendant did not make this argument in the state court below); United States v. Jones, 565 U.S. ___, 132 S.Ct. 945, 132 S.Ct. 945, 181 L.Ed.2d 911, 923 (2012) (Government argument that installation of GPS device on undercarriage of Jeep was based on probable cause or reasonable suspicion held waived as argument was not raised in the appellate court below, the DC Circuit Court of Appeals); Florida v. Harris, 568 U.S. ____, 133 S.Ct. 1050 , 185 L.Ed.2d 61, 70 (2013) (Court declines to entertain defendant's argument concerning the adequacy of the training program given a narcotics-sniffing police dog, as well as the dog's performance in such program, as the defendant failed to make that argument in the state trial court below).

157. Knowles v. Iowa, 525 U.S. 113, 119 S.Ct. 484, 142 L.Ed.2d 492, 497 n. 2 (1998) (Iowa waived its *res judicata* argument that petitioner's Fourth Amendment claim was barred when petitioner failed

c. Standard of appellate review

It is settled that a trial court's findings of historical fact involving a search or seizure are reviewed on appeal under a deferential standard of *clear error*. That is, the trial court's findings of what historically happened during the search or seizure in question must be accepted on appeal unless clearly erroneous—and due weight must be given to the inferences that trial judges and local law enforcement officers draw from those facts.[158] The U.S. Supreme Court has held that a finding of fact is "clearly erroneous when although there is evidence to support it, the reviewing court on the entire evidence is left with the definite and firm conviction that a mistake has been committed."[159]

On the other hand, a trial court's *legal conclusion*, based on these historical facts, that the search or seizure in question was or was not based on probable cause or reasonable suspicion is subject to a *de novo* standard of review on appeal—and is not subject to a deferential clear error standard. That is, given the relevant historical facts, the appellate court may determine as an initial matter whether the search or seizure is or is not based on probable cause or reasonable suspicion.[160]

Similarly, in a civil suit for violation of one's Fourth Amendment rights, all reasonable factual inferences must be resolved on appeal in favor of the jury or non-jury verdict. But whether those historical facts legally amount to a violation of the Fourth Amendment is reviewed based on a *de novo* standard.[161]

d. Harmless error doctrine

If a trial court commits error in denying a motion to suppress and in admitting evidence at trial in violation of the defendant's Fourth Amendment rights, the error is *presumptively* considered reversible, thereby requiring a reversal of the criminal conviction under review and a remand with directions to exclude the illegally obtained evidence at a new trial. The prosecution, however, can avoid such a result by demonstrating that this constitutional error was harmless beyond a reasonable doubt—that is, that there is no reasonable possibility that the admission of the complained-of evidence contributed to the defendant's conviction.[162] In that event, the appellate court is required to affirm the defendant's conviction, notwithstanding the trial court's error in admitting evidence at trial in violation of the defendant's Fourth Amendment rights.

---

to seek certiorari review of a companion conviction in which an identical Fourth Amendment claim was rejected by the Iowa Supreme Court—because Iowa failed to raise the point in its brief in opposition to the petition for certiorari and raised it for first time in its brief on the merits).

158. Ornelas v. United States, 517 U.S. 690, 116 S.Ct. 1657, 134 L.Ed.2d 911, 920 (1996); see also Lustig v. United States, 338 U.S. 74, 77, 69 S.Ct. 1372, 93 L.Ed. 1819, 1822–23 (1949), and cases collected at "Searches and Seizures" §§ 195.1, 200, 201 West Key Nos.

159. Pullman-Standard v. Swint, 456 U.S. 273, 284, n.14, 102 S.Ct. 1781, 72 L.Ed.2d 66, 77 n. 14 (1982) (internal citation omitted); 6 Wayne LaFave, Search and Seizure § 11.7(c) at 557–558 (5th ed. 2012).

160. Ornelas v. United States, 517 U.S. 690, 116 S.Ct. 1657, 134 L.Ed.2d 911, 920 (1996).

161. Muehler v. Mena, 544 U.S. 93, 125 S.Ct. 1465, 1470, n. 1, 161 L.Ed. 2d 299 (2005).

162. "We prefer the approach of this Court in deciding what was harmless error in our recent case of Fahy v. Connecticut, 375 U.S. 85, 84 S.Ct. 229, 11 L.Ed.2d 171 (1963). There we said: 'The question is whether there is a reasonable possibility that the evidence complained of might have contributed to the conviction.' Id., at 86–87, 11 L.Ed.2d at 173. * * * We therefore do no more that adhere to the meaning of our Fahy Case when we hold, as we do now, that before a federal constitutional error can be held harmless, the court must be able to declare a belief that it was harmless beyond a reasonable doubt." Chapman v. California, 386 U.S. 18, 23–24, 87 S.Ct. 824, 17 L.Ed.2d 705, 710 (1967).

The Court has cautioned, however, that the harmless error doctrine can work very unfair and mischievous results when, for example, highly important and persuasive evidence, though legally forbidden, finds its way into a trial in which the question of guilt or innocence is a close one.[163] It is only where the evidence of guilt in the case, aside from the illegally obtained evidence, is so powerful and so convincing that the court can declare beyond a reasonable doubt that the subject illegal evidence could not reasonably have contributed to the defendant's conviction—that the subject error can be declared harmless and the defendant's conviction affirmed.[164]

Moreover, the test is *not* whether the evidence, aside from the illegally obtained evidence, was *legally sufficient* to convict the defendant. Evidence that is technically sufficient evidence to convict, so as to survive a defense directed-verdict motion at trial, need not necessarily be convincing evidence to a trier of fact. The additional illegally seized evidence, which is often very powerful evidence, may very well be needed to persuade the fact-finder that the defendant is guilty beyond a reasonable doubt. The test is whether the illegally seized evidence *contributed* to the conviction, not whether its presence was *legally necessary* in order to defeat a defense motion for a directed verdict. To apply the test, the appellate court must examine the weight and persuasive force of the prosecution's untainted evidence, the strength of any defense or any impeachment evidence offered in the case, and the persuasive force of the illegally obtained evidence. It is usually in the so-called "slam-dunk" cases—where a guilty verdict was the only reasonable result the trier of fact could have returned based on the untainted evidence—that the appellate court can conclude beyond a reasonable doubt that the tainted evidence did not contribute to the conviction. Obviously, this is a judgment call that is often difficult to make based on a cold appellate record, but all reasonable doubts on the issue must be resolved in favor of the defendant.

e. Adequate-and-independent state ground doctrine

When a state court *expressly* interprets its state constitution or statutes on search and seizure to give greater rights to the individual than that guaranteed by the Fourth Amendment, as it is free to do, such a decision is insulated from U.S. Supreme Court review under the adequate-and-independent state ground doctrine upon a petition for certiorari review filed by the state. This result is not changed by the fact that the state court rests its decision on *both* the Fourth Amendment and state law as alternative grounds—so long as the decision contains a plain statement to that effect. On the other hand, where, as is often the case, the state court decision cites and discusses both federal and state cases and does *not* contain a plain statement that its decision is based in whole or in part on state law grounds, the Court assumes that the state court decided the case the way it did because it believed that federal law required it to do so, and is free to assume jurisdiction in the cause.[165]

---

163. Chapman v. California, 386 U.S. 18, 22, 87 S.Ct. 824, 17 L.Ed.2d 705, 710 (1967); Whitely v. Warden, Wyo. Penitentiary, 401 U.S. 560, 569 n. 13, 91 S.Ct. 1031, 28 L.Ed.2d 306, 314 n. 13 (1971) (error in admitting illegally seized burglary tools and the fruits of a burglary in a prosecution for burglary and habitual criminal status held not harmless, even though there was criminal accomplice testimony in the case).

164. For a thorough discussion of the *Chapman* harmless error doctrine, see 6 Wayne LaFave, Search and Seizure § 11.7(f) (5th ed. 2012).

165. Michigan v. Long, 463 U.S. 1032, 103 S.Ct. 3469, 77 L.Ed.2d 1201, 1214, 1216 (1983). For cases in which the state court decision *fails* to contain a plain statement that its decision is based on its state constitution and law on search and seizure, thereby giving the Court jurisdiction to review the case, see Ohio v. Robinette, 519 U.S. 33, 117 S.Ct. 417, 136 S.Ct. 347, 353 (1996); Illinois v.

f. Retroactive application of Fourth Amendment appellate decisions[166]

An issue sometimes arises as to whether a given Fourth Amendment decision of the U.S. Supreme Court should be applied to a pending case when the subject decision had *not* been decided at the time of the search or seizure involved in the case, but was instead an intervening decision decided *after* the search but before the trial. It is sometimes argued that this new decision should play no part in the trial or appellate court's decision in the pending case, and should not be retroactively applied. The issue becomes particularly difficult when the intervening decision drastically changes the law on the subject.

The Court has followed a zig-zag course in deciding this issue.[167] Without reciting all the Court's twists and turns, the current law is that when a U.S. Supreme Court decision announces a "new" constitutional rule of criminal procedure,[168] the new rule is generally prospective only—i.e., it applies only (1) to *trials* conducted *after* the new rule was announced, and (2) to cases pending on direct review at the time the new rule was announced. But the new rule does *not* apply retroactively to any case that became "final"[169] before the new rule was announced; it therefore is generally inapplicable to collateral attack proceedings, such as a federal habeas corpus action that seeks to overturn a state criminal conviction.[170] The states, nonetheless, are free to apply or not apply a new Fourth Amendment rule retroactively in a state collateral attack proceeding. There are, however, two situations where such a new rule of constitutional criminal procedure *must* be applied retroactively, neither of which are applicable to Fourth Amendment claims: where the

---

Rodriguez, 497 U.S. 177, 110 S.Ct. 2793, 111 L.Ed.2d 148, 157 (1990): New York v. Class, 475 U.S. 106, 106 S.Ct. 960, 89 L.Ed.2d 81, 88 (1986); Arizona v. Evans, 514 U.S. 1, 115 S.Ct. 1185, 131 L.Ed.2d 34, 42–43 (1995); California v. Carney, 471 U.S. 386, 105 S.Ct. 2066, 85 L.Ed.2d 406, 412 n. 1 (1985).

166. See also Chapter 7, Section 3c, supra, of this work.

167. For a discussion of the Court's line of decisions on this issue, see generally 6 Wayne LaFave., Search and Seizure § 11.5 (5h ed. 2012). It all began with Linkletter v. Walker, 381 U.S. 618, 85 S.Ct. 1731, 14 L.Ed.2d 601 (1965), in which the Court held that the rule of Mapp v. Ohio did *not* apply retroactively and thus was inapplicable to any post-conviction collateral attack proceeding. This was done primarily because of the enormous disruptive effect on the administration of justice if the Mapp exclusionary rule were retroactively applied to finalized convictions in the 24 states that had no exclusionary rule prior thereto.

168. "In general, however, a case announces a new rule when it breaks new ground or imposes a new obligation on the States or Federal Government. [citations omitted]. To put it differently, a case announces a new rule if the result was not dictated by precedent existing at the time the defendant's conviction became final." Teague v. Lane, 489 U.S. 288, 301, 109 S.Ct. 1060, 103 L.Ed.2d 334, 349 (1989). "And a holding is not so dictated ... unless it would have been apparent to all reasonable jurists." Chaidez v. United States, 568 U.S. ___, 133 S.Ct. 1103, 185 L.Ed.2d 149, 156 (2013) (internal citation and quotation marks omitted).

169. The Court has defined "final" to mean when the judgment of conviction has been rendered, the availability of appeal exhausted, and the time for a petition to the U.S. Supreme Court has either elapsed or such certiorari petition has been denied. Linkletter v. Walker, 381 U.S. 618, 85 S.Ct. 1731, 14 L.Ed.2d 601, 608, n. 8 (1965); see Allen v. Hardy, 478 U.S. 255, 258 n.1, 106 S.Ct. 2878, 92 L.Ed.2d 199, 204 n.1 (1986) (adopting the aforesaid Linkletter definition of "final").

170. As an aside, Fourth Amendment issues can *only* be raised by a state prisoner in a federal habeas corpus proceeding where the state has not accorded the prisoner an opportunity for a full and fair litigation of his or her Fourth Amendment claim in state court.; otherwise, such issues are precluded from federal habeas corpus review. Stone v. Powell, 428 U.S. 465, 96 S.Ct. 3037, 49 L.Ed.2d 1067 (1976).

new rule places certain individual conduct beyond the power of a state to proscribe, or a watershed rule that implicates the fundamental fairness of a criminal trial.[171]

On the other hand, where the U.S. Supreme Court decision announces no new constitutional rule of criminal procedure but merely applies settled precedents to a new and different factual situation, the decision is fully retroactive.[172] Finally, it would appear that all pre-*Teague* precedents on the issue of retroactivity remain intact.[173]

g. Alternative civil remedy: *Bivens* suit and § 1983 suit

In addition to the exclusionary rule, the U.S. Supreme Court has fashioned another remedy to enforce Fourth Amendment freedoms in accord with the original intention of the Framers. In *Bivens v. Six Unknown Named Agents of Federal Bureau of Narcotics*,[174] the Court held that a civil suit for money damages lies against a federal officer for any injuries suffered by a person as a result of the officer's violation of the person's Fourth Amendment

---

171. "New constitutional rules announced by this Court that place certain kinds of primary individual conduct beyond the power of the States to proscribe, as well as 'watershed' rules of criminal procedure must be applied in all future trials, all cases on direct review, and all federal habeas corpus proceedings. All other new rules of criminal procedure must be applied in future trials and in cases pending on direct review, but may not be the basis for a federal collateral attack on a state conviction. This is the substance of the 'Teague' rule described by Justice O'Connor in her plurality opinion in Teague v. Lane, 489 U.S. 288, 109 S.Ct. 1060, 103 L.Ed.2d 334 (1989). The question in this case is whether Teague constrains the authority of the state courts to give broader effect to new rules of criminal procedure than is required by that opinion. We have never suggested that it does, and now hold that it does not." Danforth v. Minnesota, 552 U.S. 264, 128 S.Ct. 1029, 1032–33, 169 L.Ed.2d 859 (2008) (footnote omitted in which the Court notes that the Teague rule has since been adopted by Perry v. Lynaugh, 492 U.S. 302, 313, 109 S.Ct. 2934, 106 L.Ed.2d 256 (1989)).

"Justice O'Connor [in Teague] endorsed a general rule of nonretroactivity for cases on collateral review stating that unless they fall within an exception to the general rule, new constitutional rules of criminal procedure will not be applicable to those cases that become final before the new rules are announced. The opinion defined two exceptions: rules that render types of primary conduct beyond the power of the criminal law-making authority to proscribe, and watershed rules that implicate the fundamental fairness of the trial." Danforth v. Minnesota, 128 S.Ct. at 1037–38 (internal citations and quotation marks eliminated).

172. "First, when a decision of this Court merely has applied settled precedents to new and different factual situations, no real question has arisen as to whether the later decision should apply retroactively. In such cases, it is a foregone conclusion that the rule of the later case applies in earlier cases, because the later decision has not in fact altered that rule in any material way. [citations omitted]." United States v. Johnson,457 U.S. 537, 549, 102 S.Ct. 2579, 73 L.Ed.2d 202, 213 (1982). "[A] case does not announce a new rule when it is merely an application of the principle that governed a prior decision to a different set of facts." Chaidez v. United States, 568 U.S. ___, 133 S.Ct. 1103, 185 L.Ed.2d 149, 156 (2013) (internal citation and quotation marks omitted).

As a caveat, however, the Fourth Amendment exclusionary rule may not apply even though the new decision applies retroactively to a case on direct review. This may occur, for example, where law enforcement officers reasonably rely on a binding appellate precedent that validates their search, but which the later new decision overrules. In that event, the "good faith" exception to the exclusionary is applicable. Davis v. United States, 564 U.S. ___ 131 S.Ct. 2419, 180 L.Ed.2d 285 (2011). See Section 5c(6) of this chapter on the "good faith" exception.

173. Compare United States v. Johnson, 457 U.S. 537, 549, 102 S.Ct. 2579, 73 L.Ed.2d 202, 213 (1982) (leaving intact all pre-1982 retroactivity decisions). See, e.g., Desist v. United States, 394 U.S. 244, 89 S.Ct. 1030, 22 L.Ed.2d 248 (1969)(the rule of Katz v. United States is not retroactive); Williams v. United States, 401 U.S. 646, 91 S.Ct. 1148, 28 L.Ed.2d 388 (1971) (the rule of Chimel v. United States is not retroactive); United States v. Peltier, States,422 U.S. 531, 95 S.Ct. 2313, 45 L.Ed.2d 374 (1975) (rule of Almeida-Sanchez v. United States is not retroactive).

174. 403 U.S. 388, 91 S.Ct. 1999, 29 L.Ed.2d 619 (1971).

rights while the officer was acting under color of his or her authority.[175] "The purpose of *Bivens* is to deter individual federal officers from committing constitutional violations."[176] This civil remedy would have been quite familiar to the Framers as this was the procedural device by which the victims of the English General Warrant vindicated their rights in the Wilkes lawsuits of the 1760s, which the American colonists so applauded.[177] Such an officer, however, has a qualified immunity defense to such a suit if at the time of the search or seizure in question a reasonable officer could have believed that he or she was not in violation of the "clearly established" legal rights of the plaintiff under the Fourth Amendment.[178]

---

175. To date, the *Bivens* action has been limited to suits against offending federal officials. Indeed, the Court has declined to extend the action so as to permit a suit against a private corporation which was running a half-way house under a contract with the Federal Bureau of Prisons. Correctional Services Corp. v. Malesko, 534 U.S. 61, 122 S.Ct. 515, 151 L.Ed.2d 456 (2001).

176. Correctional Services Corp. v. Malesko, 534 U.S. 61, 122 S.Ct. 515, 521, 151 L.Ed.2d 456 (2001). For a classic critique, however, on the limitations of the civil tort action to deter future Fourth Amendment violations by the police, see Wolf v. Colorado., 338 U.S. 25, 41–47, 69 S.Ct. 1359, 93 L.Ed. 1782, 1792–95 (1949) (Murphy J. dissenting).

177. See Chapter 3, Sections 2 & 3 of this work.

178. "The doctrine of qualified immunity protects government officials from liability for civil damages insofar as their conduct does not violate clearly established statutory or constitutional rights of which a reasonable person would have known. Qualified immunity gives government officials breathing room to make reasonable but mistaken judgments, and protects all but the plainly incompetent or those who knowingly violate our law. Whether an official protected by qualified immunity may be held personally responsible for an allegedly unlawful official activity generally turns on the objective legal reasonableness of the action, assessed in light of the legal rules that were clearly established at the time it was taken." Messerschmidt v. Millender, 565 U.S. ___, 132 S.Ct. 1235, 182 L.Ed.2d 47, 58 (2012) (internal citations and case quotations omitted).

"An officer conducting a search is entitled to qualified immunity where clearly established law does *not* show that the search violated the Fourth Amendment. (citation omitted). This inquiry turns on the 'objective legal reasonableness of the action, in light of the legal rules that were clearly established at the time it was taken.' (citations omitted). * * * The principles of qualified immunity shield an officer from personal liability when an officer reasonably believes that his or her conduct complies with the law. Police officers are entitled to rely on existing lower court cases without facing personal liability for their actions." Pearson v. Callahan, 555 U.S. 223, 129 S.Ct. 808, 822, 833, 172 L.Ed.2d 565 (2009) (§ 1983 action) (emphasis added).

"To be established clearly, however, there is no need that 'the very action in question [have] previously been held unlawful.' The unconstitutionality of outrageous conduct obviously will be unconstitutional, this being the reason, as Judge Posner has said, that the '[t]he easiest cases don't even arise. But even as to action less than an outrage, officials can still be on notice that their conduct violates established law ... in novel factual circumstances.'" Safford Unified School District v. Redding, 557 U.S. 364, 129 S.Ct. 2633, 2643, 174 L.Ed.2d 354 (2009) (internal citations omitted) (qualified immunity shown as lower federal court decisions were divided on how the TLO standard applies to strip searches as here).

"No decision of this Court has found a Fourth Amendment violation on facts even roughly comparable to those present in this case. On the contrary some of our opinions may be read as pointing in the opposite direction. * ** A reasonable police officer could read these decisions to mean that the Fourth Amendment permits an officer to enter a residence if the officer has a reasonable basis for concluding that there is an imminent threat of violence." Ryburn v. Huff, 565 U.S. ___, 132 S.Ct. 987, 181 L.Ed.2d 966, 970 (2012) (qualified immunity shielded from suit defendant police officers who entered homeowner's residence investigating a threatened mass shooting at a public school after student's mother rushed into house when asked by police whether there were any guns in the house).

Anderson v. Creighton, 483 US. 635, 107 S.Ct. 3034, 97 L.Ed 2d 523 (1987); see also Hunter v. Bryant, 502 U.S. 224, 112 S.Ct. 534, 116 L.Ed.2d 589 (1991) (federal tort claims suit); Mitchell v. Forsyth, 472 U.S 511, 105 S.Ct. 2806, 86 L.Ed.2d 411 (1985) (U.S. Attorney General domestic security wiretaps). For a thorough discussion of *Bivens* suits, see 1 Wayne LaFave, Search and Seizure § 1.10(b) (5th ed. 2012).

A two fold inquiry is involved in determining whether a qualified immunity defense is applicable in a given case, to wit:

(1) Taken in the light most favorable to the party asserting the Fourth Amendment injury, do the facts alleged show the law enforcement officer's conduct violated a Fourth Amendment right of the party complaining?

(2) If so, was this right "clearly established" in the specific factual context of the case, so that it would be clear to a reasonable officer that his conduct was unlawful under the Fourth Amendment in the factual situation that he or she confronted?[179]

If the answer to *either* question is "no," the officer is entitled to a summary judgment based on qualified immunity; if the answer to *both* questions is "yes," a summary judgment based on this defense does *not* lie and should be denied.[180] As in all summary judgment motions, all conflicts in the evidence and all reasonable inferences therefrom must be resolved in favor of the non-moving party.[181]

---

179. "A court required to rule upon the qualified immunity issue must consider, then, this threshold issue: [1] Taken in the light most favorable to the party asserting the injury, do the facts alleged show the officer's conduct violated a constitutional right? *** If no constitutional right would have been violated, there is no necessity for further inquiries concerning qualified immunity. [2] On the other hand, if a violation could be made out on a favorable view of the party's submissions, the next sequential step is to ask whether the right was clearly established." Saucier v. Katz, 533 U.S. 194, 121 S.Ct. 2151, 2155–56, 150 L.Ed.2d 272 (2001) (bracketed numbers added).

"In resolving questions of qualified immunity at summary judgment, courts engage in a two-fold inquiry. The first asks whether the facts, taken in the light most favorable to the party asserting injury shows the officer's conduct violated a federal right. When a plaintiff alleges excessive force during an investigation or arrest, the federal right at issue is the Fourth Amendment right against unreasonable seizures. The inquiry into whether this right was violated requires a balancing of the nature and quality of the intrusion on the individual's Fourth Amendment interests against the importance of the governmental interests alleged to justify the intrusion.

The second prong of the qualified-immunity analysis asks whether the right in question was 'clearly established' at the time of the violation. Governmental actors are shielded from liability for civil damages if their actions did not violate clearly established statutory or constitutional rights of which a reasonable person would have known. The salient question is whether the state of the law at the time of the incident provided fair warning to the defendants that their alleged conduct was unconstitutional." Tolan v. Cotton, 572 U.S. ___, 134 S.Ct. 1861, 188 L.Ed.2d 895 (2014) (internal citations and case quotations omitted).

180. For example, it has been held that the lead officer who executed a search warrant that contained no description whatever of the things to be seized, and no search warrant language incorporating by reference such a description in any supporting documents, could not rely on a qualified immunity defense in a *Bivens* civil suit brought against the officer. The Court reached this conclusion because (a) the officer violated a Fourth Amendment right of the plaintiff requiring such a description, and (b) that right was "clearly established" at the time of the search. A summary judgment in favor of the officer based on this defense was improperly entered. Groh v. Ramirez, 540 U.S. 551, 124 S.Ct. 1284, 157 L.Ed.2d 1068 (2004).

An opposite result, however, has been reached in a § 1983 action and a summary judgment for the officer was approved where the officer shot and wounded a fleeing felon attempting to escape arrest in a motor vehicle which arguably threatened the safety of other people in the immediate vicinity. The Court concluded that the defendant officer did not violate a "clearly established" Fourth Amendment right of the plaintiff at the time of the shooting. Brosseau v. Haugen, 543 U.S. 194 125 S.Ct. 596, 160 L.Ed.2d 583 (2004).

181. Tolan v. Cotton, 572 U.S. ___, 134 S.Ct. 1861, 188 L.Ed.2d 895 (2014) (summary judgment for a defendant police officer in an excessive use of force 1983 suit, claiming 4th Amendment violations; case arose from a late night police shooting of an unarmed young man in his front yard in the presence of his parents; summary judgment reversed because the circuit court below failed to view the evidence in a light most favorable to the plaintiff; conflicts in the evidence existed as to the events leading up to the shooting; cause remanded to the circuit court to apply the proper summary judgment standard and determine whether, based on the evidence most favorable to the plaintiff, the officer was entitled

Although permissible and certainly appropriate in many cases, the *sequence* of this two-fold inquiry is not mandatory, but discretionary depending on the facts and circumstances of the case.[182] This means that a trial or appellate court, for example, has the sound discretion to skip the first inquiry and solely address the second inquiry—if the answer thereto would otherwise be dispositive in sustaining the qualified immunity defense.[183] Of course, the courts are free to follow the two-step inquiry sequence should they so choose, but they are not required to do so.[184] Moreover, when the defendant officer asserts a qualified immunity defense, a ruling on that issue should be made early in the

---

to summary judgment).

"But under either prong [of the qualified immunity requirements], courts may not resolve genuine disputes of fact in favor the party seeking summary judgment. This is not a rule specific to qualified immunity; it is simply an application of the more general rule that a judge's function at summary judgment is not to weigh the evidence and determine the truth of the matter but to determine whether there is a genuine issue for trial. Summary judgment is appropriate only if 'the movant shows there is no genuine issue of material fact and the movant is entitled to judgment as a matter of law.' Fed. Rule Civ. Proc. 56(a). In making that determination, a court must view the evidence in the light most favorable to the opposing party. * * *

In holding that [the officer's] actions did not violate clearly established law, the Fifth Circuit failed to view the evidence at summary judgment in the light most favorable to [the plaintiff] with respect to the central facts of this case. By failing to credit evidence that contradicted some of the key factual conclusions, the court improperly weighed the evidence in favor of the moving party." (internal citations and case quotations omitted). 134 S.Ct. at 1866 (internal citations and case quotations omitted).

182. "[W]e conclude that, while the sequence set forth there [in *Saucier*] is often appropriate, it should no longer be regarded as mandatory. The judges of the district courts and courts of appeals should be permitted to exercise their sound discretion which of the two prongs of the qualified immunity analysis should be addressed first in light of the circumstances in the particular case at hand." Pearson v. Callahan, 555 U.S. 223, 129 S.Ct. 808, 818, 172 L.Ed.2d 565(2009). "Courts have discretion to decide the order in which to engage in these two [qualified immunity] prongs." Tolan v. Cotton, 572 U.S. ___, 134 S.Ct. 1861, 1866, 188 L.Ed.2d 895 (2014).

"When confronted with such [qualified immunity] arguments, we held in *Saucier v. Katz*, 533 U.S. 194, 200 (2001), that the 'first inquiry must be whether a constitutional right would have been violated on the facts alleged.' Only after deciding that question, we concluded, may an appellate court turn to the question whether the right at issue was clearly established at the relevant time. *Ibid.*

"We subsequently altered this rigid framework in *Pearson* [555 U.S. 223 (2009)], declaring that '*Saucier's* procedure should not be regarded as an inflexible requirement.' 555 U.S., at 227. At the same time, however, we noted that the *Saucier* procedure 'is often beneficial' because 'it promotes the development of constitutional precedent and is especially valuable with respect to questions that do not frequently arise in cases in which a qualified immunity defense is unavailable.' 555 U.S., at 236. *Pearson* concluded that courts 'have discretion to decide whether that [*Saucier*] procedure is worthwhile in particular cases.' *Id.*, at 242." Plumhoff v. Rickard, 572 U.S. ___, 134 S.Ct. 2012, 2020, 188 L.Ed.2d 1056 (2014) (both qualified immunity prongs analyzed; qualified immunity defense upheld on both prongs).

183. "There are cases in which it is plain that a constitutional right is not clearly established but far from obvious whether in fact there is such a right." Pearson v. Callahan, 555 U.S. 223, 129 S.Ct. 808, 818, 172 L.Ed.2d 565 (2009); see also Scott v. Harris, 550 U.S. 372, 127 S.Ct. 1769, 1774, 167 L.Ed.2d 686 (2007).

184. "Although we now hold that the *Saucier* protocol should not be regarded as mandatory in all cases, we continue to believe that it is often beneficial * * * Our decision does not prevent the lower courts from following the *Saucier* procedure; it simply recognizes that those courts should have the discretion to decide whether that procedure is worthwhile in particular cases." Pearson v. Callahan, 555 U.S. 223, 129 S.Ct. 808, 821, 818, 172 L.Ed.2d 565 (2009).

The court, for example, may deem it important to "the development of constitutional precedent" that it be understood that the officer's conduct did, in fact, violate the complaining party's Fourth Amendment rights—although the Fourth Amendment right asserted was not clearly established at the time of the search, and thus a qualified privilege would lie. 129 S.Ct. at 818. Moreover, "[i]t often may be difficult to decide whether a Fourth Amendment right is clearly established without deciding proceedings so that the costs and expenses of trial are avoided where the defense is dispositive.[185] And a pretrial order denying a motion for summary judgment based on a qualified immunity defense is appealable interlocutory order.[186]

In addition, 42 U.S.C. § 1983 provides, inter alia, that a search or seizure victim may bring suit for any Fourth Amendment violation committed against such victim by state officials.[187] Accordingly, "[b]oth Bivens [as to federal officers] and § 1983 [as to state officers] allow a plaintiff to seek money damages from government officials who have violated his [or her] Fourth Amendment rights."[188] There is also a qualified immunity defense for these officers if their conduct did not violate clearly established Fourth Amendment rights of which a reasonable person should have known,[189] as "under both § 1983 and Bivens, the qualified immunity analysis is identical under either cause of action."[190]

Where law enforcement officers conduct a search pursuant to a warrant issued by a neutral and detached magistrate [and the officers are not themselves guilty of misconduct in obtaining the warrant], the magistrate's authorization is generally the clearest indication that the officers acted in an objectively reasonable manner when they conduct a search under the warrant, even if invalid. Accordingly, the officers are entitled to a qualified immunity from a civil rights suit under *Bivens* or 42 U.S.C. § 1983. There is one limited exception to this general rule—to wit: qualified immunity does *not* lie when it is obvious that no reasonably competent officer would have concluded that the warrant was valid, despite the magistrate's approval. The threshold for establishing this exception, however, is a high one. This is so because in the ordinary case a lay law enforcement officer cannot be expected to question the magistrate's decision to issue the warrant, as it is the magistrate's

---

precisely what that constitutional right is"—thereby requiring the court to answer both inquiries in certain cases, regardless of whether the qualified immunity defense be sustained or not. 129 S.Ct. at 818, quoting from Lyons v. Xenia, 417 F.3d 565, 581 (6th Cir. 2005) (Sutton, J. concurring).

185. Saucier v. Katz, 533 U.S. 194, 121 S.Ct. 2151, 2156, 150 L.Ed.2d 272 (2001).

186. Plumhoff v. Rickard, 572 U.S. ___. 134 S.Ct. 2012, 2018–2020, 188 L.Ed. 2d 1056 (2014).

"An order denying a motion for summary judgment is generally not a final decision within the meaning of § 1291 and is thus generally not immediately appealable. But that general rule does not apply when the summary judgment motion is based on a claim of qualified immunity. Qualified immunity is an immunity from suit rather than a mere defense to liability. As a result, pretrial orders denying qualified immunity generally fall within the collateral order doctrine [and are therefore appealable]. This is so because such orders conclusively determine whether the defendant is entitled to immunity from suit; this immunity issue is both important and completely separate from the merits of the action and could not be effectively reviewed on appeal from a final judgment because by that time the immunity from standing trial will have been irretrievably lost." 134 S.Ct. at 2018–2019 (internal citations and quotations from past cases omitted) (bracketed material added).

187. See, e.g., Monroe v. Pape, 365 U.S. 167, 81 S.Ct. 473, 5 L.Ed. 2d 492 (1961).

188. Wilson v. Layne, 526 U.S. 603, 119 S.Ct. 1692, 143 L.Ed.2d 818, 826–27 (1999).

189. "An official sued under § 1983 is entitled to qualified immunity unless it is shown that the official violated a statutory or constitutional right that was 'clearly established' at the time of the challenged conduct. And a defendant cannot be said to have violated a clearly established right unless the right's contours were sufficiently definite that any reasonable official in the defendant's shoes would have understood that he was violating it. In other words, existing precedent must have placed the statutory or constitutional question confronted by the official beyond debate." Plumhoff v. Rickard, 572 U.S. ___, 134 S.Ct. 2012, 2023, 188 L.Ed.2d 1056 (2014).

See also Harlow v. Fitzgerald, 457 U.S. 800, 102 S.Ct. 2727, 73 L.Ed.2d 396 (1982); Malley v. Briggs, 475 U.S. 335, 106 S.Ct. 1092, 89 L.Ed.2d 271 (1986). For a thorough discussion of these § 1983 actions, see 1 Wayne LaFave, Search and Seizure § 1.10(a) (5th ed. 2012).

190. Wilson v. Layne, 526 U.S. 603, 119 S.Ct. 1692, 143 L.Ed.2d 818, 827 (1999); cf. Brosseau v. Haugen, 543 U.S. 194, 125 S.Ct. 596, 160 L.Ed.2d 583 (2004)

responsibility is to pass on the probable cause and other related warrant issues—not the officer.[191]

Nonetheless, a comprehensive treatment of this subject is beyond the scope of this work. Accordingly, only the fundamental principles have been covered.[192]

---

191. "Where the alleged Fourth Amendment violation involves a search or seizure pursuant to a warrant, the fact that a neutral magistrate has issued a warrant is the clearest indication that the officers acted in an objectively reasonable manner or, as we have sometimes put it, in 'objective good faith.' (citation omitted). Nonetheless, under our precedents, the fact that a neutral magistrate has issued a warrant authorizing the allegedly unconstitutional search or seizure does not end the inquiry into objective reasonableness. Rather we have recognized an exception allowing suit when 'it is obvious that no reasonably competent officer would have concluded that a warrant should issue.' (citation omitted). The 'shield of immunity' otherwise conferred by the warrant (citation omitted) will be lost, for example, where the warrant was 'based on an affidavit so lacking in indicia of probable cause as to render official belief in its existence entirely unreasonable.' (citation omitted).

"Our precedents make clear, however, that the threshold for establishing this exception is a high one, and it should be. As we explained in *Leon*, '[i]n the ordinary case, an officer cannot be expected to question the magistrate's probable cause determination' because 'it is the magistrate's responsibility to determine whether the officer's allegations establish probable cause and, if so, to issue a warrant comporting in form with the requirements of the Fourth Amendment.' (citation omitted)." Messerschmidt v. Millender, 565 U.S. ___, 132 S.Ct. 1235, 182 L.Ed.2d 47, 58–59 (2012).

In *Messerschmidt*, the petitioner police officers were held entitled to qualified immunity from a home dweller's 42 U.S.C. § 1983 civil rights suit involving a house search with a warrant. Even if the warrant was invalid as lacking in probable cause, the officers were reasonably entitled to believe that there was probable cause for the warrant to order the seizure of all firearms and gang-related materials on the premises—and thus were entitled to qualified immunity from suit. As the Court held, this is so because of: (a) the home resident's gang membership and long violent gun-related criminal record, (b) his prior deadly assault with a firearm on his girl friend for calling the police on him [which arguably was triggered to conceal his gang activity]; (c) his threat to kill his girl friend [which arguably could be accomplished with other possible weapons on the premises], and (d) the approval by a district attorney and supervising police officers of the warrant, made prior to warrant's issuance.

As an aside, the U.S. Supreme Court has stated that "the same standard of objective reasonableness that we applied in the context of a suppression hearing in Leon [v. United States] defines the qualified immunity accorded an officer who obtained or relied on an allegedly invalid warrant." Messerschmidt v. Millender, 565 U.S. ___, 132 S.Ct. 1235, 182 L.Ed.2d 47, 58 n. 1 (2012) (internal case quotation omitted); see Ch. 17, Sec. 5c(2), of this work on the *Leon* search warrant exception to the exclusionary rule.

192. For a treatment of *Bivens* and § 1983 actions, see 2 John Wesley Hall, Search and Seizure §§ 64.04 et. seq. (5th ed. 2013).

Appendix

I. Chief Justice Thomas Hutchinson's Draft of a General Writ of Assistance for the Boston Customs Official Charles Paxton: Massachusetts Bay Province[1] December 1761

Prov. of) George the third by the grace of God of Great Britain
Mass. Bay) France and Ireland King Defender of the faith &c.
To all and singular our Justices of the Peace Sheriffs
Constables and to all other our Officers and Subjects
within our said Province and to each of you Greeting.

Know ye that whereas in and by an Act of Parliament mad in the (thir) fourteenth year of the reign of the late King Charles the second (it is declared) the Officers of our Customs and their Deputies are authorized and impowered to go and enter aboard any Ship or Vessel outward or inward bound for the Purposes in the said Act mentioned and it is (also) in and by the said Act further enacted and declared that it shall be unlawful to or for any person or persons authorized by Writs of assistants under the seal of our Court of Exchequer to take a Constable Headborough or other Publick Officer inhabiting near unto the Place and in the day time to enter and to go into any House Shop Cellar Warehouse or Room or other Place and case of resistance to break open doors chests trunks and other package there to seize and from them to bring any kind of goods or merchandize whatsoever prohibited and uncustomed and to put and secure the same in (his Majestys) our Store house in the port next to the place where such seizure shall be made.

And where as in and by an Act of Parliament in the seventh and eighth year of the reign of the late King William the third there is granted to the Officers for collecting and managing our Revenue and inspecting the Plantation trade in any of our Plantations the same powers, and authority for visiting and searching of Ships and also to enter houses or warehouses to search for and seize any Prohibited or uncustomed goods as are provided for the Officers of our Customs in England by the said last mentioned Act made in the fourteenth year of the reign of King Charles the second, and the like assistance is required

1. Source: 2 Legal Papers of John Adams 144–47 (L. Kinvin Wroth and Hiller B. Zobel eds. 1965). "Hutchinson's draft was undoubtedly used as the basis for all subsequent writs issued." Id. at 145, n. 151. Written in Hutchinson's hand. Adams Papers, Microfilms, Reel No. 185.

to be given to the said Officers in the execution of their office as by the said last mentioned Act is provided for the Officers in England.

And whereas in and by an Act of our Province of Massachusetts by made in the eleventh year of the reign of the late King William the third it is enacted and declared that our Superior Court of Judicature Court of Assize and General Goal delivery for our said Province shall have cognizance of all matters and things within our said Province as fully and amply to all intents and purposes as our Courts of King's Bench Common Pleas and Exchequer within our Kingdom of England and have or ought to have.

And whereas our Commissioners for managing and causing to be levied and collected our customs subsidies and other duties have by Commission or Deputation under their hands and seal dated at London the 22d. day of May in the first year of our Reign deputed and impowered Charles Paxton Esqr. to be Surveyor and Searcher of all the rates and duties arising and growing due to us at Boston in our Province aforesaid and in and by said Commission or Deputation have given him power to enter into any Ship Bottom Boat or other Vessel and also into any Shop House Warehouse Hostery or other Place whatsoever to make diligent search into any trunk chest pack case truss or any other parcell or package whatsoever for any goods wares or merchandizes prohibited to be imported or exported or whereof the Customs or other Duties have not been duly paid and the same to seize to our use In all things proceeding as the Law directs.

Therefore we strictly Injoin and Command you and every one of you that, all excuses apart, you and every one of you permit the said Charles Paxton according to the true intent and form of the said commission or deputation and the laws and statutes in that behalf made and provided, *as well by night as by day from time to time to enter and go on board any Ship Boat or other Vessel riding lying or being within or coming to the said Port of Boston* or any Places or Creeks thereunto appertaining such Ship Boat or Vessel *then and there found to search and oversee* and the persons therein being strictly to examine touching the Premises aforesaid and also (according to the form effect and true intent of the said commission or deputation) *in the day time to enter and go into the vaults cellars warehouses shops and other places where any prohibited goods wares or merchandizes or goods wares or merchandizes for which the customs or other duties shall not have been duly and truly satisfied* and paid lye concealed or are suspected to be concealed, according to the true intent of the law *to inspect and oversee and search for the said goods wares and merchandizes*, And further to do and execute all things which of right and according to the laws and statutes in this behalf shall be to be done. *And we further strictly Injoin and Command you and every one of you that to the said Charles Paxton Esqr. you and every one of you from time to time be aiding assisting and helping in the execution of the premises as is meet.* And you or any one of you in no wise omit at your Perils. Witness Thomas Hutchinson Esq. at Boston the day of December in the Second year of our Reign Annoque Dom. 1761. [emphasis added].

by order of Court
N.H. Cler.

[emphasis added].

II. Legal Argument of James Otis Jr. against the General Writs of Assistance Petition of Lechmere: February 1761[2]

May it please your Honours,

I was desired by one of the court to look into the books, and consider the question now before the court, concerning Writs of Assistance. I have accordingly considered it, and now appear not only in obedience to your order, but also in behalf of the inhabitants of this town, who have presented another petition, and out of regard to the liberties of the subject. And I take this opportunity to declare, that whether under a fee or not, (for in such a cause as this I despise a fee) *I will to my dying day oppose with all the powers and faculties God has given me, all such instruments of slavery on the one hand, and villainy on the other, as this writ of assistance is. It appears to me (may it please your honours) the worst instrument of arbitrary power, the most destructive of English liberty, and the fundamental principles of the constitution, that ever was found in an English law-book.* I must therefore beg your honours patience and attention to the whole range of an argument, that may perhaps appear uncommon in many things, as well as points of learning, that are more remote and unusual, that the whole tendency of my design may the more easily be perceived, the conclusions better descend, and the force of them better felt.

I shall not think much of my pains in this cause as I engaged in it from principle. I was sollicited to engage on he other side. I was sollicited to argue this cause as Advocate-General, and because I would not, I have been charged with a desertion of my office; to this charge I can give a very sufficient answer, I renounced that office, and I argue this case from the same principle; and I argue it with the greater pleasure as it is in favor of British liberty, at a time, when we hear the greatest monarch upon earth declaring from his throne that he glories in the name of Briton, and that the privileges of his are dearer to him that the most valuable prerogatives of his crown. And as it is in opposition to a kind of power, the exercise of which in former periods of English history, cost one king of England his head and another his throne. I have taken more pains in this than I will ever take again: Although my engaging in this and another popular cause has raised much resentment; but I think I can sincerely declare, that I cheerfully submit myself to every odious name for conscience sake; and from my should I despise all those whose guilt, malice or folly has made my foes. Let the consequences be what they will, I am determined to proceed. The only principles of public conduct that are worthy of a gentleman, or a man, are to sacrifice estate, ease, health and applause, and even life itself to the sacred calls of his country. These manly sentiments in private life make the good citizen, in public life, the patriot and the hero.—I do not say, when brought to the test, I shall be invincible; I pray God I may never be brought to melancholy trial; but if ever I should, it would be then known, how far I can reduce to practice principles I know founded in truth.—In the mean time I will proceed to the subject of the writ. *In the first, may it please your Honours, I will admit, that writs of one kind, may be legal, that is, special writs, directed to special officers, and to search certain houses, &c. especially set forth in the writ, may be granted by the Court of Exchequer at home, upon oath made before the Lord Treasurer by the person, who asks, that he suspects such goods to be concealed in* THOSE VERY PLACES

2. Source: 2 Legal Papers of John Adams 139–144 (L. Kinvin Wroth and Hiller B. Zobel eds. 1965). Taken almost entirely from the Massachusetts Spy, April 29, 1773, p. 3, vols. 1–3.

HE DESIRES TO SEARCH. The Act of 14th Car. II which Mr. Gridley mentions proves this. And in this light the writ appears like a warrant from a justice of the peace to search for stolen goods. Your Honours will find in the old book, concerning the office of a justice of the peace, precedents of general warrants to search suspected houses. But in more modern books you will find only special warrants to search such and such houses specially named, in which the complainant has before sworn he suspects his goods are concealed; and you will find it adjudged that special warrants only are legal. In the same manner I rely on it, that the writ prayed for in this petition being general is illegal. It is a power that places the liberty of every man in the hands of every petty officer. I say I admit that special writs of assistance to search special houses, may be granted to certain persons on oath; but I deny that the writ now prayed for can be granted, for I beg leave to make some observations on the writ itself before I proceed to other Acts of Parliament.

In the first place the writ is UNIVERSAL, being directed "to all and singular justices, sheriffs, constables and all other officers and subjects&c." So that in short it is directed to every subject in the king's dominions; every one with this writ may be a tyrant: If this commission is legal, a tyrant may, in legal manner also, controul, imprison or murder any one within the realm.

In the next place, IT IS PERPETUAL; there's no return, a man is accountable to no person for his doings, every man may reign secure in his petty tyranny, and spread terror and desolation around him, until the trump of the arch angel shall excite different emotions in his soul.

In the third place, a person with this writ, IN THE DAY TIME may enter all houses, shops, &c. AT WILL, and command all to assist.

Fourth, by this not only deputies, &c. but even THEIR MENIAL SERVANTS ARE ALLOWED TO LORD IT OVER US—What is this but to have the curse of Canaan with a witness on us, to be the servant of servants, the most despicable of God's creation. *Now one of the most essential branches of English liberty, is the freedoms of one's house. A man's house is his castle; and while he is quiet, he is as well guarded as a prince in his castle. This writ, if it should be declared legal, would totally annihilate this privilege. Customs house officers may enter our houses when they please—we are commanded to permit their entry—their menial servants may enter—may break locks, bars and every thing in their way—and whether they break through malice or revenge, no man, no court can inquire—bare suspicion without oath is sufficient.* This wanton exercise of this power is no chimerical suggestion of a heated Brain—I will mention some facts. Mr. Pew had one of these writs, and when Mr. Ware succeeded him, he endorsed this writ over to Mr. Ware, so that THESE WRITS ARE NEGOTIABLE from one officer to another, and so your Honours have no opportunity of judging the persons to whom this vast power is delegated. Another instance is this.—Mr. Justice Wally had called this same Mr. Ware before him by a constable, to answer for a breach of the Sabbath day acts, or that of profane swearing. As soon as he had done, Mr. Ware asked him if he had done, he replied, yes. Well then, says he, I will shew you a little of my power—I command you to permit me to search your house for uncustomed goods; and went on to search his house from the garret to the cellar, and then served the constable in the same manner. But to shew another absurdity in this writ, if it should be established, I insist upon it EVERY PERSON by 14th of Car. II. HAS THIS POWER as well as Custom-house officers; the words are"it shall be lawful for any person or persons authorized, &c." What a scene does this open! Every man prompted by revenge, ill humour or wantonness to inspect the inside of his neighbour's house, may get a writ of assistance; others may ask it from self-defence; one arbitrary exertion will provoke another, until society will be involved in tumult and in blood. Again these writs ARE NOT RETURNED.

Writs in their nature are temporary things; when the purposes for which they are issued are answered, they exist no more; but these monsters in the law live forever, no one can be called to account. Thus reason and the constitution are both against this writ. Let us see what authority there is for it. No more than one instance can be found of it in all our law books, and that was in the zenith of arbitrary power, viz. In the reign of Car. II. when Star-chamber powers were pushed in extremity by some ignorant clerk of the Exchequer. But had this writ been in any book whatever it would have been illegal. ALL PRECEDENTS ARE UNDER THE CONTROUL OF THE PRINCIPLES OF THE LAW. Lord Talbot says, it is better to observe these than any precedents though in the House of Lords, the last resort of the subject. *No Acts of Parliament can establish such a writ; Though it should be made in the very words of the petition it would be void, "AN ACT AGAINST THE CONSTITUTION IS VOID."* Vid. Viner. *But these prove no more that what I before observed, that special writs may be granted on oath and probable suspicion. The Act of 7th and 8th William III. that the officers of the plantations shall have the same powers, &c. is confined in this sense that an officer should show probable grounds, should take his oath on it, should do this before a magistrate, and that such magistrate, if he thinks proper should issue a special warrant to a constable to search the places.* That of 6th Anne can prove no more.

It is the business of this court to demolish this monster of oppression, and to tear into rags this remnant of Starchamber tyranny -&c.

The court suspended the absolute determination of this matter. I have omitted many authorities; also many fine touches in the order of reasoning, and numberless Rhetorical and popular flourishes. [underlining added; all other emphasis, including capitals, in original].

[emphasis added]

III. The English General Warrants

A. The Monitor General Warrant Issued to the Kings Messengers for the Arrest of John Entick and Search of his Books and Papers November 1762[3]

George Montague Dunk, earl of Halifax, viscount Sunbury, and baron Halifax, on of the lords of his majesty's honourable privy council, lieutenant general of his majesty's forces, lord lieutenant general and general governor of the kingdom of Ireland, *and principal secretary of state, &c. these are in his majesty's name to authorize, to make strict and diligent search for John Entick, the author, or one concerned in writing of several weekly very seditious papers, entitled the Monitor, or British Freeholder*, No. 357, 358, 360, 373, 376, 379, and 380, London, printed for J. Wilson and J. Fell in Pater Noster Row, which contain gross and scandalous reflections and invectives upon his majesty's government, and upon both houses of parliament; *and him, having found you are to seize and apprehend, and to bring, together with his books and papers, in safe custody before me to be examined concerning the premises, and further dealt with according to law*; in the due execution

3. Source: Entick v. Carrington, 19 Howell's State Trials 1030, 1034 (1765) (Lord Camden's opinion).

whereof all mayors, sheriffs, justices of the peace, constables, and other his majesty's officers civil and military, and loving subjects whom it may concern, are to be aiding and assisting to you as there may be occasion; and for so doing this shall be your warrant. *Given at St. James the 6th day of November 1762, in the third year of his majesty's reign, Dunk Halifax. To Nathan Carrington, James Watson, Thomas Ardran and Robert Blackmore, four of his majesty's messengers in ordinary.*

[emphasis added]

B. The North Briton General Warrant Issued to the Kings Messengers for the Arrest and Search of the Authors, Printers and Publishers of the North Briton No. 45 April 1763[4]

George Montague Dunk, earl of Halifax, viscount Sunbury, and baron Halifax, one of the lords of his majesty's most honourable privy council, lieutenant-general of his majesty's forces, and *principal secretary of state, & These are in his majesty's name to authorize and require you, taking a constable to your assistance, to make strict and diligent search for the authors, printers and publishers of a seditious and treasonable paper, entitled, "The North Briton, No. 45"* Saturday 23, 1763, printed for G. Kearsly in Lungate Street, London; *and them or any of them having found, to apprehend and seize, together with their papers, and to bring into safe custody before me, to be examined concerning the premises, and further dealt with according to law.* In the due execution whereof, all mayors, sheriffs, justices of the peace, constables and all others his majesty's officers civil and military, and loving subjects whom it may concern, are to be aiding and assisting to you, as there shall be occasion. And for your so doing, this shall be your warrant. *Given at St. James's, the 26th day of April 1763, in the third year of his majesty's reign Dunk Halifax. To Nathan Carrington, James Money, James Watson, and Robert Blackmore, four of his messengers in ordinary.*

[emphasis added].

4. Source: Leach v. Mooney, 19 Howell's State Trials 1002, 1008 (1765) (Lord Mansfield's opinion).

Bibliographical Note on Fourth Amendment Historical Sources

The historical background of the Fourth Amendment is covered at Chapters 2–6 of this work. For a more detailed treatment of this subject, however, the reader should consult a variety of leading works.

The earliest work, which also contains some valuable historical documents, was written in 1865 by Horace Gray, Jr., later an Associate Justice of the United States Supreme Court.[1] The recognized modern work on the subject was written in 1937 by Nelson B. Lasson and is often cited in leading decisions of the United States Supreme Court on the Fourth Amendment.[2] There are, in addition, other established historical works on the subject authored by Jacob W. Landynski,[3] O.M. Dickerson,[4] Telford Taylor,[5] and Leonard Levy.[6] There are also two extensive, unpublished doctoral dissertations on this subject by Joseph R. Frese[7] and William Cuddihy,[8] a discussion and compilation of original documents in the 1761 Boston Writs case,[9] an extensive study of the case itself,[10] and a work dealing, in part, with the general warrant in English constitutional history.[11] Moreover, Robert Rutland[12] and Bernard Schwartz[13] have provided a general historical background of the American Bill of Rights—with many important historical documents included in Schwartz's work. There are, of course, many other important scholarly works and articles on the Fourth Amendment, the Constitution, and the Bill of Rights—some of which will be

1. Horace Gray, Jr., Quincy's Massachusetts Reports 1761–72, App. I 395–540 (1865).

2. Nelson Lasson, The History and Development of the Fourth Amendment to the United States Constitution (1937).

3. Jacob Landynski, Search and Seizure and the Supreme Court (1966); see also Jacob Landynski, "Search and Seizure," The Rights of the Accused (Nagel ed. 1972).

4. O.M. Dickerson, "Writs of Assistance as a Cause of the Revolution," The Era of the American Revolution (Richard Morris ed. 1939); see also O.M. Dickerson, The Navigation Acts and the American Revolution (1951).

5. Telford Taylor, Two Studies in Constitutional Interpretation (1969).

6. Leonard Levy, Original Intent and the Framers' Constitution, ch. 11 (1988); see also Leonard Levy, Origin of the Bill of Rights (1999).

7. Joseph R. Frese, "Writs of Assistance in the American Colonies 1660–1776" (Harvard Univ. Doctoral Dissertation 1951); see also Joseph R. Frese, "James Otis and the Writs of Assistance," 30 N.Eng.Q. 498 (1957).

8. William Cuddihy, "The Fourth Amendment: Origins and Original Meaning, 602–1791," (Claremont Graduate School Doctoral Dissertation 1990).

9. L. Kinvin Wroth and Hiller B. Zobel, 2 Legal Papers of John Adams 106–23 (1965).

10. M.H. Smith, The Writs of Assistance Case (1978).

11. Fredrick Siebert, Freedom of the Press in England 1476–1776, ch. 18 (1952).

12. Robert Rutland, The Birth of the Bill of Rights (rev. ed 1983).

13. I & I Bernard Schwartz, The Bill of Rights: A Documentary History (1971); see also The Complete Bill of Rights, ch. 6 (Neil Cogan ed. 1997).

referred to in this work. But the foregoing are some of the leading works that attempt to lay out in some detail the historical background of the Fourth Amendment and the Bill of Rights.

Besides these scholarly historical works, there are also a number of relevant documents of the period that should be consulted for a rudimentary understanding of Fourth Amendment history: a sample American colonial writ of assistance, James Otis Jr.'s legal argument against the writs of assistance in the 1761 Boston Writs case, and the 1762–63 English general warrants involved in the Wilkes litigation. These documents are found in a scattered variety of sources and are collected in the appendix to this book for ready reference.

Table of Cases

C

D

E

F

K

L

M

Index

Note: *n* indicates footnote.